D0212208

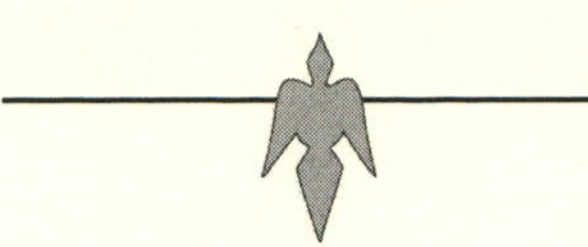

Native Americans

Volume I

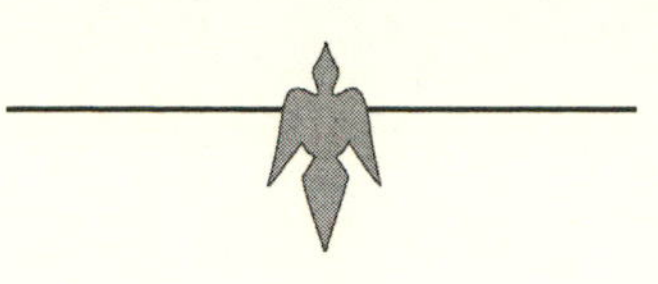

Native Americans

An Encyclopedia of History, Culture, and Peoples

Volume I

Barry M. Pritzker

ABC-CLIO

Santa Barbara, California
Denver, Colorado
Oxford, England

Library of Congress Cataloging-in-Publication Data
Pritzker, Barry.
Native Americans : an encyclopedia of history, culture, and peoples / Barry M. Pritzker.
p. cm.
Includes bibliographical references and idex.
ISBN 0-87436-836-7 (alk. paper)
1. Indians of North America. I. Title.
E77.P89 1998
970.004'97—DC21 98-21718
CIP

05 04 03 02 01 00 99 10 9 8 7 6 5 4 3 2

ABC-CLIO, Inc.
130 Cremona Drive, P.O. Box 1911
Santa Barbara, California 93116-1911

Typesetting by Letra Libre

This book is printed on acid-free paper ♾.
Manufactured in the United States of America

To Carol Batker,
for her love and encouragement,
and to our children, Olivia and Aaron,
for their patience

Contents

Preface

This encyclopedia is an attempt to illuminate in a comprehensive yet readable way some of the complex cultures of the native peoples of North America. In school, I learned that America was a pristine "wilderness" waiting for the so-called right people to come along and build a "civilization." Of course, the truth is that millions of people were already living here. In fact, they had been here for thousands—perhaps tens of thousands—of years before Eriksson, Cabot, and Coronado. Adapting over millennia to diverse climatic and physiographic environments, Native Americans created and continue to build an astonishing range of complex cultures to fulfill both their material and their spiritual needs.

I have always felt a share of responsibility concerning the basic methods—thievery and murder—that brought this rich land under the control of what we now know as the United States and Canada. As a citizen of the United States, I am implicated in and benefit from the long process of expropriation. It was this awareness, in part, that led to my interest in Indians. A teaching stint at the Taos Pueblo Day School and a fellowship at the Summer Institute of the Newberry Library's D'Arcy McNickle Center for the History of the American Indian reinforced my awareness of Native American cultures.

Today, American Indians still struggle to overcome a complicated legacy of destruction. They have been left with a tiny fraction of their aboriginal domain (many groups remain landless altogether). Neither the U.S. nor the Canadian government has hastened to redress grievances. Yet Indians and Inuit are revitalizing their cultures. In the United States, they are an important part of many local and regional economies. In Canada, native people are reclaiming their land as well as their heritage, as the creation of the new territory of Nunavut so clearly illustrates. Indians and Inuit still face daunting challenges in their efforts to

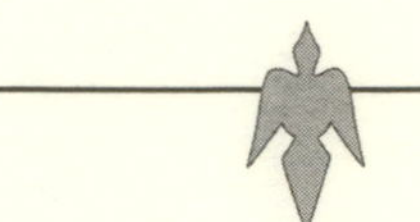

retain a native identity and reestablish sovereignty in the face of relentless assimilationist pressures, but many are meeting these challenges head-on and with success.

It is not too late to learn from Native Americans. In light of past and ongoing injustices and the momentum of Indian and Inuit self-determination movements, I would say that an understanding of Indian and Inuit cultures and concerns is essential. The past cannot be changed, but we can recognize aspects of history commonly deemed unimportant, such as the dynamics of native cultures as well as the vital contributions of Native Americans to contemporary society. We can also create a present and a future in which people work together based on mutual understanding and respect. These are my ultimate goals in writing this encyclopedia.

My research is based on a variety of primary and secondary sources. Most primary information on early native cultures comes from the records of explorers, traders, missionaries, and scientists. There are also anthropological studies of native cultures, including interviews with elders and other tribal members. Native art and other material "texts" are also important source material, as are company and government records. More recent primary information includes native-written books, articles, and electronic texts as well as material culture. I have tried to use official, tribally based material whenever possible. Although accuracy has always remained my primary concern, this encyclopedia doubtless contains errors of omission and commission. For these I take full responsibility and extend a preemptive apology to those who might be offended or misguided by any such flaws.

I would also like to thank those people who (knowingly or unknowingly) inspired me and/or helped make it possible for me to undertake and complete this project: the children, staff, and community of the Taos Pueblo Day School in the fall of 1977; Professor Carol Batker, for careful reading and editing and help with perspective; John Bowman, for inspiration and technical assistance; Professor Emma Cappeluzzo, for initiating the University of Massachusetts program that enabled students to teach at New Mexico pueblos; Karen Turple and Pierre Beaudreau at Indian and Northern Affairs Canada as well as Bill Armstrong at the British Columbia Ministry of Aboriginal Affairs for providing documents and other information; and Professor Lawana Trout, the former director of the D'Arcy McNickle Center for the History of the American Indian's Summer Institute. I would also like to thank ABC-CLIO editors Jeff Serena and Todd Hallman for their invaluable guidance, support, and direction. Connie Oehring, Libby Barstow, and Liz Kincaid saw to the encyclopedia's production, including copyediting and artwork, in a most able, professional, and friendly manner.

Finally, I would like formally to acknowledge and to honor the North American Indians and Inuit, who have struggled, and continue to struggle, in the face of hardship and oppression to retain their cultures and traditions and to live dignified lives. I also hope this encyclopedia may be of some service to people who seek to understand and appreciate the cultures of Native Americans in particular and the marvel of human diversity in general.

Barry M. Pritzker

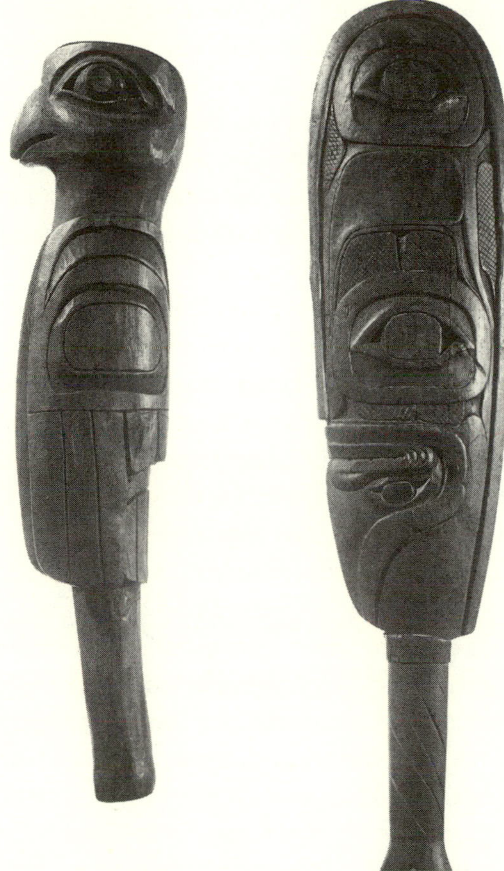

Introduction

Indians[1] have lived in North America for a long time. There is no agreement on the precise length of time or even on how and when they first appeared on the continent. According to many Indian creation stories, the people[2] have always been here, having originated either below the earth or, less commonly, in some other nonterrestrial zone. The most widely accepted theory states that ancestral Native Americans walked across the Bering Strait when frozen ocean conditions created a land bridge between what is now Siberia and Alaska. That may have occurred anywhere from 15,000 to 40,000 or more years ago. Some people speculate that even without a land bridge, ancient people may have crossed the Bering Strait in boats. Finally, there is a theory, based on certain fossils found in New Mexico, that ancient people arrived here directly from Europe, via Iceland and Greenland.

In any case, the ancestors of at least some groups were living in their historic territories in 10,000 B.C.E.[3] Over the millennia, people adapted to dramatic climate changes by creating new technologies and migrating when necessary. Some early groups hunted species of big game that are now extinct. People gradually filled in new territory as the glaciers withdrew from northern North America. The Great Plains became populated, depopulated, and then repopulated. Some groups settled down to farm the great American triad of corn, beans, and squash while others continued primarily to hunt and/or fish and/or gather wild plant foods.

Some Indian peoples developed complex mythologies and religions, whereas others made do with relatively simple beliefs. Some groups built great cities, with tens of thousands of residents, whereas others preferred living in small groups. Fighting was endemic among some groups, whereas others lived in relative peace. Many Native Americans were deeply knowledgeable about the land itself. Some groups discovered literally hundreds of plants that could be used for medicinal

purposes. Indians were no strangers to travel. Some coastal peoples built sturdy, seagoing vessels that took them 60 or more miles out to sea to hunt marine life. Extensive trade networks were set up, so that items both popular and necessary, as well as ideas, could be exchanged over distances of hundreds and even thousands of miles.

Indians learned to stay reasonably cool in the heat of desert summers and, along with the Inuit, reasonably warm in the frozen northern winters. Many groups had brilliant material arts traditions, and many more raised drama and storytelling to artistic heights. In the realm of government, too, Indians fashioned complex responses to various local situations. Some groups developed councils, some were run by clan associations, and some had separate war and peace governments. Groups had strong leaders, weak leaders, or even no real leaders at all. Confederacies such as the Creek and Iroquois developed particularly sophisticated governmental models. One trait that stands out in this area, however, is the near-universal tendency among Native Americans to make decisions by consensual agreement rather than majority rule.

By now the reader should begin to understand the degree of cultural diversity present among the millions of aboriginal American Indian and Inuit people. Why, then, are Native Americans so often depicted as just a handful of people without any culture at all? One reason has to do with myth: It was, and is, convenient for non-natives to pretend that they did not have to take the land from others. Another concerns population. The aboriginal population of North America is variously estimated at between about 2 million and 18 million at its peak. However, diseases such as smallpox, cholera, typhoid, and measles, brought by non-natives,[4] decimated Indian communities. Many suffered population losses of up to 90 percent or more even before non-natives actually arrived, because the germs far outran explorers, traders, missionaries, and settlers. So it was that so many non-natives spoke of the land as open, pristine, and virgin.

Furthermore, literary and historical depictions of Indians as savage, barbarous, and primitive have distorted the clash between the different Indian and Euro-American ways of being in the world. The Spanish sought gold and other forms of riches. They also demanded conversions to Christianity and were perfectly willing to kill and enslave Indians to get what they wanted. The British wanted land above all and were also interested in religious as well as cultural conversions. The French had their share of missionaries but in general were more willing to accept Indian cultures on their own terms, a fact that accounts for the relatively high rates of interracial marriage in New France.

In the far north, the Russians, too, sent missionaries to convert the Indians, but mainly launched a program of brutal enslavement in order to force Indians and Inuit to acquire pelts for Russian trade companies. Indians, for their part, were happy to trade with the newcomers and even to cede some land willingly. They were not, however, prepared for a wholesale onslaught on their land and way of life. These sorts of struggles are often couched in moralistic dualities, such as "savage" and "civilized," but even the introductory student must move beyond simplistic, ethnocentric explanations in order to achieve any real understanding of cultural conflict.

Indian and Inuit groups encountered non-natives at vastly different times. The Norse probably appeared in the extreme northeast around 1000; Basque and other European fishermen arrived in roughly the same area in the early sixteenth century, about the time of Spanish contact in the south. In contrast, some bands in California and the Plateau region did not directly encounter non-natives until the nineteenth century, and in parts of Arctic America there was no direct interracial contact until the early twentieth century.

The experience of Indian groups with non-natives differed according to time and place, but in general there was a greater or lesser degree of aggression on the part of the latter and resistance on the part of the former. Many Indian groups underwent dramatic transformations during the historical period. The need for increased centralization to fight the newcomers and the need to adapt to the loss of freedom altered governmental structures. New alliances were effected, as Indian groups took sides in the great colonial struggles and became heavily involved in the fur trade. Native manufacture of certain items fell away as people tended to become

dependent on non-native goods. Religion changed too, as Christianity mixed with and in many cases subsumed traditional beliefs. Perhaps the two biggest developments to influence the lives of Indians were the introductions of the horse and of firearms. As already mentioned, diseases from abroad also took a great toll on native populations, as did, increasingly, warfare as well as venereal disease and alcohol.

While individuals were busy seizing Indians' territory and destroying their resources, both the United States and Canada, having coalesced as nations, developed official policies that forced Indian groups to give up vast amounts of land. Many were forcibly removed far from their homelands at a tremendous cost in life and suffering. In the United States, treaties made with sovereign Indian nations were broken almost as soon as they were concluded. Some groups in the United States were resettled on ever-shrinking reservations, which may or may not have been located within their ancestral lands. Patriot leaders (not to mention warriors and noncombatants) were killed or otherwise neutralized, and compliant, ersatz leaders were often installed in their place. Canada favored the creation of numerous small reserves generally within aboriginal territory.

In both countries, Indians were placed under tremendous pressure to abandon their heritage and assimilate into non-native society. Various methods were used to achieve these goals, such as forcible removal of children for education at boarding schools, banning aspects of traditional culture such as language and religious practice, and mandatory participation by nomadic groups in farming schemes. These methods went far to erode strong family bonds and tribal traditions. Officials in charge of Indian affairs were notoriously corrupt, a situation that added to the difficulties of Native Americans.

Both countries also passed a series of laws designed to further their assimilationist goals. In the United States, the General Allotment (Dawes) Act (1887) sought to break up the reservation system and tribalism. Among its provisions were those that called for the government to negotiate with tribes with the goal of allotting Indian lands in severalty. Those lands remaining after certain individuals had received their share would be released for sale to or use by non-natives. Although tribes were able to negotiate under this framework, as a group they lost roughly 90 million acres of land—about two-thirds of the total land base—either through the alienation of "surplus" land or because individual allotments were subsequently lost through mechanisms such as tax foreclosure. By forcibly eliminating so much common land, the United States succeeded in dealing a serious blow to tribal identity and cohesion.

Canada concluded a series of numbered treaties with Indian groups, beginning in 1871. These called on native people to exchange land for reserves, payments, and other considerations. In 1876, Canadian officials consolidated their policies under a single Indian Act. Based on earlier laws aimed at eradicating "Indianness" through the enfranchisement of Indian men, the act empowered the federal government to control native people, even to the point of defining who was an Indian and who was not. Under the act, Indian leaders functioned essentially as government agents. Subsequent amendments expanded the concept of enfranchisement, making it involuntary, and outlawed certain rituals, such as the potlatch. They also allowed the government to seize Indian land the government decided was not being sufficiently exploited economically by the tribes. In the far north, the North-West Mounted Police built posts from which they regulated many aspects of Inuit life.

By the early twentieth century, many Indians and Inuit had fallen into conditions of severe poverty and dependence. Although many resisted it, the United States granted citizenship to Indians in 1924. In 1934, U.S. officials overturned Dawes-era policies and passed the Wheeler-Howard Indian Reorganization Act (IRA). Under the IRA, allotment was halted, and Indians were encouraged to create constitutional, majority-rule–style tribal governments. Decisions made by such governments were, of course, subject to approval by the Bureau of Indian Affairs (BIA). The tribes were also given such presumptive incentives as the opportunity to join in non-native development schemes. Despite the best hopes of policy makers, many tribes rejected the IRA as being antithetical to their customs and beliefs as well as a violation of treaty-protected sovereignty.

It was not long, however, before reaction set in, and New Deal policies were in turn reversed: In the

1950s, the federal government set about severing the special relationship between Indian tribes and the United States in a process known as termination. Related policies also encouraged Indians to leave reservations and live in cities. There, instead of jobs and assimilation, many found only poverty, loneliness, and alienation. At the same time the reservations lost thousands of young people who would have provided the next generation of leadership.

Meanwhile, Indians, led in part by war veterans, were creating important pan-tribal organizations. In 1944, the National Congress of American Indians (NCAI) took the lead in advocating for Indian self-determination. Younger activists created the National Indian Youth Conference in 1961. Both of these groups were instrumental in shaping an Indian agenda for political and social action. What ultimately stopped termination, in fact, in addition to the horrific experience of two terminated tribes, the Menominee and Klamath, was the ability of Indian leaders to convince Congress of the importance of maintaining the government's treaty obligations and of the potential gains in allowing Indians themselves to determine the course of their own futures.

In Canada, as well, the postwar period marked the emergence of Indian organizations determined to break the cycle of dependence and neglect. The far north took on great strategic importance in the early Cold War period, leading to official attention for the first time. Inuit and some Subarctic Indians were still in the process of consolidating their populations around permanent settlements and abandoning, however unwillingly, their traditional lifestyles. In 1969, Canada proposed its own version of termination, but native resistance forced the government to kill the policy before it was even enacted. Quickly, Canada withdrew Indian agents from all reserves and began funding aboriginal organizations preparatory to entering into serious discussions on aboriginal rights. Among the reforms that followed were local control of education, a process that continues today. In 1995, for instance, 98 percent of on-reserve schools were under the control of First Nations. In the far north, organizations like the Inuit Tapirisat of Canada, founded in 1971, began carving out a path toward self-determination.

The Canadian government formally recognized classes of native claims in 1973. Major concords such as the James Bay and Northern Quebec Agreement of 1975 and the Cree-Naskapi Act of 1984 helped establish the principle that the government would negotiate seriously with Indian groups concerning self-determination. Progress in this area may be illustrated in many ways but perhaps most clearly by the agreement between Canada and the Nisga'a Tribal Council on what amounts to a government-to-government basis. Also, in 1985, Parliament removed the most offensive and discriminatory sections of the Indian Act. Finally, sections recognizing Indian, Inuit, and Métis[5] rights were included in the constitution in 1982.

In the United States, a revolution of rising expectations, combined with the growing militancy of the period, produced the "Red Power" movement of the late 1960s and 1970s. Activist organizations included the Native American Civil Rights Council and the American Indian Movement. The most visible manifestations of direct action were the occupation of Alcatraz Island in 1969 and of the Bureau of Indian Affairs in 1972 and the standoff at Wounded Knee, South Dakota, in 1973. Northwestern and then Great Lakes tribes fought hard, visibly, and ultimately successfully for their fishing rights, guaranteed by treaty but denied in practice.

Progress was also made toward reaching the goal of self-determination. Indians scored important, though still limited, legal victories during the period, winning passage of several bills, including the Indian Civil Rights Act (1968), the Alaska Native Claims Settlement Act (1971), and the Indian Self-Determination and Educational Assistance Act (1975). Some tribes gained greater control over extensive mineral holdings (although leases often remained terribly exploitative). Along with Red Power came Red Pride, as people rediscovered their heritage in language, art, and spirituality. Younger people, especially, began increasingly to embrace the teachings of their elders.

Although poverty and poor health remain endemic to many Indian communities, the worst abuses of the early twentieth century have passed, and Indian populations are generally increasing. The U.S. Census recorded roughly two million Indians in 1990.

There were 287 reservations composed of 56 million acres of land. More than 300 tribal governments were officially recognized by the federal government, plus over 200 in Alaska, with over 100 more either seeking recognition or considering such a move. Slightly more than 50 percent of Indians in the United States live in urban areas. According to the 1991 Canada census, there were 1,002,675 self-identified Indians, 608 First Nations Councils (bands), 66 Inuit communities, and 2,370 reserves totaling 7.4 million acres. In 1993 there were 626,000 status[6] Indians, 212,650 Métis, and 49,225 Inuit. Almost half of all status Indians live on a reserve.

All over North America, Native American groups continue to press for self-sufficiency and self-determination, including control over natural resources, fulfillment of treaty rights, just compensation for—or the return of—land, and legal jurisdiction. In the United States, organizations such as the Council of Energy Resource Tribes (CERT) take a leading role in managing Indian energy and natural resources. Although gaming is controversial for a number of reasons, many Indian tribes have made it a centerpiece of their new economies—in the mid-1990s there were over 100 high-stakes operations and over 60 casinos taking in roughly $6 billion a year. Child welfare is largely under Indian control. Indian groups are engaged in cultural revitalization on any number of fronts. Nevertheless, unemployment, poverty, and suicide rates remain higher among Indian people than among any other single racial or ethnic group.

In 1995 there were roughly 18,000 native-owned businesses in Canada. Inuit people maintain active cooperatives, some based on art and craft production, as alternative ways to make a living. They have also developed radio and television programming in their native language (Inuktitut). There is a major effort on the part of local Inuit to prepare for the creation of Canada's newest territory, the mainly Inuit Nunavut, in 1999, and other native groups in Canada are busy working out their own versions of cultural revitalization, economic sufficiency, and political self-determination. In 1995, First Nations and the federal government began formulating a strategy designed ultimately to replace the Indian Act with local self-government.

Once independent sovereign nations, later treated as domestic dependent nations, native North Americans are once again on the road to controlling their own destinies. They face daunting and yet exciting challenges in their quest to create new political, social, and economic structures and ways of being based very much on the old ones. Furthermore, despite the long legacy of oppression, dependence, hatred, and fear, Native Americans and non-natives are working together effectively to resolve old conflicts. The success of these efforts will be based, at least in part, on a thorough understanding of the past and a firm commitment to move forward as full and equal partners into the future.

A few explanatory words about this volume are in order. The relatively little information I provide about early prehistory will be found mainly in the introductions to the regional chapters. The study of ancient aboriginal cultures is more technical and conjectural than that of their late prehistory or history. It is beyond the scope of this encyclopedia to discuss theoretical archaeology or anthropology or to delve deeply into the early prehistory of North America. That said, I hope that in the chapter introductions and in the "History" category of the individual entries I have provided enough information about prehistory for the reader to understand that Indian cultures did evolve over time. Readers who desire to learn more about the ancient North American past might find the information I have provided a helpful starting place from which to expand their research.

Material in the first section of each entry, "Historical Information," is meant to apply to precontact life, except as noted in the text. For example, when discussing the diet of Pueblo Indians I have excluded references to items such as melons, a non-native crop grown in early postcontact southwestern gardens. However, it is also true that in many cases no firm line can be drawn between "aboriginal" and "postcontact." Some groups were radically altered shortly following—or, in some cases, even prior to—direct contact with non-natives, whereas others continued relatively unchanged for decades or even centuries after they met non-natives or felt their influence. This being the case, and since

much of the early source material comes from non-native observers, the reader must keep in mind that what is meant to be a snapshot portrait of traditional society may in fact include some nonaboriginal elements.

Similarly, my use of the word "traditional" generally refers to the late prehistoric period, even when, strictly speaking, the prehistoric period might not be very traditional at all. An example: Even though many groups changed slowly and gradually between the period of their ancient past and the time when they first met non-natives, the Lakota altered their culture dramatically in the late prehistoric or even the early historic period as they moved from the forests and prairies onto the plains. Although they were Eastern Woodlands denizens for a far longer period than they were masters of the Great Plains, I have chosen to label the latter period as "traditional" because they are so clearly identified as a Plains group. Another way to think about this is that "traditional" generally refers to the named groups at around the time of contact, even though many of those groups did not technically exist as tribes in the ancient past.

The word "tribe" also requires some explanation. Most people are in the habit of referring to Indian groups, past and present, as tribes. This is partly because many Indians are grouped as tribes today and partly because the word denotes a form of social organization in opposition—with connotations implying both "inferior" and "outmoded"—to that of non-native communities. However, the word "tribe" represents a specific form of social organization. Tribes generally share descent, territory, political authority, history, and culture and consider themselves, to varying degrees, as a single, sovereign people.

Many traditional Indian societies were not tribes at all, in that they may have been highly decentralized or did not conceive of themselves as a unified entity. Many groups were actually organized as bands or as extended families. To refer to all aboriginal groups as tribes is to impose a modern idea retroactively on the past. Most, although not all, tribes were created in the postcontact period, under pressure to develop more centralized, European-style political structures. Although many Indians today use the word "tribe" to refer to their larger political structure, many also use words like "nation" and "people." I have tried to use the appropriate term wherever possible.

For space considerations I have generally excluded extinct groups, but I have included some for their particular historical significance. The Natchez and Yana, for instance, fall into this category, whereas groups like the Apalachee, though important, were omitted. Where I have discussed extinct peoples, I have merely sketched the traditional culture and omitted any reference to the nonexistent present. For tribes such as the Lumbee, about which only postcontact information is known, I have discussed the group's precontact antecedents under the "History" heading and proceeded directly to the contemporary information.

I have also omitted any discussion of mythology, an important and fascinating aspect of native cultures. Mythology occupies a vital place in the worldview of most people, perhaps particularly among those without written traditions. Mythology was essentially indistinguishable from what modern people might call "reality" or "history." Often tied to religious belief, mythology can be a window into the past and the means by which people make sense of the present. It seemed to me that I could discuss Native American religious beliefs and practices reasonably clearly and succinctly, but the task of conveying an understanding of mythology in the space of a few sentences seemed far more elusive. Unable to do justice to the topic, I chose to omit a discussion of mythology altogether. Instead, I commend the interested reader to sources that treat this subject with appropriate depth and perspective.

I would also like to point out that this encyclopedia is biased in favor of Indian groups that reside in the United States. Information on native Canadians is far less accessible, although this is beginning to change with the growth of electronic resources. Furthermore, although I have been able to provide very specific information about some topics, for others I have been less detailed and definitive. In such circumstances I hope the reader will find my material a helpful starting point for further research among more specialized resources. Finally, my aspirations to accuracy notwithstanding, caution is always advised regarding the interpretation of any data. Facts are usually appropriate only to a precise

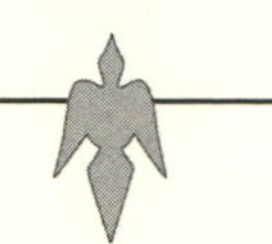

time and place, and the temptation to generalize is often irresistible. My choice of words and selection of material reflect my own particular perspective and biases.

Notes

1. The word "Indian" is, of course, technically a misnomer. Christopher Columbus thought he had reached India when he landed on the island of Hispaniola, so he called the natives Indians. There are many other terms by which the people refer to themselves, such as Native American, American Indian, native, band, and First Nation (used mainly in Canada). The use of one word or another sometimes implies a particular political position. Since the words "Indian" and "Native American" have gained widespread acceptance among the people to whom they refer, I generally use them to the exclusion of other labels.

2. "The people" is another term I often use when referring to Native Americans, since many aboriginal self-designations may be translated in this way.

3. B.C.E. stands for Before the Common Era. It replaces the conventional designation and its religious implications.

4. The term "non-native" is admittedly awkward. However, other words typically used to refer to those people who came to America after 1000 or 1492, such as "whites," Europeans," "Euro-Americans," and so forth, are factually misleading, and words like "invader" are too emotionally charged. "Non-native," at least, has the advantages of being both reasonably neutral and accurate.

5. Métis (Mā tā) are descendants of Indian women and non-native fur traders. In Canada they are officially considered nonstatus Indians and, with Indians and Inuit, constitute one of the three recognized categories of Native American people. On the prairies they combined Indian-style hunting and the settled habits of their European forebears. Today, most live in Manitoba, Canada, and among Chippewa communities in Montana.

6. Under the Indian Act, Canadian law recognizes several categories of Native Americans. "Status," or official Indians, are those registered under the Indian Act. However, not all Indians are registered; these people are "nonstatus" Indians. Status Indians may also be separated into "treaty" or "nontreaty" Indians, depending on the history of their particular group.

Chapter One

The Southwest

Above: A Navajo couple of the mid-1880s wears silver jewelry and traditionally styled clothing made of nontraditional materials. *Above, right:* Pimas lived in small, round, flat-topped, pole-framed structures, covered with grass and mud

Above: Mojave women carried babies on the hip, never on the back. *Right:* A group of Laguna men and women in the mid-1880s.

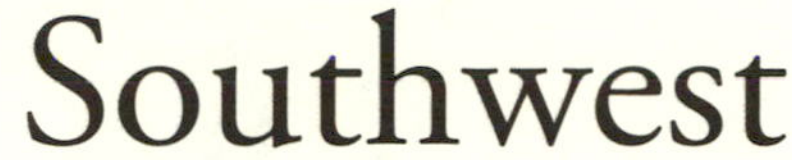

Southwest

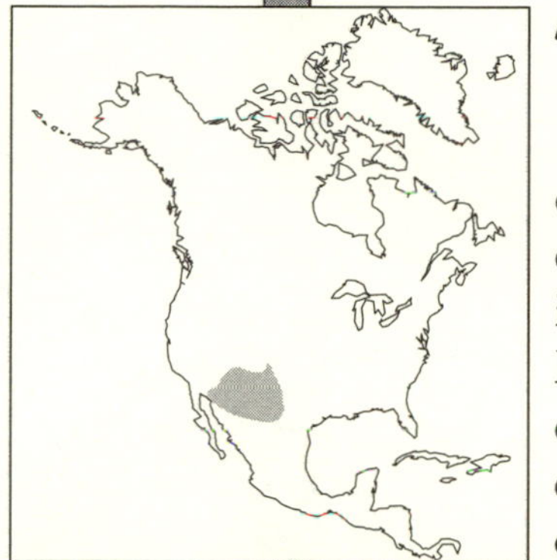

The southwestern United States, site of the continent's longest continuous human habitation outside of Mesoamerica, is also its most environmentally diverse region. Roughly including the states of Arizona and New Mexico, extreme southwest Colorado, extreme southern Utah and Nevada, and extreme southeast California, the region contains three major river basins: the Rio Grande, Colorado, and San Juan. It features colorful canyons, mesas, buttes, deserts, bluffs, rock formations, caves, plateaus, forests, and some of the highest mountains in the United States. Although some parts receive regular rainfall, the Southwest as a whole is distinguished by its aridity.

In addition to its great topographical variation, the region contains a striking divergence of climate, soils, and plant and animal life. Consequently, people living there evolved numerous traits to adapt to their specific local environment in order to survive and prosper. In time, different cultures grew out of these local adaptations. Thus, the region's environmental diversity is matched by an extraordinary linguistic and cultural mix.

Paradoxically, Southwest Indian cultures, although very diverse, also share several unifying factors. The most notable is a farming tradition and the use of ceramics; also important is the absence, in general, of state-level societies and large urban centers. Southwest Indians today take particular pride in their tenacity in retaining their land, religion, institutions, languages, and aesthetic traditions in the face of vigorous efforts over the centuries to eradicate indigenous culture, not to mention the people themselves.

The first people in what was to become the southwestern United States arrived between roughly 23,000 and 10,000 B.C.E. In about 9500 B.C.E. people hunted mammoth, giant bison, and other big game species now extinct. By around 5000 B.C.E.,

Native Americans of the Southwest

Four tribes of Arizona Indians, the Navajos, Papagos, Apaches, and Hopis, through their head men at an Indian conclave have banned the use of the traditional swastika symbol from all designs in their basket weaving and blanket making as a protest against Nazi "acts of oppression." Fred Kaboti, Hopi (left), and Miguel Flores, Apache, are about to sign a parchment document proclaiming the ban in 1940.

human activity had switched to hunting small desert animals and gathering seeds and wild plants. Both baskets and a flat milling stone were in use. Approximately 4,000 years ago, corn and other cultivated crops began coming into the region from Mesoamerica.

The Indians had completed a gradual process of agricultural transformation by roughly 500 C.E.; by that time squash, cotton, and beans had been introduced, and pottery was being produced. Farming had little immediate impact on the Southwest, but it did set in motion dramatic social and economic changes. Many peoples settled in villages, at first living in pit houses and later in buildings made of wood and/or adobe. (The pit houses, called kivas, continued to be used for ceremonial purposes, as they still are today.) As village life developed, people used pits and pottery to store foodstuffs, replaced spears and darts with bows and arrows, and used wells for water storage. With these adaptations, the four major southwestern cultural groups, each heavily influenced by Mesoamerican civilizations, were in place and poised to begin their major phases of development. These groups were the Anasazi, the Mogollon people, the Hohokam people, and the Hakataya.

The Anasazi lived on the sandstone plateaus and in the narrow canyons and broad valleys of the present-day Four Corners region, where northeast Arizona,

northwest New Mexico, and extreme southeast Utah and southwest Colorado meet. Since the region contains little water, the Anasazi refined techniques for dry farming. After their absorption of another cultural group, the Mogollon, the Anasazi built the well-known cliff dwellings at Mesa Verde, Chaco Canyon, and other sites. By around 1400, the Anasazi had abandoned most such sites, including the cliff dwellings, in the western part of their range in favor of the well-watered highland regions, Colorado Plateau waterways, and the Rio Grande Valley. Archaeologists have proposed several theories to explain why the Anasazi abandoned these sites. These include environmental factors (the region experienced a severe drought in the twelfth century), overfarming, decentralization, and natural migration patterns. The so-called Pueblo Indians of today are descended from the Anasazi.

On the edge of the Colorado Plateau, among the forested mountains, grasslands, and streams of present-day eastern Arizona to southwest New Mexico, lived the Mogollon people. Between roughly 900 to 1200, the Mimbres culture, part of the Mogollon, produced some of the best pottery north of Mexico. Some Mogollon people practiced irrigation. After about 1000, Mogollon culture underwent rapid changes in housing, arts, tools, and ceremonies, in part influenced by the Anasazi. By the fifteenth century, the dominant Anasazi had completely absorbed the Mogollon culture.

Sedentary farming based on large-scale irrigation distinguished the Hohokam people, who entered present-day southern Arizona around 300 B.C.E. They lived in the low desert west of the continental divide, primarily along the Gila and Salt Rivers. This region has extremely hot, dry summers and mild-to-cool winters with light rains. Only cactus and hardy trees like mesquite can survive in this desert. As early as several centuries B.C.E., the Hohokam had constructed an extensive and efficient system of irrigation canals. Unlike other southwestern societies, Hohokam houses were scattered according to no discernible plan. For much of their existence, the Hohokam built and occupied relatively large villages and towns, such as Snaketown (located in present-day Pinal County, Arizona), which was occupied roughly from 300 B.C.E. to at least 1100 C.E. Well-developed platform mounds and ball courts, used for religious and gaming purposes, suggest social ties to Mesoamerica. Concurrent with other southwestern peoples, the Hohokam underwent a significant population contraction around 1400 and, for undetermined reasons, vanished shortly thereafter. Their descendants are thought to be the present-day Pimas.

Finally, the Hakataya occupied an extensive area on both sides of the lower Colorado River. These deserts are even lower and hotter than those in Hohokam territory, although the region as a whole features extensive temperature variation. The Hakataya lived in small camps or villages of scattered units or in pueblos with small farm plots. Most of their structures were made of rock, in contrast to the Hohokam, who favored dirt. Relatively mobile, the Hakataya were culturally influenced by the Hohokam and other peoples. The Indian tribes that have occupied this territory in historic times, such as the Havasupai and the Mojave, probably descended from the Hakataya.

A fifth major southwestern cultural group, the Southern Athapaskans, arrived in the region from their ancestral home in west-central Canada late in the prehistoric period, probably in the 1400s, as bison-hunting nomads. These people settled in abandoned areas formerly populated by the Anasazi and Mogollon, although they eventually crowded other groups out of hunting and potential farming areas. Both Navajos and Apaches, the main groups of Southern Athapaskans, continued their nomadic occupations until the nineteenth century and later. The Navajos took up sheepherding, whereas the Apaches, having been pushed off the plains during the eighteenth century by the Comanche, became the most feared raiders of the Southwest.

Corn, beans, squash, cotton, and tobacco constituted the most important crops among prehistoric southwestern tribes. People living near rivers also ate fish as a major part of their diets. Cacti, mescal, screwbeans, mesquite, and grasses were important food sources in the south of the region; deer, mountain sheep, and small mammals were more important in the north. Those who produced little food or who had limited regular access to food raided, traded, or received agricultural products as gifts. The Athapaskans dominated hunting in the Southwest,

but only the Navajo hunted more than they gathered, and even for them, hunting was less important than farming as a source of food. Since growing food in the Southwest often required the use of many different environmental niches, a certain degree of mobility often accompanied even farming-based economies.

Southwestern tribes exchanged goods on a large scale throughout the historic and prehistoric periods. Food, shell beads, turquoise and other minerals, silver jewelry, buckskins, baskets and blankets, ritual items, and even spouses, ritualists, dancers, and medicine people were exchanged both within the region and with tribes in neighboring regions. Means of exchange included trade, mutual assistance, gambling and gaming, ceremonial redistribution, and raiding and plundering. Interestingly, although tribes did engage in localized raiding, they fought few or no organized wars, at least through the prehistoric period. In short, southwestern Indians devised complex systems of exchange to ensure, without risk to their independence and basic egalitarianism, that each community received approximately what it needed to survive and prosper.

The religious beliefs of southwestern Indians were, and are, rooted in the natural environment, as are the belief systems of other Native Americans. Some regional themes include the idea of a multilayered worldview, or cosmos, and a concept that the balance between natural and supernatural forces may be maintained through a specialist's access to power. According to this view, an intimate relationship exists between the natural and supernatural worlds. Time and space organize the former in such a way that it becomes endowed with supernatural, or sacred, meaning. Thus time may be thought of not only as linear but also spiritual, and place becomes something far more than where a certain "thing" is located.

Southwestern Indians probably developed complex annual ceremonies, with the goal of maintaining and promoting both individual and community health, as far back as 2,000 years ago. Such ceremonies, usually performed or orchestrated by specialists, were, and are, often accompanied by chanting, dancing, and music. A shaman might acquire special powers to communicate with and influence the supernatural by way of visions, dream-trances, or learning rituals. Such an approach offers a confrontation with the supernatural away from the human realm.

Conversely, sandpaintings and katsina performances, central to the ceremonialism of tribes such as the Navajo and Hopi, are designed to bring the supernatural into the human sphere. Katsinas are beings or spirits that live in or near water and may bring blessings such as rain, crops, and healing. According to tradition, katsinas visit various villages seasonally and inspire dances in their honor. Masks also figure prominently in katsina dancing and in other forms of southwestern Indian ceremonialism. Masking traditions are probably both of indigenous and of European origin. Typical ritual objects among Southwest Indians include feathers, tobacco, and corn pollen or meal.

As mentioned earlier, the fourteenth and fifteenth centuries saw the end of major residential use of large areas of the Southwest and significant population redistribution. New and colorful ceramics were also produced and distributed at this time. However, the following century was no less dramatic. In 1540, Francisco Vasquez de Coronado's northern expedition, seeking fabled golden cities, encountered the Zuñi pueblo of Hawikuh and established the first European presence in what is now the United States. Coronado retreated two years later, and no further Spanish exploration occurred until 1581. However, by the middle of the seventeenth century, the precontact southwestern Indian population of several hundred thousand or more had been reduced by 75 to 80 percent as a result of new diseases introduced by the Spaniards.

New Spain established its first regional colony in the Rio Grande Valley in 1598 and began to demand religious conversion, monetary tribute, and slave labor of the Indians. Such abuses led to revolts, culminating in the Pueblo revolt of 1680, led by Popé, which succeeded in expelling the Spanish from the valley for 12 years. When they returned, the Spanish had learned to moderate their demands somewhat, and the Pueblo Indians had learned to practice their own religion in secret while adopting a form of Catholicism.

Unlike the British colonists of North America, the Spanish did not attempt, at least initially, to settle

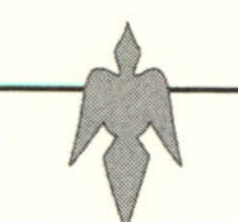

on Indian lands. Still, the Spanish influence throughout the region was enormous. In addition to Catholicism and a legacy of oppression, the Spaniards introduced a variety of technological innovations into the area, such as domestic animals, wool and textiles, wheat and other crops, metal tools, and firearms. Spanish subjugation of Southwest Indians ended in 1821 with the declaration of the modern state of Mexico. However, Mexico soon found itself in conflict with the new United States over land, a situation that led to war in 1845 and the Mexican cession between 1848 and 1853 of what is now the southwestern United States.

In short order, but especially following the Civil War, the United States began a military campaign to confine all Indians to reservations. By the 1880s it had largely achieved this goal. The more settled tribes, such as the Pueblos, fared the best during this period, retaining at least part of their traditional lands and largely avoiding the starvation, mass deportations, and attendant suffering that were the fate of the more nomadic and defiant tribes such as the Apaches and Navajos. Loss of land and liberty was almost always accompanied by new religious persecution, this time at the hands of Protestant missionaries.

Twentieth-century efforts to force southwestern Indians deeper into the margins of U.S. society have been realized in part. Statehood for the western states and the accompanying pressure to "open up" the reservations cut into the land base of many tribes. Government policies specifically encouraging the destruction of Indian identity, such as forced attendance at boarding schools and the criminalization of some ceremonies, presaged a decline of tribal structures as well as of weaving, ceramic arts, and other traditional crafts. Especially since World War II, subsistence-based economies have come under attack, and such limited wage work as exists, such as mining, is often associated with environmental degradation and its attendant health problems. Poverty and substance abuse remain endemic among Southwest Indians. The federal government remains reluctant to honor its treaty obligations.

On balance, however, Indian identity remains relatively strong in the late-twentieth-century southwestern United States. To a greater degree than Indians in most other regions, Southwest Native Americans have retained strong, secure reservations and pueblos, which provide the basis of a continuing and vital culture. The influx of non-Indians into the region has also aided the economy by bringing a boom in Native American arts and crafts. Mining leases often remain exploitative, yet they are an important source of income for many tribes, and Indians continue to seek more favorable lease terms. After decades of struggle, Indian education is coming more under local control, and the federal government is committed to some form of Indian self-determination. Indian populations are on the rise; the Navajo, at roughly 220,000, are the second-largest and one of the fastest-growing U.S. Indian tribes.

The Indians of the Southwest still grapple with the challenges of living and trying to succeed in an increasingly dominant Anglo/Hispanic culture while retaining their own heritage. Pressures on the youth are particularly acute. However, as they have for generations past, these people still demonstrate a marked ability to adapt, accepting what they will, or must, and rejecting much else. It is this dynamism, along with relatively unbroken access to their traditions and culture, that remains the key to their ongoing survival and growth.

Acoma Pueblo

Acoma (`Ä kə mä) is from the Acoma and Spanish *Acoma,* or Acú, meaning "the place that always was" or "People of the White Rock." "Pueblo" is from the Spanish for "village." It refers both to a certain style of Southwest Indian architecture, characterized by multistory buildings made of stone and adobe, and to the people themselves. The Rio Grande pueblos are known as eastern Pueblos; Zuñi, Hopi, and sometimes Acoma and Laguna are known as western Pueblos.

Location Acoma is located roughly 60 miles west of Albuquerque, New Mexico. The reservation consists of three main communities: Sky City (Old Acoma), Acomita, and McCartys. The traditional lands of Acoma Pueblo encompassed roughly five million acres. Of this, roughly 10 percent is included in the reservation.

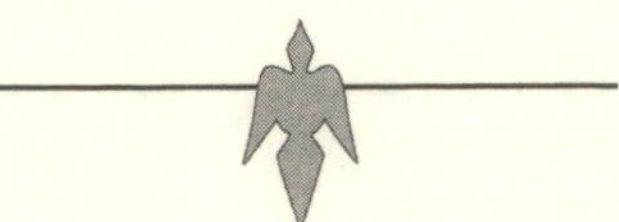

Population The pueblo's population was perhaps 5,000 in 1550. In 1990, 2,548 Indians lived at Acoma Pueblo; the tribal enrollment was roughly 4,000.

Language Acoma is a Western Keresan dialect.

Historical Information

History All Pueblo people are thought to be descended from Anasazi and perhaps Mogollon and several other ancient peoples. From them they learned architecture, farming, pottery, and basketry. Larger population groups became possible with effective agriculture and the development of ways to store food surpluses. Within the context of a relatively stable existence, the people devoted increasing amounts of time and attention to religion, arts, and crafts.

In the 1200s, the Anasazi abandoned their traditional canyon homelands in response to climatic and social upheavals. A century or two of migrations ensued, followed in general by the slow reemergence of their culture in the historic pueblos. Acoma Pueblo was established at least 800 years ago.

Acoma Pueblo was first visited by non-Indians in 1539, probably by Estevan, an advance scout of the Coronado expedition. The following year the people welcomed Hernando de Alvarado, also a member of Coronado's group. In 1598, Juan de Oñate arrived in the area with settlers, founding the colony of New Mexico. However, that year Acomas killed some of his representatives, for which they faced a Spanish reprisal in 1599: The Spanish killed 800 people, tortured and enslaved others, and destroyed the pueblo. The survivors rebuilt shortly thereafter and began a process of consolidating several farming sites near Acoma, which were later recognized by the Spanish as two villages.

Oñate carried on the process, already underway, of subjugating the local Indians; forcing them to pay taxes in crops, cotton, and work; and opening the door for Catholic missionaries to attack the Indians' religion. The Spanish renamed the pueblos with saints' names and began a program of church construction. At the same time, they introduced such new crops as peaches, wheat, and peppers into the region. In 1620, a royal decree created civil offices at each pueblo; silver-headed canes, many of which remain in use today, symbolized the governor's authority. In 1629, the Franciscan Juan Ramirez founded a mission at Acoma and built a huge church there.

The Pueblo Indians organized and instituted a general revolt against the Spanish in 1680. For years, the Spaniards had routinely tortured Indians for practicing traditional religion. They also forced the Indians to labor for them, sold Indians into slavery, and let their cattle overgraze Indian land, a situation that eventually led to drought, erosion, and famine. Popé of San Juan Pueblo and other Pueblo religious leaders planned the revolt, sending runners carrying cords of maguey fibers to mark the day of rebellion. On August 10, 1680, a virtually united stand on the part of the Pueblos drove the Spanish from the region. The Indians killed many Spaniards but refrained from mass slaughter, allowing them to leave Santa Fe for El Paso.

The Pueblos experienced many changes during the following decades: Refugees established communities at Hopi, guerrilla fighting continued against the Spanish, and certain areas were abandoned. By the 1700s, excluding Hopi and Zuñi, only Taos, Picuris, Isleta, and Acoma Pueblos had not changed locations since the arrival of the Spanish. Although Pueblo unity did not last, and Santa Fe was officially reconquered in 1692, Spanish rule was notably less severe from then on. Harsh forced labor all but ceased, and the Indians reached an understanding with the Church that enabled them to continue practicing their traditional religion. Acoma resisted further Spanish contact for several years thereafter, then bowed to Spanish power and accepted a mission.

In general, the Pueblo eighteenth century was marked by smallpox epidemics and increased raiding by the Apache, Comanche, and Ute. Occasionally Pueblo Indians fought with the Spanish against the nomadic tribes. The people practiced their religion, more or less in secret. During this time, intermarriage and regular exchange between Hispanic villages and Pueblo Indians created a new New Mexican culture, neither strictly Spanish nor Indian, but rather somewhat of a blend between the two.

Mexican "rule" in 1821 brought little immediate change to the Pueblos. The Mexicans stepped up what had been a gradual process of appropriating Indian

land and water, and they allowed the nomadic tribes even greater latitude to raid. As the presence of the United States in the area grew, it attempted to enable the Pueblo Indians to continue their generally peaceful and self-sufficient ways and recognized Spanish land grants to the Pueblos. Land disputes with neighboring Laguna Pueblo were not settled so easily, however.

During the nineteenth century, the process of acculturation among Pueblo Indians quickened markedly. In an attempt to retain their identity, Pueblo Indians clung even more tenaciously to their heritage, which by now included elements of the once-hated Spanish culture and religion. By the 1880s, railroads had largely put an end to the traditional geographical isolation of the pueblos. Paradoxically, the U.S. decision to recognize Spanish land grants to the Pueblos denied Pueblo Indians certain rights granted under official treaties and left them particularly open to exploitation by squatters and thieves.

After a gap of more than 300 years, the All Indian Pueblo Council began to meet again in the 1920s, specifically in response to a congressional threat to appropriate Pueblo lands. Partly as a result of the Council's activities, Congress confirmed Pueblo title to their lands in 1924 by passing the Pueblo Lands Act. The United States also acknowledged its trust responsibilities in a series of legal decisions and other acts of Congress. Still, especially after 1900, Pueblo culture was increasingly threatened by highly intolerant Protestant evangelical missions and schools. The Bureau of Indian Affairs also weighed in on the subject of acculturation, forcing Indian children to leave their homes and attend culture-killing boarding schools. In 1922, most Acoma children had been sent away to such schools.

Following World War II, the issue of water rights took center stage at most pueblos. Also, the All Indian Pueblo Council succeeded in slowing the threat against Pueblo lands as well as religious persecution. Making crafts for the tourist trade became an important economic activity during this period. Since the late nineteenth century, but especially after the 1960s, Pueblos have had to cope with onslaughts by (mostly white) anthropologists and seekers of Indian spirituality. The region is also known for its major art colonies at Taos and Santa Fe.

Religion In traditional Pueblo culture, religion and life are inseparable. To be in harmony with all of nature is the Pueblo ideal and way of life. The sun is seen as the representative of the Creator. Sacred mountains in each direction, plus the sun above and the earth below, define and balance the Pueblo world. Many Pueblo religious ceremonies revolve around the weather and are devoted to ensuring adequate rainfall. To this end, Pueblo Indians evoke the power of katsinas, sacred beings who live in mountains and other holy places, in ritual and dance. Each pueblo contains one or more kivas, religious chambers that symbolize the place of original emergence into this world.

In addition to the natural boundaries, Pueblo Indians created a society that defined their world by providing balanced, reciprocal relationships within which people connect and harmonize with each other, the natural world, and time itself. According to tradition, the head of each pueblo is the religious leader, or *cacique,* whose primary responsibility it is to watch the sun and thereby determine the dates of ceremonies. Especially in the eastern pueblos, most ceremonies are kept secret.

Government Pueblo governments derived from two traditions. Elements that are probably indigenous include the cacique, or head of the Pueblo, and the war captain, both chosen for life. These officials were intimately related to the religious structures of the pueblo and reflected the essentially theocratic nature of Pueblo government. A parallel but in most cases distinctly less powerful group of officials was imposed by the Spanish authorities. They generally dealt with external matters and included a governor, two lieutenant governors, and a council. In addition, the All Indian Pueblo Council, dating from 1598, began meeting again in the twentieth century.

Customs One mechanism that works to keep Pueblo societies coherent is a pervasive aversion to individualistic behavior. Children were traditionally raised with gentle guidance and a minimum of discipline. Pueblo Indians were generally monogamous, and divorce is relatively rare. The dead were prepared ceremonially and quickly buried. A vigil of four days and nights was generally observed.

Acoma Pueblo recognized roughly 20 matrilineal clans. The economy was basically a socialistic one, whereby labor was shared and produce was distributed equally. In modern times photography by outsiders is discouraged. At Acoma, a formal, traditional education system under the direction of the kiva headmen includes courses on human behavior, human spirit, human body, ethics, astrology, child psychology, oratory, history, music, and dance.

Dwellings Acoma Pueblo featured three rows of three-story, apartment-style dwellings, facing south on top of a 350-foot-high mesa. The lower levels were reserved mainly for storage. The buildings were constructed of adobe (earth and straw) bricks, with beams across the roof that were covered with poles, brush, and plaster. The roof of one level served as the floor of another. The levels were interconnected by ladders. As an aid to defense, the traditional design included no doors or windows; entry was through the roof. Baking ovens stood outside the buildings. Water was primarily obtained from two natural cisterns. Acoma also features seven rectangular pit houses, or kivas, for ceremonial chambers and clubhouses. The village plaza is the spiritual center of the village, where all the balanced forces of the world come together.

Diet Before the Spanish arrived, people living at Acoma Pueblo ate primarily corn, beans, and squash. *Mut-tze-nee* was a favorite thin corn bread. They also grew sunflowers and tobacco and kept turkeys. They hunted deer, antelope, and rabbits and gathered a variety of wild seeds, nuts, berries, and other foods. Favorite foods as of circa 1700 included a blue corn drink, corn mush, pudding, wheat cake, corn balls, paper bread, peach-bark drink, flour bread, wild berries, and prickly pear fruit. The Acomas also raised herds of sheep, goats, horses, and donkeys after the Spanish introduced these animals into the region.

Key Technology Irrigation techniques included dams and terraces. Pottery was an important technological adaptation, as was weaving baskets and cotton and tanning leather. Farming implements were made of stone and wood. Corn was ground using manos and metates.

Trade All Pueblos were part of extensive Native American trading networks that reached for a thousand miles in every direction. With the arrival of other cultures, Pueblo Indians also traded with the Hispanic American villages and then U.S. traders. At fixed times during summer or fall, enemies declared truces so that trading fairs might be held. The largest and best known was at Taos with the Comanche. Nomads exchanged slaves, buffalo hides, buckskins, jerked meat, and horses for agricultural and manufactured pueblo products. Pueblo Indians traded for shell and copper ornaments, turquoise, and macaw feathers. Trade along the Santa Fe Trail began in 1821. By the 1880s and the arrival of railroads, the Pueblos were dependent on many American-made goods, and the Native American manufacture of weaving and pottery declined and nearly died out.

Notable Arts In the Pueblo way, art and life are inseparable. Acoma women produced excellent pottery; men made fine weavings as well as silver necklaces. Songs, dances, and dramas also qualify as traditional arts. Many Pueblos experienced a renaissance of traditional arts in the twentieth century, beginning in 1919 with San Ildefonso pottery.

Transportation Spanish horses, mules, and cattle arrived at Acoma Pueblo in the seventeenth century.

Dress Men wore cotton kilts and leather sandals. Women wore cotton dresses and sandals or high moccasin boots. Deer and rabbit skin were also used for clothing and robes.

War and Weapons Though often depicted as passive and docile, most Pueblo groups regularly engaged in warfare. Weapons included clubs, darts, spears, and stones. The great revolt of 1680 stands out as the major military action, but they also skirmished at other times with the Spanish and defended themselves against attackers such as Apaches, Comanches, and Utes. They also contributed auxiliary soldiers to provincial forces under Spain and Mexico, which were used mainly against raiding Indians and to protect merchant caravans on the Santa Fe Trail. After the raiding tribes

An Acoma Pueblo woman (1910). Acoma women produced excellent pottery, while men made fine weavings as well as silver necklaces. Women wore cotton dresses and sandals or high moccasin boots.

began to pose less of a threat in the late nineteenth century, Pueblo military societies began to wither away, with the office of war captain changing to civil and religious functions.

Contemporary Information

Government/Reservations Acoma Pueblo, located on the aboriginal site in central New Mexico, has been continuously occupied for at least 800 years. The pueblo consists of roughly 500,000 acres of mesas, valleys, arroyos, and hills, with an average altitude of about 7,000 feet and roughly 10 inches of rain per year. Several major land purchases have added considerably to the land base since 1977. Only tribal members may own property; almost all enrolled members live on the pueblo. Acoma has been a member of the All Indian Pueblo Council since 1680. The *cacique* (a theological appointment, from the Antelope clan) appoints tribal council members, the governor, and his staff.

Economy Acomas grow alfalfa, oats, wheat, corn, chilies, melon, squash, vegetables, and some fruits. They also raise cattle. Acoma has coal, geothermal, and natural gas resources. Nearby uranium mines served as major employers until the 1980s. Since then, the tribe has provided most jobs. Tribal income is generated through fees charged tourists to enter Sky City (Old Acoma) as well as the associated visitor's center, and the tribe has plans to develop the tourist trade further. Arts and crafts (pottery, silverwork, leatherwork, and beadwork) also generate some individual income.

Legal Status The Pueblo of Acoma is a federally recognized tribal entity.

Daily Life Although the project of retaining a strong Indian identity is a difficult one in the late twentieth century, Pueblo people have strong roots, and in many ways the ancient rhythms and patterns continue. Many Pueblo Indians, though nominally Catholic, have fused pieces of Catholicism onto a core of traditional beliefs. Since the 1970s control of schools has been a key in maintaining their culture. Health problems, including alcoholism and drug use, continue to plague the Pueblos. Indian Health Service hospitals often cooperate with native healers.

At Acoma, many of the old ceremonies are still performed; the religion and language are largely intact, and there is a palpable and intentional continuity with the past. Nineteen clans remain, each organized by social function. Almost all people speak Acoma and English; many older people speak Spanish as well. Many people live in traditional adobe houses, with outside ovens, but increasingly one finds cement-block ranch and frame houses with exterior stucco. Most people live below the mesa, in the villages of Acomita or McCartys.

Acoma remains a relatively closed society, like other Keresan pueblos, especially as regards religious matters. Acoma shares a junior/senior high school and a full-service hospital with neighboring Laguna Pueblo. Since the uranium mines closed, Acoma has suffered high unemployment rates. The mines have also left a legacy of radiation pollution, resulting in some health problems and the draining of the tribal fishing lake.

Apache, Chiricahua

Chiricahua (Chē rə `kä wä), a name taken from their stronghold in the Chiricahua Mountains, in southeast Arizona, and Apache (U `pa chē), from the Zuñi word *Apachu,* meaning "enemy." The Apache call themselves *Ndee,* or *Dine'é* (Di `nə), "the People."

Location The Apache arrived in the Southwest from present-day Canada around 1400. By the early 1600s, the Chiricahua were living in southwestern New Mexico, southeastern Arizona, and northern Mexico. Late-twentieth-century Chiricahua communities include the Mescalero Apache Reservation in southeastern New Mexico and a presence at Fort Sill, Oklahoma.

Population Approximately 3,000 Chiricahua Apache lived in their region in the early seventeenth century. Of roughly 25,000 Apaches nationwide in 1992, some 3,500, including Chiricahua, Mescalero, and Lipan Apache, lived on the Mescalero Reservation. Several hundred lived off-reservation. A small number of Chiricahua Apaches still live in Oklahoma.

Language Apaches speak Southern Athapaskan, or Apachean.

When soldiers killed a White Mountain Apache medicine man in 1881, Geronimo, a Southern Band shaman pictured here in 1886, led a group of Chiricahua away from the disease-ridden San Carlos Reservation.

Historical Information

History Ancestors of today's Apache Indians began the trek from Asia to North America relatively late, in roughly 1000 B.C.E. Most of this group, which included the Athapaskans, was known as the Nadene. By 1300, the group that was to become the Southern Athapaskans (Apaches and Navajos) broke away from other Athapaskan tribes and began migrating southward, reaching the American Southwest around 1400 and crystallizing into separate cultural groups.

The Apaches generally filtered into the mountains surrounding the Pueblo-held valleys. This process ended in the 1600s and 1700s, with a final push southward and westward by the Comanches. Before contact with the Spanish, the Apaches were relatively peaceful and may have engaged in some agricultural activities.

Thrust into contact with the Spanish, the Apaches, having acquired horses, began raiding Spanish and Pueblo settlements. This dynamic included trading as well as raiding and warfare, but the Spanish habit of selling captured Apaches into slavery led to Apache revenge and increasingly hostile conditions along the Spanish frontier. After 1821, the Mexicans put a bounty on Apache scalps, increasing Apache enmity and adding to the cycle of violence in the region.

Following the war between Mexico and the United States (1848), the Apaches, who did their part to bring misery to Mexico, assumed that the Americans would continue to be their allies. They were shocked and disgusted to learn that their lands were now considered part of the United States and that the Americans planned to "pacify" them. Having been squeezed by the Spanish, the Comanches, the

Mexicans, and now miners, farmers, and other land-grabbers from the United States, the Apache were more than ever determined to protect their way of life.

Some Chiricahua bands tried to stay out of trouble in the 1850s by planting fields under the supervision of federal agents, but when raiding resumed as a result of broken promises of food and protection, all sides were caught in a spiral of violence. Mangas Coloradas, a peaceful Mimbreño chief, turned to war after he was bullwhipped by U.S. miners in 1860. Cochise, son-in-law of Mangas Coloradas and leader of the Central Band of Chiricahua, began a guerrilla war along the Butterfield Trail after whites killed some of his men. Cochise began as Central Band war chief, but by force of personality and integrity he eventually claimed authority over other Chiricahua bands as well. Resistance continued until 1874, when Cochise, hungry and exhausted, surrendered. He could no longer control other Chiricahua bands, though, and their raiding continued.

Meanwhile, the U.S. policy of concentration via forced marches resulted in thousands of Chiricahua and Western Apaches living on the crowded and disease-ridden San Carlos Reservation. There, a handful of dissident chiefs, confined in chains, held out for the old life of freedom and self-respect. Victorio fled in 1877, taking 350 Indians with him. He battled the army and Apache scouts until he was killed in Mexico in 1880. Nana, his successor, continued the raids until joining the Mescalero Reservation.

When soldiers killed a White Mountain Apache medicine man in 1881, Geronimo, a Southern Band shaman, led a group of Chiricahua away from San Carlos. In 1883 he agreed to return peacefully, but two years later, when soldiers banned the Indians' ceremonial drink, called "tiswin," the Chiricahua fled again. In 1886 Geronimo surrendered in Mexico but on the way back to the United States escaped with 36 other Apaches. Their final surrender, and the effective end of Apache military resistance, came several months later: General Nelson Miles and one-quarter of the U.S. Army, plus Apache scouts, were needed to find and capture them. Geronimo regretted his surrender until his death as a prisoner of war in 1909.

As punishment for the freedom-fighting activities of some of their group, the U.S. government sent all the Chiricahuas, including those who had been living peacefully at San Carlos, to prison in Alabama and Florida, where roughly one-quarter of them died over the following few years. Since the citizens of New Mexico opposed the return of the Apaches to San Carlos, those Chiricahuas who remained alive were sent in 1894 to the Kiowa Reservation at Fort Sill, Oklahoma, where they took up cattle raising and farming. In 1913, the Chiricahua were granted full freedom, although no reservation. Although some remained at Fort Sill, most moved back to New Mexico and life on the Mescalero Reservation.

Cattle raising and timber sales proved lucrative in the early twentieth century. Eventually, day schools replaced the hated, culture-killing boarding schools. By the late 1940s, every family had a house, and the economy at Mescalero was relatively strong. The reservation is managed cooperatively with the Mescalero and the Lipan Apache.

Religion Apache religion is based on a complex mythology and features numerous deities. The sun is the greatest source of power. Culture heroes, like White-Painted Woman and her son, Child of the Water, also figure highly, as do protective mountain spirits *(ga'an)*. The latter are represented as masked dancers (probably evidence of Pueblo influence) in certain ceremonies, such as the four-day girls' puberty rite. (The boys' puberty rite centered on raiding and warfare.)

Supernatural power is both the goal and the medium of most Apache ceremonialism. Shamans facilitate the acquisition of power, which could be used in the service of war, luck, rainmaking, or life-cycle events. Power could be evil as well as good, however, and witchcraft, as well as incest, was an unpardonable offense. Finally, Apaches believe that since other living things were once people, we are merely following in the footsteps of those who have gone before.

Government Traditionally, the Chiricahua knew little tribal cohesion and no central political authority. They were a tribe based on common territory, language, and culture. As much central authority as existed was

found in the local group (35 to 200 people), composed of extended families. Its leader, or chief, enjoyed authority because of personal qualities, such as persuasiveness and bravery, often in addition to ceremonial knowledge. (All the famous Apache "chiefs" were local group leaders.) Decisions were taken by consensus. One of the chief's most important functions was to minimize friction among his people.

Local groups joined to form three Chiricahua bands. One was the Eastern, or Cihene (Red Paint People), also known as Mimbreños, Coppermine, Warm Spring, or Mogollon Apaches; the second was the Central (Chokonen). The third band was the Southern (Nednai, Enemy People, also called Pinery or Bronco Apaches), who lived mainly in Mexico. Some intermarriage occurred between bands.

Customs Women were the anchors of the Apache family. Residence was matrilocal. Besides the political organization, society was divided into a number of matrilineal clans. Apaches in general respected the elderly and valued honesty above other qualities.

Gender roles were clearly defined but not rigidly enforced. Women gathered, prepared, and stored food; built the home; carried water; gathered fuel; cared for the children; tanned, dyed, and decorated hides; and wove baskets. Men hunted, raided, and waged war. They also made weapons and were responsible for their horses and equipment. They also made musical instruments.

Girls as well as boys practiced with the bow and arrow, sling, and spear, and both learned to ride expertly. Although actual marriage ceremonies were brief or nonexistent, the people practiced a number of formal preliminary rituals, designed to strengthen the idea that a man owed deep allegiance to his future wife's family. Out of deference, married men were not permitted to speak directly with their mothers-in-law. Divorce was relatively easy to obtain.

All Apaches had a great fear of ghosts. Chiricahua who died had their faces painted red and were buried the same day. Their personal possessions were burned or destroyed, including their house and favorite horse.

Dwellings Chiricahua Apaches lived in dome-shaped brush wikiups, which they covered with hides in bad weather. The doors always faced east. Eastern Chiricahua sometimes used tipis.

Diet Chiricahua Apaches were primarily hunters and gatherers. They hunted buffalo prior to the sixteenth century, and afterward they continued to hunt deer, elk, antelope, rabbits, and other game. They did not eat bear, turkey, or fish.

Wild foods included agave; cactus shoots, flowers, and fruit; berries; seeds; nuts; honey; and wild onions, potatoes, and grasses. Nuts and seeds were often ground into flour. The agave or century plant was particularly important. Baking its base in rock-lined pits for several days yielded mescal, a sweet, nutritious food, which was dried and stored.

Traditional farm crops were obtained from the Pueblos by trade or raid. The Chiricahua, particularly the Eastern Band, also practiced some agriculture: Corn, for instance, was used to make tiswin, a weak beer.

Key Technology Items included baskets (pitch-covered water jars, cradles, storage containers, and burden baskets); gourd spoons, dippers, and dishes; and a sinew-backed bow. The people made musical instruments out of gourds and hooves. The so-called Apache fiddle, a postcontact instrument, was played with a bow on strings. Moccasins were sewn with plant fiber attached to mescal thorns.

Trade Trading partners included Pueblo and Hispanic villages, as well as some Plains tribes, especially before the sixteenth century.

Notable Arts Traditional arts included fine basketry, pottery, and tanned hides.

Transportation The horse was introduced into the region in the seventeenth century.

Dress The Chiricahua traditionally wore buckskin clothing and moccasins. As they acquired cotton and later wool through trading and raiding, women tended to wear two-piece calico dresses, with long, full skirts and long blouses outside the skirt belts. They occasionally carried knives and, later, ammunition belts. Girls wore their hair over their ears, shaped around two willow hoops. Some older women wore their hair Plains-style, parted in the middle with two braids. Men's postcontact styles included calico shirts, muslin breechclouts with belts, cartridge belts, moccasins, and headbands.

War and Weapons Historically, the Apache made formidable enemies. Raiding was one of their most important activities. The main purpose of raiding, in which one sought to avoid contact with the enemy, was to gain wealth and honor. It differed fundamentally from warfare, which was undertaken primarily for revenge. Chiricahua Apaches did not generally take scalps, not did they maintain formal warrior societies.

Contemporary Information

Government/Reservations Most Chiricahua Apaches live on the Mescalero Reservation, in southeast New Mexico. The reservation contains roughly 460,000 acres of land and is home in addition to the Mescalero and Lipan Apaches. The 1992 population was 3,511. Residents gained title to the land in 1922. After 1934, the tribal business committee began functioning as a tribal council. In 1964, a new constitution defined the Mescalero tribe without reference to the original band.

Roughly 100 (as of 1992) Chiricahua Apaches still live at Fort Sill, Oklahoma. They are represented by an elected seven-member business committee formed under the auspices of the Indian Reorganization Act (IRA).

Economy Important industries include logging, cattle raising, and the Inn of the Mountain Gods.

Legal Status Federally recognized tribal entities include the Mescalero Apache Tribe; the Apache Tribe of Oklahoma; and the Fort Sill Apache Tribe of Oklahoma.

Daily Life Intermarriage between Mescalero and Lipan Apaches has tended to blur the distinction between the once-separate tribes on the Mescalero reservation. Up to three-quarters of the people still speak Apache, although the dialect is more Mescalero than Chiricahua or Lipan. The written Apache language is also taught in reservation schools. Some young women still undergo the traditional puberty ritual, and there is a marked interest in crafts and other traditions. The reservation confronts relatively few social problems, despite its high un- and underemployment. Traditional dancing by costumed mountain spirits now coincides with the July Fourth celebration and rodeo. Fort Sill Apaches participate in pan-Indian activities.

Wendall Chino has been the most important leader of the Mescalero tribe since the 1950s. He is mainly known for diversifying the tribal economy, particularly with a ski slope and a resort. In an extremely controversial 1991 decision, he agreed to study the possibility of accepting high-level nuclear waste on the reservation.

Apache, Cibecue

See Apache, Western

Apache, Fort Sill

See Apache, Chiricahua

Apache, Jicarilla

Jicarilla (Hē kä `rē ä) is from the Spanish for "little basket," or "chocolate basket," and Apache is from the Zuñi word *Apachu,* meaning "enemy." The Apache call themselves *Ndee,* or *Dine'é* (Di `nə), "the People."

Location The Apache arrived in the Southwest from present-day Canada around 1400. By the early 1600s, the Jicarilla were living from the Chama Valley in present-day New Mexico east to present-day western Oklahoma. The Jicarilla Reservation is located in northwest New Mexico, west of the Chama Valley.

Population Approximately 800 Jicarilla Apaches lived in their region in the early seventeenth century. Of roughly 25,000 Apaches nationwide, roughly 3,000 Jicarilla lived on their reservation in 1992.

Language Jicarillas spoke a dialect of Southern Athapaskan, or Apachean.

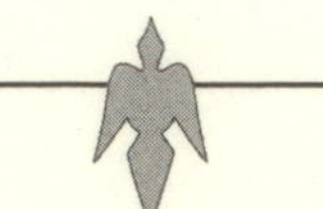

Historical Information

History Ancestors of today's Apache Indians began the trek from Asia to North America in roughly 1000 B.C.E. Most of this group, which included the Athapaskans, was known as the Nadene. By 1300, the group that was to become the Southern Athapaskans (Apaches and Navajos) broke away from other Athapaskan tribes and began migrating southward, reaching the American Southwest around 1400 and crystallizing into separate cultural groups. Before contact with the Spanish, the Apaches were relatively peaceful and may have engaged in some agricultural activities.

In the mid–eighteenth century, the Apache asked for Spanish protection against the Comanche, who were pressing them from the north and east. Despite a promise to settle down and become Christian, the Spanish refused the request. The Comanche, who had acquired guns from the French (the Spanish did not officially sell or trade guns to Indians), so disrupted Apache agriculture and life on the plains that the Apache migrated into the mountains surrounding the Pueblo-held valleys. One Jicarilla group continued to live as far south as the Texas plains until around 1800.

Having acquired horses, the Apache increased their contact with Spanish and Pueblo settlements. This dynamic included trading as well as raiding and warfare, but the Spanish habit of selling captured Apaches into slavery led to Apache revenge and increasingly hostile conditions along the Spanish frontier, effectively establishing the northern limit of New Spain at about Santa Fe. After 1821, the Mexicans put a bounty on Apache scalps, increasing Apache enmity and adding to the cycle of violence in the region.

In an effort to settle its northern areas, Mexico in the early nineteenth century made large land grants to its citizens. In 1841, one such grant delivered 1.7 million acres of Jicarilla land to two Mexicans. U.S. recognition of this grant was to complicate the establishment of a Jicarilla reservation later in the century.

Following the war between Mexico and the United States (1848), the Apaches, who did their part to bring misery to Mexico, assumed that the Americans would continue as allies. They were shocked and disgusted to learn that their lands were now considered part of the United States and that the Americans planned to "pacify" them. Having been squeezed by the Spanish, the Comanches, the Mexicans, and now miners, farmers, and other land-grabbers from the United States, the Apache were more than ever determined to protect their way of life.

Increased military activity led to a treaty in 1851 that called for the cessation of hostilities on all sides and, in exchange for aid, bound the Jicarilla to remain at least 50 miles from all settlements. When U.S. promises of food and protection went unkept, however, the Jicarilla returned to raiding, and the region was plunged into a spiral of violence. Another treaty in 1855 created agencies: Options for the Jicarilla now included either begging for food at the agency or raiding.

In the 1860s, the tribe escaped confinement at the deadly Bosque Redondo (Fort Sumner) only because the camp failed before they could be rounded up. By 1873 they were the only southwestern tribe without an official reservation. At about this time, leaders of the two Jicarilla bands, the Ollero and the Llanero, began consulting with each other, creating a new tribal consciousness. They sent a joint delegation to Washington, D.C., where they lobbied for a reservation, but in 1883 the tribe was moved to the Mescalero Reservation. Finding all the good land already taken, the Jicarilla began shortly to drift back north to their old lands. In 1887, the government granted them an official home.

Unfortunately, the climate on the new reservation was unfavorable for farming, and in any case non-Indians owned whatever good arable land existed. This, plus the existence of individual allotments and centralized government control, slowed economic progress. The tribe sold some timber around the turn of the century. In 1903, the government established a boarding school in Dulce, the reservation capital, but turned it into a sanatorium in 1918 following a tuberculosis epidemic (90 percent of the Jicarilla had tuberculosis by 1914). The Dutch Reformed Church of America opened a school in 1921.

A major addition to the reservation in 1907 provided the Jicarilla with land appropriate to herding sheep. They began this activity in the 1920s, and the tribe soon realized a profit. Livestock owners and the

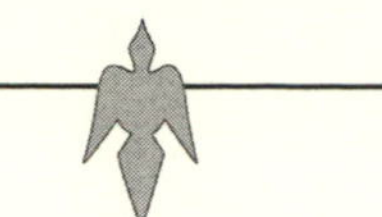

"progressive," proacculturation group tended to be Ollero, whereas the Llaneros were the farmers, the conservatives, and guardians of tradition. In the early 1930s bad weather wiped out most of the sheep herd, although by 1940 it had largely been rebuilt. Also by this time the people were generally healthy again, and acculturation quickened.

The postwar years saw a huge increase in tribal income from oil and gas development. With part of this money the tribe bought out most non-Indian holdings on the reservation. Education levels, health, and morale all rose. In the 1950s, a decline in the sheep industry brought much of the population to live in Dulce. The tribe began per capita payments at that time, partly to offset a lack of economic opportunities in Dulce. This action kept families going until more help arrived with the federal programs of the 1960s as well as an increasingly diversified economy. In the 1970s the tribe won $9 million in land claims.

Religion Apache religion is based on a complex mythology and features numerous deities. Most deities are seen as personifications of natural forces. The sun is the greatest source of power. Culture heroes, like White-Painted Woman and her son, Child of the Water, also figure highly, as do protective mountain spirits *(ga'an)*. The latter are represented as masked dancers (probably a sign of Pueblo influence) in certain ceremonies, such as the girls' puberty rite. Apaches believe that since other living things were once people, we are merely following in the footsteps of those who have gone before.

Supernatural power is both the goal and the medium of most Apache ceremonialism. They recognize two categories of rites: personal/shamanistic and long-life. In the former, power is derived from an animal, a celestial body, or another natural phenomenon. When power appears to a person and is accepted, rigorous training as a shaman follows. Shamans also facilitate the acquisition of power, which may be used in the service of war, luck, rainmaking, or life-cycle events. Power may be evil as well as good, however, and sickness and misfortune could be caused by the anger of a deity or by not treating properly a natural force. Witchcraft, as well as incest, was an unpardonable offense.

Long-life rites were taught by elders and connected to mythology. The most difficult was the bear dance, a curing rite that lasts for four days and nights and features a bear impersonator, shamans, songs, sacred clowns, and dancing. Another such ceremony is the (young boys') relay race, actually a combined ceremony and harvest festival. It derives from mythological concepts of sun and moon and also the duality of the food supply. The race is between the Olleros—sun—animals and the Llaneros—moon—plants. Other important ceremonies include the four-day girls' puberty ceremony, a five-day holiness or curing ceremony, and hunting, cultivation, and rainmaking ceremonies.

Government Traditionally, the Jicarilla knew little tribal cohesion and no central political authority. They were a tribe based on common territory, language, and culture. As much central authority as existed was found in the local group, composed of extended families. Local groups were loosely associated as bands, which made up the tribe. Local group leaders, or chiefs, enjoyed authority because of personal qualities, such as persuasiveness and bravery, often in addition to ceremonial knowledge. Decisions were taken by consensus. One of the chief's most important functions was to mitigate friction among his people.

Beginning around the nineteenth century, the Jicarilla recognized two distinct bands. The Llanero lived in the eastern Sangre de Cristo Mountains in adobe houses with nearby farms. From the pueblos, especially Taos, they learned pottery and social and religious customs. The Ollero gave up plains life somewhat later. In addition to hunting buffalo, they had picked up some Plains technology, such as tipis, parfleches, and travois.

Customs Women were the anchors of the Apache family. Residence was matrilocal. Besides the political organization, society was divided into a number of matrilineal clans. Apaches in general respected the elderly and valued honesty above most other qualities. The Jicarilla more than most Apaches were influenced by the Plains and Pueblo tribes.

Gender roles were clearly defined but not rigidly enforced. Women gathered, prepared, and stored food; built the home; carried water; gathered fuel; cared for the children; tanned, dyed, and decorated hides; and wove baskets. Men hunted, raided, and waged war. They also made weapons, were responsible for their horses and equipment, and made musical instruments. For boys, training for the hunt began early; the first hunt was roughly equal to a puberty ceremony.

Girls as well as boys practiced with the bow and arrow, sling, and spear, and both learned to ride expertly. Although actual marriage ceremonies were brief or nonexistent, the people practiced a number of formal preliminary rituals, designed to strengthen the idea that a man owed deep allegiance to his future wife's family. Out of deference, married men were not permitted to speak directly with their mothers-in-law. Divorce was unusual though relatively easy to obtain. The mother's brother played an important role in the raising of his nephews and nieces.

All Apaches had a great fear of ghosts. Jicarilla who died were buried the same day. Their personal possessions were burned or destroyed, including their house and favorite horse. They pictured the afterworld as divided into two sections, a pleasant land for good people and a barren one for witches.

Dwellings Jicarilla Apaches lived in dome-shaped, pole-framed wikiups, covered with bark or thatch and with skins in cold weather. They also used hide tipis when on a buffalo hunt.

Diet Jicarilla Apaches were primarily hunters and gatherers. They hunted buffalo into the seventeenth century, and afterward they continued to hunt deer, mountain sheep, elk, antelope, rabbits, and other game. They did not eat bear, turkey, or fish.

Wild foods included agave shoots, flowers, and fruit; berries; seeds; nuts; honey; and wild onions, potatoes, and grasses. Nuts and seeds were often ground into flour. The agave or century plant was particularly important. Baking its base in rock-lined pits for several days yielded mescal, a sweet, nutritious food, which was dried and stored.

In the late 1600s they learned farming from pueblos, and by the early nineteenth century they farmed river bottomlands and built irrigation ditches, growing some corn, beans, squash, pumpkins, peas, wheat, and melons. When supplies ran low, crops were obtained from the Pueblos by trade or raid.

Key Technology Items included baskets (pitch-covered water jars, cradles, storage containers, and burden baskets); gourd spoons, dippers, and dishes; and a sinew-backed bow. The people made musical instruments out of gourds and hooves. The so-called Apache fiddle, a postcontact instrument, was played with a bow on strings. Moccasins were sewn with plant fiber attached to mescal thorns. The Jicarilla used a sinew-backed bow, which was more effective than the Pueblo wooden bow.

Trade Trading partners included Pueblo and Hispanic villages, as well as some Plains tribes, especially before the seventeenth century.

Notable Arts Traditional arts included fine basketry, pottery, and tanned hides. The Jicarilla also excelled in beadwork, buckskin tanning, leather work, pottery, and making ceremonial clay pipes.

Transportation The horse was introduced into the region in the seventeenth century.

Dress The Jicarilla traditionally wore buckskin clothing decorated with beadwork and whitened, Plains-style moccasins. As they acquired cotton and later wool through trading and raiding, women tended to wear two-piece calico dresses, with long, full skirts and long blouses outside the skirt belts. They occasionally carried knives and ammunition belts. Girls wore their hair over their ears, shaped around two willow hoops. Some older women wore hair Plains-style, parted in the middle with two braids. Male hairstyles included a middle part, braids, and bangs with a back knot, Pueblo-style. Men also liked large earrings.

War and Weapons Historically, the Apache made formidable enemies. Raiding was one of their most important activities. The main purpose of raiding, in which one sought to avoid contact with the enemy, was to gain wealth, such as horses, and honor. It differed fundamentally from warfare, which was

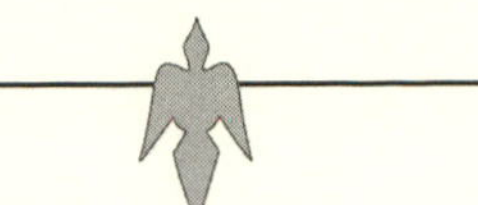

undertaken primarily for revenge. Jicarilla war leaders occasionally took scalps but only after the leaders had been ritually purified. Formal warrior societies did not exist. Like hunting, raiding and warfare were accompanied by complex rituals and rules, to which boys were introduced early. The Jicarillas' traditional enemies included the Comanche, Cheyenne, Arapaho, and Navajo; allies included the Utes and Pueblo peoples.

Contemporary Information

Government/Reservations The Jicarilla Reservation, established in 1887, is located in northwest New Mexico, west of Chama. It contains about 742,000 acres of land. The 1992 population was 3,100. The reservation headquarters is in Dulce. The tribe organized a formal government and adopted a constitution in 1937. Its first elected tribal council consisted mostly of traditional leaders.

Economy Oil and gas resources, which the tribe is moving to buy, still provide much income. Other important economic assets include sheep, timber, and big game. The tribe and the government provide some employment opportunities.

Legal Status The Jicarilla Apache are a federally recognized tribal entity.

Daily Life Roughly 70 percent of Jicarillas still practice some form of traditional religion. Fewer than half speak Jicarilla, and most who do are older. There has been some revival of traditional pottery and basketry arts, but Dulce and the reservation are increasingly part of the regional economy. Recreation facilities include an Olympic-sized, heated indoor pool. A large number of Jicarillas are Christian. Indians in Dulce live in relatively modern homes or trailers, with water and sewer hookups. Most tribal members live on the reservation.

Apache, Lipan

Lipan (`Lē pan) may mean "warriors of the mountains." Apache comes from the Zuñi word *Apachu,* meaning "enemy." The Apache call themselves *Ndee,* or *Dine'é* (Di `nə), "the People."

Location The Apache arrived in the Southwest from present-day Canada around 1400. By about 1700, the Lipan were living on the south-central Texas plains, as far south as Texas's Colorado River. Today they live on the Mescalero Reservation, in southeast New Mexico.

Population Approximately 100 Lipan Apache lived in their region around 1900, although possibly up to ten times as many lived there prior to contact with non-natives. Of roughly 25,000 Apaches nationwide in 1990, 3,500, including Chiricahua, Mescalero, and Lipan Apache, lived on the Mescalero Reservation; several hundred lived off-reservation.

Language The people spoke a dialect of Southern Athapaskan, or Apachean.

Historical Information

History Ancestors of today's Apache Indians began the trek from Asia to North America in roughly 1000 B.C.E. Most of this group, which included the Athapaskans, was known as the Nadene. By 1300, the group that was to become the Southern Athapaskans (Apaches and Navajos) broke away from other Athapaskan tribes and began migrating southward, reaching the American Southwest around 1400 and crystallizing into separate cultural groups.

Before contact with the Spanish, the Apaches were relatively peaceful and may have engaged in some agricultural activities. By about 1700 the Lipan had become separated from the Jicarilla and had migrated into the central and south Texas plains. They had also acquired horses and had become expert buffalo hunters and raiders of the western plains from Kansas to Mexico. Caddoan villages felt the wrath of Lipan raiders and slavers until they acquired guns from French traders and were able to drive the Lipan back into Texas.

A Lipan request for Spanish protection against the Comanche, who were pressing them from the north and east, resulted in the establishment of a mission in 1757, which the Comanche promptly destroyed the following year. By the late eighteenth century, the Comanche had forced most Lipans from Texas into New Mexico to join other Apache bands there.

By the early nineteenth century, the remaining Lipans had established good terms with the Texans, serving as their scouts, guides, and trading partners. Following the war between Mexico and the United States (1848), the Apaches, who did their part to bring misery to Mexico, assumed that the Americans would continue as allies. Instead, the Texans adopted an extermination policy, and those Lipans who escaped went to live in Mexico. In the late 1870s, some Lipans fought with the Chiricahua leader Victorio in his last stand against the United States and captivity. He and they were killed in Mexico.

In 1873, the U.S. government had granted the Mescalero Apache a small reservation surrounding the Sierra Blanca Mountains. The Mescaleros absorbed Apache refugees and immigrants in hopes that the increased numbers would help them gain the elusive title to their land. In 1903, 37 Mexican Lipan Apaches arrived, followed in 1913 by 187 Chiricahuas from Fort Sill, Oklahoma. Eventually, largely through intermarriage, these peoples evolved into the modern Mescalero community.

The United States engaged in extreme repression and all-out assault on traditional culture at the end of the nineteenth century. Cattle raising and timber sales proved lucrative in the early twentieth century. Eventually, day schools replaced the hated, culture-killing boarding schools. By the late 1940s, every family had a house, and the Mescalero economy was relatively stable. The reservation is managed cooperatively with the Mescalero and the Chiricahua Apache.

Religion Apache religion is based on a complex mythology and features numerous deities. Most deities are seen as personifications of natural forces. The sun is the greatest source of power. Culture heroes, like White-Painted Woman and her son, Child of the Water, also figure highly, as do protective mountain spirits *(ga'an)*. The latter are represented as masked dancers (probably an indication of Pueblo influence) in certain ceremonies, such as the girls' puberty rite. Apaches believe that since other living things were once people, we are merely following in the footsteps of those who have gone before.

Supernatural power, which pervades the universe, may be utilized for human purposes through ritual procedures and personal revelations. It is both the goal and the medium of most Apache ceremonialism. The ultimate goal of supernatural power was to facilitate the maintenance of spiritual strength and balance in a world of conflicting forces. Apaches recognize two categories of rites: personal/shamanistic and long-life. In the former, power is derived from an animal, a celestial body, or another natural phenomenon. When power appears to a person and is accepted, rigorous training as a shaman follows. Shamans also facilitate the acquisition of power, which may be used in the service of war, luck, rainmaking, or life-cycle events. Power may be evil as well as good, however, and sickness and misfortune could be caused by the anger of a deity or by not treating properly a natural force. Witchcraft, as well as incest, was an unpardonable offense.

Long-life rites were taught by elders and connected to mythology. They were also closely associated with various song cycles. Among the most important and complex is the girls' puberty ceremony. Lasting for four days and nights, this ceremony involved masked dancers, feasting, games, rituals in a ceremonial tipi, and a long and intricate song cycle. Other important rites included cradle, first steps, first haircut, and boys' puberty ceremonies. Once common, the Native American Church has now declined in popularity.

Government Traditionally, the Lipan knew little tribal cohesion and no central political authority. They were a tribe based on common territory, language, and culture. As much central authority as existed was found in the local group (composed of extended families). Its leader, or chief, enjoyed authority because of personal qualities, such as persuasiveness and bravery, often in addition to ceremonial knowledge. (All the famous Apache "chiefs" were local group leaders.) Decisions were taken by consensus. One of the chief's most important functions was to mitigate friction among his people.

Customs Women were the anchors of the Apache family. Residence was matrilocal. Besides the political organization, society was divided into a number of matrilineal clans. Apaches in general respected the elderly and valued honesty above most other qualities.

Gender roles were clearly defined but not rigidly enforced. Women gathered, prepared, and stored food; built the home; carried water; gathered fuel; cared for the children; tanned, dyed, and decorated hides; and wove baskets. Men hunted, raided, and waged war, although women sometimes took part in antelope hunts and rabbit surrounds. The men also made weapons and were responsible for their horses and equipment. The male puberty ceremony revolved around war and raiding. Girls as well as boys practiced with the bow and arrow, sling, and spear, and both were expert riders.

Although actual marriage ceremonies were brief or nonexistent, the people practiced a number of formal preliminary rituals, designed to strengthen the idea that a man owed deep allegiance to his future wife's family. Out of deference, married men were not permitted to speak directly with their mothers-in-law. Divorce was relatively easy to obtain. The mother's brother played an important role in the life of his sister and her children.

All Apaches had a great fear of ghosts. Death was repressed as much as possible. So great was their fear of the dead that outsiders sometimes buried their dead. Perhaps paradoxically, however, the elderly were venerated. The afterlife was pictured as twofold in nature: a pleasant land for the good but a barren one for witches. The Lipan pictured the underworld, home of the dead, as the place of their original emergence.

Dwellings Lipan Apaches generally lived in hide tipis. Occasionally, and especially when they were moved off the plains, they used dome-shaped brush wikiups, which they covered with grass thatch or with hides in bad weather.

Diet Lipan Apaches were primarily hunters and gatherers. They hunted buffalo into the eighteenth century, and afterward they continued to hunt deer, elk, antelope, rabbits, and other game. They ate few birds and did not eat fish, coyote, snake, or owl.

Wild foods included agave; cactus shoots, flowers, and fruit; berries; seeds; nuts; honey; and wild onions, potatoes, and grasses. Nuts and seeds were often ground into flour. The agave or century plant was particularly important. Baking its base in rock-lined pits for several days yielded mescal, a sweet, nutritious food, which was dried and stored. The Lipan moved often to follow animal migrations as well as the ripening of their wild foods. Traditional farm crops were obtained by trade or raid and by practicing some agriculture.

Key Technology Like the Plains tribes, the Lipan used hide rather than baskets or pottery for most receptacles. Most of their tools were also buffalo based.

Trade Trading partners included Plains tribes and Hispanic villages, especially before the eighteenth century. At that time their main surplus item was buffalo meat and hides.

Notable Arts Traditional arts included tanned hides and some basketry.

Transportation Lipans acquired horses in the seventeenth century. Prior to that time dogs had drawn the travois. To ford rivers, they used rafts or boats of skins stretched over a wooden frame.

Dress Men wore buckskin shirts, breechclouts, leggings, and hard-soled, low-cut moccasins. They braided and wrapped their hair. Women also dressed in buckskin and braided their hair. They also plucked their eyebrows.

War and Weapons Historically, the Apache made formidable enemies. After they acquired horses, raiding became one of their most important activities. The main purpose of raiding, in which one sought to avoid contact with the enemy, was to gain wealth and honor. It differed fundamentally from warfare, which was undertaken primarily for revenge and which, like hunting, was accompanied by complex rituals and rules. From the sixteenth century on, the Lipan were in periodic conflict with Utes, Comanches, Spanish, and Mexicans. The Lipan were less concerned than other Apache about contamination from a dead enemy, and, like Plains Indians, they considered it a virtue to be the first to strike a fallen foe (count coup). Military equipment included shields with painted buckskin covers, bows and arrows, quivers, bow

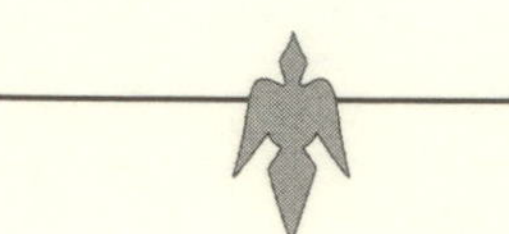

covers, wrist guards, spears, rawhide slings, flint knives, and war clubs.

Contemporary Information

Government/Reservations The Mescalero Reservation, in southeast New Mexico, contains roughly 460,000 acres of land and is home to the Chiricahua and Mescalero Apaches in addition to the Lipan. The 1992 population was 3,511. After 1934, the tribal business committee began functioning as a tribal council. In 1964, a new constitution defined the Mescalero tribe without reference to the original band.

Economy Important industries include logging, cattle raising, and the Inn of the Mountain Gods.

Legal Status The Mescalero are a federal corporation and a federally recognized tribal entity. They obtained title to the reservation in 1922.

Daily Life Intermarriage has tended to blur the distinction between the once-separate tribes on the Mescalero Reservation. Up to three-quarters of the people still speak Apache, although the dialect is more Mescalero than Chiricahua or Lipan. The written Apache language is also taught in reservation schools. Some young women still undergo the traditional puberty ritual, and there is a marked interest in crafts and other traditions. The reservation confronts relatively few social problems, despite its high un- and underemployment. Traditional dancing by costumed mountain spirits now coincides with the July Fourth celebration and rodeo. Many Mescaleros are Catholic. Children have attended public schools since 1953. A tribal scholarship fund exists to help with college expenses. The Lipan language is virtually extinct.

Apache, Mescalero

Mescalero (Mes kä `lē rō), from mescal, a food derived from the agave or century plant and an important part of their diet. Apache comes from the Zuñi *Apachu,* or "enemy." The Apache call themselves *Ndee,* or *Dine'é* (Di `nə), "the People."

Location The Mescalero traditionally lived from east of the Rio Grande to the Pecos and beyond to the west Texas plains. The Mescalero Reservation is located in southeast New Mexico, northeast of Alamogordo.

Population Perhaps 3,000 Mescaleros lived in the region prior to contact with non-natives. Of roughly 25,000 Apaches nationwide in 1990, 3,500, including Chiricahua, Mescalero, and Lipan Apaches, lived on the Mescalero Reservation; several hundred lived off-reservation.

Language Mescalero is a Southern Athapaskan, or Apachean dialect.

Historical Information

History Ancestors of today's Apache Indians began the trek from Asia to North America in roughly 1000 B.C.E. Most of this group, which included the Athapaskans, was known as the Nadene. By 1300, the group that was to become the Southern Athapaskans (Apaches and Navajos) broke away from other Athapaskan tribes and began migrating southward, reaching the American Southwest around 1400 and crystallizing into separate cultural groups.

The Apaches generally filtered into the mountains surrounding the Pueblo-held valleys. This process ended in the 1600s and 1700s, with a final push southward and westward by the Comanches. Before contact with the Spanish, the Apaches were relatively peaceful and may have engaged in some agricultural activities.

Thrust into contact with the Spanish, the Apaches, having acquired horses, began raiding Spanish and Pueblo settlements. This dynamic included trading as well as raiding and warfare, but the Spanish habit of selling captured Apaches into slavery led to Apache revenge and increasingly hostile conditions along the Spanish frontier. After 1821, the Mexicans put a bounty on Apache scalps, increasing Apache enmity and adding to the cycle of violence in the region.

The Mescalero had moved into southern New Mexico by the early sixteenth century and had acquired horses at about the same time. They and the Jicarilla raided (and traded with) Spanish settlements and pueblos on the Rio Grande, and after 1680 they controlled the Camino Real, the main route from El Paso to Santa Fe. They hunted buffalo on the southern plains and were its de facto masters.

After 1725, the Comanche (who had access to French guns) forced the Apaches into the mountains, ending their life on the plains and inaugurating an era of semipoverty. Still, they battled the Spanish, who alternately tried to fight and settle them. An 1801 treaty, reaffirmed by the Mexicans in 1832, granted the Mescalero rations and the right to land in Mexico and New Mexico. Even so, their relations with the Mexicans were tenuous.

Following the Mexican War (1848), during which they had sided with the Texans, the Mescalero assumed that the Americans would continue as allies. They were shocked and disgusted to learn that their lands were now considered part of the United States and that the Americans planned to "pacify" them. Having been squeezed by the Spanish, the Comanches, the Mexicans, and now miners, farmers, and other land-grabbers from the United States, they were more than ever determined to protect their way of life.

Some Mescalero bands tried to stay out of trouble in the 1850s by planting fields under the supervision of federal agents, but when raiding resumed owing to broken promises of food and protection, all sides became caught up in a spiral of violence. By 1863, General James Carleton forced them off their informal reservation in the Sierra Blanca Mountains to Fort Sumner, at Bosque Redondo, on the Pecos. It was a concentration camp: Living with 9,000 Navajos, the Mescalero endured overcrowding, disease, bad water, and starvation. Two years later they escaped into the mountains, where they lived for seven years.

In 1873, the U.S. government granted the Mescalero a small reservation surrounding the Sierra Blanca, which included their traditional summer territory. This land made a harsh home in winter, however, and in any case it was too small for hunting and gathering. That decade was marked by disease, white incursions, and violence directed against them. In 1880, in retaliation after some Mescaleros joined the Chiricahua in their wars against the United States, the army placed the Mescaleros under martial law, disarmed them, and penned them in a corral filled deep with manure.

By the mid-1880s, gambling had replaced the traditional raiding. Missionaries arrived, as did a day school, which the Indians hated for separating the children from their elders. Meanwhile, their population plummeted from 3,000 in 1850 to 431 in 1888. These were years marked by dependency, agent thievery, tyranny, disease, starvation and malnourishment, and uncertainty about the status of their reservation. Still, they survived the epidemics and efforts to steal their reservation by turning it into a national park (a move that proved unsuccessful in the long run).

The Mescaleros had absorbed Apache refugees and immigrants in hopes that increased numbers would help them gain the elusive title to their land. In 1883, the Jicarilla arrived, although they left by 1887. In 1903, 37 Lipan Apaches arrived, followed in 1913 by 187 Chiricahuas from Fort Sill, Oklahoma. Eventually, largely through intermarriage, all evolved into the modern Mescalero community.

The United States engaged in extreme repression and all-out assault on traditional culture at the end of the nineteenth century. Cattle raising and timber sales proved lucrative in the early twentieth century. Eventually, day schools replaced the hated, culture-killing boarding schools. By the late 1940s, every family had a house, and the reservation economy was relatively strong. The reservation is managed cooperatively with the Chiricahua and the Lipan Apache.

Religion Apache religion is based on a complex mythology and features numerous deities. Most deities are seen as personifications of natural forces. The sun is the greatest source of power. Culture heroes, like White-Painted Woman and her son, Child of the Water, also figure highly, as do protective mountain spirits *(ga'an)*. The latter are represented as masked dancers (probably a sign of Pueblo influence) in certain ceremonies, such as the girls' puberty rite. Apaches believe that since other living things were once people, we are merely following in the footsteps of those who have gone before.

Supernatural power is both the goal and the medium of most Apache ceremonialism. The ultimate goal of supernatural power was to facilitate the maintenance of spiritual strength and balance in a world of conflicting forces. Apaches recognize two

categories of rites: personal/shamanistic and long-life. In the former, power is derived from an animal, a celestial body, or another natural phenomenon. When power appears to a person and is accepted, rigorous training as a shaman follows. Shamans also facilitate the acquisition of power, which may be used in the service of war, luck, rainmaking, or life-cycle events. Power may be evil as well as good, however, and sickness and misfortune could be caused by the anger of a deity or by not treating properly a natural force. Witchcraft, as well as incest, was an unpardonable offense.

Long-life rites were taught by elders and connected to mythology. Among the most important and complex was the girls' puberty ceremony. Lasting for four days and nights, this ceremony involved masked dancers, feasting, games, rituals in a ceremonial tipi, and a long and intricate song cycle. Other important rites included cradle, first steps, first haircut, and boys' puberty ceremonies. The Native American Church has recently declined in popularity.

Government Traditionally, the Mescalero knew little tribal cohesion and no central political authority. They were a tribe based on common territory, language, and culture. As much central authority as existed was found in the local group (not more than 30 extended families). Its leader, or chief, enjoyed authority because of personal qualities, such as persuasiveness and bravery, often in addition to ceremonial knowledge. (All the famous Apache "chiefs" were local group leaders.) Decisions were taken by consensus. One of the chief's most important functions was to mitigate friction among his people.

Customs Women were the anchors of the Apache family. Residence was matrilocal. Besides the political organization, society was divided into a number of matrilineal clans. Apaches in general respected the elderly and valued honesty above most other qualities.

Gender roles were clearly defined but not rigidly enforced. Women gathered, prepared, and stored food; built the home; carried water; gathered fuel; cared for the children; tanned, dyed, and decorated hides; and wove baskets. Men hunted, raided, and waged war. They also made weapons and were responsible for their horses and equipment. The male puberty ceremony revolved around war and raiding. Girls as well as boys practiced with the bow and arrow, sling, and spear, and both were expert riders.

Although actual marriage ceremonies were brief or nonexistent, the People practiced a number of formal preliminary rituals, designed to strengthen the idea that a man owed deep allegiance to his future wife's family. Out of deference, married men were not permitted to speak directly with their mothers-in-law. Divorce was relatively easy to obtain.

All Apaches had a great fear of ghosts. Death was repressed as much as possible. Mescaleros who died had their faces painted red and were buried quickly. Their personal possessions were burned or destroyed, including their house and favorite horse, and their names were not spoken again. The afterworld was pictured as a paradise.

Dwellings Mescalero Apaches lived in dome-shaped brush wikiups, which they covered with grass thatch or with hides in bad weather. The doors always faced east. When on the plains they used tipis.

Diet Mescalero Apaches were primarily hunters and gatherers. They hunted buffalo into the eighteenth century, and afterward they continued to hunt deer, elk, antelope, rabbits, and other game. They did not eat fish, coyote, snake, or owl.

Wild foods included agave shoots, flowers, and fruit; berries; seeds; nuts; honey; and wild onions, potatoes, and grasses. Nuts and seeds were often ground into flour. The agave or century plant was particularly important. Baking its base in rock-lined pits for several days yielded mescal, a sweet, nutritious food, which was dried and stored.

Traditional farm crops were obtained from the Pueblos by trade or raid. The Mescalero also practiced some agriculture: Corn, for instance, was used to make tiswin, a weak beer.

Key Technology Items included baskets (pitch-covered water jars, cradles, storage containers, and burden baskets); gourd spoons, dippers, and dishes; leaf brushes; sheep-horn ladles; rock pounders; and a sinew-backed bow. The people made musical instruments out of gourds and hoofs. The one-stringed, so-called Apache fiddle, a postcontact

instrument, was played with a bow. Moccasins were sewn with plant fiber attached to mescal thorns. Mescaleros also used parfleches, which they originally acquired from Plains tribes.

Trade Trading partners included Pueblo and Hispanic villages, as well as some Plains tribes, especially before the eighteenth century. At that time their main surplus item was buffalo meat and hides.

Notable Arts Traditional arts included fine basketry, pottery, and tanned hides.

Transportation Mescaleros acquired horses in the sixteenth century. Prior to that time dogs had drawn the travois. To ford rivers, the Mescalero used rafts or boats of skins stretched over a wooden frame.

Dress Men wore buckskin shirts, breechclouts, leggings, and hard-soled, low-cut moccasins. They braided and wrapped their hair. Women also dressed in buckskin and braided their hair. They also plucked their eyebrows.

War and Weapons Historically, the Apache made formidable enemies. After they acquired horses, raiding became one of their most important activities. The main purpose of raiding, in which one sought to avoid contact with the enemy, was to gain wealth and honor. It differed fundamentally from warfare, which was undertaken primarily for revenge and which, like hunting, was accompanied by complex rituals and rules. Only the war leader, who had undergone a special purifying ritual, took scalps. The Mescalero did not maintain formal warrior societies. Military equipment included shields with painted buckskin covers, bows and arrows, quivers, bow covers, wrist guards, spears, rawhide slings, flint knives, and war clubs.

Contemporary Information

Government/Reservations The Mescalero Reservation, in southeast New Mexico, contains roughly 460,000 acres of land and is home in addition to the Chiricahua and Lipan Apaches. The 1992 population was 3,511. After 1934, the tribal business committee began functioning as a tribal council. In 1964, a new constitution defined the Mescalero tribe without reference to the original band.

Economy Important industries include logging, cattle raising, and the Inn of the Mountain Gods.

Legal Status The Mescalero are a federal corporation and a federally recognized tribal entity. They obtained title to the reservation in 1922.

Daily Life Intermarriage has tended to blur the distinction between the once-separate tribes on the Mescalero Reservation. Up to three-quarters of the people still speak Apache, although the dialect is more Mescalero than Chiricahua or Lipan. The written Apache language is also taught in reservation schools. Some young women still undergo the traditional puberty ritual, and there is a marked interest in crafts and other traditions. The reservation confronts relatively few social problems, despite its high un- and underemployment. Traditional dancing by costumed mountain spirits now coincides with the July Fourth celebration and rodeo. Many Mescaleros are Catholic. Children have attended public schools since 1953. A tribal scholarship fund exists to help with college expenses.

Apache, Mimbreño

See Apache, Chiricahua

Apache, Northern Tonto

See Apache, Western

Apache, San Carlos

See Apache, Western

Apache, Southern Tonto

See Apache, Western

Apache, Western

Apache comes from the Zuni *Apachu,* meaning "enemy." These people are properly known as *Ndee,* or *Dineé* (Di `nə), "the People." Western Apache is a somewhat artificial designation given to an Apache tribe composed, with some exceptions, of bands living in Arizona. After 1850 these bands were primarily the San Carlos, White Mountain, Tonto (divided into Northern and Southern Tonto by anthropologists), and Cibecue.

Location Traditionally, Western Apache bands covered nearly all but the northwesternmost quarter of Arizona. Their territory encompassed an extreme ecological diversity. Today's reservations include Fort Apache (Cibecue and White Mountain); San Carlos (San Carlos); Camp Verde, including Clarkdale and Middle Verde (mostly Tonto; shared with the Yavapai); and Payson. Tonto also live in the Middle Verde, Clarkdale, and Payson communities.

Population Perhaps 5,000 Western Apaches (all groups) lived in Arizona around 1500. In 1992 the populations were as follows: San Carlos, 7,562 (including some Chiricahuas); Fort Apache, 12,503; Camp Verde, 650 (with the Yavapai); Payson, 92; Fort McDowell (Apache, Mojave, Yavapai), 765.

Language Apaches spoke Southern Athapaskan, or Apachean.

Historical Information

History Ancestors of today's Apache Indians began the trek from Asia to North America in roughly 1000 B.C.E. Most of this group, which included the Athapaskans, was known as the Nadene. By 1300, the group that was to become the Southern Athapaskans (Apaches and Navajos) broke away from other Athapaskan tribes and began migrating southward, reaching the American Southwest around 1400 and crystallizing into separate cultural groups.

The Apaches generally filtered into the mountains surrounding the Pueblo-held valleys. This process ended in the 1600s and 1700s, with a final push southward and westward by the Comanches. Before contact with the Spanish, the Apaches were relatively peaceful and may have engaged in some agricultural activities. The Western Apache bands avoided much contact with outsiders until the mid–eighteenth century. The People became semisedentary with the development of agriculture, which they learned from the Pueblos.

Having acquired the horse, the Western Apache groups established a trading and raiding network with at least a dozen other groups, from the Hopi to Spanish settlements in Sonora. Although the Spanish policy of promoting docility by providing liquor to Native Americans worked moderately well from the late eighteenth century through the early nineteenth, Apache raids remained ongoing into the nineteenth century. By 1830, the Apache had drifted away from the presidios and resumed a full schedule of raiding.

Following the war between Mexico and the United States (1848), the Apaches, who did their part to bring misery to Mexico, assumed that the Americans would continue to be their allies. The Apaches were shocked and disgusted to learn that their lands were now considered part of the United States and that the Americans planned to "pacify" them. Having been squeezed by the Spanish, the Comanches, the Mexicans, and now miners, farmers, and other land-grabbers from the United States, some Apaches were more than ever determined to protect their way of life.

Throughout the 1850s most of the anti-Apache attention was centered on the Chiricahua. The White Mountain and Cibecue people never fought to the finish with the Americans; out of range of mines and settlements, they continued their lives of farming and hunting. When Fort Apache was created (1863), these people adapted peacefully to reservation life and went on to serve as scouts against the Tontos and Chiricahuas.

The Prescott gold strike (1863) heralded a cycle of raid, murder, and massacre for the Tonto. By 1865 a string of forts ringed their territory; they were defeated militarily eight years later. A massacre of San Carlos (Aravaipa) women in 1871 led to Grant's "peace policy," a policy of concentration via forced marches. The result was that thousands of Chiricahuas and Western Apaches lived on the crowded and disease-ridden San Carlos Reservation. There, a handful of dissident chiefs, confined in chains, held out for the old life of freedom and self-respect. The Chiricahua Victorio bolted with 350 followers and remained at large and raiding for years. More fled in 1881. By 1884 all had been killed or had returned, at least temporarily. In general, the Western Apaches remained peaceful on the reservations while corrupt agents and settlers stole their best land.

The White Mountain people joined Fort Apache in 1879. As the various bands were spuriously lumped together, group distinctions as well as traditional identity began to break down. A man named Silas John Edwards established a significant and enduring religious cult at Fort Apache in the 1920s. Though not exactly Christian, it did substitute a new set of ceremonies in place of the old ones, contributing further to the general decline of traditional life. In 1918 the government issued cattle to the Apaches; lumbering began in the 1920s. In 1930, the government informed the Apaches that a new dam (the Coolidge) would flood old San Carlos. All residents were forced out, and subsistence agriculture ended for them. The Bureau of Indian Affairs (BIA) provided them with cattle and let all Anglo leases expire; by the late 1930s these Indians were stockmen.

Religion Apache religion is based on a complex mythology and features numerous deities. The sun is the greatest source of power. Culture heroes, like White-Painted Woman and her son, Child of the Water, also figure highly, as do protective mountain spirits *(ga'an).* In fact, the very stories about these subjects are considered sacred. The latter are represented as masked dancers (probably evidence of Pueblo influence) in certain ceremonies, such as the four-day girls' puberty rite. (The boys' puberty rite centered on raiding and warfare.)

Supernatural power, inherent in certain plants, animals, minerals, celestial bodies, and weather, is both the goal and the medium of most Apache ceremonialism. These forces could become involved, for better or worse, in affairs of people. The ultimate goal of supernatural power was to facilitate the maintenance of spiritual strength and balance in a world of conflicting forces. Shamans facilitated the acquisition of power, which could, by the use of songs, prayers, and sacred objects, be used in the service of war, luck, rainmaking, or life-cycle events. Detailed and extensive knowledge was needed to perform ceremonials; chants were many, long, and very complicated. Power could also be evil as well as good and was to be treated with respect. Witchcraft, as well as incest, was an unpardonable offense. Finally, Apaches believed that since other living things were once people, we are merely following in the footsteps of those who have gone before.

Government Each of the Western Apache tribes was considered autonomous and distinct, although intermarriage did occur. Tribal cohesion was minimal; there was no central political authority. A "tribe" was based on a common territory, language, and culture. Each was made up of between two and five bands of greatly varying size. Bands formed the most important Apache unit, which were in turn composed of local groups (35–200 people in extended families, themselves led by a headman) headed by a chief. The chief lectured his followers before sunrise every morning on proper behavior. His authority was based on his personal qualities and perhaps his ceremonial knowledge. Decisions were taken by consensus. One of the chief's most important functions was to mitigate friction among his people.

Customs Women were the anchors of the Apache family. Residence was matrilocal. Besides the political organization, society was divided into a number of matrilineal clans, which further tied families together. Apaches in general respected the elderly and valued honesty above most other qualities. Gender roles were clearly defined but not rigidly enforced. Women gathered, prepared, and stored food; built the home; carried water; gathered fuel; cared for the children; tanned, dyed, and decorated hides; and wove baskets. Men hunted, raided, and waged war. They also made weapons, were responsible for their horses and equipment, and made musical instruments. Western Apaches generally planted crops and gathered food in summer, harvested and hunted in fall, and returned to winter camps for raiding in winter.

Girls as well as boys practiced with the bow and arrow, sling, and spear, and both learned to ride expertly. The four-day girls' puberty ceremony was a major ritual (at which mountain spirits appeared) as well as a major social event. Traditional games, such as hoop and pole, often also involved supernatural powers. Marriages were often arranged, but the couple had the final say. Although actual marriage ceremonies were brief or nonexistent, the people practiced a number of formal preliminary rituals, designed to strengthen the idea that a man owed deep allegiance to his future wife's family. Out of deference, married men were not permitted to speak directly with their mothers-in-law. Divorce was relatively easy to obtain.

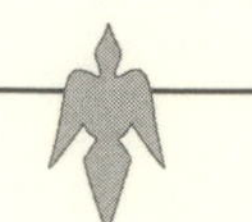

All Apaches had a great fear of ghosts. A dead person's dwelling was abandoned, and his or her name was never spoken again. Burial followed quickly.

Dwellings Women built the homes. Most Western Apache people lived in dome-shaped wikiups, made of wood poles covered with bear grass, which they covered with hides in bad weather. Brush ramadas were used for domestic activities.

Diet Western Apache groups were primarily hunters and gatherers. They hunted buffalo prior to the sixteenth century, and afterward they continued to hunt deer, antelope, mountain lion, elk, porcupine, and other game. They did not eat bear, turkey, or fish.

Wild foods included agave shoots, flowers, and fruit; berries; seeds; nuts; honey; and wild onions, potatoes, and grasses. Nuts and seeds were often ground into flour. The agave or century plant was particularly important. Baking its base in rock-lined pits for several days yielded mescal, a sweet, nutritious food, which was dried and stored. About one-quarter of their diet (slightly more among the Cibecue) came from agricultural products (corn, beans, and squash), which they both grew and raided the pueblos for. They also drank a mild corn beer called *tulupai.*

Key Technology Items included excellent baskets (pitch-covered water jars, cradles, storage containers, and burden baskets); gourd spoons, dippers, and

Most Western Apache lived in dome-shaped wickiups made of wood poles covered with bear grass. Outside this brush hut are Apache baskets. Other fine arts included cradle boards and pottery.

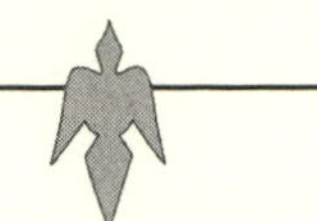

dishes; and a sinew-backed bow. Storage bags were also made of buckskin. The People made musical instruments out of gourds and hooves. The so-called Apache fiddle, a postcontact instrument, was played with a bow on strings. Moccasins were sewn with plant fiber attached to mescal thorns.

Trade By the mid–eighteenth century, the horse had enabled the Apache to establish a trading and raiding network with at least a dozen other groups, from the Hopi and other Pueblos to Spanish settlements in Sonora. From the Spanish, the Apache acquired (in addition to the horse) the lance, saddle and stirrup, bridle, firearms, cloth, and playing cards.

Notable Arts Fine arts included basketry (bowls, storage jars, burden baskets, and pitch-covered water jugs) designed with vegetable dyes, hooded cradle boards, and black or dark gray pottery.

Transportation Dogs served as beasts of burden before Spanish horses arrived in the seventeenth century.

Dress The Western Apache traditionally wore buckskin clothing and moccasins. As they acquired cotton and later wool through trading and raiding, women tended to wear two-piece calico dresses, with long, full skirts and long blouses outside the skirt belts. They occasionally carried knives and ammunition belts. Girls wore their hair over their ears, shaped around two willow hoops. Some older women wore hair Plains-style, parted in the middle with two braids. Men's postcontact styles included calico shirts, muslin breechclouts with belts, cartridge belts, thigh-high moccasins, and headbands; women wore Mexican-style cloth dresses. Blankets as well as deerskin coats were used in winter.

War and Weapons Historically, the Apache made formidable enemies. Raiding was one of their most important activities. The purpose of raiding, in which one sought to avoid contact with the enemy, was to gain wealth and honor as well as to assist the needy. It differed fundamentally from warfare, which was undertaken primarily for revenge. Western Apaches raided the Maricopa, Pai, O'odham, and Navajo (trading and raiding). Their allies included the Quechan, Chemehuevi, Mojave, and Yavapai. Since the Apache abhorred mutilation, scalping was not a custom, although a killing required revenge. At least one shaman accompanied all war parties. Mulberry, oak, or locust bows were sinew backed; arrow tips were of fire-hardened wood or cane. Other weapons included lances, war clubs, and rawhide slings.

Contemporary Information

Government/Reservations San Carlos (1871; 1.87 million acres) and Fort Apache (1871; 1.66 million acres) Reservations were divided administratively in 1897. Both accepted reorganization under the Indian Reorganization Act (1934) and elect tribal councils. Other Western Apache reservations and communities include Camp Verde (shared with the Yavapai; 640 acres), Fort McDowell (a Yavapai reservation also shared with Mojave Indians; 24,680 acres), Clarkdale, and Payson (Yavapai-Apache; 85 acres; established 1972).

Economy Important economic activities at San Carlos include cattle ranching, farming, logging, mining (asbestos and other minerals) leases, basket making, and off-reservation wage work. In general the economy at San Carlos is depressed. At Fort Apache the people engage in cattle ranching, timber harvesting, agriculture, operating the Sunrise resort, selling recreation permits, and leasing summer cabins. Unemployment at Fort Apache is relatively low. Recreation is the main resource at Camp Verde.

Legal Status The San Carlos Apache Tribe, run as a corporation; the Tonto Apache Indians; and the White Mountain Apache Tribe are federally recognized tribal entities. The Payson Community of Yavapai-Apache Indians is a federally recognized tribal entity.

Daily Life San Carlos remains poor, with few jobs. Still, even if it means continuing in poverty, many Apaches resist acculturation: The ability to remain with family and friends remains paramount. The language and many traditions and ceremonies remain an important part of people's daily lives. Increasing off-reservation work, however, has opened the door to additional serious social problems. Management of San Carlos has remained in BIA hands, leaving Indians with the usual problem of being stripped of their heritage

Measuring cloth during a government issue at the San Carlos Reservation in Arizona (1887).

and institutions with no replacement or training or responsibility for their own affairs. The people of San Carlos are fighting a University of Arizona telescope bank on their sacred Mount Graham.

The Cibecue are the most traditional people at conservative Fort Apache. Nuclear families are now more important than extended families and local groups, but clans remain key, especially for the many extant ceremonies. Alcoholism and drug use are a large problem on the reservation. Public schools at both reservations have strong bilingual programs; educated leaders are a high need and priority (education levels remain quite low on both reservations). The Tonto have intermarried extensively with the Yavapai.

Apache, White Mountain

See Apache, Western

Chemehuevi

Chemehuevi (Che mə `wā vē) is Yuman for "nose-in-the-air-like-a-roadrunner," referring to a running style of the original settlers of the Chemehuevi Valley. These Indians traditionally called themselves *Nuwu,* "the People," or *Tantáwats,* "Southern Men."

Location Since the late nineteenth and early twentieth centuries, the people have lived in the Chemehuevi Valley, California (part of the Colorado River Valley east of Joshua Tree National Monument, and southwestern California. Their traditional territory was located in southwestern Utah, the Mojave Desert, and finally the Chemehuevi Valley, near the present Lake Havasu.

Population There were perhaps 500 Chemehuevis in 1600. In 1990, there were 95 Indians at Chemehuevi and 2,345 at the Colorado River Reservation (out of these, perhaps 600 identified themselves as Chemehuevi).

Language Chemehuevis spoke Paiute, a group of the Shoshonean branch of the Uto-Aztecan language family.

Historical Information

History Toward the end of the eighteenth century, the Chemehuevi and the Las Vegas band of Southern

Paiutes may have exterminated the Desert Mojave. In the mid–nineteenth century, the Chemehuevi took over their territory as well as that of the Pee-Posh (Maricopa) Indians, who had been driven away by the Mojave Indians and had gone to live on the Gila River. The Mojave either actively or passively accepted the Chemehuevi. On the Colorado River, the Chemehuevi developed a crop-based economy and at the same time began to think of themselves as a distinct political entity. They also became strongly influenced in many ways by the Mojave, notably in their interest in warfare and their religious beliefs. Some Chemehuevis raided miners in northern Arizona from the 1850s through the 1870s.

In 1865 the Chemehuevi and Mojave fought each other. The Chemehuevi lost and retreated back into the desert. Two years later, however, many returned to the California side of the Colorado River, where they resumed their lives on the Colorado River Reservation, established two years earlier. Many Chemehuevi also remained in and around the Chemehuevi Valley, combining wage labor and traditional subsistence. By the turn of the century, most Chemehuevis were settled on the Colorado River Reservation and among the Serrano and Cahuilla in southern California. In 1885, after a particularly severe drought, a group moved north to farm the Chemehuevi Valley. When a reservation was established there, in 1907, the tribal split became official.

The creation of Hoover Dam in 1935 and Parker Dam in 1939 spelled disaster for the Chemehuevi. The Hoover stopped the seasonal Colorado River floods, which the Chemehuevi people had depended upon to nourish their crops. The Parker Dam created Lake Havasu, placing most of the Chemehuevi Valley under water. At that point, most Indians in the Chemehuevi Valley moved south again to join their people at the Colorado River Reservation. A government relocation camp operated on the reservation from 1942 to 1945.

By the end of World War II, 148 Navajo and Hopi families had also colonized the reservation; they, with the Chemehuevi and Mojave, became known as the Colorado River Indian Tribes (CRIT). As a result of a 1951 lawsuit, the Chemehuevi were awarded $900,000 by the United States for land taken to create Lake Havasu. The tribe was not formally constituted until they adopted a constitution in 1971. At about that time, some Chemehuevis began a slow return to the Chemehuevi Valley, where they remain today, operating a resort on their tribal lands.

Religion After migrating to the Colorado River Valley, the Chemehuevi became strongly influenced by Mojave beliefs. Specifically, they acquired both interest and skill in dreaming and in using the power conferred by dreams to cure illness and spiritual imbalance. The Chemehuevi also adopted some of the Mojave song cycles, which referred to dreams as well as mythological events.

Government Before their move to the Colorado River, the Chemehuevi had little tribal consciousness or government per se. They roamed their territory in many bands, each with a relatively powerless chief. They assumed a tribal identity toward the mid–nineteenth century. At the same time, the chief, often a generous, smart, wealthy man succeeded by his eldest son, assumed a stronger leadership role.

Customs After the early nineteenth century, the Chemehuevi burned the body and possessions of their dead, following preparations by relatives. At this time, they also adopted many Mojave and Quechan customs, such as floodplain farming, dwelling type, an emphasis on dreams, and specific war-related customs. New parents rested on a hot bed for several days. Their mourning ceremony, or "cry," in which a wealthy family gave a feast and destroyed goods, had its roots in Southern Paiute culture.

Dwellings The traditional Chemehuevi shelter consisted of small, temporary huts covered with dirt.

Diet Following their move to the river, a diet based on foods obtained by hunting and by gathering desert resources was partially replaced by crops such as corn, beans, pumpkins, melons, grasses (semicultivated), and wheat. The Chemehuevi also ate fish from the river; game, including turtles, snakes, and lizards; and a variety of wild plants, such as mesquite beans (a staple) and piñon nuts.

Key Technology Chemehuevi technology in the nineteenth century consisted largely of adaptations of

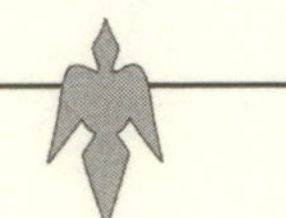

Mojave items, such as reed rafts, baskets and pottery, a headring for carrying, gourds for storage and rattles, planting sticks and wooden hoes, and fish and carrying nets. They also adopted Mojave floodplain irrigation methods.

Trade In the nineteenth century, the Chemehuevi participated in the general regional trade, extending into southern California, which saw the exchange of agricultural products for shells, feathers, and other items.

Notable Arts The Chemehuevi made excellent baskets. They also learned pottery arts from the Mojave.

Transportation In addition to horses (acquired while they were still leading a nomadic existence in the desert) for basic mobility on land, the Chemehuevi used reed or log rafts for river travel, as well as large pots to hold provisions or even small children for short travels in the water.

Dress After contact with the Mojaves, men began wearing their hair in thin "ropes" that hung down the back. Generally, men and women wore double aprons. Women also wore willow-bark aprons. Both went barefoot except when traveling, when rawhide sandals were worn.

War and Weapons The Chemehuevi did not shy away from fighting. Traditional allies included the Mojave (especially), Quechan, Yavapai, and Western Apache. Enemies included the Cocopah, Pima, O'odham, Pee-Posh, and on occasion their allies, the Mojave. Warriors generally clubbed their sleeping victims in predawn raids. They also used the bow and arrow.

Contemporary Information

Government/Reservations The Chemehuevi have their own reservation in the Chemehuevi Valley, California. It was created in 1907 and contained 36,000 acres, almost 8,000 of which were subsequently lost to Lake Havasu. Most Chemehuevis live on the Colorado River Reservation, created in 1865, and are members of CRIT. This reservation contains roughly 270,000 acres. It is governed under a constitution approved in 1937 and is dominated politically by the Mojave tribe.

Chemehuevis are also represented on the Morongo, Cabazon, and Agua Caliente Reservations (Cahuilla) in California.

Economy The tribal resort on Lake Havasu provides most of the employment and income for members of that reservation. CRIT, which boasts notably low unemployment (10 percent in 1985), features an 11,000-acre farming cooperative (primarily cotton, alfalfa, melons, and lettuce), a sheep herd, a resort (Aha Quin Park), and employment with the tribe, the Bureau of Indian Affairs, numerous small and large businesses, and the local health center. Long-term leases provide further income. There are also hydroelectric, oil, and uranium resources.

Legal Status Federally recognized tribal entities include the Chemehuevi Indian Tribe of the Chemehuevi Reservation, California, and the Colorado River Indian Tribes of the Colorado River Indian Reservation, Arizona and California.

Daily Life Intermarriage on the Colorado River Reservation has tended to blur the identities of the individual constituent tribes of CRIT, with the possible exception of the Mojave, which dominate by their sheer numbers. The other tribes both concede Mojave domination and search for ways to maintain their individuality. Toward this end, a museum has been built that details the heritage of the separate tribes. The Colorado River Reservation features motorboat races and a rodeo. Children from both reservations attend public schools.

Cochiti Pueblo

Cochiti (Kō `chē tē) from the original Keresan via a Spanish transliteration. The word "pueblo" comes from the Spanish for "village." It refers both to a certain style of Southwest Indian architecture, characterized by multistory, apartmentlike buildings made of adobe, and to the people themselves. Rio Grande pueblos are known as eastern Pueblos; Zuñi, Hopi, and sometimes Acoma and Laguna are known as western Pueblos.

Location Cochiti Pueblo has been located roughly 25 miles southwest of Santa Fe for at least several centuries.

Population In 1990, 666 Cochitis lived on the pueblo, with perhaps at least as many living off; about 500 Cochitis lived there in 1700.

Language Cochiti is a Keresan dialect.

Historical Information

History All Pueblo people are thought to be descended from Anasazi and perhaps Mogollon and several other ancient peoples, although the precise origin of the Keresan peoples is unknown. From them they learned architecture, farming, pottery, and basketry. Larger population groups became possible with effective agriculture and ways to store food surpluses. Within the context of a relatively stable existence, the people devoted increasing amounts of time and attention to religion, arts, and crafts.

In the 1200s, the Anasazi abandoned their traditional canyon homelands in response to climatic and social upheavals. A century or two of migrations ensued, followed in general by the slow reemergence of their culture in the historic pueblos. For a time the Cochiti lived with the San Felipe people but divided before the Spanish arrived.

In 1598, Juan de Oñate arrived in the area with settlers, founding the colony of New Mexico. Oñate carried on the process, already underway in nearby areas, of subjugating the local Indians; forcing them to pay taxes in crops, cotton, and work; and opening the door for Catholic missionaries to attack their religion. The Spanish renamed the Pueblos with saints' names and began a program of church construction (such as San Buenaventura mission at Cochiti). At the same time, the Spanish introduced such new crops as peaches, wheat, and peppers into the region. In 1620, a royal decree created civil offices at each pueblo; silver-headed canes, many of which remain in use today, symbolized the governor's authority.

The Pueblo Indians, including Cochiti Pueblo, organized and instituted a general revolt against the Spanish in 1680. For years, the Spaniards had routinely tortured Indians for practicing traditional religion. They also forced the Indians to labor for them, sold Indians into slavery, and let their cattle overgraze Indian land, a situation that eventually led to drought, erosion, and famine. Popé of San Juan Pueblo and other Pueblo religious leaders planned the revolt, sending runners carrying cords of maguey fibers to mark the day of rebellion. Antonio Malacate of Cochiti Pueblo was also a prominent leader. On August 10, 1680, a virtually united stand on the part of the Pueblos drove the Spanish from the region. The Indians killed many Spaniards but refrained from mass slaughter, allowing them to leave Santa Fe for El Paso. The Cochiti abandoned their pueblo from 1683 to 1692, joining other Keresan people at the fortified town of Potrero Viejo.

The Pueblos experienced many changes during the following decades: Refugees established communities at Hopi, guerrilla fighting continued against the Spanish, and certain areas were abandoned. By the 1700s, excluding Hopi and Zuñi, only Taos, Picuris, Isleta, and Acoma Pueblos had not changed locations since the arrival of the Spanish. Although Pueblo unity did not last, and Santa Fe was officially reconquered in 1692, Spanish rule was notably less severe from then on. Harsh forced labor all but ceased, and the Indians reached an understanding with the Church that enabled them to continue practicing their traditional religion.

In general, the Pueblo eighteenth century was marked by smallpox epidemics and increased raiding by the Apache, Comanche, and Ute. Occasionally Pueblo Indians fought with the Spanish against the nomadic tribes. The people practiced their religion but more or less in secret. During this time, intermarriage and regular exchange between Hispanic villages and Pueblo Indians created a new New Mexican culture, neither strictly Spanish nor Indian, but rather somewhat of a blend between the two.

Mexican "rule" in 1821 brought little immediate change to the Pueblos. The Mexicans stepped up what had been a gradual process of appropriating Indian land and water, and they allowed the nomadic tribes even greater latitude to raid. As the presence of the United States in the area grew, it attempted to enable the Pueblo Indians to continue their generally peaceful and self-sufficient ways, and recognized Spanish land grants to the Pueblos.

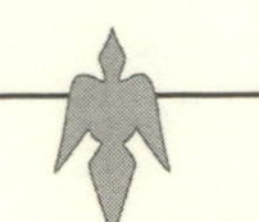

During the nineteenth century the process of acculturation among Pueblo Indians quickened markedly. In an attempt to retain their identity, Pueblo Indians clung even more tenaciously to their heritage, which by now included elements of the once-hated Spanish culture and religion. By the 1880s, railroads had largely put an end to the traditional geographical isolation of the pueblos. Paradoxically, the U.S. decision to recognize Spanish land grants to the Pueblos denied Pueblo Indians certain rights granted under official treaties and left them particularly open to exploitation by squatters and thieves.

After a gap of more than 300 years, the All Indian Pueblo Council began to meet again in the 1920s, specifically in response to a congressional threat to appropriate Pueblo lands. Partly as a result of the Council's activities, Congress confirmed Pueblo title to their lands in 1924 by passing the Pueblo Lands Act. The United States also acknowledged its trust responsibilities in a series of legal decisions and other acts of Congress. Still, especially after 1900, Pueblo culture was increasingly threatened by highly intolerant Protestant evangelical missions and schools. The Bureau of Indian Affairs also weighed in on the subject of acculturation, forcing Indian children to leave their homes and attend culture-killing boarding schools.

In the 1930s, a concrete dam just north of Cochiti made possible new irrigation canals. With a sure water supply, ceremonialism largely based on the uncertainties of local agriculture declined steeply. Completion of a larger dam in 1975 flooded important archaeological sites as well as the best sources of potters' clay and some acreage; however, farming had declined anyway.

Following World War II, the issue of water rights took center stage on most pueblos. Also, the All Indian Pueblo Council succeeded in slowing the threat against Pueblo lands as well as religious persecution. Making crafts for the tourist trade became an important economic activity during this period. Since the late nineteenth century, but especially after the 1960s, Pueblos have had to cope with onslaughts by (mostly white) anthropologists and seekers of Indian spirituality. The region is also known for its major art colonies at Taos and Santa Fe.

Religion In traditional Pueblo culture, religion and life are inseparable. To be in harmony with all of nature is the Pueblo ideal and way of life. The sun is seen as the representative of the Creator. Sacred mountains in each direction, plus the sun above and the earth below, define and balance the Pueblo world. Many Pueblo religious ceremonies revolve around the weather and are devoted to ensuring adequate rainfall. To this end, Pueblo Indians evoke the power of katsinas, sacred beings who live in mountains and other holy places, in ritual and dance. All Cochiti men belonged to katsina societies. Cochiti Pueblo contained two circular kivas, religious chambers that symbolize the place of original emergence into this world, and their associated societies, Squash and Turquoise.

In addition to the natural boundaries, Pueblo Indians created a society that defined their world by providing balanced, reciprocal relationships within which people connect and harmonize with each other, the natural world, and time itself. According to tradition, the head of each pueblo is the religious leader, or *cacique,* whose primary responsibility it is to watch the sun and thereby determine the dates of ceremonies. Much ceremonialism is also based on medicine societies, and shamans used supernatural powers for curing, weather control, and ensuring the general welfare. Especially in the eastern pueblos, most ceremonies are kept secret.

Government Pueblo governments derived from two traditions. Elements that are probably indigenous include the *cacique,* or head of the Pueblo, and the war captains. These officials are intimately related to the religious structures of the pueblo and reflected the essentially theocratic nature of Pueblo government. A parallel but in most cases distinctly less powerful group of officials was imposed by the Spanish authorities. Appointed by the traditional leadership, they generally dealt with external and church matters and included the governor, lieutenant governor, and *fiscales.* In addition, the All Indian Pueblo Council, dating from 1598, began meeting again in the twentieth century.

Customs One mechanism that works to keep Pueblo societies coherent is a pervasive aversion to

individualistic behavior. Children were traditionally raised with gentle guidance and a minimum of discipline. Pueblo Indians were generally monogamous and divorce is relatively rare. The dead were prepared ceremonially and quickly buried with clothes, beads, food, and other items. A vigil of four days and nights was generally observed. Cochiti Pueblo recognized matrilineal clans, associated with the seasons, as well as two patrilineal kiva groups, which in turn were associated with clans and medicine societies. The economy was basically a socialistic one, whereby labor was shared and produce was distributed equally. In modern times photography by outsiders is discouraged.

Dwellings In the sixteenth century, Cochiti Pueblo featured two- to three-story, apartment-style dwellings as well as individual houses, facing south. The buildings were constructed of adobe (earth and straw) bricks, with beams across the roof that were covered with poles, brush, and plaster. Floors were of wood plank or packed earth. The roof of one level served as the floor of another. The levels were interconnected by ladders. As an aid to defense, the traditional design included no doors or windows; entry was through the roof. Pit houses, or kivas, served as ceremonial chambers and clubhouses. The village plaza, around which all dwellings were clustered, is the spiritual center of the village where all the balanced forces of world come together.

Diet Cochitis were farmers. Before the Spanish arrived, they ate primarily corn, beans, and pumpkins. They also grew sunflowers and tobacco. They hunted deer, mountain lion, bear, antelope, and rabbits. Occasionally, men from Cochiti and Santo Domingo Pueblos would travel east to hunt buffalo. Cochitis also gathered a variety of wild seeds, nuts, berries, and other foods. The Spanish introduced wheat, alfalfa, sheep, cattle, and garden vegetables, which soon became part of the regular diet.

Key Technology Precontact farming implements were wooden. Traditional irrigation systems included ditches as well as floodwater collection at arroyo mouths *(ak chin)*. The Spanish introduced metal tools and equipment.

Trade All Pueblos were part of extensive Native American trading networks. With the arrival of other cultures, Pueblo Indians also traded with the Hispanic American villages and then U.S. traders. At fixed times during summer or fall, enemies declared truces so that trading fairs might be held. The largest and best known was at Taos with the Comanche. Nomads exchanged slaves, buffalo hides, buckskins, jerked meat, and horses for agricultural and manufactured pueblo products. Pueblo Indians traded for shell and copper ornaments, turquoise, and macaw feathers. Trade along the Santa Fe Trail began in 1821. By the 1880s and the arrival of railroads, the Pueblos were dependent on many American-made goods, and the Native American manufacture of weaving and pottery declined and nearly died out.

Notable Arts In the Pueblo way, art and life are inseparable. Cochiti arts included pottery, baskets, drums, and shell and turquoise ornaments. Songs, dances, and dramas also qualify as traditional arts. Many Pueblos experienced a renaissance of traditional arts in the twentieth century, beginning in 1919 with San Ildefonso pottery.

Transportation Spanish horses, mules, and cattle arrived at Cochiti Pueblo in the seventeenth century.

Dress Men wore cotton kilts and leather sandals. Women wore cotton dresses and sandals or high moccasin boots. Deer and rabbit skin were also used for clothing and robes, and sandals were made of yucca.

War and Weapons Though often depicted as passive and docile, most Pueblo groups regularly engaged in warfare. The great revolt of 1680 stands out as the major military action, but they also skirmished at other times with the Spanish and defended themselves against attackers such as Apaches, Comanches, and Utes. They also contributed auxiliary soldiers to provincial forces under Spain and Mexico, which were used mainly against raiding Indians and to protect merchant caravans on the Santa Fe Trail. After the raiding tribes began to pose less of a threat in the late nineteenth century, Pueblo military societies began to wither away, with the office of war captain changing to civil and religious functions.

Contemporary Information

Government/Reservations Cochiti Pueblo consists of over 50,000 acres. Although there is no constitution, the tribal council abandoned consensus-style decision making after World War II in favor of majority rule. Other than that, the Pueblo is governed according to tradition. Headmen of the three medicine societies (one of whom is the *cacique,* leader of the pueblo) annually select from the two kiva groups the war captain and his lieutenant, the governor and his lieutenant, and the *fiscale* and his lieutenant.

Economy Some people still farm, although more work for wages in nearby cities. In 1986, the tribe bought out a bankrupt company with whom they had signed very controversial long-term leases and contracts to develop businesses and schools. A lake associated with this development provides some recreational and other facilities; however, it has not brought a hoped-for prosperity to the tribe. Cochitis are particularly known for their fine aspen and cottonwood drums, ceremonial and tourist, as well as their excellent pottery, silver jewelry, and other arts. Unemployment in the early 1990s hovered around 20 percent.

Legal Status The Pueblo of Cochiti is a federally recognized tribal entity.

Daily Life Although the project of retaining a strong Indian identity is a difficult one in the late twentieth century, Pueblo people have strong roots, and in many ways the ancient rhythms and patterns continue. Many Pueblo Indians, though nominally Catholic, have fused parts of Catholicism onto a core of traditional beliefs. Since the 1970s control of schools has been a key in maintaining their culture. Health problems, including alcoholism and drug use, continue to plague the pueblos.

Primarily as a result of intermarriage and the general acculturation process, few Cochitis still speak Keresan or Spanish (before World War II many were trilingual). Furthermore, a growing number of Cochitis live off the pueblo, contributing to a general loss of language, traditions, and culture. Since the 1960s, children have attended a nearby day school, with children of nearby Latino communities; this has also affected the community's homogeneity. Cochitis attend high school in Bernalillo, where they graduate in relatively high numbers. Most houses on the pueblo are built of adobe walls, beam and board under adobe roofs, and packed earth or wood plank floors. Some concrete block and frame housing is beginning to appear. Most houses have running water, sewers, telephones, and televisions.

Occasional clan ceremonies are still held, and two of the three traditional medicine societies remain. The office of *cacique* also remains, though in a weakened form. Traditional medicine has largely given way to modern health centers. Most Cochitis are practicing Catholics. Some still observe traditional ceremonies, but more and more as entertainment than for strictly religious reasons. The principal ceremony and major feast day is San Buenaventuras Day. Except for katsina dances, the tribe generally admits the public for its ceremonies.

Cocopah

Cocopah (`Kō kō pä) from the Mojave kwi-ka-pah. The Cocopah called themselves *Xawil Kunyavaei,* "Those Who Live on the River."

Location The traditional home of the Cocopah is near the Colorado River delta. Presently, many tribal members live in northwestern Mexico and on a reservation near Somerton, Arizona.

Population There may once have been as many as 5,000 Cocopahs. In 1993 there were 712, excluding at least 200 Mexican Cocopahs living in Baja California and Sonora.

Language Cocopahs spoke River Yuman, a member of the Hokan-Siouan language family.

Historical Information

History Ancestors of the Cocopah probably migrated from the north during the first millennium. By 1540 the Mojave and Quechan Indians had forced

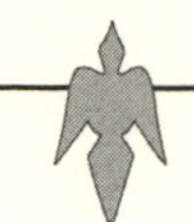

them down the Colorado River, to a place where they farmed 50,000 acres of delta land, made rich by the annual spring floods. The Cocopah encountered Spanish soldiers and travelers during the mid–sixteenth century but remained in place and relatively unaffected by contact with the Europeans until U.S. dams stopped the Colorado from flooding in the late nineteenth century.

In 1853, the Gadsden Treaty separated the four bands of Cocopah: Two remained in Mexico, and two moved north to near Somerton, Arizona. By the mid-1800s, with the cessation of warfare with their ancient enemies, the Quechans, the Cocopah lost a certain sense of purpose. A generation of men obtained employment as river pilots and navigators along the Colorado River, whetting their appetite for American goods and foods. Riverboat traffic ended when the railroad reached Yuma in 1877. In 1905, an accidental diversion of the Colorado River (the Salton Sea debacle) led to the Cocopahs' final displacement. Lacking strong political, religious, or social leadership, they quickly fell further into disintegration and impoverishment.

Thanks mainly to the work of Frank Tehanna, the U.S. government established a reservation in 1917 for Cocopahs and some Quechans and Pee-Posh. The government then almost completely abandoned them for the next 60 years. By the end of World War II, fewer than 60 Cocopahs remained on the desolate reservation; the rest lived elsewhere, generally in even worse poverty. In the 1960s, the tribe organized and won electricity and improved housing. It built its first tribal building and rewrote its constitution.

In 1986, the tribe received an additional 615 acres, now known as the North Reservation. In the 1970s and 1980s, the tribe made improvements in education as well as other social and cultural programs. That period also witnessed a revival of crafts such as beadwork and the development of fine arts.

Religion The Cocopah creation myth, like that of other Yumans, mentions twin gods living under the waters who emerged to create the world. Cocopahs revered the sun. They believed that life is directed by dreams in nearly every regard and relied on the dreams of shamans for success in war and curing. Most ceremonies, including *karuk,* a six-day mourning rite featuring long, "dreamed" song cycles, centered around death. The onset of puberty was also an occasion for ceremonies.

Government The Cocopah traditionally maintained little political leadership. They lived in small settlements, or rancherias, of 10 to 12 families. Society was organized into clans, with each clan having a leader. Other quasi officials included dance and war leaders and funeral orators. Leadership was generally determined by experience, ability, and, as with everything else, dreams.

Customs The Cocopah cremated their dead, including their possessions, following a special rite. Relatives cut off their hair in mourning, and the name of the dead person was never spoken. Marriage and divorce ceremonies were informal. Deer-bone blades hung on cords from the arms were used to wipe off perspiration. Dogs were kept as pets.

Dwellings Originally concentrated in nine rancherias, the Cocopah built two different types of homes. In winter they built conical, partially excavated (later four-post rectangular) structures, covering the walls of sticks with earth. In summer they built oval-domed, brush-covered huts. They also used a circular, unroofed ramada for dwelling and/or cooking and small granaries with elevated floors for storing food.

Diet Corn, beans, black-eyed peas, pumpkins, and later melons were planted, usually in July. Gathered food, such as the seeds of wild saltgrass, roots, fruits, eggs, and especially mesquite, were also important, as was fish (such as mullet and bass) from the river and the Gulf of California. Wild game included deer, boar, and smaller animals. Much of the food was dried and stored for the winter. In general, the women gathered and cooked food, and the men hunted.

Key Technology The Cocopah planted seeds in holes rather than rows in order to preserve topsoil. They used pottery (jars, seed-toasting trays), crude baskets, fire drills, vegetable-fiber fishing nets, clubs and bow and arrow for warfare, stone and wooden

mortars, and stone and clamshell tools. Their musical instruments included a scraped and drummed basket, gourd rattles, and cane flutes and whistles. They also used small earthen dikes for irrigation.

Trade Trade contacts stretched west to the Pacific, northwest to northern California, northeast to much of Arizona, and southeast well into the Sonoran Desert.

Notable Arts Women made pottery that was mostly utilitarian, as was the basketry (made by men and women and used for storage, carrying, and cradles). In later historic times the Cocopah also learned loom weaving.

Transportation Cottonwood dugouts (the larger ones featured clay floors) or tule or brush rafts were used for river travel. Large baskets were used to transport small items or children on the river.

Dress Men wore tanned skin loincloths. Women wore bundles of feathers or willow-bark skirts in front and back. For both, clothing was minimal. People wore rabbit-skin robes or blankets in cold weather. Both men and women painted their faces and bodies for ornamental and ritual purposes. Men wore shell ornaments in pierced ears. Sandals were made of untanned skins. Men wore their hair long and braided. In the early twentieth century they tucked it under a bandanna. Women wore their hair long and straight, with bangs.

War and Weapons Warfare united the Cocopah. They observed formalized war patterns and respected special war leaders. They prepared for war by dreaming, fasting, and painting their bodies and underwent purification rituals upon their return. Traditional enemies included the Mojave and the Quechan; allied peoples included the O'odham, Pee-Posh, and Pai. Their weapons were the war club, bow and arrow, lance, and deerskin shield.

Contemporary Information

Government/Reservations The Cocopah Reservation (established in 1917, roughly 1,700 acres) is located near Somerton, Arizona. The tribe adopted a constitution and elected a tribal council in 1964.

Economy A few people practice subsistence farming, but most Indians work off-reservation for wages. Much land is leased to non-Indian farmers. The Cocopah Bend recreational vehicle park provides numerous public recreation facilities. There are also a bingo hall and casino on the reservation. Unemployment peaked at around 90 percent in the 1970s. Tourists buy fry-bread and crafts such as beadwork and reproductions of ceremonial clothing.

Legal Status The Cocopah tribe is a federally recognized tribal entity. In 1985, the tribe received 4,000 acres in land claims settlements. American Cocopahs are working to restore dual citizenship for their kin in Mexico.

Daily Life Most Cocopahs speak their language. They still burn and otherwise dispose of the possessions of their dead and perform the mourning ceremony. Children attend public schools. A small health clinic on the reservation attempts to cope with the people's numerous health problems. Local housing, formerly grossly substandard (consisting of cardboard hovels as late as the 1970s), is now generally considered adequate. Elders may live in special housing on the reservation. After at least a thousand years of living on the river, the Cocopah are effectively no longer river people.

Colorado River Indian Tribes (CRIT)

See Chemehuevi; Hopi; Mojave; Navajo

Havasupai

Havasupai (Hä vä `sū pī) is a name meaning "People of the Blue-Green Water." With the Hualapai, from whom they may be descended, they are also called the Pai (Pa'a) Indians ("the People"; Hualapai are Western Pai, and Havasupai are Eastern Pai). With the Hualapai and the Yavapai, the Havasupai are also

Upland Yumans, in contrast to River Yumans such as the Mojave and Quechan.

Location Since approximately 1100, the Havasupai have lived at Cataract Canyon in the Grand Canyon as well as on the nearby upland plateaus.

Population Of roughly 2,000 Pai, perhaps 250 Havasupai Indians lived at Cataract Canyon in the seventeenth century. Approximately 400 lived there in 1990.

Language The Havasupai spoke Upland Yuman, a member of the Hokan-Siouan language family.

Historical Information

History The Havasupai probably descended from the prehistoric Cohoninas, a branch of the Hakataya culture. Thirteen bands of Pai originally hunted, farmed, and gathered in northwest Arizona along the Colorado River. By historic times, the Pai were divided into three subtribes: the Middle Mountain People; the Plateau People (including the Blue Water People, also called Cataract Canyon Band, who were ancestors of the Havasupai); and the Yavapai Fighters.

The Blue Water People were comfortable in an extreme range of elevations. They gathered desert plants from along the Colorado River at 1,800 feet and hunted on the upper slopes of the San Francisco peaks, their center of the world, at 12,000 feet. With the possible exception of Francisco Garces, in 1776, few if any Spanish or other outsiders disturbed them into the 1800s. Spanish influences did reach them, however, primarily in the form of horses, cloth, and fruit trees through trading partners such as the Hopi.

In the early 1800s, a trail was forged from the Rio Grande to California that led directly through Pai country. By around 1850, with invasions and treaty violations increasing, the Pai occasionally reacted with violence. When mines opened in their territory in 1863, they perceived the threat and readied for war. Unfortunately for them, the Hualapai War (1865–1869) came just as the Civil War ended. After their military defeat by the United States, some Pai served as army scouts against their old enemies, the Yavapai and the Tonto Apache.

Although the Hualapai were to suffer deportation, the United States paid little attention to the Havasupai, who returned to their isolated homes. At this point the two tribes became increasingly distinct. Despite their remote location, Anglo encroachment eventually affected even the Havasupai, and an 1880 executive order established their reservation along Havasu Creek. The final designation in 1882 included just 518 acres within the canyon; the Havasupai also lost their traditional upland hunting and gathering grounds (some people continued to use the plateau in winter but were forced off in 1934, when the National Park Service destroyed their homes).

The Havasupai intensified farming on their little remaining land and began a wide-scale cultivation of peaches. In 1912 they purchased cattle. Severe epidemics in the early twentieth century reduced their population to just over 100. At the same time the Bureau of Indian Affairs, initially slow to move into the canyon, proceeded with a program of rapid acculturation. By the 1930s, Havasupai economic independence had given way to a reliance on limited wage labor. Traditional political power declined as well, despite the creation in 1939 of a tribal council.

Feeling confined in the canyon, the Havasupai stepped up their fight for permanent grazing rights on the plateau. The 1950s were a grim time for the people, with no employment and little tourism. Conflict over land led to deep familial divisions, which in turn resulted in serious cultural loss. Food prices at the local store were half again as high as those in neighboring towns. In the 1960s, however, an infusion of federal funds provided employment in tribal programs as well as modern utilities. Still, croplands continued to shrink, as more and more land was devoted to the upkeep of pack animals for the tourists, the tribe's limited but main source of income. In 1975, after an intensive lobbying effort, the government restored 185,000 acres of land to the Havasupai.

Religion The Havasupai performed at least three traditional ceremonies a year, the largest coming in the fall at harvest time and including music, dancing, and speechmaking. They often invited Hopi, Hualapai, and Navajo neighbors to share in these celebrations. One important ceremony was cremation (burial from the late nineteenth century) and mourning of the dead, who were greatly feared. Although the Hopi influenced the Havasupai in many ways, such as the use of masked dancers, the rich Hopi ceremonialism did not generally become part of Havasupai life. Curing was accomplished by means of shamans, who acquired their power from dreams. The Havasupai accepted the Ghost Dance in 1891.

Government Formal authority was located in chiefs, hereditary in theory only, of ten local groups. Their only real power was to advise and persuade. The Havasupai held few councils; most issues were dealt with by men informally in the sweat lodge.

Customs The Havasupai were individualists rather than band or tribe oriented. The family was the main unit of social organization. In place of a formal marriage ceremony, a man simply took up residence with a woman's family. The couple moved into their own home after they had a child. Women owned no property. Babies stayed mainly on basket cradle boards until they were old enough to walk. With some exceptions, work was roughly divided by gender.

Leisure time was spent in sweat lodges or playing games, including (after 1600 or so) horse racing. The Havasupai often sheltered Hopis in times of drought. Both sexes painted and tattooed their faces. Only girls went through a formal puberty ritual.

Dwellings In winter and summer, dwellings consisted of domed or conical wikiups of thatch and dirt over a pole frame. People also lived in rock shelters. Small domed lodges were used as sweat houses and clubhouses.

Diet In Cataract Canyon the people grew corn, beans, squash, sunflowers, and tobacco. During the winter they lived on the surrounding plateau and ate game such as mountain lion and other cats, deer, antelope, mountain sheep, fowl, and rabbits, which were killed in communal hunting drives. Wild foods included piñon nuts, cactus and yucca fruits, agave hearts, mesquite beans, and wild honey.

Key Technology Traditional implements included stone knives, bone tools, bows and arrows, clay pipes for smoking, and nets of yucca fiber. The Havasupai tilled their soil with sticks. Baskets and pottery were used for a number of purposes. Grinding was accomplished by means of a flat rock and rotary mortars.

Trade The Havasupai often traded with the Hopi and other allied tribes, exchanging deerskins, baskets, salt, lima beans, and red hematite paint for food, pottery, and cloth. They also traded with tribes as far away as the Pacific Ocean.

Notable Arts Baskets, created by women, were especially well made. They were used as burden baskets, seed beaters and parching trays, pitch-coated water bottles, and cradle hoods. Brown and unpainted pottery was first dried in the sun, then baked in hot coals.

Transportation Horses entered the region in the seventeenth century.

Dress Buckskin, worked by men, was the main clothing material. Women wore a two-part dress, with a yucca-fiber or textile belt around the waist, and trimmed with hoof tinklers. In the nineteenth century they began wearing ornamental shawls. Moccasins, when worn, were made with a high upper wrapped around the calf. Men wore shirts, loincloths, leggings, headbands, and high-ankle moccasins. Personal decoration consisted of necklaces, earrings of Pueblo and Navajo shell and silver, and occasionally painted faces.

War and Weapons This peaceful people needed no war chiefs or societies. In the rare cases of defensive fighting, the most competent available leader took charge. Traditional allies included the Hualapai and Hopi; enemies included the Yavapai and Western Apache.

Contemporary Information

Government/Reservations The Havasupai Reservation was established from 1880 to 1882, near Supai, Arizona, along the Colorado River, 3,000 feet

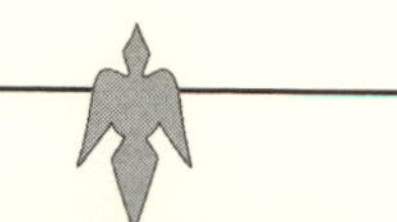

A group of students at the Havasupai Reservation in Arizona. Established between 1880 and 1882 along the Colorado River, 3,000 feet below the rim of the Grand Canyon, the reservation consists of roughly 188,000 acres.

below the rim of the Grand Canyon. It now consists of roughly 188,000 acres, with year-to-year permits issued for grazing in Grand Canyon National Park and the adjacent National Forest. The tribe adopted a constitution and by-laws in 1939 and a tribal corporate charter in 1946. Men and women serve on the elected tribal council. In 1975, the tribe regained a portion (185,000 acres) of their ancestral homeland along the South Rim of the Grand Canyon.

Economy Tourism constitutes the most important economic activity. The tribe offers mule guides, a campground, a hostel, a restaurant, and a lodge, and they sell baskets and other crafts. Farming has almost entirely disappeared. The tribe owns a significant cattle herd. Some people work for wages at Grand Canyon Village or in federal or tribal jobs. Fearing contamination from a new uranium mine, the tribe has banned mining on tribal lands.

Legal Status The Havasupai are a federally recognized tribal entity.

Daily Life Life among the Havasupai remains a mixture of the old and the new. Unlike many Indian tribes, their reservation includes part of their ancestral land. Most children entering the tribal school (self-administered since 1975) speak only Pai; again, unlike many tribes that focus on learning tribal identity, Havasupai children are encouraged to learn more about the outside world. Students attend school on the reservation through the eighth grade, then move to boarding school in California or to regular public schools.

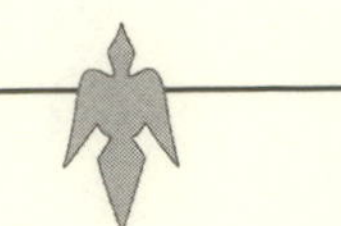

People continue to celebrate the traditional fall "peach festival," although the time has been changed to accommodate the boarding school schedule. Some people never leave the canyon; many venture out no more than several times a year. The nearest provisions are 100 miles away. Many still ride horses exclusively, although they may be listening to a portable music player at the time. Havasupai people often mix with tourists who wind up in the village at the end of the Grand Canyon's Hualapai Trail. Some people own satellite dishes and videocassette recorders, but much remains of the old patterns, and intermarriage beyond the Hualapai remains rare. Variants of traditional religion remain alive, while at the same time Rastafarianism is also popular, especially among young men. The people are fighting an ongoing legal battle over uranium pollution of a sacred site in the Kaibab National Forest.

Hopi

Hopi (`Hō pē) from *Hopituh Shi-nu-mu,* "Peaceful People." They were formerly called the Moki (or Moqui) Indians, a name probably taken from a Zuñi epithet.

Location The Hopi are the westernmost of the Pueblo peoples. First, Second, and Third Mesas are all part of Black Mesa, located on the Colorado Plateau between the Colorado River and the Rio Grande, in northeast Arizona. Of the several Hopi villages, all but Old Oraibi are of relatively recent construction.

Population Hopi population was perhaps 2,800 in the late seventeenth century. It was roughly 7,000 in 1990.

Language Hopi, a Shoshonean language, is a member of the Uto-Aztecan language family.

Historical Information

History The Hopi are probably descended from the prehistoric Anasazi culture. Ancestors of the Hopi have been in roughly the same location for at least 10,000 years. During the fourteenth century, Hopi became one of three centers of Pueblo culture, along with Zuñi/Acoma and the Rio Grande pueblos. Between the fourteenth and sixteenth centuries, three traits in particular distinguished the Hopi culture: a highly specialized agriculture, including selective breeding and various forms of irrigation; a pronounced artistic impulse, as seen in mural and pottery painting; and the mining and use of coal (after which the Hopi returned to using wood for fuel and sheep dung for firing pottery).

The Hopi first met non-native Americans when members of Coronado's party came into their country in 1540. The first missionary arrived in 1629, at Awatovi. Although the Spanish did not colonize Hopi, they did make the Indians swear allegiance to the Spanish Crown and attempted to undermine their religious beliefs. For this reason, the Hopis joined the Pueblo rebellion of 1680. They destroyed all local missions and established new pueblos at the top of Black Mesa that were easier to defend. The Spanish reconquest of 1692 did not reach Hopi land, and the Hopis welcomed refugees from other pueblos who sought to live free of Spanish influence. In 1700, the Hopis destroyed Awatovi, the only village with an active mission, and remained free of Christianity for almost 200 years thereafter.

During the nineteenth century the Hopi endured an increase in Navajo raiding. Later in the century they again encountered non-natives, this time permanently. The U.S. government established a Hopi reservation in 1882, and the railroad began bringing in trading posts, tourists, missionaries, and scholars. The new visitors in turn brought disease epidemics that reduced the Hopi population dramatically.

Like many tribes, the Hopi struggled to deal with the upheaval brought about by these new circumstances. Following the Dawes Act (1887), surveyors came in preparation for parceling the land into individual allotments; the Hopis met them with armed resistance. Although there was no fighting, Hopi leaders were imprisoned. They were imprisoned as well for their general refusal to send their children to the new schools, which were known for brutal discipline and policies geared toward cultural genocide. Hopi children were kidnapped and sent to the schools anyway.

Factionalism also took a toll on Hopi life. Ceremonial societies split between "friendly" and

"hostile" factions. This development led in 1906 to the division of Oraibi, which had been continuously occupied since at least 1100, into five villages. Contact with the outside world increased significantly after the two world wars. By the 1930s, the Hopi economy and traditional ceremonial life were in shambles (yet the latter remained more intact than perhaps that of any other U.S. tribe). Most people who could find work worked for wages or the tourist trade. For the first time, alcoholism became a problem.

In 1943, a U.S. decision to divide the Hopi and Navajo Reservations into grazing districts resulted in the loss of most Hopi land. This sparked a major disagreement between the tribes and the government that continues to this day. Following World War II, the "hostile" traditionalists emerged as the caretakers of land, resisting cold war policies such as mineral development and nuclear testing and mining. The official ("friendly") tribal council, however, instituted policies that favored exploitation of the land, notably permitting Peabody Coal to strip-mine Black Mesa, beginning in 1970.

Religion According to legend, the Hopi agreed to act as caretakers of this Fourth World in exchange for permission to live here. Over centuries of a stable existence based on farming, they evolved an extremely rich ceremonial life. The Hopi Way, whose purpose is to maintain a balance between nature and people in every aspect of life, is ensured by the celebration of their ceremonies.

The Hopi recognize two major ceremonial cycles, masked (January or February until July) and unmasked, which are determined by the position of the sun and the lunar calendar. The purpose of most ceremonies is to bring rain. As the symbol of life and well-being, corn, a staple crop, is the focus of many ceremonies. All great ceremonies last nine days, including a preliminary day. Each ceremony is controlled by a clan or several clans. Central to Hopi ceremonialism is the kiva, or underground chamber, which is seen as a doorway to the cave world from whence their ancestors originally came.

Katsinas are guardian spirits, or intermediaries between the creator and the people. They are said to dwell at the San Francisco peaks and at other holy places. Every year at the winter solstice, they travel to inhabit people's bodies and remain until after the summer solstice. Re-created in dolls and masks, they deliver the blessings of life and teach people the proper way to live. Katsina societies are associated with clan ancestors and with rain gods. All Hopis are initiated into katsina societies, although only men play an active part in them.

Perhaps the most important ceremony of the year is Soyal, or the winter solstice, which celebrates the Hopi worldview and recounts their legends. Another important ceremony is Niman, the harvest festival. The August Snake Dance has become a well-known Hopi ceremony.

Like other Pueblo peoples, the Hopi recognize a dual division of time and space between the upper world of the living and the lower world of the dead. Prayer may be seen as a mediation between the upper and lower, or human and supernatural, worlds. These worlds coexist at the same time and may be seen in oppositions such as summer and winter, day and night, life and death. In all aspects of Hopi ritual, ideas of space, time, color, and number are all interrelated in such a way as to provide order to the Hopi world.

Government Traditionally, the Hopi favored a weak government coupled with a strong matrilineal, matrilocal clan system. They were not a tribe in the usual sense of the word but were characterized by an elaborate social structure, each village having its own organization and each individual his or her own place in the community. The "tribe" was "invented" in 1936, when the non-native Oliver La Farge wrote their constitution. Although a tribal council exists, many people's allegiance remains with the village *kikmongwi (cacique)*. A *kikmongwi* is appointed for life and rules in matters of traditional religion. Major villages include Walpi (First Mesa), Shungopavi (Second Mesa), and Oraibi (Third Mesa).

Customs Hopi children learn their traditions through katsina dolls, including scare-katsinas, as well as social pressure, along with an abundance of love and attention. This approach tends to encourage friendliness and sharing in Hopi children. In general, women owned (and built) the houses and other

Hopi children learn their traditions through katsina dolls (pictured here), as well as social pressure, along with an abundance of love and attention. These dolls, carved out of cottonwood, represent the various masked katsinas.

material resources while men farmed and hunted away from the village. Special societies included katsina and other men's and women's organizations concerned with curing, clowning, weather control, and war.

Following a death, the deceased's hair was washed with yucca suds and decorated with prayer feathers. The face was covered with a mask of raw cotton, to evoke the clouds. He or she was then wrapped in a blanket and buried in a sitting position, with food and water. Cornmeal and prayer sticks were also placed in the grave, with a stick for a spirit ladder.

Dwellings Distinctive one- or two-floor pueblo housing featured sandstone and adobe walls and roof beams of pine and juniper, gathered from afar. The dwellings were entered via ladders through openings in the roofs and were arranged around a central plaza. This architectural arrangement reflects and reinforces cosmological ideas concerning emergence from an underworld through successive world levels.

Diet Hopis have been expert dry farmers for centuries, growing corn, beans, squash, cotton, and tobacco on floodplains and sand dunes or, with the use of irrigation, near springs. The Spanish brought crops such as wheat, chilies, peaches, melons, and other fruit. Men were the farmers and hunters of game such as deer, antelope, elk, and rabbits. The Hopi also kept domesticated turkeys. Women gathered wild food and herbs, such as pine nuts, prickly pear, yucca, berries, currants, nuts, and seeds. Crops were dried and stored against drought and famine.

Key Technology Farming technology included digging sticks (later the horse and plow), small rock or brush-and-dirt dams and sage windbreaks, and an accurate calendar on which each year's planting time was based. Grinding tools were made of stone. Men wove clothing and women made pottery, which was used for many purposes. Men also hunted with the bow and arrow and used snares and nets to trap animals.

Trade The Hopi obtained gems, such as turquoise, from Zuñi and Pueblo tribes. Shell came from the Pacific Ocean and the Gulf of Mexico. They also traded for sheep and wool from the Navajo, buckskins from the Havasupai, and mescal from various tribes.

Notable Arts Fine arts included pottery decorated with designs based on ancient geometric patterns, made by women. Men spun and wove cotton into costumes and clothing, for domestic use and for trade. Designs were generally asymmetrical but balanced between objects and color to render an idea of harmony. Other fine arts included silversmithing, introduced by the Navajo in 1890; weaving baskets and blankets; painting; and creating katsina dolls.

Transportation Horses arrived with the Spanish in the sixteenth century.

Dress Clothing was usually made of cotton and included long dresses for women and loincloths for men. Both wore leather moccasins and rabbit-skin robes as well as blankets and fur capes for warmth. Unmarried women wore their hair in the shape of a squash blossom; braids were preferred after marriage.

War and Weapons The annual war society ceremony is now obsolete.

These unmarried Hopi women wear their hair in the shape of a squash blossom (1912); braids were preferred after marriage.

Contemporary Information

Government/Reservations The Hopi Reservation was established in 1882. Consisting originally of almost 2.5 million acres, the total land base stood at just over 1.5 million acres in 1995. Thirteen Hopi villages now stand on three mesas. A tribal council was created in 1936, although only two of the villages were represented in 1992.

Hopis are also members of the Colorado River Indian Tribes Reservation (*see* Mojave).

Economy As they have for centuries, Hopis continue to farm for their food. They also raise sheep and cattle. Crafts for the tourist trade—especially silver jewelry, katsina dolls, and pottery—bring in some money. Seventy percent of the tribe's operating budget comes from coal leases, but mineral leases remain exploitative, and their effects include strip mining, radiation contamination, and depletion of precious water resources. The tribal council has also invested in factories and in a cultural center/motel/museum complex.

Legal Status The Hopi are a federally recognized tribal entity, as are the Colorado River Indian Tribes (CRIT), where some Hopis settled after World War II. The Hopi Reservation was carved in 1882 from traditional Hopi lands plus three villages of Navajos living on Hopi lands (settlers and refugees from U.S. Indian wars).

A major dispute has emerged within the tribe and among the Hopi tribal council, the Navajos, and the U.S. government over the lands around the part of

These Hopi women are shown building adobe houses. Distinctive one- or two-floor pueblo housing featured sandstone and adobe walls and roof beams of pine and juniper, gathered from afar. The dwellings were entered via ladders through openings in the roofs and were arranged around a central plaza.

the reservation known as Big Mountain. Technically the land belongs to the Hopis, but it has been homesteaded since the mid–eighteenth century by Navajos because, in their view, the Hopis were just "ignoring" it. The Hopi council wants the land for mineral exploitation. Hopi traditionalists want the Navajos to remain, out of solidarity, friendship with their old enemies, and their inclination to share. They would prefer that the land remain free of mineral exploitation.

In 1986, the United States recognized the squatters' rights by proclaiming 1.8 million acres of "joint use area": Each tribe got half, and those on the "other" side were to move. In effect, the Hopis lost half of their original reservation to the Navajo. More than 100 Hopis moved, but many Navajos remained. This conflict remains ongoing, with the Hopis still trying to hold onto their land. Many Indians believe that coal company profits are at the root of the dispute and forced relocations.

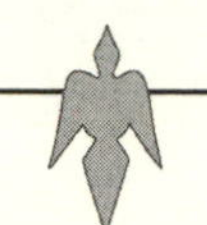

Daily Life The Hopi way continues; they are among the most traditional of all Indians in the United States. Hopis maintain a strong sense of the continuity of life and time. The split between "progressive" and "traditional" factions continues. Hopi High School, between Second and Third Mesas, opened in 1986 with an entirely local board. The school emphasizes Hopi culture and a new written language as well as computers and contemporary American curricula. The first dictionary of written Hopi is in preparation. The Hopi are making progress in solving not only the land dispute with the Navajo but also a host of social problems, including substance abuse and suicide.

Most Hopis live in the traditional pueblos, many of which now have glass windows. Perhaps 1,500 Hopis live and work off the reservation, although many return for ceremonies. Especially in some of the modern villages, houses contain plumbing and electricity and are constructed of cement blocks without benefit of a central plaza.

Hopi-Tewa

The Hopi-Tewa are a small group (roughly 700) of Native Americans living mostly on the Hopi Reservation. These Indians are descended from immigrants who settled at First Mesa (Tewa Village [Hano] and Polacca) following the Pueblo rebellion, around 1700. They speak a variety of Tewa, a Tanoan language, and have some distinct cultural attributes.

See also Hopi.

Hualapai

Hualapai (`Wä lä pī), or Walapai *(Xawálapáiya),* "Pine Tree People," were named after the piñon pine nut. With the Havasupai, they are called the Pai (Pa'a) Indians ("the People": the Hualapai are the Western Pai, and the Havasupai are the Eastern Pai). They are also described, with the Havasupai and the Yavapai, as Upland Yumans, in contrast to the River Yumans, such as the Mojave and Quechan.

Location Hualapai territory is located along the middle course of the Colorado River in present-day northwestern Arizona. Today, most Hualapai live near Peach Springs, Arizona, which is located near the Grand Canyon.

Population Roughly 1,100 prior to contact with non-natives, the 1993 Hualapai population was 1,872.

Language Hualapais spoke Upland Yuman, a member of the Hokan-Siouan language family.

Historical Information

History The Pai Indians, who traditionally considered themselves one people, probably descended from the prehistoric Patayans of the ancient Hakataya culture. Thirteen bands of Pai originally ranged in northwest Arizona along the Colorado River, hunting, farming, and gathering. By historic times, three subtribes had been organized: the Middle Mountain People, the Plateau People, and the Yavapai Fighters. Each subtribe was further divided into several bands, which in turn were divided into camps and families.

Although the Pai encountered non-natives in 1540, or perhaps as late as 1598, neither the Spanish nor the Mexicans developed Hualapai country, which remained fairly isolated until the 1820s. Around that time, a trail was blazed from the Rio Grande to California that led directly through Pai country. After the Mexican cession (1848), Hualapais began working in white-owned mines. With Anglo invasions and treaty violations increasing and the mines ever exploitative, the Hualapai, in 1865, met violence with violence. A warrior named Cherum forced a key U.S. retreat but later scouted for his old enemy. Later, the United States selected Hualapai Charley and Leve Leve as principal chiefs because they were amenable to making peace. The Hualapai war ended in 1869.

As the Eastern Pai played a minor role in the war, they were allowed to return home afterward; it was at this juncture that the two "tribes," Hualapai and Havasupai, became increasingly separate. The army forced those Hualapai who failed to escape to march in 1874 to the Colorado River Reservation. There, the low altitude combined with disease and poor rations brought the Hualapai much suffering and death. When they filtered back home several years later, they found their land in non-native hands. Still,

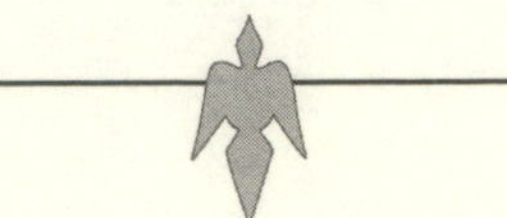

they applied for and received official permission to remain, and a reservation was established for them in 1883.

The reservation consisted of 1 million acres on the South Rim of the Grand Canyon, a fraction of their original land. Before long, overgrazing by non-Indians had ruined the native food supply, and ranchers and cattlemen were directly threatening the Indians with physical violence. A series of epidemics struck the Hualapai. Most Hualapai lived off the reservation, scrambling for wage work and sending their children to Anglo schools. As the Hualapai formed an underclass of cheap, unskilled labor, their way of life began to vanish. The railroad depot at Peach Springs became the primary Hualapai village. The railroad brought dislocation, disease, and some jobs. Their new condition strengthened their differences with the still-isolated Havasupai.

The Hualapai began herding cattle in 1914, although their herds were greatly outnumbered by those of non-natives. Extensive prejudice against the Indians diminished somewhat after World War I, out of respect for Indian war heroes. Through the middle twentieth century the Hualapai retained a strong sense of their culture, although economic progress was extremely slow.

Religion According to the Hualapai creation myth, a spirit prayed life into canes cut from along the Colorado River near Spirit Mountain, in present-day Nevada. An unseen world of gods and demons are in part responsible for the dreams that gave male and female shamans their power to cure. This they accomplished by singing, shaking gourds, and pretending to suck out disease with a tube and herbs. They also used their power to control the weather. If successful with a cure, shamans were paid in buckskins, but they might be killed if a patient died. In general, the Hualapai had few ceremonies or dances. They did accept the Ghost Dance in the 1890s.

Government Traditional political authority was decentralized. Headmen of both a camp (roughly 20 people) and a band (roughly 85–200 people) led by fostering consensus. They served as war chiefs and spokespeople when necessary. The position of headman was occasionally hereditary but more often based on personality and ability. There was little or no tribal identity until the early twentieth century, when the Hualapai created a fledgling tribal council. In the 1930s they adopted a constitution and elected their first tribal president.

Customs The Hualapai cremated their dead and burned their homes and belongings as well. In the nineteenth century they adopted the Mojave mourning ceremony, in which aspects of warfare were staged to honor the dead. They observed no formal marriage ceremony. Divorce was frequent and easy to obtain.

Dwellings Dome-shaped brush wikiups as well as rock shelters served as the major dwelling. The people (men, by and large) also used sweat lodges for curing and as clubhouses.

Diet Occasionally the Hualapai grew the standard American crops (corn, beans, and squash) near springs and ditches. Corn was made into mush, soup, and bread; pumpkins were dried in long strips. In the main, however, they obtained their food by hunting and gathering, leaving their summer camps to follow the seasonal ripening of wild foods. The women gathered piñon nuts, cactus and yucca fruits, agave (mescal) hearts, mesquite beans, and other plants. The men hunted deer, antelope, mountain sheep, rabbits (in drives), and small game. Meat was dried and stored in skin bags. The Hualapai also ate fish.

Key Technology The Hualapai practiced a number of traditional irrigation techniques, such as ditch digging, crop location near water sources, and flood runoff *(ak chin)*. They used flat pounding-grinding rocks and rotary mortars for grinding. Baskets as well as pottery were used for conveyance and storage.

Trade The Hualapai were part of an extensive system of exchange that stretched from the Pacific Ocean to the Pueblos. Shell decorations and horses came from the Mojave and the Quechan. Rich red ocher pigment was a key trade item, as were baskets and dried mescal and dressed skins. Meat and skins went for crops; lima beans for Hopi peaches.

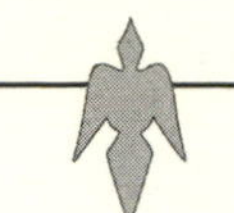

Notable Arts Baskets and pottery, including pots, dishes, jars, and pipes, have been made for centuries.

Transportation The Hualapai obtained horses in the seventeenth century.

Dress Clothing was generally made from buckskin or juniper bark. Men wore shorts and breechcloths. Women wore skirts or aprons. Both wore moccasins or yucca sandals. Rabbit-skin robes and blankets were used in cold weather. In addition, the Hualapai painted their faces for decoration (women tattooed their chins), and both sexes wore shell necklaces.

War and Weapons Traditional enemies included the Mojave and the Yavapai; their main ally was the Havasupai. The Hualapai fought with mulberry bows, clubs, and hide shields.

Contemporary Information

Government/Reservations The Hualapai Reservation consists of almost 1 million acres near Peach Springs, Arizona. The tribe adopted a constitution and by-laws in 1938 and a corporate charter in 1943. A new constitution was ratified in 1970. The tribal council consists of nine elected members and one hereditary chief, although the Bureau of Indian Affairs must still approve all ordinances.

Economy The Hualapai Reservation is marked by very high unemployment (more than 80 percent). U.S. Interstate 40 bypasses the reservation, limiting opportunities for tourism. Important economic activities include forestry and raising cattle, along with some hunting and farming. The people sell some baskets to tourists, and they lease land for mining and lumbering. The tribe also controls hydroelectric, natural gas, oil, and uranium resources. Their hope for economic development based on a proposed Bridge Canyon dam was defeated in 1968 by the Central Arizona Project. The Hualapai plan to develop further what is now small-scale tourism, such as permits and guides, related to the Grand Canyon. Many Hualapai work for wages off the reservation.

Legal Status The Hualapai are a federally recognized tribal entity.

Daily Life Many Hualapai speak English, but many also retain their native tongue. Most Hualapai who live on the reservation live in individual, modern homes. The shift from extended family to nuclear family living contributed to cultural breakdown. One response to this situation has been the development by Peach Springs Elementary School of a nationally recognized model bilingual/bicultural program. With children grounded in their own culture, their self-esteem has risen, which has translated directly into higher graduation rates. A summer memorial powwow honors the dead, whose clothes are still burned, but now they are buried rather than cremated. There are four active Christian churches on the reservation.

Isleta Pueblo

Isleta (Ēs `lā tä) from the Spanish missions San Antonio de la Isleta and San Augustin de la Isleta (*isleta* means "little island"). The word "pueblo" comes from the Spanish for "village." It refers both to a certain style of Southwest Indian architecture, characterized by multistory, apartmentlike buildings made of adobe, and to the people themselves. The pueblos along the Rio Grande are known as eastern Pueblos; Zuñi, Hopi, and sometimes Acoma and Laguna are known as western Pueblos. The Tiwa name for Isleta Pueblo is *Shiewhibak,* meaning "flint kick-stick place."

Location Since at least the eighteenth century, Isleta Pueblo has been located on the Rio Grande several miles south of Albuquerque. The pueblo consists of a main village (San Agustín) and two farm villages (Chikal and "town chief") 3 miles to the south.

Population In 1990, 2,700 Isletas lived on the pueblo, out of a total population of 2,900. Perhaps 410 lived there in 1790.

Language Isletas spoke Southern Tiwa, a Kiowa-Tanoan language.

Historical Information

History All Pueblo people are thought to be descended from Anasazi and perhaps Mogollon and

several other ancient peoples, although the precise origin of the Keresan peoples is unknown. From their ancestors they learned architecture, farming, pottery, and basketry. Larger population groups became possible with effective agriculture and ways to store food surpluses. Within the context of a relatively stable existence, the people devoted increasing amounts of time and attention to religion, arts, and crafts.

In the 1200s, the Anasazi abandoned their traditional canyon homelands in response to climatic and social upheavals. A century or two of migrations ensued, followed in general by the slow reemergence of their culture in the historic pueblos. The Tiwas were probably the first of the Tanoan Pueblo people to enter the northern Rio Grande region. Isleta itself grew from several prehistoric villages in the area, including Puré Tuay. The Spanish made contact with Isleta in the late sixteenth century, establishing a mission in 1613. Modern Isleta is perhaps an eighteenth-century settlement; many disruptions occurred as a result of constant conquistador attacks.

In 1598, Juan de Oñate arrived in the area with settlers, founding the colony of New Mexico. Oñate carried on the process, already underway in nearby areas, of subjugating the local Indians; forcing them to pay taxes in crops, cotton, and work; and opening the door for Catholic missionaries to attack their religion. The Spanish renamed the Pueblos with saints' names and began a program of church construction. At the same time, the Spanish introduced such new crops as peaches, wheat, and peppers into the region. In 1620, a royal decree created civil offices at each pueblo; silver-headed canes, many of which remain in use today, symbolized the governor's authority.

Isleta did not participate in the general Pueblo revolt against the Spanish in 1680, either out of fear of the Spanish or perhaps a reluctance to take the unusual step of joining an all-Pueblo alliance. They, the Spanish refugees, and people from some pueblos south of Albuquerque went to El Paso. Some Isletas reoccupied the pueblo in 1681; at that time, Spanish troops attacked and burned it and took hundreds of prisoners back to El Paso. Their descendants live today at Tigua Pueblo (Ysleta del Sur), south of El Paso. Some Southern Tiwas who did not go to El Paso went instead to Hopi and established a village (Payupki) on Second Mesa. Two Spanish friars escorted over 400 Tiwa back from Hopi in 1742; the permanent occupation of Isleta Pueblo may date from that time.

The Pueblos experienced many changes during the following decades: Refugees established communities at Hopi, guerrilla fighting continued against the Spanish, and certain areas were abandoned. By the 1700s, excluding Hopi and Zuñi, only Taos, Picuris, Isleta and Acoma Pueblos had not changed locations since the arrival of the Spanish. Although Pueblo unity did not last, and Santa Fe was officially reconquered in 1692, Spanish rule was notably less severe from then on. Harsh forced labor all but ceased, and the Indians reached an understanding with the Church that enabled them to continue practicing their traditional religion.

In general, the Pueblo eighteenth century was marked by smallpox epidemics and increased raiding by the Apache, Comanche, and Ute. Occasionally Pueblo Indians fought with the Spanish against the nomadic tribes. The people practiced their religion but more or less in secret. During this time, intermarriage and regular exchange between Hispanic villages and Pueblo Indians created a new New Mexican culture, neither strictly Spanish nor Indian, but rather somewhat of a blend between the two.

Mexican "rule" in 1821 brought little immediate change to the Pueblos. The Mexicans stepped up what had been a gradual process of appropriating Indian land and water, and they allowed the nomadic tribes even greater latitude to raid. As the presence of the United States in the area grew, it attempted to enable the Pueblo Indians to continue their generally peaceful and self-sufficient ways, in part by recognizing Spanish land grants to the Pueblos.

During the nineteenth century the process of acculturation among Pueblo Indians quickened markedly. In an attempt to retain their identity, Pueblo Indians clung even more tenaciously to their heritage, which by now included elements of the once-hated Spanish culture and religion. By the 1880s, railroads had largely put an end to the traditional geographical isolation of the pueblos. Paradoxically, the U.S. decision to recognize Spanish land grants to the Pueblos denied Pueblo Indians certain rights granted under official treaties and left

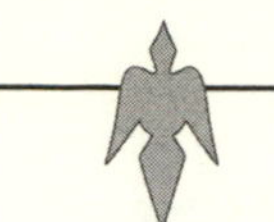

them particularly open to exploitation by squatters and thieves.

Since the 1700s, Isleta had been without katsina masks owing to the presence and active interference of the Spanish. Shortly after Laguna Pueblo divided around 1880 over factional differences, Isleta accepted a number of Lagunas into their village. Isleta traded homes and land for ceremonial invigoration. Within a few years, most of the Lagunas had returned to a village near their pueblo, but the katsina chief remained, as did his descendants, the masks, and the rituals.

After a gap of more than 300 years, the All Indian Pueblo Council began to meet again in the 1920s, specifically in response to a congressional threat to appropriate Pueblo lands. Partly as a result of the Council's activities, Congress confirmed Pueblo title to their lands in 1924 by passing the Pueblo Lands Act. The United States also acknowledged its trust responsibilities in a series of legal decisions and other acts of Congress. Still, especially after 1900, Pueblo culture was increasingly threatened by highly intolerant Protestant evangelical missions and schools. The Bureau of Indian Affairs also weighed in on the subject of acculturation, forcing Indian children to leave their homes and attend culture-killing boarding schools. Pablo Abeita, a member of the reorganized All Indian Pueblo Council, fought to defeat the Bursum Bill, a plan to appropriate the best Pueblo lands.

The dynamic tension between Catholicism and traditional beliefs remains in flux at Isleta: As recently as 1965 the Indians evicted a priest regarded as insufficiently sensitive to their traditions. Since the late nineteenth century, but especially after the 1960s, Pueblos have had to cope with onslaughts by (mostly white) anthropologists and seekers of Indian spirituality. The region is also known for its major art colonies at Taos and Santa Fe.

Religion In traditional Pueblo culture, religion and life are inseparable. To be in harmony with all of nature is the Pueblo ideal and way of life. The sun is seen as the representative of the Creator. Sacred mountains in each direction, plus the sun above and the earth below, define and balance the Pueblo world. Many Pueblo religious ceremonies revolve around the weather and are devoted to ensuring adequate rainfall. To this end, Pueblo Indians evoke the power of katsinas, sacred beings who live in mountains and other holy places, in ritual and masked dance. The Isleta katsina cult was reestablished at Isleta around 1880 by refugees from Laguna Pueblo, when Laguna religious society heads banded together at Isleta to form a single curing organization, the Laguna Fathers.

In addition to the natural boundaries, Pueblo Indians have created a society that defines their world by providing balanced, reciprocal relationships within which people connect and harmonize with each other, the natural world, and time itself. At Isleta, each tribal division (Red Eyes/summer and Black Eyes/winter) is in charge of the pueblo's ceremonies for half a year. Each is responsible for one major dance a year. According to tradition, the head of each pueblo is the religious leader, or *cacique,* whose primary responsibility it is to watch the sun and thereby determine the dates of ceremonies. Much ceremonialism is also based on medicine societies, and shamans who derive powers from animal spirits use their supernatural powers for curing, weather control, and ensuring the general welfare. Isleta has one round prayer chamber, or kiva. Ceremonies are held either in there or in the central plaza. Especially in the eastern pueblos, most ceremonies are kept secret.

Government Pueblo governments derived from two traditions. Offices that are probably indigenous include the *cacique,* or head of the Pueblo, and the war captains. These officials are intimately related to the religious structures of the pueblo and reflected the essentially theocratic nature of Pueblo government. At Isleta, the corn group leaders appointed the town chief *(cacique),* who was never permitted to leave the pueblo. Because of his many ritual obligations he was publicly supported. The *cacique* appointed the war or bow priest. A bow rather than a cane symbolized his office. He was of roughly equal importance with the *cacique* and was primarily responsible for security. Isleta also had a hunt chief, who led rituals for assuring health of animals and directed communal hunts, as well as an advisory group called the council of *principales,* composed of all religious officers and their first assistants.

A parallel but in most cases distinctly less powerful group of officials was imposed by the Spanish authorities. Appointed by the traditional leadership, they generally dealt with external and church matters and included the governor, two lieutenant governors, and two sheriffs. The authority of their offices was symbolized by canes. Nontraditional positions also included a ditch boss, who was in charge of the irrigation ditches, as well as a town crier and sacristan. In addition, the All Indian Pueblo Council, dating from 1598, began meeting again in the twentieth century.

The last correctly installed *cacique* at Isleta died in 1896. After that date, disruptions of installation rituals caused the war chiefs to serve for decades as acting *caciques.* This situation came to a head in the 1940s, when a political revolution split the pueblo into several factions and postponed elections. With the help of the Bureau of Indian Affairs, a constitution was drawn up; elections were held and the proper officers installed in 1950.

Customs One mechanism that works to keep Pueblo societies coherent is a pervasive aversion to individualistic behavior. Children were traditionally raised with gentle guidance and a minimum of discipline. Pueblo Indians were generally monogamous, and divorce was relatively rare. The dead were prepared ceremonially and quickly buried with clothes, beads, food, and other items, their heads facing south. A vigil of four days and nights was generally observed.

Isleta Pueblo was organized into seven corn groups. Men led the groups, although there were women's auxiliaries. The groups were ritual units more similar to kiva groups, functioning for personal crises and societal ceremonies. The tribe was also divided into Red Eyes/summer and Black Eyes/winter groups. Each had a war captain and two or three assistants. Four men from each group served for life as grandfathers or disciplinarians. Each group had ceremonial, irrigation, clowning, hunting, ballplaying, and other group responsibilities.

Two medicine societies (for illness due to misbehavior or witchcraft) were the Town Fathers and the Laguna Fathers. A warrior's society consisted of people who had taken a scalp and had been ritually purified. Closely associated with the kiva, this group also had a women's component, with special duties. The economy was basically a socialistic one, whereby labor was shared and produce was distributed equally. In modern times photography by outsiders is discouraged.

Dwellings Isleta Pueblo featured apartment-style dwellings as high as five stories, as well as individual houses, facing south. The buildings were constructed of adobe (earth and straw) bricks, with beams across the roof that were covered with poles, brush, and plaster. Floors were of wood plank or packed earth. The roof of one level served as the floor of another. The levels were interconnected by ladders. As an aid to defense, the traditional design included no doors or windows; entry was through the roof. Pit houses, or kivas, served as ceremonial chambers and clubhouses. The village plaza, around which all dwellings were clustered, is the spiritual center of the village where all the balanced forces of the world come together. A track for ceremonial foot races was also part of the village.

Diet Isletas were farmers. Before the Spanish arrived, they ate primarily corn, beans, and squash. They also grew cotton and tobacco. They hunted deer, mountain lion, bear, antelope, and rabbits. Occasionally, men from Isleta would travel east to hunt buffalo. Isletas also gathered a variety of wild seeds, nuts, berries, and other foods and fished in rivers and mountain streams. The Spanish introduced wheat, alfalfa, chilies, fruit trees, grapes (often made into wine for sale to Laguna Pueblo or nearby Spanish-American villages), sheep, cattle, and garden vegetables, which soon became part of the regular diet.

Key Technology Precontact farming implements were wooden. Traditional irrigation systems used ditches to ferry water from the Rio Grande as well as floodwater collection at arroyo mouths *(ak chin).* Tanning tools were made of bone and wood. The Spanish introduced metal tools and equipment. Men hunted with bows and arrows.

Trade All Pueblos were part of extensive Native American trading networks. With the arrival of other cultures, Pueblo Indians also traded with the Hispanic

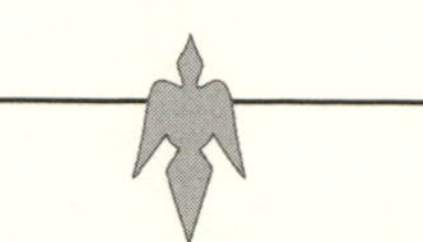

An Isleta woman dries peaches (1889). The Spanish introduced new crops such as peaches, wheat, and peppers into the region in the early seventeenth century.

American villages and then U.S. traders. At fixed times during summer or fall, enemies declared truces so that trading fairs might be held. The largest and best known was at Taos with the Comanche. Nomads exchanged slaves, buffalo hides, buckskins, jerked meat, and horses for agricultural and manufactured pueblo products. Pueblo Indians traded for shell and copper ornaments, turquoise, and macaw feathers. Isleta in particular traded for Jicarilla baskets; decorated pottery from other pueblos, especially Acoma, Zia, and Santo Domingo; and religious pictures from the Spanish, with whom they were in frequent contact. Trade along the Santa Fe Trail began in 1821. By the 1880s and the arrival of railroads, the Pueblos were dependent on many American-made goods, and the native manufacture of weaving and pottery declined and nearly died out.

Notable Arts In the Pueblo way, art and life are inseparable. Isleta arts included pottery and woven cotton items. Songs, dances, and dramas also qualify as traditional arts. Isleta pottery became strongly influenced by Laguna immigrants in the 1880s. Many Pueblos experienced a renaissance of traditional arts in the twentieth century, beginning in 1919 with San Ildefonso pottery.

Transportation Spanish horses, mules, and cattle arrived at Isleta Pueblo in the seventeenth century.

Dress Men wore shirts, leggings, and moccasins made of deer hides tanned and colored red-brown with plant dye. Women's wrapped leggings and moccasins were of white buckskin. Clothing was also made of spun cotton. Rabbit skin was also used for clothing and robes.

War and Weapons Though often depicted as passive and docile, most Pueblo groups regularly engaged in warfare. The great revolt of 1680 stands out as the major military action, but they skirmished at other times with the Spanish and defended themselves against attackers such as Apaches, Comanches, and Utes. They also contributed auxiliary soldiers to provincial forces under Spain and Mexico, which were used mainly against raiding Indians and to protect merchant caravans on the Santa Fe Trail. After the raiding tribes began to pose less of a threat in the late nineteenth century, Pueblo military societies began to wither away, with the office of war captain changing to civil and religious functions.

Contemporary Information

Government/Reservations Isleta Pueblo contains roughly 211,000 acres. Its constitution was last revised in 1970. Under it, men vote for the governor and an appointed council.

Economy Many people work for wages at the local air force base, for the tribe, or in Albuquerque. Some arts and crafts are produced, especially silver work and textiles; the pottery is produced with commercial methods and materials and is strictly for the tourist trade. There is some cattle ranching and some farming. Most Pueblo land is leased for oil testing.

Legal Status The Pueblo of Isleta is a federally recognized tribal entity.

Daily Life Although the project of retaining a strong Indian identity is a difficult one in the late twentieth century, Pueblo people have strong roots, and in many ways the ancient rhythms and patterns continue. Some people still speak Isleta, and traditional ceremonies are still performed. Children are born into ritual corn groups as well as one of the winter/summer ceremonial divisions. Many Pueblo Indians, though nominally Catholic, have fused pieces of Catholicism onto a core of traditional beliefs.

Since the 1970s control of schools has been a key in maintaining their culture. Health problems, including alcoholism and drug use, continue to plague the Pueblos. Furthermore, Isleta is the first community downstream from several highly polluting industries, including a huge landfill. Some nearby lakes have been seriously polluted.

Jemez Pueblo

Jemez (`Hē mish) from the Spanish *Jémez,* taken from the Jemez self-designation. The Jemez name for their pueblo is *Walatowa,* "at the pueblo in the cañada" or "this is the place." The word "pueblo" comes from the Spanish for "village." It refers both to a certain style of Southwest Indian architecture, characterized by multistory, apartmentlike buildings made of adobe, and to the people themselves. Rio Grande pueblos are known as eastern Pueblos; Zuñi, Hopi, and sometimes Acoma and Laguna are known as western Pueblos.

Location Jemez Pueblo is located along the east bank of the Jemez River, 25 miles north of Bernalillo, New Mexico.

Population In 1990, almost 1,750 Indians were resident, virtually the entire pueblo population. Perhaps 30,000 people lived there in 1530, and 100 in 1744.

Language The people spoke Towa, a Kiowa-Tanoan language.

Historical Information

History All Pueblo people are thought to be descended from Anasazi and perhaps Mogollon and several other ancient peoples. From them they learned architecture, farming, pottery, and basketry. Larger population groups became possible with effective agriculture and ways to store food surpluses. Within the context of a relatively stable existence, the people devoted increasing amounts of time and attention to religion, arts, and crafts.

The Jemez people lived near Stone Canyon, south of Dulce, New Mexico, around 2,000 years ago. They moved to near their present location after the arrival of the Athapaskans, around the fourteenth century. However, some of them moved to the San

Diego Canyon–Guadalupe Canyon area, south of Santa Fe, where they established numerous large fortresses and hundreds of small houses.

The Spaniards found them in 1540 and built a mission there (at Giusewa Pueblo) in the late sixteenth century. In 1621, they began another mission at the Pueblo de la Congregación, the present Jemez Pueblo. In 1628, Fray Martin de Arvide arrived at the Mission of San Diego de la Congregación with orders to unite the scattered Jemez communities, after which Jemez Pueblo became an important center for missionary activity.

Despite the pueblo's position as a missionary center, the Jemez people actively resisted Spanish efforts to undermine their religion. They joined in rebellion with the Navajo in about 1645, a crime for which 29 Jemez leaders were hanged. They also took a leading part in the Pueblo rebellion of 1680. For years, the Spaniards had routinely tortured Indians for practicing traditional religion. They also forced the Indians to labor for them, sold Indians into slavery, and let their cattle overgraze Indian land, a situation that eventually led to drought, erosion, and famine. Popé of San Juan Pueblo and other Pueblo religious leaders planned the great revolt, sending runners carrying cords of maguey fibers to mark the day of rebellion. On August 10, 1680, a virtually united stand on the part of the Pueblos drove the Spanish from the region. The Indians killed many Spaniards but refrained from mass slaughter, allowing most of them to leave Santa Fe for El Paso.

The Jemez people withdrew to sites on the top of the San Diego Mesa in 1681. When the Spanish left they descended, only to reascend in 1689 when they sighted a new Spanish force. Some returned again to the pueblo in 1692, when they, along with Keresans from Zia Pueblo, arrived at an understanding with the Spanish. Most Jemez, however, still resisted the Spanish, a situation that resulted in fighting between the Jemez and the Keresan pueblos of Zia and Santa Ana. This in turn resulted in a punitive Spanish-Keresan expedition in 1694, ending in the death or capture of over 400 Jemez people. All prisoners were pardoned after they helped the Spanish defeat the Tewas at Black Mesa.

By 1696, Jemez Pueblo had been rebuilt and reoccupied at or near the original site. The following year, however, after joining again with the Navajo in an anti-Spanish revolt, the Jemez returned to their ancestral homeland near Stone Canyon. Others went west to the Navajo country; of these, some eventually returned to Jemez but many remained with the Navajo. Some Jemez also fled to Hopi but were returned several years later by missionaries. The Jemez exile did not end until the early eighteenth century, when members of the tribe returned and settled at Walatowa, 12 miles south of their former mesa homes. At that time they built a new church, San Diego de los Jémez.

The Pueblos experienced many changes during following decades: Refugees established communities at Hopi, guerrilla fighting continued against the Spanish, and certain areas were abandoned. By the 1700s, excluding Hopi and Zuñi, only Taos, Picuris, Isleta and Acoma Pueblos had not changed locations since the arrival of the Spanish. Although Pueblo unity did not last, and Santa Fe was officially reconquered in 1692, Spanish rule was notably less severe from then on. Harsh forced labor all but ceased, and the Indians reached an understanding with the Church that enabled them to continue practicing their traditional religion.

In general, the Pueblo eighteenth century was marked by smallpox epidemics, and increased raiding by the Apache, Comanche, and Ute. Occasionally Pueblo Indians fought with the Spanish against the nomadic tribes. The people practiced their religion but more or less in secret. During this time, intermarriage and regular exchange between Hispanic villages and Pueblo Indians created a new New Mexican culture, neither strictly Spanish nor Indian, but rather somewhat of a blend between the two.

Mexican "rule" in 1821 brought little immediate change to the Pueblos. The Mexicans stepped up what had been a gradual process of appropriating Indian land and water, and they allowed the nomadic tribes even greater latitude to raid. In 1837, a political rebellion by Indians and Hispanics over the issue of taxes led to the assassination of the governor of New Mexico and the brief installation of a Taos Indian as governor. At about the same time, the last 20 or so Towa-speaking Pecos people joined the Jemez after abandoning their own pueblo due to Athapaskan raids, smallpox, factionalism, farming decreases, and

land pressures from Hispanics. As the presence of the United States in the area grew, it attempted to enable the Pueblo Indians to continue their generally peaceful and self-sufficient ways; in 1858, Congress approved the old Spanish land grant of over 17,000 acres to Jemez Pueblo.

During the nineteenth century the process of acculturation among Pueblo Indians quickened markedly. In an attempt to retain their identity, Pueblo Indians clung even more tenaciously to their heritage, which by now included elements of the once-hated Spanish culture and religion. By the 1880s, railroads had largely put an end to the traditional geographical isolation of the pueblos. Paradoxically, the U.S. decision to recognize Spanish land grants to the Pueblos denied Pueblo Indians certain rights granted under official treaties and left them particularly open to exploitation by squatters and thieves.

After a gap of more than 300 years, the All Indian Pueblo Council began to meet again in the 1920s, specifically in response to a congressional threat to appropriate Pueblo lands. Partly as a result of the Council's activities, Congress confirmed Pueblo title to their lands in 1924 by passing the Pueblo Lands Act. The United States also acknowledged its trust responsibilities in a series of legal decisions and other acts of Congress. Still, especially after 1900, Pueblo culture was increasingly threatened by highly intolerant Protestant evangelical missions and schools. The Bureau of Indian Affairs also weighed in on the subject of acculturation, forcing Indian children to leave their homes and attend culture-killing boarding schools.

Following World War II, the issue of water rights took center stage on most pueblos. Also, the All Indian Pueblo Council succeeded in slowing the threat against Pueblo lands as well as religious persecution. Making crafts for the tourist trade became an important economic activity during this period. Since the late nineteenth century, but especially after the 1960s, Pueblos have had to cope with onslaughts by (mostly white) anthropologists and seekers of Indian spirituality. The region is also known for its major art colonies at Taos and Santa Fe.

Religion In traditional Pueblo culture, religion and life are inseparable. To be in harmony with all of nature is the Pueblo ideal and way of life. The sun is seen as the representative of the Creator. Sacred mountains in each direction, plus the sun above and the earth below, define and balance the Pueblo world. Many Pueblo religious ceremonies revolve around the weather and are devoted to ensuring adequate rainfall. To this end, Pueblo Indians evoke the power of katsinas, sacred beings who live in mountains and other holy places, in ritual and masked dance. There is no katsina organization per se at Jemez, but men and women do perform masked dances personifying supernaturals to bring rain.

In addition to the natural boundaries, Pueblo Indians have created a society that defines their world by providing balanced, reciprocal relationships within which people connect and harmonize with each other, the natural world, and time itself. According to tradition, the head of each pueblo is the religious leader, or *cacique,* who serves for life and whose primary responsibility it is to watch the sun and thereby determine the dates of ceremonies. Much ceremonialism is also based on medicine societies: About 20 men's and women's religious societies, such as curing, hunter, warrior, and clown, form the social and religious basis of Jemez society. Shamans, who derive powers from animal spirits, use their supernatural powers for curing, weather control, and ensuring the general welfare. Each person also belongs to two patrilineal kiva groups, Squash and Turquoise.

Government Pueblo governments derived from two traditions. Offices that are probably indigenous include the *cacique* and the war captains. These officials are intimately related to the religious structures of the pueblo and reflected the essentially theocratic nature of Pueblo government. At Jemez, the leaders of the various religious societies appointed the *cacique* for a lifetime term.

A parallel but in most cases distinctly less powerful group of officials was imposed by the Spanish authorities. Appointed by the traditional leadership, they generally dealt with external and church matters and included, at Jemez, a governor, lieutenant governor, and *fiscales.* The authority of their offices was symbolized by canes. In addition, the All Indian Pueblo Council, dating from 1598, began meeting again in the twentieth century.

Customs One mechanism that works to keep Pueblo societies coherent is a pervasive aversion to individualistic behavior. Children were raised with gentle guidance and a minimum of discipline. Pueblo Indians were generally monogamous and divorce was relatively rare. Intertribal marriage was also rare before World War II. Afterward, and especially after the Bureau of Indian Affairs (BIA)–sponsored relocation program in 1952, the population became more heterogenous. The dead were buried after being sprinkled with water, cornmeal, and pollen. Two days after death, a prayer feather ceremony was held to send the spirit to the land of the katsinas.

The Jemez tribe recognized two divisions, or kiva groups: Squash and Turquoise. The people were further arranged into matrilineal clans with specific ceremonial functions. In modern times photography by outsiders has been discouraged.

Dwellings More than any other pueblo, Jemez was built on the heights of mesas. It featured apartment-style dwellings of up to four stories, containing as many as 2,000 rooms, as well as one- and two-room houses. The buildings were constructed of adobe (earth and straw) bricks, with pine beams across the roof that were covered with poles, brush, and plaster. Floors were of wood plank or packed earth. The roof of one level served as the floor of another. The levels were interconnected by ladders. As an aid to defense, the traditional design included no doors or windows; entry was through the roof. Two rectangular pit houses, or kivas, served as ceremonial chambers and clubhouses. The village plaza, around which all dwellings were clustered, is the spiritual center of the village where all the balanced forces of the world come together. Jemez people also built cliff dwellings to guard access to important places and monitor trails.

Diet Before the Spanish arrived, Jemez people ate primarily corn, beans, and squash. They also grew cotton and tobacco. They hunted deer, mountain lion, bear, antelope, and rabbits. Twice a year, after planting and again after the harvest, men would travel east to hunt buffalo. The women also gathered a variety of wild foods including piñon seeds, yucca fruit, berries, and wild potatoes. The Spanish introduced wheat, alfalfa, chilies, fruit trees, grapes, sheep, cattle, and garden vegetables, which soon became part of the regular diet.

Key Technology Precontact farming implements were wooden. Traditional irrigation systems used ditches to ferry water from the Rio Grande as well as floodwater collection at arroyo mouths *(ak chin).* Tools were made of bone and wood. Men hunted with bows and arrows. Pottery and yucca baskets were used for a number of purposes. The Spanish introduced metal tools and equipment.

Trade All Pueblos were part of extensive Native American trading networks. With the arrival of other cultures, Pueblo Indians also traded with the Hispanic American villages and then U.S. traders. At fixed times during summer or fall, enemies declared truces so that trading fairs might be held. The largest and best known was at Taos with the Comanche. Nomads exchanged slaves, buffalo hides, buckskins, jerked meat, and horses for agricultural and manufactured pueblo products. Pueblo Indians traded for shell and copper ornaments, turquoise, and macaw feathers. During journeys east for buffalo the Jemez traded with Apaches, Comanches, and Kiowas. They also traded buffalo hides and fur blankets to the Spanish and Mexicans as well as pottery for Keresan *ollas.* Trade along the Santa Fe Trail began in 1821. By the 1880s and the arrival of railroads, the Pueblos were dependent on many American-made goods, and the native manufacture of weaving and pottery declined and nearly died out.

Notable Arts In the Pueblo way, art and life are inseparable. Jemez arts included pottery and woven cotton items. Songs, dances, and dramas also qualify as traditional arts. Many Pueblos experienced a renaissance of traditional arts in the twentieth century, beginning in 1919 with San Ildefonso pottery.

Transportation Spanish horses, mules, and cattle arrived at Jemez Pueblo in the seventeenth century.

Dress Men wore shirts made of tanned deer hides as well as cotton kilts. Women wore black cotton dresses belted with brightly colored yarn. Both wore

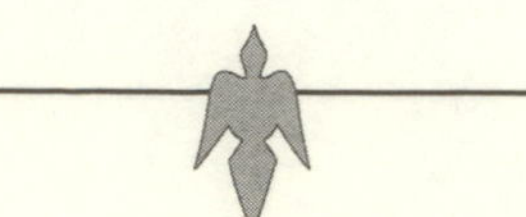

moccasins with buckskin leggings. Rabbit skin was also used for clothing and robes.

War and Weapons Though often depicted as passive and docile, most Pueblo groups regularly engaged in warfare. Every Jemez man belonged to two societies, Eagle and Arrow, related to defense and war. The great revolt of 1680 stands out as the major military action, but they also skirmished at other times with the Spanish and defended themselves against attackers such as Apaches, Comanches, and Utes. They also contributed auxiliary soldiers to provincial forces under Spain and Mexico, which were used mainly against raiding Indians and to protect merchant caravans on the Santa Fe Trail. After the raiding tribes began to pose less of a threat in the late nineteenth century, Pueblo military societies began to wither away, with the office of war captain changing to civil and religious functions.

Contemporary Information

Government/Reservations Jemez Pueblo consists of over 90,000 acres. Walatowa is the main village. The traditional government is intact. The *cacique* is the head of the pueblo, followed by a war chief and his assistants. These are lifetime positions. The positions of war captain, lieutenant war captain, and assistant war captain are filled annually by the *cacique* and war chief and their staffs and are responsible for policing the pueblo and supervising the social activities of the two divisions.

The Spanish-style civil government is also in place. A governor and his staff (two lieutenants, a sheriff, aides, and *fiscales*) are selected annually by the *cacique* and his staff; all serve without salary. Spanish, Mexican, and Lincoln canes remain symbols of authority.

Economy Many Jemez people work for wages in Los Alamos, Santa Fe, and Albuquerque. Especially since World War II and the Indian arts revival, Jemez artists have been making excellent pottery, yucca baskets, weaving, embroidery, and painting. Many people keep gardens and grow chilies, some corn and wheat, and alfalfa for animals. The Pueblo owns hydroelectric, natural gas, oil, and uranium resources. There are also jobs with the government and the tribe.

Legal Status The Pueblo of Jemez is a federally recognized tribal entity. In the 1980s, the tribe successfully fought a geothermal development in the Jemez Mountains that threatened their religious practice. Jemez and Pecos Pueblos were formally consolidated in 1936 and maintain a special connection to the land around abandoned Pecos village, now Pecos National Historic Park.

Daily Life Although the project of retaining a strong Indian identity is a difficult one in the late twentieth century, Pueblo people have strong roots, and in many ways the ancient rhythms and patterns continue. At Jemez, most of the religious societies are still extant and active. Their ceremonialism is largely intact, as is their language. The two divisions, Squash and Turquoise, still race and dance. These ceremonies are generally closed to outsiders, but other dances, with strong Catholic elements, tend to be open to tourists. The people of Jemez still recognize an honorable governor of Pecos Pueblo.

Farming, including grape growing, has dwindled, mainly because of drought, government programs to discourage farming, the people's increasing skills in other areas, welfare, and water usurpation. Children generally attend the BIA day school, mission school, or public school. The Jemez people have been particularly successful in voting tribal members onto the local school board. English has replaced Spanish as a second language. There is a recent tradition of producing first-rate long-distance runners, and the tribe has also produced some notable artists.

Laguna Pueblo

Laguna (Lə `gū nä), Spanish for "lake," refers to a large pond near the pueblo. The word "pueblo" comes from the Spanish for "village." It refers both to a certain style of Southwest Indian architecture, characterized by multistory, apartmentlike buildings made of adobe, and to the people themselves. The Pueblos along the Rio Grande are known as eastern Pueblos; Zuñi, Hopi, and sometimes Acoma and Laguna are known as western Pueblos. The Lagunas call their pueblo *Kawaika,* "lake."

Location Laguna Pueblo is made up of six major villages in central New Mexico, 42 miles west of Albuquerque.

Population Roughly 330 people lived on the pueblo in 1700, plus about 150 more in four nearby villages. In 1990, 3,600 Lagunas lived on the reservation, with perhaps almost as many living away.

Language The people spoke a Keresan dialect similar to that of Acoma Pueblo.

Historical Information

History All Pueblo people are thought to be descended from Anasazi and perhaps Mogollon and several other ancient peoples, although the precise origin of the Keresan peoples is unknown. From them they learned architecture, farming, pottery, and basketry. Larger population groups became possible with effective agriculture and ways to store food surpluses. Within the context of a relatively stable existence, the people devoted increasing amounts of time and attention to religion, arts, and crafts.

In the 1200s, the Anasazi abandoned their traditional canyon homelands in response to climatic and social upheavals. A century or two of migrations ensued, followed in general by the slow reemergence of their culture in the historic pueblos. Laguna and Acoma Pueblos have a unique descent. They have lived continuously in the area since at least 3000 B.C.E. Tradition has it that their ancestors inhabited Mesa Verde. In any case, Laguna's prehistory is closely connected with, if not identical to, that of Acoma.

In 1598, Juan de Oñate arrived in the area with settlers, founding the colony of New Mexico. Oñate carried on the process, already underway, of subjugating the local Indians; forcing them to pay taxes in crops, cotton, and work; and opening the door for Catholic missionaries to attack their religion. The Spanish renamed the Pueblos with saints' names and began a program of church construction. At the same time, the Spanish introduced such new crops as peaches, wheat, and peppers into the region. In 1620, a royal decree created civil offices at each pueblo; silver-headed canes, many of which remain in use today, symbolized the governor's authority.

The Pueblo Indians, including Laguna, organized and instituted a general revolt against the Spanish in 1680. For years, the Spaniards had routinely tortured Indians for practicing traditional religion. They also forced the Indians to labor for them, sold Indians into slavery, and let their cattle overgraze Indian land, a situation that eventually led to drought, erosion, and famine. Popé of San Juan Pueblo and other Pueblo religious leaders planned the revolt, sending runners carrying cords of maguey fibers to mark the day of rebellion. On August 10, 1680, a virtually united stand on the part of the Pueblos drove the Spanish from the region. The Indians killed many Spaniards but refrained from mass slaughter, allowing them to leave Santa Fe for El Paso.

Although Pueblo unity did not last, and Santa Fe was officially reconquered in 1692, Spanish rule was notably less severe from then on. Harsh forced labor all but ceased, and the Indians reached an understanding with the Church that enabled them to continue practicing their traditional religion. Still, the pueblos of Cochiti, Cieneguilla, Santo Domingo, and Jemez rebelled again in 1692. Over 100 people sought refuge at Acoma and Zuñi and then some continued on to found the present village of Old Laguna at the very end of the century. Peace with Spain was finally achieved in 1698. At that time, the Spanish officially recognized Laguna Pueblo, but questions of boundary, especially with Acoma Pueblo, persisted for over two centuries.

The Pueblos experienced many changes during the following decades: Refugees established communities at Hopi, guerrilla fighting continued against the Spanish, and certain areas were abandoned. By the 1700s, excluding Hopi and Zuñi, only Taos, Picuris, Isleta and Acoma Pueblos had not changed locations since the arrival of the Spanish. In general, the Pueblo eighteenth century was marked by smallpox epidemics and increased raiding by the Apache, Comanche, and Ute. Occasionally Pueblo Indians fought with the Spanish against the nomadic Athapaskan and Plains tribes. The people practiced their religion but more or less in secret. During this time, intermarriage and regular exchange between Hispanic villages and Pueblo Indians created a new New Mexican culture, neither strictly Spanish nor

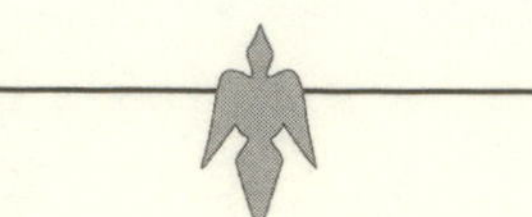

Indian, but rather somewhat of a blend between the two.

Mexican "rule" in 1821 brought little immediate change to the Pueblos. The Mexicans stepped up what had been a gradual process of appropriating Indian land and water, and they allowed the nomadic tribes even greater latitude to raid. By this time, sheep, horses, and mules had become important economically at Laguna. As the presence of the United States in the area grew, it attempted to enable the Pueblo Indians to continue their generally peaceful and self-sufficient ways and recognized Spanish land grants to the Pueblos. Land disputes with neighboring Acoma Pueblo were not settled so easily, however.

By the 1880s, several factors had combined to create a cultural and political explosion at Laguna. These included Spanish settlement in 1700s, Anglo settlement in the 1800s, the proximity to railroad lines, and the presence of Protestant whites living and working on the pueblo as teachers, missionaries, surveyors, and traders. Some of these people married into the tribe. Impatient with Catholic and native traditions, they wrote a constitution and were soon serving as tribal governors. These changes inflamed simmering factionalism and led to charges and countercharges of witchcraft. An Anglo governor in the 1870s had the two big kivas torn down. In the late 1870s, a group of traditionalists moved away to the nearby location of Mesita; some relocated to neighboring Isleta Pueblo.

After a gap of more than 300 years, the All Indian Pueblo Council began to meet again in the 1920s, specifically in response to a congressional threat to appropriate Pueblo lands. Partly as a result of the Council's activities, Congress confirmed Pueblo title to their lands in 1924 by passing the Pueblo Lands Act. The United States also acknowledged its trust responsibilities in a series of legal decisions and other acts of Congress. Still, especially after 1900, Pueblo culture was increasingly threatened by Protestant evangelical missions and schools. The Bureau of Indian Affairs also weighed in on the subject of acculturation, forcing Indian children to leave their homes and attend culture-killing boarding schools.

Following World War II, the issue of water rights took center stage on most pueblos. Also, the All Indian Pueblo Council succeeded in slowing the threat against Pueblo lands as well as religious persecution. Making crafts for the tourist trade became an important economic activity during this period. In 1950 the Laguna sheep herd stood at 15,000, reduced from 52,000 by government edict in the 1930s as a response to overgrazing. Since the late nineteenth century, but especially after the 1960s, Pueblos have had to cope with onslaughts by (mostly white) anthropologists and seekers of Indian spirituality. The Jackpile Uranium Mine opened at Laguna in 1953, creating an economic boom until it closed in 1982.

Religion In traditional Pueblo culture, religion and life are inseparable. To be in harmony with all of nature is the Pueblo ideal and way of life. The sun is seen as the representative of the Creator. Sacred mountains in each direction, plus the sun above and the earth below, define and balance the Pueblo world. Many Pueblo religious ceremonies revolve around the weather and are devoted to ensuring adequate rainfall. To this end, Pueblo Indians evoke the power of katsinas, sacred beings who live in mountains and other holy places, in ritual and dance. At Laguna, all boys were initiated into the katsina society. Laguna Pueblo featured two above-ground kivas, religious chambers that symbolize the place of original emergence into this world.

In addition to the natural boundaries, Pueblo Indians have created a society that defines their world by providing balanced, reciprocal relationships within which people connect and harmonize with each other, the natural world, and time itself. According to tradition, the head of each pueblo is the religious leader, or *cacique,* whose primary responsibility it is to watch the sun and thereby determine the dates of ceremonies. Laguna ceremonialism was controlled by shamans and medicine societies. Each had a specialty, though all participated in ceremonies. Particularly important ceremonies included winter solstice, fertility (which also ensured general health by clowning and making fun of evil spirits), reproduction of game animals and general hunting successes, war and precipitation, and curing.

Government Pueblo governments derived from two traditions. One was indigenous and included, at Laguna, the town chief—"holding the prayer stick"—or *cacique* (although Lagunas speak of all leaders as *caciques*). This official is the overall pueblo leader as well as the religious leader, reflecting the essentially theocratic nature of Pueblo government. Other indigenous officials included the "outside chief" or "white hands," the war captains, and the hunt chief. A parallel but in most cases distinctly less powerful group of officials was imposed by the Spanish authorities. Appointed by the religious hierarchy, they generally dealt with external and church matters and included, at Laguna, a governor, two lieutenant governors, *capitanes,* and *fiscales.* In addition, the All Indian Pueblo Council, dating from 1598, began meeting again in the twentieth century.

Customs One mechanism that works to keep Pueblo societies coherent is a pervasive aversion to individualistic behavior. Children were raised with gentle guidance and a minimum of discipline. Pueblo Indians were generally monogamous and divorce was relatively rare. At Laguna, the dead were prepared ceremonially and quickly buried, heads facing east, with food and other items. A vigil of four days and nights was generally observed. Laguna Pueblo recognized seven matrilineal clans, important in marriage control and other secular activities. The clans also owned all farm land. As herd workers, Lagunas often used Navajo "slaves," or people offered by their parents as children, raised with Laguna children, and freed as adults. In modern times photography by outsiders is discouraged.

Dwellings Laguna Pueblo featured multistory, apartment-style dwellings. The lower levels were reserved mainly for storage. The buildings were constructed of adobe (earth and straw) bricks, with beams across the roof that were covered with poles, brush, and plaster. The roof of one level served as the floor of another. The levels were interconnected by ladders. As an aid to defense, the traditional design included no doors or windows; entry was through the roof. Baking ovens stood outside the buildings. Water was primarily obtained from two natural cisterns. Laguna also features two rectangular pit houses, or kivas, for ceremonial chambers and clubhouses. Herders stayed in caves, small rectangular houses, logs in a horseshoe shape covered with brush, or dugouts. The village plaza is the spiritual center of the village where all the balanced forces of the world come together.

Diet Before the Spanish arrived, people living at Laguna Pueblo ate primarily corn, beans, and squash. They also grew sunflowers and tobacco and kept turkeys. They hunted deer, antelope, and rabbits and gathered a variety of wild seeds, nuts, berries, and other foods. Favorite foods as of circa 1700 included a blue corn drink, corn mush, pudding, wheat cake, corn balls, paper bread, peach-bark drink, flour bread, wild berries, and prickly pear fruit. The Lagunas also raised herds of sheep, goats, horses, and donkeys after the Spanish introduced these animals into the region.

Key Technology Lagunas practiced dry farming and ditch irrigation technology. They used mica for window lights. Fine white clay yielded excellent pottery, and wicker baskets were fashioned of red willow shoots.

Trade All Pueblos were part of extensive Native American trading networks that reached for a thousand miles in every direction. With the arrival of other cultures, Pueblo Indians also traded with the Hispanic American villages and then U.S. traders. At fixed times during summer or fall, enemies declared truces so that trading fairs might be held. The largest and best known was at Taos with the Comanche. Nomads exchanged slaves, buffalo hides, buckskins, jerked meat, and horses for agricultural and manufactured pueblo products. Pueblo Indians traded for shell and copper ornaments, turquoise, and macaw feathers. Lagunas traded black woolen dresses as well as curing fetishes. Trade along the Santa Fe Trail began in 1821. By the 1880s and the arrival of railroads, the Pueblos were dependent on many American-made goods, and the Native American manufacture of weaving and pottery declined and nearly died out.

Notable Arts In the Pueblo way, art and life are inseparable. Laguna women produced excellent pottery; men made fine weavings as well as silver necklaces. Songs, dances, and dramas also qualify as

traditional arts. Many Pueblos experienced a renaissance of traditional arts in the twentieth century, beginning in 1919 with San Ildefonso pottery.

Transportation Spanish horses, mules, and cattle arrived at Laguna Pueblo in the seventeenth century.

Dress Men wore cotton kilts and leather sandals. Women wore cotton dresses and sandals or high moccasin boots. Deer and rabbit skin were also used for clothing and robes.

War and Weapons Though often depicted as passive and docile, most Pueblo groups regularly engaged in warfare. The great revolt of 1680 stands out as the major military action, but they also skirmished at other times with the Spanish and defended themselves against attackers such as Apaches, Comanches, and Utes. They also contributed auxiliary soldiers to provincial forces under Spain and Mexico, which were used mainly against raiding Indians and to protect merchant caravans on the Santa Fe Trail. After the raiding tribes began to pose less of a threat in the late nineteenth century, Pueblo military societies began to wither away, with the office of war captain changing to civil and religious functions.

Contemporary Information

Government/Reservations Laguna Pueblo consists of six major villages on 528,079 acres in central New Mexico, bisected by route I-40. Although part of a whole, the villages enjoy some autonomy. The Indian

A group of Laguna men and women in the mid-1880s. The men wear cloth headbands, silver jewelry, cotton shirts, and trousers with woven belts, as well as leather leggings gartered at the knee. Two women wear dark wool mantas over cotton blouses and woven belts and blankets.

Reorganization Act (IRA) constitution was most recently revised in 1984. Paid secular officials are elected annually.

Economy Lagunas still practice agriculture as well as sheep and cattle herding. Contemporary arts and crafts include fine embroidery, pottery, and yucca basketry. Wage work is provided by a nearby electronics factory, a commercial center, Laguna Industries, and programs paid for by the tribe and the government. The Pueblo owns coal, natural gas, oil, and uranium resources.

Legal Status Laguna Pueblo is a federally recognized tribal entity.

Daily Life Laguna is considered a relatively wealthy and highly acculturated pueblo. Most people live in new or remodeled homes. Although the project of retaining a strong Indian identity is a difficult one in the late twentieth century, Pueblo people have strong roots, and in many ways the ancient rhythms and patterns continue. Many Pueblo Indians, though nominally Catholic, have fused pieces of Catholicism onto a core of traditional beliefs. Since the 1970s control of schools has been a key in maintaining their culture. Health problems, including alcoholism and drug use, continue to plague the Pueblos. Indian Health Service hospitals often cooperate with native healers.

The Lagunas never replaced their religious hierarchy after the schism in the 1870s, although there is a growing interest in ceremonialism, and the people have built a modern "kiva." Each village annually holds feast days honoring patron saints as well as sacred ceremonial dances. Facilities include an elementary school, public junior/senior high, outpatient clinic, and outdoor pool. The tribe also maintains a scholarship fund. From 1953 to 1982, the Anaconda Mineral Company (uranium) provided 800 well-paying jobs and brought much money to the tribe. However, yellow radioactive clouds drifted over the pueblo during those years, and people built roads and houses with radioactive ore and crushed rock from the mine. Today the groundwater is contaminated, and cancer rates are rising.

Maricopa

See Pee-Posh

Mojave or Mohave

Originally Tzi-na-ma-a. Mojave (Mō `hä vē) is a Hispanicization of the Yuman *Aha-makave,* meaning "beside the water."

Location The Mojave traditionally lived in the Mojave Valley and along the northern lower Colorado River. Today, Mojave Indians live primarily on the Fort Mojave Reservation (Arizona) and on the Colorado River Indian Reservation (Arizona and California).

Population Roughly 20,000 Mojaves lived along the river in the early sixteenth century. Their number was reduced to 3,000 by 1770. The 1990 census showed roughly 600 Indians living at Fort Mojave (of a tribal enrollment of 967) and roughly 2,350 Indians living on the Colorado River Reservation, a majority of whom identified themselves as Mojave.

Language Mojaves spoke River Yuman, a member of the Hokan-Siouan language family.

Historical Information

History Ancestors of the modern Mojave Indians settled the Mojave Valley around 1150. These people farmed soil enriched from sediment left by the annual spring floods. The Mojave may have encountered non-natives as early as 1540. Although they served as scouts for Father Francisco Garces's Grand Canyon expedition in 1776, among others, they generally resisted Spanish interference and maintained their independence.

Contact with non-natives remained sporadic until the nineteenth century. At about that time they began raiding Anglo-American fur trappers. They also allowed a band of Paiute Indians called the Chemehuevi to settle in the southern portion of their territory. The Mexican cession and discovery of gold in California brought more trespassers and led to more raids. In 1857, the Mojave suffered a decisive military loss to their ancient enemies, the Pima and Pee-Posh (Maricopa) Indians. Two years later, the United States

Mojave women carried babies on the hip, never on the back. This 1903 photograph by Edward S. Curtis emphasizes the simplicity of the Mojaves' desert life.

built Forts Mojave and Yuma to stem Mojave raiding. By this time, however, the Mojave, defeated in battle and weakened by disease, settled for peace.

In 1865, the Mojave leader Irrateba (or Yara Tav) convinced a group of his followers to relocate to the Colorado River Valley area. The same year, Congress created the Colorado River Reservation for "all the tribes of the Colorado River drainage," primarily the Mojave and Chemehuevi. Roughly 70 percent of the Mojaves had remained in the Mojave Valley, however, and they received a reservation in 1880. This split occasioned intratribal animosities for decades.

The early twentieth century was marked by influenza epidemics and non-Indian encroachment. The first assimilationist government boarding school had opened at the Colorado River Reservation in 1879. Legal allotments began in 1904. Traditional floodplain agriculture disappeared in the 1930s when the great dams tamed the Colorado River. During World War II, many U.S. citizens of Japanese heritage were interned on the Colorado River Reservation: For this operation the United States summarily appropriated 25,000 acres of Indian land.

For 19 years after the war, until 1964, the Bureau of Indian Affairs (BIA) opened the reservation to Hopi and Navajo settlement (tribal rejection of this rule in 1952 was ignored by the BIA). Now all members of four tribes call the reservation home, having evolved into the CRIT (Colorado River Indian Tribes) Indians, a difficult development for the few remaining Mojave elders. In 1963 a federal court case guaranteed the tribes title to federal water rights. They received a deed to the reservation the following year.

Religion The Mojaves believed, as did all Yumans, that they originally emerged into this world from a place near Spirit Mountain, Nevada. Dreaming was the key to Mojave religious experience. Dreams were seen as visits with ancestors. There were omen dreams and, more rarely, great dreams, which brought power to cure, lead in battle, orate a funeral, or do almost anything. However, dreams were considered of questionable authenticity unless they conferred success. Dreams permeated every aspect of Mojave culture. They were constantly discussed and meditated upon. Shamans had the most elaborate great dreams, which were considered to have begun in the womb. Shamans could cause disease as well as cure it, a situation that made for a precarious existence for them.

The Mojaves performed few public ceremonies or rituals. Instead, they sang song cycles for curing, funerals, and entertainment. The cycles consisted of dreams and tribal mythology and were accompanied by people shaking rattles and beating sticks on baskets. A complete cycle could take a night or more to sing, and the Mojave knew about 30 cycles, each with 100–200 songs.

Government Positions of authority such as subchiefs or local leaders derived from dreaming or oratory. Hereditary chiefs in the male line did exist, although with obscure functions. Despite their loose division into bands and local groups, the Mojave thought of themselves as a true tribe; that is, they possessed a national consciousness, and they came together for important occasions such as warfare.

Customs Men planted the crops and women harvested them. Leaders addressed the people from rooftops in the morning about proper ways of living. Hunters generally gave away what they killed. Both men and women tattooed and painted their bodies. The dead were cremated, and their possessions and homes were also burned after a special ceremony during which mourners sang song cycles. No formal

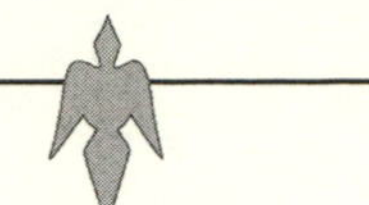

marriage ceremony existed: Marriages were arranged by the couple, and divorce was easy and common. Women carried babies on the hip, never on the back. Mojaves often traveled widely for trade and fun, covering up to 100 miles by foot in a day.

Dwellings Bands and families lived in scattered rancherias, or farms. In warm weather they lived in flat-roofed, open-sided structures. Cold weather dwellings were low and rectangular, with roofs of thatch-covered poles; sand and earth or river mud were piled over the exterior. Doors faced south against the cold north winds. The people also used cylindrical granaries with flat roofs.

Diet Crops such as corn, beans, and pumpkins (and wheat and melons after the Spanish arrived) constituted 50 percent of the Mojave diet. They also caught fish; hunted game such as rabbits and beaver with bows and arrows, traps, or deadfalls; and gathered wild foods. Mesquite beans in particular were a staple, used for food, drink, flour (pith from pods), shoes and clothing (bark), hair dye, instruments (roots), glue (sap), fuel for firing pottery, and funeral pyres.

Key Technology Mojaves used reed rafts to cross the river; headrings for carrying; gourds for storage of seeds and water and, with wooden handles fastened with greasewood and arrowweed, for rattles; bows and arrows; planting sticks and wooden hoes; and assorted pottery and baskets. They also caught fish using drip and drag fish nets, traps, and basketry scoops.

Trade Mojaves traded agricultural products with tribes near the Gulf of California and the Pacific Ocean for shells and feathers. They also acted as brokers between a number of tribes for various indigenous items.

Notable Arts Men and women working together made coiled pottery, dull red when heated, in an open wood fire. In more recent times Mojaves were known for making glass beadwork.

Transportation Reed or log rafts were used for long river trips. Also, swimmers used "ferrying pots" to push food or small children ahead of them while they swam.

Dress Men and women wore loincloths; women also wore willow-bark aprons. Both went barefoot except when traveling, when they wore badger-hide sandals. Rabbit-skin blankets and robes kept them warm in winter. Both sexes wore their hair long; women's hung loose, and men rolled theirs into strands. Both tattooed their chins and painted their faces.

War and Weapons The Mojaves were fierce fighters. A warrior society *(kwanamis)* led three different fighting groups: archers, clubbers, and stick (or lance) men. In addition to those three types of weapons, they also used deer-hide shields, mesquite or willow bows, and arrows in coyote or wildcat quivers. War leaders experienced dreams conferring power in battle. Traditional enemies included the Pima, O'odham, Pee-Posh, and Cocopah; allies included the Quechan, Chemehuevi, Yavapai, and Western Apache. The Mojave often took girls or young women as prisoners, giving them to old men as an insult to the enemy.

Contemporary Information

Government/Reservations Most Mojave Indians live on two reservations. The Colorado River Reservation (1865), containing roughly 270,000 acres, has an active tribal council (1937) and several subcommittees. The Fort Mojave Reservation (1870), within sight of Spirit Mountain and on ancestral lands, contains 32,697 acres, exclusive of about 4,000 acres in Nevada. Each reservation has its own tribal council. Both contain extremely irrigable land. Mojaves also live on the Fort McDowell Reservation in Arizona (24,680 acres, 765 population in 1992). The last traditional Mojave chief died in 1947.

Economy Farming remains important on the Colorado River Reservation, where unemployment stood at 10 percent in 1985. An 11,000-acre farming cooperative produces mainly cotton, alfalfa, wheat, melons, and lettuce. Tourism is also important: Facilities include a marina, resort (the Aha Quin Park), gift shop, and restaurant. Motorboat races are held in the spring and a rodeo in November. Some people herd sheep or work for the BIA or the public

health service. Long-term leases provide significant income, as do numerous large and small businesses, such as a 10-acre recycling plant that opened in 1992.

Although agriculture (primarily cotton) remains important at Fort Mojave, that reservation is harder to irrigate successfully because it contains a checkerboard of private lands. Unemployment there hovers around 50 percent. There are plans to build a huge residential and commercial development, including a casino, in the Nevada part of the reservation. Fort Mojave also leases some land and caters to a small tourist trade. Some opportunities exist in and around the reservation for wage labor.

Legal Status The Colorado River Indian Tribes and the Fort Mojave Indian Tribe are federally recognized tribal entities. The latter has the status of a sovereign Indian nation.

Daily Life Both groups of Mojaves still cremate their dead and mourn them with some of the old songs and ceremonies. Few other myths or song cycles are remembered. Although many Mojaves are Christians, over half speak their native language. The Fort Mojave Reservation maintains a police force and court system. A hospital at CRIT struggles to provide adequate health care. The tribes support education with scholarship funds as well as land donations. A tribal museum helps to preserve the cultural heritages of the individual Colorado Indian tribes. Children attend public schools. Both communities are fighting a proposed "low-level" radioactive waste dump for nearby Ward Valley, an environmentally sensitive area on ground sacred to local tribes.

Nambé Pueblo

Nambé (Näm `bā) is a Spanish rendition of a similar-sounding Tewa name, loosely interpreted as "rounded earth." The word "pueblo" comes from the Spanish for "village." It refers both to a certain style of Southwest Indian architecture, characterized by multistory, apartmentlike buildings made of adobe, and to the people themselves. The pueblos along the Rio Grande are known as eastern Pueblos; Zuñi, Hopi, and sometimes Acoma and Laguna are known as western Pueblos.

Location Nambé Pueblo is located about 15 miles north of Santa Fe, New Mexico.

Population In 1993 there were 487 enrolled tribal members living on Nambé Pueblo, out of a total enrollment of 630. The total number of Pueblo residents in 1990 was about 1,400. Roughly 350 people lived there in 1600.

Language Nambé people spoke a dialect of Tewa, a Kiowa-Tanoan language.

Historical Information

History All Pueblo people are thought to be descended from Anasazi and perhaps Mogollon and several other ancient peoples. From them they learned architecture, farming, pottery, and basketry. Larger population groups became possible with effective agriculture and ways to store food surpluses. Within the context of a relatively stable existence, the people devoted increasing amounts of time and attention to religion, arts, and crafts. In the 1200s, the Anasazi abandoned their traditional canyon homelands in response to climatic and social upheavals. A century or two of migrations ensued, followed in general by the slow reemergence of their culture in the historic pueblos.

In 1598, Juan de Oñate arrived in the area with settlers, founding the colony of New Mexico. Oñate carried on the process, already underway in nearby areas, of subjugating the local Indians; forcing them to pay taxes in crops, cotton, and work; and opening the door for Catholic missionaries to attack their religion. The Spanish renamed the Pueblos with saints' names and began a program of church construction: The first church at Nambé was established in the early 1600s. At the same time, the Spanish introduced such new crops as peaches, wheat, and peppers into the region. In 1620, a royal decree created civil offices at each pueblo; silver-headed canes, many of which remain in use today, symbolized the governor's authority.

The Pueblo Indians, including those at Nambé, organized and instituted a general revolt against the Spanish in 1680. For years, the Spaniards had routinely tortured Indians for practicing traditional religion. They also forced the Indians to labor for

them, sold Indians into slavery, and let their cattle overgraze Indian land, a situation that eventually led to drought, erosion, and famine. Popé of San Juan Pueblo and other Pueblo religious leaders planned the revolt, sending runners carrying cords of maguey fibers to mark the day of rebellion. On August 10, 1680, a virtually united stand on the part of the Pueblos drove the Spanish from the region. The Indians killed many Spaniards but refrained from mass slaughter, allowing them to leave Santa Fe for El Paso.

The Pueblos experienced many changes during following decades: Refugees established communities at Hopi, guerrilla fighting continued against the Spanish, and certain areas were abandoned. By the 1700s, excluding Hopi and Zuñi, only Taos, Picuris, Isleta, and Acoma Pueblos had not changed locations since the arrival of the Spanish. Although Pueblo unity did not last, and Santa Fe was officially reconquered in 1692, Spanish rule was notably less severe from then on. Harsh forced labor all but ceased, and the Indians reached an understanding with the Church that enabled them to continue practicing their traditional religion.

In general, the Pueblo eighteenth century was marked by smallpox epidemics and increased raiding by the Apache, Comanche, and Ute. Occasionally Pueblo Indians fought with the Spanish against the nomadic tribes. The people practiced their religion but more or less in secret. During this time, intermarriage and regular exchange between Hispanic villages and Pueblo Indians created a new New Mexican culture, neither strictly Spanish nor Indian, but rather somewhat of a blend between the two.

Mexican "rule" in 1821 brought little immediate change to the Pueblos. The Mexicans stepped up what had been a gradual process of appropriating Indian land and water, and they allowed the nomadic tribes even greater latitude to raid. A political rebellion by Indians and Hispanics in 1837 over the issue of taxes led to the assassination of the New Mexican governor and the brief installation of a Plains/Taos Indian as governor. As the presence of the United States in the area grew, it attempted to enable the Pueblo Indians to continue their generally peaceful and self-sufficient ways and recognized Spanish land grants to the Pueblos.

During the nineteenth century the process of acculturation among Pueblo Indians quickened markedly. In an attempt to retain their identity, Pueblo Indians clung even more tenaciously to their heritage, which by now included elements of the once-hated Spanish culture and religion. By the 1880s, railroads had largely put an end to the traditional geographical isolation of the pueblos. Paradoxically, the U.S. decision to recognize Spanish land grants to the Pueblos denied Pueblo Indians certain rights granted under official treaties and left them particularly open to exploitation by squatters and thieves.

After a gap of over 300 years, the All Indian Pueblo Council began to meet again in the 1920s, specifically in response to a congressional threat to appropriate Pueblo lands. Partly as a result of the Council's activities, Congress confirmed Pueblo title to their lands in 1924 by passing the Pueblo Lands Act. The United States also acknowledged its trust responsibilities in a series of legal decisions and other acts of Congress. Still, especially after 1900, Pueblo culture was increasingly threatened by Protestant evangelical missions and schools. The Bureau of Indian Affairs also weighed in on the subject of acculturation, forcing Indian children to leave their homes and attend culture-killing boarding schools. Since the late nineteenth century, but especially after the 1960s, Pueblos have had to cope with onslaughts by (mostly white) anthropologists and seekers of Indian spirituality. The region is also known for its major art colonies at Taos and Santa Fe.

Religion In traditional Pueblo culture, religion and life are inseparable. To be in harmony with all of nature is the Pueblo ideal and way of life. The sun is seen as the representative of the Creator. Sacred mountains in each direction, plus the sun above and the earth below, define and balance the Pueblo world. Many Pueblo religious ceremonies revolve around the weather and are devoted to ensuring adequate rainfall. To this end, Pueblo Indians evoke the power of katsinas, sacred beings who live in mountains and other holy places, in ritual and masked dance. One round kiva, or ceremonial chamber, stands at Nambé.

In addition to the natural boundaries, Pueblo Indians have created a society that defines their world by providing balanced, reciprocal relationships within which people connect and harmonize with each other, the natural world, and time itself. According to tradition, the head of each pueblo is the religious leader, or *cacique,* whose primary responsibility it is to watch the sun and thereby determine the dates of ceremonies. Much ceremonialism is also based on medicine societies, and shamans who derive powers from animal spirits use their supernatural powers for curing, weather control, and ensuring the general welfare. Especially in the eastern pueblos, most ceremonies are kept secret.

Government Pueblo governments derived from two traditions. Offices that are probably indigenous include the *cacique,* or head of the Pueblo, and the war captains. These officials are intimately related to the religious structures of the pueblo and reflected the essentially theocratic nature of Pueblo government. At Nambé, summer and winter *caciques* were the religious and the political leaders of the pueblo.

A parallel but in most cases distinctly less powerful group of officials was imposed by the Spanish authorities. Appointed by the traditional leadership, they generally dealt with external and church matters and included the governor, two lieutenant governors, and two sheriffs. The authority of their offices was symbolized by canes. Nontraditional positions also included a ditch boss, who was in charge of the irrigation ditches, as well as a town crier and sacristan. In addition, the All Indian Pueblo Council, dating from 1598, began meeting again in the twentieth century.

Customs One mechanism that works to keep Pueblo societies coherent is a pervasive aversion to individualistic behavior. Children were raised with gentle guidance and a minimum of discipline. Pueblo Indians were generally monogamous, and divorce was relatively rare. The dead were prepared ceremonially and quickly buried with clothes, beads, food, and other items. A vigil of four days and nights was generally observed.

At Nambé, in contrast with most other pueblos, seasons were traditionally delineated not so much by the solstice as by the actual change in seasons. Formerly a summer and a winter *cacique,* appointed for life, oversaw the pueblo. Society was divided into two groups, summer (associated with the Squash kiva) and winter (associated with the Turquoise kiva); membership in a group was patrilineal. These groups were further divided into clans. A number of secret societies also existed. For instance, the warrior society was concerned with hunting, war, crops, fertility, and curing. Each society had its own dances and ritual paraphernalia.

Dwellings Nambé people built small, irregular dwellings clustered around a central plaza. The buildings were constructed of adobe (earth and straw) bricks, with beams across the roof that were covered with poles, brush, and plaster. Floors were of wood plank or packed earth. Pit houses, or kivas, served as ceremonial chambers and clubhouses. The village plaza, around which all dwellings were clustered, is the spiritual center of the village where all the balanced forces of the world come together.

Diet Before the Spanish arrived, people from Nambé Pueblo ate primarily corn, beans, and squash. They also grew cotton and tobacco. They hunted deer, mountain lion, antelope, and rabbits and gathered a variety of wild seeds, nuts, berries, and other foods. The Spanish introduced wheat, alfalfa, chilies, fruit trees, grapes, sheep, cattle, and garden vegetables, which soon became part of the regular diet.

Key Technology Musical instruments included various rattles, drums, and flutes. Irrigation techniques included canals, dams and ditches, and gravity flow. Pottery was an important technological adaptation, as was weaving baskets and cotton. Farming implements were made of stone and wood. Corn was ground using manos and metates.

Trade All Pueblos were part of extensive Native American trading networks. With the arrival of other cultures, Pueblo Indians also traded with the Hispanic American villages and then U.S. traders. At fixed times during summer or fall, enemies declared truces so that trading fairs might be held. The largest and best known was at Taos with the Comanche. Nomads exchanged slaves, buffalo hides, buckskins, jerked meat, and horses

for agricultural and manufactured Pueblo products. Pueblo Indians traded for shell and copper ornaments, turquoise, and macaw feathers. Trade along the Santa Fe Trail began in 1821. By the 1880s and the arrival of railroads, the Pueblos were dependent on many American-made goods, and the native manufacture of weaving and pottery declined and nearly died out.

Notable Arts In the Pueblo way, art and life are inseparable. Nambé artists specialized in making embroidered dresses. Songs, dances, and dramas also qualify as traditional arts. Many Pueblos experienced a renaissance of traditional arts in the twentieth century, beginning in 1919 with San Ildefonso pottery.

Transportation Spanish horses, mules, and cattle arrived at Nambé Pueblo in the sixteenth century.

Dress Men wore cotton and buckskin shirts and kilts. Womens' traditional dress featured spun cotton dresses and sandals or high moccasin boots. Rabbit skin was also used for clothing and robes.

War and Weapons Though often depicted as passive and docile, most Pueblo groups regularly engaged in warfare. The great revolt of 1680 stands out as the major military action, but they also skirmished at other times with the Spanish and defended themselves against attackers such as Apaches, Comanches, and Utes. They also contributed auxiliary soldiers to provincial forces under Spain and Mexico, which were used mainly against raiding Indians and to protect merchant caravans on the Santa Fe Trail. After the raiding tribes began to pose less of a threat in the late nineteenth century, Pueblo military societies began to wither away, with the office of war captain changing to civil and religious functions.

Contemporary Information

Government/Reservations Nambé Pueblo consists of roughly 19,000 acres. Like most other pueblos, Nambé has no written constitution. An elected governor and four other officials serve for two-year terms. Voting on tribal decisions is restricted to a group of past governors. Children of male, but not female, members of the tribe who have married outside the pueblo are automatically enrolled.

Economy Wage work may be found primarily at Los Alamos, with local businesses, or with the tribe or the government. Nambé Falls is a tourist attraction, although few craftspeople cater to the tourist trade. The tribe also operates a trailer park. There is some subsistence farming as well as grazing on leased lands. In addition, the tribe earns interest on land claims compensation funds.

Legal Status Nambé Pueblo is a federally recognized tribal entity. The people are currently seeking the return of roughly 45,000 acres of land near the Santa Fe Ski Basin.

Daily Life Since the Tewas retain fewer traditions than most other pueblos, they are not always successful in preserving a palpable and intentional continuity with the past. Most people, especially the younger ones, speak English and Spanish but little Tewa; the trend is toward only English. Children are bused to schools in nearby towns.

Most Nambé Pueblo Indians are at least nominally Catholic. The festival of Saint Francis, in October, is the only ceremony still performed at Nambé (not including one for the tourists in July at Nambé Falls). The last *cacique* died in 1970. No medicine or other societies remain extant. Clans have virtually disappeared; the basic social unit is now the nuclear family. There is a very high rate of marriage with non-Indians; few marry within the Pueblo or even Tewa Indians. Virtually all people complete high school. Since the 1970s, control of schools has been a key in maintaining their culture. Health problems, including alcoholism and drug use, continue to plague the Pueblos.

Navajo

Navajo (`Nä və hō) is a Tewa word meaning "planted fields." The Navajo call themselves *Dine'é* (Di `nə), "the People." Like the Apache, they are of Athapaskan descent.

Location Dinetah, the traditional Navajo homeland, is located on the lower Colorado Plateau, between the San Juan and Little Colorado Rivers, about 75 miles northwest of Santa Fe. Today's Navajo

Nation occupies a 28,800-square-mile reservation in northern Arizona and New Mexico and southern Utah. This land is mostly plateau (above 5,000 feet) and is marked by deep, sheer-walled canyons. The winters are cold, the summers are hot, and there is little water.

Population The Dine'é are the most numerous Indian tribe in the United States. In 1990, 144,000 Indians lived on the Navajo Reservation, plus 1,177 at Cañoncito and 191 at Ramah (see "Government/ Reservations" under "Contemporary Information"). Many thousands also live off-reservation. More than 200,000 Indians now qualify for membership in the Navajo Nation (officially 219,198 in 1990). Perhaps 6,000 Navajos lived in the Dinetah in 1800.

Language Navajo is an Athapaskan language.

Historical Information

History Roughly 3,000 years ago, the Athapaskans, along with others (all called the Nadene), began a new wave of Asian migration into North America. Nomadic hunter-gatherers, the Southern Athapaskans arrived in the Southwest in roughly 1400 and filled in the mountains around the Pueblo-held valleys. The Northern Athapaskans remained in the subarctic.

To the Athapaskans, Spanish influence (early seventeenth century) meant primarily horses, guns, and places to raid. Consequently their interest in raiding grew, and they effectively established the northern Spanish frontier. Spanish missionaries had little success with the Navajo. Navajos also raided Pueblo Indians for food, women, slaves, and property. Between raids, Navajo and Pueblo people traded with each other. From this contact, the Navajo adopted some Pueblo habits, arts, and customs, especially farming, and settled down. The Navajo became farmers, then herders of sheep, goats, and horses.

Navajos helped the Pueblo people in their great revolt against the Spanish (1680), mainly by accepting, occasionally on a permanent basis, fugitives and refugees. Throughout much of the eighteenth century, the Navajo came in greater contact with Pueblo people and adopted more and more of their ways. Dine'é-Pueblo "pueblitas" became almost a distinct culture in parts of the Dinetah. What is now considered the traditional Navajo culture arose out of this cultural mix.

Animal husbandry, agriculture, hunting, gathering, and weaving wool were the economic base of the Navajo as they began slowly to spread west and south. The early nineteenth century saw much reciprocal raiding with Mexicans, Spaniards, and early travelers on the Santa Fe Trail. Faced with the Mexicans' better firepower, Navajos, especially children, became targets of slave traders during the first half of the nineteenth century. At this time the Navajo possessed no tribal consciousness. They traveled with their livestock in clans (there were over 60) to summer and winter hogans.

In the 1840s, the Navajos held out against U.S. troops in their sacred stronghold, Canyon de Chelly. However, treaties signed then did not stop conflict over grazing lands; white abuses of Indians, including the slave trade; and U.S. Army depredations. Following the Mexican cession (1848), the Navajo were shocked to learn that the United States considered itself as the "owner" of all traditional Navajo territory. In the face of Navajo resistance, the United States determined to take the land by force.

The great warrior and war chief Manuelito attacked and almost took Fort Defiance in 1860. Kit Carson defeated the Navajos in 1864 through a scorched-earth policy: He destroyed their fields, orchards, and livestock and then invaded Canyon de Chelly. Band by band the Navajos surrendered. Manuelito surrendered in 1866. The United States then forcibly relocated 8,000 Navajos to Bosque Redondo (Fort Sumner) in eastern New Mexico, with plans to transform them into farmers. Hundreds of Navajos died on the 400-mile walk, and 2,000 more died in a smallpox epidemic the following year. Those Navajos who had not been captured hid in and around Navajo country.

In 1868 the Navajos were allowed to return and were granted 3.5 million acres of land for a reservation. Although the treaty called for a U.S. government–appointed tribal chief, local headmen retained their power. Manuelito returned home to serve as a Bureau of Indian Affairs (BIA)–appointed subchief and then head chief of the Navajo. He also served as the head of the "Navajo Cavalry," the local police dedicated to ending Navajo raiding. After their

return, the Navajo turned successfully to horse and sheepherding. Navajo culture changed quickly at that time: Trading posts opened, rug weaving for tourists began to take the place of traditional blanket weaving, children were sent to U.S. boarding schools (although this was fiercely resisted at first), Navajos began working for the railroads, missionaries arrived in force, and non-native health care made inroads into traditional cultural practices.

By 1886 the reservation had grown from 3.5 to 11.5 million acres, although much of the best land was taken for railroad rights of way. Tremendous sheep and goat herds made the Navajo relatively prosperous and independent until the mid-1890s, when economic and natural disasters combined to reduce the herds by 75 percent. Following this period the Navajo switched from subsistence herding to raising stock for market.

The Navajo remained organized primarily by band into the twentieth century and thus knew little or no true tribal consciousness until a business council began to meet in 1922. Local business councils, the first and most important community-level political entities, had been created in 1904 (well over 100 chapters of the councils now exist). In 1915, the BIA divided the Navajo Reservation into six districts (which were in turn reorganized in 1955), each with a non-Indian superintendent. These communities retain their character as government towns. In 1923 the secretary of the Interior appointed a tribal commissioner and a tribal council. In 1923 Henry Chee Dodge, who had assumed the position of head chief after Manuelito, became the first tribal chair. He provided the tribe with valuable leadership until his death in 1947.

Overgrazing was the key issue in the 1930s; a BIA-mandated stock reduction at that time led to dramatically lower standards of living. It also led to rejection by the tribe of the Indian Reorganization Act (IRA), of which the stock reduction plan was a part. World War II was a watershed for the tribe: Navajos traveled off the reservation in numbers for the first time, and those who returned came home not only with some money but also with a sense of honor gained from fighting as well as from using their language as a code the enemy was unable ever to break. Still, a crisis of unemployment, and even starvation, marked the immediate postwar years for the Navajo.

The 1950s brought large-scale energy development and with it jobs, money, and new social problems. Coal, oil, and uranium were the most important resources. The number of tribal programs increased dramatically, as did the power of the tribal council. The tribe adopted its own court system and legal code in 1959. The new programs culminated in 1965 with the Office of Navajo Economic Opportunity (ONEO), led by Peter MacDonald. The ONEO funneled tens of millions of dollars into social programs. MacDonald dominated Navajo politics for 20 years, both as head of the ONEO and as tribal chairman in 1970, 1974, 1978, and 1986.

However, the coal leases of the 1960s included provisions for massive strip mining. Soon the once-pristine region was seriously polluted, and by the late 1970s there was strong sentiment against further development. MacDonald himself was convicted in 1990 and 1992 of several felony corruption-related crimes and later jailed. Peterson Zah served as tribal chairman in 1982, as president of the Navajo Nation in 1990, and as chair of the nation in 1992. The controversy over the degree and type of economic development continues today, the Navajo having achieved a large degree of self-determination.

Religion *"Sa'ah Naaghei Bik'en Hozho,"* which may be characterized as being grounded to the earth, whole, and in harmony with life, is the Navajo Way. Everything is sacred and interrelated. For instance, religion equals identity equals clan equals place. The chief role of ceremonialism is to maintain or restore this harmony. Therefore, most ceremonies are for curing illness, broadly defined as being off balance for any number of reasons, such as contact with non-natives, ghosts, witches, or the dead.

According to legend, Navajos (and all other beings) came to this world 600 to 800 years ago through a progression of underworlds. They were assisted by powerful and mysterious spiritual beings such as coyote, changing woman, spider woman, spider man, and the hero twins. These beings exist in the natural and supernatural worlds and may be called upon for help with curing. Most ceremonies are held when needed, not according to a calendar.

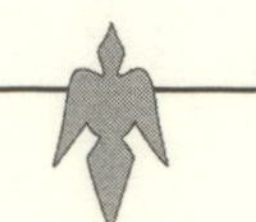

Many important aspects of Navajo ceremonialism, such as the use of masked dancers, feathered prayer sticks, altars, dry (sand) painting, cornmeal, and pollen, were borrowed from the Hopi and other Pueblo people. Traditional Navajo religion excludes organized priesthoods or religious societies. Instead, ceremonies are conducted by "singers" who have mastered one or more of 24 chantway systems. The systems are divided into six main groups: blessingway, war, gameway (hunting), and the three curing ceremonials—holyway, evilway (ghostway), and lifeway. Each group might be composed of 50 or more chants, which in turn might have hundreds of songs or prayers. Specific sandpaintings and social functions often accompany each chant.

As part of the ceremony, the singers use bundles containing items such as rattles, feathered wands and brushes, various stones, and herbal medicines. The most important is the mountain earth bundle, which contains pinches of soil from the tops of the four sacred (bordering) mountains. Around 1940, the Native American Church took its place in Navajo religious practice.

Government Traditionally, the Navajo were organized in a number of bands, each led by a headman (appointed for life) and a clan leader, who were assisted by one or more war leaders. The leaders met formally only every few years. Decisions were taken by consensus.

Customs In general, the individual takes precedence over the group. Property ownership is individual. The residence group, which was organized around a head mother, a sheep herd, and a customary land-use area, was the largest traditional Navajo organization. Clans were both matrilineal and matrilocal. Men were not allowed to see or talk with their mothers-in-law, so families lived near the wife's mother but in their own homes. The Navajo had a great fear of death. After the dead were buried, their belongings were destroyed.

The extended family was an important economic and social unit, as was the "outfit" in later times, a grouping that consisted of two or more extended families. Home, crops, pottery, and livestock belonged to women and were considered women's work; men made jewelry and represented the family in public and at ceremonials. A four-day girls' puberty ceremony ranked among the most important occasions.

Dwellings Navajos lived in hogans. At first they were cone-shaped structures, framed with logs and poles and covered with earth and bark. Later the hogans had six or eight sides and were covered with stone and adobe. Doorways always faced east. The hogans were grouped in rancherias, or small settlements. Other structures included sweat lodges, brush corrals, and ramadas.

Diet Before the Spanish influence, the Navajo grew corn, beans, and squash. Afterward they added fruit trees, oats, and wheat. They hunted antelope, deer, and bear and gathered wild foods such as pine nuts, cactus fruit, wild potatoes, greens, seeds, and herbs. Grazing by sheep, goats, and cattle, acquired from the Spanish in the sixteenth century, destroyed much of their wild food.

Key Technology The Navajo used traps and snares for hunting. After the introduction of livestock, they learned to spin and weave. In the nineteenth century they learned silver work from the Mexicans.

Trade Navajos were part of an extensive Native American trading system. In particular, they traded meat, hides, blankets, and minerals to Pueblo Indians for ceramics and cloth. Extensive trade began after the Civil War, with traders acting in many cases as primary links to the outside world as well as bankers, via a pawn system.

Notable Arts The arts were traditionally seen as ways to relate to and influence spiritual beings and to be closer to the ancestors; as such they were integrated into Navajo ceremonialism. Oral chants told history, traditions, and mythology and were accompanied by music. The Navajo knew several categories of traditional music, from personal/pleasurable to deeply sacred. The people made paintings on clean sand of mineral powders and pollens, which they destroyed at the end of a ceremony. Weaving, done by women, was learned from Pueblo people around 1700; Navajo weavers created a golden age in the early nineteenth century.

Weaving, done by women, as shown in this 1893 photograph, was learned from Pueblo people around 1700. Navajo weavers created a golden age in the early nineteenth century, and rugs began to replace blankets after 1890.

Rugs began to replace blankets after 1890. Women also made pottery. Basketry was more utilitarian than artistic. The Navajo learned the art of making silver and turquoise jewelry in the mid-1800s.

Transportation The Navajo acquired horses from the Spanish in the sixteenth century.

Dress Navajos traditionally dressed in aprons and breechcloths of woven yucca, later buckskin, with feathered headgear. Moccasins were made of juniper bark and yucca, later deerskin and cowhide. By the eighteenth century, women wore belted, black wool dresses with stripes of red, yellow, or blue. Men wore buckskin shirts, leggings, and moccasins. From the 1860s on, women wore long, full, colorful skirts and velveteen blouses. Men wore cotton pants and velveteen shirts. Pendleton blankets became regular items of clothing in the nineteenth century; silver and turquoise jewelry in the twentieth.

War and Weapons The Navajo first made points of stone for items such as arrows and lance tips; later they used metal. They made bows of oak and juniper and first acquired guns in the seventeenth century. Beginning about that time the Navajo became inveterate raiders. Their traditional targets included the Spanish and the Ute and Pueblo Indians.

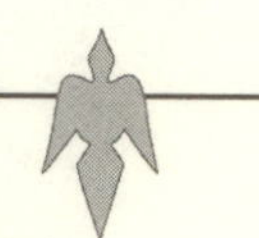

A Navajo couple of the mid-1880s wears silver jewelry and traditionally styled clothing made of nontraditional materials.

Contemporary Information

Government/Reservations The Navajo Reservation, established in 1868, consists of almost 14 million acres (28,800 square miles) plus several nearby satellite communities. Cañoncito Reservation (1868; 76,813 acres) near Laguna Pueblo is one such satellite, where roughly 1,700 people (1990) are descended from generally proassimilation, Christian Navajos who moved south in the early nineteenth century under Spanish pressure. Other satellite communities include Utah (6,000 people), Ramah (1868; 146,953 acres; 1,500 people), and Puertocito, or Alamo (1868; 63,109 acres; 2,000 people). Thirty thousand Navajos also live on the "checkerboard" in New Mexico, a region in which each alternate square mile is Indian owned. Navajos are also represented among the Colorado River Indian Tribes (*see* Mojave).

Other official Navajo communities include the following: Aneth, Baca, Becenti, Beclabito, Bread Springs, Burnham, Cameron, Casamero, Cheechilgeetho, Chilchinbeto, Chinle, Church Rock, Coalmine, Copper Mine, Cornfields, Coyote Canyon, Crownpoint, Crystal, Dalton Pass, Dennehotso, Forest Lake, Fort Defiance, Ganado, Greasewood, Houck, Huerfano, Inscription House, Iyanbit, Jeddito, Kaibito, Kayenta, Kinlichee, Klagetoh, Lake Valley, Lechee, Leupp, Little Water, Low Mountain, Lukachukai, Lupton, Manuelito, Many Farms, Mariano, Mexican Springs, Mexican Waters, Nageezi, Naschitti, Navajo Mountain, Nazlini, Nenahnezad, Oak Springs, Oljatoh, Pinedale, Piñon, Pueblo Plaintado, Red Lake, Red Mesa, Red Rock, Rock Point, Rock Springs, Rough Rock, Round Rock, St. Michaels, Sanostee, Sawmill, Sheep Springs, Shiprock, Shonto, Smith Lake, Standing Rock, Steamboat, Sweetwater, Teecnospos, Teesto, Thoreau, Tohatchi, Tolani Lake, Torreon and Star Lake, Tsaile-Wheatfields, Tsayatoh, Tselani, Tuba City, Twin Lakes, Two Grey Hills, Upper Fruitland, White Cone, White Rock, Wide Ruins, and Whitehorse Lake as well as Dilkon Community and Ojo Encino.

Twenty-five energy-producing tribes, including the Navajo, created the Council of Energy Resource Tribes (CERT) in 1976 to help tribes exert control over their mineral resources. Despite their array of lawyers, the tribes have found it difficult to resist pressure from the major energy companies to sign exploitative leases.

The U.S. government still officially controls the Navajo tribal government. Elections for the tribal council are held every four years. In 1936 the council adopted a set of rules that serve as a constitution (they formally rejected organization under the IRA). The "Navajo Nation" was formally adopted in 1969. In 1990, the government was reorganized to coincide with the U.S. model, and the offices of president and vice-president replaced those of chair and vice-chair.

Economy Peabody Coal remains the largest single employer of Navajos. Mineral (oil, gas, coal, uranium) exploitation continues, although not without some controversy. Navajo Agricultural Products Industries and Navajo Forests Products Industries are also large employers. Some people still farm, herd, and produce

wool. Many are engaged in making arts and crafts, especially weavings, jewelry, baskets, pottery, and commercial sandpaintings. There is some retail business as well as some off-reservation employment. One-third of the tribal workforce is often unemployed.

Legal Status The following are federally recognized tribal entities: Navajo Tribe of Arizona, New Mexico, and Utah; Navajo Tribe of Arizona, New Mexico, and Utah (Alamo); Navajo Tribe of Arizona, New Mexico, and Utah (Cañoncito); Navajo Tribe of Arizona, New Mexico, and Utah (Ramah). The Cañoncito Band of Navajos had petitioned for federal recognition as of 1993.

A land dispute with the Hopi dates back to 1882. At that time, the Hopi Reservation included at least 300 Navajos. The Navajos asked for title to the lands in light of Hopi "nonuse": the issue was Hopi "homesteading" versus Navajo "aggressive exploitation." The Hopi refused. A 1962 district court decision *(Healing* v. *Jones)* ruled that each tribe had joint interest in most of the 1882 Hopi Reservation.

In 1974 Congress passed the Navajo-Hopi Land Settlement Act, under which each tribe was to receive half of 1.8 million acres of jointly held land. Those people on the "wrong" side were to move. One hundred Hopis moved. Thousands of Navajos did too, but many refused to leave, and the issue is still in dispute. The Hopi refuse money for land. Traditional leaders among both tribes oppose the act, preferring to keep the land in question open and unspoiled. They have formed a unity council to resolve the situation and consider the ongoing tension the work of energy companies and prodevelopment factions on both tribal councils.

The Navajos also have other land conflicts outstanding with the Hopi as well as with the recently recognized San Juan Paiutes.

Daily Life Navajo children attend community schools, private schools, and reservation high schools; some of the curricula are in the Navajo language. The Rough Rock Demonstration School (1964), the first to operate under a contract from the BIA, demonstrated the wisdom of local control. Since 1969, the reservation has been home to Navajo Community College (the first tribally controlled college); since 1972, to the College of Ganado (Presbyterian). Many Navajos live away from the reservation, although ties between urban Navajos and the reservation remain generally close. Within the context of traditional Navajo identity, new ideas and types of knowledge continue to be taught. Though many Navajos are Christian, the traditional beliefs and the Native American Church are even more popular.

Economically, herders often depend upon a family member with a local wage job. Older Navajos in particular experience chronic under- and unemployment. The tribe has plans to develop a marina, an electronics assembly plant, shopping centers, and motels. Tourism is a high priority. Energy resources are a mixed blessing: They bring in money, but the leases remain exploitative, and their development is often accompanied by political dissension as well as the ravages of strip mining and radiation poisoning.

Life in the late twentieth century remains a balancing act for all. Some (up to 25,000) traditional people speak only or mostly Navajo, some are thoroughly acculturated, and many are uncomfortably in the middle. Today, native healers practice alongside modern doctors. The reservation was scheduled to receive complete telephone service in 1995 but was still waiting as of early 1998. Homes look more modern every year, but the hogan remains the spiritual center and the only place for ceremonies. Women have generally continued their traditional matriarchal roles. Alcoholism is widespread, and suicide rates are high. The Navajo religion is alive and strong, although, with singers and dancers to be paid and food, baskets, and other equipment to be bought, some ceremonials can be very expensive. The Native American Church has a strong presence on the reservation, as does Christianity. Radio stations broadcast programs in Navajo.

Papago

See Tohono O'odham

Pecos Pueblo

See Jemez Pueblo

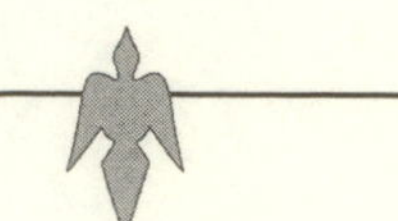

Pee-Posh

Pee-Posh (`Pē Posh) or "*Pipatsje,*" "the People." These people are also known as the Maricopa. (*See also* Pima.)

Location The Pee-Posh lived for centuries along the lower Colorado River and then began migrating to the Gila River region in the 1600s. Today the majority of Pee-Posh live outside of Arizona and California, although the greatest concentrations live with the Pima on the Gila River and Salt River Reservations in Arizona (none live on the Maricopa Reservation).

Population Perhaps 2,500 Pee-Posh and related groups (see "History") migrated to the Gila River region in early historical times. There were roughly 800 Pee-Posh nationwide in 1990.

Language The Pee-Posh spoke a dialect of River Yuman, a Hokan-Siouan language.

Historical Information

History Those people whom the Spanish called the Opa or the Cocomaricopa were one of several small Yuman tribes (including the related groups—the Halchidoma, Kahwan, Kavelchadom, and the Halyikwamai) who lived along the lower Colorado River. Contact with the Spanish was minimal and sporadic. By the early eighteenth century, these peoples had relocated up the Gila River, owing to an escalation of attacks by the Quechan and Mojave. The Pima offered them land and protection, and the two groups soon formed a confederation. By the early nineteenth century, the Pee-Posh had all but absorbed the smaller tribes.

The Pima-Maricopa confederacy went a long way toward making non-Indian settlement of that part of the desert possible, protecting Anglos from Apaches, starvation, and thirst. For example, the Indians used much of their surplus wheat to provide food for the so-called forty-niners on their way to California. (By 1870, their wheat production had reached 3 million pounds, an achievement that aroused the wrath of Anglo wheat farmers.) The Indians also sold wheat to the U.S. Army. In 1857, the confederacy decisively defeated the Quechans and Mojaves at Maricopa Wells, marking the last major formal battle between Indian nations in the Southwest. Beginning in the 1840s, and continuing throughout the century, epidemics took a heavy toll on the Indian population.

In recognition of its alliance with the confederation, the U.S. government established a reservation on the Gila River in 1863 for the Pima and the Pee-Posh. However, river water levels shortly began to fall so low as a result of upstream diversions by non-natives that a group of Indians moved to the confluence of the Gila and Salt Rivers. Now known as Laveen, this community was first called Maricopa Colony. Halchidoma descendants soon relocated to the Salt River, around the present site of Lehi. In 1879, the original reservation was enlarged, and the Salt River Reservation was established.

During that decade several factors conspired to ruin the Indians' thriving economy: a decline in rainfall, a doubling of the population, and, in particular, huge diversions of Gila River water by non-Indians. By the 1880s, Indian crops routinely failed and famine threatened. Many Pimas and Pee-Posh were forced into the wage economy at the lowest levels. With the loss of the river, the heart of their culture also disappeared. The U.S. government continued to ignore the key problem of water rights, and Pima and Pee-Posh impoverishment continued well into the twentieth century.

In the late nineteenth century, the Bureau of Indian Affairs (BIA) began a campaign to assimilate local Indians. With its blessing, the Presbyterian Church became very active at Gila River, beginning a day school and in general imposing a religious structure on the tribes. The issue of Christianity proved to be a very divisive one on the reservation. In 1914, allotment hit both reservations (against active Indian opposition), scattering the people and further disrupting community life. In 1926, the BIA formed a Pima Advisory Council in an effort to create a formal body that spoke for the tribe. In 1934, the Pimas created a constitution, which was revised by the Pima and Pee-Posh community two years later.

By 1930, non-native water diversions had effectively ended Gila River surface water flowing to the Pee-Posh. Rather than redress the situation, the BIA forced the Indians to use brackish well water. This water was only suitable for growing cotton and some grains, however, and the people could no longer grow edible crops. Several other factors worked to cancel any benefits that might have come with the well water, including a dependency of Indians on wage work, continued ongoing water shortages, and the hated allotments (heirships), which had destroyed their effective land base.

In 1934, the Pima and the Pee-Posh accepted the Indian Reorganization Act (IRA) and formed the Gila River Indian Community. Following World War II, many Pee-Posh (encouraged by the BIA's relocation program) moved away from the reservation. For years outsiders thought that the Pee-Posh had died out and become a subgroup of the Pima Indians.

Religion In general, ceremonialism among River Yumans was not especially well developed, except to honor the dead or to celebrate war exploits. Pee-Posh people believed in the power of dreams to direct life and to reveal the potential for special skills and abilities. Shamans had special powers to cure, control the weather, and detect thieves and enemies.

Government Nominal village chiefs exerted little influence. Recognized specialists had the true authority, as curers, calendar-stick keepers, singers, potters, and dancers. All obtained their power from dreams.

Customs Entire villages moved when someone died, after the body, residence, and possessions had been burned. Special singers sang elaborate song cycles for funerals and transmitted legends, such as ancestral wanderings or conflicts with other groups. Girls celebrated a special puberty ceremony, after which they were tattooed. Both sexes cultivated a high tolerance of pain. As was true for other River Yumans, farming, including ownership of the farm site, was essentially an individual activity. Boundary disputes were solved by mediation or by controlled fighting. The Pee-Posh recognized patrilineal clan as well as village divisions.

Dwellings Flattened-dome houses were built with a frame of mesquite or cottonwood uprights and covered with willow ribs and arrowweed thatch. Walls were packed with earth. Rectangular ramadas often adjoined the houses. All dwellings faced east. Other structures included storage sheds, woven basket granaries, and sweat lodges.

Diet The Pee-Posh used floodwater agriculture in their farming. Their staples were mesquite beans and corn. Men planted and cultivated and women harvested. Much food was also gathered, including seeds, berries, nuts, cactus fruit, honey, caterpillars, and beans. The people also ate jackrabbits and fish (caught with nets or bare hands).

Key Technology All River Yumans share a similar material culture. Clay for pottery was shaped between a curved paddle and a stone anvil or pottery mold. Grinding stones came from granite or sandstone. Wooden mortars, made by hollowing the end of a cottonwood or mesquite log, were used with stone pestles to pulverize mesquite beans. The people used hides for thongs, quivers, shield coverings, and, occasionally, sandals. After the early 1800s, brush dams and ditches replaced floodwater farming as irrigation methods. O'odham-derived calendar sticks told of ancestors, travels, fights, and deaths.

Trade Trails linked the Pee-Posh with the Mojave and other southern desert peoples. With them, they traded for goods from the Pacific Ocean and the Gulf of California. Trade articles included hand nets and weirless traps for fishing, Pima baskets, and, after the 1700s, Spanish horses and captives. In times of need, food could be obtained from the O'odham literally for a song.

Notable Arts Women made a wide variety of pottery, including cooking pots, bowls, and water jars. Both men and women wove blankets, cradle ties, headbands, belts, and skirts for girls' puberty ceremonies. Baskets were made and obtained in trade from the Pima.

Transportation The Pee-Posh began using horses in the seventeenth century.

Dress Men wore breechclouts. Women wore fringed skirts of woven willow bark. Both used cotton and

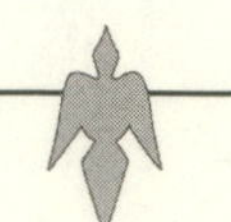

rabbit-skin garments in bad weather and sandals for long journeys.

War and Weapons The Pee-Posh fought primarily defensive wars. Their weapons included mesquite or ironwood bows, short clubs, and hide shields.

Contemporary Information

Government/Reservations The Pee-Posh live on the Salt River Reservation (1879; 50,506 acres), near Lehi, and on the Gila River Reservation (1859; 371,933 acres), west of Laveen ("District Seven" of the reservation, the old Maricopa Colony). They share a tribal government with the Pimas; constitutions and by-laws were approved in 1940 (Salt River) and 1936 (Gila River). It is the Ak-chin O'odham who live on the Maricopa Reservation.

Economy The possibility of subsistence farming was lost because individual allotments mandated by the Dawes Act (1887) divided the land into parcels too small to be farmed. Most reservation land is now leased to non-native farmers, and the reservation suffers from a high unemployment rate. Still, the Maricopa Indian Cooperative Association farms about 1,200 acres. Some Indians work off-reservation for wages, generally in Phoenix. Some pottery, not of original Indian concept, is made for the tourist trade. Industrial and mineral development (Gila River) is growing slowly.

Legal Status Recognized tribal entities include the Gila River Pima-Maricopa Indian Community and the Salt River Pima-Maricopa Indian Community.

Daily Life The ethnic identities of the other River Yuman people who followed the Pee-Posh east remain important. Despite the loss of many pre-Pima traditions, the Pee-Posh think of themselves as a united nation and remain in many ways distinct from the Pimas. They are relatively well educated and attend public school. Most speak only English, though a few still speak Pee-Posh. Water rights and health issues, including substance abuse and diabetes, are ongoing concerns. The cremation and mourning ceremonies remain important. A trade fair is held on the reservation every year.

Frame and cement block houses are replacing a few "Pima-style sandwich houses" of adobe packed between slats and timbers. Some Pee-Posh also live in surplus houses of all kinds, including Japanese internment buildings and trailers. Pee-Posh housing is generally considered substandard.

Picuris Pueblo

Picuris (`Pē kur `ēs) comes from the Spanish *Picurís,* "at the mountain gap." The word "pueblo" comes from the Spanish for "village." It refers both to a certain style of Southwest Indian architecture, characterized by multistory, apartmentlike buildings made of adobe, and to the people themselves. Rio Grande pueblos are known as eastern Pueblos; Zuñi, Hopi, and sometimes Acoma and Laguna are known as western Pueblos. The people call their pueblo *Pingultha,* which means either "mountain warrior place" or "mountain pass place."

Location Picuris Pueblo is located on the western slopes of the Sangre de Cristo Mountains, 18 miles south of Taos Pueblo. The average elevation is about 7,000 feet, which makes for a relatively short and somewhat precarious growing season.

Population There were perhaps 2,000 residents of Picuris Pueblo in 1630. In 1990, 147 Indians lived on the reservation out of a total population of 1,882.

Language People from Picuris spoke a dialect of Northern Tiwa, a Tanoan language.

Historical Information

History All Pueblo people are thought to be descended from Anasazi and perhaps Mogollon and several other ancient peoples. From them they learned architecture, farming, pottery, and basketry. Larger population groups became possible with effective agriculture and ways to store food surpluses. Within the context of a relatively stable existence, the people devoted increasing amounts of time and attention to religion, arts, and crafts.

In the 1200s, the Anasazi abandoned their traditional canyon homelands in response to climatic and social upheavals. A century or two of migrations

ensued, followed in general by the slow reemergence of their culture in the historic pueblos. The Tiwas were probably the first of the Tanoan Pueblo people to enter the northern Rio Grande region. Initial settlement of Picuris Pueblo occurred in the twelfth century. It reached its prehistoric peak in the sixteenth century, then declined, probably as a result of the arrival of the Athapaskans.

In 1598, Juan de Oñate arrived in the area with settlers, founding the colony of New Mexico. Oñate carried on the process, already underway in nearby areas, of subjugating the local Indians; forcing them to pay taxes in crops, cotton, and work; and opening the door for Catholic missionaries to attack their religion. The Spanish renamed the Pueblos with saints' names and began a program of church construction, constructing the Mission of San Lorenzo at Picuris in 1621. At the same time, the Spanish introduced such new crops as peaches, wheat, and peppers into the region. In 1620, a royal decree created civil offices at each pueblo; silver-headed canes, many of which remain in use today, symbolized the governor's authority.

Picuris joined the Pueblo rebellion of 1680. For years, the Spaniards had routinely tortured Indians for practicing traditional religion. They also forced the Indians to labor for them, sold Indians into slavery, and let their cattle overgraze Indian land, a situation that eventually led to drought, erosion, and famine. Popé of San Juan Pueblo and other Pueblo leaders, including Tupatu or Luis Picuri, planned the great revolt, sending runners carrying cords of maguey fibers to mark the day of rebellion. On August 10, 1680, a virtually united stand on the part of the Pueblos drove the Spanish from the region. The Indians killed many Spaniards but refrained from mass slaughter, allowing most of them to leave Santa Fe for El Paso.

When the northern pueblos again revolted in 1696, the Picuris abandoned their pueblo and went to live for 20 years on the plains with the Apaches. Between 1680 and 1716, the Picuris population declined by 90 percent. By the 1700s, excluding Hopi and Zuñi, only Taos, Picuris, Isleta, and Acoma Pueblos had not changed locations since the arrival of the Spanish. Although Pueblo unity did not last, and Santa Fe was officially reconquered in 1692, Spanish rule was notably less severe from then on. Harsh forced labor all but ceased, and the Indians reached an understanding with the Church that enabled them to continue practicing their traditional religion.

In general, the Pueblo eighteenth century was marked by smallpox epidemics and increased raiding by the Apache, Comanche, and Ute. The people practiced their religion but more or less in secret. During this time, intermarriage and regular exchange between Hispanic villages and Pueblo Indians created a new New Mexican culture, neither strictly Spanish nor Indian, but rather somewhat of a blend between the two. In the early part of the century the Picuris fought with the Spanish against the Apaches, Utes, and Comanches. They also welcomed a French trading party to the pueblo in 1739, having first encountered French goods through trade with Plains tribes 80 years earlier. By the late eighteenth century they had achieved peace with the Comanche. Partly as a result, Spanish settlement grew, and Picuris Pueblo became surrounded by Spanish-Americans.

Mexican "rule" in 1821 brought little immediate change to the Pueblos. The Mexicans stepped up what had been a gradual process of appropriating Indian land and water, and they allowed the nomadic tribes even greater latitude to raid. As the presence of the United States in the area grew, it attempted to enable the Pueblo Indians to continue their generally peaceful and self-sufficient ways and recognized Spanish land grants to the Pueblos (the grant to 600-year-old Picuris was recognized in 1858). Picuris spent much of the nineteenth century fighting encroachment. To help them, the people turned to non-native civil authorities (Spanish, Mexican, and U.S.). They achieved some success but lost political autonomy in the process.

The relative isolation of Picuris delayed the assimilationist pressures faced by other pueblos. However, a government day school, in which children learned Anglo ways and values, opened in 1899. Adults were encouraged to engage in wage work off the pueblo. Timber operations also began, damaging the fragile irrigation system. In an attempt to retain their identity, Pueblo Indians clung even more tenaciously to their heritage, which by now included elements of the once-hated Spanish culture and religion. By the 1880s, railroads had largely put an end to the traditional geographical isolation of the pueblos. Paradoxically, the U.S. decision to recognize Spanish land grants to the Pueblos denied Pueblo Indians certain rights granted under official treaties and left them particularly open to exploitation by squatters and thieves.

By the 1920s, land disputes had claimed the people's traditional friendliness toward Spanish-Americans. By the 1930s, government wage work and food had largely replaced the subsistence life. Also, the Bureau of Indian Affairs (BIA) was actively intervening in the people's political affairs. After a gap of over 300 years, the All Indian Pueblo Council began to meet again in the 1920s, specifically in response to a congressional threat to appropriate Pueblo lands. Partly as a result of the Council's activities, Congress confirmed Pueblo title to their lands in 1924 by passing the Pueblo Lands Act. The United States also acknowledged its trust responsibilities in a series of legal decisions and other acts of Congress. Still, especially after 1900, Pueblo culture was increasingly threatened by Protestant evangelical missions and schools. The BIA also weighed in on the subject of acculturation, forcing Indian children to leave their homes and attend culture-killing boarding schools.

Since the late nineteenth century but especially after the 1960s, Pueblos have had to cope with onslaughts by (mostly white) anthropologists and seekers of Indian spirituality. The region is also known for its major art colonies at Taos and Santa Fe.

In 1947, the adult men of Picuris voted to change the name of the pueblo to San Lorenzo; however, the name Picuris was again adopted in 1955.

Religion In traditional Pueblo culture, religion and life are inseparable. To be in harmony with all of nature is the Pueblo ideal and way of life. The sun is seen as the representative of the Creator. Sacred mountains in each direction, plus the sun above and the earth below, define and balance the Pueblo world. Many Pueblo religious ceremonies revolve around the weather and are devoted to ensuring adequate rainfall. To this end, Pueblo Indians evoke the power of katsinas, sacred beings who live in mountains and other holy places, in ritual and masked dance.

In addition to the natural boundaries, Pueblo Indians have created a society that defines their world by providing balanced, reciprocal relationships within which people connect and harmonize with each other, the natural world, and time itself. At Picuris, people were divided into two patrilineal ceremonial groups, Northside and Southside. Each had a kiva, or prayer chamber. There were also a number of ceremonial organizations, such as Spring People (responsible for the first of three summer rain ceremonies), Fall People (responsible for the second ceremony), and Winter People (responsible for the third ceremony). All used a round house in the north pueblo for ceremonies, except the Winter People, whose ceremonies took place in the "ice kiva." Other ceremonial organizations included water clowns, a mountain group, a *cacique*'s group, and a women's group.

According to tradition, the head of each pueblo is the religious leader, or *cacique,* whose primary responsibility it is to watch the sun and thereby determine the dates of ceremonies. Much ceremonialism is also based on medicine societies, and shamans who derive powers from animal spirits use their supernatural powers for curing, weather control, and ensuring the general welfare. Especially in the eastern pueblos, most ceremonies are kept secret. The mission church at Picuris also served local Spanish-Americans until the late 1800s.

Government Pueblo governments derived from two traditions. Offices that are probably indigenous include the *cacique,* or head of the Pueblo, and the war captains. These officials are intimately related to the religious structures of the pueblo and reflected the essentially theocratic nature of Pueblo government. At Picuris, a Council of *Principales,* composed of the headmen of ceremonial groups and respected elders, made policy, judged offenses, and appointed civil officers.

A parallel but in most cases distinctly less powerful group of officials was imposed by the Spanish authorities. Appointed by the traditional leadership, they generally dealt with external and church matters and included the governor and four assistant governors. The authority of their offices was symbolized by canes. In 1950, Picuris men voted in the pueblo's first election for governor and other civil officials. At that time, the

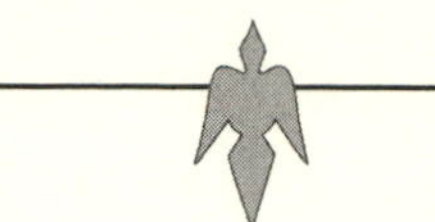

governor replaced the *cacique* as head of the pueblo. During the 1950s and 1960s, the All Indian Pueblo Council (of eastern villages) became increasingly active in asserting rights and solving problems.

Customs One mechanism that works to keep Pueblo societies coherent is a pervasive aversion to individualistic behavior. Children were raised with gentle guidance and a minimum of discipline. Pueblo Indians were generally monogamous, and divorce was relatively rare. After birth, the baby remained in bed with the mother for 30 days. Children were christened during this time and then confirmed in church between ages 6 and 12. Girls tended to marry in their late teens or early twenties; men about four years later. A new couple established a new household. At Picuris, the dead were ceremonially prepared (black mica on the face and a prayer feather in each hand), death songs were sung, and a wake and Christian hymns followed. Burial, with a food bag, occurred quickly, followed by a four-day vigil. In modern times photography by outsiders is discouraged.

Dwellings Picuris Pueblo featured apartment-style dwellings as high as nine stories. The buildings were constructed of adobe (earth and straw) bricks, with beams across the roof that were covered with poles, brush, and plaster. Floors were of wood plank or packed earth. The roof of one level served as the floor of another. The levels were interconnected by ladders. As an aid to defense, the traditional design included no doors or windows; entry was through the roof. Pit houses, or kivas, served as ceremonial chambers and clubhouses. The village plaza, around which all dwellings were clustered, is the spiritual center of the village where all the balanced forces of world come together.

Diet Before the Spanish arrived, Picuris people ate primarily corn, beans, and squash. They also grew cotton and tobacco. They hunted deer, mountain lion, bear, antelope, and rabbits. Occasionally, men from Picuris would travel east to hunt buffalo. The people also gathered a variety of wild seeds, nuts, berries, and other foods and fished in rivers and mountain streams. The Spanish introduced wheat, alfalfa, chilies, fruit trees, grapes, sheep, cattle, and garden vegetables, which soon became part of the regular diet.

Key Technology Precontact farming implements were wooden. Traditional irrigation systems included ditches as well as floodwater collection at arroyo mouths *(ak chin).* Tanning tools were made of bone and wood. The Spanish introduced metal tools and equipment. Men hunted with juniper bows and arrows.

Trade All Pueblos were part of extensive Native American trading networks. With the arrival of other cultures, Pueblo Indians also traded with the Hispanic American villages and then U.S. traders. At fixed times during summer or fall, enemies declared truces so that trading fairs might be held. The largest and best known was at Taos with the Comanche. Nomads exchanged slaves, buffalo hides, buckskins, jerked meat, and horses for agricultural and manufactured pueblo products. Pueblo Indians traded for shell and copper ornaments, turquoise, and macaw feathers. Trade along the Santa Fe Trail began in 1821. By the 1880s and the arrival of railroads, the Pueblos were dependent on many American-made goods, and the native manufacture of weaving and pottery declined and nearly died out.

The Picuris served as a link between Pueblo and Plains tribes. In particular, they were generally friendly with the Jicarilla Apache, exchanging both trade items and visits during ceremonies. Despite the proximity of Taos Pueblo (18 miles by trail), the two peoples interacted relatively infrequently and traded little but mountain plants. Picuris enjoyed generally good relations and trade with the Tewa-speaking pueblos, especially San Juan. Picuris also traded with Spanish-Americans, by whom they were surrounded from the eighteenth century on. They also occasionally worked for wages in Spanish-American fields.

Notable Arts In the Pueblo way, art and life are inseparable. Picuris arts included pottery, baskets, and woven cotton items. Songs, dances, and dramas also qualify as traditional arts. Many Pueblos experienced a renaissance of traditional arts in the twentieth century, beginning in 1919 with San Ildefonso pottery.

Transportation Spanish horses, mules, and cattle arrived at Picuris Pueblo in the seventeenth century.

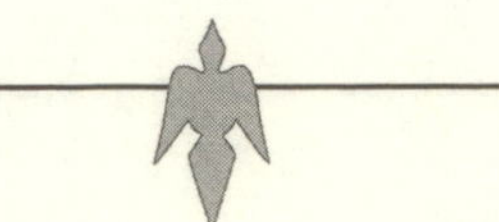

Dress Men wore shirts, leggings, and moccasins made of deer hides tanned and colored red-brown with plant dye. Womens' wrapped leggings and moccasins were of white buckskin. Clothing was also made of spun cotton. Rabbit skin was also used for clothing and robes.

War and Weapons Though often depicted as passive and docile, most Pueblo people regularly engaged in warfare. The great revolt of 1680 stands out as the major military action, but they also skirmished at other times with the Spanish and defended themselves against attackers such as Apaches, Comanches, and Utes. They also contributed auxiliary soldiers to provincial forces under Spain and Mexico, which were used mainly against raiding Indians and to protect merchant caravans on the Santa Fe Trail. After the raiding tribes began to pose less of a threat in the late nineteenth century, Pueblo military societies began to wither away, with the office of war captain changing to civil and religious functions.

Contemporary Information

Government/Reservations Picuris Pueblo contains almost 15,000 acres. Tribal officers are elected for two-year terms. The tribe is headed by a governor rather than a *cacique.*

Economy Most of the jobs at Picuris Pueblo are with federal and tribal programs. Little remains of the subsistence economy. Some people make pottery for the tourist trade, which is also served by a restaurant and a small museum and cultural center. The tribe also allows a college to hold an anthropological field school in the pueblo. There are also jobs fighting forest fires with the U.S. Forest Service. In 1991, the tribe opened a major hotel in Santa Fe, backed by non-Indian partners and the BIA. Many people leave the pueblo for outside jobs.

Legal Status Picuris Pueblo is a federally recognized tribal entity.

Daily Life The project of retaining a strong Indian identity is a difficult one in the late twentieth century. Although Picuris people have strong roots and the rebuilding of four kivas has characterized a renewed interest in traditional celebrations, the pueblo is largely acculturated. Children attend local public schools. San Lorenzo's Day, on August 10, is the main feast day; during the races, the traditional division between Northside and Southside people is largely ignored. The pueblo also holds a mountain dance in late September as well as some other dances under direction of the war captain.

Pima

Pima (`Pē mä), from *pi-nyi-match,* "I don't know" (a reply to early questioners). The Pima were originally called Akimel O'odham, or River People, and they are also known as One Villagers because of their relatively settled lives. The O'odham Indians include the Pima, Tohono O'odham (Papago, or Desert People, also known as Two Villagers because of their traditional migration patterns), Sand Papago (Hia C-ed O'odham, or No Villagers because of their more or less constant migrations in search of food), and the Ak-chin O'odham.

Location Traditionally, the Pima lived in rancherias in present-day southern Arizona and northern Sonora, Mexico (the Sonoran Desert). The Spanish categorized them as the Pima Alto (Upper Pima, who lived near the Gila and Salt Rivers) and the Pima Bajo (or Nevones, Lower Pima, who lived along the Yaqui and Sonora Rivers). Today's (upper) Pima reservations are located in southern Arizona.

Population There were roughly 50,000 Pimas in 1500 and perhaps 3,000 in 1700. The 1990 Pima-Maricopa Reservation population was roughly 12,600. There were also at least several hundred Pimas living on the Ak-chin Reservation and off-reservation.

Language Piman is a language of the Uto-Aztecan family.

Historical Information

History The Pima are probably descended from ancient Hohokam Indians. They lived and farmed in permanent settlements (rancherias) near rivers on the northern edge of the Spanish frontier, which at the time was at present-day Tucson. The first non-Indian

to visit the Pimas was Marcos de Niza (1589). In 1684, Father Eusebio Kino organized several missions and introduced livestock, wheat, and metal tools into the region.

An accommodation between the Pima and Spanish masked resentments over religious, political, and cultural imperialism, not to mention forced labor. In 1695 the Lower Pima, under Luis Oacpicagigua and others, revolted against the Spanish, and in 1751 the Upper Pima rebelled. The latter had little support from other tribes or even a majority of Pimas, however, and peace was soon established.

Around 1800 the Pee-Posh (Maricopa) Indians came to live near the Upper Pima. At the same time the area came under more frequent attack by Apache raiders. The twin factors of winter wheat production plus increased conflict with the Apache led to a thorough transformation of Pima society. Pima bands engaged in closer cooperation and began to produce agricultural surpluses. This led in turn to an increased integration of their society. By the mid–nineteenth century the position of governor had become hereditary, and the Pima had become a true tribe. They were also the only effective force in the area against the Apache as well as an important economic power.

Despite Pima food assistance to so-called forty-niners and the U.S. Army, Anglo settlers along the Gila River took the best farmland and diverted water for their own use. After the Gadsden Purchase (1853) split O'odham country in two, Anglos began using the term "Pima" for residents on the Gila River and "Papago" for Piman speakers south of the Gila. The United States established a Pima-Maricopa reservation on the Gila River in 1859. However, as a result of failing water supplies, many Indians moved north, where another reservation was established in 1879 on the Salt River. From the 1850s on, three generations of the Azul family led the Pima-Maricopa confederation.

By 1870, Pima wheat production had reached 3 million pounds. Non-natives reacted to this achievement with fear, envy, and retaliation. Major Anglo water diversions soon left the Pima with little water for their crops. Combined with a drought and population increases, this led to Pima impoverishment in the late nineteenth century and early twentieth century. Many Pimas were forced into the wage economy at the lowest levels. The U.S. government ignored the key problem of Pima water rights.

The loss of the river and the growing influence of Presbyterians brought about a severe decline in Pima culture and traditional religion. The Presbyterians replaced the Pima religious structure with one of their own creation. The Presbyterian Church and the Bureau of Indian Affairs (BIA) opened day and boarding schools respectively. Allotment hit the reservation in 1914, breaking up tribal land patterns and further disrupting community life.

In 1926, the BIA created a Pima Advisory Council to meet the bureau's need for a body that spoke for the tribe. Eight years later the Pimas adopted a constitution and tribal council, which remained quite powerless, as the Pima "tribe" had virtually disappeared. The Pima and Maricopa community revised the constitution and by-laws in 1936. In the 1930s the San Carlos Project began returning irrigation water to the Pimas, but several factors worked to cancel its benefits, including the dependency of Indians on wage work (at that point they were reluctant to return to subsistence farming), a complex water-management bureaucracy that mandated required crops, chronic ongoing water shortages, and the fact that allotments (heirship) had destroyed their effective land base. The postwar period has been a time for Pimas once again to assume a degree of control over their own resources and lives.

Religion Pimas worshiped several deities, the most important of which were Earthmaker and Elder Brother *(I'itoi)*. The harvest and victory after battle provided the best occasions for ceremonies. Many O'odhams became Catholics in the eighteenth century, but theirs was a Catholicism with important native variations.

Government A civil leader and one or more shamans presided over economically and politically independent villages. Village ceremonial leaders were known as "keepers of the smoke." Village chiefs elected a tribal chief, who ran council meetings. His other responsibilities included overseeing farm projects and defending against Apache raiders. In the

mid–nineteenth century, the chieftainship went from a position of power and no wealth to one of wealth and no power. In 1936 the adoption of a new constitution under the Indian Reorganization Act marked the beginning of the Pima battle for legal rights.

Customs Each village was divided into two groups, Red Ant and White Ant, who opposed each other in games and other ceremonial functions. The groups were further divided into patrilineal clans. In general, men farmed, fished, hunted, built the houses, and wove cotton; women gathered food and made baskets, pottery, and clothing. They also carried firewood and food on their backs in burden baskets. The Pima used a lunar calendar. Their year began with the rainy season and the appearance of flowers on certain plants, such as the saguaro cactus. *Viikita* was a celebration held every fourth harvest to celebrate and ensure the favor of the gods. The Pima buried their dead in rock crevices or in stone huts, with weapons, tools, and food. The deceased's house was burned. For traveling long distances, the Pima preferred running to walking; a ball was kept in motion to maintain the pace.

Dwellings Pimas lived in small, round, flat-topped, pole-framed structures, covered with grass and mud. In warmer weather they moved into simple open-sided brush arbors. They also built cylindrical bins in which they stored mesquite beans. Ramadas, used for clubhouses, also dotted each village.

Diet Farm products such as corn, squash (cut into strips and dried), and tepary beans accounted for up to 60 percent of the Pima diet. The people also grew tobacco and cotton and, after the Spanish arrived, wheat (winter wheat ensured against starvation and made farms very productive) and alfalfa. Wild foods included cactus fruit, mesquite beans, greens, chilies, and seeds, which, with corn, were ground into meal on a cottonwood mortar and used in gruel and cakes. Pimas also ate fish and hunted deer, rabbit, mountain sheep, antelope, and reptiles. They drank saguaro wine for ceremonial purposes.

Key Technology To irrigate their crops, Pimas diverted water from rivers with dams of logs and brush. They also built canals and feeder ditches. Farm tools consisted of digging sticks and a flat board used for hoeing and harvesting. Hunting bows were made of Osage orange or willow. After a great meteor shower in 1833, the people used calendar sticks—saguaro ribs with cuts—to mark certain events. The Spanish brought horse- and oxen-drawn wagons and plows and metal picks and shovels into the region.

Pima women grew their hair long, wore ear pendants of turquoise and other stones, and tattooed and painted their bodies. This woman's elaborate face paint may denote her family or simply be ornamental.

Trade Pimas traded salt, seashells, and ceremonies for River Yuman pottery and food. They also traded with the Lower Pimas for hides, mescal, and pepper.

Notable Arts Women made highly prized baskets with abstract designs out of black devil's claw. They also made red-and-black pottery. Men made equally good cotton belts and blankets.

Transportation The O'odham traveled by foot until the introduction of Spanish horses in the seventeenth century.

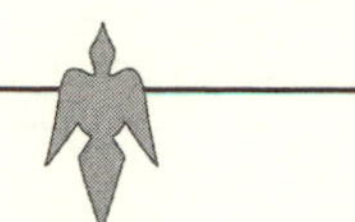

Pimas lived in small, round, flat-topped, pole-framed structures, covered with grass and mud (pictured here in 1892). In warmer weather they moved into simple open-sided brush arbors.

Dress Men wore cotton or deerskin breechcloths. Women wore cloth, willow bark, or deerskin wraparound skirts. Both sexes used hide or fiber sandals and cotton and rabbit-skin blankets. They also grew their hair long, wore ear pendants of turquoise and other stones, and tattooed and painted their bodies.

War and Weapons Pimas placed a high value on peace yet became more oriented toward war with the growing Apache threat after the mid–eighteenth century. Traditional enemies also included Quechans and Yavapais; their main allies were the Pee-Posh. Pimas also fought against Apaches with the Spanish, Mexicans, and U.S. troops. Pimas fought in all U.S. wars beginning with the Civil War. Warriors who had killed an enemy underwent a 16-day purification rite. War bows were made of mulberry. Other weapons included clubs and shields.

Contemporary Information

Government/Reservations The Gila River Reservation was established in 1859. It consists of roughly 370,000 acres. A community council of 17 members governs by way of various committees; the governing structure also contains an executive and a judicial element. The Salt River Reservation was established in 1879, in Maricopa County, and contains roughly 52,600 acres. Its constitution and by-laws were adopted in 1940. Some Pimas also live among the Tohono O'odham on the Ak-chin Reservation.

Economy Almost all farmland is leased to non-Indians for industrial parks and agribusiness, although Gila River Farms produces a number of crops, and the Salt River Reservation has roughly 12,000 acres under cultivation. There is some wage work in the cities and with the tribe. There is also a large retail center on the reservation. Other sources of income include apiary licenses, traders' licenses, industrial parks, a large motor racing park, and sand and gravel sales. Additional highway development may bring in some money. The Gila River Arts and Crafts Center, which includes a restaurant and a museum, is a focus for the local tourist trade.

Legal Status The Gila River Pima-Maricopa Community of the Gila River Indian Reservation and the Salt River Pima-Maricopa Community of the Salt

River Indian Reservation are federally recognized tribal entities.

Daily Life Faced with the need to store calories against periodic famines, Pimas traditionally ate in what might today be called binges. The combination of the absence of famine and a diet that contains many highly processed, low-fiber, and junk foods has left Pimas with a marked tendency toward diabetes. A number of health centers, including the private Native American Dialysis Center, help with these problems. The Fiesta de Magdalena, held in the fall in Sonora, Mexico, remains the most powerful connection between the Arizona and Mexican O'odham. Water rights remain a pressing issue—the water table in their area has been lowered some 300 feet over the years—as does creeping urban and suburban sprawl.

Most Pimas are Presbyterians and are relatively assimilated into mainstream U.S. life. Few live any longer in extended families. The loss of most traditions has been difficult for some people: It led in part to the death of Ira Hayes, one of six men who raised the U.S. flag on Iwo Jima during World War II. The Pima hold annual fairs, particularly the *mul-chu-tha* festival, in March as well as a rodeo and parades. Some Pimas continue to make baskets. There is a net outflow of population off the reservations. Students attend BIA schools on the reservations (Gila River) as well as public schools. The Salt River Reservation contains a number of recreational and cultural facilities.

Pojoaque Pueblo

Pojoaque (Pō `hwä kā) is an adaptation of the Tewa *Posuwaegeh,* meaning "drink-water place." The word "pueblo" comes from the Spanish for "village." It refers both to a certain style of Southwest Indian architecture, characterized by multistory, apartment-like buildings made of adobe, and to the people themselves. Rio Grande pueblos are known as eastern Pueblos; Zuñi, Hopi, and sometimes Acoma and Laguna are known as western Pueblos.

Location Pojoaque Pueblo is located 16 miles north of Santa Fe; it is the smallest of the six Tewa villages.

Population In 1990, 177 Indians lived on the pueblo out of an overall population of roughly 2,500; 79 lived there in 1712 and possibly as many 500 in 1500.

Language Tewa is a Kiowa-Tanoan language.

Historical Information

History All Pueblo people are thought to be descended from Anasazi and perhaps Mogollon and several other ancient peoples. From them they learned architecture, farming, pottery, and basketry. Larger population groups became possible with effective agriculture and ways to store food surpluses. Within the context of a relatively stable existence, the people devoted increasing amounts of time and attention to religion, arts, and crafts. In the 1200s, the Anasazi abandoned their traditional canyon homelands in response to climatic and social upheavals. A century or two of migrations ensued, followed in general by the slow reemergence of their culture in the historic pueblos. Occupation of the Pojoaque area has been constant since about 900, and it grew to be a major political and cultural center.

In 1598, Juan de Oñate arrived in the area with settlers, founding the colony of New Mexico. Oñate carried on the process, already underway in nearby areas, of subjugating the local Indians; forcing them to pay taxes in crops, cotton, and work; and opening the door for Catholic missionaries to attack their religion. The Spanish renamed the Pueblos with saints' names and began a program of church construction. At the same time, the Spanish introduced such new crops as peaches, wheat, and peppers into the region. In 1620, a royal decree created civil offices at each pueblo; silver-headed canes, many of which remain in use today, symbolized the governor's authority.

Pojoaque took an active part in the 1680 Pueblo revolt against the Spanish. For years, the Spaniards had routinely tortured Indians for practicing traditional religion. They also forced the Indians to labor for them, sold Indians into slavery, and let their cattle overgraze Indian land, a situation that eventually led to drought, erosion, and famine. Popé of San Juan Pueblo and other Pueblo religious leaders planned the revolt, sending runners carrying cords of

maguey fibers to mark the day of rebellion. On August 10, 1680, a virtually united stand on the part of the Pueblos drove the Spanish from the region. The Indians killed many Spaniards but refrained from mass slaughter, allowing them to leave Santa Fe for El Paso.

Pojoaque suffered greatly in the aftermath of the revolt. Spanish recolonizers took much of their best land. The tribe became decimated and scattered but was able to reestablish itself in 1706. However, by then most of their population had been absorbed by other pueblos. Although Pueblo unity did not last, and Santa Fe was officially reconquered in 1692, Spanish rule was notably less severe from then on. Harsh forced labor all but ceased, and the Indians reached an understanding with the Church that enabled them to continue practicing their traditional religion.

In general, the Pueblo eighteenth century was marked by smallpox epidemics and increased raiding by the Apache, Comanche, and Ute. Occasionally Pueblo Indians fought with the Spanish against the nomadic tribes. The people practiced their religion but more or less in secret. During this time, intermarriage and regular exchange between Hispanic villages and Pueblo Indians created a new New Mexican culture, neither strictly Spanish nor Indian, but rather somewhat of a blend between the two.

Mexican "rule" in 1821 brought little immediate change to the Pueblos. The Mexicans stepped up what had been a gradual process of appropriating Indian land and water, and they allowed the nomadic tribes even greater latitude to raid. A political rebellion by Indians and Hispanics in 1837 over the issue of taxes led to the assassination of the New Mexican governor and his brief replacement by a Plains/Taos Indian. As the presence of the United States in the area grew, it attempted to enable the Pueblo Indians to continue their generally peaceful and self-sufficient ways.

During the nineteenth century the population at Pojoaque became so small (it was recorded as 32 in 1870) that the people could no longer hold their ceremonies. A steady loss of their land base contributed to the tribe's degeneration. Many people left to live at other pueblos or to make their way in the outside world. At the same time, documents attesting to Spanish land grants and water rights were lost, although the United States did confirm their holding in 1858; shortly afterward, leaders traveled to Washington to receive the patent as well as a silver-headed Lincoln cane. Paradoxically, the U.S. decision to recognize Spanish land grants to the Pueblos denied Pueblo Indians certain rights granted under official treaties and left them particularly open to exploitation by squatters and thieves.

By the early twentieth century, Pojoaque Pueblo was all but abandoned, although it had become a small Spanish-American settlement by the 1930s. At that time a handful of Pojoaque families returned, evicted non-Indians, and fenced the land. Antonio José Tapia was instrumental in reestablishing the pueblo during this period. Government payment for losses suffered over the years acted as an incentive for other Pojoaques to return. Partly because of lobbying from the All Indian Pueblo Council, Congress confirmed Pueblo title to their lands in 1924 by passing the Pueblo Lands Act. The United States also acknowledged its trust responsibilities in a series of legal decisions and other acts of Congress. Still, the Bureau of Indian Affairs (BIA) forced Indian children to leave their homes and attend culture-killing boarding schools and in general tried its best to undermine Indian identity and survival.

Religion In traditional Pueblo culture, religion and life are inseparable. To be in harmony with all of nature is the Pueblo ideal and way of life. The sun is seen as the representative of the Creator. Sacred mountains in each direction, plus the sun above and the earth below, define and balance the Pueblo world. Many Pueblo religious ceremonies revolve around the weather and are devoted to ensuring adequate rainfall. To this end, Pueblo Indians evoke the power of katsinas, sacred beings who live in mountains and other holy places, in ritual and masked dance.

In addition to the natural boundaries, Pueblo Indians have created a society that defines their world by providing balanced, reciprocal relationships within which people connect and harmonize with each other, the natural world, and time itself. According to tradition, the head of each pueblo is the religious leader, or *cacique,* whose primary responsibility it is to watch the sun and thereby determine the dates of ceremonies. Much

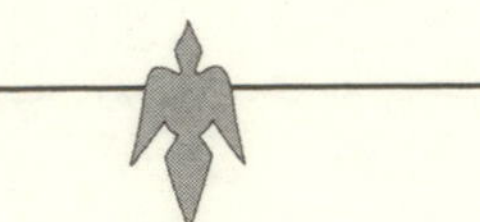

ceremonialism is also based on medicine societies, and shamans who derive powers from animal spirits use their supernatural powers for curing, weather control, and ensuring the general welfare. Especially in the eastern pueblos, most ceremonies are kept secret.

Government Pueblo governments derived from two traditions. Offices that are probably indigenous include the *cacique,* or head of the Pueblo, and the war captains. These officials are intimately related to the religious structures of the pueblo and reflected the essentially theocratic nature of Pueblo government. Pojoaque had both summer and winter *caciques.*

A parallel but in most cases distinctly less powerful group of officials was imposed by the Spanish authorities. Appointed by the traditional leadership, they generally dealt with external and church matters and included the governor, two lieutenant governors, and two sheriffs. The authority of their offices was symbolized by canes. Nontraditional positions also often included a ditch boss, who was in charge of the irrigation ditches, as well as a town crier and sacristan. In addition, the All Indian Pueblo Council, dating from 1598, began meeting again in the twentieth century.

Customs One mechanism that works to keep Pueblo societies coherent is a pervasive aversion to individualistic behavior. Children were raised with gentle guidance and a minimum of discipline. Pueblo Indians were generally monogamous, and divorce was relatively rare. The dead were prepared ceremonially and quickly buried with clothes, beads, food, and other items. A vigil of four days and nights was generally observed.

At Pojoaque, in contrast with most other pueblos, seasons were traditionally delineated not so much by the solstice as by the actual change in seasons. Formerly a summer and a winter *cacique,* appointed for life, oversaw the pueblo. Society was divided into two groups, summer (associated with the Squash kiva) and winter (associated with the Turquoise kiva); membership in a group was patrilineal. These groups were further divided into clans. A number of secret societies also existed. For instance, the warrior society was concerned with hunting, war, crops, fertility, and curing. Each society had its own dances and ritual paraphernalia.

Dwellings Most Pueblos (possibly including Pojoaque) originally featured multistory apartment-style dwellings constructed of adobe (earth and straw) bricks, with pine beams across the roof that were covered with poles, brush, and plaster. Floors were of wood plank or packed earth. The roof of one level served as the floor of another. The levels were interconnected by ladders. As an aid to defense, the traditional design included no doors or windows; entry was through the roof. Pit houses, or kivas, served as ceremonial chambers and clubhouses. The village plaza, around which the church and all dwellings were clustered, was the spiritual center of the village where all the balanced forces of the world come together.

Diet Before the Spanish arrived, people from Pojoaque Pueblo ate primarily corn, beans, and squash. They also grew cotton and tobacco. They hunted deer, mountain lion, antelope, and rabbits. They also gathered a variety of wild seeds, nuts, berries, and other foods. The Spanish introduced wheat, alfalfa, chilies, fruit trees, grapes, sheep, cattle, and garden vegetables, which soon became part of the regular diet.

Key Technology Pojoaque people used irrigation ditches from a time well before the arrival of the Spanish.

Trade All Pueblos were part of extensive Native American trading networks. With the arrival of other cultures, Pueblo Indians also traded with the Hispanic American villages and then U.S. traders. At fixed times during summer or fall, enemies declared truces so that trading fairs might be held. The largest and best known was at Taos with the Comanche. Nomads exchanges slaves, buffalo hides, buckskins, jerked meat, and horses for agricultural and manufactured pueblo products. Pueblo Indians traded for shell and copper ornaments, turquoise, and macaw feathers. Trade along the Santa Fe Trail began in 1821. By the 1880s and the arrival of railroads, the Pueblos were dependent on many American-made goods, and the

Native American manufacture of weaving and pottery declined and nearly died out.

Notable Arts In the Pueblo way, art and life are inseparable. Traditional arts at Pojoaque include weaving, songs, dances, and dramas. Many Pueblos experienced a renaissance of traditional arts in the twentieth century, beginning in 1919 with San Ildefonso pottery.

Transportation Spanish horses, mules, and cattle arrived at Pojoaque Pueblo in the sixteenth century.

Dress Men wore cotton and buckskin shirts and kilts. Womens' traditional dress featured spun cotton dresses and sandals or high moccasin boots. Rabbit skin was also used for clothing and robes.

War and Weapons Though often depicted as passive and docile, most Pueblo groups regularly engaged in warfare. The great revolt of 1680 stands out as the major military action, but they also skirmished at other times with the Spanish and defended themselves against attackers such as Apaches, Comanches, and Utes. They also contributed auxiliary soldiers to provincial forces under Spain and Mexico, which were used mainly against raiding Indians and to protect merchant caravans on the Santa Fe Trail. After the raiding tribes began to pose less of a threat in the late nineteenth century, Pueblo military societies began to wither away, with the office of war captain changing to civil and religious functions.

Contemporary Information

Government/Reservations Pojoaque Pueblo consists of roughly 11,600 acres, with some still in dispute. The governor, who may be—and has been—a woman, is elected annually. The tribal council, which may also contain women, meets at least every two weeks.

Economy Many people work for wages in Santa Fe or Española. The tribe owns valuable frontage on U.S. Route 285 and is planning long-term commercial development. It also operates La Mesita restaurant, Nambé Mills (pottery), the Poeh Cultural Center and Museum, and several other businesses, including a shopping center. It owns forestry leases in addition to commercial ones. Uranium is found on the pueblo. Income is divided among all tribal members. To limit excessive development, the council has insisted on ten-year leases; it also insists that Indians have the top priority for jobs. There is very little farming or livestock activity, but there is some craft activity, especially pottery. Pojoaque Pueblo boasts relatively low unemployment.

Legal Status Pojoaque Pueblo is a federally recognized tribal entity.

Daily Life Pojoaque is largely assimilated into the local Hispanic-Anglo culture. Nothing remains of the old pueblo. Nor do any traditional ceremonies or the office of *cacique* remain (the last *cacique* died around 1900); cultural identity is maintained through participation in other pueblos' ceremonies, particularly those at Santa Clara.

Most people, especially the younger ones, speak English and possibly Spanish but little Tewa; the trend is toward only English. Most Pojoaque Indians are at least nominally Catholic. An excellent school complex educates both local Indian and non-Indian children, and the tribe provides some scholarships for postsecondary education. Health care is available in Española and Santa Fe. Despite the lack of traditional cultural attributes, Pojoaque is slowly regaining its former position as a center of Tewa culture.

Quechan

Quechan (`Kē chan) from *xam kwatcan,* "another going down" (a reference to their ancestral migration). Quechans are also known as Yuma Indians; Yuma is an O'odham word for "People of the River."

Location The Quechan lived in several small settlements, or rancherias, along the bottomlands of the Colorado River, near the mouth of the Gila. Many Quechans now live on the Fort Yuma Reservation as well as on the Cocopah Reservation with Pee-Posh and Cocopas, having once been allied with these tribes.

Population Perhaps 4,000 Quechans lived on the Colorado River in the sixteenth century. Almost

1,200 Quechans lived at Fort Yuma in 1990; others lived on the Cocopah Reservation and off-reservation. The 1990 Quechan population was roughly 3,000.

Language Quechan is a dialect of River Yuman.

Historical Information

History Quechan farmers began using floodwaters of the Colorado River for irrigation beginning around 2,500 years ago. The Quechans first encountered a non-native person in 1540, in the person of Hernando de Alarcón. Father Eusebio Kino arrived in 1698 and Father Francisco Garces in 1775. The Quechans generally resisted Spanish missions and settlements. A rebellion in 1781 ended Spanish control of a key river crossing, and the Quechans were able to continue their traditional way of life.

In the mid–nineteenth century, Quechans occasionally raided overland travelers (on the Southern Overland Trail, or Butterfield Route), partly in retaliation for crop thievery. The number of non-Indians passing through their territory increased greatly in and after 1849, due to the California gold rush. At that time, the Quechans provided a ferry service across the Colorado. When Anglos attempted to open a competing service, the Quechans blocked the passage. When the U.S. Army intervened to keep the passage open, the Quechans fought back, driving the U.S. forces away for a year. In 1852, the soldiers returned and built Fort Yuma, effectively ending Quechan resistance in the area. Five years later, the Quechan and their Mojave allies were defeated by the Pima and Maricopa in the last big intra-Indian fight near the Colorado River.

In 1853 the United States established the Fort Yuma Reservation with 45,000 acres, on the California side of the Colorado. Steamship and railroad travel as well as the town of Yuma boomed in the following decades. Quechans worked as steamship pilots and woodcutters until railroads ended the industry and then as laborers and domestics.

By the end of the century the tribe, devastated by disease, was in a state of cultural eclipse. Factionalism also weakened the tribe, and Anglos took the opportunity to appoint Quechan leaders unilaterally. Clan and village affiliations broke down when youths were taken away forcibly to boarding school. The Quechan relinquished most of their land in 1893 and lost the best of what was left to Anglos by 1910. Upstream dams prevented natural flooding, and Quechan farmers, people of the river for centuries, found themselves in the position of having to pay for irrigation water.

Quechans lived in poverty well into the twentieth century. Mandated allotment of their land in 1912 led to endless subdivision and rendered it useless for agriculture; most was leased to non-Indians. The federal War on Poverty arrived in the 1960s, and with it new opportunities for decent housing and economic development. In 1978 the government returned 25,000 acres (minus the vital water rights) and paid for even more in the 1980s.

Religion Like those of all Yumans, Quechan religion and knowledge were based on dreaming. Dreams were seen as visits with ancestors. The most powerful dreamer was their religious leader. Dreams also brought power to lead in battle, orate a funeral, or do almost anything. However, dreams were considered of questionable authenticity unless they conferred success. Shamans were specialists who were able to cure using supernatural powers acquired through very powerful dreams, perhaps begun in the womb. They also controlled the weather.

Quechans sang extended song cycles for curing, funerals, and entertainment. The cycles consisted of dreams and tribal mythology and were accompanied by people shaking rattles and beating sticks on baskets. Important Quechan ceremonies included a four-day-long girls' puberty rite and a boy's nose-piercing ceremony (at age seven, which also included racing and fasting). A mesquite harvest festival in summer and a crop harvest festival in fall both featured games, contests, gambling, and songs. Quechans also observed a four-day-long mourning ceremony.

Government All political authority was based on dreams, as was the authority of singers, speakers, and curers. Each rancheria had one or more headmen: Although they might meet in council to discuss tribal matters, decision making was by concensus. Other offices included the war leader and funeral orator.

Customs The Quechan were organized into patrilineal clans. Little or no status differences existed between family groups. Rancheria leaders addressed the people from rooftops on correct behavior. All possessions of the deceased, even the house, were given away or destroyed. Dung was burned to keep away mosquitoes.

Dwellings Rectangular, open, earth-covered structures served as summer houses; in winter people lived in semisubterranean houses covered with sand. Other structures included sunshades and woven granaries.

Diet Quechans mainly farmed for their food. They grew corn, beans, and pumpkins and, after the Spanish arrived, melons and wheat. They also grew tobacco and gourds. They used the seasonal flooding of the river to irrigate their fields, predicting the occurrence of the floods with astrological knowledge. They also fished with nets, traps, and bows and arrows. They hunted small game such as rabbits and gathered foods such as mesquite, screwbeans, nuts, and seeds. They parched the nuts and seeds in trays and then ground them to meal or flour. Squash and pumpkins were cut into strips and dried.

Key Technology Sowing was accomplished by means of digging sticks. Musical instruments included flutes and gourd and deer hoof rattles. Nets attached to headbands were used for carrying burdens on the back. Women made pottery bowls, dippers, and cooking pots as well as basket trays and storage containers.

Trade Among other items, the Quechan received blankets from the Hopi and Navajo. They traded agricultural products with tribes near the Gulf of California and the Pacific Ocean for shells and feathers.

Notable Arts Pottery and basketry ranked among Quechan fine arts.

Transportation The Quechan used rafts of cottonwood logs or tule reeds for river travel. They floated children and goods in large pots. Horses arrived in their area by the late eighteenth century.

Dress Quechan dress was minimal. Women wore willow-bark aprons, and men occasionally wore buckskin or bark breechclouts. Both wore rawhide sandals. Domestically manufactured blankets were of rabbit skin or woven bark. Both sexes kept their hair long (men wore long rolls of hair) and painted their faces for decoration. Men also wore nose and/or ear rings.

War and Weapons Quechans considered war essential to the acquisition and maintenance of their spiritual power. They distinguished between raiding, an activity whose main purpose was to acquire horses or captives, and warfare, the purpose of which was revenge. The Mojave were traditional allies; enemies included the Cocopah, Pee-Posh, and Pima. The Quechan warrior hierarchy included the leader, then spearmen and clubmen, archers, horsemen (after contact) with spears, and finally women with clubs. For weapons they used mesquite bows, clubs, stone knives, hide shields, and spears.

Contemporary Information

Government/Reservations The Fort Yuma Reservation (1884) consists of 43,561 acres. Many Quechans also live on the Cocopah Reservation (6,000 acres; established 1917) near Summerton, Arizona. They adopted an Indian Reorganization Act constitution in 1936 and began electing tribal council two years later. Both men and women are represented in leadership positions.

Economy Tribal businesses include sand and gravel operations, recreational vehicle parks, a bingo parlor, and an irrigation project. Still, there are few jobs on the reservation; federal funding of tribal projects accounts for most economic activity. The tribe would like to establish a closed economy, with no need for jobs in Yuma. Future farming depends on establishing water rights and obtaining water for irrigation. Most prime farming land remains leased to non-Indian interests. Legal fights over these matters are pending. In addition, the Indians of the Cocopah Reservation recently signed an agreement to build a large recreational vehicle park.

Legal Status The Quechan Tribe of the Fort Yuma Indian Reservation is a federally recognized tribal entity.

Daily Life Older Quechans still speak the language. The mourning ceremony remains, as do some of the songs and dances. Most Quechans still prefer to be cremated along with much of their personal property. A small hospital attempts to cope with many cases of diabetes and substance abuse. The elderly are still revered, as are eloquent speakers of the native language. Children attend local public schools. Quechans are largely acculturated and have high hopes for survival in the modern world.

Sandia Pueblo

Sandia (Sän `dē ä) from the Spanish for "watermelon," referring to the size, shape, and color of the nearby Sandia Mountains. The word "pueblo" comes from the Spanish for "village." It refers both to a certain style of Southwest Indian architecture, characterized by multistory, apartmentlike buildings made of adobe, and to the people themselves. Rio Grande pueblos are known as eastern Pueblos; Zuñi, Hopi, and sometimes Acoma and Laguna are known as western Pueblos. The Tiwa name for Sandia Pueblo is *Napeya* or *Nafiat,* "at the dusty place."

Location Sandia Pueblo is located 15 miles north of Albuquerque, on the east bank of the Rio Grande. The altitude ranges from 5,000 to 10,670 feet, and the land contains good farmland, game, and wild foods.

Population There were roughly 3,000 people living on Sandia Pueblo in 1680 and 350 people in 1748. The 1993 tribal enrollment was 481; 266 people lived on the pueblo.

Language Southern Tiwa is a Kiowa-Tanoan language.

Historical Information

History All Pueblo people are thought to be descended from Anasazi and perhaps Mogollon and several other ancient peoples. From them they learned architecture, farming, pottery, and basketry. Larger population groups became possible with effective agriculture and ways to store food surpluses. Within the context of a relatively stable existence, the people devoted increasing amounts of time and attention to religion, arts, and crafts.

In the 1200s, the Anasazi abandoned their traditional canyon homelands in response to climatic and social upheavals. A century or two of migrations ensued, followed in general by the slow reemergence of their culture in the historic pueblos. The Tiwas were probably the first of the Tanoan Pueblo people to enter the northern Rio Grande region. Sandia Pueblo was founded around 1300.

Francisco Vasquez de Coronado probably visited Sandia Pueblo in 1540. In 1598, Juan de Oñate arrived in the area with settlers, founding the colony of New Mexico. Oñate carried on the process, already underway in nearby areas, of subjugating the local Indians; forcing them to pay taxes in crops, cotton, and work; and opening the door for Catholic missionaries to attack their religion. The Spanish renamed the Pueblos with saints' names and began a program of church construction, constructing the Mission of San Francisco Sandia in 1617. At the same time, the Spanish introduced such new crops as peaches, wheat, and peppers into the region. In 1620, a royal decree created civil offices at each pueblo; silver-headed canes, many of which remain in use today, symbolized the governor's authority.

Sandia joined the Pueblo rebellion of 1680. For years, the Spaniards had routinely tortured Indians for practicing traditional religion. They also forced the Indians to labor for them, sold Indians into slavery, and let their cattle overgraze Indian land, a situation that eventually led to drought, erosion, and famine. Popé of San Juan Pueblo and other Pueblo religious leaders planned the great revolt, sending runners carrying cords of maguey fibers to mark the day of rebellion. On August 10, 1680, a virtually united stand on the part of the Pueblos drove the Spanish from the region. The Indians killed many Spaniards but refrained from mass slaughter, allowing most of them to leave Santa Fe for El Paso.

The Spanish burned Sandia Pueblo after the revolt. It was then reoccupied but later burned or abandoned several times in the 1680s and 1690s; the pueblo was in ruins in 1692. The Sandias first fled to the nearby mountains and then lived for a time at Hopi. Sandia Pueblo was permanently reoccupied in 1748 by a mixed group of refugees from various pueblos. Meanwhile, Santa Fe was officially reconquered in 1692, although Spanish rule was notably less severe from then on. Harsh forced labor all but ceased, and the Indians reached an understanding with the Church that enabled them to continue practicing their traditional religion.

In general, the Pueblo eighteenth century was marked by smallpox epidemics and increased raiding by the Apache, Comanche, and Ute. During this time, intermarriage and regular exchange between Hispanic villages and Pueblo Indians created a new New Mexican culture, neither strictly Spanish nor Indian, but rather somewhat of a blend between the two. Mexican "rule" in 1821 brought little immediate change to the Pueblos. The Mexicans stepped up what had been a gradual process of appropriating Indian land and water, and they allowed the nomadic tribes even greater latitude to raid.

As the presence of the United States in the area grew, it attempted to enable the Pueblo Indians to continue their generally peaceful and self-sufficient ways and recognized Spanish land grants to the Pueblos. However, Sandia lost thousands of acres during this process as a result of filing, surveying, and other errors. In an attempt to retain their identity, Pueblo Indians clung even more tenaciously to their heritage, which by now included elements of the once-hated Spanish culture and religion. By the 1880s, railroads had largely put an end to the traditional geographical isolation of the pueblos. Still, Sandia Pueblo avoided much Anglo-American influence until after World War II. Paradoxically, the U.S. decision to recognize Spanish land grants to the Pueblos denied Pueblo Indians certain rights granted under official treaties and left them particularly open to exploitation by squatters and thieves.

Sandia and other pueblos had suffered significant population decline by 1900 as a result of wars, disease, and resource loss. After a gap of over 300 years, the All Indian Pueblo Council began to meet again in the 1920s, specifically in response to a congressional threat to appropriate Pueblo lands. Partly as a result of the Council's activities, Congress confirmed Pueblo title to their lands in 1924 by passing the Pueblo Lands Act. The United States also acknowledged its trust responsibilities in a series of legal decisions and other acts of Congress.

Still, especially after 1900, Pueblo culture was increasingly threatened by Protestant evangelical missions and schools. The Bureau of Indian Affairs also weighed in on the subject of acculturation, forcing Indian children to leave their homes and attend culture-killing boarding schools. Since the late nineteenth century, but especially after the 1960s, Pueblos have had to cope with onslaughts by (mostly white) anthropologists and seekers of Indian spirituality.

Religion In traditional Pueblo culture, religion and life are inseparable. To be in harmony with all of nature is the Pueblo ideal and way of life. The sun is seen as the representative of the Creator. Sacred mountains in each direction, plus the sun above and the earth below, define and balance the Pueblo world. Many Pueblo religious ceremonies revolve around the weather and are devoted to ensuring adequate rainfall. To this end, Pueblo Indians evoke the power of katsinas, sacred beings who live in mountains and other holy places, in ritual and masked dance.

In addition to the natural boundaries, Pueblo Indians have created a society that defines their world by providing balanced, reciprocal relationships within which people connect and harmonize with each other, the natural world, and time itself. At Sandia, people were divided into two patrilineal ceremonial groups, Squash (summer) and Turquoise (winter). Each had a rectangular kiva, or prayer chamber. There were also a number of ceremonial organizations.

According to tradition, the head of each pueblo is the religious leader, or *cacique,* whose primary responsibility it is to watch the sun and thereby determine the dates of ceremonies. At Sandia the *cacique* served for life. Much ceremonialism is also based on medicine societies, and shamans who derive powers from animal spirits use their supernatural powers for curing, weather control, and ensuring the general welfare. Especially in the eastern pueblos, most ceremonies are kept secret.

Government Pueblo governments derived from two traditions. Offices that are probably indigenous

include the *cacique,* or head of the Pueblo, and the war captains. These officials are intimately related to the religious structures of the pueblo and reflected the essentially theocratic nature of Pueblo government.

A parallel but in most cases distinctly less powerful group of officials was imposed by the Spanish authorities. Appointed by the traditional leadership, they generally dealt with external and church matters and included the governor and four assistant governors. The authority of their offices was symbolized by canes. During the 1950s and 1960s, the All Indian Pueblo Council (of eastern villages) became increasingly active in asserting rights and solving problems.

Customs One mechanism that works to keep Pueblo societies coherent is a pervasive aversion to individualistic behavior. Children were raised with gentle guidance and a minimum of discipline. Pueblo Indians were generally monogamous, and divorce was relatively rare. At Sandia the dead were ceremonially prepared and then buried quickly. Burial was followed by a four-day vigil. In modern times photography by outsiders is discouraged.

Dwellings Sandia Pueblo featured multistoried apartment-style dwellings constructed of adobe (earth and straw) bricks, with beams across the roof that were covered with poles, brush, and plaster. Floors were of wood plank or packed earth. The roof of one level served as the floor of another. The levels were interconnected by ladders. As an aid to defense, the traditional design included no doors or windows; entry was through the roof. Pit houses, or kivas, served as ceremonial chambers and clubhouses. The village plaza, around which all dwellings were clustered, is the spiritual center of the village where all the balanced forces of the world come together.

Diet Before the Spanish arrived, Sandia people ate primarily corn, beans, and squash. They also grew cotton and tobacco. They hunted deer, mountain lion, bear, antelope, and rabbits. The people also gathered a variety of wild seeds, nuts, berries, and other foods but ate little or no fish. The Spanish introduced wheat, alfalfa, chilies, fruit trees, grapes, sheep, cattle, and garden vegetables, which soon became part of the regular diet.

Key Technology Precontact farming implements were wooden. Traditional irrigation systems included ditches as well as floodwater collection at arroyo mouths *(ak chin).* Tanning tools were made of bone and wood. The Spanish introduced metal tools and equipment.

Trade All Pueblos were part of extensive aboriginal trading networks. With the arrival of other cultures, Pueblo Indians also traded with the Hispanic American villages and then U.S. traders. At fixed times during summer or fall, enemies declared truces so that trading fairs might be held. The largest and best known was at Taos with the Comanche. Nomads exchanged slaves, buffalo hides, buckskins, jerked meat, and horses for agricultural and manufactured pueblo products. Pueblo Indians traded for shell and copper ornaments, turquoise, and macaw feathers. The Sandias enjoyed particularly close ties with Zia, Santa Ana, San Felipe, and Laguna Pueblos. They also had frequent contact with Isleta Pueblo, especially at ceremony times.

Trade along the Santa Fe Trail began in 1821. By the 1880s and the arrival of railroads, the Pueblos were dependent on many American-made goods, and the Native American manufacture of weaving and pottery declined and nearly died out.

Notable Arts In the Pueblo way, art and life are inseparable. Sandia arts included pottery and willow baskets. Songs, dances, and dramas also qualify as traditional arts. Many Pueblos experienced a renaissance of traditional arts in the twentieth century, beginning in 1919 with San Ildefonso pottery.

Transportation Spanish horses, mules, and cattle arrived at Sandia Pueblo in the seventeenth century.

Dress Men wore shirts, leggings, and moccasins made of deer hides tanned and colored red-brown with plant dye. Womens' wrapped leggings and moccasins were of white buckskin. Clothing was also made of spun cotton. Rabbit skin was also used for clothing and robes.

War and Weapons Though often depicted as passive and docile, most Pueblo groups regularly engaged in warfare. The great revolt of 1680 stands out as the major military action, but they also skirmished at other times with the Spanish and defended themselves against attackers such as Apaches, Comanches, and Utes. They also contributed auxiliary soldiers to provincial forces under Spain and Mexico, which were used mainly against raiding Indians and to protect merchant caravans on the Santa Fe Trail. After the raiding tribes began to pose less of a threat in the late nineteenth century, Pueblo military societies began to wither away, with the office of war captain changing to civil and religious functions.

Contemporary Information

Government/Reservations Sandia Pueblo contains roughly 23,000 acres. The *cacique* is considered the village's true leader—the "mother of his people." He has several assistants, one of which will succeed him. The *cacique* and the assistants annually choose officials such as the governor, who has control over aspects that relate to the outside world, and the war captain, who has authority at ceremonial functions. There is also a council, or advisory body, made up of former governors and war chiefs, as well as several other appointed administrative positions.

Economy Important sources of income include sand and gravel leases, a trading post, a bingo parlor, and several small businesses. Many people work for wages in Albuquerque and Bernalillo and for the tribe itself. They also make jewelry on the pueblo. The Pueblo is also purchasing the local Coronado Airport. Aspects of the traditional economy that remain include gathering piñon nuts and hunting deer and rabbits. Unemployment is quite low, owing in part to the community's highly educated work force.

Legal Status The Pueblo of Sandia is a federally recognized tribal entity. The Pueblo is also seeking title for traditional forest lands that contain a number of sacred sites. They are opposed by the U.S. Forest Service.

Daily Life Traditional religion and culture remain vital at Sandia. Many of the old ceremonies are still performed, and there is a palpable and intentional continuity with the past. The major feast day, the Feast of Saint Anthony (June 13), is celebrated with a corn dance. The people hold many other dances as well during the year. Sandias guard their traditional religious practices carefully. Catholicism exists, too, but with little or no conflict with traditional religion. The two ceremonial groups, Turquoise and Pumpkin (Squash), have permanent leaders and are responsible for dances. There are also kiva organizations, Corn groups, and curing groups. Once enemies, the Navajo are now welcomed visitors at fiesta time.

Pueblo facilities include a community center, a swimming pool, and tribal offices. Most people live in modern, single-family houses, complete with modern amenities and utilities. Only a few people remain in the old village, although many maintain a home there that they use on feast days. In order to help assure that the people have clean water for religious and health purposes, the Pueblo has both sued the government to make it enforce the Clean Water Act and developed its own EPA-approved water quality standards. Health problems, including diabetes, alcoholism, and drug use, continue to plague the Pueblo, which is planning to build both a clinic and a wellness center.

Since the 1970s, control of schools has been a key in maintaining their culture. Sandia's students are supported by tribal scholarship funds and achieve relatively high education levels. However, well over 50 percent of the people speak no Sandia, and there is much marriage out of the Pueblo. A number of language preservation programs are in place. The traditional clans have largely disappeared. Few people wear traditional dress. There is a large Sandia community in California.

Sand Papago, or Hia C-ed O'odham

See Tohono O'odham

San Felipe Pueblo

The Spanish assigned the patron saint San Felipe (San Fə `lē pā) Apóstol to this Pueblo in 1598. The word "pueblo" comes from the Spanish for "village." It

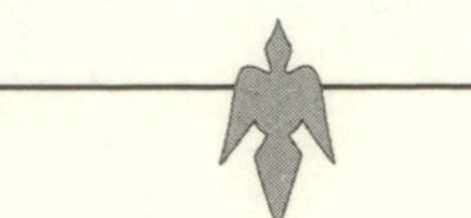

refers both to a certain style of Southwest Indian architecture, characterized by multistory, apartment-like buildings made of adobe, and to the people themselves. Rio Grande pueblos are known as eastern Pueblos; Zuñi, Hopi, and sometimes Acoma and Laguna are known as western Pueblos. The native name for this Pueblo is *Katishtya.*

Location San Felipe Pueblo is located at the foot of Santa Ana Mesa on the west bank of the Rio Grande, 6 miles north of its junction with the Jemez River (25 miles north of Albuquerque). One or more other San Felipe pueblos may have existed in the area prior to the sixteenth century.

Population The Pueblo population in 1680 was roughly 600. In 1990, 1,859 Indians lived on the Pueblo, out of a total population of almost 2,500.

Language San Felipe people spoke a dialect of Keresan.

Historical Information

History All Pueblo people are thought to be descended from Anasazi and perhaps Mogollon and several other ancient peoples, although the precise origin of the Keresan peoples is unknown. From them they learned architecture, farming, pottery, and basketry. Larger population groups became possible with effective agriculture and ways to store food surpluses. Within the context of a relatively stable existence, the people devoted increasing amounts of time and attention to religion, arts, and crafts.

Keresans have been traced to an area around Chaco Canyon north to Mesa Verde. In the 1200s, the Keresans abandoned their traditional canyon homelands in response to climatic and social upheavals. A century or two of migrations ensued, followed in general by the slow reemergence of their culture in the historic pueblos. For a time the San Felipe people lived with the Cochitis at several locations, but the pueblos divided before the Spanish arrived.

Francisco Vasquez de Coronado may have visited San Felipe Pueblo. In 1598, Juan de Oñate arrived in the area with settlers, founding the colony of New Mexico. Oñate carried on the process, already underway in nearby areas, of subjugating the local Indians; forcing them to pay taxes in crops, cotton, and work; and opening the door for Catholic missionaries to attack their religion. The Spanish renamed the Pueblos with saints' names and began a program of church construction. Oñate found two pueblos at San Felipe, on either side of the river. A church was built at the eastern village around 1600. At the same time, the Spanish introduced such new crops as peaches, wheat, and peppers into the region. In 1620, a royal decree created civil offices at each pueblo; silver-headed canes, many of which remain in use today, symbolized the governor's authority.

The San Felipes took an active part in the 1680 Pueblo revolt against the Spanish. For years, the Spaniards had routinely tortured Indians for practicing traditional religion. They also forced the Indians to labor for them, sold Indians into slavery, and let their cattle overgraze Indian land, a situation that eventually led to drought, erosion, and famine. Popé of San Juan Pueblo and other Pueblo religious leaders planned the revolt, sending runners carrying cords of maguey fibers to mark the day of rebellion. On August 10, 1680, a virtually united stand on the part of the Pueblos drove the Spanish from the region. The Indians killed many Spaniards but refrained from mass slaughter, allowing them to leave Santa Fe for El Paso.

The San Felipe people abandoned their pueblo in 1681, when the Spanish attempted a reconquest. They fled to the top of Horn Mesa southwest of Cochiti, and the Spanish sacked San Felipe. The people agreed to return and accept baptism in 1692. At that time they lived on top of Santa Ana Mesa. Their friendship with the Spanish alienated them from other pueblos. After 1696, they descended from the mesa top to the site of the present pueblo.

The Pueblos experienced many changes during the following decades: Refugees established communities at Hopi, guerrilla fighting continued against the Spanish, and certain areas were abandoned. By the 1700s, excluding Hopi and Zuñi, only Taos, Picuris, Isleta, and Acoma Pueblos had not changed locations since the arrival of the Spanish. Although Pueblo unity did not last, and Santa Fe was officially reconquered in 1692, Spanish rule was notably less severe from then on. Harsh forced labor

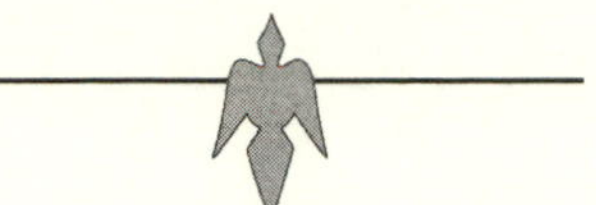

all but ceased, and the Indians reached an understanding with the Church that enabled them to continue practicing their traditional religion.

In general, the Pueblo eighteenth century was marked by smallpox epidemics and increased raiding by the Apache, Comanche, and Ute. Occasionally Pueblo Indians fought with the Spanish against the nomadic tribes. The people practiced their religion but more or less in secret. During this time, intermarriage and regular exchange between Hispanic villages and Pueblo Indians created a new New Mexican culture, neither strictly Spanish nor Indian, but rather somewhat of a blend between the two.

Mexican "rule" in 1821 brought little immediate change to the Pueblos. The Mexicans stepped up what had been a gradual process of appropriating Indian land and water, and they allowed the nomadic tribes even greater latitude to raid. A political rebellion by Indians and Hispanic poor in 1837 over the issue of taxes led to the assassination of the New Mexican governor and the brief installation of a Plains/Taos Indian as governor. As the presence of the United States in the area grew, it attempted to enable the Pueblo Indians to continue their generally peaceful and self-sufficient ways and recognized Spanish land grants to the Pueblos. San Felipe remained fairly isolated, and there are few references to the Pueblo in the eighteenth or early nineteenth centuries.

During the nineteenth century the process of acculturation among Pueblo Indians quickened markedly. In an attempt to retain their identity, Pueblo Indians clung even more tenaciously to their heritage, which by now included elements of the once-hated Spanish culture and religion. By the 1880s, railroads had largely put an end to the traditional geographical isolation of the pueblos. Paradoxically, the U.S. decision to recognize Spanish land grants to the Pueblos denied Pueblo Indians certain rights granted under official treaties and left them particularly open to exploitation by squatters and thieves.

After a gap of over 300 years, the All Indian Pueblo Council began to meet again in the 1920s, specifically in response to a congressional threat to appropriate Pueblo lands. Partly as a result of the Council's activities, Congress confirmed Pueblo title to their lands in 1924 by passing the Pueblo Lands Act. The United States also acknowledged its trust responsibilities in a series of legal decisions and other acts of Congress.

Still, especially after 1900, Pueblo culture was increasingly threatened by highly intolerant Protestant evangelical missions and schools. In 1943, a U.S. senator from New Mexico tried, ultimately unsuccessfully, to survey the central plaza at San Felipe as part of plans to build a dam there. The Bureau of Indian Affairs (BIA) also weighed in on the subject of acculturation, forcing Indian children to leave their homes and attend culture-killing boarding schools.

Following World War II, the issue of water rights took center stage on most pueblos. Also, the All Indian Pueblo Council succeeded in slowing the threat against Pueblo lands as well as religious persecution. Since the late nineteenth century, but especially after the 1960s, Pueblos have had to cope with onslaughts by (mostly white) anthropologists and seekers of Indian spirituality. The region is also known for its major art colonies at Taos and Santa Fe.

Religion In traditional Pueblo culture, religion and life are inseparable. To be in harmony with all of nature is the Pueblo ideal and way of life. The sun is seen as the representative of the Creator. Sacred mountains in each direction, plus the sun above and the earth below, define and balance the Pueblo world. Many Pueblo religious ceremonies revolve around the weather and are devoted to ensuring adequate rainfall. To this end, Pueblo Indians evoke the power of katsinas, sacred beings who live in mountains and other holy places, in ritual and dance. All San Felipe men belonged to Katsina societies. San Felipe Pueblo contained two circular kivas, religious chambers that symbolize the place of original emergence into this world, and their associated societies, Squash and Turquoise.

In addition to the natural boundaries, Pueblo Indians have created a society that defines their world by providing balanced, reciprocal relationships within which people connect and harmonize with each other, the natural world, and time itself. According to tradition, the head of each pueblo is the religious leader, or *cacique,* whose primary responsibility it is to watch the sun and thereby determine the dates of

ceremonies. Much ceremonialism was also based on medicine societies, and shamans used supernatural powers for curing, weather control, and to ensure the general welfare. Especially in the eastern pueblos, most ceremonies are kept secret.

Government Pueblo governments derived from two traditions. Elements that are probably indigenous include the *cacique,* or head of the Pueblo, and the war captains (one from each kiva group at San Felipe). These officials were intimately related to the religious structures of the pueblo and reflected the essentially theocratic nature of Pueblo government. At San Felipe the *cacique* served for life and was not required to support himself or his family. He chose two war chiefs annually (one from each kiva group), who exercised his power. In turn, the first war chief selected new *caciques.* Pueblo Indians did not typically seek to hold office.

A parallel but in most cases distinctly less powerful group of officials was imposed by the Spanish authorities. Appointed by the traditional leadership, they generally dealt with external and church matters and included the governor, lieutenant governor, and *fiscales.* There was also an advisory council of *principales,* composed of former officeholders. In 1934, San Felipe adopted the Indian Reorganization Act, although without a formal constitution. In addition, the All Indian Pueblo Council, dating from 1598, began meeting again in the twentieth century to assert rights and help solve problems.

Customs One mechanism that works to keep Pueblo societies coherent is a pervasive aversion to individualistic behavior. Children were raised with gentle guidance and a minimum of discipline. Pueblo Indians were generally monogamous, and divorce was relatively rare. The dead were prepared ceremonially and quickly buried with clothes, beads, food, and other items; their possessions were destroyed. A vigil of four days and nights was generally observed.

Matrilineal clans with recognized heads were very important at San Felipe in governing and ceremonies. Various groups acted to hold the pueblo together, including medicine societies (curing, including witch purging; public welfare; and weather); a hunters' society; a warriors' society; and katsina societies, associated with the two patrilineal kiva groups, Squash and Turquoise, which held masked rain dances. In modern times photography by outsiders is discouraged.

Dwellings In the sixteenth century, San Felipe Pueblo featured two- to three-story, apartment-style dwellings, as well as up to 200 individual houses. The buildings were constructed of adobe (earth and straw) bricks, with beams across the roof that were covered with poles, brush, and plaster. Floors were of wood plank or packed earth. The roof of one level served as the floor of another. The levels were interconnected by ladders. As an aid to defense, the traditional design included no doors or windows; entry was through the roof. Pit houses, or kivas, served as ceremonial chambers and clubhouses. The village plazas, around which all dwellings were clustered, was the spiritual center of the village where all the balanced forces of world came together.

Diet Before the Spanish arrived, San Felipe people ate primarily corn, beans, and pumpkins. They also grew sunflowers and tobacco. They hunted deer, mountain lion, bear, antelope, and rabbits. They also gathered a variety of wild seeds, nuts, berries, and other foods. The Spanish introduced wheat, alfalfa, sheep, cattle, and garden vegetables, which soon became part of the regular diet. San Felipe fruit orchards date from after the Spanish contact.

Key Technology Precontact farming implements were wooden. Traditional irrigation systems included ditches as well as floodwater collection at arroyo mouths *(ak chin).* The Spanish introduced metal tools and equipment. San Felipes built a bridge spanning the Rio Grande by sinking wooden braces into the riverbed and placing over them rock-filled wicker-woven basketry cribs.

Trade All Pueblos were part of extensive aboriginal trading networks. With the arrival of other cultures, Pueblo Indians also traded with the Hispanic American villages and then U.S. traders. At fixed times during summer or fall, enemies declared truces so that trading fairs might be held. The largest and

best known was at Taos with the Comanche. Nomads exchanged slaves, buffalo hides, buckskins, jerked meat, and horses for agricultural and manufactured pueblo products. Pueblo Indians traded for shell and copper ornaments, turquoise, and macaw feathers. Trade along the Santa Fe Trail began in 1821. By the 1880s and the arrival of railroads, the Pueblos were dependent on many American-made goods, and the Native American manufacture of weaving and pottery declined and nearly died out.

Notable Arts In the Pueblo way, art and life are inseparable. San Felipe arts included pottery, baskets, and wooden masks. Songs, dances, and dramas also qualify as traditional arts. Many Pueblos experienced a renaissance of traditional arts in the twentieth century, beginning in 1919 with San Ildefonso pottery.

Transportation At least as early as the 1600s, San Felipe people used rafts to cross the Rio Grande. They also used canoes, paddled, and hauled by rope, at least as early as the 1700s. Spanish horses, mules, and cattle arrived at San Felipe Pueblo in the seventeenth century.

Dress Men wore cotton kilts and leather sandals. Women wore cotton dresses and sandals or high moccasin boots. Deer and rabbit skin were also used for clothing and robes, and sandals were made of yucca.

War and Weapons Though often depicted as passive and docile, most Pueblo groups regularly engaged in warfare. The great revolt of 1680 stands out as the major military action, but they also skirmished at other times with the Spanish and defended themselves against attackers such as Apaches, Comanches, and Utes. They also contributed auxiliary soldiers to provincial forces under Spain and Mexico, which were used mainly against raiding Indians and to protect merchant caravans on the Santa Fe Trail. After the raiding tribes began to pose less of a threat in the late nineteenth century, Pueblo military societies began to wither away, with the office of war captain changing to civil and religious functions.

Contemporary Information

Government/Reservations San Felipe Pueblo contains almost 49,000 acres, mostly on the east side of the Rio Grande. The Pueblo is governed in the traditional manner.

Economy Many people work in Albuquerque or Bernalillo. San Felipe also produces some art and crafts, including baskets, woven sashes and belts, and pueblo moccasins with deerskin uppers and cowhide soles. Both large- and small-scale farming is practiced, the latter in combination with other subsistence activities such as hunting, picking piñon nuts, and trading.

Legal Status San Felipe Pueblo is a federally recognized tribal entity.

Daily Life The project of retaining a strong Indian identity is a difficult one in the late twentieth century, yet Pueblo people have strong roots, and in many ways the ancient rhythms and patterns continue. Many San Felipe people have fused pieces of Catholicism onto a core of traditional beliefs. Their religion, ceremonialism, and social structure are largely intact. Since the 1970s control of schools has been a key in maintaining their culture. Smaller children attend BIA day schools or public schools and either a tribally run or a public high school. Stubbornly high unemployment is partially responsible for the health problems, including alcoholism and drug use, that are present on the pueblo. Many San Felipe people still speak Keresan. There is relatively little intermarriage outside the Pueblo. Most people live in the old pueblo, in traditional adobe houses, and in new government-built frame houses. San Felipe is considered to be one of the most culturally conservative pueblos.

San Ildefonso Pueblo

San Ildefonso (San Ēl dä `fän sō) is the name of the Spanish mission established in 1617. The Tewa name for the Pueblo, *Powhoge,* means "where the water runs through." The word "pueblo" comes from the Spanish for "village." It refers both to a certain style of Southwest Indian architecture, characterized by multistory, apartmentlike buildings made of adobe, and to the people themselves. Rio Grande pueblos are known as eastern Pueblos; Zuñi, Hopi, and

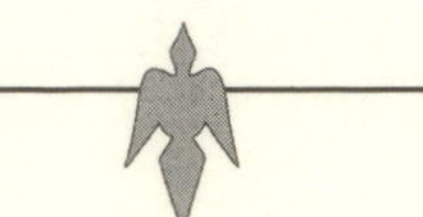

sometimes Acoma and Laguna are known as western Pueblos.

Location Located roughly 22 miles northwest of Santa Fe, San Ildefonso shares a common boundary with Santa Clara Pueblo.

Population In 1990, approximately 350 Indians lived on the pueblo, out of a total population of 1,500. Perhaps 800 people lived there in 1680.

Language San Ildefonso people spoke a dialect of Tewa, a Kiowa-Tanoan language.

Historical Information

History All Pueblo people are thought to be descended from Anasazi and perhaps Mogollon and several other ancient peoples. From them they learned architecture, farming, pottery, and basketry. Larger population groups became possible with effective agriculture and ways to store food surpluses. Within the context of a relatively stable existence, the people devoted increasing amounts of time and attention to religion, arts, and crafts. In the 1200s, the Anasazi abandoned their traditional canyon homelands in response to climatic and social upheavals. A century or two of migrations ensued, followed in general by the slow reemergence of their culture in the historic pueblos. San Ildefonso has been occupied at its present site since before the Spanish arrived.

In 1598, Juan de Oñate arrived in the area with settlers, founding the colony of New Mexico. Oñate carried on the process, already underway in nearby areas, of subjugating the local Indians; forcing them to pay taxes in crops, cotton, and work; and opening the door for Catholic missionaries to attack their religion. The Spanish renamed the Pueblos with saints' names and began a program of church construction. At the same time, the Spanish introduced such new crops as peaches, wheat, and peppers into the region. In 1620, a royal decree created civil offices at each pueblo; silver-headed canes, many of which remain in use today, symbolized the governor's authority.

San Ildefonso played a leading role in the 1680 Pueblo revolt against the Spanish. For years, the Spaniards had routinely tortured Indians for practicing traditional religion. They also forced the Indians to labor for them, sold Indians into slavery, and let their cattle overgraze Indian land, a situation that eventually led to drought, erosion, and famine. Popé of San Juan Pueblo as well as a San Ildefonso official named Francisco and other Pueblo leaders planned the revolt, sending runners carrying cords of maguey fibers to mark the day of rebellion. On August 10, 1680, a virtually united stand on the part of the Pueblos drove the Spanish from the region. The Indians killed many Spaniards but refrained from mass slaughter, allowing them to leave Santa Fe for El Paso.

San Ildefonso was also a leader in the resistance to the Spanish reconquest under Diego de Vargas. The people of San Ildefonso and members of other pueblos moved to the top of Black Mesa and held out there until 1694, two years longer than most other pueblos. In 1696, San Ildefonso staged another uprising, killing two priests; this was the last of the Pueblo armed resistance. Although Pueblo unity did not last, and Santa Fe was officially reconquered in 1692, Spanish rule was notably less severe from then on. Harsh forced labor all but ceased, and the Indians reached an understanding with the Church that enabled them to continue practicing their traditional religion.

In general, the Pueblo eighteenth century was marked by smallpox epidemics and increased raiding by the Apache, Comanche, and Ute. Occasionally Pueblo Indians fought with the Spanish against the nomadic tribes. The people practiced their religion but more or less in secret. During this time, intermarriage and regular exchange between Hispanic villages and Pueblo Indians created a new New Mexican culture, neither strictly Spanish nor Indian, but rather somewhat of a blend between the two.

Mexican "rule" in 1821 brought little immediate change to the Pueblos. The Mexicans stepped up what had been a gradual process of appropriating Indian land and water, and they allowed the nomadic tribes even greater latitude to raid. A political rebellion by Indians and Hispanics in 1837 over the issue of taxes led to the assassination of the New Mexican governor and his brief replacement by a Plains/Taos Indian. As the presence of the United States in the area grew, it attempted to enable the Pueblo Indians to continue

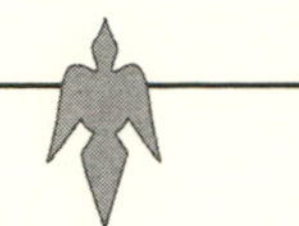

their generally peaceful and self-sufficient ways. Paradoxically, however, the U.S. decision to recognize Spanish land grants to the Pueblos denied Pueblo Indians certain rights granted under official treaties and left them particularly open to exploitation by squatters and thieves.

After the Pueblo revolt, and contrary to tradition, San Ildefonso relocated to the north. In 1923, when mortality rates rose and prosperity fell, the *cacique* led a small group of people back to the original southern village. By this time, however, a flu epidemic had reduced part of the tribe, the winter people (see "Customs"), to two families, so the other division (summer people) divided and absorbed what was left of the winter people. This situation gave rise to intense factionalism that greatly affected the pueblo. The traditional summer-winter division was virtually replaced by an ersatz north-south split. Each group, organized around a plaza, became autonomous but incomplete. By the late 1930s, some offices and societies had been discontinued, and some ritual had been forgotten. Secular authority remained in the hands of the north side for decades, and the situation turned violent in the 1930s when kivas were raided and burned.

Partly because of lobbying from the All Indian Pueblo Council, Congress confirmed Pueblo title to their lands in 1924 by passing the Pueblo Lands Act. The United States also acknowledged its trust responsibilities in a series of legal decisions and other acts of Congress. Still, the Bureau of Indian Affairs (BIA) forced Indian children to leave their homes and attend culture-killing boarding schools and in general tried its best to undermine Indian identity and survival. Beginning in the 1920s, traditional subsistence agriculture at San Ildefonso began to fail, primarily because of a population decrease and land incursions by non-natives, and malnutrition became a serious problem. At that time the San Ildefonso economy became increasingly based on cash, especially cash derived from the sale of arts and crafts.

Religion In traditional Pueblo culture, religion and life are inseparable. To be in harmony with all of nature is the Pueblo ideal and way of life. The sun is seen as the representative of the Creator. Sacred mountains in each direction, plus the sun above and the earth below, define and balance the Pueblo world. Many Pueblo religious ceremonies revolve around the weather and are devoted to ensuring adequate rainfall. To this end, Pueblo Indians evoke the power of katsinas, sacred beings who live in mountains and other holy places, in ritual and masked dance.

In addition to the natural boundaries, Pueblo Indians have created a society that defines their world by providing balanced, reciprocal relationships within which people connect and harmonize with each other, the natural world, and time itself. According to tradition, the head of each pueblo is the religious leader, or *cacique,* whose primary responsibility it is to watch the sun and thereby determine the dates of ceremonies. Much ceremonialism is also based on medicine societies, and shamans who derive powers from animal spirits use their supernatural powers for curing, weather control, and to ensure the general welfare. Especially in the eastern pueblos, most ceremonies are kept secret. San Ildefonso was among the Pueblos least receptive to Christianity, which was not established there until well into the nineteenth century.

Government Pueblo governments derived from two traditions. Offices that are probably indigenous include the *cacique,* or head of the Pueblo, and the war captains. San Ildefonso had both summer and winter *caciques.* These officials are intimately related to the religious structures of the pueblo and reflected the essentially theocratic nature of Pueblo government.

A parallel but in most cases distinctly less powerful group of officials was imposed by the Spanish authorities. Appointed by the traditional leadership, they generally dealt with external and church matters and included the governor, two lieutenant governors, and two sheriffs. The authority of their offices was symbolized by canes. Nontraditional positions also often included a ditch boss, who was in charge of the irrigation ditches, as well as a town crier and sacristan. The Spanish canes, plus canes given them by President Lincoln, continue to be a symbol of authority. In addition, the All Indian Pueblo Council, dating from 1598, began meeting again in the twentieth century.

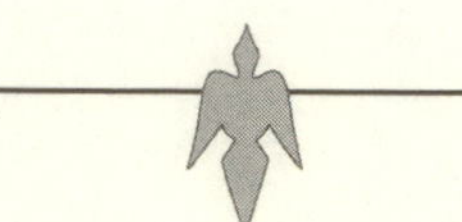

Customs One mechanism that works to keep Pueblo societies coherent is a pervasive aversion to individualistic behavior. Children were raised with gentle guidance and a minimum of discipline. Pueblo Indians were generally monogamous, and divorce was relatively rare. The dead were prepared ceremonially and quickly buried, feet to the north (the original place of emergence). Their possessions were broken and placed on the grave, along with food, to help them on their journey to the spirit land. A vigil of four days and nights was generally observed.

At San Ildefonso, in contrast with most other pueblos, seasons were traditionally delineated not so much by the solstice as by the actual change in seasons. Formerly a summer and a winter *cacique,* appointed for life, oversaw the pueblo. Society was divided into two groups, summer (associated with the Squash kiva) and winter (associated with the Turquoise kiva); membership in a group was patrilineal. These groups were further divided into clans. A number of secret societies also existed. For instance, the warrior society was concerned with hunting, war, crops, fertility, and curing. Each society had its own dances and ritual paraphernalia.

Dwellings San Ildefonso Pueblo originally featured two- and three-story apartment-style dwellings constructed of adobe (earth and straw) bricks, with pine beams across the roof that were covered with poles, brush, and plaster. Floors were of wood plank or packed earth. The roof of one level served as the floor of another. The levels were interconnected by ladders. As an aid to defense, the traditional design included no doors or windows; entry was through the roof. Three pit houses, or kivas, two rectangular and one round, served as ceremonial chambers and clubhouses. The village plaza, around which the church and all dwellings were clustered, was the spiritual center of the village, a place where all the balanced forces of world came together. The multilevel dwelling was replaced in historic times at San Ildefonso by one- and two-story adobe houses.

Diet Before the Spanish arrived, people from San Ildefonso Pueblo ate primarily corn, beans, and squash. They also grew cotton and tobacco. They hunted deer, mountain lion, antelope, and rabbits. They also gathered a variety of wild seeds, nuts, berries, and other foods. The Spanish introduced wheat, alfalfa, chilies, fruit trees, grapes, sheep, cattle, and garden vegetables, which soon became part of the regular diet.

Key Technology San Ildefonso people used irrigation ditches long before the arrival of the Spanish.

Trade All Pueblos were part of extensive aboriginal trading networks. With the arrival of other cultures, Pueblo Indians also traded with the Hispanic American villages and then U.S. traders. At fixed times during summer or fall, enemies declared truces so that trading fairs might be held. The largest and best known was at Taos with the Comanche. Nomads exchanged slaves, buffalo hides, buckskins, jerked meat, and horses for agricultural and manufactured pueblo products. Pueblo Indians traded for shell and copper ornaments, turquoise, and macaw feathers. Trade along the Santa Fe Trail began in 1821. By the 1880s and the arrival of railroads, the Pueblos were dependent on many American-made goods, and the Native American manufacture of weaving and pottery declined and nearly died out.

Notable Arts In the Pueblo way, art and life are inseparable. Traditional arts at San Ildefonso included pottery, weaving, songs, dances, and dramas. In 1919, San Ildefonso kicked off a major Pueblo arts revival with its pottery, based on prehistoric designs and styles, and its painting.

Transportation Spanish horses, mules, and cattle arrived at San Ildefonso Pueblo in the sixteenth century.

Dress Men wore cotton and buckskin shirts and kilts. Womens' traditional dress featured spun cotton dresses and sandals or high moccasin boots. Rabbit skin was also used for clothing and robes.

War and Weapons Though often depicted as passive and docile, most Pueblo groups regularly engaged in warfare. The great revolt of 1680 stands out as the major military action, but they also skirmished at other times with the Spanish and defended themselves

against attackers such as Apaches, Comanches, and Utes. They also contributed auxiliary soldiers to provincial forces under Spain and Mexico, which were used mainly against raiding Indians and to protect merchant caravans on the Santa Fe Trail. After the raiding tribes began to pose less of a threat in the late nineteenth century, Pueblo military societies began to wither away, with the office of war captain changing to civil and religious functions.

Contemporary Information

Government/Reservations San Ildefonso Pueblo contains roughly 26,000 acres. The *cacique* (summer group) appoints the governor, who is confirmed by the Council of Principales. The governor is assisted by a lieutenant and a 12-member council.

Economy The wage economy is based on work in surrounding cities as well as the sale of art and crafts, particularly pottery and painting.

Legal Status San Ildefonso is a federally recognized tribal entity.

Daily Life Although the project of holding on to their identity is a strong challenge, Pueblo people have strong roots, and in many ways the ancient rhythms and patterns continue. The tribal schism was formally healed in the 1960s with regard to civil authority, when houses dividing the two plazas were removed, but ceremonialism remains disrupted and diminished. Still, many public and closed ceremonies take place throughout the year. Traditional religion has also merged in some degree with Catholicism; for example, the Pueblo feast day for their patron saint is also celebrated with the buffalo-deer dance and a Comanche dance. Many people are married with both Catholic and traditional ceremonies.

Control of local schools since the 1970s has been a key in maintaining the Pueblo culture. Health problems, including alcoholism and drug abuse, continue to plague the pueblos. Indian Health Service hospitals often cooperate with native healers from two medicine societies. Many people still speak Tewa, and English has served as a common second language since the 1960s. Children attend the pueblo day school and then either the public high school or private (Catholic and tribally run) high schools. Most people live in either the old pueblo, in homes around two plazas, or in outlying adobe-style houses. The houses have modern utilities and conveniences.

San Juan Pueblo

The Tewa name for San Juan (San `Hwän) Pueblo is *Ohke,* the meaning of which is unknown. The word "pueblo" comes from the Spanish for "village." It refers both to a certain style of Southwest Indian architecture, characterized by multistory, apartment-like buildings made of adobe, and to the people themselves. Rio Grande pueblos are known as eastern Pueblos; Zuñi, Hopi, and sometimes Acoma and Laguna are known as western Pueblos. A sacred metaphorical phrase meaning "village of the dew-bedecked corn structure" also refers to the San Juan Pueblo.

Location San Juan Pueblo is located about 25 miles north of Santa Fe, on the east bank of the Rio Grande. The land includes river bottomlands and mountains.

Population In 1990, almost 1,300 Indians lived on the Pueblo, out of a total population of 5,200. Roughly 300 people lived there in 1680.

Language The people spoke a dialect of Tewa.

Historical Information

History All Pueblo people are thought to be descended from Anasazi and perhaps Mogollon and several other ancient peoples. From them they learned architecture, farming, pottery, and basketry. Larger population groups became possible with effective agriculture and ways to store food surpluses. Within the context of a relatively stable existence, the people devoted increasing amounts of time and attention to religion, arts, and crafts. In prehistoric times, the Tewa were generally north and west of their present locations and have inhabited numerous prehistoric villages on both sides (though mostly the west side) of the Rio Grande and the Rio Chama. In the 1200s, the Anasazi abandoned their traditional canyon homelands in response to climatic and social upheavals. A century or two of migrations ensued,

followed in general by the slow reemergence of their culture in the historic pueblos.

When the Spanish arrived in the 1540s, the San Juan people were living at the present pueblo and at a more westerly pueblo. The appearance of Gaspar Castaño de Sosa in 1591 marked the first contact between San Juan and non-natives. In 1598, Juan de Oñate arrived in the area with settlers, founding the colony of New Mexico. Oñate carried on the process, already underway in nearby areas, of subjugating the local Indians; forcing them to pay taxes in crops, cotton, and work; and opening the door for Catholic missionaries to attack their religion. The Spanish renamed the Pueblo San Juan Bautista; it was also known as San Juan de los Caballeros. At the same time, they introduced such new crops as peaches, wheat, and peppers into the region. In 1620, a royal decree created civil offices at each pueblo; silver-headed canes, many of which remain in use today, symbolized the governor's authority.

In 1680 Pueblo Indians organized and carried out a revolt against the Spanish. For years, the Spaniards had routinely tortured Indians for practicing traditional religion. They also forced the Indians to labor for them, sold Indians into slavery, and let their cattle overgraze Indian land, a situation that eventually led to drought, erosion, and famine. Popé of San Juan Pueblo and other Pueblo religious leaders planned the revolt, sending runners carrying cords of maguey fibers to mark the day of rebellion. On August 10, 1680, a virtually united stand on the part of the Pueblos drove the Spanish from the region. The Indians killed many Spaniards but refrained from mass slaughter, allowing them to leave Santa Fe for El Paso.

Although Pueblo unity did not last, and Santa Fe was officially reconquered in 1692, Spanish rule was notably less severe from then on. Harsh forced labor all but ceased, and the Indians reached an understanding with the Church that enabled them to continue practicing their traditional religion.

In general, the Pueblo eighteenth century was marked by smallpox epidemics and increased raiding by the Apache, Comanche, and Ute. Occasionally Pueblo Indians fought with the Spanish against the nomadic tribes. The people practiced their religion but more or less in secret. During this time, intermarriage and regular exchange between Hispanic villages and Pueblo Indians created a new New Mexican culture, neither strictly Spanish nor Indian, but rather somewhat of a blend between the two.

Mexican "rule" in 1821 brought little immediate change to the Pueblos. The Mexicans stepped up what had been a gradual process of appropriating Indian land and water, and they allowed the nomadic tribes even greater latitude to raid. A political rebellion by Indians and Hispanics in 1837 over the issue of taxes led to the assassination of the New Mexican governor and his brief replacement by a Plains/Taos Indian. As the presence of the United States in the area grew, it attempted to enable the Pueblo Indians to continue their generally peaceful and self-sufficient ways. Paradoxically, however, the U.S. decision to recognize Spanish land grants to the Pueblos (they recognized the grant to San Juan in 1858) denied Pueblo Indians certain rights granted under official treaties and left them particularly open to exploitation by squatters and thieves.

San Juan's reputation as a center of trade was enhanced when a general store opened on the Pueblo in 1863 (see "Trade"). Farming and cattle raising were the other economic mainstays of the pueblo during this period.

Partly because of lobbying from the All Indian Pueblo Council, Congress confirmed Pueblo title to their lands in 1924 by passing the Pueblo Lands Act. The United States also acknowledged its trust responsibilities in a series of legal decisions and other acts of Congress. Still, the Bureau of Indian Affairs (BIA) forced Indian children to leave their homes and attend culture-killing boarding schools and in general tried its best to undermine Indian identity and survival. Until the 1940s, the San Juan economy remained almost completely subsistence based.

Since the late nineteenth century, but especially after the 1960s, Pueblos have had to cope with onslaughts by (mostly white) anthropologists and seekers of Indian spirituality. For about 20 years beginning in the 1960s, the people used a number of federal grants to construct various facilities as well as to support a number of social, economic, and cultural programs.

Religion In traditional Pueblo culture, religion and life are inseparable. To be in harmony with all of

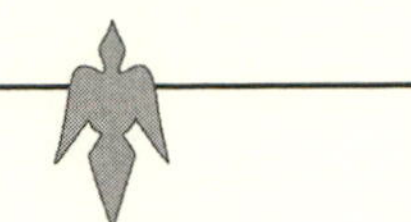

nature is the Pueblo ideal and way of life. The sun is seen as the representative of the Creator. Sacred mountains in each direction, plus the sun above and the earth below, define and balance the Pueblo world. Many Pueblo religious ceremonies revolve around the weather and are devoted to ensuring adequate rainfall. To this end, Pueblo Indians evoke the power of katsinas, sacred beings who live in mountains and other holy places, in ritual and masked dance. *Cikumu* (Chicoma Mountain) is a particularly sacred location for the people of San Juan.

In addition to the natural boundaries, Pueblo Indians have created a society that defines their world by providing balanced, reciprocal relationships within which people connect and harmonize with each other, the natural world, and time itself. According to tradition, the head of each pueblo is the religious leader, or *cacique,* whose primary responsibility it is to watch the sun and thereby determine the dates of ceremonies. Much ceremonialism is also based on medicine societies, and shamans who derive powers from animal spirits use their supernatural powers for curing, weather control, and ensuring the general welfare. Especially in the eastern pueblos, most ceremonies are kept secret. Since at least the seventeenth century, Catholicism has strongly influenced traditional religion and ceremonialism.

Winter (Turquoise) and summer (Squash) groups divided the pueblo. Each had a cacique and a kiva. There were also eight ceremonial societies, including curing, clowning, hunting, and defense. The *caciques* and the heads of societies, or priests, ran the religious and the political life of the pueblo. All rituals were performed within the winter-summer context. Also, all children were initiated into the masked dance society, Ohuwa.

Government Pueblo governments derived from two traditions. Offices that are probably indigenous include the *cacique* (two at San Juan), or head of the Pueblo, and the war captains. These officials are intimately related to the religious structures of the pueblo and reflected the essentially theocratic nature of Pueblo government.

A parallel but in most cases distinctly less powerful group of officials was imposed by the Spanish authorities. Appointed by the traditional leadership, they generally dealt with external and church matters and included the governor, two lieutenant governors, two sheriffs, and four *fiscales.* The authority of their offices was symbolized by canes. Nontraditional positions also often included a ditch boss, who was in charge of the irrigation ditches, as well as a town crier and sacristan. The Spanish canes, plus canes given them by President Lincoln, were a symbol of authority. In addition, the All Indian Pueblo Council, dating from 1598, began meeting again in the twentieth century.

Customs One mechanism that works to keep Pueblo societies coherent is a pervasive aversion to individualistic behavior. Children were raised with gentle guidance and a minimum of discipline. Pueblo Indians were generally monogamous, and divorce was relatively rare. The dead were prepared ceremonially and quickly buried. Their possessions were broken and placed on the grave, along with food, to help them journey to the spirit land. A vigil of four days and nights was generally observed.

At San Juan, a summer and a winter *cacique,* appointed for life, oversaw the pueblo. Society was divided into two groups, summer (associated with the Squash kiva) and winter (associated with the Turquoise kiva); membership in a group was patrilineal. These groups were further divided into more than 30 clans. A number of secret societies also existed. For instance, the warrior society was concerned with hunting, war, crops, fertility, and curing. Each society had its own dances and ritual paraphernalia. Numerous life-cycle rites, as well as songs, crafts, and communal activities such as maintenance of irrigation canals and performing dances, also ensured that one spent one's life "becoming" a Tewa.

People of San Juan further classified themselves into three categories: ordinary earth people, youths, and made people (priests of eight separate priesthoods, half of which admit women as full members). Similarly, their physical world was divided into three corresponding categories. Village, farmlands, and other nearby lowlands, accessible to all and particularly the woman's domain, were delineated by four shrines to ancestors. Hills, mesas, and washes, defined by four sacred mesas and in the spiritual

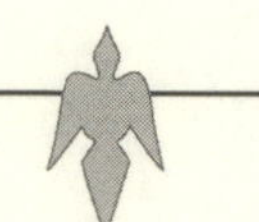

charge of the "youths," were a mediating environment in spatial, social, sexual, spiritual, and even subsistence terms. Mountains, a male realm of hunting and male religious pilgrimages, were in the charge of the made people.

Dwellings San Juan Pueblo originally featured multistory apartment-style dwellings constructed of adobe (earth and straw) bricks, with pine beams across the roof that were covered with poles, brush, and plaster. Floors were of wood plank or packed earth. The roof of one level served as the floor of another. The levels were interconnected by ladders. As an aid to defense, the traditional design included no doors or windows; entry was through the roof. Pit houses, or kivas, served as ceremonial chambers and clubhouses. The village plaza, around which the church and all dwellings were clustered, was the spiritual center of the village, a place where all the balanced forces of the world came together.

Diet Before the Spanish arrived, people from San Juan Pueblo ate primarily corn, beans, and squash. They also grew cotton and tobacco. They hunted deer, mountain lion, antelope, and rabbits. They also gathered a variety of wild seeds, nuts, berries, and other foods. The Spanish introduced wheat, alfalfa, chilies, fruit trees, grapes, sheep, cattle, and garden vegetables, which soon became part of the regular diet.

Key Technology San Juan people used irrigation ditches from well before the arrival of the Spanish.

Trade All Pueblos were part of extensive aboriginal trading networks. Many, such as San Juan, visited nearby Pueblos regularly to attend festivals and occasionally to intermarry. With the arrival of other cultures, Pueblo Indians also traded with the Hispanic American villages and then U.S. traders. At fixed times during summer or fall, enemies declared truces so that trading fairs might be held. The largest and best known was at Taos with the Comanche. Nomads exchanged slaves, buffalo hides, buckskins, jerked meat, and horses for agricultural and manufactured Pueblo products. Pueblo Indians traded for shell and copper ornaments, turquoise, and macaw feathers.

Trade along the Santa Fe Trail began in 1821. The trader Samuel Eldodt opened a general store at San Juan in 1863. Until it burned down in 1973, it was the oldest continuously operated store in New Mexico and furthered San Juan's reputation as a trade center. By the 1880s and the arrival of railroads, the Pueblos were dependent on many American-made goods, and the native manufacture of weaving and pottery declined and nearly died out.

Notable Arts In the Pueblo way, art and life are inseparable. Traditional arts at San Juan included pottery, weaving, masks, songs, dances, and dramas. The great Pueblo arts revival, begun at San Ildefonso in 1919, came to San Juan in the 1930s.

Transportation Spanish horses, mules, and cattle arrived at San Juan in the sixteenth century.

Dress Men wore cotton and buckskin shirts and kilts. Womens' traditional dress featured spun cotton dresses and sandals or high moccasin boots. Rabbit skin was also used for clothing and robes.

War and Weapons Though often depicted as passive and docile, most Pueblo peoples regularly engaged in warfare. The great revolt of 1680 stands out as the major military action, but they also skirmished at other times with the Spanish and defended themselves against attackers such as Apaches, Comanches, and Utes. They also contributed auxiliary soldiers to provincial forces under Spain and Mexico, which were used mainly against raiding Indians and to protect merchant caravans on the Santa Fe Trail. After the raiding tribes began to pose less of a threat in the late nineteenth century, Pueblo military societies began to wither away, with the office of war captain changing to civil and religious functions.

Contemporary Information

Government/Reservations San Juan Pueblo contains roughly 12,000 acres. The *cacique* still oversees religious and political matters, appointing the various governmental leaders. The church officers still function as an important level of government. Women's role in pueblo government and religious affairs is severely circumscribed. There is also a tribal court.

Economy Many people work in nearby cities and towns or on the pueblo for federal or tribal programs. Crafts, especially pottery, are an important economic activity. The Pueblo hosts the self-sustaining Oke Oweenge Cooperative for artists. It also collects rent for leased land and buildings. The tribe also owns a gas station near Española, a recreation center, and a bingo operation and contains gas and oil resources.

Legal Status The Pueblo of San Juan is a federally recognized tribal entity.

Daily Life Although the project of holding on to their identity is a strong challenge, Pueblo people have strong roots, and in many ways the ancient rhythms and patterns continue. Despite the absence of the older generation—still the most important transmitters of traditional culture—in today's nuclear families, many of the old ceremonies are still performed, and the religion and language are largely intact. There is a palpable and intentional continuity with the past. Since the 1950s, San Juan people have also attended festivals as far away as the Plains, the West, and the Midwest. Traditional religion has also merged to some degree with Catholicism.

Control of local schools since the 1970s has been a key in maintaining the Pueblo culture. The San Juan Day School included a fine bilingual and bicultural program until funding was cut off in 1990. Many people still speak Tewa, and English has served as a common second language since the 1960s. However, increasing rates of intermarriage (already high with the Hispanic community) with other Indians and non-natives threaten the culture to some degree; most of these couples live away from San Juan. Health problems, including alcoholism and drug abuse, continue to plague the Pueblos, and there is no professional health care at San Juan Pueblo. Indian Health Service hospitals often cooperate with native healers. The nuclear family is the basic social and economic unit. Several legal cases regarding water rights remain ongoing.

Santa Ana Pueblo

Santa Ana (`San tä `Ä nä) people call their Old Pueblo *Tamaya.* The word "pueblo" comes from the Spanish for "village." It refers both to a certain style of Southwest Indian architecture, characterized by multistory, apartmentlike buildings made of adobe, and to the people themselves. Rio Grande pueblos are known as eastern Pueblos; Zuñi, Hopi, and sometimes Acoma and Laguna are known as western Pueblos. (See "Location" and see "Daily Life" under "Contemporary Information.")

Location The Old Pueblo (Tamaya) is located 27 miles northwest of Albuquerque, on the north bank of the Jemez River 8 miles northwest of its junction with the Rio Grande. This fairly isolated location traditionally kept residents from much contact with non-Indians. The pueblo was all but abandoned in historic times because of low-quality arable land. The people then bought land and moved to a location (Los Ranchitos) about 10 miles to the southeast and just north of Bernalillo.

Population As of 1990, 480 Indians lived on the reservation; roughly 340 lived there in 1700.

Language The people spoke a dialect of Keresan.

Historical Information

History All Pueblo people are thought to be descended from Anasazi and perhaps Mogollon and several other ancient peoples, although the precise origin of the Keresan peoples is unknown. From them they learned architecture, farming, pottery, and basketry. Larger population groups became possible with effective agriculture and ways to store food surpluses. Within the context of a relatively stable existence, the people devoted increasing amounts of time and attention to religion, arts, and crafts.

Keresans have been traced to an area around Chaco Canyon north to Mesa Verde. In the 1200s, the Keresans abandoned their traditional canyon homelands in response to climatic and social upheavals. A century or two of migrations ensued, followed in general by the slow reemergence of their culture in the historic pueblos. Old Santa Ana was probably established in the late sixteenth century.

Francisco Vasquez de Coronado may have visited Santa Ana Pueblo. In 1598, Juan de Oñate arrived in the area with settlers, founding the colony of New

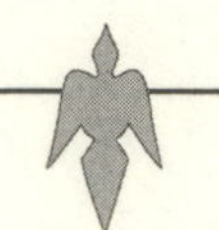

Mexico. Oñate carried on the process, already underway in nearby areas, of subjugating the local Indians; forcing them to pay taxes in crops, cotton, and work; and opening the door for Catholic missionaries to attack their religion. The Spanish renamed the Pueblos with saints' names and began a program of church construction. At the same time, they introduced such new crops as peaches, wheat, and peppers into the region. In 1620, a royal decree created civil offices at each pueblo; silver-headed canes, many of which remain in use today, symbolized the governor's authority.

The Santa Anas took part in the 1680 Pueblo revolt against the Spanish. For years, the Spaniards had routinely tortured Indians for practicing traditional religion. They also forced the Indians to labor for them, sold Indians into slavery, and let their cattle overgraze Indian land, a situation that eventually led to drought, erosion, and famine. Popé of San Juan Pueblo and other Pueblo religious leaders planned the revolt, sending runners carrying cords of maguey fibers to mark the day of rebellion. On August 10, 1680, a virtually united stand on the part of the Pueblos drove the Spanish from the region. The Indians killed many Spaniards but refrained from mass slaughter, allowing them to leave Santa Fe for El Paso.

Shortly after the onset of the revolt, the residents had abandoned Santa Ana and were living in the Jemez Mountains. The Spanish burned Santa Ana Pueblo in 1687. By 1693, the Santa Anas had rebuilt their pueblo. They also joined with the Spanish against Pueblo and other Indians after this time.

The Pueblos experienced many changes during the following decades: Refugees established communities at Hopi, guerrilla fighting continued against the Spanish, and certain areas were abandoned. By the 1700s, excluding Hopi and Zuñi, only Taos, Picuris, Isleta, and Acoma Pueblos had not changed locations since the arrival of the Spanish. Although Pueblo unity did not last, and Santa Fe was officially reconquered in 1692, Spanish rule was notably less severe from then on. Harsh forced labor all but ceased, and the Indians reached an understanding with the Church that enabled them to continue practicing their traditional religion.

In general, the Pueblo eighteenth century was marked by smallpox epidemics and increased raiding by the Apache, Comanche, and Ute. Occasionally Pueblo Indians fought with the Spanish against the nomadic tribes. The people practiced their religion but more or less in secret. During this time, intermarriage and regular exchange between Hispanic villages and Pueblo Indians created a new New Mexican culture, neither strictly Spanish nor Indian, but rather somewhat of a blend between the two. Santa Anas began buying and cultivating fields at Ranchitos and spent more and more time there into the next century.

Mexican "rule" in 1821 brought little immediate change to the Pueblos. The Mexicans stepped up what had been a gradual process of appropriating Indian land and water, and they allowed the nomadic tribes even greater latitude to raid. A political rebellion by Indians and Hispanic poor in 1837 over the issue of taxes led to the assassination of the New Mexican governor and the brief installation of a Plains/Taos Indian as governor. As the presence of the United States in the area grew, it attempted to enable the Pueblo Indians to continue their generally peaceful and self-sufficient ways and recognized Spanish land grants to the Pueblos.

During the nineteenth century the process of acculturation among Pueblo Indians quickened markedly. In an attempt to retain their identity, Pueblo Indians clung even more tenaciously to their heritage, which by now included elements of the once-hated Spanish culture and religion. By the 1880s, railroads had largely put an end to the traditional geographical isolation of the pueblos. Paradoxically, the U.S. decision to recognize Spanish land grants to the Pueblos denied Pueblo Indians certain rights granted under official treaties and left them particularly open to exploitation by squatters and thieves. Fierce epidemics swept through Santa Ana around the turn of the century. Those children who escaped the sickness were forced to attend a new Bureau of Indian Affairs (BIA)–sponsored day school designed to strip them of their Indian heritage.

After a gap of over 300 years, the All Indian Pueblo Council began to meet again in the 1920s, specifically in response to a congressional threat to appropriate Pueblo lands. Partly as a result of the

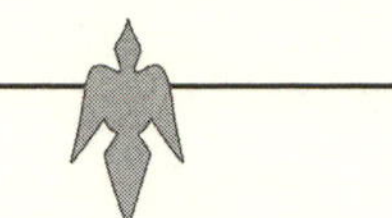

Council's activities, Congress confirmed Pueblo title to their lands in 1924 by passing the Pueblo Lands Act. The United States also acknowledged its trust responsibilities in a series of legal decisions and other acts of Congress. Still, especially after 1900, Pueblo culture was increasingly threatened by Protestant evangelical missions and schools. The BIA also weighed in on the subject of acculturation, forcing Indian children to leave their homes and attend culture-killing boarding schools.

Following World War II, the issue of water rights took center stage on most pueblos. Also, the All Indian Pueblo Council succeeded in slowing the threat against Pueblo lands as well as religious persecution. Making crafts for the tourist trade became an important economic activity during this period. Since the late nineteenth century, but especially after the 1960s, Pueblos have had to cope with onslaughts by (mostly white) anthropologists and seekers of Indian spirituality. The region is also known for its major art colonies at Taos and Santa Fe.

Religion In traditional Pueblo culture, religion and life are inseparable. To be in harmony with all of nature is the Pueblo ideal and way of life. The sun is seen as the representative of the Creator. Sacred mountains in each direction, plus the sun above and the earth below, define and balance the Pueblo world. Many Pueblo religious ceremonies revolve around the weather and are devoted to ensuring adequate rainfall. To this end, Pueblo Indians evoke the power of katsinas, sacred beings who live in mountains and other holy places, in ritual and dance. All Santa Ana men belonged to Katsina societies. Santa Ana Pueblo contained two circular kivas, religious chambers that symbolize the place of original emergence into this world, and their associated societies, Squash and Turquoise.

In addition to the natural boundaries, Pueblo Indians have created a society that defines their world by providing balanced, reciprocal relationships within which people connect and harmonize with each other, the natural world, and time itself. According to tradition, the head of each pueblo is the religious leader, or *cacique,* whose primary responsibility it is to watch the sun and thereby determine the dates of ceremonies. Much ceremonialism is also based on medicine societies, and shamans used supernatural powers for curing, weather control, and ensuring the general welfare. Important ceremonies at Santa Ana included the winter solstice, several winter dances, San Antonio Day, the summer solstice, San Juan's Day, Santiago's Day, and the harvest dance. Especially in the eastern pueblos, most ceremonies are kept secret.

Government Pueblo governments derived from two traditions. Elements that are probably indigenous include the *cacique,* or head of the Pueblo, and the war chiefs. These officials were intimately related to the religious structures of the pueblo and reflected the essentially theocratic nature of Pueblo government. At Santa Ana the *cacique* served for life and was not required to support himself or his family. He authorized all rituals and made yearly appointments, including two war chiefs (one from each kiva group) who exercised his power. In turn, the first war chief chose new *caciques.* Other traditional offices included the war chiefs' assistants and a ditch boss who, by means of ritual and duties, presided over the Pueblo irrigation system. Pueblo Indians did not typically seek to hold office.

A parallel but in most cases distinctly less powerful group of officials was imposed by the Spanish authorities. Appointed annually by the traditional leadership, they generally dealt with external and church matters and included the governor, lieutenant governor, captains, and *fiscales* (church officials). In addition, a sacristan (another church official) and a *kahéra* (drum roller for certain ceremonies) served for life. There was also an advisory council of *principales,* composed of former office holders. In 1934, Santa Ana adopted the Indian Reorganization Act, although without a formal constitution. In addition, the All Indian Pueblo Council, dating from 1598, began meeting again in the twentieth century to assert rights and help solve problems.

Customs One mechanism that works to keep Pueblo societies coherent is a pervasive aversion to individualistic behavior. Children were raised with gentle guidance and a minimum of discipline. Pueblo Indians were generally monogamous, and divorce was relatively rare. The dead were prepared ceremonially and quickly buried with clothes, beads, food, and other items; their possessions were destroyed, and they were said to become katsinas in the land of the dead. A vigil of four days and nights was generally observed.

Matrilineal clans with recognized heads determined kiva membership and regulated marriage. Various other groups acted to hold the pueblo together, including medicine societies (curing, including witch purging, which was open to men only; public welfare; and weather); a hunters' society; a clown society; a warriors' society (open to men who had killed or scalped an enemy in battle); and katsina societies, associated with the two patrilineal kiva groups, Squash and Turquoise, which held masked rain dances. At Santa Ana the katsina society was voluntary and open to both sexes. In modern times photography by outsiders is discouraged.

Dwellings In the sixteenth century, Santa Ana Pueblo featured two- to three-story, apartment-style dwellings as well as individual houses arranged around several plazas. The buildings were constructed of adobe (earth and straw) bricks, with beams across the roof that were covered with poles, brush, and plaster. Floors were of wood plank or packed earth. The roof of one level served as the floor of another. The levels were interconnected by ladders. As an aid to defense, the traditional design included no doors or windows; entry was through the roof. Two pit houses, or kivas, served as ceremonial chambers and clubhouses. The village plazas, around which all dwellings were clustered, was the spiritual center of the village where all the balanced forces of the world came together.

Diet Before the Spanish arrived, Santa Ana people ate primarily corn, beans, and pumpkins, using dry farming methods and ditch irrigation. They also grew sunflowers and tobacco. They hunted deer, mountain lion, bear, antelope, and rabbits. They also gathered a variety of wild seeds, nuts, berries, and other foods. The Spanish introduced wheat, alfalfa, sheep, cattle, and garden vegetables, which soon became part of the regular diet.

Key Technology Precontact farming implements were wooden. Traditional irrigation systems included ditches as well as floodwater collection at arroyo mouths *(ak chin)*. Textiles were woven of cotton. Other items included baskets, pottery, and leather goods. In more recent times, Santa Anas made jewelry and straw-inlay work. The Spanish introduced metal tools and equipment.

Trade All Pueblos were part of extensive aboriginal trading networks. With the arrival of other cultures, Pueblo Indians also traded with the Hispanic American villages and then U.S. traders. At fixed times during summer or fall, enemies declared truces so that trading fairs might be held. The largest and best known was at Taos with the Comanche. Nomads exchanged slaves, buffalo hides, buckskins, jerked meat, and horses for agricultural and manufactured pueblo products. Santa Anas traded for numerous daily and ceremonial items, including drums, tortoise rattles, buffalo robes, abalone shell jewelry, bows, arrows, quivers, pottery, and blankets. Trade along the Santa Fe Trail began in 1821. By the 1880s and the arrival of railroads, the Pueblos had become dependent on many American-made goods, and the native manufacture of weaving and pottery declined and nearly died out.

Notable Arts In the Pueblo way, art and life are inseparable. Santa Ana arts included pottery, baskets, and wooden masks. Songs, dances, and dramas are other traditional arts. Santa Anas learned the art of silversmithing from the Navajo around 1890. Many Pueblos experienced a renaissance of traditional arts in the twentieth century, beginning in 1919 with San Ildefonso pottery.

Transportation At least as early as the 1700s, Santa Ana people used canoes to cross the Rio Grande. Spanish horses, mules, and cattle arrived at Santa Ana Pueblo in the seventeenth century.

Dress Men wore cotton kilts and leather sandals. Women wore cotton dresses and sandals or high moccasin boots. Deer and rabbit skin were also used for clothing and robes, and sandals were made of yucca.

War and Weapons Though often depicted as passive and docile, most Pueblo groups regularly

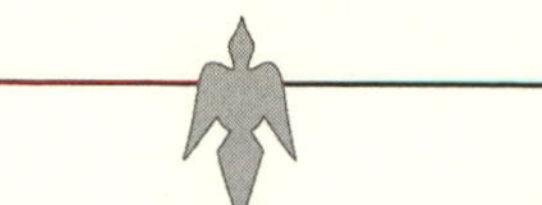

engaged in warfare. The great revolt of 1680 stands out as the major military action, but they also skirmished at other times with the Spanish and defended themselves against attackers such as Apaches, Comanches, and Utes. They also contributed auxiliary soldiers to provincial forces under Spain and Mexico, which were used mainly against raiding Indians and to protect merchant caravans on the Santa Fe Trail. After the raiding tribes began to pose less of a threat in the late nineteenth century, Pueblo military societies began to wither away, with the office of war captain changing to civil and religious functions. At Santa Ana, the old warrior society is now made up of men who have killed a bear, mountain lion, or eagle.

Contemporary Information

Government/Reservations Santa Ana Pueblo contains roughly 62,000 acres. It is governed in the traditional manner with the addition of a modern administrative structure. Most people live at Ranchitos.

Economy Most people work either in Albuquerque or on federal and tribal projects. Farming was revived beginning in the mid-1980s as a commercial endeavor. Products from their Blue-Corn Mill and greenhouse complex are marketed internationally. There are also some crafts as well as a golf course and restaurant, a smoke shop, and some commercial offices. The Pueblo contains geothermal resources.

Legal Status Santa Ana Pueblo is a federally recognized tribal entity.

Daily Life The project of retaining a strong Indian identity is a difficult one in the late twentieth century, yet Pueblo people have strong roots, and in many ways the ancient rhythms and patterns continue. Santa Ana is more religiously conservative than most pueblos, although Santa Ana people have in general fused pieces of Catholicism onto a core of traditional beliefs. Their religion, ceremonialism, and religious and social structure are largely intact. Many Santa Ana people still speak Keresan. Since the 1970s control of schools has been a key in maintaining their culture. Children attend a nearby pubic school. Facilities at Ranchitos include a clinic, offices, a swimming pool, and a community center.

Tamaya features parallel rows of single-story houses grouped around several plazas, two circular kivas, and an eighteenth-century church. The houses are built of adobe and contain no modern utilities. Tamaya is reserved for ceremonial use, though most families have a home there as well as at Ranchitos. Housing at Ranchitos includes independent adobe structures with modern facilities as well as small, modern wood-frame houses.

Santa Clara Pueblo

The Tewa name for Santa Clara (`San tä `Clä rä) Pueblo is *Capo,* variously translated. The word "pueblo" comes from the Spanish for "village." It refers both to a certain style of Southwest Indian architecture, characterized by multistory, apartmentlike buildings made of adobe, and to the people themselves. Rio Grande pueblos are known as eastern Pueblos; Zuñi, Hopi, and sometimes Acoma and Laguna are known as western Pueblos.

Location Santa Clara Pueblo is located on the west bank of the Rio Grande, about 25 miles north of Santa Fe.

Population The Pueblo population was roughly 650 in 1780 and perhaps several thousand in 1500. In 1990, 1,245 Indians lived on the Pueblo out of a total population of over 10,000. Total tribal enrollment was over 2,000.

Language The people spoke a dialect of Tewa.

Historical Information

History All Pueblo people are thought to be descended from Anasazi and perhaps Mogollon and several other ancient peoples. From them they learned architecture, farming, pottery, and basketry. Larger population groups became possible with effective agriculture and ways to store food surpluses. Within the context of a relatively stable existence, the people devoted increasing amounts of time and attention to religion, arts, and crafts. In prehistoric times, the Tewa were generally north and west of their present locations and have inhabited numerous prehistoric villages on both sides (though mostly the west side) of the Rio Grande and the Rio Chama.

In the 1200s, the Anasazi abandoned their traditional canyon homelands in response to climatic and social upheavals. A century or two of migrations ensued, followed in general by the slow reemergence of their culture in the historic pueblos. According to tradition, Santa Claras lived previously in two sites north of the present pueblo. Francisco Vasquez de Coronado found them in the pueblo's present location in 1540.

In 1598, Juan de Oñate arrived in the area with settlers, founding the colony of New Mexico. Oñate carried on the process, already underway in nearby areas, of subjugating the local Indians; forcing them to pay taxes in crops, cotton, and work; and opening the door for Catholic missionaries to attack their religion. The Spanish renamed the Pueblos with saints' names and began a program of church construction. At the same time, the Spanish introduced such new crops as peaches, wheat, and peppers into the region. In 1620, a royal decree created civil offices at each pueblo; silver-headed canes, many of which remain in use today, symbolized the governor's authority.

In 1680 Pueblo Indians organized and carried out a major revolt against the Spanish. For years, the Spaniards had routinely tortured Indians for practicing traditional religion. They also forced the Indians to labor for them, sold Indians into slavery, and let their cattle overgraze Indian land, a situation that eventually led to drought, erosion, and famine. Popé of San Juan Pueblo and other Pueblo religious leaders planned the revolt, sending runners carrying cords of maguey fibers to mark the day of rebellion. On August 10, 1680, a virtually united stand on the part of the Pueblos drove the Spanish from the region. The Indians killed many Spaniards but refrained from mass slaughter, allowing them to leave Santa Fe for El Paso.

Although Pueblo unity did not last, and Santa Fe was officially reconquered in 1692, Spanish rule was notably less severe from then on. Harsh forced labor all but ceased, and the Indians reached an understanding with the Church that enabled them to continue practicing their traditional religion.

In general, the Pueblo eighteenth century was marked by smallpox epidemics and increased raiding by the Apache, Comanche, and Ute. Occasionally Pueblo Indians fought with the Spanish against the nomadic tribes. The people practiced their religion but more or less in secret. During this time, intermarriage and regular exchange between Hispanic villages and Pueblo Indians created a new New Mexican culture, neither strictly Spanish nor Indian, but rather somewhat of a blend between the two.

Mexican "rule" in 1821 brought little immediate change to the Pueblos. The Mexicans stepped up what had been a gradual process of appropriating Indian land and water, and they allowed the nomadic tribes even greater latitude to raid. As the presence of the United States in the area grew, it attempted to enable the Pueblo Indians to continue their generally peaceful and self-sufficient ways. Paradoxically, however, the U.S. decision to recognize Spanish land grants to the Pueblos denied Pueblo Indians certain rights granted under official treaties and left them particularly open to exploitation by squatters and thieves.

Especially after 1821, the Pueblos underwent a steady acculturation. Toward the late nineteenth century, the United States reintroduced religious repression. The government and Protestant missionaries branded Indian religious practices as obscene and immoral, and the Bureau of Indian Affairs forcibly removed Indian children to culture-killing boarding schools.

Partly because of lobbying from the All Indian Pueblo Council, Congress confirmed Pueblo title to their lands in 1924 by passing the Pueblo Lands Act. The United States also acknowledged its trust responsibilities in a series of legal decisions and other acts of Congress. Following World War II, the issue of water rights took center stage on most pueblos. Also, the All Indian Pueblo Council succeeded in slowing the threat against Pueblo lands as well as religious persecution. Making crafts for the tourist trade became an important economic activity during this period. Since the late nineteenth century, but especially after the 1960s, Pueblos have had to cope with onslaughts by (mostly white) anthropologists and seekers of Indian spirituality. The region is also known for its significant art colonies at Taos and Santa Fe.

Religion In traditional Pueblo culture, religion and life are inseparable. To be in harmony with all of nature is the Pueblo ideal and way of life. The sun is seen as the representative of the Creator. Sacred mountains in each direction, plus the sun above and the earth below, define and balance the Pueblo world. Many Pueblo religious ceremonies revolve around the weather and are devoted to ensuring adequate rainfall. To this end, Pueblo Indians evoke the power of katsinas, sacred beings who live in mountains and other holy places, in ritual and masked dance.

In addition to the natural boundaries, Pueblo Indians have created a society that defines their world by providing balanced, reciprocal relationships within which people connect and harmonize with each other, the natural world, and time itself. According to tradition, the head of each pueblo is the religious leader, or *cacique,* whose primary responsibility it is to watch the sun and thereby determine the dates of ceremonies. Much ceremonialism is also based on medicine societies, and shamans who derive powers from animal spirits use their supernatural powers for curing, weather control, and ensuring the general welfare. Especially in the eastern pueblos, most ceremonies are kept secret. Since at least the seventeenth century, Catholicism has strongly influenced traditional religion and ceremonialism.

Winter (Turquoise) and summer (Squash) groups divided the pueblo. Each had a *cacique* and a kiva. Ceremonial societies included curing, clowning, hunting, and defense. The *caciques* and the heads of societies, or priests, ran the religious and the political life of the pueblo. All rituals were performed within the winter-summer context.

Government Pueblo governments derived from two traditions. Offices that are probably indigenous include the *cacique,* or head of the Pueblo, and the war captains. At Santa Clara, both summer and winter *caciques* "ruled" by consensus among the pueblo leaders, meeting in the kiva and having the final say in all matters. Each traded village control every six months. These officials were intimately related to the religious structures of the pueblo and reflected the essentially theocratic nature of Pueblo government.

A parallel but in most cases distinctly less powerful group of officials was imposed by the Spanish authorities. Appointed by the traditional leadership, they generally dealt with external and church matters and included the governor, two lieutenant governors, sheriffs, and *fiscales.* The authority of their offices was symbolized by canes. Nontraditional positions also often included a ditch boss, who was in charge of the irrigation ditches, as well as a town crier and sacristan. Also, a council of *principales* (present and former officers) had justice-related responsibilities. The Spanish canes, plus canes given them by President Lincoln, were a symbol of authority. In addition, the All Indian Pueblo Council, dating from 1598, began meeting again in the twentieth century.

Santa Clara Pueblo experienced a major political schism in the 1890s. The winter division, the more "progressive" for much of the nineteenth century, had resisted the rigid dictates of pueblo life and advocated a separation of religious from secular life. In 1894, the summer division and some winter people applied for and received recognition from the Indian agency in Santa Fe as the legitimate governing authority at the Pueblo. For the next 30 years, the summer division elected all secular officials except the lieutenant governor and tried to enforce the traditionally rigid sacred-secular connection. The winter group resisted and openly defied them.

In the 1930s, each division split along progressive and conservative lines; now there were four factions, each allied with a like-minded group. Their government in shambles, the Pueblo requested arbitration by the Indian Service in Santa Fe, with the result that the Pueblo incorporated under the Indian Reorganization Act (IRA) and turned to a constitution and an elected government. Thus religious and secular affairs were finally split, and participation in ceremonies was made voluntary.

Customs One mechanism that works to keep Pueblo societies coherent is a pervasive aversion to individualistic behavior. Children were raised with gentle guidance and a minimum of discipline. Pueblo Indians were generally monogamous, and divorce was relatively rare. The dead were prepared ceremonially and quickly buried. Their possessions were broken and placed on the grave, along with food, to help them journey to the spirit land. A vigil of four days and nights was generally observed.

At Santa Clara, a summer and a winter *cacique,* appointed for life, oversaw the pueblo. Society was divided into two groups, summer (associated with the Squash kiva) and winter (associated with the Turquoise kiva); membership in a group was patrilineal. These groups were further divided into clans. A number of secret societies also existed. For instance, the warrior society was concerned with hunting, war, crops, fertility, and curing. Each society had its own dances and ritual paraphernalia. Numerous life-cycle rites, as well as songs, crafts, communal activities such as maintenance of irrigation canals, prayer retreats, and performing dances, also ensured that one spent one's life "becoming" a Tewa.

People of Santa Clara further classified themselves into three categories: ordinary earth people, youths, and made people (priests of eight separate priesthoods, half of which admit women as full members). Similarly, their physical world was divided into three corresponding categories. Village, farmlands, and other nearby lowlands, accessible to all and particularly the woman's domain, were delineated by four shrines to ancestors. Hills, mesas, and washes, defined by four sacred mesas and in the spiritual charge of the "youths," were a mediating environment in spatial, social, sexual, spiritual, and even subsistence terms. Mountains, a male realm of hunting and male religious pilgrimages, were in the charge of the made people.

Dwellings Santa Clara Pueblo originally featured apartment-style dwellings of up to five stories constructed of adobe (earth and straw) bricks, with pine beams across the roof that were covered with poles, brush, and plaster. Floors were of wood plank or packed earth. The roof of one level served as the floor of another. The levels were interconnected by ladders. As an aid to defense, the traditional design included no doors or windows; entry was through the roof. Pit houses, or kivas, served as ceremonial chambers and clubhouses. The village plaza, around which the church and all dwellings were clustered, was the spiritual center of the village, a place where all the balanced forces of the world came together.

Diet Before the Spanish arrived, people from Santa Clara Pueblo ate primarily corn, beans, and squash. They also grew cotton and tobacco. They hunted deer, buffalo, mountain lion, antelope, and rabbits, and they also fished. They also gathered a variety of wild seeds, nuts, berries, and other foods. The Spanish introduced wheat, alfalfa, chilies, fruit trees, grapes, sheep, cattle, and garden vegetables, which soon became part of the regular diet.

Key Technology Santa Clara people traditionally diverted water from the Rio Grande via irrigation ditches. They used wood shovels and hoes, stone axes, and woven fiber baskets. They fished with pointed sticks and yucca-fiber nets.

Trade All Pueblos were part of extensive aboriginal trading networks. With the arrival of other cultures, Pueblo Indians also traded with the Hispanic American villages and then U.S. traders. At fixed times during summer or fall, enemies declared truces so that trading fairs might be held. The largest and best known was at Taos with the Comanche. In the seventeenth and eighteenth centuries, Santa Clara Pueblo traded primarily with other Pueblos, Comanches, Kiowas, Jicarillas, and Utes. They traded cornmeal, wheat flour, bread, and woven goods for jerked meat, buffalo robes, pipe pouches, tortoise shells, buckskins, and horses. They also traded for baskets, Navajo blankets, shell and copper ornaments, turquoise, and macaw feathers. Santa Claras sometimes acted as middlemen between Plains tribes and more southern pueblos. Trade along the Santa Fe Trail began in 1821. By the 1880s and the arrival of railroads, the Pueblos were dependent on many American-made goods, and the native manufacture of weaving and pottery declined and nearly died out.

Notable Arts In the Pueblo way, art and life are inseparable. Traditional arts at Santa Clara included pottery, weaving, masks, songs, dances, and dramas. The great Pueblo arts revival, begun at San Ildefonso in 1919, came to Santa Clara in the 1930s and 1940s.

Transportation Spanish horses, mules, and cattle arrived at Santa Clara in the sixteenth century.

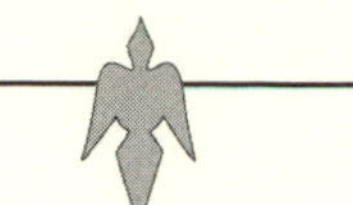

Dress Men wore cotton and buckskin shirts and kilts. Womens' traditional dress featured spun cotton dresses and sandals or high moccasin boots. Rabbit skin was also used for clothing and robes.

War and Weapons Though often depicted as passive and docile, most Pueblo peoples regularly engaged in warfare. The great revolt of 1680 stands out as the major military action, but they also skirmished at other times with the Spanish and defended themselves against attackers such as Apaches, Comanches, and Utes. They also contributed auxiliary soldiers to provincial forces under Spain and Mexico, which were used mainly against raiding Indians and to protect merchant caravans on the Santa Fe Trail. Tewas occasionally raided Navajos for goods. After the nomadic tribes began to pose less of a threat in the late nineteenth century, Pueblo military societies began to wither away, with the office of war captain changing to civil and religious functions.

Contemporary Information

Government/Reservations Santa Clara Pueblo consists of almost 46,000 acres. The Pueblo adopted a constitution in 1935. They elect six officials annually, nominated by the kiva groups, plus a tribal council. The *cacique* still runs sacred matters.

Economy Many Santa Clara Indians work in Santa Fe, Española, and Los Alamos or for federal and tribal programs. Arts and crafts, including textiles, embroidery, and especially pottery, also bring in money. Tourism is an important economic activity. The cliff dwellings at Puye (an ancestral home) and Santa Clara Canyon are well-developed tourist sites, and dances for tourists are held in July. The tribe leases pumice and timber resources.

Legal Status Santa Clara Pueblo is a federally recognized tribal entity.

Daily Life Although the project of holding on to their identity is a strong challenge, Pueblo people have strong roots, and in many ways the ancient rhythms and patterns continue. Many of the old ceremonies are still performed; the religion is largely intact, and there is a palpable and intentional continuity with the past. Traditional religion has also merged to some degree with Catholicism.

Change has come to Santa Clara Pueblo, but thanks in part to effective political leadership, disruption has been minimal. Control of local schools since the 1970s has been another key in maintaining Pueblo culture. Santa Clara maintains a relatively high regard for Western education. Many people still speak Tewa, and English has served as a common second language since the 1960s. Health problems, including alcoholism and drug abuse, continue to plague the Pueblos. There is a small hospital at Santa Clara. The nuclear family is the basic social and economic unit. A new senior citizens community center helps elders remain vital and purposeful.

Santo Domingo Pueblo

The Santo Domingo (`San tō Dō `mēn gō) people call their pueblo *Kiuw.* The word "pueblo" comes from the Spanish for "village." It refers both to a certain style of Southwest Indian architecture, characterized by multistory, apartmentlike buildings made of adobe, and to the people themselves. Rio Grande pueblos are known as eastern Pueblos; Zuñi, Hopi, and sometimes Acoma and Laguna are known as western Pueblos.

Location Santo Domingo Pueblo is situated on the east bank of the Rio Grande, 30–35 miles southwest of Santa Fe, near the Camino Real and modern highways.

Population About 3,000 Indians lived in this largest of the eastern Keresan pueblos in 1990. Roughly 150 people lived there in 1680.

Language The people spoke a Keresan dialect.

Historical Information

History All Pueblo people are thought to be descended from Anasazi and perhaps Mogollon and several other ancient peoples, although the precise origin of the Keresan peoples is unknown. From them they learned architecture, farming, pottery, and basketry. Larger population groups became possible with effective agriculture and ways to store food

surpluses. Within the context of a relatively stable existence, the people devoted increasing amounts of time and attention to religion, arts, and crafts.

Keresans have been traced to an area around Chaco Canyon north to Mesa Verde. In the 1200s, the Keresans abandoned their traditional canyon homelands in response to climatic and social upheavals. A century or two of migrations ensued, followed in general by the slow reemergence of their culture in the historic pueblos. The original Santo Domingo people lived in at least two villages called Gipuy, several miles north of the present location. These sites were eventually destroyed by flooding, and the people established a village called Kiwa, about a mile west of the present pueblo.

In 1598, Juan de Oñate arrived in the area with settlers, founding the colony of New Mexico. Oñate carried on the process, already underway in nearby areas, of subjugating the local Indians; forcing them to pay taxes in crops, cotton, and work; and opening the door for Catholic missionaries to attack their religion. The Spanish renamed the Pueblos with saints' names and began a program of church construction. Santo Domingo (Saint Dominic) replaced the Pueblo's original name, Gipuy, in 1691. At the same time, the Spanish introduced such new crops as peaches, wheat, and peppers into the region. In 1620, a royal decree created civil offices at each pueblo; silver-headed canes, many of which remain in use today, symbolized the governor's authority.

The Santo Domingos took an active part in the 1680 Pueblo revolt against the Spanish. For years, the Spaniards had routinely tortured Indians for practicing traditional religion. They also forced the Indians to labor for them, sold Indians into slavery, and let their cattle overgraze Indian land, a situation that eventually led to drought, erosion, and famine. Popé of San Juan Pueblo as well as Alonzo Catiti from Santo Domingo Pueblo and other Pueblo leaders planned the revolt, sending runners carrying cords of maguey fibers to mark the day of rebellion. On August 10, 1680, a virtually united stand on the part of the Pueblos drove the Spanish from the region. The Indians killed many Spaniards but refrained from mass slaughter, allowing them to leave Santa Fe for El Paso. The Santo Domingos were forced to retreat north with other Keresan peoples to the fortified town of Potrero Viejo. They returned in 1683, although sporadic rebellion continued until 1696.

The Pueblos experienced many changes during the following decades: Refugees established communities at Hopi, guerrilla fighting continued against the Spanish, and certain areas were abandoned. By the 1700s, excluding Hopi and Zuñi, only Taos, Picuris, Isleta, and Acoma Pueblos had not changed locations since the arrival of the Spanish. Several floods destroyed the original site of Santo Domingo Pueblo; the present pueblo was established in the early eighteenth century. Although Pueblo unity did not last, and Santa Fe was officially reconquered in 1692, Spanish rule was notably less severe from then on. Harsh forced labor all but ceased, and the Indians reached an understanding with the Church that enabled them to continue practicing their traditional religion.

In general, the Pueblo eighteenth century was marked by smallpox epidemics and increased raiding by the Apache, Comanche, and Ute. Occasionally Pueblo Indians fought with the Spanish against the nomadic tribes. The people practiced their religion but more or less in secret. During this time, intermarriage and regular exchange between Hispanic villages and Pueblo Indians created a new New Mexican culture, neither strictly Spanish nor Indian, but rather somewhat of a blend between the two.

Mexican "rule" in 1821 brought little immediate change to the Pueblos. The Mexicans stepped up what had been a gradual process of appropriating Indian land and water, and they allowed the nomadic tribes even greater latitude to raid. A political rebellion by Indians and Hispanic poor in 1837 over the issue of taxes led to the assassination of the New Mexican governor and the brief installation of a Plains/Taos Indian as governor. As the presence of the United States in the area grew, it attempted to enable the Pueblo Indians to continue their generally peaceful and self-sufficient ways and recognized Spanish land grants to the Pueblos (in 1858, the United States recognized a 1689 Spanish land grant to Santo Domingo Pueblo of roughly 70,000 acres).

During the nineteenth century the process of acculturation among Pueblo Indians quickened markedly. In an attempt to retain their identity, Pueblo Indians clung even more tenaciously to their

heritage, which by now included elements of the once-hated Spanish culture and religion. By the 1880s, railroads had largely put an end to the traditional geographical isolation of the pueblos. Paradoxically, the U.S. decision to recognize Spanish land grants to the Pueblos denied Pueblo Indians certain rights granted under official treaties and left them particularly open to exploitation by squatters and thieves. In 1886, Kiwa was destroyed by floods, and the people moved to their present location.

After a gap of over 300 years, the All Indian Pueblo Council began to meet again in the 1920s, specifically in response to a congressional threat to appropriate Pueblo lands. Partly as a result of the Council's activities, Congress confirmed Pueblo title to their lands in 1924 by passing the Pueblo Lands Act. The United States also acknowledged its trust responsibilities in a series of legal decisions and other acts of Congress. Still, especially after 1900, Pueblo culture was increasingly threatened by Protestant evangelical missions and schools. The Bureau of Indian Affairs also weighed in on the subject of acculturation, forcing Indian children to leave their homes and attend culture-killing boarding schools.

Following World War II, the issue of water rights took center stage on most pueblos. Also, the All Indian Pueblo Council succeeded in slowing the threat against Pueblo lands as well as religious persecution. Making crafts for the tourist trade became an important economic activity during this period. Since the late nineteenth century, but especially after the 1960s, Pueblos have had to cope with onslaughts by (mostly white) anthropologists and seekers of Indian spirituality. The region is also known for its major art colonies at Taos and Santa Fe.

Religion In traditional Pueblo culture, religion and life are inseparable. To be in harmony with all of nature is the Pueblo ideal and way of life. The sun is seen as the representative of the Creator. Sacred mountains in each direction, plus the sun above and the earth below, define and balance the Pueblo world. Many Pueblo religious ceremonies revolve around the weather and are devoted to ensuring adequate rainfall. To this end, Pueblo Indians evoke the power of katsinas, sacred beings who live in mountains and other holy places, in ritual and dance. All Santo Domingo men belonged to katsina societies. Santo Domingo Pueblo contained two circular kivas, religious chambers that symbolize the place of original emergence into this world, and their associated societies, Squash and Turquoise.

In addition to the natural boundaries, Pueblo Indians have created a society that defines their world by providing balanced, reciprocal relationships within which people connect and harmonize with each other, the natural world, and time itself. According to tradition, the head of each pueblo is the religious leader, or *cacique,* whose primary responsibility it is to watch the sun and thereby determine the dates of ceremonies. Much ceremonialism is also based on medicine societies, and shamans used supernatural powers for curing, weather control, and ensuring the general welfare. As at other pueblos, much doctrine and ritual of the Catholic Church has been integrated into the native religion at Santo Domingo. Important ceremonies include church days such as Easter, Christmas, and saints' days as well as corn and harvest dances and other ceremonies related to agriculture and legend. Especially in the eastern pueblos, most ceremonies are kept secret.

Government Pueblo governments derived from two traditions. Elements that are probably indigenous include the *cacique,* or head of the Pueblo, and the war chiefs. These officials were intimately related to the religious structures of the pueblo and reflected the essentially theocratic nature of Pueblo government. At Santo Domingo the *cacique* was the head medicine man; he represented the Corn Mother and was sometimes referred to as *yaya,* or mother. He authorized all rituals and made yearly appointments, including two war chiefs (one from each kiva group) who exercised his power. In turn, the first war chief chose new *caciques.* Other traditional offices included the war chiefs' assistants and a ditch boss who, by means of ritual and duties, presided over the Pueblo irrigation system. Pueblo Indians did not typically seek to hold office.

A parallel but in most cases distinctly less powerful group of officials was imposed by the Spanish authorities. Appointed annually by the traditional leadership, they generally dealt with external and church matters and included the governor, lieutenant governor, captains, and *fiscales* (church officials). Young men were groomed for certain positions. There was also an advisory council of *principales,* comprised of former office holders. In addition, the All Indian Pueblo Council, dating from 1598, began meeting again in the twentieth century to assert rights and help solve problems.

Customs One mechanism that works to keep Pueblo societies coherent is a pervasive aversion to individualistic behavior. Children were raised with gentle guidance and a minimum of discipline. Pueblo Indians were generally monogamous, and divorce was relatively rare. The dead were prepared ceremonially and quickly buried with clothes, beads, food, and other items; their possessions were destroyed, and they were said to become katsinas in the land of the dead. A vigil of four days and nights was generally observed.

Matrilineal clans also existed at Santo Domingo, although their functions remain unclear. Various other more or less secret societies including medicine, hunters, clown, warriors, and katsina (associated with the two patrilineal kiva groups, Squash and Turquoise) acted to hold the pueblo together. The societies are said to have gained power from supernatural animals, through fetishes and figurines. Santo Domingo societies were traditionally so strong that other pueblos came to them if theirs needed revitalization. Most traditional customs remained relatively intact at Santo Domingo well into the 1940s. In modern times photography by outsiders is discouraged.

Dwellings In the seventeenth century, Santo Domingo Pueblo probably contained multistory apartment-style dwellings constructed of adobe (earth and straw) bricks, with beams across the roof that were covered with poles, brush, and plaster. Floors were of wood plank or packed earth. The roof of one level served as the floor of another. The levels were interconnected by ladders. As an aid to defense, the traditional design included no doors or windows; entry was through the roof. Two pit houses, or kivas, served as ceremonial chambers and clubhouses. The village plaza, around which all dwellings were clustered, was the spiritual center of the village where all the balanced forces of the world came together. Floods destroyed previous settlements; the present village dates from 1886.

Diet Before the Spanish arrived, Santo Domingo people ate primarily corn, beans, and pumpkins. They also grew sunflowers and tobacco. They hunted deer, mountain lion, bear, antelope, and rabbits. They also gathered a variety of wild seeds, nuts, berries, and other foods. The Spanish introduced wheat, alfalfa, sheep, cattle, and garden vegetables, which soon became part of the regular diet.

Key Technology Precontact farming implements were wooden. Traditional irrigation systems included ditches as well as floodwater collection at arroyo mouths *(ak chin).* Textiles were woven of cotton. Other items included baskets, pottery, and leather goods. The Spanish introduced metal tools and equipment.

Trade All Pueblos were part of extensive aboriginal trading networks. With the arrival of other cultures, Pueblo Indians also traded with the Hispanic American villages and then U.S. traders. At fixed times during summer or fall, enemies declared truces so that trading fairs might be held. The largest and best known was at Taos with the Comanche. Nomads exchanged slaves, buffalo hides, buckskins, jerked meat, and horses for agricultural and manufactured pueblo products. Trade along the Santa Fe Trail began in 1821. By the 1880s and the arrival of railroads, the Pueblos were dependent on many American-made goods, and the Native American manufacture of weaving and pottery declined and nearly died out.

Notable Arts In the Pueblo way, art and life are inseparable. Santo Domingo arts included pottery, baskets, and turquoise necklaces. They also excelled at making pump-drilled *heishi* beads. Songs, dances, and dramas are other traditional arts. Santo Domingos may have taught turquoise work to the Navajos in the 1880s.

Transportation Spanish horses, mules, and cattle arrived at Santo Domingo Pueblo in the seventeenth century.

Dress Men wore cotton kilts and leather sandals. Women wore cotton dresses and sandals or high moccasin boots. Deer and rabbit skin were also used for clothing and robes, and sandals were made of yucca.

War and Weapons Though often depicted as passive and docile, most Pueblo groups regularly engaged in warfare. The great revolt of 1680 stands out as the major military action, but they also skirmished at other times with the Spanish and defended themselves against attackers such as Apaches, Comanches, and Utes. They also contributed auxiliary soldiers to provincial forces under Spain and Mexico, which were used mainly against raiding Indians and to protect merchant caravans on the Santa Fe Trail. After the raiding tribes began to pose less of a threat in the late nineteenth century, Pueblo military societies began to wither away, with the office of war captain changing to civil and religious functions.

Contemporary Information

Government/Reservations Santo Domingo Pueblo contains roughly 70,000 acres. It is governed in the traditional manner, and there is no written constitution.

Economy The Pueblo hosts an annual arts fair; it also contains a service station and a small museum/visitor center. Many Santo Domingos work in nearby cities. Many are also active artists, specializing in traditional turquoise and shell necklace, pottery, other jewelry, woven belts, and leather moccasins and leggings. Santo Domingo people trade widely throughout the Southwest. In keeping with their conservative values, much of their work is unsigned. Farming and grazing are also important economic activities.

Legal Status Santo Domingo Pueblo is a federally recognized tribal entity.

Daily Life Santo Domingo remains one of the most conservative pueblos. The religion, ceremonialism, and social structure of the Pueblo are largely intact, and the society remains proud and vital. Most Santo Domingo people still speak Keresan, along with English and some Spanish. Many people marry within the pueblo. Changes since World War II include a greater reliance on hospitals, improved sanitation, and fewer school disruptions for religious or ceremonial reasons. Although their appreciation for Western education has increased, high school drop-out rates remain very high, in part because of continued opposition from pueblo leaders. They fear that non-Indian education opens up the potential for undesirable, far-reaching change; an example would be to have women sitting on the tribal council. Santo Domingos are well represented in the leadership of pan-Pueblo political organizations.

Taos Pueblo

Also known as San Geronimo de Taos. Taos (`Tä ōs) is from a Tiwa word meaning "in the village." The word "pueblo" comes from the Spanish for "village." It refers both to a certain style of Southwest Indian architecture, characterized by multistory, apartment-like buildings made of adobe, and to the people themselves. Rio Grande pueblos are known as eastern Pueblos; Zuñi, Hopi, and sometimes Acoma and Laguna are known as western Pueblos. The Taos name for their Pueblo is *Tecuse* or *Ilaphai,* "at the mouth of Red-Willow Canyon."

Location The northernmost, highest (with Picuris, at about 7,000 feet), and one of the most isolated of the eastern pueblos, Taos is 70 miles north of Santa Fe.

Population In 1990, 1,200 Indians lived at Taos; the tribal enrollment stood at roughly 1,800. Roughly 2,000 people lived there in the late seventeenth century.

Language Taos Indians spoke Northern Tiwa, a Kiowa-Tanoan language.

Historical Information

History All Pueblo people are thought to be descended from Anasazi and perhaps Mogollon and several other ancient peoples. From them they learned architecture, farming, pottery, and basketry. Larger population groups became possible with effective agriculture and ways to store food surpluses. Within the context of a relatively stable existence, the people devoted increasing amounts of time and attention to religion, arts, and crafts. The Anasazi pueblo of Chaco, in northwest New Mexico, is thought by some to be the ancestral home of the Taos Indians.

In the 1200s, the Anasazi abandoned their traditional canyon homelands in response to climatic and social upheavals. A century or two of migrations ensued, followed in general by the slow reemergence of their culture in the historic pueblos. The Tiwas were probably the first of the Tanoan Pueblo people to enter the northern Rio Grande region. The earliest archaeological sites near Taos date from 1000 to 1200; these are not at the site of the present pueblo, however, and most remain unexcavated. "Modern" Taos dates from roughly 1400.

Francisco Vasquez de Coronado visited Taos in 1540. In 1598, Juan de Oñate arrived in the area with settlers, founding the colony of New Mexico. Oñate carried on the process, already underway in nearby areas, of subjugating the local Indians; forcing them to pay taxes in crops, cotton, and work; and opening the door for Catholic missionaries to attack their religion. The Spanish renamed the Pueblos with saints' names and began a program of church construction, establishing the mission of San Geronimo at Taos in the early seventeenth century. At the same time, the Spanish introduced such new crops as peaches, wheat, and peppers into the region. In 1620, a royal decree created civil offices at each pueblo; silver-headed canes, many of which remain in use today, symbolized the governor's authority.

Taos played a leading role in the Pueblo rebellion of 1680. For years, the Spaniards had routinely tortured Indians for practicing traditional religion. They also forced the Indians to labor for them, sold Indians into slavery, and let their cattle overgraze Indian land, a situation that eventually led to drought, erosion, and famine. Popé of San Juan Pueblo and other Pueblo religious leaders planned the great revolt at Taos, sending runners carrying cords of maguey fibers to mark the day of rebellion. On August 10, 1680, a virtually united stand on the part of the Pueblos drove the Spanish from the region. The Indians killed many Spaniards but refrained from mass slaughter, allowing most of them to leave Santa Fe for El Paso.

Santa Fe was officially reconquered in 1692, after which the Taos fled to the mountains and to their Plains friends, the Kiowa. The Spanish sacked Taos Pueblo in 1693, after which the Indians returned and rebuilt. Another short-lived rebellion occurred in 1696. Although Pueblo unity did not last, Spanish rule was notably less severe from then on. Harsh forced labor all but ceased, and the Indians reached an understanding with the Church that enabled them to continue practicing their traditional religion. By the 1700s, excluding Hopi and Zuñi, only Taos, Picuris, Isleta, and Acoma Pueblos had not changed locations since the arrival of the Spanish.

In general, the Pueblo eighteenth century was marked by smallpox epidemics and increased raiding by the Apache, Comanche, and Ute. The people practiced their religion but more or less in secret. During this time, intermarriage and regular exchange between Hispanic villages and Pueblo Indians created a new New Mexican culture, neither strictly Spanish nor Indian, but rather somewhat of a blend between the two.

Mexican "rule" in 1821 brought little immediate change to the Pueblos. The Mexicans stepped up what had been a gradual process of appropriating Indian land and water, and they allowed the nomadic tribes even greater latitude to raid. As the presence of the United States in the area grew, it attempted to enable the Pueblo Indians to continue their generally peaceful and self-sufficient ways and recognized Spanish land grants to the Pueblos. A political rebellion by Indians and poor Hispanics in 1837 over the issue of taxes led to the assassination of the governor of New Mexico and his brief replacement by a Plains/Taos Indian. In 1845, a few Tiwas from Taos, along with local Hispanics, killed the U.S. governor and attacked several officials over depredations committed by U.S. troops as well as long-standing land issues. The troops replied with a slaughter.

In an attempt to retain their identity, Pueblo Indians clung even more tenaciously to their heritage, which by now included elements of the once-hated Spanish culture and religion. By the 1880s, railroads had largely put an end to the traditional geographical isolation of the pueblos. Paradoxically, the U.S.

decision to recognize Spanish land grants to the Pueblos denied Pueblo Indians certain rights granted under official treaties and left them particularly open to exploitation by squatters and thieves.

After a gap of over 300 years, the All Indian Pueblo Council began to meet again in the 1920s, specifically in response to a congressional threat to appropriate Pueblo lands. Partly as a result of the Council's activities, Congress confirmed Pueblo title to their lands in 1924 by passing the Pueblo Lands Act. The United States also acknowledged its trust responsibilities in a series of legal decisions and other acts of Congress. Still, especially after 1900, Pueblo culture was increasingly threatened by Protestant evangelical missions and schools. The Bureau of Indian Affairs also weighed in on the subject of acculturation, forcing Indian children to leave their homes and attend culture-killing boarding schools.

In 1906, the U.S. government included Taos's holiest site, the Blue Lake region in the Sangre de Cristo Mountains, as part of a national forest. Under the leadership of longtime governor Severino Martinez and others, the tribe fought to get it back. In 1965 they received title to the land and were offered a cash payment, but they held out for the land. In 1970 the government returned Blue Lake, along with 48,000 surrounding acres. Since the late nineteenth century, but especially after the 1960s, the Pueblos have had to cope with onslaughts by (mostly white) anthropologists and seekers of Indian spirituality. The region is also known for its major art colonies at Taos and Santa Fe.

Religion In traditional Pueblo culture, religion and life are inseparable. To be in harmony with all of nature is the Pueblo ideal and way of life. The sun is seen as the representative of the Creator. Sacred mountains in each direction, mountain lakes and other natural places, plus the sun above and the earth below, define and balance the Taos Pueblo world. Many Pueblo religious ceremonies revolve around the weather and are devoted to ensuring adequate rainfall. To this end, Pueblo Indians evoke the power of katsinas, sacred beings who live in mountains and other holy places, in ritual and masked dance.

In addition to the natural boundaries, Pueblo Indians have created a society that defines their world by providing balanced, reciprocal relationships within which people connect and harmonize with each other, the natural world, and time itself. Unlike the situation in most Pueblos, the heads of the kiva societies, rather than the *cacique,* were the most important religious leaders. In fact, the *cacique* had both religious and secular duties.

Seven kiva or ceremonial societies were active at Taos. Each had special functions and separate religious knowledge. Feathers of birds such as eagles, hawks, and ducks, as well as wildflowers, were important ceremonially. Traditionally, all preteen boys underwent religious training, and a select few were chosen for an 18-month initiation, culminating in a pilgrimage to Blue Lake, into one of the kiva societies. Only initiated men could move from "boys" to "elders" and hold secular office.

Much ceremonialism is also based on medicine societies, and shamans who derive powers from animal spirits use their supernatural powers for curing, weather control, and ensuring the general welfare. Corn dances are held in summer and animal dances in winter. Most ceremonies at Taos are still kept secret from outsiders. Although most Taos Indians consider themselves Catholics, it is a form of Catholicism that coexists with their traditional religion. The Native American Church was introduced at Taos in 1907. Although controversial, it remains active.

Government Pueblo governments derived from two traditions. Offices that are probably indigenous include the *cacique,* or head of the Pueblo, and the war captains. These officials are intimately related to the religious structures of the pueblo and reflected the essentially theocratic nature of Pueblo government. At Taos, the *cacique* plus the tribal council (kiva society heads plus secular officials) ruled religious matters.

A parallel but in most cases distinctly less powerful group of officials was imposed by the Spanish authorities. Appointed by the traditional leadership, they generally dealt with external and church matters and included the governor, assistant governors, and *fiscales.* The authority of their offices was symbolized by canes. Community announcements were called out from the roof of the governor's house. During the 1950s and 1960s, the

All Indian Pueblo Council (of eastern villages) became increasingly active in asserting rights and solving problems.

Customs One mechanism that works to keep Pueblo societies coherent is a pervasive aversion to individualistic behavior. Children were raised with gentle guidance and a minimum of discipline. A high value is placed on generosity and reciprocity. Pueblo Indians were generally monogamous, and divorce was relatively rare.

Taos Indians enjoyed regular contact with other Pueblos and Plains Indians, and they have borrowed freely from other cultures over the centuries. However, they are very protective of their own society and have maintained a fundamental cultural isolation. Most people who married out of the Pueblo have stayed away.

Corpses were dressed in their best clothes and buried with food. Household members observed a four-day vigil, after which they set out prayer feathers and cornmeal for the spirit of dead. In modern times photography by outsiders is discouraged.

Dwellings Taos was formerly walled, as a defense against the Comanche raids of the 1700s. The Pueblo features two clusters of apartment-style buildings, as high as six stories, on either side of Taos Creek. The buildings are constructed of adobe (earth and straw) bricks, with beams across a roof covered with poles, brush, and plaster. Floors are of wood plank or packed earth. The roof of one level serves as the floor of another. The levels are interconnected by ladders. As an aid to defense, the traditional design included no doors or windows; entry was through the roof. There were also a number of adobe houses scattered around the Pueblo. Seven pit houses, or kivas, serve as ceremonial chambers and clubhouses. The village plaza, around which all dwellings are clustered, is the spiritual center of the village where all the balanced forces of world come together. A racetrack is part of the village, built to accommodate ceremonial footraces.

Diet Before the Spanish arrived, Taos people ate primarily corn, beans, and squash. They also grew cotton and tobacco. A relatively short growing season necessitated a greater dependence on hunting and gathering. They hunted deer, mountain lion, bear, antelope, and rabbits. Men from Taos also traveled east to hunt buffalo. The people also gathered a variety of wild seeds, nuts, berries, and other foods and fished in rivers and mountain streams. The Spanish introduced wheat, alfalfa, chilies, fruit trees, grapes, sheep, cattle, and garden vegetables, which soon became part of the regular diet.

Key Technology Precontact farming implements were wooden. Most pottery was basically utilitarian. Tanning tools were made of bone and wood. Musical instruments included drums of animal hide. Men hunted with juniper bows and arrows. The Spanish introduced metal tools and equipment.

Trade All Pueblos were part of extensive aboriginal trading networks. With the arrival of other cultures, Pueblo Indians also traded with the Hispanic American villages and then U.S. traders. Taos Indians traded for cotton since they could not grow it themselves. At fixed times during summer or fall, enemies declared truces so that trading fairs might be held. The largest and best known was at Taos with the Comanche. In fact, Taos served as a Pueblo trade gateway to the Plains tribes north and east. Nomads exchanged slaves, buffalo hides, buckskins, jerked meat, and horses for agricultural and manufactured pueblo products. Pueblo Indians traded for shell and copper ornaments, turquoise, and macaw feathers.

Despite the proximity of Picuris Pueblo (18 miles by trail), the two peoples interacted relatively infrequently and traded little but mountain plants. Trade along the Santa Fe Trail began in 1821. By the 1880s and the arrival of railroads, the Pueblos were dependent on many American-made goods, and the Native American manufacture of weaving and pottery declined and nearly died out.

Notable Arts In the Pueblo way, art and life are inseparable. Taos arts included moccasins, drums, songs, dances, and dramas. Many Pueblos experienced a renaissance of traditional arts in the twentieth century, beginning in 1919 with San Ildefonso pottery.

Transportation Spanish horses, mules, and cattle arrived at Taos Pueblo in the seventeenth century. Horses were especially important at Taos.

Dress Men wore Plains-style fringed and beaded buckskin shirts, leggings, and moccasins. Women wore deerskin dresses and white buckskin moccasins (married women). Rabbit skin and buffalo hide were also used for blankets and robes.

War and Weapons Though often depicted as passive and docile, most Pueblo groups regularly engaged in warfare. The great revolt of 1680 stands out as the major military action, but they also skirmished at other times with the Spanish and defended themselves against attackers such as Apaches, Comanches, and Utes. They also contributed auxiliary soldiers to provincial forces under Spain and Mexico, which were used mainly against raiding Indians and to protect merchant caravans on the Santa Fe Trail. After the raiding tribes began to pose less of a threat in the late nineteenth century, Pueblo military societies began to wither away, with the office of war captain changing to civil and religious functions.

Contemporary Information

Government/Reservations Taos Pueblo contains roughly 95,000 acres. Twenty-two civil officers are appointed annually by the traditional religious leadership. The all-male council consists of roughly 60 members (1990).

Economy Most people obtain money by working in Taos and by making and/or selling arts and crafts, especially drums and moccasins but also woodcarvings, weavings, pottery, and rabbit-skin blankets. Tourists also pay parking and camera fees to the Pueblo. There is also some work available with the tribe.

Legal Status Taos Pueblo is a federally recognized tribal entity.

Daily Life Although holding on to their identity is increasingly a challenge, Pueblo people have deep roots. In general, change has come very slowly to Taos. Many of the old ceremonies are still performed; the religion is largely intact, as is the language and entire worldview; and there is a very palpable and intentional continuity with the past. Community duties include cleaning irrigation ditches, repairing fences, plastering the church, and dance and other ceremonial activities. English is replacing Spanish as the Pueblo's second language. Control of their own day school since the 1970s has been a key in maintaining their culture, although most students go to high school in the town of Taos. Taos Pueblo copes with a number of health problems, including diabetes, alcoholism, and drug use.

Since the 1930s, the traditional multistoried pueblos have contained glass windows and some doorways, although no electricity or running water. Now fewer than 100 people live there, and the buildings are falling into disrepair. Most people live in single-family adobe houses, more and more of which include commercial building materials. Buildings outside the old walls have been electrified since 1971, although indoor toilets are still unusual. Some so-called crackerbox houses put up by the Department of Housing and Urban Development also dot the pueblo. The ruined village walls remain important in Taos thought: Anything within them is considered sacred. A few Indians keep summer homes in nearby towns.

Older people still wear the dress of an earlier era, such as braids, blankets, moccasins, simulated leggings, and brightly colored shawls. The extended family remains important. Birth, death, and marriage rituals reflect the Catholic influence. Divorce is becoming more frequent, and interpersonal conflicts are more likely to be handled outside of the pueblo (in state court, for example). An elaborate kiva initiation for boys begins between ages 7 and 10. San Geronimo Day (September 29–30) is the major harvest/feast day. Taos Indians maintain frequent contact with their non-Indian neighbors, yet they retain firm cultural boundaries.

Tesuque Pueblo

Tesuque (Te `sū kē) is a Hispanicization of the Tewa word *tecuge,* which means "structure at a narrow place" or "dry, spotted place." The word "pueblo" comes from the Spanish for "village." It refers both to a certain style of Southwest Indian architecture, characterized by multistory, apartmentlike buildings

Two members of the Tesuque tribe at Tesuque Pueblo in the late nineteenth century. Today, Tesuque Pueblo contains roughly 17,000 acres. In 1993 there were 488 enrolled members of Tesuque Pueblo.

made of adobe, and to the people themselves. Rio Grande pueblos are known as eastern Pueblos; Zuñi, Hopi, and sometimes Acoma and Laguna are known as western Pueblos.

Location Tesuque Pueblo is located 9 miles north of Santa Fe, on the Tesuque River.

Population Perhaps 200 people lived at Tesuque Pueblo in 1680. In 1990, 232 Indians lived there, out of a total population of almost 700. There were 488 enrolled members of Tesuque Pueblo in 1993.

Language Tesuque Indians spoke Tewa, a member of the Kiowa-Tanoan language family.

Historical Information

History All Pueblo people are thought to be descended from Anasazi and perhaps Mogollon and several other ancient peoples. From them they learned architecture, farming, pottery, and basketry. Larger population groups became possible with effective agriculture and ways to store food surpluses. Within the context of a relatively stable existence, the people devoted increasing amounts of time and attention to religion, arts, and crafts. In prehistoric times, the Tewa were generally north and west of their present locations and have inhabited numerous prehistoric villages on both sides (though mostly the west side) of the Rio Grande and the Rio Chama.

In the 1200s, the Anasazi abandoned their traditional canyon homelands in response to climatic and social upheavals. A century or two of migrations ensued, followed in general by the slow reemergence of their culture in the historic pueblos. Tesuque Pueblo had at least one (unknown) location previous to its present site, which dates from 1694.

In 1598, Juan de Oñate arrived in the area with settlers, founding the colony of New Mexico. Oñate carried on the process, already underway in nearby areas, of subjugating the local Indians; forcing them to pay taxes in crops, cotton, and work; and opening the door for Catholic missionaries to attack their religion. The Spanish renamed the Pueblos with saints' names and began a program of church construction, establishing a mission known as San Lorenzo at Tesuque in the early seventeenth century. At the same time, the Spanish introduced such new crops as peaches, wheat, and peppers into the region. In 1620, a royal decree created civil offices at each pueblo; silver-headed canes, many of which remain in use today, symbolized the governor's authority.

In 1680 Pueblo Indians organized and carried out a major revolt against the Spanish. For years, the Spaniards had routinely tortured Indians for practicing traditional religion. They also forced the Indians to labor for them, sold Indians into slavery, and let their cattle overgraze Indian land, a situation that eventually led to drought, erosion, and famine. Popé of San Juan Pueblo and other Pueblo religious leaders planned the revolt, sending runners carrying cords of maguey fibers to mark the day of rebellion. The revolt began on August 10, 1680, probably at Tesuque. A virtually united stand on the part of the Pueblos drove the Spanish from the region. The Indians killed many Spaniards but refrained from mass slaughter, allowing them to leave Santa Fe for El Paso.

Although Pueblo unity did not last, and Santa Fe was officially reconquered in 1692, Spanish rule was notably less severe from then on. Harsh forced labor all but ceased, and the Indians reached an understanding with the Church that enabled them to continue practicing their traditional religion. Tesuque Indians abandoned their pueblo after 1680 but rebuilt it on the present site in 1694.

In general, the Pueblo eighteenth century was marked by smallpox epidemics and increased raiding by the Apache, Comanche, and Ute. Occasionally Pueblo Indians fought with the Spanish against the nomadic tribes. The people practiced their religion but more or less in secret. During this time, intermarriage and regular exchange between Hispanic villages and Pueblo Indians created a new New Mexican culture, neither strictly Spanish nor Indian, but rather somewhat of a blend between the two.

Mexican "rule" in 1821 brought little immediate change to the Pueblos. The Mexicans stepped up what had been a gradual process of appropriating Indian land and water, and they allowed the nomadic tribes even greater latitude to raid. A political rebellion by Indians and Hispanic poor in 1837 over the issue of taxes led to the assassination of the governor of New Mexico and his brief replacement by a Plains/Taos Indian. As the presence of the United States in the area grew, it attempted to enable the Pueblo Indians to continue their generally peaceful and self-sufficient ways. Paradoxically, however, the U.S. decision to recognize Spanish land grants to the Pueblos denied Pueblo Indians certain rights granted under official treaties and left them particularly open to exploitation by squatters and thieves.

Especially after 1821, the Pueblos underwent a steady acculturation. Toward the late nineteenth century, the United States reintroduced religious repression. The government and Protestant missionaries branded Indian religious practices as obscene and immoral, and the Bureau of Indian Affairs forcibly removed Indian children to culture-killing boarding schools. As part of the effort to retain their traditions, Indians more deeply embraced customs once seen as alien, such as Catholicism. By the 1880s, railroads had ended the traditional isolation of most pueblos. Instead of treaties, the United States recognized old Spanish land "grants" of pueblo land. Ironically, this put them outside official treaty rights and left them particularly open to exploitation by squatters and thieves.

Tesuque ran out of water in the early twentieth century as a result of diversions by recent Anglo settlers. A series of dams and basins restored much of their water by 1935. Partly because of lobbying from the All Indian Pueblo Council, Congress confirmed Pueblo title to their lands in 1924 by passing the Pueblo Lands Act. The United States also acknowledged its trust responsibilities in a series of legal decisions and other acts of Congress. In the late 1950s, Tesuque Pueblo received no tribal income other than the interest from funds on deposit with the government. Since the late nineteenth century, but especially after the 1960s, Pueblos have had to cope with onslaughts by (mostly white) anthropologists and seekers of Indian spirituality. The region is also known for its significant art colonies at Taos and Santa Fe.

Religion In traditional Pueblo culture, religion and life are inseparable. To be in harmony with all of nature is the Pueblo ideal and way of life. The sun is seen as the representative of the Creator. Sacred mountains in each direction, plus the sun above and the earth below, define and balance the Pueblo world. Many Pueblo religious ceremonies revolve around the weather and are devoted to ensuring adequate rainfall. To this end, Pueblo Indians evoke the power of katsinas, sacred beings who live in mountains and other holy places, in ritual and masked dance.

In addition to the natural boundaries, Pueblo Indians have created a society that defines their world by providing balanced, reciprocal relationships within which people connect and harmonize with each other, the natural world, and time itself. According to tradition, the head of each pueblo is the religious leader, or *cacique,* whose primary responsibility it is to watch the sun and thereby determine the dates of ceremonies. Much ceremonialism is also based on medicine societies, and shamans who derive powers from animal spirits use their supernatural powers for curing, weather control, and ensuring the general welfare. Especially in the eastern pueblos, most ceremonies are kept secret. Since at least the

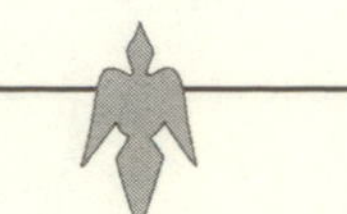

eighteenth century, Catholicism has strongly influenced traditional religion and ceremonialism.

Winter (Turquoise) and summer (Squash) groups divided the pueblo. Each had a *cacique* and a kiva. Ceremonial societies included katsina, curing, clowning, hunting, and defense. The *caciques* and the heads of societies, or priests, ran the religious and the political life of the pueblo. All rituals were performed within the winter-summer context.

Government Pueblo governments derived from two traditions. Offices that are probably indigenous include the *cacique,* or head of the Pueblo, and the war captains. These officials are intimately related to the religious structures of the pueblo and reflected the essentially theocratic nature of Pueblo government.

A parallel but in most cases distinctly less powerful group of officials was imposed by the Spanish authorities. Appointed by the traditional leadership, they generally dealt with external and church matters and included the governor, two lieutenant governors, sheriffs, and *fiscales.* The authority of their offices was symbolized by canes. Nontraditional positions also often included a ditch boss, who was in charge of the irrigation ditches, as well as a town crier and sacristan. Also, a council of *principales* (present and former officers) had justice-related responsibilities. The Spanish canes, plus canes given them by President Lincoln, were a symbol of authority. In addition, the All Indian Pueblo Council, dating from 1598, began meeting again in the twentieth century.

Customs One mechanism that works to keep Pueblo societies coherent is a pervasive aversion to individualistic behavior. Children were raised with gentle guidance and a minimum of discipline. Pueblo Indians were generally monogamous, and divorce was relatively rare. The dead were ceremonially prepared and quickly buried. Their possessions were broken and placed on the grave, along with food, to help them journey to the spirit land. A vigil of four days and nights was generally observed.

At Tesuque, a summer and a winter *cacique,* appointed for life, oversaw the pueblo. Society was divided into two patrilineal groups, summer (associated with the Squash kiva) and winter (associated with the Turquoise kiva), which united in times of crisis and for the welfare of the Pueblo. These groups were further divided into relatively weak and ill-defined clans. A number of secret societies also existed. For instance, the warrior society was concerned with hunting, war, crops, fertility, and curing. Each society had its own dances and ritual paraphernalia. Numerous life-cycle rites, as well as songs, crafts, communal activities such as maintenance of irrigation canals, prayer retreats, and performing dances, also ensured that one spent one's life "becoming" a Tewa.

Dwellings Tesuque Pueblo originally featured apartment-style dwellings of up to five stories constructed of adobe (earth and straw) bricks, with pine beams across the roof that were covered with poles, brush, and plaster. Floors were of wood plank or packed earth. The roof of one level served as the floor of another. The levels were interconnected by ladders. As an aid to defense, the traditional design included no doors or windows; entry was through the roof. Pit houses, or kivas, served as ceremonial chambers and clubhouses. The village plaza, around which the church and all dwellings were clustered, was the spiritual center of the village, a place where all the balanced forces of the world came together.

Diet Before the Spanish arrived, people from Tesuque Pueblo ate primarily corn, beans, and squash. They also grew cotton and tobacco. They hunted deer, mountain lion, and antelope, and they also fished. They also gathered a variety of wild seeds, nuts, berries, and other foods. The Spanish introduced wheat, alfalfa, chilies, fruit trees, grapes, sheep, cattle, and garden vegetables, which soon became part of the regular diet.

Key Technology Tesuque people traditionally diverted water from the Rio Grande via irrigation ditches. They used wood shovels and hoes, stone axes, and woven fiber baskets. They fished with pointed sticks and yucca-fiber nets.

Trade All Pueblos were part of extensive aboriginal trading networks. With the arrival of other cultures, Pueblo Indians also traded with the Hispanic

American villages and then U.S. traders. At fixed times during summer or fall, enemies declared truces so that trading fairs might be held. The largest and best known was at Taos with the Comanche. In the seventeenth and eighteenth centuries, Tesuque Pueblo traded primarily with other Pueblos, Navajos, and Plains tribes. They traded cornmeal, wheat flour, bread, and woven goods for jerked meat, buffalo robes, pipe pouches, tortoise shells, buckskins, and horses. They also traded for baskets, Navajo blankets, shell and copper ornaments, turquoise, and macaw feathers. Trade along the Santa Fe Trail began in 1821. By the 1880s and the arrival of railroads, the Pueblos were dependent on many American-made goods, and the native manufacture of weaving and pottery declined and nearly died out.

Notable Arts In the Pueblo way, art and life are inseparable. Traditional arts at Tesuque included pottery, weaving, masks, songs, dances, and dramas. Tesuque joined in the great Pueblo arts revival, begun at San Ildefonso in 1919.

Transportation Spanish horses, mules, and cattle arrived at Tesuque in the sixteenth century.

Dress Men wore cotton and buckskin shirts and kilts. Womens' traditional dress featured buckskin or spun cotton dresses and leather sandals or high moccasin boots. Rabbit skin was also used for clothing and robes.

War and Weapons Though often depicted as passive and docile, most Pueblo peoples regularly engaged in warfare. The great revolt of 1680 stands out as the major military action, but they also skirmished at other times with the Spanish and defended themselves against attackers such as Apaches, Comanches, and Utes. They also contributed auxiliary soldiers to provincial forces under Spain and Mexico, which were used mainly against raiding Indians and to protect merchant caravans on the Santa Fe Trail. Tewas occasionally raided Navajos for goods. After the nomadic tribes began to pose less of a threat in the late nineteenth century, Pueblo military societies began to wither away, with the office of war captain changing to civil and religious functions.

Contemporary Information

Government/Reservations Tesuque Pueblo contains roughly 17,000 acres. Government is by tradition, with officers elected annually by the division chiefs. At Tesuque, the office of governor rotates between four men. The *fiscales* have responsibilities outside of the church. The Tesuques have no sheriff, unlike the other Tewa pueblos. The council, consisting of the officers, past governors, and the war chief, acts as liaison to the outside world. Tesuque is a member of the Eight Northern Indian Pueblos Council.

Economy Many people work in Santa Fe or Los Alamos. Some good pottery is produced, but there is generally little art or crafts. Subsistence farming, the basis of the economy into the 1960s, still exists, as does grazing and sales of timber. Income is also derived from leasing land to non-Indian businesses as well as from a bingo parlor.

Legal Status Tesuque Pueblo is a federally recognized tribal entity.

Daily Life Although the project of holding on to their identity is a strong challenge, Pueblo people have deep roots, and in many ways the ancient rhythms and patterns continue. Many of the old ceremonies are still performed; the religion is largely intact, and there is a palpable and intentional continuity with the past. Almost all Tesuques are Catholic. Tesuque was one of the first pueblos to have electricity and housing put up by the Department of Housing and Urban Development in addition to the traditional adobe houses.

Tesuque is traditionally the most conservative of the Tewa pueblos. Many people still speak Tewa, and English has served as a common second language since the 1960s. Children attend a day school on the reservation and public or private high school in Santa Fe. Health problems, including alcoholism and drug abuse, continue to plague the Pueblos. Indian Health Service hospitals often cooperate with native healers. The annual katsina dance in October is closed to outsiders. In 1970, the pueblo entered into an extremely controversial, long-term lease with a non-native company to develop thousands of acres of tribal lands. They also gave up some water rights. After years

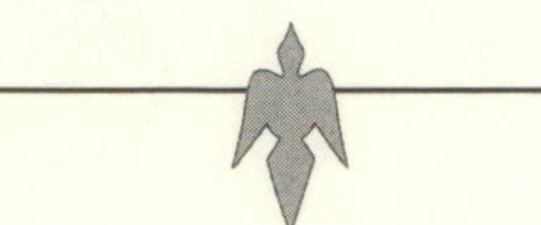

of litigation, Tesuque canceled the lease in 1976. The annual feast day is November 12.

Tigua

This tribe lives on Ysleta del Sur Pueblo, "Isleta of the South," a reference to the ancestral Isleta Pueblo in New Mexico. The Pueblo was formerly known as Tigua (`Tē wä) Reservation. The word "pueblo" comes from the Spanish for "village." It refers both to a certain style of Southwest Indian architecture, characterized by multistory, apartmentlike buildings made of adobe, and to the people themselves. (*See also* Isleta Pueblo.)

Location Ysleta del Sur Pueblo is located within the southern boundary of El Paso, Texas.

Population The original—late-seventeenth-century—population of Ysleta del Sur Pueblo may have ranged from 500 to about 1,500. In 1990, 211 Indians out of a total population of 292 lived at Tigua. Tribal enrollment in the mid-1990s was around 1,500.

Language The native language of the Tigua people is Southern Tiwa.

Historical Information

History Ysleta del Sur Pueblo was founded in 1682 by Pueblo refugees from the rebellion of 1680. Its original inhabitants included Indians from Isleta Pueblo as well as Piro, Manso, Apache, Suma, and Tompiro Indians, none of whom joined the revolt. These Indians retreated south with the fleeing Spaniards. They built a church at Tigua, dedicated to Saint Anthony, in 1682. Following the 1692 Spanish reconquest, in which these Indians participated, Governor Diego de Vargas planned to resettle them in their New Mexico homelands, but most preferred to remain. The Piros eventually became absorbed into Tigua Pueblo or the local Spanish-American population. At some point, the Ysleta Indians received a land grant from the king of Spain.

For the next two centuries, Tigua people practiced farming on irrigated fields. Tiguas scouted for El Paso settlements against Comanche and Apache raiders. Tiguas also scouted for the Texas Rangers and the U.S. cavalry during the Indian campaigns. After 1848, however, Tiguas were subject to "legal" and extralegal abuses from rapacious Anglos, and much of their land was lost. When President Lincoln acknowledged the New Mexican Pueblo land grants with a second set of silver-headed canes, Tigua, standing in the Confederacy, was ignored. In any case, since Texas retained its public lands, the U.S. government was unable to create a reservation for the Tigua.

In the late nineteenth century and into the 1920s the tribe virtually faded away, mixing with the local populace and living in extreme poverty. In 1967, the state of Texas recognized the Ysleta Indian community; federal recognition followed the next year. The receipt of federal money and recognition revitalized the tribe and provided the means through which it was able to reclaim its identity.

Religion Tiguas practice Catholicism, with some native elements. The Pueblo's patron saint is Anthony, who was the patron of Isleta Pueblo before the 1680 revolt. A small core of people practice a more traditional religion, featuring a katsinalike entity known as the *awelo,* or grandfather, who oversees all behavior. The tribe also possesses buffalo *awelo* masks and an ancient ceremonial drum.

Government The tribal government is Spanish-style civil. There is a *cacique,* a *cacique teniente* (lieutenant *cacique,* or governor), an *alguacil* or sergeant at arms, a *capitán de guerra* or war captain, and four assistant captains. Except for the first and the last, all are elected annually. Ysleta del Sur Pueblo also possesses the old Spanish canes, symbols of political authority, that were carried by the original settlers.

Customs Tribal ceremonial items are stored in a *tusla,* generally the home of a tribal officer, where celebrations are often held. There is a high rate of intermarriage with outsiders, particularly with Mexicans and other Indians. The Tigua enjoy a close relationship with Isleta Pueblo, New Mexico, 250 miles away. They are also associated with the Tortugas community of Las Cruces, New Mexico, a Tigua community founded in the late nineteenth century

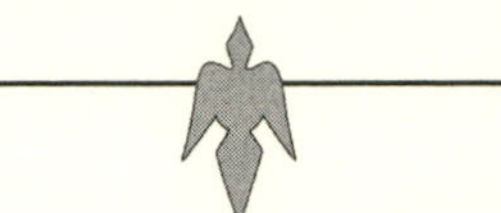

and composed of Tigua, Piro, and Manso Indians. The Tiguas also have relatives in Mexico, at the former Piro pueblo of Senecú, near Juarez. There may have been a clan system in earlier days.

Dwellings Originally, adobe houses were arranged around a church plaza. The general neighborhood is shared with Mexican American and Anglo neighbors.

Diet Traditional crops included corn, beans, and squash. The people also hunted buffalo and other wild game.

Key Technology Women made pottery into the twentieth century. They also made willow baskets, and men wove blankets and braided rope.

Trade Tiguas traded corn, wheat, fruit, and salt as well as crafts. Most arts and crafts were sold in El Paso and Juarez, although some were traded in Chihuahua City.

Notable Arts Women made pottery until the last traditional potter died in 1930. Before the early twentieth century, men wove blankets and braided rope, and women made willow baskets.

Transportation Baskets were used to transport goods.

Dress Men wore cotton kilts and leather sandals. Women wore cotton dresses and sandals or high moccasin boots. Buckskin and rabbit skin were also used for clothing and robes.

War and Weapons Tiguas supplied soldiers to help the Spanish reconquer New Mexico in the 1680s and 1690s. They also fought against Comanches and Apaches during most of the eighteenth and nineteenth centuries.

Contemporary Information

Government/Reservations Ysleta del Sur Pueblo, established in 1682, contains 66 acres. The state of Texas is trustee for all tribal lands. Men elect all officials including the *cacique,* war captain, and governor. There is no constitution.

Economy Most people work in El Paso and surrounding cities. Some beadwork, pottery, and other crafts are produced and sold to tourists. Texas has initiated a program to turn the reservation into a tourist attraction. A Tigua tribal museum, restaurant, and gift shop already exist. Gaming is seen as the way of the future.

Legal Status Ysleta del Sur Pueblo is a federally recognized tribal entity. A land claims case for prehistoric Huenco lands, of great religious significance to the Tigua, is pending.

Daily Life The Tigua community is an urban enclave. In the early 1900s, Spanish largely replaced Tiwa on the Pueblo, with English as a second language. Some tribal revitalization has occurred since the 1960s, including ceremonies, language, and hunts, but the population is overwhelmingly assimilated. Tribal rolls closed in 1984 with 1,124 certified members. The Tiguas use their tribal drum, brought from New Mexico 300 years ago, on the Feast of Saint Anthony.

The officially unrecognized Tortuga community (Gualalupe Indian Village) still exists in Las Cruces, on 40 acres owned by their own incorporated organization. Land is privately owned. No one speaks the native language, but several traditional ceremonies, such as the Rabbit Hunt, attended by the people of Ysleta del Sur Pueblo, are still performed.

Tohono O'odham

Tohono O'odham (Tō hō nō `Ō dəm) are also known as Papago or Desert People. The name Papago is derived from the Pima word *Papahvio-Otam,* meaning "bean people." They are also known as Two Villagers, owing to their traditional migration patterns (see "History" under "Historical Information"). They, along with the Pima (Akimel O'odham, or River People, also known as One Villagers because of their relatively settled lives), the Sand Papago (Hia-ced O'odham, also known as No Villagers, because of their more or less constant migrations in search of food), and the Ak-Chin ("mouth of the arroyo") O'odham, constitute the O'odham Indians.

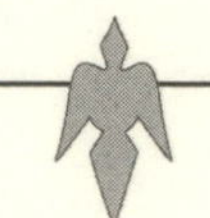

Location The Tohono O'odham lived originally in the Sonoran Desert near the Gulf of California. (The Sand Papago lived in the western and most arid parts of the Sonoran Desert.) Today they live in four reservations in southern Arizona (see "Government/ Reservations" under "Contemporary Information").

Population Up to 50,000 Tohono O'odham probably lived in the region in 1500, although their numbers had shrunk to about 3,000 by 1700. In 1990, approximately 8,500 people lived on the main reservation. Another 400 lived at Ak Chin, almost 1,100 lived at San Xavier, about 500 lived at Gila Bend, and several thousand lived off-reservation. The enrolled membership in 1991 was 17,589.

Language The native language of the Tohono O'odham is Piman, a Uto-Aztecan language.

Historical Information

History The O'odham are probably descended from the ancient Hohokam Indians. Unlike the Hohokam or the Pima, the Tohono O'odham were seminomadic. They generally spent summers in their "field villages" in the desert, usually at the mouth of an arroyo, where flash floods would provided needed water. Winters were spent in "well villages," by mountain springs.

The Tohono O'odham may have first met non-natives in the 1500s. They experienced extensive contact with the Spanish in late 1600s when Father Eusebio Kino established numerous Catholic missions and introduced cattle, horses, and wheat (1684). The Spanish also established a series of presidios against the growing Apache threat. Although too isolated to have had to endure harsh forced labor and agricultural taxes as did the Pima, some Tohono O'odham, such as Luis Oacpicagigua and others, participated in the Pima revolt of 1751.

Apaches constituted the major threat from the eighteenth century through the mid–nineteenth century. During this time, the Sand Papago died off or became assimilated with the Spanish or surrounding tribes. From 1840 to 1843, the Papago fought and lost a war against Mexico in an attempt to stop the usurpation of their lands. With the Gadsden Purchase (1853), the Tohono O'odham lost the part of their territory that remained in Mexico, although they tended to ignore the international border for many years. Despite tighter border restrictions today, Tohono O'odham Indians living in Sonora and the United States remain in contact.

In the 1860s, the Papago fought with the Pima, Pee-Posh, and U.S. troops against the Apaches. Still, Anglos appropriated their water holes and grazing land, resulting in conflict and some violence. San Xavier Reservation was founded in 1874, with Gila Bend Reservation following in 1882. The Papago Reservation was established in 1916 and 1917, albeit without most of the Tohono O'odhams' best lands.

The railroad came to Tucson in the 1880s, bringing an increase of cattlemen and miners into O'odham territory. The cattle lost by these people began important O'odham herds. By the end of the century, countless Papago (and other Indian) girls were working as domestics for whites through Bureau of Indian Affairs (BIA) programs at the Phoenix Indian School. About this time, and concurrent with the rise of many Christian schools, the O'odham culture declined markedly.

A field camp at Vecol Wash became the permanent settlement of the Ak Chin O'odham in the 1870s; Pimas and Maricopas lived there too. In the early wage economy, O'odham potters sold and traded water-cooling *ollas;* men cut firewood; basket makers sold baskets. Cotton picking became the most important economic activity through the 1950s. In the 1970s, a severe drought killed many cattle, reducing the Papago to near starvation.

Religion The Tohono O'odham worshiped Earth Maker *(Tcuwut Makai)* and Elder Brother *(I'itoi,* or *Se'ehe),* the heroes of their creation story, whose sacred home is Baboquivari Peak in southern Arizona. Ceremonies encouraged these spirits to bring the rain that made food possible. The people also made annual pilgrimages to salt flats near the Gulf of California, home of the rain spirits, to pray to them.

Their most sacred ceremony was *Nawait,* or the new year's rain ceremony, which they celebrated with saguaro wine. Other important ceremonial occasions included puberty (especially for girls), funerals, the summer cactus wine feast, the "naming" (to honor and entertain other groups), purification following childbirth, sickness, the corn harvest, the deer hunt, the early winter harvest, purification for an eagle killing, warfare, and the annual salt expeditions.

Shamans, both men and older women, derived curing power from dreams. Although many Papagos became Catholic in the eighteenth century, having clustered around Spanish presidios and missions to escape the Apache, it was a Catholicism heavily mixed with traditional beliefs.

Government The Tohono O'odham were organized into autonomous villages. Although each village had a chief (there was no tribal chief), decisions were taken by consensus. Each village also had shamans, a headman who set the agenda for meetings and mediated conflict, and an all-male council. They also recognized a ceremonial leader, akin to the headman, called Keeper of the Smoke. Other officials included a village crier, war leader, hunt leader, game leader, and song leader.

Customs A universal O'odham concept of the way of life *(Himdag)* centers on family, community, generosity, and modesty. The Papago made annual visits to relatives on the Gila River or in the Sonora River Valleys. In times of famine, families often moved to Pima villages along the Gila River. Every four years the Papago and Pima together celebrated *Viikita,* a holiday dedicated to ensuring their continued fortune, with dancers and clowns dressed in masks and costumes.

Each Tohono O'odham village was divided into two clans, Buzzard and Coyote. Their year began when the cactus fruit ripened. Gifts and wagering were major forms of exchange. Games and races also held cultural importance. With the exception of warriors, who were cremated, the dead were dressed in their best clothing and buried with their personal property in caves, crevices, or stone houses.

Dwellings Like those of the Pimas, everyday Papago houses were circular and constructed of saguaro and ocotillo ribs and mesquite covered with mud and brush. Ceremonial houses were similar, but larger. Wall-less ramadas provided shelter for most outdoor activities in good weather. Sand Papagos used small rings of stone as temporary windbreaks.

Diet The key to survival in the desert was diversification. The goal of the Papago was security rather than surpluses. Men grew corn, beans, and squash. Later the Spanish introduced cowpeas, melons, and wheat. Winter wheat especially provided an edge against starvation. The people also hunted, primarily in the winter. Wild foods such as mescal, mesquite beans, ironwood and paloverde seeds, cactus fruits, amaranth and other greens, wild chilies, acorns, and sand root provided about three-quarters of their diet. Saguaro wine was used on ceremonial occasions. During hard times the Papago "hired out" to Pima Indians, exchanging labor for food. The Sand Papago ate shellfish from the Gulf of California, reptiles, insects, and small mammals. A staple was the parasitic plant sand root.

Key Technology The Desert People baked in pit ovens. They used long poles called kuibits to knock down saguaro fruit. The use of calendar sticks, with carved dots and circles to record important ceremonies, began in the early 1830s. Notches referred to secular events, such as earthquakes or Apache attacks. Other equipment included carrying nets, frame backpacks, and cradle boards. In characteristic *ak chin* farming, men built dams to channel water runoff into one major arroyo. When the flash floods arrived, they would water the fields by erecting brush spreader dams across the arroyo. After contact with the Spanish, the Desert People adopted picks, shovels, and horse- and oxen-drawn plows and wagons.

Trade Trade occurred mostly in the fall and winter. The Tohono O'odham traded meat, baskets, pottery, salt, shells, mineral pigments, and macaws for corn and, later, wheat from Pimas and Quechans. The Sand Papago also traded with Yuman peoples on the Colorado River.

Notable Arts Specialized arts included coiled willow, devil's claw, yucca, and bear grass baskets. Older people made a traditional red pottery.

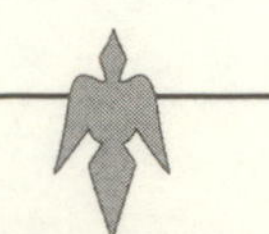

In this roofless Papago kitchen a young girl scrapes corn; the woman inside is cooking tortillas (1895).

Transportation Baskets were used for transporting goods.

Dress Men wore cotton or deerskin breechcloths. Women wore cloth, willow bark, or deerskin wraparound skirts. Both sexes used hide or fiber sandals and cotton and rabbit-skin blankets. They also grew their hair long, wore ear pendants of turquoise and other stones, and tattooed and painted their bodies.

War and Weapons Traditional enemies of the Papago included the Mojave and the Apache.

Contemporary Information

Government/Reservations The Tohono O'odham live on four reservations in southern Arizona, with a combined acreage of over 2.8 million: San Xavier (1874); Gila Bend (1882, although most of this reservation was lost by flooding caused by the Painted Rock Dam); Ak Chin (1912); and Papago, or Sells (1874). The people are in regular communication with O'odham living in Mexico.

A tribal constitution and by-laws were ratified in 1937, and an elected tribal council, from the Papago Reservation plus San Xavier and Gila Bend, runs tribal political affairs. Decision making is decentralized, with district tribal councils acting to preserve the interests of the community. A 1986 constitutional revision created a tripartite form of government. The BIA still maintains direct influence over the tribe.

Economy Important economic activities include mining (mostly copper) and chemical businesses;

license fees paid by traders and hunters; farming; cattle, including both individual subsistence herds and large herds owned by wealthy families; bingo; and fire fighting. Wage work is also provided by the tribe, the BIA, the health service, and businesses in nearby cities and towns. Arts and crafts include world-famous baskets, pottery, wooden bowls, horsehair miniatures, and lariats. The San Xavier Reservation has recently opened an industrial park. Unemployment often remains above 30 percent.

Legal Status The Ak Chin Indian Community of Papago Indians and the Tohono O'odham Nation of Arizona (formerly the Papago Tribe of the Sells, Gila Bend, and San Xavier Reservations) are federally recognized tribal entities. The Sand Papago won recognition in 1980s but own no land to date.

Daily Life With the advent of drilled wells and a dependable water supply, the O'odham no longer migrate to mountain well villages; thus has their immemorial relationship with their environment and their world been changed forever. The Fiesta de Magdalena, a combination harvest, trade, and religious festival held every fall in Sonora, Mexico, remains the most powerful connection of the Arizona O'odham to Mexico. English has largely replaced Spanish as a second language.

Many O'odham still live in extended families, and they still strive for consensus decision making. More than three-quarters of O'odham Indians are at least nominally Catholic. Schools use local resources to teach native language and culture; the main reservation contains both schools and a hospital. In addition, the tribe works closely with the University of Arizona to develop and institute a wide variety of educational programs available to tribal members. A rodeo and fair are held at Sells in October; the Saguaro Festival is also celebrated. Many, perhaps a majority, of O'odham Indians live off-reservation.

At San Xavier, allotment policies in 1890 gave most of the land to individuals. With division by inheritance, 400–500 people may own an acre today, making individual land use almost impossible. These people practice cooperative farming. The Ak-chin O'odham speak a distinct dialect and consider themselves neither Tohono O'odham nor Pima. Having abandoned subsistence farming in the 1930s, they now operate a cotton cooperative. Acculturation at Ak-chin is far advanced.

Tortugas

See Tigua

Walapai

See Hualapai

Yaqui

Yaqui (`Yä kē) is a name established by Jesuit missionaries in the early seventeenth century. It was taken from the name of a nearby river. The traditional Yaqui name for themselves is *Yoeme.*

Location The Yaqui originated in the northwestern Mexican state of Sonora. They have lived in southern and southwest Arizona from the late nineteenth century.

Population The Yaqui population stood at perhaps 30,000 at contact (1533), the largest native tribal population in northwest New Spain. Roughly 6,000 now live in U.S. villages out of a total U.S. tribal enrollment (1992) of almost 10,000. About 25,000 Yaquis live in Sonora, Mexico.

Language Yaquis spoke a dialect of Cahita, a member of the Uto-Aztecan language family.

Historical Information

History The aboriginal land of the Yaquis consisted of roughly 6,000 square miles in Sonora, Mexico, approximately between the Rio Mátapa and the Arroyo de Cocoraqui. The Yaqui believe their boundaries were made sacred by singing angels *(batnaataka)* who traversed them in mythological times. Although the Sonora region is primarily a desert, Yaqui lands in the river basin were quite fertile as a result of the annual flood cycles.

A party of Spaniards first encountered the Yaqui in 1533 but were prevented by force from trespassing on Yaqui territory. In 1609, after defeating the

Spanish for the third time, the Yaquis arrived at an accommodation with them and accepted Jesuit missionaries in 1617. Over the next seven years almost all Yaquis converted to Catholicism.

The next 150 years were a period of creative cultural and economic growth for the Yaqui. Transformations in agriculture and technology led to increasing agricultural surpluses and economic diversification (mining and sheep herding for the Spanish wool trade). In 1740, the Yaqui staged a major revolt as a result of growing tensions over land incursions, Spanish attempts to secularize and control the missions, and missionary abuses. The Indians' defeat strengthened both Spanish colonial power and the Jesuit missions, until the latter were expelled from the New World in 1767.

The 1800s were a time of semiautonomy, with gradual loss of land and continual resistance against the Mexicans. Juan Ignacio Jusacamea, also known as Juan de la Cruz Banderas or Juan Banderas, emerged as the uncontested leader of the Yaquis and their allies in the early Mexican rebellions until his capture and execution in 1833. Further periodic revolts culminated in the so-called Cajeme era (1875–1885), a period of Yaqui cultural and economic renewal during which Yaqui society made a final defensive stand against Mexico under José María Leyva, called Cajeme.

The defeat of Cajeme in 1885 was followed by military occupation, repression, and mass deportation under the regime of Porfirio Diaz, although Yaqui bands continued guerrilla resistance in the Bacatete Mountains into the twentieth century. Most Yaquis not exiled to the Yucatan dispersed throughout rural Sonora, assisting the guerrillas and working in the mines, on the railroads, and on haciendas. Many also headed north to the United States to begin new Yaqui communities there.

The Mexican Revolution of 1910 offered the Yaqui a chance to regroup and reestablish their identity, with the formation of their own revolutionary army. Following the wars, Yaquis began a gradual return to their traditional lands and a reconstruction of their culture. For Yaquis living in Mexico, the last half of the twentieth century has been marked by the integration, albeit at the lowest levels, into that country's economy. In 1964, the U.S. Congress gave 202 acres of land to the Pascua Yaqui Association. This grant became the basis of New Pascua, which became officially recognized in 1978.

Religion The Yaqui Indians have been practicing a heavily Christian-influenced religion for nearly 400 years. They recognize a two-part universe: one is town and church, whose dwellers are mortal; the other is the *Huya Aniya,* spirit world and source of spiritual power, whose dwellers are immortal. The two worlds are integrated ritually. Every Christian ceremony requires participation of ceremonialists, such as Pascola and Deer Dancers, whose power derives from the *Huya Aniya.*

Other important religious elements include honoring of and concern for ancestors, the sharing of accumulated wealth for help in curing (healing), maintaining and distributing the benevolent power of Our Mother (the supernatural), honoring the patron saints of the eight towns (see "Dwellings"), and affirming the sacred relationships between the Yaqui and their traditional territory.

In addition to a number of feast days, the most important and elaborate ceremony of the year is the *waehma,* or the reenactment during Holy Week of Christ's (the great curer) final days. A central theme is the accumulation of evil in the town and the destruction of that evil during a ceremonial battle on Holy Saturday, through the ritual use of flowers, followed by a great celebration.

Government The largest political unit was the town. Authority consisted of five groups: church, civil governors, military, "custom authorities" *(kohtumbre),* and fiesta makers *(Pahkome).* Each had its own clearly defined jurisdiction, but they worked together on matters of the public good. Decision making was by consensus in town meeting except in time of military emergency, and even then the military leader's power in nonmilitary affairs was highly circumscribed. A constant process of interaction and sharing promoted continuity among the towns.

Customs Traditional Yaqui households consisted of any number of nuclear families related in a variety of ways. Yaqui elders were respected as the tribal spokespeople and maintained schools for young men.

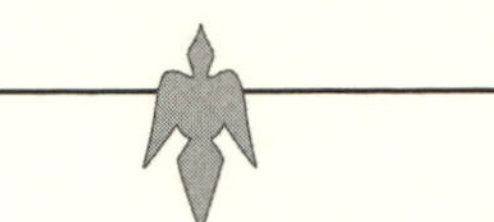

The godparent system, introduced by the Jesuits, has evolved into a highly complex and important institution.

Dwellings Prior to 1617 the Yaqui lived in roughly 80 rancherias, most containing fewer than 250 people, consisting of clusters of dome-shaped, cane mat–covered adobe houses with flat or gently sloping roofs. Consolidation under the Jesuits of the scattered rancherias into eight towns, each with between 2,000 and 4,000 people, occurred by the mid-1600s. Each town was built around an adobe-walled church, with new civil, military, and ceremonial organizations grouped around the church and central plaza. Houses built near churches always included ramadas as well as walled rooms, surrounded by a cane fence. After 1887, the Mexicans succeeded in imposing the grid plan of settlement on Yaqui towns.

Diet Cultivated crops such as corn, squash, beans, and amaranth were supplemented by abundant wild foods such as mesquite beans, cactus fruits, succulent roots, grass seeds, wild game (including deer and rabbits), and many kinds of shellfish and large saltwater fish from the Gulf of California. By the late seventeenth century, the Jesuits had introduced wheat, pomegranates, peaches, figs, and other crops as well as cattle (including oxen for plowing) and horses.

Key Technology Rudimentary irrigation ditches were improved by the Jesuits, who also introduced the plow to the region. The Yaquis traditionally fashioned cane into a great number of articles, including mats for roof and wall materials, household compound fences, sleeping mats, cutting instruments, spoons, and shelves as well as numerous ceremonial items.

Trade Yaquis generally had many items to trade, including crops, cane items, and woven articles.

Notable Arts Yaqui traditional arts consist of ritual dance (all male) and religious drama, music, wood mask carving, cane mat making, and blanket and mat weaving in both cotton and wool.

Transportation Horses were introduced into the region in the seventeenth century.

Dress Yaquis wore cotton and wool clothing and blankets as well as special ceremonial kilts, masks, rattles, stuffed deer heads, and red ribbons (symbolizing flowers).

War and Weapons Members of the military society served for life and had their own rituals, which included flag-bearing ceremonies and dances. Although the elected captains generally tended to dominate Yaqui society in the eighteenth and nineteenth centuries because of the continual state of crisis, community leaders were always consulted for important decisions.

Contemporary Information

Government/Reservations Significant U.S. Yaqui communities are located in and around Phoenix and Tucson, Arizona (Guadaloupe, Eloy, Old Pascua, New Pascua Pueblo [Yaqui Reservation; population 2,737 in 1992], and Barrio Libre). Village organization is church oriented and controlled by the ceremonial groups. A Bureau of Indian Affairs–approved Yaqui constitution (1988) calls for an elected tribal council. In Mexico, an unofficial tribal structure, created by the Mexican government and loosely based on and operating with the traditional government, has been in existence since the 1930s.

Economy In the United States, tribal members participate in the local economy in a number of urban occupations and professions and as farm or construction workers. In addition, the tribe runs a landscape nursery, a charcoal-packing business, and a bingo enterprise. Unemployment remains very high. In Mexico, government water diversions and rapid development have removed the possibility of subsistence farming.

Legal Status The Yaqui received official U.S. government recognition in 1978, primarily through the leadership of Anselmo Valencia; the Pascua Yaquis are a federally recognized tribal entity. Many Mexican Yaquis live on their reservation and in the "original eight" and other small towns.

Daily Life Wherever Yaquis have settled, they have maintained some degree of devotion to the ideal of life

in the eight towns. Religion remains a distinct blend of Catholic and native beliefs, and the ceremonial cycle still follows the life of Christ. Saints' days are celebrated with fireworks, feasting, and entertainment, such as masked dancing and musicians. Lenten and Holy Week ceremonies remain especially elaborate, culminating in the unique Passion Play.

Yaquis living in the United States enjoy close contact with the Tohono O'odham (Papago) tribe, including mutual attendance of ceremonies and festivals. Children attend public school, where they have access to Yaqui language preservation programs. Contemporary issues include obtaining decent health care and housing, in addition to solving the high unemployment rate. Yaqui arts especially include music, dance, and painting. Rural houses in the United States are built primarily of adobe. Most houses feature a fenced-in yard, with a few trees, small plots of green grass, and flowers. Open ramadas serve as the main living spaces and also as gathering places at fiesta time. Typically, a small white church sits at one end of the village plaza with a fiesta ramada at the other end. Over 50 homes at Old Pascua were rebuilt in the 1980s.

In Mexico, Yaquis are still relatively isolated and more traditional than other Indian groups. In clothing and material culture they are nearly identical to rural Mexican mestiso peasant farmers.

Yavapai

Yavapai (`Yä vä pī) from the Mojave *Enyaéva Pai,* "People of the Sun." They are sometimes confused with the Apaches, as a result of their long association together, and are occasionally (and erroneously) referred to as Mojave Apaches or Yuma Apaches.

Location Traditionally, the Yavapai controlled roughly 10 million acres in present-day west-central Arizona. This transitional area between the Colorado Plateau and the lower deserts provided them with a salubrious mixture of desert, mountain, and plateau plants and animals. Today, Yavapai Indians live on the Fort McDowell, the Camp Verde, and the Yavapai Reservations, Arizona.

Population In 1992 there were approximately 1,550 enrolled Yavapais on the three reservations. Resident population in 1990 was as follows: Six hundred and forty lived at Fort McDowell, 650 lived at Camp Verde, 130 lived at Prescott, and some lived off-reservation. Roughly 1,500 Yavapai lived in their area in 1500.

Language Yavapais spoke a dialect (similar to Pai) of Upland Yuman, a Hokan-Siouan language (though culturally and historically the Yavapai were more closely related to the Tonto Apache).

Historical Information

History The nomadic Yavapai were probably descended from the ancient Hakataya peoples.

In the nineteenth century, the Yavapai scouted for the U.S. Army against the Chiricahua Apaches. This scout wears an officer's coat, helmet, and sword in a commercial studio portrait taken in Wyoming Territory circa 1881.

Traditionally they consisted of four major divisions: the Kewevkapaya (southeastern), the Wipukpaya (northeastern), the Tolkepaye (western), and the Yavepe (central). Each was further divided into local bands.

Contact between the Spanish and the Yavapais occurred in 1582. After Father Francisco Garces lived with them in 1776, contact became more frequent. Nevertheless the Yavapais lived traditionally until the 1850s, largely because their country was too rough for the Spaniards, Mexicans, or Americans. Some bands, especially the Kewevkapaya, raided with the Apaches. After the Mexican cession, more non-Indian travelers and miners frequented the region, although the Yavapai tried to avoid conflict, owing primarily to their poor weaponry.

Gold was discovered in 1863. Shortly thereafter the frontier arrived and brought the permanent disruption of Yavapai traditional life. Hungry and under continuous attack, the Yavapai fought back. In 1872–1873, General George Crook's bloody Tonto Basin campaign against the Tonto Apaches and Yavapais (won with a heavy reliance on Pai scouts) ended with a massacre of Yavapais. Forced onto the Camp Verde reservation after disease had killed an additional one-third of their number, the Yavapai and Tonto Apaches dug a 5-mile irrigation ditch using discarded army tools and brought in a good harvest. For this they were forcibly relocated (again) in 1875 and settled with the Apaches on the San Carlos Reservation, 180 miles to the east. Many died or were killed on the "March of Tears" (within 25 years, their population fell from 1,500 to 200).

At San Carlos the Yavapai again tried farming. They also scouted for the army against the Chiricahua Apaches and acquired cattle. However, flooding ruined their ditches, miners and ranchers took their land, and they still wanted to go home. By 1900, most Yavapais had left San Carlos. Some returned to the Verde Valley and some to Forts McDowell and Whipple. In 1903, Fort McDowell became a reservation, inhabited mostly by the Kewevkopaya band. Camp Verde (Weepukapa) reservation was established in 1910, with outlying communities such as Middle Verde, Clarkdale, and Rimrock added during the following 60 years. Fort Whipple became a reservation (Yavapai-Prescott) in 1935. The western Yavapai (Tolkepaye) received no reservation and have nearly disappeared.

The Verde River ran through Fort McDowell. The Yavapai tried farming once again, but they were soon involved in a struggle for water rights. Instead of providing funds to improve irrigation and guard against floods, the government wanted to remove the Yavapai to the Salt River Pima Reservation. Largely owing to the efforts of Carlos Montezuma they were able to remain, but they secured little money or water. During this period cattle grazing and wage work, both on and off the reservation, became important sources of income. From the 1950s through the 1980s, the Yavapai also fought off a dam (Orme) that would have flooded most of the Fort McDowell Reservation, refusing $33 million in compensation. Finally, in 1990, the Yavapai won passage of a law granting them sufficient water rights from the Verde River as well as $25 million in compensatory funds.

Yavapais and Apaches leaving San Carlos settled at Camp Verde around the turn of the century. Camp Verde is more Apache than Yavapai in character. Unable to make a living on the inadequate reservation lands, most people worked in the nearby copper industry until the 1930s and 1940s.

In 1935 a separate reservation, primarily inhabited by the Yavepe band, was created north of Prescott. Rather than organize under the Indian Reorganization Act, this group maintained the traditional governing structure until 1988. Their land base is surrounded by the city of Prescott.

Religion Like other Yumans, veneration of the sun, dream omens, and shamanism were key aspects of Yavapai religion. Knowledge of all kinds was acquired by each person through dreaming. Shamans conducted healing rituals by singing, smoking tobacco, and sucking out bad blood. Some Yavapai rituals included the use of sandpaintings. Singing, dancing, and eagle feathers were part of every ritual, as were certain plants and musical instruments such as rattles, drums, and flutes. "Little people" or spirits living in the mountains were thought to help people. The Yavapai place of emergence was considered to be at Montezuma Well, near Sedona.

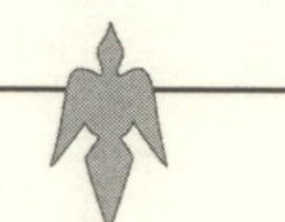

Government The closest the Yavapai came to centralized authority was each local group's "civic leader." This person would orate each morning on proper ideas and behavior. Leadership was based on personal merit (wisdom, personality, and ability in war).

Customs The Yavapai were a nomadic people who followed the ripening of wild foods. Bands camped in groups of up to ten families; winter gatherings were even larger. Elders or group leaders orated each morning from the roof of a hut, instructing people on the proper way to live. Social dances were held on occasion. Until the early 1900s the dead were customarily cremated (the house and possessions were also burned). Polygyny was rare, as was divorce. The Yavapai practiced formal puberty rites for women and men.

Dwellings People lived in caves or dome-shaped huts, framed with poles and covered with brush, thatch, or mud. Other structures included ramadas and sweat lodges.

Diet Mescal was a staple, along with other wild plants such as cactus fruit, mesquite beans, greens, acorns, piñon nuts, walnuts, seeds, and berries. Women gathered wild foods. Game included deer, quail, fox, antelope, and rabbits; people also ate lizards, caterpillars, yellowjacket nests, and turkeys. Small amounts of corn, beans, and squash were grown or traded, mostly by the western band.

Key Technology Tools included bows and arrows, baskets, clubs, buckskin ponchos, grinding stones and other stone tools, throwing sticks, and snares or traps for hunting. Food was boiled in clay pots.

Trade The Yavapai were active traders in a large local trade network. Baskets were the primary currency. They traded mescal and buckskin to the Navajo for blankets and to the Hopi for jewelry. They occasionally obtained corn from the Pima and the O'odham.

Notable Arts Women made pottery, but baskets were one of the most highly developed arts. Color came not from dyes or artificial materials but from the shoots of cottonwood and mulberry trees, the roots of yucca or soapwood, or devil's claw.

Transportation Women made baskets for carrying goods.

Dress The Yavapai painted their bodies. Ornaments included necklaces, bracelets, and ear and nose rings (especially warriors). Bangs were worn to the eyebrows. Men wore hide breechclouts, leggings, and moccasins, and blankets or skin ponchos in winter (also boots and mittens). Women wore two buckskins draped over a belt and a buckskin top and moccasins (of buckskin or possibly yucca fiber). Some women tattooed their faces. Men dressed the skins for clothing.

War and Weapons Each local group decided for itself whether or nor to join a war. Yavapai traditional enemies included the Pai, Pima, Pee-Posh, and O'odham. Their allies included the Quechan, Mojave, and Apache. Unlike the Apaches, the Yavapais used few guns; instead, they mostly made do with hunting tools to fight the U.S. Army. Other weapons included clubs, hide shields, mulberry bows, and cane arrows with obsidian points. Although they were inclined toward war, they proved to be more flexible than the Apaches regarding change, adaptation, and coexistence.

Contemporary Information

Government/Reservations Yavapai reservations are at Prescott (1935; almost 1,400 acres), Fort McDowell (1901–1904; almost 25,000 acres; 28 miles northeast of Phoenix), and Camp Verde (1914; 1,092 acres in two sections, shared with the Tonto Apache). At Camp Verde intermarriage has produced a new tribe, the Yavapai-Apaches, organized in 1937. Clarkdale (1969; 60 acres, also shared with the Apache) and Payson (Yavapai and Tonto Apache, 1972; 85 acres) are associated with Camp Verde, which, with Fort McDowell, elects a tribal council.

Economy At Fort McDowell, a gambling establishment brings in much money and provides employment, as does the tribal farm. There is also a

large sand and gravel operation and several small businesses. Some people work in surrounding cities and towns, raise stock, or, in a few cases, practice subsistence farming. Under- and unemployment often exceeds 50 percent. A water settlement (1990) provided for both water rights and $25 million in compensatory funds. There is potential for economic development near the Beeline Highway. Some women also produce coiled baskets for the tourist trade.

Verde places most economic hope in tourism associated with Montezuma Castle National Monument; some people also work off-reservation. At Prescott there is an industrial park, a commercial park, a shopping center, a bingo operation, and a hotel complex, and there are plans for a museum. People also raise stock and work off-reservation.

Legal Status The Fort McDowell Mohave-Apache Indian Community, Fort McDowell Band of Mohave Apache Indians, Yavapai-Apache Indian Community, and the Yavapai-Prescott Tribe are all federally recognized tribal entities.

Daily Life Acculturation is well established; the last big Yavapai dance was held in 1924. The language is all but lost. Children attend public schools. Camp Verde is negotiating the purchase of 6,500 additional acres. Some women still make high-quality baskets. The tribes cosponsor Ba'ja days, a cultural celebration. Yavapai-Prescott has also developed a cultural program with a professional staff.

Ysleta del Sur Pueblo

See Tigua

Yuma

See Quechan

Zia Pueblo

Zia (`Tsē ä, or `Sē ä) from the Spanish spelling of its Keresan name. The word "pueblo" comes from the Spanish for "village." It refers both to a certain style of Southwest Indian architecture, characterized by multistory, apartmentlike buildings made of adobe, and to the people themselves. Rio Grande pueblos are known as eastern Pueblos; Zuñi, Hopi, and sometimes Acoma and Laguna are known as western Pueblos.

Location Zia Pueblo is located on the Jemez River, 30 miles north of Albuquerque, New Mexico.

Population At least 5,000 and as many as 20,000 Indians may have lived on the pueblo in 1540, although fewer than 300 remained in 1690 and fewer than 100 in 1890. In 1990, 637 Zia Indians lived on the pueblo, with perhaps as many living outside of it.

Language Zia Indians spoke a dialect of Keresan.

Historical Information

History All Pueblo people are thought to be descended from Anasazi and perhaps Mogollon and several other ancient peoples, although the precise origin of the Keresan peoples is unknown. From them they learned architecture, farming, pottery, and basketry. Larger population groups became possible with effective agriculture and ways to store food surpluses. Within the context of a relatively stable existence, the people devoted increasing amounts of time and attention to religion, arts, and crafts.

Keresans have been traced to an area around Chaco Canyon north to Mesa Verde. In the 1200s, the Keresans abandoned their traditional canyon homelands in response to climatic and social upheavals. A century or two of migrations ensued, followed in general by the slow reemergence of their culture in the historic pueblos. Six thirteenth-century archaeological sites have been identified with Zia. Five of these were occupied between the sixteenth and eighteenth centuries. Antonio de Espejo, who visited in 1583, called these sites Punames and described a large city with eight plazas, over 1,000 two- to three-story houses, and a population of at least 5,000 and perhaps as many as 20,000.

In 1598, Juan de Oñate arrived in the area with settlers, founding the colony of New Mexico. Oñate carried on the process, already underway in nearby areas, of subjugating the local Indians; forcing them to pay taxes in crops, cotton, and work; and opening the door for Catholic missionaries to attack their

religion. The Spanish renamed the Pueblos with saints' names and began a program of church construction; the mission at Zia was built about 1610. At the same time, the Spanish introduced such new crops as peaches, wheat, and peppers into the region. In 1620, a royal decree created civil offices at each pueblo; silver-headed canes, many of which remain in use today, symbolized the governor's authority.

The Zians participated in the 1680 Pueblo revolt against the Spanish. For years, the Spaniards had routinely tortured Indians for practicing traditional religion. They also forced the Indians to labor for them, sold Indians into slavery, and let their cattle overgraze Indian land, a situation that eventually led to drought, erosion, and famine. Popé of San Juan Pueblo and other Pueblo religious leaders planned the revolt, sending runners carrying cords of maguey fibers to mark the day of rebellion. On August 10, 1680, a virtually united stand on the part of the Pueblos drove the Spanish from the region. The Indians killed many Spaniards but refrained from mass slaughter, allowing them to leave Santa Fe for El Paso.

Zia suffered a bloody military defeat by Spanish forces in 1687: Six hundred were killed, and many were held captive for ten years. In 1689 Zia received a royal land grant from Spain. In 1692 Zia accepted mass baptism and collaborated with the Spanish in their campaigns against other pueblos throughout the rest of the decade.

The Pueblos experienced many changes during the following decades: Refugees established communities at Hopi, guerrilla fighting continued against the Spanish, and certain areas were abandoned. By the 1700s, excluding Hopi and Zuñi, only Taos, Picuris, Isleta, and Acoma Pueblos had not changed locations since the arrival of the Spanish. Although Pueblo unity did not last, and Santa Fe was officially reconquered in 1692, Spanish rule was notably less severe from then on. Harsh forced labor all but ceased, and the Indians reached an understanding with the Church that enabled them to continue practicing their traditional religion.

In general, the Pueblo eighteenth century was marked by smallpox epidemics and increased raiding by the Apache, Comanche, and Ute. Occasionally Pueblo Indians fought with the Spanish against the nomadic tribes. The people practiced their religion but more or less in secret. During this time, intermarriage and regular exchange between Hispanic villages and Pueblo Indians created a new New Mexican culture, neither strictly Spanish nor Indian, but rather somewhat of a blend between the two.

Mexican "rule" in 1821 brought little immediate change to the Pueblos. The Mexicans stepped up what had been a gradual process of appropriating Indian land and water, and they allowed the nomadic tribes even greater latitude to raid. A political rebellion by Indians and Hispanic poor in 1837 over the issue of taxes led to the assassination of the New Mexican governor and the brief installation of a Plains/Taos Indian as governor. As the presence of the United States in the area grew, it attempted to enable the Pueblo Indians to continue their generally peaceful and self-sufficient ways and recognized Spanish land grants to the Pueblos.

During the nineteenth century the process of acculturation among Pueblo Indians quickened markedly. In an attempt to retain their identity, Pueblo Indians clung even more tenaciously to their heritage, which by now included elements of the once-hated Spanish culture and religion. By the 1880s, railroads had largely put an end to the traditional geographical isolation of the pueblos. Paradoxically, the U.S. decision to recognize Spanish land grants to the Pueblos denied Pueblo Indians certain rights granted under official treaties and left them particularly open to exploitation by squatters and thieves.

After a gap of over 300 years, the All Indian Pueblo Council began to meet again in the 1920s, specifically in response to a congressional threat to appropriate Pueblo lands. Partly as a result of the Council's activities, Congress confirmed Pueblo title to their lands in 1924 by passing the Pueblo Lands Act. The United States also acknowledged its trust responsibilities in a series of legal decisions and other acts of Congress. Still, especially after 1900, Pueblo culture was increasingly threatened by Protestant evangelical missions and schools. The Bureau of Indian Affairs also weighed in on the subject of acculturation, forcing Indian children to leave their homes and attend culture-killing boarding schools.

Until World War II, however, much of Zia's traditional life remained substantially unchanged. Almost all Zians lived on the pueblo, and all adult members participated in community events. Herding dominated the economy in the mid–twentieth century, although there was a shift from sheep to cattle. Since the late nineteenth century, but especially after the 1960s, Pueblos have had to cope with onslaughts by (mostly white) anthropologists and seekers of Indian spirituality. The region is also known for its major art colonies at Taos and Santa Fe.

Religion In traditional Pueblo culture, religion and life are inseparable. To be in harmony with all of nature is the Pueblo ideal and way of life. The sun is seen as the representative of the Creator. Sacred mountains in each direction, plus the sun above and the earth below, define and balance the Pueblo world. Many Pueblo religious ceremonies revolve around the weather and are devoted to ensuring adequate rainfall. To this end, Pueblo Indians evoke the power of katsinas, sacred beings who live in mountains and other holy places, in ritual and dance. Zia Pueblo contained two circular kivas on its south side, religious chambers that symbolize the place of original emergence into this world. The kiva societies were Wren and Turquoise.

In addition to the natural boundaries, Pueblo Indians have created a society that defines their world by providing balanced, reciprocal relationships within which people connect and harmonize with each other, the natural world, and time itself. According to tradition, the head of each pueblo is the religious leader, or *cacique,* whose primary responsibility it is to watch the sun and thereby determine the dates of ceremonies. Religious societies were central to the Pueblo's social structure; they helped to ensure the fertility of crops and people, triumph over evil, success in hunting, physical and spiritual curing, and good relations between the living and their dead ancestors. Shamans also used supernatural powers for curing, weather control, and ensuring the general welfare. Especially in the eastern pueblos, most ceremonies are kept secret.

Government Pueblo governments derived from two traditions. Elements that are probably indigenous include the *cacique,* or head of the Pueblo, and the war chiefs. These officials were intimately related to the religious structures of the pueblo and reflected the essentially theocratic nature of Pueblo government. The *tiyamunyi* were the supreme priests of Zia from legendary times until about 1900. Since then, proper installation rituals have been forgotten, and this office has been replaced by the former first assistant, who is now called *cacique.* Freed from other work, he mostly meditates and invests annual officers.

A parallel but in most cases distinctly less powerful group of officials was imposed by the Spanish authorities. Appointed annually by the traditional leadership, they generally dealt with external and church matters and included the governor, lieutenant governor, captains, and *fiscales* (church officials). There was also an advisory council of *principales,* composed of former officeholders. In 1863, President Lincoln presented Pueblo leaders with ebony canes, which were then used with the older Spanish canes as symbols of authority. The All Indian Pueblo Council, dating from 1598, began meeting again in the twentieth century to assert rights and help solve problems.

Customs One mechanism that works to keep Pueblo societies coherent is a pervasive aversion to individualistic behavior. Children were raised with gentle guidance and a minimum of discipline. Pueblo Indians were generally monogamous, and divorce was relatively rare. The dead were prepared ceremonially and quickly buried with clothes, beads, food, and other items; their possessions were destroyed, and they were said to become katsinas in the land of the dead. A vigil of four days and nights was generally observed. Matrilineal clans existed but were not linked to memberships in kiva or religious societies. Various other groups acted to hold the pueblo together, including medicine and other religious societies. In modern times photography by outsiders is discouraged.

Dwellings In the sixteenth century, Zia Pueblo featured two- to three-story, apartment-style dwellings arranged around eight plazas. The buildings were constructed of adobe (earth and straw) bricks, with beams across the roof that were covered with poles,

brush, and plaster. Floors were of wood plank or packed earth. The roof of one level served as the floor of another. The levels were interconnected by ladders. As an aid to defense, the traditional design included no doors or windows; entry was through the roof. Two pit houses, or kivas, served as ceremonial chambers and clubhouses. The village plazas, around which all dwellings were clustered, was the spiritual center of the village where all the balanced forces of the world came together.

Diet Before the Spanish arrived, Zians ate primarily corn, beans, and pumpkins, using the floodwaters of the Jemez River as both irrigation and fertilizer. They also grew sunflowers and tobacco. They hunted deer, mountain lion, bear, antelope, and rabbits. They gathered a variety of wild seeds, nuts, berries, and other foods. The Spanish introduced wheat, alfalfa, sheep, cattle, and garden vegetables, which soon became part of the regular diet.

Key Technology Precontact farming implements were wooden. Textiles were woven of cotton. Other items included baskets, pottery, and leather goods. The Spanish introduced metal tools and equipment.

Trade All Pueblos were part of extensive aboriginal trading networks. With the arrival of other cultures, Pueblo Indians also traded with the Hispanic American villages and then U.S. traders. At fixed times during summer or fall, enemies declared truces so that trading fairs might be held. The largest and best known was at Taos with the Comanche. Nomads exchanged slaves, buffalo hides, buckskins, jerked meat, and horses for agricultural and manufactured pueblo products. Zians traded for numerous daily and ceremonial items, including drums, tortoise rattles, buffalo robes, abalone shell jewelry, bows, arrows, quivers, pottery, and blankets. Trade along the Santa Fe Trail began in 1821. By the 1880s and the arrival of railroads, the Pueblos were dependent on many American-made goods, and the Native American manufacture of weaving and pottery declined and nearly died out.

Notable Arts In the Pueblo way, art and life are inseparable. Zia arts included pottery, baskets, and wooden masks. Songs, dances, and dramas are other traditional arts. Many Pueblos experienced a renaissance of traditional arts in the twentieth century, beginning in 1919 with San Ildefonso pottery.

Transportation Spanish horses, mules, and cattle arrived at Zia Pueblo in the seventeenth century.

Dress Men wore cotton kilts and leather sandals. Women wore cotton dresses and sandals or high moccasin boots. Deer and rabbit skin were also used for clothing and robes, and sandals were made of yucca.

War and Weapons Though often depicted as passive and docile, most Pueblo groups regularly engaged in warfare. The great revolt of 1680 stands out as the major military action, but they also skirmished at other times with the Spanish and defended themselves against attackers such as Apaches, Comanches, and Utes. They also contributed auxiliary soldiers to provincial forces under Spain and Mexico, which were used mainly against raiding Indians and to protect merchant caravans on the Santa Fe Trail. According to tradition, a Zian who touched a dead enemy or anything that belonged to him was required to scalp the corpse and bring the scalp back for purification; he then joined the warriors' society. After the raiding tribes began to pose less of a threat in the late nineteenth century, Pueblo military societies began to wither away, with the office of war captain changing to civil and religious functions.

Contemporary Information

Government/Reservations Zia Pueblo occupies roughly 121,080 tribally owned acres. There are two all-male tribal councils: one concerned with secular matters, the other the more important and secret religious council. There is also an administrative staff.

Economy With wage jobs, sheep and cattle raising is the most important economic activity. Stock raising is conducted by cattle and sheep groups based on clan membership. Many people work in surrounding cities. Arts and crafts, especially wool kilts (men) and pottery (women) occupy an important economic

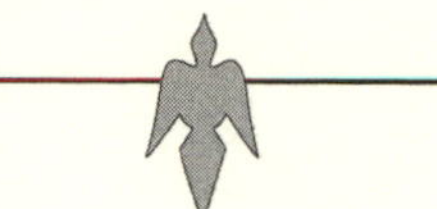

niche. Agriculture is served by modern irrigation systems. Major crops include corn, wheat, alfalfa, oats, beans, chilies, melons, and fruits. Most produce is sold on the open market. The Pueblo contains geothermal, natural gas, and oil resources.

Legal Status Zia Pueblo is a federally recognized tribal entity.

Daily Life The project of retaining a strong Indian identity is a difficult one in the late twentieth century, yet Pueblo people have deep roots, and in many ways the ancient rhythms and patterns continue. At Zia, men must still participate in the dances, take care of the *cacique's* field and food needs, sweep the village plaza, and clean and repair the irrigation ditches. Many Zia people still speak Keresan.

The older Pueblo now has ground-level entries and glass windows, and most homes have electricity and running water. Floors are of packed earth under linoleum. Interior walls are whitewashed. Each household owns a beehive oven. The seventeenth-century mission church is still standing. Modern houses have also been built along and across the river. As of the mid-1990s, a new village located to the east was under construction.

Zia religion and ceremonial and social structure are largely intact, though since World War II Zia has been marked by relatively increased social breakdown, with fewer people belonging to religious societies. The governor's power has grown at the expense of the *cacique's*. Increasing numbers of Zians live off-reservation. Some of the traditional societies, like the katsina, hunters, and warrior societies, now exist much devoid of their former knowledge.

The household is now the primary economic and social unit. Six modern clans still exist. Many Zians have fused pieces of Catholicism onto a core of traditional beliefs. They distinguish between Indian and Catholic marriages: The former are formed through cohabitation and are easily dissolved, whereas the latter go through the Church and are difficult to dissolve. There has been a written form of the Zia dialect of Keresan since 1990. Facilities include a community building, museum and cultural center, clinic, gymnasium, and offices.

Zuñi

Zuñi (`Zūn yē or `Zū nē), from the Spanish, is the name of both a people and a pueblo. This Pueblo's original name was *Ashiwi,* which might have meant "the flesh."

Location Zuñi consisted of six pueblos along the north bank of the upper Zuni River, in western New Mexico, at least 800 years ago. It is presently in the same location.

Population In 1990, 7,073 Indians lived at Zuñi. Perhaps as many as 20,000 lived there in 1500.

Language Zuni is a language unlike that spoken at other pueblos. Scientists speculate as to a possible link to the Penutian language family.

Historical Information

History Zuñis and their ancestors, the Mogollon and the Anasazi, and perhaps Mexican Indians as well have lived in the Southwest for well over 2,000 years. By the eleventh century, the "village of the great kiva," near Zuñi, had been built. In the fourteenth and fifteenth centuries a large number of villages existed in the Zuni Valley. By 1650 the number of Zuñi villages had shrunk to six.

Zuñi was probably the first native North American village visited by Spaniards, who had heard tales of great wealth in the "Kingdom of Cibola." In 1539, Estavinico, a black man in the advance guard of Fray Marcos de Niza's party, visited Zuñi. He was killed as a spy, and his group quickly retreated. The following year, Francisco Vasquez de Coronado visited the pueblos, ranging all the way to present-day Kansas in search of the mythical Cibola. The Zuñis resisted his demands and fled to a nearby mesa top. Other Spanish came in Coronado's wake. The first mission was established at Hawikuh in 1629. In 1632, Zuñis attacked and killed a number of missionaries, but the Spanish built a new mission, Halona, in 1643.

Zuñi participated in the Pueblo revolt of 1680. Their main grievances were being forced to supply the Spanish with corn, women, and labor and being punished harshly for practicing their religion. At that time the Zuñis lived in three of the original six pueblos. They fled to escape the Spanish, and in 1693

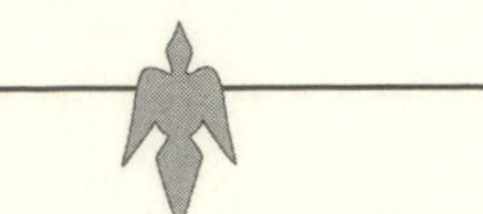

returned to the village at Halona on the Zuni River. A new church was built there, but shortly abandoned, the Zuñis preferring their own religion to Christianity. The ancient site of Halona is now modern Zuñi.

Left on their own by the Spanish, Zuñi was open to raids from Apaches, Navajos, and Plains tribes. Zuñi was still self-sufficient as of 1850, although it was on important trade routes and was increasingly raided by both Indians and Anglos. The U.S. government officially recognized a Zuñi reservation in 1877, although one far too small to support traditional agriculture. Three outlying summer villages established in the early nineteenth century became permanent in the 1880s, and a fourth such village was established in 1912 or 1914. In the late nineteenth and early twentieth centuries the Zuñi economy shifted from agriculture to sheep and cattle herding. With the decline of warfare, their Bow society turned to warfare against supposed Zuñi witches. The Bureau of Indian Affairs soon called in troops to suppress witchcraft trials, destroying the power of the Bow priests and the entire traditional government.

The opposition of tribal members as well as the failure of the government's Black Rock Reservation and Dam combined to block implementation of the allotment process at Zuñi. Erosion of arable land has been a considerable problem, especially since the debacle of counterproductive, government-mandated canal irrigation projects in the early twentieth century. By the 1930s, the government was promoting livestock as an alternative to agriculture. After World War II, the continuing shift in political power from priests to politicians led to the growth of political parties and the increased importance of the tribal council.

Religion Religion, including membership in religious and ceremonial organizations, was at the core of Zuñi existence. The sun priest was highly revered: In charge of solstice ceremonies as well as the calendar, he was held responsible for the community's welfare. The Zuñi recognized six points of orientation, which corresponded to the cardinal directions as well as mythological events. Each had its own color, position, kiva group, medicine societies and priesthoods, and ceremonies. Kivas were rectangular and above ground.

Katsinas, or benevolent guardian spirits, played a key part in Zuñi religion. Katsinas represented the rain gods as well as Zuñi ancestors. All boys between the ages of 11 and 14 underwent initiation into the katsina cult. At death, one was said to join the katsinas, especially if one was closely associated with the cult. Both men and women could join the curing cult of the beast gods. Its focus was animals of prey who lived in the east.

The Zuñi new year began at the winter solstice. A 20-day period during this time was known as *Itiwana,* or cleansing and preparing the village for the new year. Winter dances took place from February through April. Summer dances began at the solstice and lasted into September, concluding with the fertility ritual called *Olowishkia.* In late November or early December the Zuñis celebrated *Shalako,* a reenactment by katsina priests of the creation and migration of the Zuñi people. The people built six to eight Shalako houses and attended the Shalako katsinas—giant-sized messengers of the rain gods. This festival was accompanied by spectacular dancing and closed the Zuñi year. *Molawai,* or the ritual dramatization of the loss and recovery of corn maidens, immediately followed Shalako.

Government Ruled by heads of various priesthoods and societies, Zuñi was a theocracy. Bow priests enforced the rules from at least the seventeenth century on. A tribal council played a minor role in the nineteenth century but a more powerful one in the twentieth century. Zuñi accepted the Indian Reorganization Act (IRA) and an elected tribal council in 1934 (they ratified a constitution in 1970).

During the eighteenth century, a parallel, secular government developed at Zuñi to handle mundane problems. Based on the Spanish model, it was appointed by and responsible to the religious leaders. Offices included a governor, two lieutenant governors, a sheriff, and *fiscales* (church assistants). These officers acted as liaisons between the pueblo and the outside world and kept order within the pueblo. Metal-topped canes with a Spanish cross served as symbols of authority. Through the years, these were augmented by more Spanish canes, Mexican canes, and then canes given by President Lincoln to reward the pueblo for its neutrality in the Civil War.

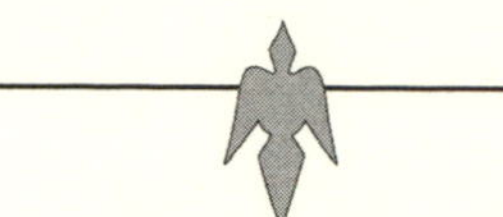

Customs Zuñi was divided into two groups, people of the north (also characterized as winter or rain) and people of the south (also characterized as summer or sun). Matrilineal clans affected ceremonial roles and certain behaviors. In general, however, ritual activity went through the father's family, and economic activity went through the mother's. There were also a number of secret cults and societies, some highly complex, each responsible for certain ceremonies. Zuñis traditionally cremated their dead. In modern times the dead are buried, with their possessions burned or buried after four days, following a ceremony that includes prayer sticks and cornmeal. With the exception of certain clan and family taboos, marriage was a matter between the two people involved and was traditionally preceded by a trial period of cohabitation. Divorce was simple and easy.

Dwellings Like other Pueblo Indians, Zuñis lived in multistoried houses (pueblos). Men built the structures of stone and plaster, not the adobe bricks used in the pueblos to the east. Ladders led to the upper stories. Floors were of packed adobe and roofs of willow boughs, brush, and packed earth. Women kept the outsides whitewashed. Tiny windows and outside beehive ovens were introduced in the sixteenth century.

Diet Farming was the chief Zuñi mode of subsistence. Men grew at least six varieties of corn plus beans, squash, and cotton. The Spanish introduced crops such as wheat, chilies, oats, and peaches. Zuñis used dams and sage windbreaks for irrigation. Corn was dried, ground into flour or meal, and served as mush or baked into breads. Food was also obtained by hunting (deer, antelope, and rabbits), fishing, and gathering wild plants (women were the gatherers, and they also kept small garden plots).

Key Technology Zuñis used dams and sage windbreaks for irrigation.

Trade The Zuñi traded in pottery, baskets, textiles, and shell and turquoise ornaments, among other items.

Notable Arts Traditional arts included pottery, weaving, and basketry (of willow and yucca leaves). In the 1830s they added brass and copper jewelry, which was in turn replaced around 1870 by silver (a skill learned from the Navajo). The Zuñi began using turquoise around 1890.

Transportation Women made baskets to transport goods.

Dress Men wove cotton into ceremonial costumes and clothing. Women wore one-piece black cotton dresses, belted at the waist. Both wore moccasins and deerskin leggings.

War and Weapons Zuñis who killed an enemy could join the Bow priesthood, which served as an important part of the religious hierarchy. The warrior society has deteriorated in recent years.

Contemporary Information

Government/Reservations Zuñi is located at the ancient site of the old village of Halona, in McKinley and Valencia Counties, New Mexico. A continuation of the 1689 Spanish land grant, the main reservation was established in 1877. Three other tracts were added later. Despite the return of their most sacred site, Katsina Village, in 1984, the reservation's 636 square miles is less than 3 percent of the tribe's original holdings. Most tribal members live on the reservation.

Zuñis elect their own governors and tribal councils, yet the religious leaders remain powerful. Tribal officers' terms begin during the first week of January and last for two years. Since 1970 the Zuñis have controlled their own reservation.

Economy The most important economic activities on Zuñi Pueblo are tribal employment and silver and turquoise jewelry manufacture, begun in earnest in the 1920s. People also make pottery, weavings, and baskets. Some Zuñis still farm and raise livestock, although by 1900 the tribe had lost 80 percent of its land base to Anglo settlers. Zuñi Cultural Resources Enterprise provides local archaeological services, and several individuals have established small businesses. There is also work off-reservation, particularly in Gallup, the nearest city. The tribe received $50 million in land claims settlements in 1990. Various

Like other Pueblo Indians, Zuñis lived in multistoried pueblos. As shown in this photograph, ladders led to the upper stories, as there were no stairs inside. Tiny windows and outside beehive ovens were introduced in the sixteenth century.

water rights cases remain ongoing, as does planning for economic development.

Legal Status Zuñi Pueblo is a federally recognized tribal entity.

Daily Life Most Zuñis live in the old pueblo, which has been rebuilt as single-story houses. There are also almost 1,000 houses in nearby settlements. Modern and traditional associations, such as the Lions Club, American Legion, clans, kiva groups, priesthoods and medicine societies, school boards, and cattle, farm, and irrigation associations all coexist at Zuñi. The result is a modern but close and cohesive community in which heritage remains vital. Much of the traditional religion, customs, social structure, and language remains intact.

Radio stations broadcast programs in Zuñi. Zuñis control their educational system (they received a school district in 1980), in which native language and culture figures prominently. The tribe also provides basic social services. Shalako, celebrating in late fall the connections between modern Zuñis and the spirits of their ancestors, remains a major ceremony. Races are still held between clans and ceremonial groups. An arts and crafts fair is held in mid-May.

Chapter Two

California

Left: A Pomo woman weaving a basket. Pomo baskets were of extraordinarily high quality.
Below: This Wiyot woman is basket weaving in the dunes near Eureka.
Far right: A selection of finely crafted California Indian baskets.

Above: Yurok warriors wore headdresses such as this at their annual Jump Dance.
Right: A Yokuts shaman displays his baskets and some of his medicine equipment.

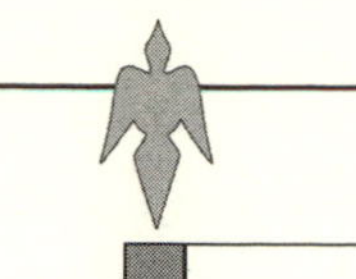

California

"California," in the context of this chapter, corresponds approximately to the present state of California. It omits the southeastern deserts because the Indian cultures of those deserts are usually considered part of the Southwest. Nor does it cover the region east of the Sierra Nevada (Great Basin), the extreme northeast of the state (Plateau), or Baja California (Mexico). The region contains two great mountain ranges, the Coastal and the Sierra Nevada; two major rivers, the Sacramento and the San Joaquin, and many minor river systems; roughly 1,100 miles of coast; interior semidesert; and, at least before the nineteenth century, huge areas of grassland in the central valleys. Much of California's climate may be categorized as Mediterranean, with the north, west, and highlands in general receiving more precipitation than the south, east, and lowlands.

Today's references to pre-twentieth-century "tribes," such as "Pomo" or "Cahuilla," are nothing more than contemporary conventions. Few, if any, of the roughly 300,000 California Indians (eighteenth century) were organized into true tribes. Instead, the most common form of political organization and the largest autonomous group was the tribelet, or cluster of satellite villages around one or more permanent villages. Perhaps 500 of these groups existed in aboriginal California. Tribelets shared a language, culture, and history. Each contained from some 50 to 500 people. They were often presided over by a headman, or chief, who controlled economic resources and activity. Chiefs were generally very wealthy and greatly respected. Different tribelets were occasionally named and even spoke varying dialects. Members of a tribelet were often related through the male line. Tribelets in northwestern California were, as a rule, less cohesive than in other parts of the region.

Native Americans of California

A selection of finely crafted California Indian baskets.

With perhaps the highest pre-Columbian population density north of Mexico, California Indians spoke over 300 different dialects of some 100 languages. The three main language families were the Hokan (from the Great Plains), Penutian (possibly from British Colombia and/or the Yucatan), and Uto-Aztecan (from the Southwest). Algonquian (eastern North America), Athapaskan (from Canada), and Yukian (origin unknown) languages were also spoken in California.

Though in many ways quite diverse, California Indians tended to share a number of cultural similarities. Foremost among these perhaps was a dependence on acorns as a staple food. Others included the use of shamans as religious leaders and doctors, especially doctors who cure by sucking; political organization by tribelet; an emphasis on individual wealth and private property; a reliance on such foods as fish, deer, elk, antelope, buckeye, sage seed, and epos root in addition to the primary food of acorns; the manufacture of numerous types of finely crafted baskets; and the use of datura in religious or rite-of-passage ceremonies. Many California people were subjected to strong mission influences in the eighteenth and nineteenth centuries.

In general, although California Indians suffered terribly from contact with the Spanish, they fared even worse at the hands of non-natives around the time of the gold rush and after. The population of Native Americans in the region fell by more than 90 percent, from upward of 200,000 in the mid–nineteenth century to roughly 15,000, within the span of a generation or two. Today, the descendants of these people, still in the process of regrouping, are fashioning renewed lives and identities as Indians of California.

California being relatively isolated geographically, its original occupation by people was probably not the result of mass migrations of major cultures but rather the slow trickling in of a number of small groups over a long period of time. Archaeologists have determined that people were

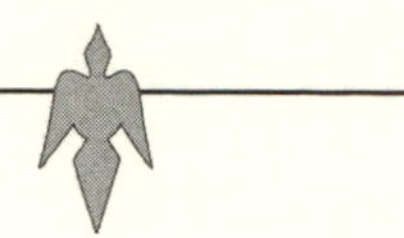

present in some parts of California at least 19,000 years ago. Some believe that human occupation goes back 50,000 years. About 9000 B.C.E., native peoples began the transition from an economy based mainly on hunting to one that also depended heavily on seed collecting. By about 2000 B.C.E., people had adjusted to local environments to the point that they had evolved several different subsistence patterns.

During the hunting period, people probably used darts powered by throwing sticks to bring down ancient species of camel, bison, and horse as well as several species of big game that still exist. They also hunted smaller mammals and fowl, fished, and ate some shellfish and plant food. They lived in open-air dwellings, although they may also have used caves for shelter. The transition to seed collecting took place between roughly 6000 and 3000 B.C.E., particularly along the south coast. In some areas the changeover evolved directly from the hunting economy, whereas in others it seems to have been a function of the westward migration of interior seed-gathering peoples. Milling stones served as the gatherers' primary tool. During this time, settlements seem to have increased in both size and stability.

After about 3000 B.C.E., Native Americans in California began to show a more pronounced economic and cultural diversity in response to fine-tuned regional and local adaptations. In general, a variety of subsistence strategies was practiced, with one predominating. Tools became more varied, numerous, and well made. At this time, the Windmiller culture flourished in the lower Sacramento Valley. Those people were accomplished artists and craftspeople, having made a number of stone, bone, and wooden tools as well as beads from shells acquired in trade from coastal tribes. They also made pottery, twined baskets, and, most notably, finely crafted charmstones, the exact purpose of which is unclear. The dead were buried prone, with faces down and oriented toward the west. They were decorated with shells and pendants and accompanied by a variety of goods.

Regional and local diversification was sufficiently advanced that by roughly 500 C.E., and in some cases much earlier, the basic patterns and customs of many historical peoples had been established. Population shifts and, in general, increases in village size and complexity also continued during this time, as people continued to take better advantage of food resources. As already mentioned, most California Indians depended on the acorn as a staple food. Acorns were collected on special autumn expeditions organized specifically for this purpose. After removing the kernels from the shell, sun drying them and pounding them into flour, Indian women leached out the bitter tannic acid by a variety of methods, most commonly by repeatedly pouring hot water over the flour. The meal was then boiled into soup or mush or baked into bread. Other common foods, which of course varied depending on the availability of resources, included big game such as deer, elk, antelope, and bear; fish such as salmon and trout; smaller mammals; a huge diversity of seeds, nuts, berries, roots, bulbs, tubers, and greens; insects and their larvae; waterfowl; sea mammals; shellfish and mollusks. The only cultivated crop was tobacco.

From as early as 1000 B.C.E., many California Indian groups created rock art. Most such art was probably made for ceremonial purposes, such as hunting or puberty rituals. Indians either carved or pecked the rock face (petroglyphs) or painted it (pictographs) to make their drawings. Most designs featured geometric patterns such as crosses, stars, wheels, triangles, and dots as well as stylized representations of people and animals.

Trade was well developed in California. Most trade occurred between close neighbors, although long-distance trading was not uncommon either, as an extensive and continuous trail system crisscrossed the entire region. Items were either bartered or purchased with money such as dentalium shells, clamshell disk beads, and magnesite beads. Among the chief items traded were foods, especially salt, acorns, and fish; shell beads; baskets; hides and pelts; obsidian; and bows. Trading generally took place either as part of friendly visits or on ceremonial occasions.

Organized warfare was rare among California Indians. Reasons for conflict ranged from physical offenses such as murder and rape to trespass and sorcery to simple insult. Surprise attacks were often the preferred method of fighting; in any case, pitched battles were generally avoided, and casualties remained low. Armed conflict was generally resolved after a brief period of fighting, with the headmen of

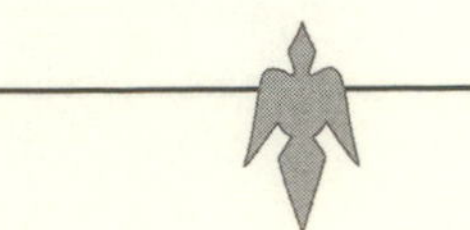

each party forming a peace commission to work out the details. Most groups agreed to compensate the other for all damages incurred, such as loss of life and property.

Ceremonialism played an important role in the lives of most California Indians. For most groups, shamans were the religious leaders as well as the curers, obtaining their powers through intercourse with supernatural spirits. Some peoples had secret religious societies, such as those associated with the Kuksu cult. This cult involved a lengthy and complex instructional period and, by referencing and impersonating supernatural spirits, symbolically restored the group to an original, perfect state. Other groups celebrated a World Renewal cycle of ceremonies, an elaboration of first salmon rituals that provided an opportunity to relate history and mythology and to display wealth.

Most groups practiced well-defined rituals centered around life-cycle events such as puberty and death. Other ceremonial occasions were related to subsistence. Shamanic preparation as well as certain initiation rites or ceremonies frequently included the use of psychotropic drugs such as datura (jimsonweed or toloache) to assist in the attainment of visions. Tobacco was also an important part of most rituals. Music and dance were an integral part of most ceremonies. Catholicism arrived by force with the Spanish. Most peoples were influenced by the Ghost Dances of the 1870s.

Marriage generally took place when the couple was recently postpubescent. Northern California Indians observed a relatively rigid and closed class system, based on wealth and perpetuated by marriage (including the bride price) and custom: People were either elite, common, or poor. Some groups also kept slaves. Chiefs and shamans often had more than one wife, as could any wealthy man. Occupational specialists included craftspeople as well as minor officials such as assistant chief, messenger, and dance manager. Games such as hoop-and-pole, the hand game, cat's cradle, shinny (a form of lacrosse), dice, and athletic contests, as well as music and dancing, were almost universal.

Indians across California first encountered non-natives at widely different times. Along the southern and central coast, Indians met Spanish and English explorers, for example, as early as the mid–sixteenth century. In some of the interior hills and valleys, face-to-face contact occurred as late as the early to mid–nineteenth century, and in some more remote desert and mountain locations not until the early twentieth century, although indirect contact had been established for some time previously in the form of trade items, diffused customs, and disease. Radical change due to contact with non-natives began in the south and central coastal regions with the establishment of the first missions and in the north and interior with the gold- and/or land-induced invasion of Indian territory.

The long-term presence of the Spanish, beginning in 1769 with the founding of a presidio and Franciscan mission in San Diego, had a profound effect on California. Immediate ramifications were of two kinds. Habitat change occurred when European grasses and weeds replaced the original seed-food grasses; overgrazing accelerated erosion and diminished the amount of available surface water; and the amount of much wild game and marine food was reduced. Direct personal change occurred when large numbers of Indians were forcibly transported and confined to Spanish missions from San Diego to San Francisco. There, disease, torture, overwork, and malnourishment, combined with a policy of cultural genocide, both drastically reduced Indian populations and destroyed many cultures. Indians resisted both actively, through occasional armed revolts, and passively, mainly by escaping into the interior, where they introduced horses, firearms, and other elements of Spanish culture. Indians in southern and central California who remained outside of mission life were generally able to adopt resistance strategies and gradually adapt their lives to the new influences.

The missions came under Mexican control in 1834 and were secularized shortly thereafter. The original intention had been to divide mission lands and wealth between the new administrators and the Indians; in practice, the former kept it all for themselves. Many mission Indians worked on the new ranchos (estates), living lives little different from those in the missions. Others drifted into lives of poverty and misery in the white settlements. Some who still had aboriginal homes returned to them, resuming traditional lives as much as possible in the face of

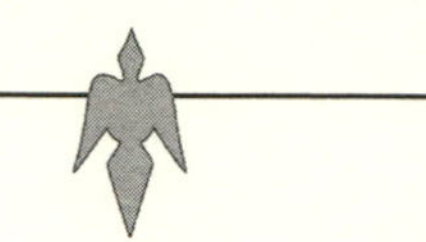

cultural dislocation and regular attacks from Mexican colonists. Many Indian groups, particularly in the Sacramento Valley, abandoned their once-peaceful ways and turned to raiding and guerrilla warfare to protect themselves. Some Indians also fought with the Yankees in the Mexican War.

Further dislocations occurred as the United States took possession of California. The 1848 Treaty of Guadalupe Hidalgo had no provisions protecting Indian land title. Many Indian peoples living in the regions of the mines as well as desirable farmlands in central and northern California were overwhelmed by the crunch of non-native immigrants and were all but exterminated. After 1850, many Indians living in interior California lost their lives to starvation and unchecked—in fact, government-subsidized—massacres. Vigilantes and other criminals kidnapped more than 10,000 Indian men, women, and children and sold them for use as virtual slaves. Furthermore, disease, in part caused by lowered resistance due to hunger and ill-treatment, probably surpassed kidnapping and murder as a cause of village abandonment. In 1833 a major malaria epidemic struck Indian populations. Later smallpox and venereal and other diseases took a huge toll.

In the early 1850s, U.S. treaty commissioners met with 400 or so chiefs and headmen, representing between one-third and one-half of California Indians. At that time several Indian groups signed 18 treaties, but the state of California, asserting its "state's rights" and preferring Indian extinction to a negotiated settlement, pressured the U.S. government not to ratify them. The United States did establish several reservations in the 1850s; however, since federal aid was siphoned off by corrupt bureaucrats, and massacres, kidnappings, and land theft continued even on the reservations themselves, most were abandoned in the following decade. Most California Indians were never restricted to reservations but were left to fend for themselves, their land taken and most of their people destroyed.

In the 1870s, federal administration of Indian affairs in the state was placed under the control of churches, which promptly moved to suppress all traditional religious practices. The United States began granting reservations to so-called Mission Indians in 1875. Throughout the last half of the nineteenth century, Indians struggled to support themselves through farming, raising livestock, and subsistence and ruthlessly exploitative wage labor while receiving few or no government services. This pattern continued well into the twentieth century. At the same time, Indians continued to resist government policies such as the abduction and forced settlement of their children at boarding schools and the breaking up of their reservations under the provisions of the hated Dawes Act (1886), all aimed at detribalization and forced assimilation. Although Indian resistance was partially successful, Anglo pressure was inexorable, and the old ways and knowledge declined steadily during the twentieth century.

Following World War II, government "termination" policies favored ending all services to California Indians, a move that resulted in plunging economic and quality-of-life indicators on the remaining reservations and rancherias. In the 1960s, federal housing, health, education, and training programs and a changing political climate combined to provide an environment within which California Indians began to take greater control over their lives. They created new political organizations to meet the new situations. Eventually, interreservation organizations proliferated to meet the needs of Indians.

Cultural change accompanied political and economic change. The establishment of several museums and language classes reflected a growing interest in native cultures. Increasing Indian interest in and control over their own education resulted in greater Indian participation in the educational process at all levels. Indian morale slowly rebounded. The Native American Historical Society led an effort to replace negative stereotypes in school texts; this organization also created a publishing house and a newspaper, *Wassaja.* Still, in the 1970s, most Indians lived with appalling housing conditions and few job opportunities and were continuing to lose their land base as a result primarily of tax and other government policies.

Today, people once thought to be extinct are in fact still very much present. Many Indian peoples have survived as recognizable, continuous entities. There is much lost ground to be recovered, yet

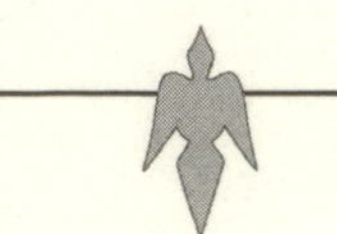

California Indians are tackling the issues of identity, housing, and land within a context of renewed self-determination and pride as well as sophisticated political organizing, economic planning, and communication skills.

Achumawi

Achumawi (Ä chū `mä wē, or Ä jū `mä wē), "River People." Also known, occasionally with the Atsugewi, as Pit River Indians, from their practice of hunting deer by means of pitfalls. These people were organized into 11 bands and shared several cultural characteristics of Indians of the Great Basin.

Location The Achumawi traditionally lived in the northeastern part of the region, from Mount Shasta and Lassen Peak to the Warner Range. This area of tremendous ecological diversity yielded a huge variety of foods, medicines, and raw materials. In the 1990s, Pit River Indians live on their own or shared reservations and rancherias, plus Pit River trust lands, in Modoc, Shasta, Mendocino, Lassen, and Lake Counties, California (see "Government/Reservations" under "Contemporary Information").

Population Roughly 3,000 Achumawi lived in California in the mid–nineteenth century. In 1990, 75 Pit River Indians lived on eight rancherias and the Pit River trust lands. Pit River Indians also lived on four reservations with other tribes. Tribal enrollment in the early 1990s was 1,350.

Language With the Atsugewi, their language made up the Palaihnihan Branch of the Hokan language family.

Historical Information

History Trappers entering Achumawi territory in 1828 made little impact. However, the flood of non-natives after the gold rush provoked Achumawi resistance, which was brutally repressed by state and private militias as well as extralegal vigilantes. By the end of the century, several hundred Achumawis had been forced onto the Round Valley Reservation. Some remained in their traditional lands, however. Their acquisition of individual allotments after 1897 helped them to retain their band ties and some subsistence activities.

Most of these allotments were lost in the early twentieth century to Pacific Gas and Electric. Major health problems plagued the Achumawi Indians in the 1920s. Seven small rancherias were created between 1915 and 1938. In 1938, some Achumawi families settled on the 9,000-acre XL Ranch. As late as the 1950s, the Achumawi still retained much of their ancient knowledge and carried on a form of their aboriginal existence. It was mostly younger people who began a new activism in the 1960s, focused on the issues of sovereignty and land usurpation. The Pit River Tribe received federal recognition in 1976.

Religion By means of vision quests, boys might attract a spirit guide, or supernatural power. Girls acquired their connection to the spirit world through ceremony. This power could strongly influence the quality of daily activities such as hunting, fighting, gambling, or shamanic responsibilities. However, supernatural power could depart at any time for any or no reason.

Shamans, or doctors, provided medical care as well as religious leadership. In fact, the two were closely related. A shaman's power, or medicine, which could be held by man or woman, was similar to the spirit guide, only more powerful. Shamans often used medicinal plants and wild tobacco, curing with the explicit aid of their spirit power. The Achumawi recognized four types of maladies: visible accidents, "bad blood," poisoning by another shaman, or soul-loss (connected with another's death).

Government The Achumawi people were composed of about nine tribelets. Though autonomous, each was connected by language, culture, and intermarriage. Chiefs were chosen on the basis of popularity, ability, and possession of supernatural powers.

Customs At puberty, boys usually went to mountain retreats in search of a spirit vision that would bestow supernatural powers. They also had their noses pierced. On the occasion of their first menstrual period, girls sang, danced, and feasted with the community all night for ten days. This activity was

repeated for nine days on the second month, eight on the third, and so on until the tenth month, when they were considered women.

Corpses were cremated and all their former possessions burned. Mourners cut their hair, darkened their faces with pitch, and refrained from speaking the name of the dead. The soul was said to head for the western mountains. When a chief died, two or three less-liked members of the tribe were sometimes killed to provide the chief with traveling companions.

When within earshot, people were generally addressed by their kin terms, not by their names. Gifts exchanged at marriage were regarded as a price for both spouses. If a married person died, the surviving spouse could still be obligated to marry another suitable person in that family. As with many North American Indians, the Achumawi played the hand game, as well as shinny, wrestling, and footraces.

Dwellings Conical three-season houses were made of tule mats over a light pole framework. Wood-frame winter houses were built partly underground and covered with grass, bark, or tule and a layer of earth. Both were entered by means of a ladder through the smoke hole.

Diet The environmentally diverse Achumawi territory, which ranged from mountains to lowland swamps, contained a great variety of foods. The Achumawi regularly burned the fir and pine uplands, meadows, and grasslands in order to augment this richness. The fires stimulated the growth of seed and berry plants, made insects available for collecting, and drove game into accessible areas.

Food staples included fish, such as salmon, trout, bass, pike, and catfish; crawfish; and mussels. Waterfowl were caught with nets, and the people ate the eggs as well. Other important foods included acorns, tule sprouts, various seeds, berries, roots and bulbs, and insects and their larvae. Game included deer, antelope, bear, beaver, badger, coyote, and a variety of small mammals.

Key Technology Bow wood was either juniper or yew. Most points and blades were made from obsidian. Other building materials included bone and stone, including antler. Baskets were made for a number of purposes, including fish traps. The Achumawi made five kinds of tule or milkweed nets, including dip, gill, seine, and waterfowl. Tule was used for many other products, including mats, twine, shoes, and rafts. Fire drills were made of juniper. Sometimes the people used a cedar rope as a slow-burning match. They also made juniper snowshoes.

Trade Achumawis had regular and friendly contact with the Atsugewi, who could speak their language. They traded occasionally with the Shasta, Yana, and Paiute.

Notable Arts Achumawi women made fine flexible twined baskets of grasses and willow, decorated with vegetable dye designs. Beginning about 1000 B.C.E., the people also made petroglyphs, or rock carvings, that were related to hunting large game.

Transportation For river travel, the Achumawi used both tule fiber balsa rafts and juniper and pine dugout canoes.

Dress Clothing included shirts, skirts, belts, caps, capes, robes, leggings, moccasins, and dresses. Clothing was made primarily of deer, badger, coyote, and antelope skin and shredded juniper bark. Colored minerals were used to decorate both objects and people.

War and Weapons The slave-raiding Modocs were a traditional enemy. Instead of retaliating in kind, the Achumawi usually hid out until the raiders went away. Weapons included elk hide armor and shields and arrows poisoned with rattlesnake venom.

Contemporary Information

Government/Reservations Achomawi/Pit River reservations include: Alturas Rancheria (1906; 20 acres; Modoc County); Big Bend Rancheria (1916; 40 acres); Big Valley Rancheria (Pomo and Pit River; Lake County); Likely Rancheria (1922; 1.32 acres); Lookout Rancheria (1913; 40 acres; Modoc County); Montgomery Creek Rancheria (1915; 72 acres; Shasta County); Redding Rancheria (31 acres; 79 Indians in 1990; Shasta County); Roaring Creek Rancheria (1915; 80 acres; Shasta County); Round Valley

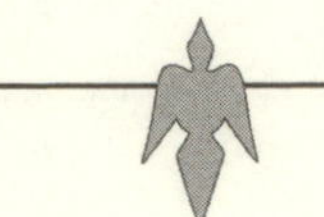

Reservation (1864; 30,538 acres; 577 Indians in 1990, Mendocino County); Susanville Rancheria (1923; 150 acres; Lassen County); and XL Ranch Reservation (1938; 9,254.86 acres; Modoc County). Most rancherias are governed by elected tribal councils.

The Pit River Tribe was formally recognized in 1976, and a constitution was adopted in 1987. The 1990 population was roughly 1,350. Each of 11 bands is represented by one vote in a tribal council.

Economy Unemployment on the reservations and rancherias remains stubbornly high. Jobs in logging and hay ranching are available at XL Ranch. There is also some money to be made in the tourism trade, especially in basket sales.

Legal Status The Alturas Indian Rancheria of Pit River Indians; the Pit River Tribe of California (including Big Bend, Lookout, Montgomery Creek, and Roaring Creek Rancherias and XL Ranch); the Big Valley Rancheria of Pomo and Pit River Indians; the Covelo Indian Community of the Round Valley Reservation; and the Susanville Indian Rancheria of Paiute, Maidu, Pit River, and Washoe Indians are all federally recognized tribal entities.

Daily Life Attempts at tribal organization have been largely unsuccessful. Ancient subdivisions are still identifiable and, despite the population decimation and scattered and inadequate land base, the people retain a strong attachment to the land and to their traditions. Pit River Indians work to oppose development of the sacred Mt. Shasta. They also hold an annual powwow.

Barbariño

See Chumash

Cahto

Cahto (ˋKä tō) is Northern Pomo for "lake," referring to an important Cahto village site. The Cahto called themselves *Djilbi,* the word in their language for that same lake and village. The Cahto are sometimes referred to as Kaipomo Indians.

Location The Cahto homeland is in northwest California, south of Rattlesnake Creek, north of the North Fork of the Ten Mile River, and between the South Fork of the Eel River and just west of the Eel River (more or less the Long and Cahto Valleys). Today, most Cahtos live in Mendocino County.

Population Roughly 1,100 Cahto Indians lived in their region in the early eighteenth century. In 1990, 129 Cahto-Pomo people lived at Laytonville. A few Cahto also lived at Round Valley Reservation.

Language Cahto was an Athapaskan language.

Historical Information

History Like other Indian people who were overwhelmed by the sheer numbers and brutality of non-native Californians in the 1850s, the Cahto fought back for a brief period before being defeated. Their population declined by some 95 percent during the nineteenth century. The town of Cahto was founded in 1856, the same year reservations were created at Round Valley and Fort Bragg, in Mendocino County. The town of Laytonville was established in 1880.

Religion Cahtos prayed frequently, in part to two original beings, *Nagaicho,* or Great Traveler, and *Tcenes,* or Thunder. They also followed the Kuksu cult, which involved the acquisition of spiritual power through direct contact with supernatural beings. Tribal and intertribal ceremonies were held in winter (such as the Acorn Dance) and summer. A host who had enough food to share invited his neighbors. Then there was dancing for a week, the creation story was told, and the headman made speeches.

Government The Cahto lived in approximately 50 villages. Although most were completely autonomous, six in Long Valley were united to the extent that they called themselves "Grass Tribe." Each village was led by a headman or two. His authority was mainly advisory, and he was generally succeeded by his son.

Customs Marriage was generally a matter between the couple involved, although girls were generally prepubescent when married. The Cahto practiced

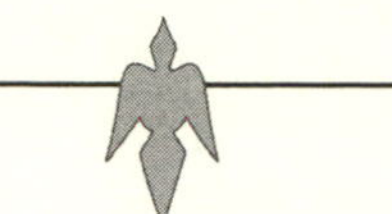

polygyny as well as the taboo that prevented a man from addressing his mother-in-law directly. Divorce was easily obtained for nearly any reason. Unlike many California Indians, pregnant Cahto women observed no food taboos. Deformed children and twins were killed at birth.

The six-day girls' puberty ceremony included dietary taboos and then a quiet life for five subsequent months. Boys, at puberty, remained in the dance house all winter to receive admonitions regarding proper behavior; "ghosts" also sang and danced for this purpose. Corpses were buried with their valuables or cremated if away from home. Both men and women mourners cut their hair, and women put pitch on their bodies.

Adult games included shinny, the grass game, stone throwing, and races. Children's games included camping, skipping rope, and playing with acorn tops. Women enjoyed singing in chorus around an evening fire. The Cahto danced the feather and *necum* dances solely for pleasure. Pets included birds, coyotes, and rabbits.

The Cahto knew three types of shamans: sucking doctors, bear doctors, and singing and dancing doctors. Bear doctors were said to be strong enough to kill enemies of the Cahto. Various ceremonies, including magic, were practiced before all important events, such as hunting, war, birth, and funerals. Men owned hunting and war items; women owned their clothing, baskets, and cooking rocks. Men generally hunted and fished. Women gathered all foods except acorns; gathering acorns was a communal activity.

Dwellings Living houses, which were privately owned by up to three families, were built over two-foot-deep pits. Slabs, bark, or earth covered wood rafters, which in turn rested on four poles. Most houses were rebuilt after two years as a vermin-control measure. Larger villages contained similarly built but larger dance houses.

Diet Acorns, salmon, and deer served as food staples. Other important foods included other fish; bear; mink, raccoon, and other small game; birds; and some insects. Meat was generally broiled over coals or on a spit. The Cahto also ate a variety of seeds, tubers, and berries. They also used domesticated dogs to help them hunt.

Key Technology Stone, bone, and shell were the primary tool materials. Baskets were usually twined but sometimes coiled. Hunting tools included traps, snares, bows, arrows, slings, nets, and harpoons. Fish were sometimes poisoned. Musical instruments included whistles, rattles, a foot drum, a musical bow, and a six-hole elderberry flute.

Trade The Cahto were particularly friendly with the Northern Pomo. Some Cahto even spoke Pomo in addition to their own language. In addition to regular trade with the Northern Pomo, the Cahto gathered shellfish and seaweed in Coast Yuki territory. They also supplied these people with hazelwood bows in exchange for items such as salt, mussels, seaweed, abalone, sea fish, clamshells, and dried kelp. They traded arrows, baskets, and clothing to the Wailaki in exchange for dentalia. They also supplied clam disk beads to the Lassik and received salt from the Northern Wintun as well as dogs from an unknown location to the north.

Notable Arts Fine arts consisted of fashioning musical instruments and singing.

Transportation The Cahto used log rafts for crossing streams.

Dress Men and women dressed in a similar fashion. They both wore tanned deerhide aprons. They also wore long hair and used iris nets. Both wore bracelets, nose and ear ornaments, and, occasionally, tattoos.

War and Weapons The Cahto seldom engaged in large-scale warfare. There were, however, frequent conflicts with the Sinkyone, Yuki, Northern Pomo, Wailaki, and Huchnom, generally over murder or trespass. When fighting occurred, close fighting was avoided whenever possible. War dances were held before each battle. Weapons included the bow and arrow, deer hide sling, and spear. All casualties were indemnified following the fighting.

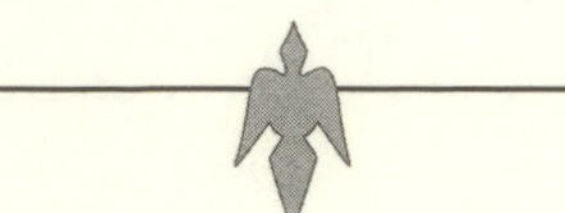

Contemporary Information

Government/Reservations Laytonville Rancheria (1906), in Mendocino County, consists of 264 acres. The tribal council consists of three people who serve a one-year term. The term "Cahto" refers to those eligible for tribal membership, even though some Cahtos personally adhere to other tribal affiliations.

Economy Some Cahtos work at a nearby lumber mill. However, unemployment remains high at Laytonville. The tribe has built the Ya-Ka-Ama Indian Center in Sonoma County.

Legal Status The Cahto Indian Tribe of the Laytonville Rancheria is a federally recognized tribal entity.

Daily Life Laytonville is not an isolated Indian community. Racial intermarriage is common, and Indians compete for scarce job opportunities with other local citizens. Educational levels among Cahtos are relatively low. Little remains of traditional culture, although there are Pomo dancers and basket weavers, and native language classes are held.

Cahuilla

Cahuilla (Kä `hwē lä), perhaps derived from the Spanish *kawiya,* or "master." The Cahuilla refer to themselves as *Iviatim,* or speakers of their native language.

Location The Cahuilla lived generally southwest of the Bernardino Mountains in the eighteenth century. They ranged over a territory including several distinct environmental zones, from mountain ranges to canyons to desert (11,000 feet to 273 feet). Today they live on ten reservations in southern California.

Population The Cahuilla population may have numbered as many as 10,000 in the seventeenth century, with roughly 5,000 remaining by the late eighteenth century. In 1990, the total Indian population of all reservations on which Cahuilla lived, including those they shared with other peoples, was 1,276.

Language Cahuilla was a language from the Cupan subgroup of the Takic division of the Uto-Aztecan language family.

Historical Information

History New diseases and elements of Spanish culture probably preceded the physical arrival of the Spanish, which occurred when the Juan Bautista de Anza expedition arrived in 1774. The Cahuilla were at first hostile to the Spanish. Since most routes to the Pacific at that time were by sea, the two groups had little ongoing contact, except that a few Cahuillas were baptized at nearby missions.

By the early nineteenth century, some Cahuillas worked seasonally on Spanish cattle ranches, and aspects of Spanish culture such as cattle, wage labor, clothing, and language had significantly changed the traditional Cahuilla lifestyle. The latter maintained their autonomy until the severe smallpox epidemic of 1863. After 1877, they moved slowly on to reservations. Although self-supporting, they grew increasingly dependent on the Americans.

After 1891 the federal government took a much more active role in their lives. Government schools trained Cahuillas to perform menial tasks; influential Protestant missionaries suppressed native religion and culture; allotment under the Dawes Act (1886) destroyed their agricultural capabilities; and Indian Service personnel controlled their political activities, under protest. From roughly 1891 through the 1930s, Cahuillas farmed, raised cattle, worked for wages, sold peat and asbestos, and leased their lands for income. Lack of water was a chronic obstacle to economic activities. Their tourist industry, especially that of the Agua Caliente Band, also dates from the 1920s.

Following World War II, partial termination and the severe curtailment of government services forced the Cahuilla to take a much more active role in their welfare. Renewed federal programs in the 1960s in combination with a vitalized tribal political structure led to a general increase in the quality of life for most Cahuillas.

Religion The Cahuilla recognized a supreme power, neither good nor bad, but unpredictable. According to their worldview, the entire universe and everything in it was interconnected. Cahuillas performed a large

number of rituals. The most significant ones were an annual mourning ceremony, the eagle ceremony (honoring a dead chief or shaman), rite-of-passage rituals, and food-related rituals. Song cycles were a key part of Cahuilla ritual. They sought to reaffirm the people's place in the universe and their connections with the past and with all things. Ceremonial implements included rattles, headdresses, wands, eagle-feathered skirts, and especially the *máyswut,* a ceremonial bundle.

Government The Cahuillas lived in about 50 villages aboriginally. The political unit was the clan, or group of between three and ten lineages. Each clan had a leader, usually hereditary, called the *nét.* This person had religious, economic, and diplomatic as well as political responsibilities. The *nét* also had an assistant.

Háwayniks knew and sang the ceremonial songs, including the long song cycles. Shamans (always male) had much power, including curing, through the control of supernatural power. They also controlled the weather; guarded against evil spirits; and, with the *néts,* exercised political authority. Strong as it was, however, the shaman's authority was only maintained by regular public displays of power.

Customs The Cahuilla recognized two societal divisions, Wildcat and Coyote, each composed of a number of patrilineal clans. Female doctors complemented male shamans as curers; their methods included the use of medicinal plants and other knowledge. When a person died, the spirit was believed to travel to the land of the dead; from there, it could still be involved in the lives of the living. Old age was venerated, largely because old people taught the traditional ways and values, which were themselves venerated.

Reciprocity and sharing were two defining values. The Cahuillas frowned upon hasty behavior; conversely, it was appropriate to do things slowly, deliberately, and cautiously. They enjoyed regular interaction, including intermarriage, with other Indian groups such as the Gabrieleño and Serrano.

Although each extended family had a village site and resource area, land away from the village could be owned by anyone. Mens' games were based on endurance and the ability to withstand physical punishment. Women's games included footraces, juggling, cat's cradle, top spinning, jackstones, and balancing objects. People often bet on games.

Cahuilla songs contained tribal history and cosmology, and they accompanied all activities. Singing was common. Bathing and cleanliness in general were important. Spouses were selected by parents from the opposite division. Divorce was difficult to obtain. Everyone observed specific rules of deference and behavior toward other people.

Dwellings Dome-shaped shelters were constructed of brush. Rectangular houses were generally made of thatch. Other structures included acorn granaries, mens' sweat houses, and ceremonial lodges.

Diet Six varieties of acorns constituted a key food source. Other gathered food included pine nuts, mesquite and screwbeans, and a huge variety of cactus, seeds, berries, roots, and greens. Other plants were used in construction and for medicinal purposes. Rabbits, deer, antelope, rodents, mountain sheep, reptiles, and fowl were all hunted, and fish were taken. Meat was roasted, boiled, or sun-dried in strips, with the bones then cracked for marrow or ground and mixed with other foods. Blood was drunk fresh or cooked and stored. Some Cahuilla bands practiced agriculture, although this was a less important activity.

Key Technology The Cahuilla used a variety of natural materials for their technological needs, including willow or mesquite wood (bows and arrows), grasses (cooking, storage, and carrying baskets), stone (mortars, pestles, manos and metates, arrow straighteners), wood (mortars), clay (pottery for cooking, storage, eating, and pipes), pine pitch (to seal storage bins for food preservation), and mescal (fibers for rope). Other technological innovations included hunting nets, snares and traps, baking ovens or pits, and musical instruments such as elder flutes, whistles, panpipes, and rattles.

Trade The Cocopah-Maricopa Trail, a major trade route, bisected Cahuilla territory. Two other trade routes, the Santa Fe and the Yuman, passed close by. Cahuillas traded mostly with the Mojave,

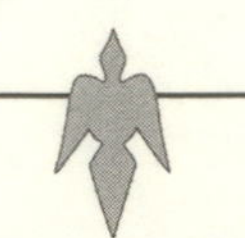

Six varieties of acorns constituted a key food source for the Cahuilla. This woman is stocking her elevated granary of acorns in the rocky mountains of southwestern California, circa 1900.

Halchidoma, Ipai, Tipai, Luiseño, Serrano, and Gabrieleño. The Cahuilla traded food products, furs, hides, obsidian, and salt for shell beads, minerals such as turquoise and tourmaline, Joshua tree blossoms, axes, and other crafts. Rituals and songs were also exchanged.

Notable Arts Petroglyphs, perhaps beginning as early as 1000 B.C.E., depicted big game hunting. Pictographs, associated with the girls' puberty ceremony, began in the fifteenth century.

Transportation Baskets were used to transport goods.

Dress Women wore basket hats as well as skirts of mescal bark, tule, or skins. Men wore breechclouts of the same material when they wore anything at all. Both men and women wore sandals of mescal fibers soaked in mud and tied with mescal fibers or buckskin. Babies wore mesquite-bark diapers. Blankets or woven rabbit-skin robes were used for warmth.

War and Weapons Cahuillas fought other Cahuillas as a last resort, usually over economic disputes. Weapons included war clubs and poison-tipped arrows.

Contemporary Information

Government/Reservations Cahuilla reservations include Agua Caliente (1896; 23,173 acres; Riverside County; 1957 constitution and by-laws), Augustine (1893; 502 acres; Thermal County), Cabazon (1876;

1,382 acres; Indio and Riverside Counties; 20 Indians; democratically elected tribal council); Cahuilla (1875; 18,884 acres; Riverside County), Los Coyotes (1889; Cahuilla and Cupeño; 25,049.63 acres; San Diego County), Morongo (1908; 32,362 acres; Cahuilla, Serrano, and Cupeño, Riverside County), Ramona (1893; 560 acres; Riverside County), Santa Rosa (1907; 11,092.6 acres; Kings County), and Torres-Martinez (1876; 24,024 acres; Imperial and Riverside Counties). Each is administered by elected business committees and/or tribal councils in conjunction with the Bureau of Indian Affairs (BIA) and is connected to the others in various formal and informal ways. None have Indian Reorganization Act constitutions.

Economy Important activities include cattle raising, farming, billboard and land leasing, and general off-reservation employment opportunities. Agua Caliente has extensive real estate holdings. The Cabazon Band operates the Fantasy Springs Casino and owns an industrial park; they have no unemployment, though income is fairly low. In general, the Cahuillas' land is far from markets, water, and jobs. Most of the reservations have job development plans. The unemployment rate at Torres-Martines was 78 percent in 1995. There is also some basket making for the tourist trade.

Legal Status The Agua Caliente Band of Mission Indians of the Agua Caliente Indian Reservation; the Augustine Band of Mission Indians of the Augustine Indian Reservation; the Cabazon Band of Mission Indians of the Cabazon Indian Reservation; the Cahuilla Band of Mission Indians of the Cahuilla Reservation; the Los Coyotes Band of Cahuilla Mission Indians of the Los Coyotes Reservation; the Morongo Band of Cahuilla Mission Indians of the Morongo Reservation; the Ramona Band or Village of Cahuilla Mission Indians; the Santa Rosa Band of Cahuilla Mission Indians of the Santa Rosa Reservation; and the Torres-Martinez Desert Cahuilla Indians are federally recognized tribal entities.

Daily Life Some traditions remain alive, although much diminished, such as the funeral ritual, foods, and kin relationships, as do values like reciprocity. Ceremonies have been greatly modified, but the patterns remain, as do traditional games, relationships with the supernatural, wagering, and songs. People, especially the young, are learning the living language. Most Cahuillas are Catholic. Institutions include the Malki Museum of Cahuilla Culture at Morongo Reservation, the Morongo Indian Health Clinic, and the Torres-Martinez Historical Society. Cahuillas are relatively well educated. Two intertribal powwows are held annually. Tribal autonomy remains an issue, as does resource management and Indian burials. Recently, Cahuillas have been forced to consider the issue of hazardous waste disposal on their lands. An Agua Caliente Cultural Museum is planned for Palm Springs.

Among the Cabazon Band, children receive education grants to attend public or private schools off the reservation. The casino plays a major role in their lives. The people are building 1,000 houses on their reservation.

At Torres-Martinez, extended families often live together. Children attend public school but also learn traditional songs and dances. Seniors meet regularly, and many converse in their native language. Diabetes and substance abuse are significant social problems. Neither the clans nor many traditional ceremonies remain. Most people live in trailers or Housing and Urban Development/BIA housing, little of which is suitable for the desert. Illegally dumped toxic sludge is a local environmental threat and the object of ongoing blockades and other protests.

Chilula

See Hupa

Chukchansi

See Yokuts

Chumash

Chumash (`Chū mash), a label chosen by an Anglo anthropologist, comes from the word used by the Coastal Chumash for either the Santa Cruz *(Mi-tcú-mac)* Indians or the Santa Rosa *(Tcú-mac)* Indians. Each Chumash regional group—Barbareño, Ynezeño, and Ventureño (Eastern Coastal); Obispeño and

Purisimeño; Island Chumash; and Interior Chumash—has its own self-designation. The Chumash are sometimes referred to as the Santa Barbara Indians.

Location Traditionally, the Chumash lived along the Pacific coast from San Luis Obispo to Malibu Canyon and inland as far as the western edge of the San Joaquin Valley. There were also Chumash Indians on the Santa Barbara Channel islands of San Miguel, Santa Rosa, Santa Cruz, and Anacapa. Today, the Santa Ynez Band lives at and near Santa Ynez, California.

Population Chumash population was between roughly 10,000 and 18,000 in the late eighteenth century. In 1990, 213 Indians lived on the Santa Ynez Reservation.

Language At least six separate groups spoke related Hokan languages: Barbareño, Ventureño, Ynezeño, Purisimeño, Obispeño, and the Island language.

Historical Information

History The Coastal Chumash were living in their traditional territory by roughly 1000. In 1542, contact was established between the Chumash and the Spanish explorers Juan Cabrillo and Bartolome Ferello. Relations were amiable, and although the Spanish soon began using the Santa Barbara Channel as a stopover for their trans-Pacific voyages, early impact on the Chumash was minimal.

In 1772 the Franciscans built San Luis Obispo mission. Other missions followed soon thereafter. The Chumash entered the mission period willingly, and many became completely missionized (turned into farmers, artisans, and Christians). However, for most Indians, missions were places of slave labor. Smallpox and syphilis were major killers, but even the common cold often turned into a deadly disease. Refusing either to give up their traditional ways or to be mistreated by the Spanish missionaries, some Chumash escaped into the hills either before or during the mission period. In 1824, Indians staged a major rebellion at several missions. Many sought sanctuary with the Yokuts Indians or at other interior communities. Although many ultimately returned to the missions, many others did not.

Mexico seized control of the missions in 1834. Indians either fled into the interior, attempted farming for themselves and were driven off the land, or were enslaved by the new administrators. Alcoholism soon became a large problem among the Chumash. Many found highly exploitative work on large Mexican ranches. After 1849 most Chumash land was lost to theft by Americans and a declining population, mainly as a result of the effects of violence and disease. The remaining Chumash began to lose their cohesive identity. In 1855, a small piece of land (120 acres) was set aside for just over 100 remaining Chumash Indians near Santa Ynez mission. This land ultimately became the only Chumash reservation, although Chumash individuals and families also continued to live throughout their former territory in southern California.

Chumash cemeteries along Santa Barbara Channel were looted extensively in the 1870s and 1880s. By 1900, disease combined with intermarriage had rendered Chumash culture virtually extinct.

Religion Little is known about traditional Chumash religion and ceremonialism. The people worshiped a deity, the nature of which is unclear, called *sup, achup,* or *chupu.* Shamans cured disease using chants, herbs, and a tube with which to suck out bad spirits. Their power derived from a guardian angel that appeared to them in a vision. Charmstones were a key part of shamans' work. The Chumash used toloache, a powerful hallucinogen, for ceremonial purposes.

Government The Chumash were organized by village rather than by tribe. Villages were led by chiefs; their limited authority was based on heredity and wealth. Coast villages maintained patrilineal descent groups. Each contained three or four captains, one of whom was head chief. Women could inherit the position of head chief. A chief's formal power was limited to leading in war, presiding at ceremonies, and granting hunting permissions.

Customs After a mourning ceremony, the dead were buried face down (face up on the islands), head to the west, and in a flexed position. Graves were

marked with rows of wood or stone. Some babies may have been killed at birth. Also, babies' noses were flattened after birth. At the onset of puberty, girls were subject to dietary restrictions, and boys were given a strong liquor to induce visions. Brides were purchased with gifts. Adultery was taboo, and only a few highly placed men could have more than one wife.

Many people smoked tobacco. Coastal people were generally gentle and slow to anger. Punishment was rare. Transvestitism was common and even esteemed. On the coast, people had more time for games, singing, and dancing

Dwellings The Chumash lived in rancheria-style villages. Their houses, some of which were as large as 50 feet in diameter, were domed. They were built on poles bent inward and covered with grass. A hole in the roof let light in and smoke out. Houses in the interior were generally smaller. Reed mats covered frame beds. Reeds were also used for floor coverings, partitions, and mattresses. Other structures included storehouses, sweat houses, and ceremonial ramadas.

Diet Live oak acorns were a staple, although fish, shellfish, and marine mammals were more important for coastal and island Chumash. The people also hunted game such as mule deer, coyote, and fox and gathered pine nuts, cherries, and a variety of roots, bulbs, seeds, and berries.

Key Technology The Chumash hunted with bow (sinew-backed) and arrow, snares, and deadfalls. They fished with seines, dip nets, and hook and line, killing larger fish and sea mammals with harpoons. They carved wood plates, bowls, and boxes; they wove water baskets and sealed them from the inside with asphaltum. Coastal residents fashioned stools of whale vertebrae.

Other cooking items and tools were made of stone, especially steatite. Musical instruments included elder wood or bone flutes, whistles, and rattles. The Chumash had no drums. For water transportation they used a *tomol,* or planked canoe (see "Transportation"). Abalone and shell were used for inlay work. In general, material culture was less developed away from the coast.

Trade Trade was active with nearby tribes. The mainland Chumash provided steatite, asphaltum, fish, wooden vessels, beads, and shells, in exchange for black pigment, antelope and elk skins, piñon nuts, obsidian, salt, beads, seeds, and herbs.

Notable Arts Fine arts included baskets, sea animals carved in wood and soapstone, and, from roughly 1000 to 1800, ceremonial rock paintings. The latter were generally abstract but also contained highly stylized life forms. The circle was a basic theme. Rock paintings were especially well developed in mountainous regions, although the arts were generally less well developed away from the coast.

Transportation The Chumash are the only native North Americans who built boats out of planks. They split cedar logs with antler or whalebone wedges and smoothed the lumber with shell and stone tools. Planks were lashed together with sinew or plant fibers and then caulked with asphaltum. The resulting boats had 12- to 30-foot double-bowed hulls and were moved with double-bladed paddles. They carried a crew of four and were quite oceanworthy; they traveled at least as far as San Nicholas Island, 65 miles offshore.

Dress Most Chumash men wore few or no clothes. Women wore knee-length buckskin skirts ornamented with snail and abalone shell. All wore additional buckskin clothing, blankets, or robes against the cold weather. Men and women tied their long hair with strings interwoven with the hair. They pierced their noses and ears, painted their bodies, and wore shell, bone, and stone necklaces.

War and Weapons Reasons for war included trespass, breach of etiquette, avenging witchcraft, or defense (interior Indian peoples occasionally attacked the Coastal Chumash). Rules of engagement were highly formalized. In general, however, the Chumash seldom engaged in actual warfare. The 1824 revolt against the Mexicans stands out as the major historical conflict.

Contemporary Information

Government/Reservations The only formal Chumash reservation is the 127-acre Santa Ynez

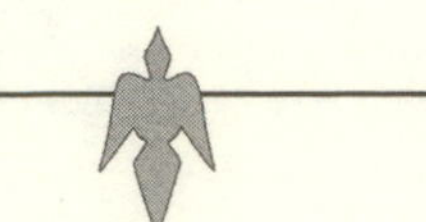

Reservation (1901; Santa Barbara County). It is governed by a five-member business council (1968 articles of incorporation).

Economy There is a campground and a bingo parlor at Santa Ynez.

Legal Status The Santa Ynez Band of Chumash Mission Indians is a federally recognized tribal entity. The Coastal Band of Chumash Indians had petitioned for federal recognition as of 1997.

Daily Life The last native speaker of a Chumash language died in 1965. Santa Ynez features a tribal hall and a clinic. Although little knowledge remains of their traditional culture, the people perform dances, songs, and storytelling and make crafts for the tourist trade as well as local cultural organizations.

Costanoan

Costanoan (Cos tä `nō än) is Spanish for "coast people." The term denotes a language family as opposed to a unified political entity such as a tribe. Costanoans are sometimes referred to as *Ohlone,* the name of one tribelet.

Location The Costanoans traditionally lived around and south of San Francisco and Monterey Bays and east to near the central valleys. Today many live in the same area and in Indian Canyon in San Benito County.

Population The Costanoan population was roughly 10,000 in the mid–eighteenth century and about 200 in the late 1970s. There were probably thousands of Costanoan descendants in the mid-1990s.

Language Costanoan, a group of about eight languages, belongs to the Penutian language family.

Historical Information

History Costanoan ancestors reached the Bay areas in roughly 500. They first encountered non-natives in the Sebastián Vizcaíno exploring expeditions of 1602. By the late eighteenth century, the Spanish had built seven missions in their territory and forced most Costanoans to join them.

In an effort to stem and reverse their cultural and physical extinction, the Costanoans in the late eighteenth century organized several incidents of armed resistance. Between 1770 and 1832, the Costanoan population fell by more than 80 percent as a result of disease, hardship, and general abuse. Their aboriginal existence disappeared during this time, as their culture and traditional practices were repressed and they mingled and mixed with other Indian peoples, including Esselen, Miwok, and Yokuts, also brought by force to the missions.

After 1835, when Mexico secularized the missions, many Costanoans worked on ranches or tried to return to a hunting and gathering existence. Most, however, had become mixed with non-natives and other Indians, establishing multiethnic Indian communities in the area. Costanoans were considered ethnologically extinct by the early twentieth century.

However, land claims cases in the 1920s and the 1960s resulted in small monetary payments and, as well, the recognition of Costanoan/Ohlone survival. Also in the 1960s, Costanoan descendants of Mission San José prevented the destruction of a burial ground that lay in the proposed path of a freeway. These people later organized as the Ohlone Indian tribe and now hold title to a cemetery in Fremont, California. A similar situation occurred in 1975, resulting in the establishment of the Pajaro Valley Ohlone Indian Council. In 1911 and again in 1988, individuals received trust allotments that became the Costanoan refuge of Indian Canyon.

Religion The sun was just one of many Costanoan deities that received offerings such as tobacco smoke as well as seeds, tobacco, shell beads, and feathers. Shamans interpreted their dreams in religious terms, which were often used as a guide for future actions. Shamans also controlled weather and cured disease by sucking out offending disease objects and through the use of herbs. They could also bestow luck in economic pursuits. Much of their power depended on the performance of dances and ceremonies, including the Medicine Man's Dance, Devil's Dance, Coyote Dance, Dove Dance, and Puberty Dance.

Government Roughly 50 tribelets, each headed by a chief and a council of elders, spoke Costanoan

languages. Each tribelet averaged about 200 people. The larger ones, of up to 500 people, had more than one permanent village.

Although men were usually chiefs, women occasionally held the office in the absence of male heirs. The position of chief was hereditary but subject to village approval. Responsibilities included directing ceremonial, economic, and war activities; feeding visitors; providing for the poor; caring for captured grizzly bears and coyotes; and leading the council of elders. All power was advisory except in time of war. An official speaker also had ceremonial and diplomatic duties.

Customs Costanoans maintained a clan structure as well as a division into two main groups, Deer and Bear. Small gifts given from groom to bride constituted the marriage formalities. The new couple lived in the groom's father's house. Men might have more than one wife. The dead and their possessions were either buried or cremated; their souls were said to journey across the sea. Widows cut or singed their hair, covered their heads with ashes or asphalt, and battered themselves, sometimes seriously.

Music often accompanied religious and mythological ritual. Both sexes underwent puberty rituals: Girls were confined to their houses and observed food taboos; boys used datura to seek visions. People played games such as ball race, shinny, hoop-and-pole, dice, and the hand game and often bet on the results.

Dwellings Most houses were conical in shape and built of tule, grass, or ferns around pole frames. Some Costanoan people substituted redwood slabs or bark. Sweat houses, used by men and women, were dug into the side of a stream. Large houses or brush enclosures served as dance sites.

Diet Costanoans hunted deer using deer-head disguises. They also hunted elk, antelope, bear, mountain lion, waterfowl, small mammals, and reptiles. They caught fish, especially salmon, steelhead, sturgeon, and lamprey in nets and traps. Fish were also speared by the light of a bonfire. Gathered foods included acorns, seeds, berries, nuts, insects, grapes, roots, greens, and honey. The people also ate shellfish as well as beached whales and sea lions.

Costanoans also practiced land management by controlled burning. This activity promoted the growth of seed-bearing plants, consumed dead plant material (a fire hazard), increased the grazing area for game, and facilitated acorn gathering.

Key Technology Technological innovations included the use of tule balsa canoes; twined baskets; musical instruments, including bird-bone whistles, alder flutes, rattles, and a musical bow; earth ovens (for roasting meat, especially sea lion and whale); a variety of nets for catching rabbits, fish, and fowl; and cagelike traps to capture quail. Milkweed, hemp, or nettle fiber was used for cordage. Bedding was of tule mats and animal skins.

Trade Significant trading partners included Plains Miwok, Sierra Miwok, and Yokuts Indians. Costanoans supplied mussels, abalone shells, dried abalone, salt, and olivella shells and imported piñon nuts and possibly clamshell beads.

Notable Arts Arts included music, usually connected with ritual or myth (instruments included whistles, rattles, and flutes) as well as dances and basket making.

Transportation Tule balsa canoes were used for fishing and duck hunting.

Dress Men often wore no clothes; women wore tule or buckskin aprons. Rabbit-skin, deerskin, duck feather, or otter-skin robes were worn in cold weather. Some men wore beards but most plucked facial hair with wooden tweezers or a pair of mussel shells or singed it with a hot coal. Both sexes painted and tattooed their bodies. Ornaments were worn in pierced ears and around the neck.

War and Weapons War was not uncommon among the different tribelets and between the Costanoan and the Esselen, Salinan, and Northern Valley Yokuts. Trespass often provoked hostilities, which began either by prearrangement or by surprise attack. Captives, except young women, were usually killed, their heads displayed on a pike in the village. Raiding parties burned enemy villages. The main weapon was the bow and arrow.

Contemporary Information

Government/Reservations The (corporate) Ohlone Indian Tribe holds title to a cemetery in Fremont, California. In 1988, a Mutsun descendant acquired land (Indian Canyon) by allotment.

Economy There is complete integration into the mainstream economy.

Legal Status The Amah Band of Ohlone/Costanoan Indians, the Costanoan Band of Carmel Mission Indians, the Indian Canyon Band of Costanoan/Mutsun Indians and the Ohlone/Costanoan/Muwekma Tribe are all recognized by the state of California. As of 1997, they had not yet attained federal recognition.

In 1971, descendants of the Costanoans formed the Ohlone Indian Tribe, which is still unrecognized. The Pajaro Valley Ohlone Indian Council was formed in the mid-1970s.

Daily Life All Costanoan languages are virtually extinct, although some people are trying to revive Mutsun. Some Costanoans engage in Indian-related activities such as crafts and the recognition struggles of tribes and local sacred sites. *Noso-n* (Mutsun for "in breath as it is in spirit") is a newsletter for the contemporary community of Costanoans and neighboring peoples. In 1989, Stanford University agreed to return all of its Native American skeletal remains to local Ohlone/Costanoan people for reburial. Costanoan descendants established the Carmel Valley Indian Center to promote cultural programs and exhibits about local Indians.

Cupeño

Cupeño (Kū `pā n yō) is Spanish for "a person who comes from *Kúpa.*"

Location The Cupeño traditionally lived in a mountainous area at the headwaters of the San Luis Rey River and the San Jose de Valle Valley. Today most Cupeños live on Pala Reservation in San Diego County.

Population Fewer than 750 Cupeños lived in their region in the mid–eighteenth century. In 1990, 563 Indians lived on the Pala Reservation, some of whom were Cupeño.

Language Cupeño belongs to the Cupan subgroup of the Takic family of Uto-Aztecan languages.

Historical Information

History Specific Cupeño customs and identity were derived from neighboring Cahuilla, Luiseño, Ipai, and other groups in a process that began at least 800 years ago. Non-natives entered the area in 1795. In the early nineteenth century, the Spanish took over Cupeño lands, building a chapel, a health spa, and a meeting place and grazing their cattle. During this period, Indians worked as virtual serfs for Spanish masters.

Juan Antonio Garra, a clan leader, attempted but failed around 1850 to organize a general revolt of all southern California Indians meant to drive out or kill all non-natives. He was captured by Cahuilla Indians and later shot by a paramilitary court. His village, Kúpa, was also burned. Between 1875 and 1877, the U.S. government created thirteen separate reservations for former "Mission Indians." Around the turn of the century, despite widespread local and even national protest, the California Supreme Court ordered all 250 or so Cupeños to move from their homes at Warner's Hot Springs to the Pala Reservation (Luiseño), awarding title to the former land to a man who was once governor of California. An influential group of non-natives pressured the government in 1903 to purchase a 3,438-acre ranch for the Cupeño at Pala Valley, now known as New Pala. By 1973 fewer than 150 people claimed Cupeño descent.

Religion Death ceremonies were perhaps the Cupeños' most important. Corpses were burned almost immediately, possessions were burned several weeks or months later, and images of the dead were burned every year or two as part of an eight-day festival. Also, an annual eagle-killing ritual was held in honor of the dead.

Around the turn of the century, despite widespread local and even national protest, the California Supreme Court ordered all roughly 250 Cupeños to move from their homes at Warner's Hot Springs to the Pala Reservation (Luiseño). Here, the small Cupeño tribe of southern California is shown en route to the Pala Reservation in 1903.

Government Kúpa and Wilákalpa were the two permanent villages prior to 1902. Each was politically independent. Decisions concerning the entire village were taken by consensus of the clan leaders.

Customs Cupeños recognized two divisions, Coyote and Wildcat, and within them a number of patrilineal clans. Each clan owned productive food-gathering sites. Each had a leader, usually hereditary in the male line, as well as an assistant leader.

Sometimes leaders were also shamans. Shamans were powerful, feared, and respected. They cured, witched, and divined through supernatural powers acquired in trances and dreams. Parents arranged most marriages, with the boy's parents taking the lead in mate selection, gift-giving, and feasting. Girls around age 10 underwent a puberty ceremony. The male initiation ceremony occurred between 10 and 18 years of age and probably involved the use of toloache.

Dwellings Family houses were conical in shape, built partly underground, and covered with reeds, brush, or bark. Earth sweat houses were also semisubterranean. People used ramadas for ceremonies and domestic chores. Other structures included acorn granaries, mens' sweat houses, and ceremonial lodges.

Diet Acorns, small seeds, berries, cactus fruit, deer, quail, rabbits, and other small mammals constituted the basic Cupeño diet.

Key Technology The Cupeño used a variety of natural materials for their technological needs, including willow or mesquite wood (bows and arrows), grasses (cooking, storage, and carrying

baskets), stone (mortars, pestles, manos and metates, arrow straighteners), wood (mortars), clay (pottery for cooking, storage, eating, and pipes), pine pitch (to seal storage bins for food preservation), and mescal (fibers for rope). Other technological innovations included hunting and carrying nets, snares and traps, baking ovens or pits, and musical instruments such as elder flutes, whistles, panpipes, and rattles.

Trade The Cupeño were part of an elaborate southern California network that dealt in economic and ritual items and activities. The Cocopah-Maricopa Trail, a major trade route, as well as the Santa Fe and the Yuman Trails passed close by. The people traded food products, furs, hides, obsidian, and salt for shell beads, minerals such as turquoise and tourmaline, Joshua tree blossoms, axes, and other crafts. Rituals and songs were also exchanged.

Notable Arts Rock paintings were used in the girls' puberty ceremony. Fine arts also included pottery, coiled baskets, and sandpaintings.

Transportation Baskets were used to transport goods.

Dress Women wore basket hats as well as skirts of mescal bark, tule, or skins. Men donned breechclouts of the same material when they wore anything at all. Both wore sandals of mescal fibers soaked in mud and tied with mescal fibers or buckskin. Babies wore mesquite-bark diapers. Blankets or woven rabbit-skin robes were used for warmth.

War and Weapons Cupeño groups generally feuded over women, trespass, and sorcery. Murder also required retribution. Tactics included ambush or simply chasing away an enemy. Weapons included the bow and arrow (possibly with a poisoned tip), poniard, thrusting sticks, and war club. Forced to resist the missions and Mexican imperialism, the people became more aggressive during the early nineteenth century.

Contemporary Information

Government/Reservations An elected tribal council governs the Cupeño at Pala Reservation (New Pala, which is divided from Old Pala [Luiseño] by the San Luis Rey River). Many Cupeños also live on the Morongo and the Los Coyotes Reservations (Cahuilla) and are intermarried with those people.

Economy There is income from agricultural land and mineral resources, especially sand and gravel.

Legal Status The Cupeño are a federally recognized tribal entity.

Daily Life The Cupa Cultural Center was dedicated in 1974. Some people still speak the language (there are language instruction programs) and practice several traditions, including some games, funeral rituals, social songs (such as birdsongs), and dances. The people still live in a traditional central village. Major political issues include economic development, sovereignty, health, housing, water availability, protection of sacred sites, gaming, and toxic waste pollution.

Diegueño

See Tipai-Ipai

Hupa

Hupa (ˋHū pä), from the Yurok name for the Hoopa Valley. Their self-designation was *Natinook-wa,* "People of the Place Where the Trails Return." The Hupa were culturally and linguistically related to three neighboring groups, the Chilula, Whilkut, and the North Fork Hupa, who lived mainly to their east.

Location The Hupa lived traditionally along the lower Trinity River, a main tributary of the Klamath, and especially in the Hoopa Valley. The Hoopa Valley Reservation is in this region today.

Population Roughly 1,000 Hupa Indians lived in and near the Hoopa Valley in the early nineteenth century. In 1990, 1,732 Indians lived on the reservation out of a total enrollment of roughly 2,140 Indians.

Language Hupa is an Athapaskan language.

Historical Information

History Little is known about Hupa prehistory, although they are culturally related to the Yurok and the Karuk to the north. They arrived in northern California in roughly 1000. Being fairly isolated, they had little contact with non-natives until the mid–nineteenth century. There were few Spanish or Russian inroads or even American trappers. Even in 1849, the Hupa saw some miners but avoided the wholesale displacement experienced by other natives.

After the 1849 gold rush, settlers flooded the region, but the Hupas held their ground. The construction of a fort in 1858 resulted primarily in some liaisons between soldiers and Hupa women. The government created the Hoopa Valley Reservation in 1864. Because of the relative lack of cataclysmic disruption and the location of a reservation in their traditional homeland, the Hupa were generally able to adjust slowly but steadily to their new situation. The period following World War II brought good jobs as lumberjacks and mill workers as well as the end of the traditional subsistence economy. In the 1970s and 1980s, the United States took control of tribal funds and resources for use at the government's discretion.

Religion The Hupa celebrated annual World Renewal ceremonies, for which shamans performed secret rites and dances such as the White Deerskin Dance and the Jumping Dance. This ceremony was held in specific locations for ten days in late summer

The Hupa celebrated annual World Renewal ceremonies, for which shamans performed secret rites and performed dances such as the White Deerskin Dance and the Jumping Dance. These men are participating in the White Deerskin Dance in the 1890s.

or fall. It included a long narrative about Hupa history and the actions of the supernaturals. Wealthy families provided ceremonial regalia. The people also held other ceremonies for seasonal activities, such as the beginning of the salmon run. Two ceremonial divisions, northern and southern, came together in the ancient village of Takimildin, located in the heart of the Hoopa Valley.

Curing shamans, whose methods included sucking out illness-causing objects, were almost always women. They charged high fees, which were payable in advance but refundable if the cure failed. People also used family-owned medicines for more minor ailments. Hupas also believed that male sorcerers could find many ways in which to harm a person. They recognized many spirits and supernatural beings but gave them little ritual attention. They did observe numerous daily rituals and taboos and recognized the obligation to maintain a healthy mindset.

Government The Hupa recognized no formal political leadership. Instead, people were ranked according to their wealth. The family was a basic unit, but several patrilineally related households formed a larger grouping or a village. The 10 to 15 Hupa villages acted together informally and only for activities like holding religious ceremonies or building communal fish weirs.

Customs According to Hupa tradition, all customs were formed in an earlier, mythological period of the peoples' existence. One notable custom concerned social status, which was defined by inheritable material possessions such as albino deerskins, large obsidian blades, and headdresses decorated with redheaded-woodpecker scalps. Money, such as shell currency, was slightly different from material wealth and could be used to pay for items such as a dowry, a shaman's fee, or an indemnity to an injured party. Wealth could theoretically be obtained through hard work, but in practice property was difficult to accumulate and there was little movement through class lines. The legal code stated that every wrong had to be compensated for, usually with money but occasionally with blood. Family and individual wealth and power affected the terms of redress.

When a Hupa died, his or her body was wrapped in deerskin and buried. Clothing and utensils were placed on top of a plank-lined grave marked with a board. Close relatives cut their hair as a sign of mourning. After five days, souls departed for a dank, dark underworld (the souls of shamans and singers were fortunate to inhabit a pleasant heaven in the sky).

Hupas observed a number of life-cycle prohibitions and taboos as well as magic and religious observances. Babies remained in the cradle until they walked and were not formally named at least until age five. Children knew only mild discipline. At age eight or so a boy joined his father in the sweat lodge. Pubescent girls were considered unclean and remained secluded, although girls from wealthier families might have a party to mark the occasion. Girls married at 15 or 16; boys slightly later. A feast and an exchange of gifts marked the occasion. Only rich men could afford more than one wife. Sex was generally avoided for a number of reasons, except during the late summer and fall family camping trips. In case of divorce, which was fairly easy to obtain, the bride price was returned if the couple was childless.

Most men and women worked hard and steadily, although time was set aside for diversions. Men played the hand game; women bet on the mussel-shell toss. Other diversions included athletic contests, storytelling, and smoking at bedtime for men. The voice was the most important musical instrument, followed by wooden clappers, bone whistles, and hoof rattles.

Dwellings For most of the year, Hupas lived in cedar-planked single-family houses built around a square hole. A stone-lined fire pit sat in the center of the house. Smoke escaped through a hole in the three-pitched roof. Earthen shelves next to the walls served as storage areas. Women and children slept in the family house; men slept in semisubterranean sweat houses, which they also used as clubhouses and workshops. People lived in roofless brush shelters during the autumn acorn-gathering expeditions.

Diet Acorns and fish, especially salmon, were the staples. Women harvested and prepared the former, cooking it into mush or bread. Deer and elk were captured by stalking or driving them into a river and then pursuing them by canoe. Small game was also taken. Other fish included trout, sturgeon, and eel.

Fish was sliced thin and smoke dried for storage or broiled fresh. People also gathered a number of food plants, including berries, nuts, seeds, roots, and greens. They did not eat many birds, reptiles, amphibians (except turtles), insects, and larvae. Hupas rarely lacked for an adequate food supply.

Key Technology Women made baskets for a number of uses. Men made wooden bowls and other items as well as tools of stone and bone. Hupas fished using dip nets, gill nets, and dragnets; weirs; bone-pointed harpoon; and hook and line. Hunters used a sinew-lined bow with stone-tipped arrows. They also used iris-fiber nooses.

Trade Hupas traded acorns and food with the Coastal Yurok for canoes, dried seaweed (for salt), and ocean fish. They also traded occasionally with other groups. Products were either bartered for or purchased with shell money.

Notable Arts Fine arts included baskets (women) and horn work (men), particularly elkhorn items such as spoons for men (women used mussel-shell spoons). People made highly abstract petroglyphs from roughly 1600 on.

Transportation Hupas traveled the rivers using redwood dugout canoes and paddles.

Dress Men wore buckskin breechclouts or nothing at all. Women wore a two-piece buckskin skirt. They also had three vertical striped tattoos on their chins. Basketry caps protected their heads against burden basket tumplines. Hide robes were used for warmth. People on long journeys wore buckskin moccasins and leggings. Both sexes wore long hair and ornaments in pierced ears.

War and Weapons The Hupa never fought together as a tribe. Even villages rarely united for war, which was generally a matter for individuals or families. Hupas kept their conflicts short, few and far between, with few casualties, except for a particularly harsh war with the Yokuts in the 1830s. Favored tactics included ambushes and surprise raids. Weapons included the bow and arrow, spears, stone knives, and rocks. Wooden or hide "armor" was sometimes worn for protection.

Contemporary Information

Government/Reservations The 85,445-acre Hoopa Valley Reservation (1876; Humboldt County) is the largest and most populous Indian reservation in California. The Hupa share it with some Karuk, Chilula, Yurok, Whilkut, and other Indians. The Hoopa Valley Tribe adopted a constitution and by-laws in 1950. Some Hupas also live at Elk Valley Rancheria, Del Norte County.

Economy The reservation is generally self-sufficient. Timber, farming, and livestock constitute the main economic activities.

Legal Status The Hoopa Valley Tribe is a federally recognized tribal entity.

Daily Life Hupas maintain a strong tribal identity and sense of continuity with the past, thanks in part to a continued presence in their homeland. They still practice many traditional customs, such as hunting, fishing, acorn gathering, basket and bead making, and the two World Renewal dances. The language is still spoken, particularly by older people. Children attend public school. The people seek complete political and economic control of their own affairs.

Jamul Indians

See Tipai-Ipai

Juaneño

See Luiseño

Kamia

See Tipai-Ipai

Karuk

Karuk (`Kä ruk) means "upstream," as opposed to the word for their neighbors, Yurok, which means "downstream."

Location In the mid–nineteenth century, the Karuk lived on the middle course of the Klamath River in three main clusters of villages. Today, most Karuk live in Siskyou County, California, and in southern Oregon.

Population Karuk population in the eighteenth century is estimated to have been around 1,500. In 1990, tribal membership was pegged at 2,900, a number that included 33 Indians living on Karuk trust lands in Siskyou County, California, as well as the Karuk population of the Quartz Valley Reservation and those living in the region.

Language Karuk is a Hokan language.

Historical Information

History Contact with outsiders was largely avoided until 1850 and the great gold rush. At that time miners, vigilantes, soldiers, and assorted Anglos seized Karuk lands, burned their villages, and massacred their people. Hitherto unknown diseases also decimated their population. Many Karuk were removed to the Hoopa Valley Reservation.

Without a reservation of their own, many survivors drifted away from their traditional lands in search of work. Children were forcibly removed from their families and sent to culture-killing boarding schools. Some people did remain at home, however, and continued to live a lifestyle that included traditional subsistence and religious activities. Ceremonialism fell off after World War II but was reinvigorated beginning in the 1970s.

Religion The acorn harvest and the salmon run provided occasions for ceremony and celebration. Specific events included the World Renewal dances: the Jumping Dance, held in spring (associated with the salmon run), and the Deerskin Dances, held in fall (associated with the acorn harvest and the second salmon run). Both featured priestly rituals, displays of wealth, dancing, and singing.

Government No political organization or formal leadership existed within the three main clusters of villages, although wealthy men enjoyed a greater degree of influence. The Karuk regulated their community through shared values.

Customs Culturally, the Karuk were very similar to the neighboring Yurok and Hupa. In fact, they enjoyed especially close marriage and ceremonial ties with the Yurok. Their main values were industry, thrift, and the acquisition, mostly by hunting and gambling, of property such as dentalium shells, red woodpecker scalps, and large obsidian blades. These forms of wealth were important in and of themselves, not just for their purchasing power.

Woman doctors cured by sucking out the cause of a disease with the help of a "pain," an object, recoverable at will, that she kept within her body. Other kinds of doctors of both sexes cured by using medicinal plants. Corpses were buried in a family plot, along with shell money and valuables. Clothing and tools were hung on a fence around the grave. After five days, the soul was said to ascend to a place in the sky (the relative happiness of the afterlife was said to depend on the level of a person's wealth). A dead person's name remained taboo until or unless given to a child.

Crimes were recognized against individuals only (not against society). As such they could be atoned for by making material restitution. Refusal to pay could lead to death. The Karuk considered sex to be an enemy of wealth and did not often engage in it except during the fall gathering expeditions. Sex and children outside of marriage were acceptable in this scheme: "Legitimacy," like almost everything else, had a price. Marriage was basically a financial transaction, as was divorce. A couple lived with the man's parents.

The Karuk observed many daily magical practices and taboos. They also underwent extensive ritual preparations for the hunt, including sweating, bathing, scarification, bleeding, smoking their weapons with herbs, fasting, and sexual continence. Games included gambling with a marked stick, shinny, cat's cradle, archery, darts, and the women's dice game.

Dwellings Dwelling structures (family houses and sweat houses) were made of planks, preferably cedar. Family houses were rectangular and semisubterranean, with an outside stone-paved porch and a stone-lined

firepit inside. Doors were small and low. Males from about three years of age slept, sweat, gambled, and passed the time in sweat houses, which women, except for shaman initiates, could not enter.

Diet The Karuk diet consisted mostly of salmon, deer (caught in snares or by hunters wearing deer head masks), and acorns (as soup, mush, and bread). The people also hunted bear, elk, and small game. Meat and fish were usually roasted, although salmon and venison could be dried and stored. The only cultivated crop was tobacco. The following were never eaten: dog, coyote, wolf, fox, wildcat, gopher, mole, bat, eagle, hawk, vulture, crow, raven, owl, meadowlark, blue jay, snake, lizard, frog, caterpillar, and grasshopper.

Key Technology To catch fish, Karuks stood on fishing platforms holding large dip nets (the platforms were privately owned but could be rented). They also used harpoons and gaffs. They cut planks with stone mauls and horn wedges. Wooden implements included seats, storage boxes, spoons (for men; women used mussel-shell spoons), and hand drills for making fire. Women wove vegetable fiber baskets, containers, cradles, and caps. Bows were made of yew wood, with sinew backings and strings. Meat and bulbs were roasted in an oven of hot stones.

Trade The Coastal Yurok supplied seaweed (for salt) to nearby tribes.

Notable Arts Fine arts included woodwork, storytelling (myths, with songs), and highly abstract petroglyphs, made after approximately 1600.

Transportation Karuks purchased Yurok boats made from hollowed-out redwood logs.

Dress Hides, usually from deer, and furs were the basic clothing materials. Women wore hides with the hair on to cover their upper bodies, and they wore a double apron of fringed buckskin. They also had three vertical lines tattooed on their chins. Men wore a buckskin breechclout or nothing at all. Both sexes wore buckskin moccasins with elkhide soles and perhaps leggings for rough traveling. Both sexes also wore basketry caps and ear and nose ornaments. They decorated their ceremonial clothing with fringe, shells, and pine nuts. Snowshoes were of hazelwood with iris-cord netting and buckskin ties.

War and Weapons There was no war in a real sense, only retaliatory activity that might involve fellow villagers. Casualties were invariably light, and young women who may have been captured were usually returned at settlement time, when every injured party received full compensation. Weapons included yew bows, obsidian-tipped arrows, and elk hide or rod armor vests.

Contemporary Information

Government/Reservations The Karuk Tribe of California elects a nine-member tribal council. They adopted a constitution in 1985. Committees oversee the various programs. As of 1995, there was a land base of 300 acres.

The Quartz Valley Reservation, Siskiyou County, has a land base of 300 acres. The 1992 population was roughly 124.

Economy The tribe itself employed about 80 people in 1995. It operates three health clinics and owns a hardware store. Tribal members also work for the U.S. Forest Service. The Karuk Community Development Corporation maintains formal development plans.

Legal Status The Karuk Tribe of California has been a federally recognized tribal entity since 1979. The Quartz Valley Rancheria of Karok, Shasta, and Upper Klamath Indians is a federally recognized tribal entity.

Daily Life Although hundreds and perhaps thousands of people claim Karuk ancestry, few Karuks remain who have been in direct contact with their elders and traditions. Still, since the 1970s Karuks have revived aspects of their traditional culture, including their language and the World Renewal ceremony (Pikyavish), held in late summer and early fall. The traditional fine art of basket weaving has also been rediscovered.

Medicine men and women usually receive their authority from an elder. Many people live in extended families. Most children attend public schools, and the

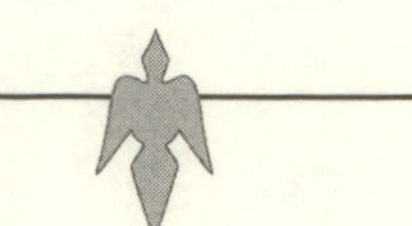

tribe provides some scholarship money for those who attend college. Several villages have been inhabited since precontact times. There is a pending land claim against the United States. Important contemporary issues include health care, water rights, proper natural resource management, and land acquisition.

Konkow

See Maidu

Konomihu

See Shasta

Lassik

See Wailaki

Luiseño

Luiseño (Lū i `sā nyō) is a name derived from the Mission San Luis Rey. Luiseño Indians associated with a nearby mission, San Juan Capistrano, were often referred to as Juaneño Indians. Both of these peoples are included among the groups of so-called Mission Indians.

Location The traditional (eighteenth-century) location of the Luiseño was a region of great environmental diversity, along the coast and inland along streams, south of present-day Los Angeles but north of the Tipai-Ipai. Today most Luiseño live on reservations in San Diego and Riverside Counties.

Population Roughly 10,000 in the late eighteenth century, the 1990 Luiseño population on their reservations stood at 1,795.

Language Luiseño and Juaneño belong to the Cupan group of the Takic division of the Uto-Aztecan language family.

Historical Information

History The Luiseño constituted a distinct culture from at least 1400 or so. They first encountered non-natives in 1796, with the Gaspar de Portolá expedition and the founding of Mission San Diego. Shortly thereafter, the Spanish built Missions San Luis Rey and San Juan Capistrano. Many Luiseños were missionized, and many died during this and succeeding Mexican and U.S. periods of hardship, disease, and murder.

After Mexican secularization of the missions in 1834, many Indians revolted against their continued exploitation by Mexican rancheros. In general, Luiseño villages maintained their traditional subsistence activities, with the addition of wheat and corn agriculture, irrigation, orchards, and animal husbandry. The United States created several Luiseño reservations in 1875; people either lived there or scattered. The 1891 Act for the Relief of Mission Indians led to the placement of federal administrative personnel on the reservations, including police, schools, and courts. The idea was to undermine the traditional power structure and move the people toward assimilation into mainstream U.S. culture.

Throughout the nineteenth and into the twentieth century, Luiseños fought to retain their land and their traditions. For instance, their resistance to government schools culminated in 1895 when a Luiseño burned the school and assassinated the teacher at Pachanga. Luiseños rejected the Indian Reorganization Act (IRA) of 1934 because it provided for too little home rule. They were finally forced to abandon once-prosperous farms and orchards after precious water supplies were taken by non-Indians living upstream.

Still, federal control of the reservations increased, as did pressure to assimilate. The 1950s brought a partial termination of federal services, which stimulated a resurgence of local self-government and self-determination. This trend accelerated in the 1960s with the arrival of various federal economic programs. Today, Luiseños are prominent in state and regional Indian groups.

Religion Ritual drama and sacred oral literature controlled their environment and confirmed Luiseños' place in the world. Ritual offices included chief, assistant chief, shamans, councilors, and members of the *Chinigchinich* society (most of the men in the village). A large number of ceremonies revolved around hunting, life-cycle, weather control, and war

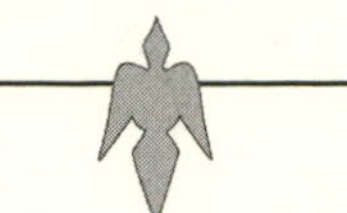

and peace. Some ceremonies involved questing for visions with the help of a drink prepared from jimsonweed (datura). Religious knowledge/power was carefully guarded.

Sandpaintings were part of the secret *Chinigchinich* cult initiation (the cult may have been in part a response to the Spanish presence): The cosmos, sacred beings, and human spiritual phases were all represented. Sandpaintings never lasted beyond the ceremony. Ritual equipment included stone grinding bowls, clay figurines, sacred wands, head scratchers, and eagle-feather headdresses. Most participants in rituals were paid.

Government The Luiseño were organized into roughly 50 patrilineal clan tribelets, each with an autonomous, semipermanent village led by a hereditary chief. Each village group also had its own food resource area; other resources (raw materials, sacred sites as well as food) could be owned individually or collectively. Trespass was by express permission only.

The chief supervised hunting, gathering, and war activities. He was aided by an assistant, shamans, and a council of advisers (all positions were hereditary). Band specialists managed natural resources using techniques such as controlled burning and water and erosion management. They also led various activities such as rabbit hunts and deer and antelope drives. In the eighteenth century, Spanish-style political offices (such as *generales* and *capitanes*) existed parallel to the traditional religious ones.

Customs In addition to food and other resource areas, private property might include capital and ritual equipment, eagle nests, and songs. Social status was important and defined by many criteria. Aside from hunting (male) and gathering (female), sexual divisions of labor were ill defined. Aged women taught children crafts, whereas older men were generally more active in ceremonial affairs, including making hunting and ceremonial paraphernalia, and in instructing initiates. Games included dice, the split stick gambling game, the ball and stick game, and cat's cradle.

The Luiseño observed various life-cycle taboos, restrictions, and ritual requirements. Puberty rituals stressed correct conduct, such as dances, ordeals, learning songs and rituals (boys), and rock painting and behavior in married life (girls). Girls married an arranged partner shortly after puberty. Divorce was possible but not easy to obtain. Death ceremonies proliferated. At different times, burning an image of the deceased, purification of the relatives, feasting and gift-giving were all practiced. A person's possessions were generally destroyed when she or he died.

Dwellings Family houses were conical in shape, built partly underground, and covered with reeds, brush, or bark. Earth sweat houses were also semisubterranean. People used ramadas for ceremonies and domestic chores.

Diet Six species of acorns served as a dietary staple. Inland groups traveled seasonally to fish along the coast; coastal groups gathered acorns inland. Luiseños also ate a wide variety of seeds, nuts, berries, bulbs, roots, mushrooms, cactus pods, and fruits. Seeds were parched, ground, and cooked into mush. Other foods included small game, deer (stalked or run down), antelope, fowl, fish, sea mammals, crustaceans, and mollusks. Teas as well as tobacco and datura were used medicinally and ceremonially. Most predators as well as reptiles were avoided. Many foods were cooked in clay jars over a fire; game was roasted in coals.

Key Technology Luiseños practiced controlled burning of certain areas to increase the yield of seed-bearing plants. They hunted with bow and arrow, throwing sticks, snares, and traps. Men used deer-antler flakes to help flake stone points. They built canoes for ocean fishing. Other fishing equipment included seines, basketry traps, dip nets, bone or shell hooks, possibly harpoons, and poison. Utilitarian items included pottery, coiled and twined baskets, carrying pouches of net or skin, stone grinding tools, cooking and eating utensils of wood and stone, and musical instruments, including bone and cane whistles, cane flutes, split-stick clappers, and turtle shell, gourd, or hoof rattles.

Trade The Luiseño imported steatite bowls (from Santa Catalina Island), obsidian (from northern or eastern neighbors), and other items.

Notable Arts Fine arts included pottery; coiled baskets, decorated with tan, red, or black geometric designs; sandpaintings; petroglyphs, perhaps associated with hunting, from about 500 B.C.E. to 1000; and pictographs, which featured straight and wavy lines, angles, and people. The pictographs were used in girls' puberty ceremonies after about 1400.

Transportation Dugout or balsa canoes were used for ocean fishing.

Dress Women wore cedar bark aprons. Men generally wore little or no clothing, although both sexes used deer, rabbit, or otter robes in colder weather. They also tattooed and painted their bodies and wore pendants of mica, bone, clay, abalone shell, and bear claws; human hair bracelets and anklets; and yucca-fiber and deerskin moccasins.

War and Weapons Trespass was a major cause for war. The Luiseño were also fairly imperialist, fighting (and marrying) to acquire territory. During war, the chief assumed commander duties along with an initiated warrior class. Weapons included the bow and arrow, small and large war clubs, lances, slings, and thrusting sticks.

Contemporary Information

Government/Reservations Luiseño reservations include Rincon (1875; 4,276 acres; 379 Indians in 1996; San Diego County), Pala (1875; 11,893 acres; San Diego County; shared with the Cupeño), Pauma and Yuima (1872; 5,877 acres; San Diego County), Soboba (1883; 5,916 acres; Riverside County), Pechanga (1882; 4,394 acres; Riverside County), La Jolla (1875; 8,541 acres; San Diego County), and Twentynine Palms (1895; 402 acres; San Bernardino County). The reservations feature elected chairs and councils, formal membership roles, and articles of association.

Economy A range of jobs may be found on or near the reservations. Many operate campgrounds, orchards, and stores. La Jolla has excellent recreation facilities that also bring in money. Pauma has hydroelectric resources. Planning for resource development is ongoing.

Legal Status The La Jolla Band, the Twentynine Palms Band, the Soboba Band, the Rincon Band, the Pechanga Band, the Pauma Band, and the Pala Band of Luiseño Mission Indians are federally recognized tribal entities. The Juaneño Band of Mission Indians had not attained federal recognition as of 1997.

Daily Life Many people still speak Luiseño, and language classes are popular among the young. Villiana Hyde has written a language text (1971). Traditional food, games, songs, and dances remain part of people's lives, as do many ideas regarding property and other cultural references. Luiseños are relatively highly educated. Although most Luiseños are Catholics, some traditional ceremonies, such as the initiation for cult members, the installation of religious chiefs, and funerals, are still performed.

Reservations feature libraries as well as senior and cultural programs. Water rights remain an ongoing issue despite the tribe's paper victory in a court case settled in 1985. In general, Luiseños have struck a balance between resisting government intrusion into their lives and becoming politically savvy enough to manipulate public and private organizations to their best benefit.

Maidu

Maidu (`Mī dū), a group of three languages (Maidu, Konkow, and Nisenan; see "Language") and in modern times a tribe of Indians. Maidu comes from their self-designation and means "person." Konkow comes from the Anglicization of their word for "meadowland." Nisenan comes from their self-designation and means "among us."

Location Traditional Maidu territory is along the eastern tributaries of the Sacramento River, south of Lassen Peak. This country features a great variation in terrain, from river and mountain valleys to high mountain meadows. Today, most Maidus live on two small reservations in Butte County and share one in Lassen County and one in Mendocino County.

Population Roughly 9,000 Maidus lived in the early nineteenth century. In 1990, two lived at Berry Creek and five at Enterprise Rancheria. Also in 1990, 154

Indians of mixed tribes, including Maidu, lived at Susanville, and 577 Maidu and other Indians lived at Covelo. The 1995 Maidu population is considered to be approximately 2,500.

Language Maiduan is a Penutian language. Its three divisions—northeastern or mountain (Maidu), northwestern or foothill (Konkow), and southern or valley (Nisenan)—were probably mutually unintelligible.

Historical Information

History Prior to about 1700, when they abandoned it to the Paiutes, Maidus also controlled territory east of Honey Lake into present-day Nevada. Maidus first met Spanish and U.S. expeditions and trappers in the early nineteenth century. Initial contact was peaceful.

The Maidu were relatively successful in avoiding missions, but many were killed in 1833 by a severe epidemic, possibly malaria. The 1849 gold rush led directly to theft of their land, disruption of their ability to acquire food, more disease, violence, and mass murder. Most survivors were forced into ranch and farm work and onto reservations. Although some groups signed a treaty in 1851, it was never ratified; each Maidu received a land claims settlement payment of about $660 in 1971.

The Konkow Reservation was established as Nome Lackee in 1854, but its residents were forced nine years later to abandon it and march to the Round Valley Reservation. The few surviving Nisenan lived near foothill towns and worked in local low-paying industries at that time. Many Maidu children attended assimilationist boarding schools around the turn of the century. Maidu culture underwent a brief revival in the 1870s under the influence of the Ghost Dance. All rancherias were purchased between 1906 and 1937 under legislation providing for "homeless" California Indians. Following the death in 1906 of the last hereditary headman, much of the people's ceremonial regalia was sold to a local museum.

Religion Maidu religion was closely related to their mythology. Konkows and Nisenans, but not the Maidu proper, practiced the Kuksu cult, a ceremonial and dance organization led by a powerful shaman. Only those properly initiated could join. Members followed a dance cycle in which dances represented different spirits.

Shamans trucked with the spirits, cured, interpreted dreams, and conducted ceremonies. Spirits were said to live in natural geographic sites. Shamans had at least one spirit as a guardian and source of power. Female shamans were assumed to be malevolent.

The Nisenan observed an annual fall mourning ceremony and other ritual dances as well. Doctors could be of either sex, although women were considered less likely to hurt a patient (doctors could also poison people). Religious specialists included religious shamans, poison shamans, singing shamans, and weather shamans.

Government Of the three main Maidu divisions, the valley people, or Nisenan, had the largest population and the most number of tribelets (permanent villages). Village communities (consisting of several villages, with size in inverse proportion to elevation) were autonomous. The central village had the largest dance or ceremonial chamber, which doubled as a home to the headman. This office, which was inheritable only among the Nisenan, was chosen by a shaman. He or she (women might become chiefs among Nisenan) was generally wealthy and served primarily as adviser and spokesperson.

Customs The Maidu observed many life-cycle taboos and restrictions. Gender roles were fairly rigidly defined. There was no formal marriage ceremony other than mutual gift-giving. Couples lived in the woman's home at first and later in a home of their own near the man's family. If a woman gave birth to twins, she and the babies were often killed. The Nisenan practiced cremation; the other two groups buried their dead with food and gifts. All three burned the house and possessions after death and held annual mourning ceremonies for several years thereafter.

Most fishing and hunting areas were held in common. Theft from a neighbor was severely punished, although theft from someone of another community was not punished by the home community. Murder and rape were dealt with by blood revenge (of the guilty party or a near friend or

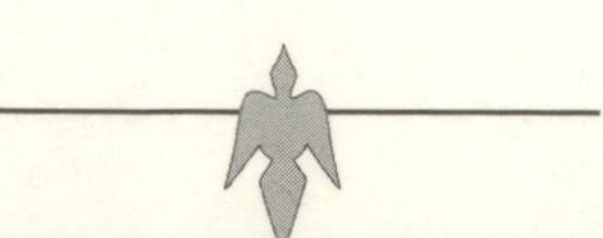

A Nisenan youth. Of the three main Maidu divisions, the valley people, or Nisenan, had the largest population and the greatest number of tribelets (permanent villages).

relative) or by payment. Lying was generally avoided. The community policed its boundaries against poachers.

Games include hoop-and-pole, tossing games, dice games, and hand games and often contained wagering, music, and song. Tobacco was their only cultivated plant. It was smoked in elderberry pipes at bedtime and during ceremonies.

Dwellings The Maidu settled in small village groups, with the headman, dance hall, and ceremonial chamber in the central village. Hill dwellings were pole-framed, brush- or skin-covered houses in winter and brush shelters in summer. Most mountain people remained in their villages during the winter. In winter, valley people lived in earth-covered, domed pit houses, with door and smoke openings in the roof. They used brush shelters in summer.

Diet Maidus were mainly hunters and gatherers. Their staple was the acorn, from which they made mush, bread, and soup. They also ate pine nuts, manzanita, roots, and insects. Game included deer (hunted in communal drives), elk, antelope, and bear (for hides). Meat was baked, dried, or roasted. Fish included eel, salmon, and trout. Taboo foods among the Maidu proper included coyote, dog, wolf, buzzard, lizard, snake, and frog. Konkows refused to eat bear and mountain lion. The Nisenan ate neither owl, condor, nor vulture. Maidus drank wild mint tea and manzanita cider.

Key Technology Nets, weirs, and spears served a fishing equipment. The people hunted with bow and arrow and stone (basalt and obsidian) spears and knives. Other tools (stone, grass, and wood) included scrapers, arrow straighteners, pestles, mortars, and pipes. They used a buckeye drill to start fires and tule mats for seats, beds, roofs, doors, skirts, rafts, and beds. Musical instruments included drums, rattles, flutes, whistles, and a bow.

Trade Little individual travel occurred between villages greater than 20 miles apart, but trade was widespread among nearby villages and groups. Goods also changed hands as a result of gambling games. The Konkow traded arrows, bows, deer hides, and foods for shell beads, pine nuts, and salmon. The Maidu proper traded bows and deer hides to enemy Achumawi for beads, obsidian, and green pigment. The Nisenan traded acorns, nuts, berries, wood, and skins for fish, roots, grasses, shells, beads, salt, and feathers. Goods could also be purchased with shell and baked magnesite cylinder beads.

Notable Arts Fine arts included baskets; necklaces; shell, bone, and feather earrings; and other bead and feather work. Petroglyphs, mostly circles and dots, with a few people or animals, were created perhaps as early as 1000 B.C.E.

Transportation Dugout and tule (rush) canoes were used for water transportation.

Dress Dress was minimal year-round. In summer, men wore nothing or a buckskin breechclout. Women wore apron skirts of buckskin, bark, or grass. Bear, deer (bird and fowl feather to the south), and mountain lion fur robes and blankets were added in cold weather. Only the northeastern group wore moccasins and snowshoes. Both sexes wore tattoos and shell, bone, feather, and wood ornaments.

War and Weapons Posting regular sentries against enemies was a common practice. Although all groups recognized foreign enemies, most warfare occurred between villages or village communities. Favored tactics included raiding and ambush. Arrows were often poisoned. Other weapons included spears, sticks, slings, and elk hide armor. The Konkow tortured captured males, whereas the Nisenan simply killed them. Women prisoners were generally kept in the household.

Contemporary Information

Government/Reservations Berry Creek (1916; 33 acres; Butte County) and Enterprise (1906; 40 acres; Butte County) are the two Maidu rancherias. Maidus also live on the Greenville Rancheria (Plumas and Tehama Counties), Shingle Springs Rancheria (El Dorado County), the Susanville Rancheria (1923; 150 acres), and the Round Valley Reservation (1864; 30,538 acres) with other tribes. Most rancherias are governed by elected tribal councils.

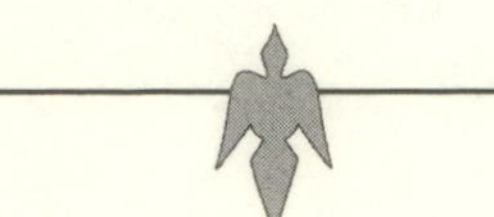

The Chico Rancheria (Mechoopda Maidu) is governed by an elected tribal government. There were about 70 residents of a population of 400 in the early 1990s.

Economy Unemployment among the Maidu community remains chronically high. Because of the small land base and limited resources, economic development remains extremely limited.

Legal Status The Berry Creek Rancheria of Maidu Indians; the Greenville Rancheria of Maidu Indians; the Enterprise Rancheria of Maidu Indians; the Mooretown Rancheria of Maidu Indians; the Shingle Springs Rancheria of Maidu Indians; the Susanville Indian Rancheria of Paiute, Maidu, Pit River, and Washoe Indians; and the Covelo Indian Community of the Round Valley Reservation are all federally recognized tribal entities. The Mechoopda Tribe of Maidu Indians was rerecognized in 1992.

The Maidu Nation and the North Maidu Tribe are currently unrecognized.

Daily Life Maidus have generally assimilated with other Indians and with the general population. A few Maidu still speak their language, make baskets, and hold ceremonies. Social problems abound: Education levels are low, whereas levels of crime, alcoholism, and suicide remain stubbornly high. Housing, sanitation, and health care is generally poor. Many Maidus suffer from diabetes. The Maidu hold an annual bear dance in Janesville, and efforts have increased to preserve the language and culture. Maidus are also active in pan-Indian activities.

Mattole

See Wailaki; Wiyot

Mission Indians

See Cahuilla; Luiseño; Serrano; Tipai-Ipai

Miwok

Miwok (`Mē wok) is a word meaning "People" in Miwokan.

Location The Miwok were originally composed of three divisions: Eastern (Sierra), Lake, and Coast. The Miwok lived in over 100 villages along the San Joaquin and Sacramento Rivers, from the area north of San Francisco Bay east into the western slope of the Sierra Nevada. The Lake Miwok lived near Clear Lake, north of San Francisco Bay.

Today the Eastern Miwok live in five rancherias, located roughly between Sacramento and Stockton, and in nearby cities. Lake Miwoks have one small settlement at Middletown Rancheria that they share with Pomo Indians.

Population Miwok population stood at about 22,000 in the eighteenth century, of whom approximately 90 percent (19,500) were Eastern Miwok. In 1990, the total Miwok population was about 3,400.

Language There were several dialects and groups of Miwokan, a California Penutian language.

Historical Information

History Lowland occupation of California by the Eastern Miwok probably began as early as 2,000 years ago or more; occupation of the Sierra Nevada is only about 500 years old. The Eastern Miwok were divided into five cultural groups: Bay Miwok, Plains Miwok, Northern Miwok, Southern Miwok, and Central Sierra Miwok. Sir Francis Drake (1579) and Sebastian Cermeño (1595) may have met the Coast Miwok, but no further record of contact exists until the late eighteenth century and the beginning of the mission period. Russians also colonized the region in the early nineteenth century.

The Spanish had established missions in Coast Miwok and Lake Miwok territory by the early nineteenth century to which thousands of Miwoks were forcibly removed and where most later died of disease and hardship. In the 1840s, Mexican *rancheros* routinely kidnapped Lake Miwok people to work on their ranches and staged massacres to intimidate the survivors. As a result of all this bloodshed, previously independent tribelets banded together and even formed military alliances with other groups such as the Yokuts, raiding and attacking from the 1820s through the 1840s.

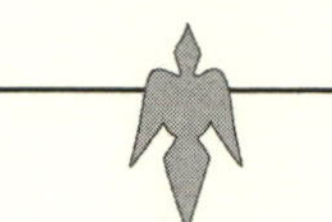

Everything changed for the Eastern Miwok in the late 1840s, when the United States gained political control of California and the great gold rush began. Most Miwoks were killed by disease, white violence, and disruption of their hunting and gathering environment. The Mariposa Indian War (1850), led by Chief Tenaya and others, was a final show of resistance by the Eastern Miwok and the Yokuts against Anglo incursions and atrocities. By the 1860s, surviving Miwoks were eking out a living by mining, farm and ranch work, and low-paying work on the edges of towns. Most Miwoks remained on local rancherias, several of which were purchased for them by the U.S. government in the early twentieth century.

Coast Miwok remained for the most part in their traditional homeland in the twentieth century, working at sawmills, as agricultural laborers, and fishing. They were officially terminated in the 1950s, but in 1992 a group called the Federated Coast Miwok created by-laws and petitioned the government for recognition.

Religion Eastern and probably also Coast Miwoks believed in the duality (land and water) of all things. Ceremonies, both sacred and secular, abounded, accompanied by dances held in great dance houses. The ceremonial role of each village in the tribelet was determined by geographical and political considerations. Lake Miwoks only allowed men in the dance houses.

Sacred ceremonies revolving around a rich mythology featured elaborate costumes, robes, and feather headdresses. The Miwok recognized several different kinds of shamans, such as spirit or sucking shamans, herb shamans (who cured and helped ensure a successful hunt), and rattlesnake, weather, and bear shamans. Shamans, whose profession was inherited patrilineally, received their powers via instruction from and personal acquisition of supernatural power gained through dreams, trances, and vision quests.

Government The main political unit was the tribelet, an independent and sovereign nation of roughly 100–500 people (smaller in the mountains). Each tribelet was composed of a number of lineages, or settlement areas of extended families. Larger tribelets, those composed of several named settlements, were led by chiefs, who were usually wealthy. Their responsibilities included hosting guests, sponsoring ceremonies, settling disputes, and overseeing the acorn harvest. In turn, chiefs were supplied with food and were expected to conduct themselves with a measure of grandness.

Among the Lake Miwok, special ceremonial officials presided over dances. Among Eastern and Lake Miwok the office of chief was hereditary and was male if possible. Other officials included the announcer (elective) and messenger (hereditary). The Coast Miwok also included two important female officials who presided over certain festivals and who supervised construction of the dance house.

Customs All Eastern Miwoks were members of one of two divisions (land or water). Both boys and girls went through puberty ceremonies. Marriage between Lake Miwok was a matter arranged by the parents through gift giving. Intermarriage between neighboring groups was common. The many life-cycle prohibitions and taboos included sex before the hunt or during a woman's period. Fourth and later infants may have been killed. The dead were cremated or buried. Widows cut their hair and rubbed pitch on their heads. Along the coast, property was burned along with the body. The name of the dead was never spoken again. There were no mourning ceremonies.

Men and occasionally women used pipes to smoke a gathered local tobacco. Miwoks possessed a strong feeling for property: Trespass was a serious offense, and virtually every transaction between two people involved payment. The profession of "poisoner" was widely recognized, and many people feared being poisoned more than they feared illness. People often danced, both for fun and ritual. Most songs were considered personal property. Both sexes played hockey, handball, and the grass game. Women also played a dice game. Children played with mud or stick dolls, acorn buzzers, and pebbles as jacks.

Dwellings Miwoks built conical houses framed with wooden poles and covered with plants, fronds, bark, or grasses. Hearths were centrally located, next to an

The Sierra Miwok and Mono peoples of the Sierra foothills built conical houses framed with wooden poles and covered with plants, fronds, bark, or grasses. Hearths were centrally located, next to an earth oven. Pine needles covered the floors; mats and skins were used for bedding. This photograph shows a woman in front of such a dwelling in 1870.

earth oven. Pine needles covered the floors; mats and skins were used for bedding. Some winter homes or dance houses, and most houses among the Lake Miwok, were partially below ground. Larger villages had a sweat lodge that served mostly as a male clubhouse.

Diet Acorns, greens, nuts, berries, seeds, and roots were some of the great variety of wild plants eaten by the Miwok. They also ate fish, especially salmon, trout, and shellfish, and hunted elk, deer, bear, antelope, fowl, and small game, especially rabbit. Deer were hunted in several ways, including driving them into a net or over a cliff, stalking while in deer disguise, shooting them from blinds, and running them down over the course of a day or so. Miwoks generally avoided eating dog, coyote, skunk, eagle, roadrunner, and snakes and frogs.

Key Technology Hunting equipment included traps, snares, and bow and arrow. A variety of baskets served many functions, such as winnowers, seed beaters, cradles, burden baskets, and storage. Fish were caught with nets, hook-and-line, and harpoon. Foods were stored either in granaries (acorns) or baskets. Foods were baked or steamed in earth ovens. Stone and bone

provided the raw material for a variety of tools. Cords and string came from plant fibers, especially milkweed and hemp. Coast and Lake Miwok used clamshell beads as money. Musical instruments included elderberry flutes, drums, cocoon rattles, clappers, and whistles. The Lake Miwok used several plants for natural dyes.

Trade Costanoans supplied the Eastern Miwok with salt. Other items of exchange included obsidian, shells, bows, and baskets. Along the coast, goods were more often purchased than traded. Lake Miwoks often traveled west to collect marine resources such as clamshells and seaweed.

Notable Arts Fine arts included baskets and representational petroglyphs, consisting mostly of circles and dots and beginning as early as 1000 B.C.E.

Transportation The Eastern Miwok used a tule balsa on navigable rivers. Log rafts were used on the coast.

Dress Eastern and Lake men wore buckskin breechclouts and shirts. Men along the coast wore little or nothing. Most women wore hide skirts and aprons, although in lower elevations they sometimes used grasses for skirts. Hide and woven rabbit-skin robes and blankets kept people warm in winter. Most people also wore ear and nose ornaments as well as face and body paint. They also practiced tattooing and head deformation (flattened heads and noses) for adornment. Young children wore no clothes. Hair was worn long except in mourning (Eastern Miwok). Lake Miwoks braided their hair.

War and Weapons The bow and arrow was the most important weapon. Coast Miwoks also used slings.

Contemporary Information

Government/Reservations Middletown Rancheria (189 acres in Lake County; 18 Indians in 1990) is a Lake Miwok and Pomo community. Eastern Miwok lands include Jackson Rancheria (1893; 331 acres in Amador County; 35–40 families in 1990; tribal council), Sheep Ranch Rancheria (1916; .92 acres [a cemetery] in Calaveras County), and Tuolomne Rancheria (1910; 336 acres in Tuolumne County; some 150 population in 1990). Other rancherias with very small Miwok populations include Shingle Springs, Buena Vista, Chicken Ranch, and Cortina.

Economy Many Miwoks work in logging and related industries. There are also some employment opportunities at Yosemite National Park. There is a bingo parlor on the Chicken Ranch Rancheria.

Legal Status The Chicken Ranch Rancheria of Me-Wuk Indians, the Jackson Rancheria of Me-Wuk Indians, the Tuolomne Band of Me-Wuk Indians, the Sheep Ranch Rancheria of Me-Wuk Indians, and the Buena Vista Rancheria are federally recognized tribal entities. The Cortina Indian Rancheria is a federally recognized tribal entity.

The American Indian Council of Mariposa County, the Calavaras Band of Mewuk, the Federated Coast Miwok Tribe, and the Ione Band of Mewuk have petitioned for federal recognition.

Daily Life There is a clinic/health center and a traditional roundhouse at Tuolumne Rancheria. Tuolumne also celebrates an acorn festival as well as a pan-Indian gathering in September. Although most of the religious traditions have been lost, young people are beginning to revive some dances and songs. Many Coast Miwoks have achieved prominence as scholars. Lake Miwoks have developed innovative educational programs in local schools. With native speakers of Miwok almost gone, the people have developed a number of programs to preserve and restore the language. Traditional basket making and weaving are also making comebacks.

Monache

See Mono

Mono

Mono (`Mō nō), or Monache, is a Yokuts term of uncertain meaning. Also known as the Western Mono, they are *Nimi,* or "People," in their own language.

Location Traditionally, the Mono lived in central California along the Sierra Nevada, higher in elevation (mainly 3,000 to 7,000 feet) then the Foothill Yokuts. Today most Mono live on Big Sandy and Cold Springs Rancherias, with other Indians on the Tule River Reservation, and in several northern California communities.

Population Mono population stood at roughly 2,500 in the late eighteenth century. In 1990, 38 lived on the Big Sandy Rancheria; 159 lived on the Cold Springs Rancheria; and probably several hundred are included with the 745 mixed Indians on the Tule River Indian Reservation and in communities in northern California.

Language Mono is a language of the western group of the Numic family of the Uto-Aztecan language stock.

Historical Information

History In the eighteenth century, the Mono included six independent tribal groups (Northfork Mono, Wobonuch, Entimbich, Michahay, Waksachi, Patwisha). They were in general culturally similar to the neighboring Foothill Yokuts. Since they lived in a region not highly desired by miners or non-native settlers, they enjoyed relatively higher survival rates in the nineteenth century than did most other California Indian peoples.

As "homeless Indians," the Mono received three rancherias from the federal government in the 1910s. Some individuals also acquired parcels of land. Many people retained their traditional subsistence gathering patterns while working as loggers, ranch hands, miners, and domestic help. As was the case with many other Indians, a large number of Mono moved to the cities after World War II.

Religion The Mono believed that spirits contained supernatural powers that might be employed by people with the proper knowledge. Supernatural powers were obtained through a connection with nature or by taking datura, a drug, as part of a ritual. Although shamans were especially skilled in these techniques, most people thought it a good idea to possess some powers for general success in life. Shamans used their powers for curing. However, they could also hurt or kill, and various evil activities were often ascribed to them.

Ceremonies included bear dances (by members of the Bear lineage) and the annual mourning ceremony. The Mono brought the Ghost Dance of 1870 west of the Sierra Nevada. This phenomenon ended by 1875, largely because it failed to bring back the dead as promised; the 1890 Ghost Dance revival had no impact on the Mono.

Government Each Mono group was composed of villages or hamlets of between one and eight huts, each led by a (usually hereditary male) chief. Patrilineal lineages, such as Eagle, Dove, Roadrunner, and Bear, were social organizations. The chief (from the Eagle lineage) arranged ceremonies, saw to the needy, and sanctioned the killing of evil shamans or others. He led by suggestion rather than by command. A messenger (Roadrunner lineage) assisted the chief and settled quarrels. They both had a symbol of office, an eight-foot-long cane with red-painted bands and string on top. Only the Northfork Mono had formal intradivision groups (Eagle and Dove), each with its own chief.

Customs After death, the soul was said to travel west for two days to the land of the dead. The dead were cremated and their remains buried. Mourning took place at the time of death and also at an annual ceremony. The Mono maintained close relations with their neighbors for activities such as trade, intermarriage, ceremonies, visiting, and resource exploitation. They observed no particular hunting or puberty rituals. Most men had only one wife (some wealthy men had more). Marriages were planned by the man's parents; the principals usually agreed. Divorce was possible for cause. Mono married each other as well as Yokuts Indians.

Dwellings The Mono built three types of houses: conical with an excavated floor, oval with a ridgepole, and conical with a center pole covered by thatch or cedar bark. Houses were arranged in a semicircle around the village. Most villages also contained a sweat house (male only), an acorn storehouse, and an open area used for dances and ceremonies.

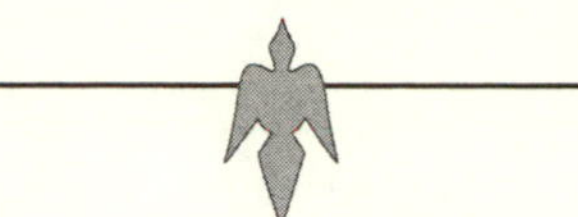

Diet Acorns were the staple food of these hunter-gatherers. They also ate roots, pine nuts, seeds, and berries (and drank cider from manzanita berries). They hunted and trapped deer, bear, rabbits, and squirrels. Good hunters shared their meat. Bears were often killed by blocking egress from their caves and then shooting them. Fish were caught with traps, weirs, nets, and spears.

Key Technology Items included a variety of fish nets and hunting traps; pottery and soapstone cookware; baskets; juniper and laurel bows; obsidian knives, scrapers, and arrow points; and various tools of stone and wood.

Trade Trade occurred mainly with the Owens Valley Paiute on the eastern side of the mountains. Most items were natural products, including acorns, obsidian, pine nuts, and rabbit skins. Mono also traded with the Yokuts.

Notable Arts Traditional arts included basket making and beadwork.

Transportation People floated babies and other valuables across rivers in basket boats. They used log rafts with brush or mat decking for crossing streams.

Dress Men and women wore deerskin or fiber aprons or breechclouts. Some groups wore moccasins. Both sexes pierced their ears and noses and tattooed their faces. Face and bodies were painted for ceremonies only. Woven rabbit-skin blankets were used in cold weather.

War and Weapons The usual cause of war was trespass or injuries to individuals (from shamans). Its intent was individual revenge; actual intertribal warfare was rare. People fought with bows and special, occasionally poisoned, arrows. The Monache generally did not take captives. Peacemaking included gifts of presents that were not considered reparations.

Contemporary Information

Government/Reservations The Mono Tribal Council is located in Dunlap, California. Formal communities include the Tule River Reservation (Tulare County, shared, with a tribal council); the Posgisa community (about 200 people) at Big Sandy Rancheria (Fresno County); the Num (about 600 people), located around the town of North Fork; the Wobonuch community at Dunlap (about 80 people); and the Holkoma community at Cold Springs Rancheria (Fresno County; 275 people; 155 acres). Populations are as of the early 1990s.

Economy The Tule River Reservation contains hydroelectric resources.

Legal Status The Tule River Indian Tribe of the Tule River Indian Reservation, the Big Sandy Rancheria of Mono Indians, the Northfork Rancheria of Mono Indians (Num community), and the Cold Springs Rancheria of Mono Indians are all federally recognized tribal entities.

As of 1997, the Dunlap Band of Mono Indians (Wobonuch community) and the Mono Lake Indian community had not attained federal recognition.

Daily Life There is a regional health center at North Fork, as well as a seniors' lunch program and a Head Start program. The Sierra Mono Museum is located at North Fork. It features displays, collections, and classes in traditional arts and language. Indian Days are held in August. The community at Big Sandy uses federal grant money for programs to preserve language and traditional culture.

Nisenan

See Maidu

Nomlaki

See Wintun

Nongatl

See Wailaki

Obispeño

See Chumash

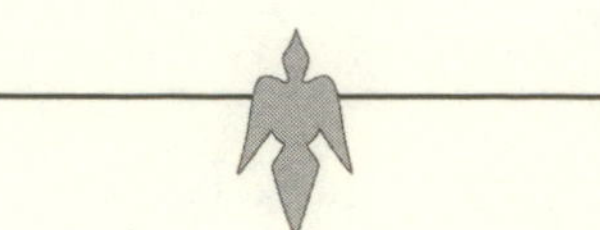

Okwanuchu

See Shasta

Patwin

See Wintun

Pit River Indians

See Achumawi

Pomo

Pomo (ˋPō mō), a group of seven culturally similar but politically independent villages or tribelets. This Pomo word means roughly "those who live at red earth hole," possibly a reference to a local mineral.

Location Traditionally, the Pomo lived about 50 miles north of San Francisco Bay, on the coast and inland, especially around Clear Lake and the Russian River. Today there are roughly 20 Pomo rancherias in northern California, especially in Lake, Mendocino, and Sonoma Counties. Pomo Indians also live in regional cities and towns.

Population Roughly 15,000 in the early nineteenth century, the Pomo population stood at 4,766 in 1990. About one-third of these lived on tribal land.

Language "Pomo" was actually seven mutually unintelligible Pomoan (Hokan) languages, including Southern Pomo, Central Pomo, Northern Pomo, Eastern Pomo, Northeastern Pomo, Southeastern Pomo, and Southwestern Pomo (Kashaya).

Historical Information

History Pomo prehistory remains murky, except that the people became a part of a regional trading system at about 1500. By the late 1700s, the Spanish had begun raiding Southern Pomo country for converts, and Hispanic influence began to be felt in Pomo country. Russian fur traders also arrived to brutalize the natives during this time. Their primary method of attracting Indian help was to attack a village and kidnap the women and children, who were then held as hostages (slaves) while the men were forced to hunt fur-bearing animals. In 1811 the Russians established a trading post at Fort Ross, on Bodega Bay (abandoned in 1841).

Hundreds of Pomos accepted the Catholic faith at local Spanish missions after 1817. In 1822, California became part of the Mexican Republic. Mexicans granted land to their citizens deep within Pomo country and enforced the land grants with strict military control. Thousands of Pomos died of disease (mainly cholera and smallpox) during the 1830s and 1840s, and Mexican soldiers killed or sold into slavery thousands more. Deaths from disease were doubly killing: Since the Pomo attributed illness to human causes, as did many native peoples, the epidemics also brought a concurrent rise in divisive suspicions and a loss of faith in traditions.

A bad situation worsened for the Pomo after 1849, when Anglos flooded into their territory, stealing their land and murdering them en masse. Survivors were disenfranchised and forced to work for their conquerors under slavelike conditions. A number of Pomos—perhaps up to 200—were killed by the U.S. Army in 1850. In 1856, the Pomo were "rounded up" and forced to live on the newly established Mendocino Indian Reserve. The government discontinued the reserve eleven years later, however, leaving the Indians homeless, landless, and with no legal rights.

Later in the century, Pomos mounted a project to buy back a land base. Toward this end, they established rancherias (settlements) and worked as cheap migrant agricultural labor, returning home in winter to carry on in a semitraditional way. By 1900, however, Pomos had lost 99 percent of these lands through foreclosure and debt. The remaining population were viewed with hatred by most whites, who practiced severe economic and social discrimination against them. This situation provided fertile ground for Ghost Dance activity and the Bole-Maru (dreamer) cult, an adaptive structure that may have helped ease their transition to mainstream values.

Missionaries in the early twentieth century worked with Indians to promote Indian rights, antipoverty activities, education, and temperance. By that time, Pomos had begun using the courts and the media to expand their basic rights and better their situation. A key Supreme Court decision in 1907

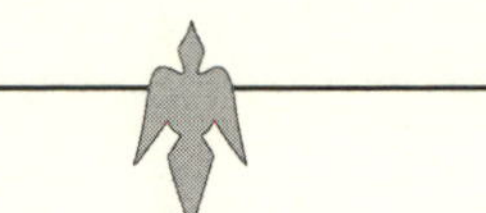

recognized the rancherias as Indian land in perpetuity. More Pomo children began going to school; although the whites kept them segregated, the people mounted legal challenges designed to win equal access. After World War I, Indian and white advocacy groups proliferated, and reforms were instituted in the areas of health, education, and welfare. Indians gained a body of basic legal rights in 1928.

During the 1930s, the Depression forced a return to more traditional patterns of subsistence, which led to a period of relative prosperity and revitalization. At the same time, contact with other, non-Indian migratory workers brought new ideas about industry and labor organization to the Pomo. Intermarriage also increased. Women gained more independence and began to assume a greater role in religious and political affairs around this time.

After World War II, the United States largely relinquished its role in local Indian affairs to the state of California, which was unprepared to pick up the slack. Several rancherias were terminated, and services declined drastically, leading to a period of general impoverishment. Since the 1950s, however, various Indian groups have been active among the Pomo in helping them to become more politically and economically savvy, and some state agencies have stepped in to provide services. The Clear Lake Pomo were involved in the takeover of Alcatraz Island in 1969–1971, reflecting their involvement in the pan-Indian movement. Beginning in the 1970s, many Pomo bands successfully sued the government for rerecognition, on the grounds that Bureau of Indian Affairs promises of various improvements had not been kept.

Religion The Kuksu cult was a secret religious society, in which members impersonated a god (kuksu) or gods in order to obtain supernatural power. Members observed ceremonies in colder months to encourage an abundance of wild plant food the following summer. Dances, related to curing, group welfare, and/or fertility, were held in special earth-covered dance houses and involved the initiation of 10- to 12-year-old boys into shamanistic, ritual, and other professional roles. All initiates constituted an elite secret ceremonial society, which conducted most ceremonies and public affairs.

Secular in nature, and older than the Kuksu cult, the ghost-impersonating ceremony began as an atonement for offenses against the dead but evolved into the initiation of boys into the Ghost Society (adulthood). A very intense and complex ceremony, especially among the Eastern Pomo, it ultimately became subsumed into the Kuksu cult.

The Bole-Maru in turn grew out of the Ghost Dances of the 1870s. The leader was a dreamer, and a doctor, who intuited new rules of ceremonial behavior. Originally a revivalistic movement like the Ghost Dance, this highly structured, four-day dance ceremony incorporated a dualistic worldview and thus helped Indians to step more confidently into a Christian-dominated society.

Other ceremonies included a women's dance, a celebration of the ripening of various crops, and a spear dance (Southeastern, involving the ritual shooting of boys). Shamans were healing or ceremonial professionals. They warded off illness, which was thought to be caused by ghosts or poisoning, from individuals as well as the community. Doctors (mostly men) were a type of curing specialist, who specialized in herbalism, singing, or sucking.

Government The Pomo were divided into tribelets, each composed of extended family groups of between 100 and 2,000 people. Generally autonomous, each tribelet had its own recognized territory. One or more hereditary, generally male, minor chiefs headed each extended family group. All such chiefs in a tribelet formed a council or ruling elite, with one serving as head chief, to advise, welcome visitors, preside over ceremonies, and make speeches on correct behavior. Groups made regular military and trade alliances between themselves and with non-Pomos. A great deal of social control was achieved through a shared set of beliefs.

Customs The Pomo ranked individuals according to wealth, family background, achievement, and religious affiliation. Most professions, such as chief, shaman, or doctor, required a sponsor and were affiliated with a secret society. The people recognized many different types of doctors. Bear doctors, for instance, who could be male or female, could acquire extraordinary power to move objects, poison, or cure.

The position was purchased from a previous bear doctor and required much training. Names were considered private property.

Boys, who were taught certain songs throughout their childhoods, were presented with a hair net and a bow and arrow around age 12. For girls, the onset of puberty was a major life event, with confinement to a menstrual hut and various restrictions and instructions. Pomos often married into neighboring villages. The two families arranged a marriage, although the couple was always consulted (a girl was not forced into marriage but could not marry against the wishes of her family). Methods of population control included birth control, abortion, sexual restrictions, infanticide, and occasionally geronticide. The dead were cremated after four days of lying in state. Gifts, and occasionally the house, were cremated along with the body.

Dwellings Along the coast, people built conical houses of redwood bark against a center pole. Inland, the houses were larger pole-framed, tule-thatched circular or elliptical dwellings. Other structures included semisubterranean singing houses for ceremonies and councils and smaller pit sweat houses.

Diet Hunters and gatherers, the Pomo mainly ate seven kinds of acorns. They hunted deer, elk, antelope, fowl, and small game. Gathered foods included buckeyes, pepperwood nuts, various greens, roots, bulbs, and berries. Most foods were dried and stored for later use. Coastal groups considered dried seaweed a delicacy. In some communities the good food sources were privately owned.

Key Technology Items included baskets (cooking pots, containers, cradles, hats, mats, games, traps, and boats); fish nets, weirs, spears, and traps; tule mats, moccasins, leggings, boots, and houses; and assorted stone, wood, and bone tools. Feathers and beads were often used for design. Hunting tools included the bow and arrow, spear, club, snares, and traps.

Trade The Pomo participated in a vast northern California trade group. Both clamshell beads and magnesite cylinders served as money. People often traded some deliberately overproduced items for goods that were at risk of becoming scarce. One group might throw a trade feast, after which the invited group was supposed to leave a payment. These kinds of arrangements tended to mitigate food scarcities.

Exchange also occurred on special trade expeditions. Objects of interest might include finished products such as baskets as well as raw materials. The Clear Lake Pomo had salt and traded it for tools, weapons, furs, and shells. All groups used money of baked and polished magnesite as well as strings of clam shell beads. The Pomo could count and add up to 40,000.

Notable Arts Pomo baskets were of extraordinarily high quality. Contrary to the custom in many tribes, men assisted in making baskets. Pomos also carved highly abstract petroglyphs beginning about 1600.

Transportation Coastal residents crossed to islands on driftwood rafts bound by vegetal fiber. The Clear Lake people used boats of tule bound with split grape leaves.

Dress Dress was minimal. Such clothing as people wore they made from tule, skins, shredded redwood, or willow bark. Men often went naked. Women wore waist-to-ankle skirts, with a mantle tied around the neck that hung to meet the skirt. Skin blankets provided extra warmth. A number of materials were used for personal decoration, including clamshell beads, magnesite cylinders, abalone shell, and feathers. Bead belts and neck and wrist bands were worn as costume accessories and as signs of wealth.

War and Weapons Poaching (trespass), poisoning, kidnapping or murder of women or children (usually for transgressing property lines), or theft constituted most reasons for warfare. Pomos occasionally formed military alliances among contiguous villages. Warfare began with ritual preparation, took the form of both surprise attacks and formal battles, and could end after the first casualty or continue all the way to village annihilation. Women and children were sometimes captured and adopted. Chiefs of the fighting groups arranged a peace settlement, which often included reparations paid to the relatives of those killed. Hunting or gathering rights might be lost

A Pomo woman weaving a basket. Pomo baskets were of extraordinarily high quality. Unlike the custom in many tribes, men also assisted in making baskets.

or won as a result of a battle. Pomos often fought Patwins, Wappos, Wintuns, and Yukis. They made weapons of stone, bone, and wood.

Contemporary Information

Government/Reservations In addition to cities and towns in and around northern California, Pomos live at the following rancherias: Big Valley (Pomo and Pit River, Lake County; 38 acres; 90 Indians), Cloverdale (Mendocino County; no formal land base; 1 resident), Dry Creek (Sonoma County; 1906; 75 acres; 38 Indians), Coyote Valley (Mendocino County), Sulphur Bank (Lake County; 1949; 50 acres; 90 Indians), Grindstone (Glenn County), Lytton (Sonoma County), Hopland (Mendocino County; 1907; 48 acres; 142 Indians), Stewart's Point (Sonoma County; 40 acres; 86 Indians [Kashia Band]), Manchester–Point Arena (Mendocino County; 1909; 363 acres; 178 Indians), Middletown (Lake County; 1910; 109 acres), Potter Valley (Mendocino County; 200 tribal members; 10 acres; 1 Indian resident), Redding (Shasta County; 31 acres; 79 Indians), Redwood Valley (Mendocino County; 58 acres; 14 Indians), Robinson (Lake County; 103 acres; 113 Indians), Sugar Bowl (Scott's Valley Band of Pomo Indians [Pomo and Wailaki], Lakeport County), Sherwood Valley (Mendocino County; 350 acres; 9 Indians), Upper Lake (Lake County; 1907; 19 acres; 28 Indians), Guidiville (Mendocino County), and Laytonville (Cahto-Pomo, Mendocino County; 200 acres; 129 Indians). They also live at the Pinoleville Reservation (1911; Mendocino County; 99 acres [almost half owned by non-natives]; 280 members) and the Round Valley Reservation (1864; 30,538 acres; Achomawi, Concow, Nomlaki, Wailaki, Wintun, Yuki, and Pomo; Mendocino County; 577

A Pomo's chin-to-hip armor, made of two layers of willow and hazel shoots, offered protection from arrows at the expense of mobility.

Indians). Population figures are as of 1995. Rancherias and reservations are generally governed by elected tribal councils.

The Pinoleville Band of Pomo Indians lives on the Pinoleville Reservation, which is located north of Ukiah, Mendocino County. The reservation was "unterminated" and its boundaries reestablished in the 1980s.

Economy Pomo country is still relatively poor. People engage in seasonal farm work as well as skilled and unskilled work. Some work with federal agencies, and some continue to hunt and gather their food.

Legal Status The Big Valley Rancheria of Pomo and Pit River Indians, the Cloverdale Rancheria of Pomo Indians, the Coyote Valley Band of Pomo Indians, the Dry Creek Rancheria of Pomo Indians, the Elem Indian Colony of Pomo Indians of the Sulphur Bank Rancheria, the Grindstone Rancheria, the Guidiville Rancheria, the Hopland Band of Pomo Indians of the Hopland Rancheria, the Kashia Band of Pomo Indians of the Stewart's Point Rancheria, the Laytonville Rancheria (Cahto-Pomo), the Lytton Rancheria, the Manchester Band of Pomo Indians of the Manchester–Point Arena Rancheria, the Middletown Rancheria of Pomo Indians, the Pinoleville Reservation of Pomo Indians, the Potter Valley Rancheria of Pomo Indians, the Redding Rancheria of Pomo Indians, the Redwood Valley Rancheria of Pomo Indians, the Robinson Rancheria of Pomo Indians, the Round Valley Reservation, the Scott's Valley Band of Pomo Indians, the Sherwood Valley Rancheria of Pomo Indians, and the Upper Lake Band of Pomo Indians of Upper Lake Rancheria are all federally recognized tribal entities.

The Sherwood Rancheria, the Yokayo Rancheria, and the Yorkville Rancheria are all privately owned; their Pomo communities are seeking federal recognition.

Daily Life Despite the years of attempted genocide and severe dislocation, Pomo culture remains alive and evolving. The extended family is still the main social unit. Pomo languages are still spoken, and some traditional customs, including ritual restrictions, traditional food feasts, some ceremonies, intercommunity ceremonial exchange, singing and dancing, and seasonal trips to the coast, are still performed. Pomo doctors cure illness caused by poisoning; non-Indian doctors are called in for some other medical problems. Pomo basket weavers enjoy an international reputation.

Many Christian Pomos practice a mixture of Christian and traditional ritual. Some Pomos would like to unite politically, but the lack of such a tradition acts as a brake on the idea. However, various transgeographic (not limited to one formal or even informal community) social and political organizations do exist to bring the Pomo people together and advance their common interests. The relatively large number of non-natives on some of the Pomo rancherias may be explained by the effects of termination and the loss of individual Pomo land (to taxes and foreclosure) and its subsequent sale to whites. The struggle continues to reacquire a land

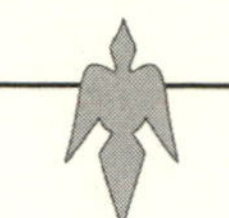

base and to win recognition (or rerecognition) for some bands. Pinoleville must deal with environmentally hazardous industries established within its borders.

The pan-Pomo Ya-Ka-Ama Indian Center features a plant nursery among other economic development, educational, and cultural projects. The intertribal Sinkyone Wilderness Council works to restore heavily logged areas using modern native techniques.

Purisimeño

See Chumash

Salinan

Salinan (Sä `lē nən) consisted of two divisions, Northern (Antoniaño) and Southern (Migueleño). A third division, extreme Coastal, may also have existed.

Location The people traditionally lived along the south-central California coast, inland to the mountains. Today's Salinan descendants live mainly in the Salinas Valley between Monterey and Paso Robles.

Population Roughly 3,000 in the late eighteenth century, the contemporary population consists of hundreds of Salinan descendants.

Language Salinan was a Hokan language.

Historical Information

History Little is known about Salinan prehistory. In 1771 the Spanish constructed San Antonia de Padua, the first mission in Salinan territory. By 1790 this was the largest mission in California. Mission San Miguel followed in 1797 and also expanded rapidly. The northern division of Salinans became associated with the former mission; the southern with the latter mission.

Under some pressure, most Salinans abandoned their aboriginal customs and became acculturated to mission life. After 1834 and the secularization of the missions, the Salinan experienced a rapid depopulation, primarily as a result of intermarriage and assimilation. Survivors either worked on the large *rancheros* or else remained in their original homeland as small-scale ranchers and hunters and gatherers. By the 1880s, most of the few remaining Salinan worked on the large cattle ranches that overspread the area, retaining a memory of their Indian heritage as well as close contact with each other. Until the 1930s there was a Salinan community not far from Mission San Antonia known as The Indians.

Religion The Salinan offered prayer to the golden eagle, the sun, and the moon. Shamans controlled the weather. Souls went to a western land of the dead. Initiation into religious societies was important, probably within the context of the Kuksu and/or the toloache cults.

Government Salinan political organization by tribelet was typical of California Indians.

Customs Clans as well as a Deer-Bear ceremonial division may have existed in aboriginal times. Although generosity with property was considered a virtue, loans of currency came with high rates of interest. Girls did not undergo a formal puberty ceremony. The boys' puberty ceremony involved the use of datura. (Datura was also used for pain relief.) Although the Salinan observed no formal marriage ceremony, marriage was formalized by gift giving and other customs. Divorce was relatively easy to obtain. The dead were cremated. The people played the bone game, shinny, ball races, games of strength, and possibly hoop-and-pole games. Shamans cured. They also poisoned and specialized in black magic. Medical treatments included bleeding, scarification, herbs, and sweat baths.

Dwellings Houses were domes, about 10 feet square, with a pole framework covered with tule or rye grass. Other buildings included communal structures and dance houses.

Diet Acorns were the staple food. The people also gathered wild oats, sage seeds, berries, mescal, and wild fruits. They hunted deer, bear, and rabbit, and they fished. They ate snakes, lizards, and frogs but not skunks.

Key Technology Both coiled and twined baskets were used for a number of purposes. Stone tools included scrapers, choppers, points, mortars, pestles, and bowls. Bone and shell tools included awls, wedges, and fish hooks. Wooden tools included mortars, combs, and spoons. Musical instruments included cocoon rattles, elderwood rattles and flutes, musical bows, rasps, bone whistles, and drums. The Salinan also had calendars, numerical and measuring systems, and some knowledge of astronomy. They cooked basket-leached acorn meal in an earth oven.

Trade Salinans and Yokuts enjoyed friendly relations, including visiting, mutual use of resources, and trade. The former traded beads and unworked shells for salt-grass salt, seeds, obsidian, lake fish, and possibly tanned hides. They also traded with other groups for wooden dishes, steatite vessels, and ornaments. Trade competition for the inland market for shells led to much enmity, particularly with the Costanoan. Beads of mussel and shell formed the basis of a local currency.

Notable Arts Pictographs, mostly angles, with some people and animals, appeared from about 1000 to 1600. Baskets were produced in aboriginal times.

Transportation Baskets were used to transport goods.

Dress Men wore few or no clothes. Women wore tule aprons, cloaks of rabbit or otter skin, and basket hats. Both sexes painted and possibly tattooed their bodies and wore abalone shell earrings.

War and Weapons Frequent combatants included Chumash and Costanoan Indians. Allies included the Yokuts. Salinans fought with sinew-backed bows and cane arrows.

Contemporary Information

Government/Reservations The Salinans have neither tribal land nor a formal organization. Most Salinan descendants live in the Salinas Valley between Monterey and Paso Robles.

Economy Salinan descendants work as ranchers and in the local economy.

Legal Status The Salinan Nation had not received federal recognition as of 1997.

Daily Life An informal network keeps Salinan identity alive. In recent years there has been a renewed interest in heritage and traditional culture.

Santa Barbara

See Chumash

Serrano

Serrano (Sə `rä nō) is a name taken from the Spanish term for "mountaineer" or "highlander."

Location In the late eighteenth century, the Serrano lived in small, autonomous villages, near water sources in the San Bernardino Mountains and Mojave Desert. Today most live mainly on two reservations in Riverside and (especially) San Bernardino Counties, California.

Population Serrano population stood at roughly 2,000 in the late eighteenth century. In 1990, 56 Indians lived on the San Manuel Reservation, and 526 Serrano and members of other tribes, mostly Cahuilla, lived on the Morongo Reservation.

Language Serrano belongs to the Takic division of the Uto-Aztecan language family and includes languages such as Kitanemuk, probably Vanyume, and possibly Tataviam.

Historical Information

History The Serrano may have encountered the Spanish as early as the 1770s, but the latter exerted little influence until 1819, when they constructed a settlement in the area. Most Western Serrano were removed by force to the missions between then and 1834; at that point, too few remained to carry on a traditional lifestyle. The Vanyume, a group associated with the Serrano and possibly living just to their north, became extinct well before 1900.

Religion The Serrano recognized a hierarchy of supernatural beings and spirits. Shamans conducted their ceremonies. They acquired their powers through dreaming and datura-induced visions.

Government Autonomous lineages, the main political unit, claimed specific local territory. Larger social units included clans, headed by *kikas* who provided political, economic, and religious leadership. *Kikas* also had assistants.

Customs All people belonged to one of two divisions, Wildcat and Coyote, each of which was composed of a number of patrilineal clans. In addition to conducting religious ceremonies, shamans also interpreted dreams and cured both by sucking out disease objects and by administering medicinal plants.

Both young men and women undertook puberty ceremonies. *Waxan,* the female ceremony, was public in the case of wealthy families and included dietary restrictions and instructions on how to be good wives. During *Tamonin,* the boys' ceremony, initiates ingested a datura drink and danced around a fire in the ceremonial house. After they experienced their visions, they learned special songs. The ceremony was followed by feasting and gift giving. A new mother and child lived in a heated pit for several days, observing food taboos. The dead were cremated, and most of their possessions were burned. A month after the death, a second burning of possessions was held, accompanied by singing and dancing. There was also an annual seven-day mourning ceremony.

Dwellings Parents, unmarried daughters, married sons, and sometimes extended family members lived in circular, domed tule-mat houses built around willow frames. Most household activities took place in nearby ramadas. Other structures included granaries, semisubterranean sweat houses, and a large ceremonial house where the *kika* lived. Men, women, and children all sweated and bathed together.

Diet Women gathered acorns, pine nuts, yucca roots, and mesquite and cactus fruit. Men hunted deer, antelope, mountain sheep, and small game using bow and arrow, traps, and curved throwing sticks. They also hunted birds, especially quail, and occasionally fished. Meat was baked in earth ovens, boiled in watertight baskets, or parching in trays with hot coals. The people also ate bone marrow. Blood was either thickened and cooked or eaten cold.

Key Technology Food utensils included flint knives, stone or bone scrapers, pottery trays and bowls, baskets, and horn and bone spoons and stirrers. Most tools, including awls, arrow straighteners, bows, arrows, fire drills, pipes, and musical instruments, were made of wood, bone, stone, shell, or plant fiber.

Trade Desert and mountain villages traded with each other for foods unavailable in the other's area.

Notable Arts The Serrano made fine decorated coiled basketry. They also carved petroglyphs, beginning perhaps as early as 1000 B.C.E., that depicted big game hunting. Pictographs, consisting of geometric designs, straight and wavy lines, and people, were painted as part of the girls' puberty ceremony as early as 1400 C.E.

Transportation Goods were carried in baskets.

Dress Serrano Indians wore little clothing except for some rabbit and otter fur blankets.

War and Weapons Their traditional enemies included the Mojave and Chemehuevi.

Contemporary Information

Government/Reservations The San Manuel Reservation (1893; San Bernardino County; 658 acres) had an early-1990s population of 25 Indians (out of 85 enrolled Serranos). Serranos also share the Morongo Reservation with other tribes, particularly the Cahuilla. Serrano descendants also live on the Soboba Reservation.

Economy People on the San Manuel Reservation work primarily at bingo facilities and other wage-paying jobs. Many Morongo people are cattlemen and farmers. They also have a bingo facility.

Legal Status The San Manuel Band of Mission Indians is a federally recognized tribal entity.

Daily Life Today's Serrano participate in pan-Indian ceremonies and events. Many residents of Morongo are Moravian. A very few people still speak Serrano. Although their culture has largely disappeared, the few people who claim Serrano ancestry remain proud of their heritage and identity. Some sacred and secular songs are sung on social occasions.

Shasta

Shasta (`Shas tə) were one of four Shastan tribes, the other three being Konomihu, Okwanuchu, and New River Shasta. The origin and meaning of the word "Shasta" is obscure. The approximate translation for their word for their homeland, *kahusariyeki,* is "among those who talk right."

Location Traditionally, the Shasta lived on both sides of the modern California-Oregon border, roughly in Oregon's Jackson and Klamath Counties and California's Siskyou County, regions mostly of mountains and forest. Today most Shastas live on the Quartz Valley Rancheria in Siskyou County, California; the Shasta Nation in Yreka, California; and among the general population.

Population Roughly 3,000 Shastas lived in their region in the eighteenth century. In 1990, 19 Indians (Karuk, Shasta, and Upper Klamath) lived at the Quartz Valley Rancheria. The Shasta had roughly 600 enrolled members at that time.

Language Shasta, Konomihu, Okwanuchu, and New River Shasta make up the Shastan division of the Hokan language family.

Historical Information

History Fur trappers in the 1820s constituted the first non-native presence in the Shasta region. Their influence was relatively benign, in sharp contrast to that of the settlers who soon followed in their wake. Although Shastas often fought each other and their neighbors, they all banded together in the 1850s to resist the Anglo invaders. In 1851, a treaty called for a Shasta reservation in Scott Valley, but the state of California refused to let the treaty be ratified. After the signing, Indians ate a meal at which the food had been poisoned with strychnine; thousands more Indians died during the ensuing attacks by white vigilantes.

The few surviving Shastas were forced onto the Grande Ronde and, later, Siletz Reservations. Among the other treaties that included Shastas was the 1864 Klamath Treaty, in which, unbeknownst to them, their aboriginal homeland was ceded. Shastas participated in the late-nineteenth-century religious revivals, including the Ghost Dance, Earth Lodge cult, and Big Head cult.

Religion The most important ceremony centered around girls' puberty. There were also war dances and doctor-making ceremonies as well as several personal rituals for luck and protection.

Government Shastas lived in villages of one or more families. Larger villages as well as each of the four divisions had a headman (loose hereditary succession) whose duties included mediating disputes among men and preaching correct behavior. The headman's wife had similar responsibilities among women.

Customs Shamans were usually women. They cured through the use of supernatural powers, which were also the source of all disease and death (except ill will). They acquired these powers through dream trances, during which a spirit or "pain" taught the shaman its song. An extended training period followed the trance experience. Each shaman acquired certain paraphernalia over the years. They diagnosed by singing, dancing, or blowing tobacco smoke and cured by sucking. If a shaman lost too many patients, she was killed. Shamans' services were also available to kill an enemy (by throwing a "pain") and to find lost or stolen objects and people. Doctors, who cured by using medicinal plants, were also women.

The Shasta observed numerous life-cycle food and behavior taboos. Puberty activities for boys included an optional vision-seeking quest, which ensured success in male activities such as hunting, fishing, gambling, and racing. The girls' puberty ceremony and dance were the group's most important. Marriage required the payment of a bride price. Wealthy men occasionally had more than one wife. Divorce was unusual. The dead were buried in family

plots; their possessions were burned or buried. Widows cut their hair (widowers singed it), covered their head and face with a pitch and charcoal mixture until remarriage, and observed several taboos. Souls were said to travel east along the Milky Way to the home of Mockingbird, a figure in Shasta mythology.

Both bitter feuds and friendships characterized Shasta intragroup relations. Payment usually resolved interpersonal differences. Families (through the male line) owned exclusive rights to specific hunting or fishing places within the village territory at large. Money and wealth were measured in olivella, haliotsis, deerskins, clamshell disks, dentalia, and woodpecker scalps. Games included ring-and-pin, shinny, target games, and the men's grass (hand) and women's many-stick games.

Dwellings Rectangular winter homes were set about three feet into the ground. With earth side walls and wood end walls, they held between one and four families. All houses faced the water. Furnishings included tule pillows and wooden stools. Some groups used tule or raccoon-skin bed coverings; others used elk or deerskin blankets or imported buffalo hides. The community house was similar, but larger. Boys past puberty and unmarried men slept in the sweat house if their village contained one. The menstrual hut was generally located on the west side of the village. Other structures included brush shelters in spring and summer and bark houses during the fall acorn-gathering season.

Diet Shastas generally ate two meals a day. Venison was a staple. Hunters also brought in bear, fowl, turtles, and various small game. Their methods included stalking and the use of drop pits and traps. Various hunting rituals and taboos included not eating one's first kill. Meat was boiled, baked (in earth ovens), broiled, or dried. Insects were parched or baked.

Men also fished for salmon, mussels, trout, and eels, using spears, nets, and traps. There were several first-fish-run rituals and taboos. Fresh salmon was generally roasted. Acorns were another staple. In addition to acorns, gathered foods included pine nuts, roots, seeds, greens, bulbs, and berries. Dried foodstuffs were ground into flour. Men were often served before women.

Key Technology Most tools were made of wood, bone, stone, and obsidian. The Shasta also used rawhide and basket containers, bowls of wood and soapstone, imported and domestic baskets, and adhesives made of fish glue, pine pitch, and chokecherry pitch.

Trade The four Shasta groups traded with each other as well as within the different villages of each group. They traded acorns (Achumawi, Wintun) and acorn paste (Rogue River Athapaskans), clamshell beads (northern peoples), and buckskin, obsidian, and dentalia (Warm Springs Indians). They obtained obsidian (Achumawi), buckskin clothing (Warm Springs Indians), otter skins (northern peoples), dentalia (Rogue River Athapaskans), and pine nut necklaces (Wintun). Trade with their northern neighbors generally excluded the Klamath and the Modoc. From their California neighbors, the Shasta received acorns, baskets, dentalia, obsidian blades, juniper, and Wintun beads.

Notable Arts The Shasta specialized in making deerskin containers. Their relatively few musical instruments included deer-hoof rattles, bone and elder flutes, and hide drums.

Transportation They used pine dugout canoes and tule rafts to navigate waterways.

Dress Clothing was made of deerskin and shredded bark. People also wore shell necklaces, ear and nose ornaments, face and body paint, and tattoos. Heads were flattened for aesthetic reasons. Caps were of basketry (women) and buckskin (men). Footgear included buckskin ankle-length moccasins and snowshoes.

War and Weapons The four groups occasionally fought with each other. They also engaged in intragroup feuds, primarily for revenge of witchcraft, murder, rape, and insult to a headman. Other occasional enemies included the Achomawi, Wintun, and Modoc (retaliation for the latter's raiding). Weapons included the bow and arrow, knives, and rod armor vests. Peace settlements included disarmament and payments. Young women occasionally

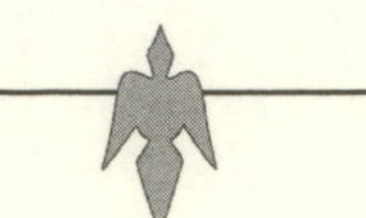

accompanied a Shasta war party. They might be taken captive but were usually returned as part of the settlement.

Contemporary Information

Government/Reservations The Quartz Valley Rancheria (1939; rerecognized in 1983; Siskiyou County) had an early-1990s Shasta population of two.

Shasta descendants also live on the Grande Ronde and Siletz Reservations (*see* Upper Umpqua entry in Chapter 3).

Economy Most people work in the timber industry or at local small businesses.

Legal Status The Shasta Nation had not received federal recognition as of 1997. The Quartz Valley Rancheria of Karok, Shasta, and Upper Klamath Indians is a federally recognized tribal entity.

Daily Life Today's Shasta have little knowledge of aboriginal culture. No Shasta languages are currently spoken. The people are primarily interested in federal recognition, archaeology, and the return of grave items. Residents of the Quartz Valley Rancheria suffer from poor health care. Some Shastas possess heirloom family artifacts.

Sinkyone

See Wailaki

Smith River Indians

See Tolowa

Tache

See Yokuts

Tipai-Ipai

Tipai-Ipai (Tē `pī-Ē `pī) is the common name since the 1950s of two linguistically related groups formerly known as Kamia (Kumeyaay) and Diegueño. Both terms mean "People." "Diegueño" comes from the Spanish mission San Diego de Alcala. "Kamia" may have meant "those from the cliffs." The Tipai-Ipai are sometimes referred to as Diegueño Mission Indians.

Location As of the late eighteenth century, the Tipai-Ipai lived in southern California and Baja California, along the coast and inland almost to the Colorado River. Today, many live on 13 reservations in San Diego County, California.

Population The late-eighteenth-century Tipai-Ipai population stood between 3,000 and 9,000. In 1990, roughly 1,200 Tipai-Ipais lived on the reservations and perhaps 2,000 more lived off-reservation.

Language Diegueño is a member of the Yuman division of the Hokan language family.

Historical Information

History People have been living in traditional Tipai-Ipai territory for roughly 20,000 years. A proto–Tipai-Ipai culture had been established by about 5000 B.C.E., and the historic Tipai-Ipai were in place about 1,000 years ago.

In 1769, the Spanish built the presidio and mission of San Diego de Alcala and began rounding up local Indians, especially those to the north and on the coast. The latter revolted regularly. In 1775, about 800 people from some 70 villages united to burn the mission. It was later rebuilt, however, and the missionization process continued. After the Mexicans secularized the missions in 1834, they treated the resident Tipai-Ipai as trespassers or rebels and continued many of the same oppressive practices that characterized mission life.

In 1852, shortly after the United States gained control of California, the Senate ratified a treaty with "the nation of Diegueño Indians," under which the latter lost their best lands. Overgrazing and water diversions soon destroyed their remaining grassland and woodland. By the late 1870s, the Tipai-Ipai were settled on about 12 small, poor reservations, although many were at least located on the site of native villages. Coastal Ipais also lived in San Diego slums or camped in nearby hills.

At the turn of the century many Tipai-Ipais could be found working for low wages on ranches and in mines and towns or starving on the inadequate

reservations. Traditional government was disrupted by Indian agents who required the Indians to select a "captain." Bitter political factions had emerged by the 1930s with the formation of the rival Mission Indian Federation and the Southern Mission Indians. Frequent cross-border visits and ceremonies became difficult after 1950 and impossible after the 1970s, owing to U.S. immigration policies. In recent times, the bands have been reviving the traditional governing structure.

Religion Shamans were the religious leaders. They performed ceremonies, interpreted dreams, controlled weather, and cured the sick. Evil shamans might also produce disease. Named song cycles were associated with certain ceremonial dances. Ground paintings, a feature illustrating the connection with southwestern cultures, featured symbols of colors and their associated directions. Their most important religious ceremony was *kaurk*. This clan-based mourning ceremony lasted from four to eight days. It included gift giving, dancing with images of the dead, and feasting and culminated with the burning of effigies of the dead. Toloache, a hallucinogenic root, was used by adolescent boys and adult men for spiritual strengthening.

Government The Tipai-Ipai consisted of over 30 autonomous bands or tribelets, usually made up of a single patrilineal clan and headed by a clan chief and an assistant. Neither the tribe nor the band had a formal name. Positions of authority were sometimes inherited by eldest sons, brothers, and, rarely, widows. Two tribal chiefs directed ceremonies, advised about proper behavior, and appointed war or gathering leaders. Band leaders and councils saw to resource management. In historic times, some chiefs ordered assistants to beat nonconformists. The Imperial Valley Tipai had a tribal chief but no clan chief.

Customs The Tipai-Ipai observed numerous life-cycle rituals, obligations, and taboos. Reaching puberty was a public affair. Girls underwent special rites; boys often had their nasal septa pierced. Most marriages, arranged by parents when children reached puberty, were monogamous. Divorce was relatively easy to effect. Twins were considered a blessing and supernaturally gifted. The dead were cremated along with their possessions. Souls were said to inhabit a region somewhere in the south. Wailing, speech making, the singing of song cycles, and gift exchange might accompany cremation. Mourners cut their hair, blackened their faces, and never mentioned the deceased's name again.

All tribal members shared certain lands. In addition, each band claimed specific communal land, some of which was apportioned to individual families, as well as the right to kill thieves and trespassers. Certain rights were also preserved for the needy. Mockingbirds and roadrunners were caged as pets. Before hunting, a man studied his dreams, fasted, and avoided women and corpses. He usually gave away his first deer.

Dwellings Dwellings varied with season and environment. In winter, people built dome-shaped houses with a pole framework, covered with bark, thatch, or pine slabs. Openings faced east. The people also lived in mountain caves. Brush shelters and pole and palm-leaf thatch houses served in the summer.

Diet The food staple was flour made from six varieties of acorn as well as from mesquite beans and seeds of sage, pigweed, peppergrass, flax, and buckwheat. Flour was cooked into mush and cakes and stewed with meat and vegetables. Other wild foods included cactus, agave, clover, cherries, plums, elderberries, watercress, manzanita berries, piñon nuts, and prickly pear. People fished where fish were available. Animal foods, which were generally roasted on coals or in ashes, included rodents and an occasional deer. The people also ate lizards, some snakes, insects, larvae, and birds. They also cultivated tobacco, which only men smoked. Imperial Valley Ipais planted maize, beans, and teparies, but they placed greater emphasis on gathering.

Key Technology Men hunted with a bow and arrow and throwing sticks. A variety of basketry and pottery items served food-related functions. Other tools were made of stone, bone, and wood.

Trade The Tipai-Ipai traded most frequently among themselves, but since major trails crossed their

territory, they also interacted with others as far inland as Zuñi. Coastal people traded salt, dried seaweed, dried greens, and abalone shells for acorns, agave, mesquite beans, and gourds. Other items traded included granite for pestles, steatite for arrow straighteners, red and black minerals for paint, and eagle feathers.

Notable Arts Tipai petroglyphs, which were produced perhaps as early as 1000 B.C.E., depicted big game hunting. The Ipai produced theirs from roughly 500 B.C.E. to A.D. 1000. Pictographs, which featured geometric designs, were used as part of the girls' puberty ceremony as early as circa 1400.

Transportation Most fishing boats were either balsa rafts or dugout canoes.

Dress Dress was minimal. Children and men often went naked. Women wore an apron. Both sexes wore caps against head-carried items and sandals of agave leaves. Bedding and robes were of rabbit skin, willow bark, or buckskin. Men plucked whiskers with their fingers. Women tattooed their chins and painted their bodies.

War and Weapons Clans generally feuded over women, trespass, murder, and sorcery. Tactics included ambush or simply chasing away an enemy. Weapons included the bow and arrow, poniard, and war club. Forced to resist the missions and the Mexicans, the people became more aggressive during the early nineteenth century.

Contemporary Information

Government/Reservations The following were Tipai-Ipai (Diegueño) reservations in 1990: Barona (1875; 5,902 acres; 450 members), Campo (1893; 15,480 acres; 213 enrolled members), Capitan Grande (1875; 15,753 acres), Cuyapaipe (1893; 4,103 acres; 16 enrolled members), Inaja and Cosmit (1875; 852 acres; 16 enrolled members), Jamul (1975; 6 acres; 120 enrolled members), LaPosta (1893; 4,500 acres; 13 enrolled members), Manzanita (1893; 3,579 acres; 52 enrolled members), Mesa Grande (1875; 1,000 acres; roughly 300 enrolled members), San Pasqual (1910; 1,379.58 acres; roughly 200 enrolled members), Santa Ysabel (1893; 15,527 acres; 950 enrolled members), Sycuan (1875; 640 acres; 120 enrolled members), and Viejas (1875; 1,609 acres; 180 members). All are located in San Diego County. Membership figures may exclude children. Most reservations are governed by elected councils and chairs. Bands are attempting to revive a tribal-level organization. Populations are as of 1990.

Economy Sycuan Reservation operates restaurants, a casino, a bingo parlor, and an off-track betting establishment. Other reservations are planning development along these lines.

Legal Status The Barona Group of Capitan Grande Band, the Campo Band, the Capitan Grande Band, the Cuyapaipe Community, the Inaja Band, the LaPosta Band, the Manzanita Band, the Mesa Grande Band, the Santa Ysabel Band, the Sycuan Band, and the Viejas Group of Capitan Grande Band of Diegueño Mission Indians are all federally recognized tribal entities. The Jamul Indian Village of California is a federally recognized tribal entity. The San Pasqual General Council is a federally recognized tribal entity.

Daily Life Major contemporary issues include sovereignty, the status of tribal land, water rights, and economic independence. Tipai-Ipai Indians are also interested in issues concerning education, housing, health care, traditional culture, and the environment. Most Indians are Catholic or observe a combination of Catholic and native religious traditions. Most religious ceremonies are closed to the public. Major feasts, such as the Fiesta de Las Cruces on November 14, celebrate the fusion of Indian, Spanish, Mexican, frontier, and contemporary American customs and beliefs. Many dialects of Diegueño are still spoken. The traditional art of basket making has been revived.

Most reservations have tribal halls, programs for seniors, and various cultural programs. Some have libraries, preschools, and police and fire departments and provide scholarship assistance to students.

Tolowa

Tolowa (ˈTo lə wä) is an Algonquian name given to these people by their southern neighbors, the Yurok.

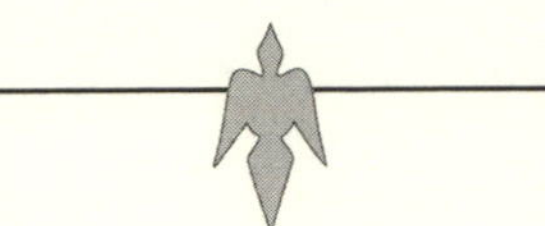

Cultural and linguistic relatives in Oregon are known as Chetco and Tututni. Tolowas are presently associated with the Tututni. Their name for themselves is *Xus,* or "person."

Location Traditionally, the Tolowa lived in approximately eight permanent villages in northwestern California, from Wilson Creek north to the Oregon border. The area included coast, rivers (especially the Smith River), and interior marshes, hills, and mountains. Today many Tolowa live in and around Humboldt and Del Norte Counties, California.

Population From perhaps 2,400 in the early nineteenth century (out of roughly 4,000 Tolowa/Chetco/Tututnis), by 1990 59 Indians lived on the Trinidad Rancheria and 32 Indians lived on the Elk Valley Rancheria (mostly Tolowa). Roughly 400 people identified themselves as Tolowa in 1990.

Language The people spoke several dialects of Tolowa, an Athapaskan language.

Historical Information

History During the late eighteenth century, probably before the Tolowa had yet encountered non-natives face to face, an epidemic contracted from non-native explorers in the region destroyed one of their villages. The first direct contact came in June 1828 in the person of Jedediah Smith and his exploring party. However, the Tolowa continued to live relatively unaffected by outside influences until about 1850.

More than half of the Tolowa population died during that decade alone from disease and the effects of Anglo mass murders. In 1860, following the Chetco/Rogue River Indian War (begun in 1852), 600 Tolowas were forced to march into reservations in Oregon. Some of those people were later removed to the Hoopa Valley Reservation. The 1870 Ghost Dance revival reached them in about 1872 and lasted about ten years.

Around the turn of the century, the Tolowa suffered further dramatic population reduction as a result of disease, mostly measles and cholera. Their population at this time had been reduced by roughly 95 percent, to some 200 people. Individual Tolowas had received a few allotments in the late nineteenth century. In 1906, the government purchased tracts of land near the mouth of the Smith River that later became the Smith River and Elk Valley Rancherias. By 1913, most Tolowas were living in and around Crescent City and on the Hoopa Valley and Siletz Reservations. Beginning in 1923 and lasting for at least 30 years, owing to the government crackdown and confiscation of regalia, people held their traditional religious observances secretly.

The Indian Shaker Movement, which supported traditional healing and spiritual practices, arrived around 1930 and remained popular for a generation. About the same time, the Del Norte Indian Welfare Association was founded as a community and self-help organization. The two rancherias were terminated in 1960, with devastating cultural results. As a response to termination, Tolowa landowners in 1973 created the Nele-chun-dun Business Council and filed for federal acknowledgment ten years later as the Tolowa Nation. The rancherias were reinstated in 1983.

Religion Most important Tolowa ceremonies were connected with diet, such as catching the season's first salmon, smelt, or sea lion. The *Naydosh* (Feather Dance) was performed as part of a World Renewal ceremony.

Government The wealthiest man in the village was usually the leader. There was no formal chief or overall political organization.

Customs Prestige, in the form of gaining and displaying wealth, or treasure (such as large obsidian knives, necklaces of dentalium shell beads, and red woodpecker scalp headdresses) was of prime concern to the Tolowa. Treasure was not normally used for utilitarian purposes except for bride prices. Besides marrying off daughters, other ways to get wealth were shrewd trading, fines and indemnities (there were many occasions for this, which were watched for carefully), infant betrothal, and gambling. Wealthy men might have several wives.

Shamans were mostly women or transvestite men. They were paid a high fee for curing disease. Their methods included dancing, trances, and

sucking with the assistance of a spiritual power, or "pain." Although Tolowa villages did not closely cooperate among themselves, intermarriage and ceremonial interaction between the Tolowa and their neighbors (Yurok, Karuk, Hupa, Tututni) was common. Male activities mostly revolved around hunting, boat building, and fishing; women generally collected and transported food, especially acorns, and prepared it for eating and storage. Corpses were removed through a loose plank in the house, wrapped in tule mats, and buried with shell beads and other objects.

Dwellings Tolowas lived in square redwood-plank houses with two-pitched roofs. The central area was slightly excavated for cooking and sleeping. An interior ground-level ledge was used for storage. Men and boys slept, gambled, and made nets and weapons in semisubterranean sweat houses. The people lived in their permanent villages about nine months a year, leaving in late summer to fish for smelt on sandy beaches and continuing on inland to catch salmon and gather acorns through the fall.

Diet Salmon, smelt, and sea lion were the staples. Other foods included seaweed, shellfish, shore bird eggs, and acorns. The people may have cultivated tobacco.

Key Technology Technological innovations included wild iris fishnets; tule mats; baskets of various fibers; stone, fiber, bone, and wooden tools such as bow and arrow, harpoons, fishing nets, woodworking wedges (antler), stone pounders, and pestles; and bone needles for weaving tule items. Deer hooves were used as musical instruments. Tolowas counted by fives.

Trade Local trading networks extended into interior California and Oregon and along the coast at least as far north as Puget Sound.

Notable Arts Highly abstract petroglyphs date from roughly 1600. Locally, complex twined basket design depended on techniques such as overlay. The design was characterized by a large variety of geometric elements and the use of three colors.

Transportation The people built and used 40-foot redwood canoes from which to fish and hunt sea lions.

Dress Men wore buckskin breechclouts or nothing at all. Women wore a two-piece buckskin skirt. They also had three vertical stripes tattooed on their chins. Basketry caps protected their heads against burden-basket tumplines. Hide robes were used for warmth. People on long journeys wore buckskin moccasins and leggings. Both sexes wore long hair and ornaments in pierced ears.

War and Weapons Each village defended its land, occasionally against other Tolowa villages. There were few pitched battles; most fights consisted of individual attacks or village raids. Young women were sometimes taken captive but usually returned at settlement time. Every injured party received a settlement, with the winners paying more than the losers.

Contemporary Information

Government/Reservations Tolowas live at the following locations: the Cher-ae Heights community of the Trinidad Rancheria (47 acres; about 60 Yurok, Wiyot, and Tolowa Indians in the mid-1990s) in Humboldt County; the Big Lagoon Rancheria (20 acres; 19 Yurok and Tolowa in 1996) in Humboldt County; the Smith River Rancheria (1906; 30 acres; 72 Indians) in Del Norte County, rerecognized in the 1980s and governed by the constitution of the Howonquet Indian Council; and the Elk Valley Rancheria (1906; Del Norte County; roughly 30 Tolowa, Yurok, and Hupa, governed by a nine-member tribal council). Tolowas also live on the Siletz Reservation (*see* Upper Umpqua entry in Chapter 3).

Economy Unemployment at Elk Valley in 1995 stood at about 40 percent. Economic activities there include casino gambling and a casket company. Access to jobs is relatively difficult.

Legal Status The Cher-ae Heights Indian Community of the Trinidad Rancheria, the Smith River Rancheria, and the Big Lagoon Rancheria are federally recognized tribal entities. The Elk Valley Rancheria of Smith River Tolowa Indians is a federally

recognized tribal entity. The Tolowa Nation, derived from the nineteenth-century Jane Hostatlas allotment and the 1973 Nele-chun-dun Business Council, had not received federal recognition as of 1997. The Tolowa-Tututni Tribe of Indians is also federally unrecognized.

Daily Life Although few know and practice the old traditions, the Tolowa do perform ceremonies such as the *Naydosh* (Feather Dance). Indian Shaker religious practices are also popular. At Elk Valley, extended families live together or nearby. Children attend public school, although the people are working toward setting up tribal schools. Health care facilities are considered inadequate, despite the presence of a clinic at Smith River. Diabetes, heart disease, and substance abuse are chronic problems. Tolowas have written dictionaries and conduct classes in their native language. Like most rural people, they garden, fish, and hunt for subsistence.

Tubatulabal

Tubatulabal (Tə `bät əl `ä bəl), "pine nut eaters." These people originally lived in three autonomous bands: the Pahkanapil, Palagewan, and Bankalachi, or Toloim.

Location In the early nineteenth century, the Tubatulabal lived in the southern Sierra Nevada and their foothills and in the Kern, South Fork Kern, and Hot Springs Valleys. Today many live on reservations in Tulare County.

Population A population of up to 1,000 Tubatulabal lived in their region in the early nineteenth century. In 1990, roughly 400 Tubatulabal Indians live in the Kern River Valley, and possibly another 500 live elsewhere.

Language Tubatulabal was a subgroup of the Uto-Aztecan language family.

Historical Information

History This group of Indians entered the region at least around 1450 and perhaps as early as 2,000 years ago. They first encountered Spanish explorers in the late eighteenth century. By the mid–nineteenth century, miners, ranchers, and settlers began taking their land. The Kern River gold rush began in 1857. In 1862, a few Tubatulabals joined the Owens Valley Paiutes in antiwhite fighting in the Owens Valley. In the following year whites massacred Tubatulabals in the Kern River Valley.

By 1875, most male survivors were working for local ranchers. In 1893, survivors of the Pahkanapil Band, the only one left of the original three, were allotted land in the Kern and South Fork Kern Valleys. The people experienced severe epidemics of measles and influenza in 1902 and 1918. During the twentieth century, many Tubatulabals moved to the Tule River Reservation and throughout California. After the last hereditary leader died in 1955, a council of elders carried on leadership through the 1960s. In the 1970s, the Tubatulabal, Kawaiisu, and Canebrake area Indians formed the Kern Valley Indian Community and Council, a goal of which is to obtain federal recognition.

Religion According to traditional belief, numerous supernatural spirits often took human or animal form. They were treated with respect, in part because they could be malevolent. Shamans used jimsonweed, believed to have special powers, as an aid in curing. They also used singing, dancing, herbs, blowing tobacco smoke, and sucking techniques, calling upon their supernatural guardian helpers for assistance. Shamans could be either men or women, but only men could cure: Female shamans were witches, the most feared members of the community (men could also be witches). Chronically unsuccessful shamans might be accused of witchcraft and killed. Shamanism was considered an inborn quality that could not be acquired.

Government The three bands were composed of several family groups, mobile throughout much of the year except during winter, when they settled in hamlets of between two and six extended families. Each band was headed by a chief, generally hereditary, occasionally female. He or she arbitrated disputes, represented the band, and organized war parties. A "dance manager" or "clown" instigated public criticism of the chief preparatory to the appointment

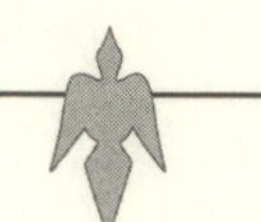

of a new chief. He also acted the clown at ceremonies. Although the three bands were politically autonomous, people often visited and intermarried.

Customs Neither men nor women underwent formal puberty rites. Marriages were formalized by gift exchanges or groom service to his in-laws. Corpses were wrapped in tule mats and buried. A six-day mourning ceremony was held within two years, during which time a tule effigy of the dead was destroyed along with most of his or her possessions.

Each band claimed formal but unexclusive possession of a specific territory. The people played several games, most of which involved gambling on the outcome. They included a women's dice game, a men's shinny game, and a men's hoop-and-pole game (in which an arrow was shot through a rolling hoop). String figure making and storytelling provided entertainment on winter evenings. Professional male dancers performed at various ceremonies and occasions. Also, both sexes danced for enjoyment.

Dwellings Winter houses were circular, dome-shaped structures of brush or mud. In summer, people used open-sided pole-and-beam brush shelters. Bedding consisted of tule mats and skins. Most villages also contained a brush-and-mud sweat house. Special structures, in which several families slept, ate, and stored supplies, were constructed at the autumn gathering grounds. These buildings were between 30 and 50 feet in diameter and featured three- to four-foot-high brush walls.

Diet Food staples were acorns, piñon nuts, and fish. People either caught fish individually or drove them into stone corrals, where other people waded in and tossed them out. Sun-dried and stored, acorns and piñons were eventually ground into meal and mixed with water to form gruel or mush. The Tubatulabal also ate seeds, berries (juniper, manzanita, goose), roots (tule, cattail), and bulbs. Plant foods were boiled, parched, roasted, or baked in pit ovens. Berries were eaten fresh, boiled, or pounded or were mixed with water, shaped into cakes, sun-dried, and stored.

Men hunted deer, bear, antelope, mountain lion, mountain sheep, birds, and small game. They also participated in annual communal antelope drives with neighboring tribes. Large game was broiled, roasted, or stewed immediately or salted and sun-dried for storage. Sugar crystals came from cane; salt from plants and rock salt. Both men and women used wild tobacco as an emetic before bed.

Key Technology The Tubatulabal made coiled and twined baskets. Coiled baskets often had human, snake, or geometric designs. Local red clay was used to make pottery. Other technological items included the sinew and self-backed bow (strung with native twine); numerous nets, snares, traps, and throwing sticks for hunting small game; fishing baskets, traps, nets, harpoons, hooks, and stone-and-wood corrals; a barrel cactus spine awl for sewing and basket making; and soaproot fiber brushes. Many such tools were made of stone. Musical instruments included rattles, quill whistles, elderberry flutes, and musical bows.

Trade Small groups of men and women traded piñons, balls of prepared tobacco, and other items for clamshell disks, which served as money. Their trading expeditions took them as far as the coast or as close as the next hamlet. During winter, when supplies were low, people bought goods with their own or borrowed lengths of disks.

Notable Arts Fine baskets were their major art. They also made pictographs on local rock faces.

Transportation Fishermen hurled harpoons from tiny floating tule platforms.

Dress In summer, men went naked, and women wore tanned deerskin aprons. Other clothing, worn during various times of the year, included deerhide moccasins, vests, aprons, and coats. Only women, clowns, and shamans decorated their bodies.

War and Weapons The Tubatulabal engaged in regular hostilities against their neighbors for revenge against previous attacks. These wars lasted between one and two days and produced only light casualties. The preferred fighting method was to attack the whole village by surprise at dawn. Peace was arranged through negotiation and was generally accompanied by mutual nonaggression promises.

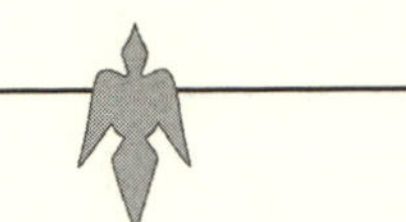

Contemporary Information

Government/Reservations Tule River Reservation (Tule River Tribe; Tulare County; 1873; 55,356 acres, shared with the Monache and the Yokuts) had a 1990 population of roughly 750. It is governed by a tribal council.

The Kern Valley Indian Community (KVIC) and Council is a member of the Confederated Aboriginal Nations of California. KVIC tribes signed four unratified treaties in 1852 and never received any compensation for their aboriginal lands.

Economy People obtain employment as cowhands, secretaries, and loggers and in local businesses. The Tule River Economic Development Council works to provide economic opportunities there. Economic resources include timber and a campground.

Legal Status The KVIC had not received federal recognition as of 1997. The Tule River Tribe is a federally recognized tribal entity.

Daily Life Outmigration and intermarriage have diminished the people's tribal identity. The lives of today's Tubatulabals are similar to those of their non-Indian neighbors. The Valley Cultural Center is a symbol of their active rebuilding of their culture and spirituality. The Monache Gathering is a three-day event that includes sweat lodge ceremonies. The Tule River Reservation has its own health center. Some elders continue to make baskets and dig for traditional roots.

Ventureño

See Chumash

Wailaki

Wailaki (`Wī lä kē) is a Wintun term meaning "north language." The tribe had three main subdivisions: Tsennahkenne (Eel River Wailaki); Bahneko (North Fork Wailaki); and Pitch Wailaki (located farther up the North Fork of the Eel River). The Wailaki are culturally related to four other small tribes—the Mattole, Lassik, Sinkyone, and Nongatl—who lived just to their north and west.

Location In aboriginal times, the Wailaki lived in northwestern California, along the Eel River and the North Fork Eel River. Today, descendants of these people live in and near Mendocino County.

Population Roughly 2,700 Wailaki lived in their region in the mid–nineteenth century; the population of all five tribes may have exceeded 13,000. In 1990, 577 Indians, including some Wailaki, lived on the Round Valley Reservation. The enrolled tribal membership in 1990 was 1,090.

Language With the Mattole, Lassik, Sinkyone, and Nongatl, the Wailaki spoke a Southern Athapaskan language.

Historical Information

History Although human occupation of the region is at least 4,000 years old, the Southern Athapaskans appear to have come to California around 900. They had little contact with non-natives until the mid–nineteenth century. The Anglo extermination raids of 1861 and 1862 were fairly successful.

Survivors fiercely resisted being placed on reservations. Most stayed in the hills working on Anglo sheep and cattle ranches. Others worked on small parcels of land. At one point around the turn of the century, so many of their young were being kidnapped and indentured that parents tattooed their children so they would always know their ancestry.

Religion The Wailaki believed that spirits were present in all objects, inanimate as well as animate. The source of shamans' power was their ability to communicate with *Katanagai* (Night Traveler), the creator god. The Wailaki recognized various types of shamans, both men and women, who might attend special schools to receive visions and practice on patients. They cured the sick by sucking or with herbs and could find lost souls. Sucking and soul-loss doctors could also foretell the future and find lost people or objects. Singing, dancing, and smoking tobacco accompanied most shamans' rituals. Other ceremonies were connected with salmon fishing, acorn gathering, and girls' puberty.

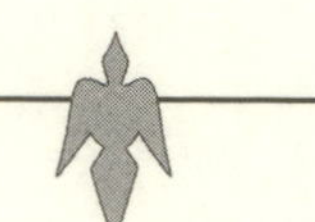

Government Traditionally, the Wailaki consisted of at least 19 tribelets and 95 villages. Tribelets were presided over by hereditary chiefs, who settled disputes and provided food for ceremonial occasions. Chiefs were entitled to extra wives.

Customs The nuclear family was the primary social unit. Gift exchange formed the basis of the marriage formalities. Mothers-in-law and sons-in-law did not speak directly to each other out of respect. Herbal abortion was practiced and probably infanticide, especially in the case of twins, one of whom was generally killed. Divorce was relatively easy to obtain for the usual reasons: unfaithful, barren, or lazy wife; unfaithful or abusive husband. Corpses were buried with their heads facing east; the grave was later piled with stones. Wives and husbands were generally buried together. The house was destroyed, and possessions were buried or otherwise disposed of.

Wealth was important but not as much as with the Klamath River people to the north. Most property except land was individually owned. Childrens' games included jumping rope, swinging, running races, dolls, tops, and buzzer or hummer toys. Adult games included shinny, archery contests, the hand game, and the women's dice game.

Dwellings In winter, people lived in circular houses with conical roofs, made of redwood slabs or bark. A cooking fire was located in the center of a dugout floor. Two or more families occupied a single house. Hide bedding was most common. Brush shelters served as summer houses. Villages also contained circular sweat houses.

Diet Acorns and game, including deer and elk, were the major food source. The Wailaki also ate fish, particularly salmon and trout. Summer was a time for migration following acorns and other ripening plant food sources.

Key Technology Women coiled and (mostly) twined hazel shoots and conifer root fibers, decorated in bear grass, into basket containers, bowls, caps, traps, and other items. Musical instruments included drums, rattles, clappers, whistles, and flutes. Elkhorn and wooden wedges with groundstone mauls were used to split wood. Spoons were made of elkhorn or deer skull. Other raw materials included hide, horn, and stone. Fire came from buckeye or willow fire drills with moss for tinder.

Trade Regular trade partners included the Yuki and Cahto Pomo.

Notable Arts Fine arts included basket making, woodworking, and the manufacture of ceremonial clothing and items.

Transportation Although the Mattole, Lassik, Sinkyone and Nongatl used dugout canoes, the Wailaki made do with log rafts. Goods and children were towed in baskets by swimmers.

Dress Clothing, especially in summer, was minimal. When they did wear clothes, men wore deer hide shirts and buckskin breechclouts. Women wore a one-piece bark skirt or a double apron of buckskin. Both sexes wore their hair shoulder length or longer, combed it with soaproot brushes, and cut it with a stone knife.

War and Weapons Retaliation or revenge for murder, witchcraft, insult, or rape could lead to war among tribelets or families. Most Southern Athapaskans fought little and then usually only among themselves. Battles consisted mainly of surprise attacks. Ceremonial dances preceded and victory dances followed hostilities. All casualties and property loss were compensated for. Weapons included the sinew-backed bow and arrow, knives, clubs, sticks, slings, spears, and rocks. The Wailaki also used elk hide armor and shields.

Contemporary Information

Government/Reservations Some Wailaki Indians live on the Round Valley Reservation (1864; 30,538 acres) as well as on the Sugar Bowl Rancheria (Lakeport County). Their constitution and by-laws were approved in 1936. Other California Southern Athapaskans also live among and have become mixed with Athapaskan Hupa or with other Indians. The Rohnerville Rancheria (Humboldt County) is home to some Southern Athapaskans.

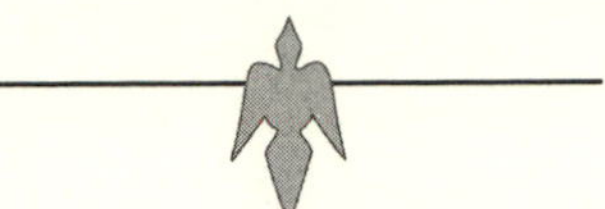

Economy Important economic activities include cattle and sheep ranching, logging, and local small business employment.

Legal Status The Covelo Indian Community of Round Valley Reservation (Wailaki, Yuki, Pit River, Achumawi, Pomo, Konkow, Nomlaki, Wintun) is a federally recognized tribal entity. The Wailaki are federally recognized as part of the Covelo Indian Community and have applied for separate recognition as well.

Daily Life Today's Wailakis are known for their healers and doctoring schools. Local plants are used in traditional arts, such as basket weaving and woodworking, as well as for curing and subsistence. They are in the process of reacquiring their own land base; part of this project includes the struggle for access to aboriginal locations.

Whilkut

See Hupa

Wintun

Wintun (`Win tun), "person." The Wintun people consisted of three subgroups: Patwin (Southern); River and Hill Nomlaki (Central); and Wintu (Northern).

Location Wintuns traditionally lived west of the Sacramento River, from the valley to the Coast Range. Today most Wintuns live on reservations and rancherias in Colusa, Glenn, Yolo, Mendocino, and Shasta Counties.

Population The eighteenth-century population of Wintuns was roughly 15,000, including perhaps 2,000 Nomlaki. In 1990, 147 Indians lived on the four Wintun rancherias, and more lived off-reservation. Also, Wintuns were among 656 Indians who lived on two other shared reservations. The enrolled membership figures were 2,244 Wintu, 332 Nomlaki, and no Patwin.

Language The three Wintun language groups—Wintu, Nomlaki, and Patwin—are Penutian languages.

Historical Information

History In aboriginal times, the Wintuns consisted of nine major groups within the three main subgroups. Some Nomlakis encountered the Spanish as early as 1808, although in general the Nomlaki were outside the sphere of Spanish influence.

By 1800, Patwins were being taken by force to the missions. Wintus first met non-natives in 1826, when the Jedediah Smith and Peter Ogden expeditions entered the region. Malaria epidemics killed roughly 75 percent of Wintuns in the early 1830s. Severe smallpox epidemics followed in 1837. By the mid–nineteenth century, most of their land had been stolen. Ranchers' cattle and sheep destroyed their main food sources. Miners polluted the fresh water. Then came the massacres. Captain John C. Frémont killed 175 Wintu and Yana in 1846; in 1850, whites gave a "friendship" feast with poisoned food, killing 100 Wintu. In 1851, 300 Indians died when miners burned the Wintu council house.

The so-called Cottonwood Treaty, ratified in 1852, acknowledged 35 square miles of Wintu land, but from 1858 to 1859, California regular and irregular troops killed at least 100 Wintus and displaced hundreds of others. Throughout the 1860s, Wintuns were hunted down and either killed or used as laborers. The 25,000-acre Nome Lackee Reservation was established in 1854 in the foothills of western Tehama County. Indians created a stable existence there based on farming, but by 1863, the reservation had been taken over by whites, and its residents were sent to Round Valley. Many surviving Nomlakis eventually returned to their old territory, working as farm hands and establishing a number of settlements, or rancherias. Most Patwins who survived the missions, military forays, raids, epidemics, and massacres either became assimilated into white society or were forced onto small reservations during the 1850s and 1860s, most of which have since been terminated.

A period of religious revival occurred in the 1870s, during which much traditional practice was replaced with Ghost Dance and, later, Big Head

ceremonies. Wintus gathered en masse for the last time at the end of the nineteenth century. Copper-processing plants around the turn of the century poisoned what decent land and water remained in the region. Cortina, Colusa, Paskenta, and Grindstone Rancherias were created between 1906 and 1909. Wintu children were formally excluded from local schools until 1928. Termination and allotment policies during 1952 and 1953 further broke up Wintun culture; only three rancherias survived this period. In the 1930s, and again in the 1970s, dam construction flooded much of their remaining land. Despite an agreement with the Wintu people, the U.S. government removed people from and destroyed the Toyon-Wintu site in 1984.

Religion The rich Wintun mythology included recognition of a supreme being as well as numerous spirits. Wintuns prayed to the sun before washing in the morning, smoking, and eating. Spirits, present in all things, could be acquired by dreaming and going to a sacred place and engaging in ritual behavior. Among the Nomlaki, they could also be influenced by prayer, charms, magic, and ritual. Shamans provided overall religious leadership. Bear shamans could destroy enemies. They received their powers during an annual five-day initiation period of fasting, dancing, and instruction from other shamans. Their curing methods included massage, soul capture, and sucking out a disease-causing object. Some Wintuns practiced the Kuksu cult, in which one or more secret societies, open by initiation to men and some high-status women, performed their own dances and rituals to restore the people to a perfect aboriginal state.

Wintuns did not adopt the 1870 Ghost Dance but rather the 1871 Earth Lodge cult, which preached return of the dead, the end of the world, and protection of the faithful. The Bole-Maru religion came in 1872, and dream dancing was popular toward the end of the century. Among the Nomlaki, virtually every activity and life-cycle phase carried with it ritual restrictions and ceremonies.

Government Like many California peoples, Wintuns were organized into tribelets. The village was the main social, economic, and political unit. Villages were autonomous and had clearly defined territory. Each village was led by a chief, often hereditary, who arbitrated disputes, hosted ceremonies and gatherings, and engaged in diplomatic relations with chiefs of other villages. The chief, who was materially supported by his followers, had to be a good singer and dancer and generally well liked. The Nomlaki recognized a secret society of higher-status men. These people had a higher degree of authority in public matters and controlled most of the skilled crafts and professions.

Customs The complex girls' puberty ritual involved seclusion for up to seven months in a special hut, a special diet and behavior, and, later, a dance. Boys had no puberty ceremony, but after killing their first deer they gave away the meat and then bathed. Marriage and cohabitation were synonymous; premarital relations were frowned upon. Wealthy men might have more than one wife. Mother-in-law taboos were present but not absolute. Both men and women observed many food and behavioral taboos related to pregnancy and birth. When a person died, mourners dressed his or her body in good clothes, removed it through a special opening in the rear of the house, and buried it with acorn meal, water, and personal items. The Patwin wrapped their dead with long hemp cords. Souls were said to travel along the Milky Way.

Murder and rape or other sexual transgressions were generally capital crimes. Most intentional crimes could be atoned for by compensating the injured party. Dances were more often social than religious and were often given when food was plentiful. Gambling was also a part of social dances; activities included the grass game (men), hand games, shinny (women), football, hoop and pole, ring and pin, and other contests of skill. Songs could also be social or religious.

Dwellings Four to seven pole-framed, bark-covered conical houses made up a village. Among the Patwin, dwellings as well as the ceremonial and domed menstrual huts were semisubterranean and earth covered. The men's clubhouse and sweat lodge was semisubterranean and circular, 15–20 feet in diameter, with one center pole. In cold weather single men also slept there.

Diet Men hunted deer and rabbits both communally in drives and individually. They also smoked bear (except grizzly) out of their dens and captured fowl, birds, and rodents. Communal drives were held to catch salmon and trout. Women gathered grubs, grasshoppers, acorns, greens, and seeds. Men and women cooperated in gathering acorns, with men shaking acorns out of trees for women to gather. The acorns were then dried and pounded into meal, after leaching them to remove their bitter taste.

Key Technology Material items included bows (seasoned yew, reinforced with shredded deer sinew and containing twisted deer backbone sinew string), arrowheads (obsidian, pressure-flaked), arrows, and fishing nets, poles, and traps. Iris, hemp, grapevine, and milkweed were used for cordage. Other tools were made from bone, horn, and stone. Baskets served a number of functions. Fire drills were made of buckeye. Grass, boughs, or deer hides served as mattresses.

Trade Trade was more frequent between villages or tribelets than with other peoples. Wintus obtained salmon flour, body paints, yew wood for bows, and obsidian for deer hides, woodpecker scalps, and salt. The Nomlaki traded for highly prized black bear pelts. They also traded in items made from Oregon to San Francisco Bay. Patwins traded freely and intermarried with some Pomo groups. Bows were a common item of exchange. In general, strings of clamshell disks, dentalia, and magnesite cylinders served as money. Men bartered mostly in clamshells and dentalia, women in baskets.

Notable Arts Basket making constituted the main Wintun fine art.

Transportation People used rafts to cross streams and floated children or supplies in large baskets. River Patwin used tule balsa boats that exceeded 20 feet in length.

Dress Dress was minimal. Adult women wore shredded maple bark aprons. Capes and blankets for warmth were of deer, fox, and rabbit skin. Decorations included earrings, headdresses, and tattooing (mainly women). The Nomlaki wore elk hide sandals.

War and Weapons In addition to fighting neighboring villages and tribelets, Wintun enemies generally included the Shasta, Klamath, Modoc, and Yana. The Nomlakis' main enemy was the Yuki. Wintus took no prisoners. Typical provocations for feuds or war included murder, theft of women, poaching, and trespass. Among the Nomlaki not all men fought; those who did underwent special practical and magical training. Seers determined the proper course of action, and poisoners used magic as a weapon. Wars were usually limited, and casualties were minimal. Weapons included the bow and arrow, clubs, spears, daggers, slings, and wooden rod armor. Hand-to-hand fighting was avoided if possible. When the fighting stopped, an assembly of important men decided on just compensation.

Contemporary Information

Government/Reservations Wintuns currently live at Grindstone Creek Rancheria (Glenn County; 1906; 80 acres), Cortina Rancheria (Colusa County; 1907; 640 acres [Miwok]), Colusa Rancheria (Colusa County; 1907; 273 acres), Redding Rancheria (Shasta County), Rumsey Rancheria ("Yocha-De-He"; Yolo County; 1907; 185 acres), and the Round Valley Reservation/Covelo Indian Community (Mendocino County; 1864; 30,538 acres [Wailaki, Yuki, Nomlaki, Pomo, Concow, Pit River, and Little Lake peoples]). The Rumsey Rancheria elects a tribal council based on a constitution and by-laws approved in 1976. Other communities are governed by tribal councils as well.

Economy The Rumsey Rancheria's diversified businesses include agricultural enterprises and a grocery store, service station, and bingo casino. They are financially self-sufficient.

Legal Status The Colusa Rancheria (Cachil DeHe Band of the Colosa Indian Community); Cortina Indian Rancheria; Grindstone Indian Rancheria (Wintun-Wailaki); and the Rumsey Indian Rancheria are federally recognized tribal entities. The Covelo

Indian Community of the Round Valley Reservation is a federally recognized tribal entity. The Hayfork Band of Nor-El-Muk Wintu Indians, the Wintoon Indians, and the Wintu Indians of Central Valley had not received federal recognition as of 1997.

Daily Life In the 1970s, the residents of Grindstone Rancheria, in combination with local non-Indians, successfully fought the Story–Elk Creek Dam. Today's Wintus work to protect ancient burial sites as well as the sacred Mt. Shasta. The Nomlaki have been forced to deal with the issue of toxic waste dumping. Although much traditional culture has been lost, their heritage, transmitted in large measure by dedicated elders, remains very important to Wintu people.

Wiyot

Wiyot (`Wē yut) is the name of one of three culturally and linguistically related groups on the Eel River Delta in the early nineteenth century. They were culturally similar to the Yurok.

Location The Wiyot traditionally inhabited the vicinity of Humboldt Bay, California, from the Little River south to the Bear River and east about 25 miles. This environment is coastal lowlands, an unusual one in California. Today, most Wiyots live in and around Humboldt County.

Population As many as 3,500 Wiyot may been living in their region in the early nineteenth century. In 1990, roughly 50 Indians who consider themselves Wiyot lived on rancherias, with perhaps another 400 in local cities and towns.

Language Wiyot was an Algonquian language related to Yurok.

Historical Information

History Humboldt Bay was first occupied around 900 by either Wiyots or Yuroks. In 1806, the first non-native explorers came into the region. The first systematic murders of Wiyots began around 1852 during the Chetco/Rogue River Indian War. Regular killings of Indians led to wholesale massacres shortly thereafter. In 1860, a massacre at Gunther Island, perpetrated by white residents of Eureka during a Wiyot religious celebration, killed as many as 250 Indians. Survivors were forced onto reservations on the Klamath and Smith Rivers. Wiyot culture never recovered from this event; their identity became mixed with whites and other local Indian peoples.

Religion The creator was known as "that old man above." The Wiyot practiced World Renewal ceremonies and dances. Although other peoples celebrated the World Renewal religion in a showy and complex manner, which involved recitations, displays of wealth, costumed dances, and various decorations, the Wiyot observed it irregularly and with less flair. Men and women also performed victory dances when an enemy was killed and conducted an elaborate girls' puberty ceremony. They did not observe a first salmon ritual. Female berdaches played an important role in Wiyot ceremonialism.

Government In place of formal tribal organization, each Wiyot group was autonomous and self-governing.

Customs Wealth was valued as the source of social stratification and prestige, although not to the degree of the Klamath River peoples. There was no debt slavery. Most of the common menstrual taboos were absent among the Wiyot. Married couples generally lived with the father's family, except in the case of "half-marriages" (when a man worked to cover part of the bride price). Corpses were carried by stretcher to the cemetery and buried in an extended position in plank-lined graves along with money and valuables. Relatives and undertakers observed various taboos following the funeral.

Both women and men hunted. Disease was considered to be caused either by the intrusion of poison objects, soul loss, or breaches of taboo. Herb doctors and especially sucking doctors (shamans) cured disease. Unlike most northwest California peoples, the Wiyots did not penalize shamans for declining a curing case.

Dwellings Two or more families, including men, slept in rectangular houses of split redwood planks. Each unnamed house had a two- or three-pitch roof and a smoke hole at the top. The sweat house, built like a dwelling, only smaller, was used for gambling, ceremony, and occasionally sleeping. The Wiyot built no separate birth or menstrual huts.

Diet Acorns were both traded for and gathered on special inland expeditions. The people also gathered berries and various other foods. Salmon, the main food staple along with other fish, was caught with traps, nets, weirs, on platforms, and with the use of fish poisons. Other foods included mollusks, sea lions, stranded whales, deer, elk, and other game. They did not eat wolf, fox, bear, and skunk.

Key Technology Tools and utilitarian items were made from bone, shell, stone, and wood. Twined baskets served a large variety of purposes.

Trade Wiyots participated in a regional trading complex.

Notable Arts Wiyot baskets were particularly well made.

Transportation The Wiyot used large redwood dugout canoes.

Wiyot baskets were particularly well made, and women generally wore twined basket hats. This Wiyot woman is basket weaving in the dunes near Eureka in 1900.

Dress Women generally wore twined basket hats and either fringed and embroidered buckskin double-aprons that hung to between the knee and the ankle or one-piece, inner-bark skirts or aprons. Men wore buckskin breechclouts. Robes were of deer hide and woven rabbit skin. Both sexes wore moccasins.

War and Weapons Murder, insult, or poaching were the typical causes of war. The Wiyot fought by surprise attack or prearranged battle and used elk hide armor, rawhide shields, and bows and arrows. Women and children were not killed in war. After the fighting, both sides paid compensation for damaged property.

Contemporary Information

Government/Reservations Today, Wiyot live on the Blue Lake Rancheria (Wiyot, Yurok, Hupa; Humboldt County), the Rohnerville Rancheria (Wiyot-Mattole; Humboldt County), the Table Bluff Rancheria (Humboldt County), and the Trinidad Rancheria (Yurok, Wiyot, Tolowa; Humboldt County). Government is by tribal council.

Economy All four rancherias are working to promote economic development. Logging and fishing are important economic activities.

Legal Status The Bear River Band of the Rohnerville Rancheria is a federally recognized tribal entity (Wiyot/Mattole). The Blue Lake Rancheria, the Trinidad Rancheria, and the Table Bluff Rancheria are federally recognized tribal entities.

Daily Life The Wiyot support the traditional culture of their neighbors. They also hold an annual vigil in memory of the victims of the 1860 massacre. There is some semitraditional basket making among the people.

Yana

Yana (`Yä nä), "People."

Location In the early nineteenth century, the Yana lived in the upper Sacramento River Valley and the adjacent eastern foothills. The elevation of their territory ranged between 300 and 10,000 feet.

Population The aboriginal population of Yana probably numbered fewer than 2,000. Few, if any, Yana remain alive today.

Language Yana was a Hokan language. Its four divisions were Northern, Central, Southern, and Yahi.

Historical Information

History Members of an 1821 Mexican expedition may have been the first non-natives to encounter the Yana. Hudson's Bay Company trappers almost certainly interacted with the Yana from about 1828 on, and some Mexicans received land grants in Yana territory during that time. The first permanent Anglo settlement in the area came in 1845.

By the late 1840s, Anglo trails crossed Yana territory. With Anglo encroachment came increased conflict: Attacks by U.S. soldiers (John C. Frémont in 1846, for example) led to retaliations, and as food became scarcer the Yana began raiding cabins. In the 1860s, Anglos set out to exterminate the Yana. Though massacres, disease, and starvation, their population was reduced by 95 percent in about 20 years.

In 1911, a Yana man named Ishi walked out of the foothills of Mt. Lassen to a nearby town, where two anthropologists were able to communicate with him. Ishi eventually communicated his story, which began at the time when Anglo invaders and murderers began to destroy the Yahi. Only about a dozen or so Yahis remained alive after a massacre in 1868, six years after Ishi's birth. These people remained in the wilderness until 1908, when only four were left. Three died shortly thereafter, leaving Ishi as the only remaining Yahi in 1911. After leaving the woods, he lived and worked at the University of California Museum of Anthropology (San Francisco), demonstrating traditional crafts, providing a wealth of information about his culture, and learning some English. Ishi died of tuberculosis in 1916.

Religion Little is known about Yana ceremonial life. They may have practiced the Kuksu cult. The few surviving Yana danced the Ghost Dance in 1871.

Government Yana tribelets consisted of a main village with several smaller satellite villages. Each

village probably had a hereditary chief or headman, who lived in the main village. Chiefs were wealthy and often had two wives. They led the dances, orated from the roof of the assembly house on proper behavior, and were the only ones permitted to keep vultures as pets. The villagers provided food for chiefs and their families.

Customs Shamans, mostly male, received their power by fasting in remote places or swimming in certain pools. Trained by older shamans, they cured by singing, dancing, or sucking. Unsuccessful shamans might be accused of sorcery and killed. Various roots and teas were also used as medicines.

Girls had a more significant puberty ritual and greater restrictions around puberty than did boys. Parents arranged most marriages. The Yana observed a strong mother-in-law taboo. Yahi dead were usually cremated; the other groups buried their dead after four days, wrapped in deerskin, along with personal items, and burned their house and other possessions.

Land was privately owned. Men played double-ball shinny (usually a woman's game). Other games included ring and pin, cat's cradle, stick throwing at a stake, and the grass or hand game.

Dwellings Northern and Central groups lived in earth-covered multifamily houses. The Southern and Yahi groups preferred smaller, conical bark-covered houses. An assembly house was located in a tribelet's main village. All groups lived in temporary brush shelters or caves while hunting.

Diet Acorns, fish, and venison were the staples. Men climbed trees to shake acorns down while women gathered, shelled, and dried them. After leaching the acorn flour, it was used for mush, bread, and a soup with meat, berries, and other foods. Women also gathered roots, tubers, bulbs, berries, pine nuts, and grasshoppers. Men stalked deer using a deer-head decoy and bow and arrow. Salmon was broiled on heated rocks, roasted over an open fire, or dried and stored. Rabbits were hunted in community drives. The Yana also took other game.

Key Technology Yanas hunted with bow (preferably of yew wood) and arrow, as well as snares. They used spears, nets, and traps to catch fish. Other technological items included stone grinding tools; baskets of hazel, willow, pine roots, and sedge; milkweed fiber, peeled bark, and hemp ropes; mahogany and oak digging sticks; and buckeye fire drills. Musical instruments included rattles and elderwood flutes.

Trade Typical exports included deer hides, salt, baskets, and buckeye fire-making drills. Imports included obsidian (Achumawi and Shasta); arrows, wildcat-skin quivers, and woodpecker scalps (Atsugewi); clam disk beads and magnesite cylinders (Maidu or Wintun); dentalium shells (Wintu); and barbed obsidian arrow points from the north.

Notable Arts Yana women made fine baskets.

Transportation People used rafts to cross streams and floated children or supplies in large baskets. Regional Indians also used dugout and tule (rush) canoes for water transportation.

Dress Women wore shredded bark or tule aprons or skirts. Wealthy women wore braids of human hair and skirts with leather and grass tassels. Men who could afford them wore buckskin leggings in winter; others made do with a simple apron. Men also wore eelskin hats and deerskin moccasins. Adornments included necklaces, feather headbands, woodpecker-scalp belts, and body paint. Hide robes provided warmth in winter. Men plucked facial hair with a split piece of wood. Both sexes pierced their ears.

War and Weapons The Yana often fought their neighbors. Poaching and avenging the abduction of women were common reasons for war.

Ynezeño

See Chumash

Yokuts

Yokuts (`Yō kutz), a linguistic term meaning "person" or "People." The three divisions were the Northern Valley Yokuts, the Southern Valley Yokuts, and the

Foothill Yokuts. Contemporary Yokuts tribes include the Choinumni, the Chukchansi, the Tachi (or Tache) and the Wukchumni.

Location The Yokuts traditionally lived along the San Joaquin Valley and the Sierra Nevada foothills. Specifically, the Southern Yokuts inhabited a lake-slough-marsh environment in the southern San Joaquin Valley; the Northern Yokuts' territory was wetlands and grassy plains in the northern San Joaquin Valley; and the Foothill Yokuts lived approximately on the western slopes between the Fresno and Kern Rivers. Today, Yokuts live on two rancherias in Tulare and Kings Counties and in nearby communities.

Population The Yokuts population stood between 18,000 and 50,000 in the early eighteenth century. They had one of the highest regional population densities in aboriginal North America. In 1990, about 1,150 Indians lived on two Yokuts rancherias. At least several hundred more live on other rancherias and are scattered nearby and around California.

Language Yokuts people spoke various dialects of Yokuts, a California Penutian language.

Historical Information

History The San Joaquin Valley has been inhabited for some 11,000 years. Yokuts culture is probably about between 600 and 2,000 years old, with direct cultural antecedents dating back perhaps 7,000 years. Aboriginal population density was extremely high, relatively speaking. The Spanish came into the region of the Southern Yokuts in the 1770s and were warmly received.

In the early nineteenth century, serious cultural destruction began as the northern valleys were drawn into the exploitative mission system. Yokuts resistance and retaliation brought further Spanish repression and even military expeditions. Foothills Yokuts communities were protected by their relative isolation, but they sheltered escapees and began raiding for horses to ride and eat, activities that they continued into the Mexican period. Yokuts became excellent cattle breeders and horse breakers during this period.

In the early 1830s, malaria and cholera epidemics killed roughly three-quarters of all Indians in the region. Mexicans established land grants in the San Joaquin Valley. By then, traditional flora, fauna, and subsistence patterns had all been severely disrupted. After the United States annexed California in 1848, its citizens began a large-scale campaign of slaughter and land theft against the Yokuts. The latter, along with their Miwok allies, resisted Anglo violence and land theft by force (such as the Mariposa Indian War of 1850–1851). In 1851, the tribes signed a treaty to relinquish their land for a reservation and payment, but pressure from the state of California kept the U.S. government from ratifying the agreement.

Dispossessed, some Yokuts worked on local ranches, where they were poorly paid and kept practically in peonage. The 1870 Ghost Dance revival provided a straw of hope to a beaten people. It lasted two years; its failure probably prevented the 1890 Ghost Dance from gaining popularity. The Tule River Reservation was established 1873. The Santa Rosa Rancheria was established in 1921.

Yokuts found minimal employment in the logging industry, as ranch hands, and as farm laborers into the twentieth century. Their children were forcibly sent to culture-killing boarding schools in the early part of the century. By the 1950s, most Indian children were in (segregated) public schools. A cultural revival took place beginning in the 1960s.

Religion The Yokuts' most important festival was their annual six-day ritual in honor of the dead. They also celebrated the arrival of the first fruit of the season. Group ceremonies were always conducted in the open and included shamanic displays of magic powers. Many men and older women also had spiritual helpers that conferred good fortune or specific abilities. The Northern Yokuts may have practiced the Kuksu cult. Men and women of this group also drank datura annually as part of a spring cleansing and curing ritual. Among the central Foothills group, datura was drunk once in a lifetime, by adolescents.

Government The Yokuts were organized into about 50 named tribelets, each with its own semipermanent

A Yokuts shaman displays his baskets and some of his medicine equipment in 1920. Shamans derived power from spirit animals via dreams or vision quests. Chronically unsuccessful shamans might be accused of sorcery and killed.

villages, territory, and dialect. Each tribelet also had several hereditary chiefs (often at least one per village, usually from among the Eagle lineage). The chief, usually a wealthy man, sponsored ceremonies, hosted guests, aided the poor, mediated disputes, and authorized hunts as well as the murder of evil people such as sorcerers. Other offices included chief's messenger.

Customs Corpses, often along with their material possessions, were traditionally cremated. Most undertakers were berdaches. Public and private mourning ceremonies were observed. The afterworld, to the west or northwest, was a mirror image of this world, only better.

Shamans derived power from spirit animals via dreams or vision quests. They cured and presided over ceremonies. Large fees were charged for cures. Chronically unsuccessful shamans might be accused of sorcery and killed.

Various patrilineal lines existed among the Yokuts. Each had a totem symbol, such as a bird or an animal, which had certain ceremonial functions. Also, many tribelets had a dual division (Eagle and Coyote).

Among both men and women, various restrictions and taboos were associated with pregnancy and childbirth. The girls' puberty ceremony also involved certain restrictions and taboos. Families arranged the marriages with the couple's consent. Most men had only one wife. After living for a year with the woman's parents, a couple lived in or near the husband's parents' home. The Yokuts observed parent-in-law taboos. Divorce was relatively easy to obtain. After their infant cradle of soft tule, babies were confined to a forked-stick frame for almost a year.

Among the Foothill Yokuts, everyone swam at least daily, with adolescents also swimming several times at night during the winter for toughening. The divisions competed against each other in games, with men and women often gambling on the results. Both sexes played the hand game. Women also threw dice or split sticks. Leisure activities also included dancing and storytelling. Men smoked tobacco, usually at bedtime. Rattles accompanied most singing, which usually occurred during rituals. Other instruments included bone and wood whistles, flutes, and a musical bow.

Dwellings The Southern Yokuts built both single-family oval-shaped and ten-family dwellings, in which each family had its own door and fireplace. Both featured tule mats covering pole frames. Mats also covered the floor and raised beds. Men sweated and sometimes slept in sweat houses.

The Northern Yokuts built similar single-family and possibly ceremonial earth lodges. Conical huts thatched with grass or bark slabs characterized dwellings of the Foothills Yokuts. Beds were of pine needles. Other structures included sweat houses, gaming courts, and mat-covered granaries and ramadas. Among Foothills Yokuts, women might use the sweat houses when no men were present.

Diet The wetland home of the Southern Valley Yokuts contained an enormous variety and quantity of wildlife. They hunted fowl, rabbits, squirrels and other rodents, turtles, and occasionally big game. They gathered tule roots, manzanita berries, pine nuts, and seeds. Seafood included lake trout, salmon,

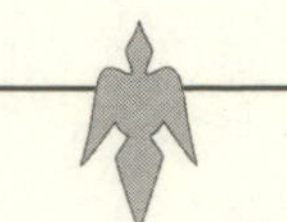

perch, and mussels. Fresh fish was broiled on hot coals or sun-dried for storage. They also raised dogs for eating but did not eat frogs. Their salt came from salt grass.

In addition to many of the above foods, Northern Valley Yokuts depended on fish, mussels, turtles, elk, antelope, and smaller mammals. Salmon and especially acorns were staples. The Foothills Yokuts ate a lot of deer, quail, acorns, and fish. They also ate pine nuts, wild oats, manzanita berries, duck, trout, wasp grubs, squirrels, and rabbits. Iris bulb and tule root were important sources of flour. Men stalked deer by using deer disguises, or they ambushed them and shot them with bow and arrow. Quail were trapped. Salmon and other fish were caught with spears, weirs, and basket traps. The Yokuts also planted tobacco and may have engaged in basic horticulture or plant management.

Key Technology Baskets alone included water bottles, seed beaters, burden baskets, cooking vessels, winnowing trays, cradles, and caps. People fished with traps, nets, baskets, and spears from scaffolds built over river banks. Other types of snares and nets were used to capture fowl, as were spring poles with underwater triggers, stuffed decoys, and special water-skimming arrows.

Cords and ropes were fashioned from milkweed fiber. Ovens were made of earth. Northern Valley Yokuts' tools were made more often of stone and bone. Foothills Yokuts used stone, obsidian, granite, and quartz, and they had basic pottery. Southern Valley Yokuts made most of their crafts of tule, although there were a few wood, stone, and bone tools. The Yokuts burned wild seed plant areas to improve the following year's crop.

Trade Yokuts Indians traded widely with peoples of different habitats. Southern Valley people imported obsidian for arrowheads and sharp tools, stone mortars and pestles, wooden mortars, and marine shells for money and decoration. Northern Valley people traded dog pups for Miwok baskets and bows and arrows. They also traded with other tribes for mussels and abalone shells. Hunting, gathering, or fishing rights were occasionally exchanged as well.

Notable Arts Basketry was considered a fine art as well as a craft. Representational petroglyphs, mostly circles and dots, were made perhaps as early as 1000 B.C.E. The Yokuts also drew pictographs, similar to those of the Chumash, into the historic period.

Transportation Valley Yokuts used wide, flat rafts made from lashed tule rushes. They floated belongings across rivers on log rafts. Some Foothills groups also used small basket boats. Women carried burdens in baskets anchored by tumplines.

Dress Dress was minimal. Men wore skin breechclouts at most. Women's clothing consisted of skin, grass, or tule aprons. Blankets and bedding were often made from the skins of rabbits or mud hens. Women tattooed their chins and used ornaments in pierced ears and noses.

War and Weapons Yokuts tribelets would occasionally fight one another or neighboring groups, but they were generally peaceful. Motives for fighting included trespass, theft of food, or the adventurous raiding by young men. They generally did not take captives. The peace conference included presents that were not considered reparations.

Contemporary Information

Government/Reservations Many Yokuts live on the Santa Rosa Rancheria (1921; 170 acres; about 400 people in 1990 [Tachi tribe]) and the Tule River Reservation (1873; 55,356 acres; 750 people in 1990 [Tule River tribe]). Both are governed by tribal councils. Some Foothills Yokuts live in hamlets or scattered dwellings on or near their former territories.

The Choinumni tribe is governed by a tribal council and affiliated with the Choinumni Cultural Association. Their 1990 population was about 250.

The Wukchumni tribe, population about 300 (1990), is governed by a tribal council.

The Picayune Rancheria (Chukchansi tribe) was founded in 1912 and "unterminated" in 1984. There is no land base for the population of about 800.

Table Mountain Rancheria (Chukchansi and Monache; 1916; 100 acres) had a 1990 population of about 100 people.

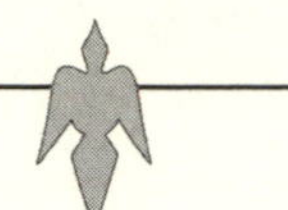

Economy Primary economic activities include lumbering; ranching, including the leasing of lands; and farming. Many people, especially off-reservation Yokuts, receive government assistance. The Tule River Economic Development Corporation is a local planning agency. There are bingo parlors on the Table Mountain and Santa Rosa Rancherias.

Legal Status The Santa Rosa Indian Community (Tachi Tribe) is a federally recognized tribal entity. The Picayune Rancheria of Chukchansi Indians is a federally recognized tribal entity. The Table Mountain Rancheria is a federally recognized tribal entity. The Tule River Indian Tribe of the Tule River Indian Reservation is a federally recognized tribal entity. The Choinumni Tribe and the Wukchumni Tribe had not received federal recognition as of 1997.

Daily Life Some Yokuts dialects are still spoken. Much of Yokuts traditional culture, other than on a scattered individual level, has disappeared. Some spiritual leaders belong to the Native American Cultural Association. Educational levels among the Yokuts is generally low, and the people suffer from recurring social and health problems. Important contemporary concerns include health care, education, land rights, the protection of sacred sites, and federal recognition.

The Tule River Reservation has its own health center. It also sponsors an elders' gathering in August and San Juan's Day in June. The Choinumni Tribe celebrates a traditional harvest gathering. The Wukchumni Tribe holds a spring dance. Chukchansi Indians are working to establish a land base. The Santa Rosa Rancheria celebrates a festival for spiritual renewal on March 1. Yokuts also attend many intertribal gatherings.

Yurok

Yurok (`Yū rək) is a Karuk word meaning "downstream" and refers to the tribe's location relative to the Karuk people. The Yurok referred to themselves as *Olekwo'l,* or "persons."

Location Traditionally, the Yurok lived in permanent villages along and near the mouth of the Klamath River, in northern California. Today, many live on several small rancherias in Humboldt County.

Population The aboriginal Yurok population was roughly 3,000 (early nineteenth century). In 1990, 1,819 Indians, not all of them Yurok, lived on four Yurok reservations. Other Yurok lived off-reservation. The official Yurok enrollment in 1991 was about 3,500.

Language Yurok is an Algonquian language.

Historical Information

History Some Yurok villages were established as early as the fourteenth century and perhaps earlier. Their first contact with non-natives came with Spanish expeditions around 1775. The first known contact was among Hudson's Bay Company trappers and traders in 1827. However, the Yurok remained fairly isolated until about 1850, when a seaport was created in Yurok territory to make travel to the gold fields more accessible. The rush of settlers after 1848 led to a wholesale slaughter and dispossession of the Yurok. An 1851 treaty that would have established a large Yurok reservation was defeated by non-Indian interests. Shortly after the first white settlement was founded, Yuroks were working there as bottom-level wage laborers.

President Franklin Pierce established the Klamath River Reservation in Yurok Territory in 1855. Congress authorized the Hoopa Valley Reservation in 1864. In 1891, the Klamath River Reservation was joined to the Hoopa Reservation in an extension now called the Yurok Reservation. This tract of land consisted of 58,168 acres in 1891, but allotment and sale of "surplus" land, primarily to Anglo timber companies, reduced this total to about 6,800 acres. Three communal allotments became the rancherias of Big Lagoon, Trinidad, and Resighini.

From the mid–nineteenth century into the twentieth, many Yuroks worked in salmon canneries. Yuroks formed the Yurok Tribal Organization in the 1930s. Indian Shakerism was introduced in 1927, and some Yuroks joined the Assembly of God in the 1950s and 1960s. In a landmark 1988 case, the U.S. Supreme Court declined to protect sacred sites of Yurok and other Indians from government road

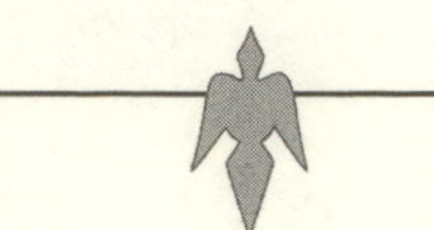

building. Also in 1988, the Hoopa-Yurok Settlement Act partly resolved a long-standing dispute over timber revenues and fishing rights.

Religion With other northern California Indians, local Yurok groups practiced the World Renewal religion and the accompanying wealth-displaying white deerskin and jumping dances. Other ceremonies included the brush dance, kick dance, ghost dance, war dance, and peace dance. People who performed religious ceremonies were drawn from the ranks of the aristocracy (see "Government"). In general, religious training was related to acquiring not spirits, as in regions to the north, but rather real items, such as dentalia or food.

Government The wealthiest man was generally the village leader. About 10 percent of the men made up an aristocracy known as *peyerk,* or "real men." Selected by elder sponsors for special training, including vision quests, they lived at higher elevations, spoke in a more elaborate style, and acquired treasures such as albino deerskins, large obsidian knives, and costumes heavily decorated with shells and seeds. They also wore finer clothing than most Yuroks, imported special food, ate with a different etiquette, hosted ceremonial gatherings, and occasionally spoke foreign languages. The *peyerk* occasionally gathered as a council to arbitrate disputes. "Real women" went through a similar training experience. Since children were considered a financial drain, "real women" and their husbands practiced family limitation by sexual abstinence.

Customs Social status was a function of individual wealth, which was itself a major Yurok preoccupation. Only individuals owned land, although other resources might be owned as well by villages and descent groups. Poor people could voluntarily submit to the status of slave in order to acquire some measure of wealth. Imported dentalia shells were a major measure of wealth; they were engraved, decorated, and graded into standard measures for use as money. Other forms of wealth included large obsidian blades (also imported), pileated woodpecker scalps, and albino deerskins.

Via prayer and elicitation of wrongdoing, women doctors cured by gaining control of "pains," small inanimate, disease-causing objects within people. The misuse of curing power (sorcery) could cause individual death or group famine. Intertribal social and ceremonial relations with neighbors were frequent and friendly. Yurok villages often competed against each other in games. Unlike most offenses, certain sex crimes may have been considered crimes against the community.

The basic unit of society was small groups of patrilineally related males. Marriage was accompanied by lengthy haggling over the bride price. Most couples lived with the husband's family. Illegitimacy and adultery, being crimes against property, were considered serious. Corpses were removed from the home through the roof and buried in a family plot. If a married person died, the spouse guarded the grave until the soul's departure for the afterworld several days after death.

Dwellings Yuroks lived in over 50 semipermanent villages; late summer and early fall were devoted to gathering expeditions. Village dwellings were small rectangular redwood-plank houses with slanted or three-pitched roofs and a central excavated pit. Platforms lined the interior. A small anteroom was located immediately inside the entrance. They housed individual biological families. Houses of people of standing were named. People lived in temporary brush shelters while away on the gathering trips.

Rectangular plank sweat houses served as dormitories for the men and boys of a kinship unit. A "rich man," or head of a paternal kin group, built this structure for himself and his male relatives. The walls lined the sides of a deep pit, within which there was a fire for providing direct heat. Men often sweated in the afternoon, alternating sweats with immersion in chilly river water, scrubbing with herbs, and reciting prayers for good fortune. Space inside the sweat house was apportioned according to rank.

Diet Acorns and salmon were riverine staples; other fish and shellfish were also eaten along the coast. Yuroks also ate sea lions, elk, deer, small game, and various roots and seeds.

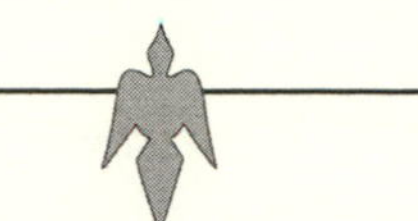

Yurok village dwellings, like the ones pictured in this 1890 photograph, were small rectangular redwood-plank houses with slanted or three-pitched roofs and a central excavated pit.

Key Technology Baskets were used for a number of purposes. Many items, including houses and canoes, were fashioned of wood. Salmon were taken with weirs, poles, and nets as well as with harpoons. Yuroks may have had systems of higher mathematics.

Trade Yuroks traded canoes to the Karuk and other neighboring peoples.

Notable Arts Baskets were particularly well made, as were wood products such as sweat house stools and headrests; dugout canoes with seats, footrests, and yokes; and hollowed treasure chests.

Transportation Yuroks traveled both river and ocean on square-ended, dugout redwood canoes.

Dress Ceremonial regalia included headdresses with up to 70 redheaded-woodpecker scalps. Every adult had an arm tattoo for checking the length of dentalia strings. Everyday dress included unsoled, single-piece moccasins, leather robes (in winter), and deerskin aprons (women). Men wore few or no clothes in summer. They generally plucked their facial hair except while mourning.

War and Weapons The Yurok were not a hostile people by nature, but they feuded constantly. An

Yurok men fish on the Klamath River (1908). Among the Yurok, acorns and salmon were riverine staples; other fish and shellfish were also eaten along the coast.

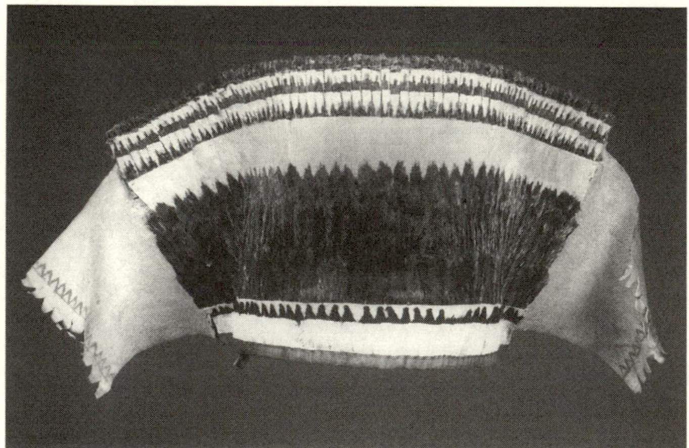

Yurok warriors wore headdresses such as this at their annual Jump Dance. The headdress, a mosaic of woodpecker scalps and bluebird feathers attached to albino deerskin, is almost 30 inches wide.

elaborate wergild system, intimately connected to social status, was used to redress grievances. In their occasional fighting among themselves or with neighboring tribes—for offenses ranging from trespass and insult to murder—they avoided pitched battles, preferring to attack individuals or raid villages. Their fighting seldom resulted in many casualties. Young women were sometimes taken captive but were usually returned at the time of settlement. All fighting ended with compensation for everyone's losses.

Contemporary Information

Government/Reservations Yuroks may be found on the Hoopa Extension (Yurok) Reservation (1891; roughly 7,800 acres), the Berry Creek Rancheria

(Butte County; 1916; 33 acres [Maidu]), the Resighini Reservation (Del Norte County; 1938; 228 acres [Coast Indian Community]), the Trinidad Rancheria (Humboldt County; 1917; 47 acres [Cher-Ae-Heights community]), the Big Lagoon Rancheria (Humboldt County; 1918; 20 acres; 19 Yurok and Tolowa in 1996), the Blue Lake Rancheria (Humboldt County), and the Elk Valley Rancheria (Del Norte County; 1906; 100 acres, with Tolowa and Hoopa). The first election for a Yurok Tribal Council was scheduled for 1997.

Economy Logging and fishing (commercial and subsistence) are the most important local economic activities. People also leave the communities for work in the Bay area and elsewhere. Trinidad Rancheria owns a bingo parlor, and Big Lagoon Rancheria has invested in a major hotel. The Yuroks also manage two fish hatcheries.

Legal Status The Yurok Tribe, the Big Lagoon Rancheria (Yurok and Tolowa), and the Coast Indian Community of Yurok Indians of the Resighini Rancheria are federally recognized tribal entities, as are the Hoopa Extension Reservation, the Trinidad Rancheria, the Blue Lake Rancheria, the Berry Creek Rancheria, and the Elk Valley Rancheria. In 1983, the Yuroks and the Tolowas won a protracted battle with the United States for control of a sacred mountainous site in the Six Rivers National Forest.

Daily Life Many Yuroks live semisubsistence lives of hunting, fishing, and gathering. Some still speak the Yurok language. Since the 1970s there has been a revival of traditional arts such as basket weaving and woodworking, along with some traditional ceremonies, such as the Jump and Brush Dances. Sumeg, a re-created traditional plank hamlet, was dedicated in 1990. The few *peyerk* who survive are almost all elderly.

The Tsurai Health Center (Trinidad Rancheria) serves the Yurok population. The application of dioxin by the U.S. Forest Service and timber companies to retard the growth of deciduous trees poses a major health problem in the area. Important ongoing issues include increasing the land base, construction of decent and affordable housing, the institution of full electrical service, protection of Indian grave sites and declining salmon stocks, and economic development.

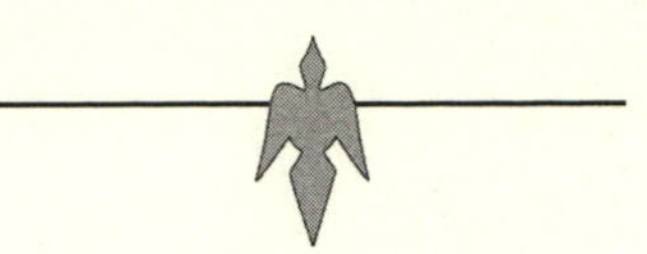

Chapter Three

The Northwest Coast

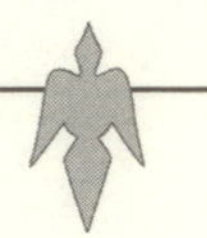

Right: The Haida were outstanding wood carvers whose masterpieces included weapons such as these carved clubs.

Above: The importance of the potlatch ceremony is denoted by this Tlingit woman's queenlike costume. Behind her is a view of the Tlingit village of Klukwan.
Below: A Chilkat Tlingit blanket.

Northwest

For the purposes of this book, the Northwest Coast geographic region extends from just north of Yakutat Bay in southwest Alaska more or less to the California-Oregon border, including lands west of the Coast and Cascade Mountains. Its length is roughly 1,500 miles, but its width averages less than 100 miles. It is a territory dominated and defined by water. Especially in the north, great sounds, inlets, and fjords bring the maritime world to people well away from the coast and islands, and numerous rivers further contextualize their liquid world. Depending on elevation and precise distance from the coast, it is an area of seemingly endless fog and rain, fierce winter storms, dense forest, and giant trees. The climate is generally moderate.

The tribes that are spoken of today are modern inventions. Aboriginally, perhaps 165,000 Indians of the Northwest Coast lived in autonomous villages; these and their lineage constituted their political identities. Thus, for example, the people now referred to as the Tlingit tribe were once about 14 separate and distinct Tlingit tribes, such as Chilkat Tlingit, Hoonah Tlingit, and Stikines Tlingit, each of whom shared a dialect, territory, natural resources, and certain inherited rights and obligations. In the north, autonomous local groups occasionally formed military and/or ceremonial alliances. Northwest Coast Indians spoke at least 40 dialects of languages in the Nadene (Athapaskan), Haida, Tsimshian, Wakashan, Chimakuan, Salishan, and Penutian language families.

Almost all Northwest Coast Indian groups shared certain aspects of material culture. Not surprisingly, the sea and/or rivers played a central role in their lives. Fish, especially salmon, was the most important food for most Northwest Coast Indians. Since transportation for most of these groups was by canoe, they were great builders of

Native Americans of the Northwest Coast

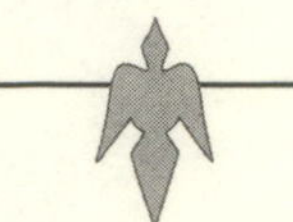

canoes as well as other finely constructed and carved wooden objects. Trees, especially the red cedar, were the raw materials for everything from canoes to clothing to plank houses. The people generally lived in permanent winter villages but had one or more small permanent, semipermanent, or seasonal villages or camping sites as well.

Aside from life's necessities, their most important activity was to acquire and maintain wealth and social status. Especially in the north, society was carefully ranked according to hereditary status. The region's classic ceremonial activity—the potlatch—was both a reflection of and a means to perpetuate this system of social inequality. Religion was based on an individual's relationship with one or more guardian spirits acquired from the nonhuman world.

With the arrival of non-natives (Spaniards, Russians, British, and, later, Americans) in the late eighteenth and the nineteenth centuries, native Northwest Coast peoples suffered a fate similar to that of other Native Americans. Across the board, populations declined by as much as 90 percent, mostly owing to disease as well as destruction and appropriation of subsistence areas. However, the effects of these changes were uneven; in general, southern and coastal peoples fared worse than northern and more interior peoples.

In the late twentieth century, longhouse kin ties had endured in many places, and tribes in general were moving toward increasing levels of self-government. In the United States, the 1974 Boldt decision (see later discussion of fishing rights in western Washington) secured native fishing rights, although the status of native rights in British Columbia is far less clear. Northwest Indians in general are full participants in contemporary U.S. and Canadian life while at the same time retaining strong native identities.

The first humans entered the Northwest Coast region about 10,000 years ago. Early prehistoric cultures probably came from the interior via the Columbia River and, somewhat later, down the coast and up the river valleys. Technology was characterized by flaked stone industries. Little else is known about the very earliest inhabitants of the region, other than that they adapted quite successfully to the region.

In southwestern Alaska, a new and much better documented stage of cultural development began around 3000 B.C.E. Items of that period, including adzes, labrets, and beads, were fashioned of ground stone and bone. These people ate shellfish and some sea mammals. Later, around 1000 B.C.E., bark mats and poles appear, as do signs of extensive fish and land mammal consumption, more complex tools, and seasonal site occupation. Items consistent with early historic culture date from roughly 1000 C.E.

In northern and central British Columbia as well, changes in the archaeological record, particularly the presence of shellfish middens, indicate that the basic subsistence technology for the following 5,000 years was in place by at least 3000 B.C.E. Sedentary villages appear around 700 B.C.E., and social ranking, woodworking, and distinctive regional art styles shortly thereafter. Intergroup trade was also well established by this time.

Southern British Columbia and northern Washington show a somewhat different pattern. Several distinct cultural periods preceded the final prehistoric pattern, which began in roughly 400 C.E., although in many respects life in the region was little changed from that around 3000 B.C.E. Cultural continuity can be demonstrated along Washington's ocean coast for at least the past 4,000 years and around Puget Sound for roughly 2,000 years.

Separate and distinct cultures evolved in the Lower Columbia and Willamette Valleys as early as 1560 B.C.E. (Lower Columbia) and 5800 B.C.E. (Willamette Valley). The former featured a fishing economy and larger villages; the latter was based on more diverse subsistence activities and smaller villages or camps. Finally, along the Oregon coast, people moved from a premarine to a marine-based economy early in the first millennium B.C.E., with the marine and riverine culture becoming fully developed by about 500 C.E.

Descriptions of traditional Northwest Coast Indian culture are heavily influenced by what non-Indians observed in the late eighteenth and the nineteenth centuries, by which time many aboriginal elements had been altered. However, what follows is a portrait of aspects probably common to many aboriginal Northwest Coast cultures.

The importance of the potlatch ceremony is denoted by this Tlingit woman's queenlike costume. The potlatch ceremony was both a reflection of and a means to perpetuate a system of social inequality.

Unidentified woman and child. The photographers' active studio in Juneau, Alaska, catered to both Indians and non-Indians.

The use of two resources above all defined Northwest Coast Indians: fish, especially salmon, and cedar. Many peoples caught all five kinds of salmon: pink, coho, chum (dog), chinook, and sockeye. Many groups celebrated rituals concerning the season's first salmon run. Up to 12 methods of salmon fishing were employed, including varieties of nets, spears, and traps. Other important fish included halibut, eulachon (candlefish), smelt, herring, and sturgeon.

Also, many groups availed themselves of abundant quantities of shellfish. Seafood was generally eaten fresh or dried and stored for the winter. Eulachon was used primarily for its oil. Other common foods, in addition to fish and shellfish, included sea mammals, some land mammals, and plants, especially berries (mashed and dried into cakes) and roots such as camas, wapato, and bracken fern. Food was generally eaten fresh, or grilled, boiled (in a basket with hot rocks), or steamed or baked in a pit oven. Mountain goat was hunted for its hair and horn.

The other primary resource, red cedar (redwood in the south), was the backbone of Northwest Coast technology. People used it for clothing, baskets, houses, and canoes as well as for art, ceremonial, and utilitarian objects such as bent-corner boxes, bowls, masks, and heraldic poles. Men worked it with tools such as adzes, chisels, wedges, hammers, drills, and knives. Blades were made of rock, shell, horn, bone, and a small amount of iron. Most carved wood objects were of extremely fine craftsmanship. Although most men could craft objects of wood, canoe making was a distinct profession. Northwest Coast Indians built several types of canoes for specialized activities.

In general, Northwest Coast Indian people fished for eulachon in late winter; gathered seaweed, cedar bark, and herring spawn and fished for halibut in early spring (May); moved to their summer camps around June, where they gathered sea bird eggs and caught salmon; fished and gathered berries, roots, and shoots throughout the summer; preserved the fish and hunted in the fall; and gathered shellfish, hunted sporadically, observed their ceremonies, gambled, told stories, wove, and carved in winter.

Most Northwest Coast societies were ranked according to social status. Status was generally inherited and carried with it certain rights and obligations. Chiefs of local (kin) groups, for instance, tended to be both wealthy and of high birth. They directed large-group activities and wore finer and special clothing. Since it concerned the interests of two kin groups, marriage was a function more of social organization than of life cycle.

Typically, four groups existed: nobility, upper class free, lower class free, and slaves (actually not members of society at all). Each individual was also ranked within the group. Because they were largely based on inheritance, the groups were fairly immutable, although some transfer was possible through acquiring (by trade, purchase, marriage, or war) some inherited rights. These rights, or privileges, owned by the kin group, included songs, dances, performances, and control of subsistence areas and were identified by crests, or design patterns, reflecting real and mythical histories of family lines and associated incidents, animals, and spirits.

This muslin dance robe, fashioned by a Clayoquot artist of the Pacific Northwest in the late nineteenth century, bears a colorful image of the mythical thunderbird. The thunderbird was an important spirit for many Indian peoples.

All such items were originally obtained by an ancestor from a supernatural spirit. All present members of an opposite division received payment to view a crest, because in so doing they legitimated both the display and the crest's associated privileges. Resource areas were often "owned" or controlled by kin groups. Among the nobility, status—indeed, the entire system of ranking and kin groups—was confirmed and reaffirmed by a ceremonial obligation called the potlatch.

Potlatching, although it probably increased in intensity during the nineteenth century, was almost certainly part of aboriginal culture. The potlatch was held on varying occasions, such as the succession of a chief, an important life-cycle event, or to save or regain face. Nobles, or chiefs, and their groups invited other chiefs and their relatives from other villages to a feast that lasted for several days. Seating was strictly according to social position. The host and his family would recite their myths and genealogies and give gifts, also according to social position, the acceptance of which also indicated acceptance of the social order.

All potlatches included feasting, socializing, speeches, songs, displays of wealth (such as hammered pieces of copper, pelts, robes, and dentalium shell) and crests, and dances. The original purpose of the institution may have been to exchange goods for food during lean times. Potlatches were held in winter.

Around the turn of the century, the "rivalry potlatch," a bitter scene in which the object was to humiliate a rival, was brought about in part because of population decline and consolidation.

Northwest Coast religion centered around the phenomenon of a guardian spirit. Such spirits came from both animate and inanimate objects. They could be individually acquired or inherited; they occasionally arrived uninvited. Individual acquisition of guardian spirits came as the result of spirit quests—bathing, fasting, and praying in remote places—that began when a person was prepubescent and culminated as many as 10 or 20 years later when the spirit power revealed itself. The spirit, associated with a particular song and dance that was displayed during the winter ceremonials, imparted some kind of skill or luck or some special knowledge. Shamans received special spirits that enabled them to cure and/or harm people.

Large rectangular plank houses were the norm along the Northwest Coast. Roof types (shed, gambrel, gable) varied according to location. Several families generally lived in a house, each partitioned off from another, with a particular family's position in the house determined by rank. Temporary seasonal shelters were built of mats, planks removed from the main house, or bark. House posts were frequently carved and painted with heraldic or crest designs. In fact, most Northwest Coast art was heraldic in nature. In addition to house posts, beams, and fronts, this kind of art was often displayed, especially in the north, in the form of totem (mortuary, memorial, portal) poles.

Weaving was an important nonwood craft. Raw materials included spruce root, cedar inner bark, cattail, tule, mountain goat and dog wool, and bird down. Most women used the twining method to weave baskets (including watertight baskets), clothing (capes, hats, robes), and mats. Coast Salish women spun wool on a full loom. Some clothing was also made of dressed skins, although these were more generally traded for than made locally.

Aboriginally, intragroup conflict was minimal, with the exception of witchcraft, which was a capital offense along with clan incest (among those groups with clans). Intergroup conflict took place within the framework of feuds and wars: The former entailed conflict for a legalistic purpose, whereas the latter existed solely for material gain (land, booty, slaves). In general, the north saw more warfare than the south. Chiefs were the nominal war commanders, and soldiers often undertook practical as well as ritual preparations before fighting. Night raids were the preferred war strategy. Victims' heads were often displayed on poles as proof of fighting prowess. Defensive tactics included the use of sentries and fortifications.

The first non-natives may have appeared on the Northwest Coast as early as the sixteenth century. However, it was not until Captain James Cook's crew realized in 1778 the enormous profit in selling Northwest Coast sea otter pelts in China that contact began in earnest. Land-based fur trade operations by Russians, Spaniards, British, and Americans followed shortly after the onset of the maritime fur trade. By about 1850 sea otter stocks had become depleted, and the great non-native fur trade era along the Northwest Coast had come and gone.

During this relatively brief period, diseases such as smallpox and malaria destroyed up to 80 percent or more of some Indian villages. Alcoholism and venereal disease killed more slowly but just as surely. Indians also acquired firearms, iron, sugar, flour, rum, and sails for their canoes during this period. Some strategically placed chiefs became wealthy by monopolizing parts of the fur trade. With the exception of the effects of depopulation, however, and the concentration of remaining populations around trading posts, basic cultural patterns were little disrupted. One significant result of the new wealth accumulated by some groups was the increase in numbers and extravagance of potlatches and the reinvigoration of material culture, including artistic expression.

Though they did not know it, non-native settlers who arrived in the mid–nineteenth century found the Indian population greatly diminished. Perhaps because of the region's relative inaccessibility, all-out war between Indians and Anglos was largely avoided on the northern Northwest Coast. The United States having only acquired Alaska from the Russians in 1867, its nonmilitary presence was minimal there until the late nineteenth century.

Still, throughout the Northwest Coast, Indians in the late nineteenth century saw further outbreaks of infectious disease as well as intensive missionary work, official efforts to encourage assimilation, severe racial prejudice, and regular anti-Indian violence. Their land was increasingly taken over by non-native squatters while the Indians were legally denied the right to squat on, and thus obtain rights to, their own land. Ultimately, their subsistence patterns and cultural traditions under severe attack, and divided among themselves over the merits of change, most Indians became involved in the wage economy, such as canneries and commercial fishing, built without their permission on their lands.

The United States and Britain fixed their western boundary in 1846 at 49 degrees north latitude. Shortly thereafter, Oregon and Washington Territories were created, and the United States set about extinguishing Indian land title. In Oregon white settlers and miners were allowed simply to dispossess Indians. In the 1850s, treaties were concluded with Washington coastal tribes, providing for land cession and removal to reservations. Reservations in Washington were near or within traditional territory. Most Oregon Indians, however, were removed to two distant reservations following the bitter Rogue River wars of 1851–1855. Conditions there were poor and many starved, and in any case the reservations were soon whittled down by the government. Even in Washington, from 1855 to 1856, a coalition of Puget Sound tribes under the leadership of the Nisqually chief Leschi rose up against their poor treatment at the hands of the whites. Education, including missionization, and agriculture were the primary methods to force the Indians to assimilate. By the early twentieth century, Indian populations were still declining, and many traditions continued to unravel.

Unlike most other North American Indians, the Indians of British Columbia were not conquered militarily, nor did they formally surrender title to their land. In 1884, 13 years after British Columbia joined the Canadian Confederation, the Canadian government simply discounted Indian land ownership and passed its first Indian Act, under which it appropriated land and exercised legal control over Indians within Canada. The first of its two main provisions established roughly 200 small reserves to accommodate the different bands. A reserve could consist of a fishing location, a cemetery, or a village site. The thinking was to permit Indians to remain self-sufficient as they made the transition to a capitalist economy, whereas in the United States policymakers forced various groups of Indians to live together on large reservations, where they were strongly encouraged to become farmers and abandon their traditional identities. The other major provision of the Indian Act outlawed the potlatch; that provision was repealed in 1954.

In 1912, a group of Tlingit and Tsimshian men and women formed the Alaska Native Brotherhood (ANB). This group, with the Native American Sisterhood formed 11 years later, was dedicated to progress as defined by non-native society: Anglo-style education, citizenship, and the abolition of native customs, especially languages and the potlatch (which persisted clandestinely despite its de jure ban). During the 1920s, the ANB broadened its activities to include working against the pervasive institutional and individual discrimination against Native Americans. Today they embrace many of their old traditions, and the ANB remains an active and influential player in Tlingit-Haida-Canadian affairs.

Groups like the Tlingit and Haida Central Council fought for years for aboriginal land claims. The landmark resolution of this fight was the Alaska Native Claims Settlement Act (1971). Under its terms, Alaska's Tlingit and Haida Indians were organized into regional corporations. In addition, the act created 200 village corporations. Indians born before 1971 were issued shares of their corporation. As of 1996, they are restricted from selling those shares on the open market unless a majority, and in some cases (Tlingit and Haida, for instance) a supermajority of the tribe agrees to do so.

Indians in western Washington have their own landmark legal case. With the rise of the Indian self-determination movement in the 1960s and 1970s, Indians in that region redoubled their efforts to safeguard their fishing rights under the various treaties. For decades, white-owned commercial fishing had been depleting fish stocks so that the Indians, who were guaranteed by treaty the right to fish at their usual places, were decreasingly able to exercise that right. Often Indians were harassed physically and

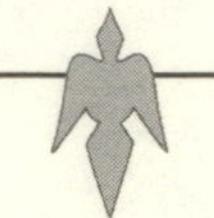

legally for attempting to fish in their usual way. In 1974, Judge George Boldt ruled definitively that the treaty Indians of western Washington were entitled under their treaties to special fishing rights at their "usual and customary" fishing places and to take 50 percent of the allowable salmon harvest in the state. The impact of this ruling has been profound. It includes an explosive growth of Indian fishing and marine-related industries as well as the reinvigoration of local Indian culture.

Since World War II, Canada has tried through federal funds and programs to increase the socioeconomic status of Indians in British Columbia. Since the 1970s, at least, those Indians have fought, with limited success, for an increased share of self-determination. Regional band organizations ("tribal councils") formed in the mid-1970s to press a range of issues, from land claims to services to national political reforms. Despite the reemergence of potlatching and other aspects of traditional culture such as language, rituals, art, performances, and songs after laws against them were removed in 1950s and 1960s, British Columbia Indians still face severe social and economic challenges.

In keeping with the relatively harsh treatment on the Oregon reservations, the federal government in the United States voted to terminate them in 1951—that is, to sell the land and end the government's relationship with the 61 tribes and bands. Many tribes supported this move. However, when it predictably led to further impoverishment, tribes petitioned for and secured restoration in the 1970s and 1980s. Also in the 1980s, Oregon tribes redoubled their efforts to secure economic development and improved housing and health services.

Bella Bella

Bella Bella (`Be lə `Be lə) is a term dating from 1834 that does not refer to an aboriginal self-designation. The Bella Bella (made up of at least three subgroups: the Kokaitk, Oelitk, and Oealitk), Haihais, and Oowekeeno are sometimes referred to as Heiltsuk. The Heiltsuk, along with the Heisla, are today identified as Bella Bella or northern Kwakiutl.

Location Traditionally, these groups lived in the vicinity of Queen Charlotte Sound, north of Vancouver Island and the Kwakiutl people, in the Canadian province of British Columbia. This is a relatively moderate, wet land marked by inlets, islands, peninsulas, mountains, and valleys.

Population Roughly 1,700 Bella Bellas lived in their territory in 1835. In 1901 the figure had shrunk to 330, but it climbed to 1,874 in 1995.

Language The Heiltsuk spoke Heiltsuk (Haihai and Bella Bella)-Oowekyala (Oowekeeno), a Wakashan language. The two component languages were virtually mutually unintelligible.

Historical Information

History Bella Bellas probably met non-Indians for the first time in 1793, when the explorers George Vancouver and Alexander Mackenzie arrived to prospect for the fur trade. Shortly thereafter, that trade brought more Anglos as well as Anglo-Indian violence. Milbanke Sound was the first local major trade center. In 1833, the Hudson's Bay Company built Fort McLoughlin on Campbell Island as a major trading post. Although it abandoned the fort ten years later, the company opened a small store on the site about 1850. During the fur trade period, the Bella Bellas emerged as middlemen, controlling access to some interior tribes and playing the Americans and British off against each other.

An 1862 smallpox epidemic set off a period of rapid change. Dramatic Indian depopulation led to village consolidation. Missionization followed, as did the growth of the commercial fishing, canning, and logging industries. In 1880, the government separated Indians from their land by unilaterally establishing reserves. The Bella Bella reserve was run by Methodist missionaries. Village centralization and consolidation continued. Around 1900, two Oowekeeno villages were established near a sawmill and a cannery. The Haihais moved from their local villages in about 1870 to Swindle Island, a fuel depot for steamships.

In the twentieth century, northern Kwakiutls were largely displaced from the logging and fishing industries owing to a combination of factors, including competition with non-natives, technological

advances, and loss of land rights. Increased unemployment and out-migration has been the result. However, ties remain strong between home communities and those people in regional cities and towns.

Religion Dancing or secret societies performed their ceremonies in winter. Initiation into the societies was by hereditary right. Dances—a first, or shamans', series, including a cannibal's dance; a "coming down again," or second, series, including war dances; and a dog-eating dance—were ranked according to the status of both the dance and the performers. Performances dramatized the encounter of an ancestor with a supernatural being. Wealthy, high-status people sponsored dances, feasts, and potlatches. A council of chiefs managed the winter dances.

Government As was generally the case along the Northwest Coast, the basic political unit was the autonomous local group or clan. Each such group was presided over by a chief. Parts of several clans often formed a village, where the highest-ranking chief had relative degrees of control over the others. For defensive purposes, some villages congregated to form loose confederations or tribes.

Customs Distinctive crests and ranked titles identified each of the four crest groups, or clans—Raven, Eagle, Orca, and Wolf. These groups also had heads, or chiefs. Resource sites could be owned by families, local groups, or crest groups and could be rented out for some form of compensation.

In general, society was divided into status-ranked groups, such as chiefs, free commoners, and slaves. Some divisions also added another free group between commoners and slaves, as well as several levels of chief. Symbols of high rank included tattoos, ornamentation, and the possession of wealth and hereditary titles. Commoners had less prestigious names, held smaller feasts, and had no inherited rights to certain dances. The low-class free were orphans or the unambitious, with no wealthy relatives.

Regular intermarriage occurred between the Bella Bella and the Bella Coola. Marriage between close cousins was condoned if it furthered one's status. The bride price was a key ingredient of a marriage; in cases of divorce it was generally refunded.

Dwellings Semipermanent winter villages were composed of rectangular cedar plank houses. Features included vertical wall planks, a gabled roof and double ridgepole, carved interior posts, an adjustable central smoke hole, and mat-lined walls in sleeping areas. Summer camp houses were of similar but less elaborate construction. When they were in small or temporary camps, people made do with bark structures.

Diet Fish, especially salmon, was the staple. Other marine foods were also important. The Bella Bella took stranded whales only for their blubber. They ate several varieties of berries and hunted deer, wolf, bear, mountain goat, small mammals, waterfowl, and most birds (except crow and raven) and their eggs. Other than in winter, when food stores were eaten, people migrated seasonally to various resource sites.

Key Technology Fishing technology included stone and wood stake weirs, traps, harpoons, dip nets, and clubs. Harpoons, clubs, and bow and arrow were used for hunting sea mammals. Land animals were hunted with the help of dogs, snares, spears, and deadfalls. Digging sticks helped people gather roots. Most woodworking tools were of stone. Women made burden and storage baskets.

Trade The Bella Bella traded shellfish and seaweed with more inland groups (such as the Bella Coola) for eulachon and eulachon products. They also obtained canoes in trade, often from the north.

Notable Arts Bentwood boxes, chests, canoes, and horn spoons and ladles were items of fine local construction. Also important were relief carved and painted ceremonial/religious items such as totem poles and masks.

Transportation The cedar dugout, a shallow-bottom canoe used with round-tipped blades, was the primary means of transportation. The Bella Bella and Haihais also used bark canoes for lake travel.

Dress In warm weather, women wore cedar-bark aprons; men went naked. Blankets of woven cedar bark, mountain goat wool or dog hair, or tanned, sewn skins kept people warm in cold weather. Women wore waterproof basket caps and cedar-bark ponchos in the rain. Both sexes wore their hair long. Those who could afford it wore abalone nose and ear pendants. High-status women also wore labrets, dentalia bracelets, necklaces, and anklets. They also deformed their babies' heads for aesthetic purposes. The people painted their bodies and faces against sunburn.

War and Weapons The Bella Bella fought regularly, mainly against the Bella Coola, Haida, Tsimshian, and Kwakiutl. They were well organized militarily. The Haihais were regularly under attack, but the Oowekeeno were more geographically isolated. Revenge, trespass, violation of custom, and seasonal shortages of food were common causes of war.

Contemporary Information

Government/Reservations The Heiltsuk Band, formerly the Bella Bella, controls 22 reserves on 1,369 hectares of land on Campbell Island. As of 1995, the population was 1,874. Elections are held under the provisions of the Indian Act, and the band is unaffiliated.

Economy Important economic activities and resources include a shipyard, cable television, fisheries, and small businesses.

Legal Status The Heiltsuk Band is a federally and provincially recognized entity.

Daily Life Throughout the twentieth century, life for the Bella Bella has been characterized by displacement from local industries, the loss of rights to their land, and slow population increase. One result of these trends has been high unemployment and out-migration, although ties between home communities and populations in Vancouver remain relatively strong. Children attend band and provincial schools. A Heiltsuk cultural-educational center facilitates the rebuilding and promotion of local culture. Other facilities include a community hall and a day care center. The old religion has been largely replaced by Christianity, and much of the traditional culture has been lost.

Bella Coola

Bella Coola (`Be lə `Cū lə) is an Anglicization of a Heiltsuk word for the speakers of the Bella Coola language. The native word for the people of the Bella Coola valley was *Nuxalkmx*. They consisted of four or five subgroups linked linguistically, territorially, and culturally, although not politically. These people are known today as the Nuxalt Nation.

Location Traditionally, several permanent villages existed south and east of the Bella Bella and the Haisla, east of the Queen Charlotte Sound coast in British Columbia. These people may also have occupied territory east of the Coastal Range. Beginning around 1800, they consolidated their villages at the mouth of the Bella Coola River. In 1936, a flood forced them to move from the north to the south shore of the river's mouth. Their traditional territory is rugged, with mountains, estuaries, and forests. The climate is cool and wet.

Population Perhaps 1,400 Bella Coolas lived in their villages in 1780. In the 1970s, roughly 600 lived on their reserves and in Northwest cities.

Language Bella Coola is a Salishan language.

Historical Information

History The Bella Coola were latecomers to the region, probably arriving around 1400. In 1793 they encountered the explorers George Vancouver and Alexander Mackenzie; the Indians traded fish and skins to them for iron, copper, knives, and other items. As the fur trade developed, Hudson's Bay Company maintained a local fort/post from 1833 to 1843. During this period, the Bella Coola prevented furs from the Carrier Indians (an eastern group) from reaching the coast, thus maintaining a trade monopoly with the whites.

Shortly after gold was discovered in their area (1851), disease, alcohol, and hunger combined to weaken and kill many Indians. A severe smallpox

epidemic in 1863 forced the abandonment of numerous villages. Hudson's Bay Company operated another local trading post from 1869 to 1882, and Protestant missionaries penetrated the Bella Coola territory in the 1870s and 1880s. In 1885, nine Bella Coolas journeyed to Germany for 13 months, dancing and singing for European audiences and inspiring the anthropologist Franz Boas to begin his lifelong study of Northwest Coast Indians. A Norwegian colony, the first local non-Indian settlement, was established in the Bella Coola Valley in 1894.

These changes, combined with the gradual transition to a commercial (fishing and logging) economy and the replacement of traditional housing with single-family structures, weakened descent groups and led to the gradual consolidation of ceremonials and the abandonment of songs. In the 1960s and 1970s, however, the people relearned the old songs, using recordings made by anthropologists. In the 1970s, the revival of traditional culture also included new masks and dances.

Religion The Bella Coola recognized four or five worlds, including a center, or human, world. A supernatural being kept this flat center world level and balanced. There were many deities and a supreme female deity, all of whom resided in the sky. All things had spirits that could intervene in the lives of people. Favorable intervention might be gained through prayer and ritual sexual intercourse.

Their extremely rich ceremonialism was dominated by two secret societies as well as the potlatch. Membership in one such society, *Sisaok,* was restricted to the children and relatives of certain chiefs. An extended period of seclusion accompanied initiation, as did songs and the display of carved masks with crests. The ceremony dramatized various kin-related legends. The other society, *Kusiut,* was based on contact with the supernaturals. Its dances, such as cannibal, scratcher, breaker, and fungus, included songs and masks representing supernatural beings. These dances dominated the ceremonial period, which lasted from November through March.

All people had the potential to become shamans; the event occurred when a supernatural being conferred power through a visit, a name, and songs. Some such power could cure sickness. Some shamans received power through ghosts and could see dead people; they cured disease caused by ghosts.

Government Aboriginally, the Bella Coola inhabited between 30 and 60 autonomous villages, each consisting of from 2 to 30 houses arranged in a row along a river or creek bank. Each village had a chief, whose status derived from his ancestral name, prerogatives, and wealth. Chiefs had little direct ruling power. A woman who had been "rebought" several times, and had thus helped her husband accumulate status, was also recognized as a chief.

Customs Descent groups probably owned fish weirs in aboriginal times. Hunting, too, could only occur in an area claimed by a descent group. Hunters, some of whose ancestral prerogatives allowed them to be known as professionals, underwent ritual preparation.

The units of social organization included the household, village, and descent group, or all those with a common ancestral mythology. A child could inherit both parents' descent groups, but residence with the father's family tended to reinforce the patrilineal line. Social status was important and clearly delineated. The ability (and obligation) to give away gifts on ceremonial occasions (potlatches) was a key component of social status. Social mobility was possible, and even slaves might obtain dance prerogatives and thus achieve some status.

Babies were born with the assistance of midwives in a birth hut in the woods. Their heads were flattened and their bodies massaged daily. Wealthy parents gave naming potlatches. Infanticide and abortion were occasionally practiced. The Bella Coola pierced the nasal septa of high-status children, both boys and girls; the occasion was accompanied by potlatches. Upon reaching puberty, girls were secluded, and their activity and diet were restricted for a year. There were no boys' puberty rituals, although their first hunted game was distributed and eaten ritually as were the first berries gathered by girls.

Although the "ancestral family" was an important source of Bella Coola identity, they did intermarry extensively with other peoples. Parents and elderly relatives arranged marriages, around which there were many rituals and opportunities to increase

status. The relatives of high-status brides were expected to "rebuy" the woman (donate goods) every time her husband gave a potlatch. Cruelty, neglect, and infidelity were considered grounds for divorce.

Corpses were buried squatting in a wooden box. Twins' coffins were placed in trees. Coffins may also have been placed in caves, on scaffolds, or on top of memorial poles. They may also have been wrapped in bearskins and left on tree stumps in the forest. Property was also buried at the funeral.

Music could be both sacred and secular. The former was sung by a choir, who used sticks and drums for a beat, and three main performers. Various wind instruments were also used to symbolize the supernaturals.

Dwellings Permanent houses were large, planked structures. They were constructed of red cedar and often built on stilts against floods and enemies. Housefronts were decorated with the owner's crest. Houses were inhabited by extended families. Entrance was through carved house posts. Some winter houses were excavated, with only the roofs showing.

Diet The Bella Coola enjoyed a fairly regular food supply. Fish were the staple, including five types of salmon plus steelhead trout, rainbow and cutthroat trout, eulachon, Pacific herring, and others. All fish was boiled, roasted, or smoke dried. Eulachon was very valuable, perhaps more for its grease than as food. The first chinook salmon and eulachon of the season were eaten ritually.

Other important foods included shellfish; seals, sea lions, and beached whales; land mammals, such as mountain goat, bear, lynx, hare, beaver, marmot, and deer; and fowl. More than 135 plants were used for foods, medicines, and raw materials. Important plant foods included berries and the cambium layer of the western hemlock (steamed with skunk cabbage leaves, pounded, dried, and mixed with eulachon grease).

Key Technology Fish were taken in weirs and also with harpoons, dip nets, rakes, and hook and line. Hunting technology included snares, traps, deadfalls, spears, and bow and arrow. General raw materials included wood and stone (dishes, containers, boxes, spoons), sheep horn (spoons), and cedar-bark (mats, clothing, baskets, rope, fishing line). Men built canoes for water transportation, and women made burden and storage cedar-bark baskets.

Trade The Bella Coola received herring eggs from the Bella Bella as well as some canoes from the Bella Bella and other Kwakiutl groups. They also traded with some Plateau Indians.

Notable Arts Wood carving was probably the preeminent Bella Coola art. Masks, entry poles, house frontal poles (with entrance through a gaping mouth), and carved posts were often painted and decorated with crest figures. They had no fully developed totem pole. They also made pictographs and petroglyphs.

Transportation The Bella Coola used several types of canoes, including long, narrow canoes of a single red cedar log for rivers (most common), plus four types of seagoing canoes. Canoes were decorated with crest designs or painted black. Hunters also wore two types of snowshoes in winter.

Dress Blankets and moccasins came from seal, sea lion, and caribou skin (although the Bella Coola usually went barefoot). They also made mountain goat wool blankets and fur robes and capes and wore long hair and shell and bone ornaments. Tattooing was common.

War and Weapons The people engaged in irregular conflict with neighbors such as the Carrier, Chilcotin, and Kwakiutl. Their lack of political centralization made retaliating against raiding parties difficult. The Bella Coola raided too, attacking at dawn, burning a village, killing all the men, and taking women and children as slaves. Weapons included moose-hide shields, wood armor, the bow and arrow, clubs, and spears.

Contemporary Information

Government/Reservations The Nuxalt Nation (known before about 1980 as the Bella Coola Band) has seven reserves on 2,024 hectares at the mouth of the Bella Coola River in British Columbia, Canada. Their population in 1995 was 1,140, of whom 718 people lived on the reserve. They are governed according to the provisions of the Indian Act and are affiliated with the Oowekeeno/Kitasoo Tribal Council.

Economy Economic activities and resources include a sawmill smoker plant, commercial fishing, and tree farm license registration.

Legal Status The Nuxalt Nation is a federally and provincially recognized entity.

Daily Life Nuxalt people retain some ceremonies and make wood carvings for sale to tourists. Children attend both band and provincial schools. The reserve contains two fire houses, a community hall, two administration buildings, a seniors' home, and a clinic. Beginning in the 1970s there was a revival of traditional culture, including new masks, songs, and dances. Their dancers perform throughout British Columbia.

Chehalis

See Salish, Southwestern Coast

Chetco

See Tolowa (Chapter 2); Upper Umpqua

Chinook

Chinook (Shin `uk or Chin `uk), one of a group of Chinookan peoples whose branches included Lower Chinookan (or Chinook proper) and Upper Chinookan. The name came from a Chehalis word for the inhabitants of and a particular village site on Baker Bay.

Location Traditionally, the Chinookan peoples lived along the Pacific Coast around the Columbia River Delta and upstream on both sides for about 150 miles. Lower Chinookans included the Shoalwater Chinook (Shoalwater or Willapa Bay and the north bank of the Columbia from Cape Disappointment to Gray's Bay) and the Clatsop (south bank of the Columbia, from Young's Bay to Point Adams). Upper Chinookans included the Cathlamet (Grays Bay to Kalama), the Multnomah (Kalama to about Portland and up the Columbia just past Government Island), and the Clackamas (southwest of Portland and roughly along the Willamette and Clackamas Rivers). Today, most Chinooks live in southwestern Washington and scattered around the Pacific Northwest.

Population In 1780, roughly 22,000 Chinookans lived in their territory, a figure that declined to less than 100 in the late nineteenth century. Chinook tribal membership stood at more than 2,000 in 1983.

Language The Chinookan family of Penutian languages was composed of Lower Chinookan (Chinook proper) and Upper Chinookan, which included the languages of Cathlamet, Multnomah, and Kiksht. In the context of historic Northwest Coast trade, "Chinook," or Oregon Trade Language (consisting of elements of Chinookan, Nootkan, French, and English), was considered a trade lingua franca from Alaska to California.

Historical Information

History Although Chinookans may have spotted Spanish ships off the Columbia River delta, it was early Anglo explorers who first encountered and spread smallpox to the Chinook in 1792. Meriwether Lewis and William Clark lived among and wrote about the Clatsops in 1805.

The fur trade began in earnest during the next decade; Astoria was founded in 1811. During the early days of the fur trade, at least, the Indians played key roles. The acquisition of goods such as musket and powder, copper and brass kettles, cloth, tobacco, and other items increased the relative prestige of downriver groups so much that they tried to monopolize trade to the exclusion of their upriver rivals. Native culture began gradually to change, owing mainly to acquisition of manufactured items and to enduring contact between Indians and Anglos.

Shortly after the initial contacts, Indians began to experience severe population declines due to disease. Alcohol-related disease and deaths took a further toll. They abandoned many village sites and consolidated others, particularly around trading sites. The number of potlatches may have increased during this time, as villages had to rerank themselves within

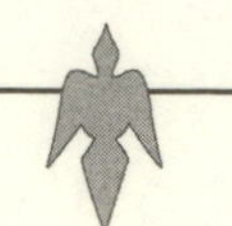

the context of the new trading society. By the 1850s, most survivors were being forced, under treaties that were never ratified, to cede their land in exchange for fishing rights. Survivors drifted to area reservations (Chehalis, Siletz, Grande Ronde, Shoalwater) or remained in their homelands.

By the twentieth century, the (Lower) Chinook had so effectively merged with the Lower Chehalis and the Shoalwater Salish that their language essentially passed out of use. Other groups also lost their identities through merger and consolidation. In 1899, the Chinooks, Clatsops, Cathlamets, and Wahkiakums (Upper Chinookans) presented a land claim to the U.S. government. They were awarded $20,000 (for almost 214,000 acres) in 1912. In 1925, the tribe established a business council to pursue its elusive treaty rights. A 1931 U.S. Supreme Court case *(Halbert v. U.S.)* held that Chinooks and other tribes had formal rights on the Quinault Reservation. Within a few years they had become that reservation's largest landholders. The Bureau of Indian Affairs (BIA), however, blocked their bid to organize a government under the Indian Reorganization Act.

In 1951, the nonreservation Chinookans combined to form the Chinook Nation and press their land claims with the newly created (1946) Indian Claims Commission. Soon, however, and without any official action, the BIA began to treat them as a terminated tribe. In 1971, this group, reconstituted in 1953 as the Chinook Indian Tribe, Inc., received an award of almost $50,000, but no land. Their petition for federal recognition, filed in 1979, is still pending.

Religion All Chinookan males and some females sought guardian spirit powers on prepubescent quests alone at night. Special songs and dances accompanied the receipt of such powers. An elaborate ceremonialism, based on the acquisition and display of spirit powers, took place during winter, the sacred period of spiritual renewal. Shamans might rent their powers to inflict harm (bodily injury or soul loss) or to cure someone. Chinookans also observed the first salmon rite.

Government Aboriginally, the Chinookans lived in more than 30 villages. Each village had a hereditary chief, but through the deployment of the proper alliances and methods a chief could exercise his authority over a wider area. The chief arbitrated quarrels, supervised subsistence activities, and provided for his village in time of need. His privileges included taking food, goods, or women at will. The chief was assisted by an orator who spoke directly to the lower-ranked people.

Customs Chinookan society was clearly stratified; status rankings included slave, commoner, and chief. High status went to those who had and could display wealth (food, clothing, slaves, canoes, high-ranked spouses), such as chiefs, warriors, shamans, and traders, as well as those with hereditary privileges. Slaves were bought, sold, or captured as property. Fishing areas were usually controlled by specific descent groups, although other subsistence areas were not so clearly controlled. Ties between villages were maintained by trade and alliances through wives. Imported dentalium shell was used for money and ornamentation. Later, beads from China were also highly prized.

All life-cycle events, at least among high-status families as well as those of chiefly succession, were marked by wealth display, gift giving, feasting, singing, and dancing. The purpose of the potlatch, a word meaning "giving" in Chinookan, was to reaffirm the lineage system as well as individual and descent group rank and social status, by conferring legitimacy on an occasion. Chinookans observed numerous taboos around girls' puberty (including seclusion for five months) and menstruation. Nonslave infants' heads were flattened at birth for aesthetic reasons. Corpses were placed in cattail mats; burial with possessions took place in canoes. A slave was sometimes killed to serve as a servant in the afterlife. Mourners cut their hair and never again spoke the name of the dead. Lacrosse was a popular game.

Dwellings Permanent winter dwellings were rectangular, gable-roofed, cedar plank houses, excavated and framed with cedar logs, with an average length of 50 feet. Decorations were of geometric, animal, and human designs. Floors were mat covered or planked, with an excavated central fireplace and a smoke hole above. Elevated bed platforms ran along the walls. Winter villages generally comprised around 20 houses. A light framework supported shelters of cattail-mat sides and cedar-bark roofs at summer fishing, hunting, or root-gathering camps.

Diet Fish—all five salmon species plus sturgeon, steelhead trout, eulachon, and herring—was the dietary staple. Chinookans fished with nets, especially seine nets, as well as scoops and spears. Fish were usually smoke dried. Rituals attended the season's first salmon run. Other marine foods included stranded whales (which also provided blubber and oil) and other mammals as well as shellfish. Men hunted deer, elk, bear, and other large game, as well as smaller game and fowl, with snares, deadfalls, traps, spears, and bow and arrow. Women gathered roots, especially the wapato tuber, and berries.

Key Technology Raw materials included wood, bone, shell, cedar bark, spruce roots, bear grass, cattail rushes, antler, and horn. These materials were carved, woven, and otherwise shaped. Especially significant were carved bent wooden boxes, dugout canoes, and twined bear grass baskets. Long poles with bunches of deer hooves served as musical instrument.

Trade Their strategic location at the mouth of the Columbia, as well as their business skills, enabled the Chinookans to dominate trade as far away as Puget Sound and areas to the west and south. The Dalles, a giant waterfall and rapids on the Columbia, was the site of a great aboriginal trade fair. Participants brought pelts, mountain sheep horn, baskets, woven rabbit-skin robes (interior tribes); slaves (Klamath and Modoc); salmon, bear grass, blubber, canoes, and berries (Chinook); and dentalia (Nootkas). Connections to this trade fair stretched ultimately as far as the Great Plains. As mentioned earlier, the existence of "Chinook jargon," the regional trade language, was testament to the central role the Chinook played in trade. Imported dentalium shells were a standard medium of exchange.

After contact, the Chinook were involved in a triangular trade in which they traded elk-hide cuirasses and other items to non-natives, who traded them to other native people for sea otter pelts, which they in turn traded in China for items such as silk and tea. Meanwhile, the Chinook traded guns, powder, and steel tools obtained from the non-natives to other Indians for fabulous profit. This trade pattern greatly increased the status of Chinook women, who played a more active trading role than men. When land-based trade in items such as beaver and other furs replaced the maritime trade, women continued their dominant roles.

Notable Arts Significant art objects included carved wooden boxes and house framework, totem poles, wrap-twined baskets, and carved and decorated mountain sheep horn bowls that were first steamed, boiled, and molded into shape.

Transportation Six types of canoes were carved from a single cedar or fir log. An elaborate manufacturing process included harrowing, carving, and painting the logs and then studding them with shells. Large canoes could hold up to 30 people.

Dress Men went naked whenever possible. Women wore at least a skirt of cedar bark or strips of silk-grass. Some wore a deerskin breechclout. In cold weather people wore robes of various furs. Some groups wore a conical rainproof cedar hat as well as tule-mat rain capes. Personal ornaments were made of shell, feathers, and beads.

War and Weapons When diplomacy failed, a regional system of reparations took effect; the system included payment, enslavement, execution, or formalized warfare. War might also serve to establish the relative rankings among villages. Following a war, the losers paid reparations to the victors.

Contemporary Information

Government/Reservations Many Chinookans live on the Chehalis Reservation, Grey's Harbor and Thurstron Counties, Washington. The reservation (1864; 2,076 acres) had a 1990 population of 307 Indians. The Chehalis Reservation is governed by a generally elected community council, which in turn elects a business committee. Chinookans also live on the Shoalwater Reservation (1866;335 acres), Pacific County, Washington. In 1990, 66 Indians lived on

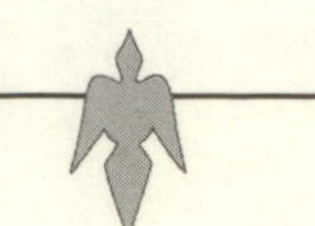

this reservation, which is governed by an elected tribal council. Chinook descendants also live on the Grand Ronde and Siletz Reservations (*see* Upper Umpqua).

Economy Chinook Indian Bingo operates on the Long Beach Peninsula. Chinooks are also active in the commercial forestry and fishing industries.

Legal Status In 1979, the Tchinouk Indians of Klamath Falls, Oregon, and the Chinook Indian Tribe of Chinook, Washington, appealed for federal recognition, based on the unratified 1851 treaty and their unofficial termination in 1955. The government rejected the Tchinouk petition in 1986; the Chinooks' was denied in early 1998.

Daily Life Chinooks are largely integrated into the mainstream. The language is not spoken. Still, tribal members are planning a museum and cultural center to keep alive their heritage and spirit. They have taken an active role in local organizations such as the Quinault Allotees Association and the Small Tribes Organization of Western Washington. Some people still speak the so-called Chinook jargon.

Comox

See Salish, Northern Coast

Coosans

Coosans (`Kū sə ns) consisted of the Coosan proper and Siuslaw peoples. The word is probably southwestern Oregon Athapaskan and refers to Coos Bay and the surrounding region. "Coos" may mean "on the south," "lake," or "lagoon." "Siuslaw" comes from the Siuslaw word for their region.

Location The Coosans lived around Coos Bay, Oregon, roughly from Twomile Creek in the south to Tenmile Lake in the north. Siuslaw speakers lived north of them along the coast and inland, to about Tenmile Creek. Except for the immediate coast, much of the area is mountainous and densely forested. Today, most of these people live in and around Coos Bay in southwestern Oregon.

Population The number of Coosans in the mid–eighteenth century may have approximated 4,000. This number had declined to roughly 465 by 1870. In the early 1990s, the Confederated Tribes of Coos, Lower Umpqua, and Siuslaw Indians had an enrolled population of 526. The Siletz Reservation had an official Indian population of 2,000 in 1991.

Language Coosans spoke two Coosan languages, Hanis and Miluk. The Siuslawans spoke the Siuslaw language, which consisted of the dialects Siuslaw proper and Lower Umpqua (Kuitch). Both Coosan and Siuslaw were Penutian languages.

Historical Information

History The first regional contact with non-natives occurred in 1792, when Upper Umpquas traded with U.S. and British ships. Occasional trade-based contacts through the 1830s were generally amicable, except for a Kuitch (Lower Umpqua) massacre of the Jedediah Smith party in 1828 and their attack on a Hudson's Bay Company fort in 1838.

Tensions increased with the major influx of non-natives in the 1850s. Although only the southernmost Coosan group, the Miluks (Lower Coquilles), participated in general in the 1855–1856 Rogue wars, all the Coosans and Siuslaws also suffered. An 1855 treaty, signed by Chief Jackson and others, though never ratified, was used to dispossess the Indians of their land and move them the following year to the Lower Umpqua River. Miluks and Kuitch were taken to the Coast (later the Siletz and the Alsea) Reservation, where about half died of starvation, exposure, and disease.

During these and subsequent years, the military continued to round up groups of Indians living in remote areas. As was the case nearly everywhere, Indian agents stole mercilessly from the Indians. Indians who practiced their traditional customs were whipped at a post. Easy access to alcohol corrupted, demoralized, and sickened the people.

In 1860, both groups were forcibly marched to the Siletz Reservation, which had been created five years earlier. In 1861, people on the southern part of Siletz, including Coos and Kuitch, were moved to or near the Yachats River on the coast, home of the Alsea Indians. They remained there until 1875, dying of

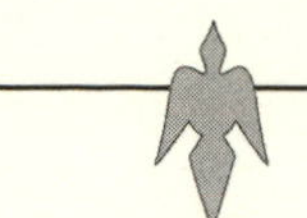

illness and starvation from trying to farm in a rain forest. In 1865, a central strip was removed from the reservation and opened for white settlement. The northern part then became the Siletz Reservation (Miluk) and the southern half became the Alsea Reservation (Coosans, Kuitch, and Alseans).

In 1875, when the Alsea Reservation was made available for non-Indian settlement, many people refused to go to Siletz. Some joined the Siuslaws while others filtered back to their original homelands and received 80-acre homesteads from the government in 1876. As their culture and language languished, tribal members worked as loggers, laborers, clam diggers, and cranberry harvesters. Women specialized in making baskets and cattail fiber mats.

Those Coosans who did live at Siletz worked at subsistence activities around the turn of the century. Indian loggers cut trees that stood on their former, plundered reservation. Siletz Indians won several small land claims judgments in the 1930s and 1950s. However, the tribe and reservation were "terminated" in the mid-1950s, with devastating result. They were restored in 1977 and given a 3,630-acre reservation three years later.

The Confederated Tribes of Coos, Lower Umpqua, and Suislaw organized formally in 1916. They have spent the rest of the century petitioning the government for compensation for their aboriginal lands, in vain to date. The Coos obtained a 6.1-acre "reservation" at Coos Bay in 1940. They were involuntarily terminated in 1954 and restored 30 years later.

The Dream Dance, a local variation of the Ghost Dance, was popular in the 1870s. By the twentieth century, most native languages were no longer spoken. In 1917, Coosans and Siuslaws created the Coos–Lower Umpqua–Siuslaw Tribal Government. A schism in the Coos tribe occurred in 1951 after a court ruled that some Miluks were eligible to share in money awarded in a land claims suit to the (Upper) Coquille (Mishikhwutmetunne) Indians. These Miluks then became affiliated with the Coquille Indian Tribe.

Religion Individuals could acquire power, mostly used to ensure luck in gaining wealth, through dreams and spirit quests. Unlike more northerly tribes, few other than shamans were actively involved with the supernatural; most people were much more interested in obtaining wealth. The most common kind of shaman was rigorously trained as a curer of disease (caused either by intrusion of a disease-causing object, often sent by a hostile shaman, or, less often, by soul loss). The second kind of shaman was more ritualistic; in addition to curing, these shamans also found thieves and promulgated evil. This type of shaman was involved in the numerous life-cycle taboos and especially in the elaborate girls' puberty ceremony and various other rituals of purification.

The people regularly held large-scale ceremonies featuring dancing, feasting, games, and gambling. Their mythology included stories of a primordial trickster, of legends, and of supernatural beings of forest and water. First salmon and first elk ceremonies were also held.

Government The basic political unit was the winter village group, usually a group of paternally related men with their families. Each major village had a chief and often an assistant chief. An informal council of wealthy men and women advised the chief. Succession was mainly hereditary, at least among the Coosans. Women might succeed if there were no eligible males. Chiefs arbitrated quarrels, supervised communal activities, and saw that no one went hungry. Villagers contributed food to the chief's family.

Customs Coosan and Siuslaw society consisted of four classes: chiefly and wealthy families, a socially respectably majority, poor people, and slaves (obtained by capture or trade). The classes enjoyed similar subsistence levels; their main difference lay in nonfood wealth and status. Marriage occurred when a groom's family paid a bride price, which was later returned in a lifelong cycle of mutual gift giving and responsibilities. The dead were buried. Their goods were broken and placed in and around the grave.

Dwellings Permanent houses ranged between 20 and 50 or more feet long and half as wide and were excavated to a depth of about 3 to 6 feet. Two or more center posts supported a single ridgepole. Rafters sloped to the ground or to side supports. Walls and gabled roofs were of lashed cedar planks. Tule mats

lined the inside walls, mat partitions divided the several families within the house, and mats or hides covered the floors. Bed platforms ran along the walls. Among the Siuslaw, two or more houses were sometimes joined together.

Camp houses were of thatched grass with a gabled or one-pitch roof. Two types of sweat houses existed. One doubled as a men's clubhouse and boys' dormitory. It was square, plank-walled, excavated, and covered with dirt. The other, for use by both men and women, was in a beehive shape and heated by steam.

Diet The staple food was fish, primarily salmon. Fishing gear, used from shore and canoes, included dip nets, clubs, weirs, and harpoons. Other important food resources included shellfish, marine mammals, deer, and elk as well as various roots, shoots, and berries, such as camas, skunk-cabbage roots, and wapato. Both Coosans and Siuslaws cultivated tobacco. Most groups wintered near the ocean and moved upstream in summer to fish for salmon, hunt, and trap.

Key Technology Women made cattail and tule mats and various twined, decorated baskets. Men made weapons and hunting and fishing gear, including canoes. Most tools were made of wood, plant fiber, shell, or bone.

Trade Both groups traded mainly with their immediate neighbors.

Notable Arts Baskets and carved wood items were the principal arts.

Transportation Most transportation was by water and therefore by canoe, of which there were three main types. One was 15–20 feet long and flat bottomed, with both ends slightly raised. Another, often obtained in trade from the north, was larger and favored for ocean fishing; it was flat bottomed, with an undercut bow and pointed prow. The third type was a shovelnose canoe for bay and river travel. Most canoes were made of red cedar.

Dress Most clothing was made by women from skins and various fibers. Both sexes wore leggings and moccasins but usually only for travel and in cold weather. On such occasions, they also wore headbands and waterproof fur or fiber capes. Men generally wore breechclouts or shorts and often shirts and caps. Women wore shirts and skirts or one-piece dresses and woven hats. Everyone wore rain capes of cattail or shredded bark. Wealthy people were likely to decorate their clothing. Some people wore tattoos, primarily for measuring dentalia strings. The Kuitch wore large beads in their noses and flattened the heads of their infants.

War and Weapons Some hunting gear doubled as weapons.

Contemporary Information

Government/Reservations The Confederated Tribes of Coos, Lower Umpqua, and Siuslaw Indians, Inc., is based in Coos Bay, Oregon. The Coos tribe adopted its first constitution and by-laws in 1938 and has its own land (6.1 acres) and cemetery.

Federal recognition was restored in 1977 to the Confederated Tribes of Siletz Indians of Oregon, and in 1980 they received 3,630 acres of federal land. The mid-1990s tribal enrollment was roughly 2,900. A nine-member Tribal Council governs these Indians.

The Coquille Indian Tribe, composed of Miluks and Upper Coquilles, is also based in Coos Bay and has a land base of 6.2 acres. The 1993 population was 630.

Economy The Confederated Tribes of Coos, Lower Umpqua, and Siuslaw Indians work with the federal government on excavating and preserving archaeological projects. Logging, lumber, fishing, and service industries constitute major economic activities. Economic activity at Siletz is overseen by the Siletz Tribal Economic Development Corporation (STEDC) and centers on the timber industry. There are also a smokehouse and a bingo parlor. A casino is in the planning stages.

Legal Status The Confederated Tribes of Coos, Lower Umpqua, and Siuslaw Indians is a federally recognized tribal entity. The Coquille Tribe received federal rerecognition in 1989. The Confederated

Tribes of the Siletz Reservation is a federally recognized tribal entity. The Coos Tribe of Indians is federally recognized within their confederation with the Lower Umpquas and the Siuslaws.

Daily Life Over the past 30 years, the Coos tribe has formed several organizations to preserve its culture, the most prominent of which may be the Oregon Coast Indian Archaeological Association. The research center/museum is open on the Confederated Tribes of Coos, Lower Umpqua, and Siuslaw Reservation, which also sponsors a salmon feast in August. With the Bureau of Land Management, they are planning a $20 million interpretive center. In the mid-1970s, Indians influenced local schools to adopt programs and curricula relating to native culture. The Siletz Reservation holds a powwow in August; a museum/archive is in the process of being established.

Coquille (Mishikhwutmetunne)

See Coosans; Upper Umpqua

Cow Creek Band of Umpqua Indians

See Upper Umpqua

Cowichan

See Salish, Central Coast

Cowlitz

See Salish, Southwestern Coast

Duwamish

See Salish, Southern Coast

Grand Ronde, Confederated Tribes of

See Upper Umpqua

Haida

Haida (`Hī dä) is an adaptation from their self-designation. In the late eighteenth century, Haidas lived in a number of towns, politically unorganized but distinguishable as six groups by geography, tradition, and speech. These groups included the Kaigani people, the people of the north coast of Graham island, the Skidegate Inlet people, the people of the west coast of Moresby Island, the people of the east coast of Moresby Island, and the southern (Kunghit) people. The west coast Pitch-town people stood outside this classification system.

Location Haida territory included the Queen Charlotte Islands and Alexander Archipelago of British Columbia. This is a region of considerable environmental variation, including coastal lowlands, plateau, and mountains. The area is fairly wet, especially in the west.

In the 1990s, most Haida live in Masset and Skidegate on the Queen Charlottes and Hydaburg (established in 1911 as a specifically acculturated Haida town) on Prince of Wales Island, Alaska. Many also live in the cities of Ketchikan, Alaska, and Seattle, Washington.

Population The Haida population was roughly 9,000–10,000 in the late eighteenth century. This number dropped by almost 95 percent, to about 550, in 1915. In 1996 there were 1,076 members of the Skidegate band, of whom 478 were a resident population; 2,300 members of the Masset band; and 342 Indians at Hydaburg. The total U.S. Haida population was about 1,800.

Language Haidas spoke various dialects, including Skidegate and Masset, of the Haida Athapaskan language.

Historical Information

History Haida country was settled more than 9,000 years ago. The natives first saw a non-Indian when the Spanish explorer Juan Pérez Hernandez arrived in 1774. Numerous trading ships followed in the late eighteenth and early nineteenth centuries. The Haida traded sea otter pelts for European and U.S. manufactured goods. They also

A Haida brass band from Howkan, Alaska, circa 1905.

began cultivating potatoes at this time. By the late eighteenth century the Haida were rich and powerful.

Early trade was generally peaceful except for some hostilities in 1791, the probable year they first contracted smallpox. The sea otter trade ended about 1830. It was replaced by land-based fur operations and the Hudson's Bay Company; its 1830s post at Fort Simpson (Coast Tsimshian country) became the central trading location for Tlingit, Haida, and Tsimshian traders for the next 40 years. The Haida also traded in Victoria beginning in 1858, drawn by the local gold rush. During this period, however, they fought with rival Kwakiutls and fell victim to drinking and prostitution. More disease, especially smallpox, hit hard in 1862 and led to widespread village abandonment and consolidation. By the mid-1870s, Haida culture was in full collapse.

Christian (Methodist) missionaries arrived in Haida country in 1829. The Anglican church was active at Masset from the early 1880s on; shortly thereafter the Haida ceased erecting grave posts and memorial totem poles. Dancing and the power of shamans also declined. In 1883, Haida villages were divided between Methodists (central and southern) and Anglican (northern) missionaries.

Under government auspices, the Presbyterian Church established Hydaburg, Alaska, around the turn of the century. It was meant to facilitate the transition among Haidas from traditional to dominant culture. In 1936, the Haida became the first Indian group in Alaska to adopt a constitution under the Indian Reorganization Act. They succeeded

Christian funeral of Chief Sonihat in 1912. Christian (Methodist) missionaries arrived in Haida country in 1829. By 1883, Haida villages were divided between Methodists (central and southern) and Anglican (northern) missionaries.

in obtaining a large reservation in 1949, but under pressure from the salmon industry, a judge invalidated the reservation several years later.

Haidas in Canada were granted almost 3,500 acres of land in 1882 and another 360 in 1913. By the twentieth century, Haidas were migrating seasonally to work in the commercial mining, fishing, and canning industries. Acculturation proceeded rapidly. The potlatch was outlawed in 1884, although many Indians continued clandestinely to observe this central aspect of their culture. Government land allotments without regard to traditional lineages undercut the latter's power, as did the growth of single-family housing.

Canada passed its first comprehensive Indian Act in 1884. Among other things, the act established numerous small reserves for Indian subsistence and other activities. In 1912, Presbyterian Tlingits formed the Alaska Native Brotherhood (the Alaska Native Sisterhood was founded 11 years later), which worked for the abandonment of tradition, the mitigation of racial prejudice, increased educational opportunities, and land rights. These organizations reversed their stand against traditional practices in the late 1960s. Severe overt economic and social discrimination against Indians continued, however, including a virtual apartheid system during the first half of the twentieth century.

After World War II, Masset experienced a brief boom in carpentry and boatbuilding. Most villagers in the 1960s worked in the canning and processing industries for half the year and were otherwise unemployed. In general, Alaska Indians campaigned for self-government and full citizenship. Canadian Indian policy favored integration into mainstream society after World War II. In the 1960s, the government granted Indians a measure of self-determination, which sparked a period of cultural

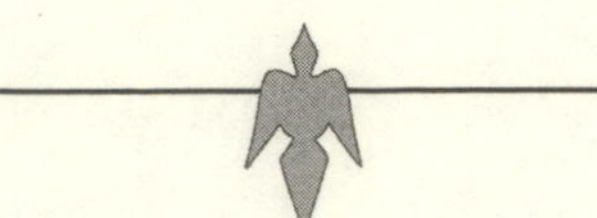

renewal. Tlingits and Haidas received a $7.5 million land claims settlement in 1970. Under the terms of the Alaska Native Claims Settlement Act (1971), the Haidas set up several corporations, although one, the Haida Corporation, declared bankruptcy in 1986.

Religion Haidas believed that animals possessed intelligence and humanlike souls, had a hierarchical ranking, lived in villages, and could change their form at will. Haidas offered prayers, grease, tobacco, and flicker feathers to the spirits of game animals. They also conceived of three worlds: sky, sea, and land. Their ceremonies were directly related to the system of social stratification. Potlatches, feasts, and dance performances, given by high-ranking people, were the main ceremonial events. Shamans, with multiple supernatural powers, were considered to be more powerful than chiefs.

Government People lived in autonomous villages, some consisting of a single lineage. The basic social and political unit was the lineage, or clan; each contained up to 12 households and was presided over by a hereditary chief. He gave permission for others to access the lineage's subsistence area and could declare war. Household chiefs (owners of plank houses) exercised control over their households, deciding when members left for fishing or hunting camps. In multilineage towns, the wealthiest, highest-ranking house chief was the town master, or town mother.

Customs The Haida divided most labor along sex and class lines. Women gathered, processed, and preserved all foods; prepared animal skins; and made clothing and baskets. Men fished, hunted, built houses and canoes, carved, and painted. Canoe making and carving, as well as sea otter hunting, were high-prestige occupations. Economically important slaves, captured during war, did much of the fishing.

Ambition, success in hunting and fishing, and industry were highly valued qualities. Haida society was divided into two matrilineal divisions, Raven and Eagle, each composed of lineages, or clans. Lineages had mythological origins and controlled property such as subsistence areas and names, dances, songs, and crest figures. Crests were the identifying symbols of lineages and an indication of personal rank within the lineage. They were carved on totem poles and other wooden items and tattooed on the body.

At feasts and potlatches, guests were seated according to their rank. Feasts, although always part of potlatches, were also held separately to name a child, at a marriage or death, to honor a visitor, or to enhance prestige. In addition to personal rank, there was a class system. Upper-class people bore many potlatch names, because when they were children their parents had given potlatches in their honor; they owned houses and were heirs to high-ranking names and chieftainships.

The Haida observed a number of life-cycle rituals and taboos. Children were regarded as reincarnated ancestors. Uncles toughened boys by, for example, making them take winter sea swims. There was no boys' puberty ceremony, but girls were secluded for a month or longer and followed many behavioral restrictions. Marriages were arranged in childhood or infancy. Property exchange and gift giving marked the marriage. Death among high-status people was a major ceremonial occasion. After bodies were washed, costumed, and painted, they lay in state for several days. Then they were placed in bent-corner coffins constructed by men of the father's lineage and removed through a hole in the wall. Burial was either in a lineage grave or in a mortuary column, followed by a potlatch and the raising of a memorial pole. Commoners had no poles erected in their honor. Slaves were thrown into the sea.

Dwellings There were two basic types of red cedar–plank houses, one with seven roof beams, a central smoke hole, and corner posts, and the other with four beams and four internal posts. Both types were roofed with cedar bark. Larger houses (houses could be as large as 60 by 100 feet) featured a centrally excavated pit and terraced tiers leading down to the base. Sleeping places were arranged by tier according to rank. Corner and interior posts were carved and painted. They were set along the tree line and facing the beach.

House names were considered personal property and might be attributes of the owner or related to the construction or physical features of the house. At one time, towns were probably composed of one lineage

This Haida chief stands before a typical dwelling called the House Where the People Want to Go (1888). House names might reflect an attribute of the owner or relate to the construction or physical features of the house. Entry into the house was either through a hole in the bottom of a totem pole or through elliptical doorways cut into the front facade.

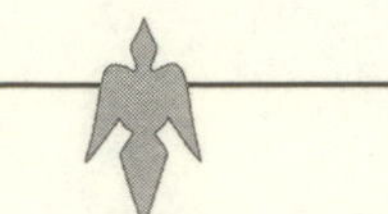

only. Many Haida towns had a "forest" of totem poles along the beachfront. Entry into the house was either through a hole in the bottom of a pole or through elliptical doorways cut into the front facade.

Diet Fish, especially halibut and salmon, and shellfish (gathered by men and women) were the staples. They were sliced and sun dried or smoked. Other important foods included sea mammals (seals, porpoises, sea otters, sea lions, and stranded whales), wild foods (seaweed, berries, and shoots), and land mammals (deer and beaver [Alaska], caribou [the Queen Charlottes], and bear). Meat was also preserved by smoking and drying. Some groups also ate birds (hunted by men and women) and their eggs. The Haida also grew tobacco.

Key Technology The Haida were a seafaring people. Fishing technology included hook and line (of gut), traps, and harpoons. Hunting equipment included snares, bows and arrows, and clubs. Women made twined basketry (for quivers and other items) of split spruce roots and cedar-bark mats and bags. Building tools included wooden wedges, stone adzes, and basalt or jade hammers. Dugout cedar canoes were up to 70 feet long and 8 feet wide, carved and painted. The Haida had a fire bow drill and began working their own iron in the late eighteenth century.

Trade At least in the early historic period, the Haida gained wealth from their skill as traders. They traded canoes, slaves, and shell to the Tlingit for copper, Chilkat blankets, and moose and caribou hides. Canoes, seaweed, chewing tobacco, and dried halibut went to the Tsimshian for eulachon grease, dried eulachons, and soapberries. They acquired slaves from the Kwakiutl. There was some intravillage trade. In the mid-1830s they traded furs, dried halibut, potatoes, and dried herring spawn to the Hudson's Bay Company for blankets, rice, flour, and other staples.

Notable Arts The Haida were outstanding wood-carvers. Their masterpieces included canoes, totem (mortuary) poles, house fronts, walls, screens, weapons, bentwood boxes, ceremonial masks, tools, and implements. Totem pole carving burgeoned during the nineteenth century with the acquisition of metal tools; the Haida built some of the best such poles in world history.

Designs included zoomorphic crest figures as well as mythological beings and events. Black, red, and blue-green were traditional colors. Other arts included basketry, especially hats, and other excellent woven items, such as robes, capes, and blankets. They may have carved argillite in prehistoric times, but certainly for the curio trade from the nineteenth century on, at which time they also took up silver engraving.

The Haida were outstanding wood-carvers. Their masterpieces included weapons such as these carved clubs, canoes, totem (mortuary) poles, house fronts, walls, screens, bentwood boxes, ceremonial masks, tools, and implements. Designs included zoomorphic crest figures as well as mythological beings and events.

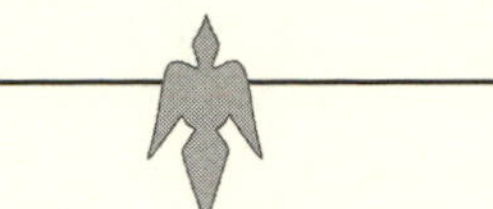

Transportation The Haida built several forms of red cedar dugout canoes.

Dress Clothing came from otter and other furs, cedar bark, and other fibers. Upper-class people wore tattoos. Wooden labrets were placed in the lips of upper-class girls at puberty; the size depended on rank and age.

War and Weapons The Haida enjoyed fighting. Their enemies included the Coast Tsimshian, Bella Bella, and Southern Tlingit as well as the Kwakiutl, Coast Salish, and Nootkans. There were also internal conflicts. Plunder and revenge were the main reasons for fighting. Weapons included the bow and arrow, bone-tipped spears, clubs, wooden helmets, and armor.

Relations with Non-natives Early trade relationships were positive, except for one violent incident directed against them in 1791 and subsequent revenge attacks. Non-native "culture" rather than weapons "triumphed" over the Haida as they fell to social vices as well as disease. Missionaries had success among the Haida, although the latter secretly retained many elements of their culture. Thorough acculturation took place during the last quarter of the nineteenth century.

Contemporary Information

Government/Reservations The centers of contemporary Haida culture are Masset and Skidegate on the Queen Charlottes, British Columbia, and Hydaburg (established in 1911 as a specifically acculturated Haida town), Alaska. A 101,000-acre reservation there was invalidated in 1952. The city of Hydaburg remains, at least for now, under the general control of Haida Indians.

In Canada, bands (an administrative entity created by the Indian Act) manage most resources. Although not self-governing, they elect councils every two years. Since the 1980s the Council of the Haida Nations, from Masset and Skidegate, has pursued common goals and interests.

The Old Masset Village Council Band, formerly known as the Masset Band and located seven kilometers west of the village of Masset, British Columbia, is commonly known as Haida Village. The band controls 26 reserves on 907 hectares. Their population in 1995 was 2,201, of which 600 people lived in 260 houses on the reserves. They are affiliated with the North Coast Tribal Council in addition to the Council of the Haida Nation. Officials are elected by custom.

The Skidegate Band is located in southeast Graham Island, British Columbia. Eleven reserves are located on 670 hectares of land. The band is affiliated with the North Coast Tribal Council as well as the Council of the Haida Nation. The 1996 population was 1,076, of which 478 people lived in 239 houses.

Economy The Sealaska Corporation, which includes Haidas since they were a party to the Alaska Native Claims Settlement Act, owns large timber, fishery, and other interests. The Haida Corporation also owns timber and oil and seafood interests. Residents of Hydaburg are engaged in subsistence economies as well as some commercial fishing and timber jobs. Most skilled jobs are held by outsiders. Unemployment among the Haida is a major problem.

Economic activities and resources of the Old Masset Village Council Band include a pizza parlor, a taxi service, a bed-and-breakfast, a jewelry casting company, stores, a boat charter, seasonal logging, and commercial fishing. Economic activities and resources of the Skidegate band include the Gwaalagaa Naay Cooperative grocery and a number of small businesses as well as seasonal logging and commercial fishing.

Hydaburg features a municipal government and a small urban economy, in addition to a reliance on the logging industry.

Legal Status The Hydaburg Cooperative Association is a federally recognized tribal entity. With the Alaska Native Claims Settlement Act (1971), hundreds of native corporations formed, including Sealaska (the Tlingit-Haida Central Council), which is a federally recognized tribal entity.

The Old Masset Village Council Band and the Skidegate Band are federally and provincially recognized entities. Tlingit and Haida native villages include Angoon, Craig, Hoonah, Hydaburg, Juneau (Juneau Fishing Village), Kake, Klawok, Klukwan, Saxman, Sitka Village, and Yakutat. The government

of British Columbia and Native Canadians continue to struggle over the issue of aboriginal rights.

Daily Life In Canada, native towns have regular and constant interaction with other nearby towns, yet life in the communities still centers around kinship, rank, and traditional ceremonial activities. The major church denominations are Anglican, Pentecostal, and United Church of Canada. The cultural renaissance of the 1970s was based in part on the emergence of several major artists.

Facilities at Masset include offices, a community hall, a counseling center, a warehouse, a longhouse, an elders' center, and a group home. Those at Skidegate include a community hall, a recreation hall, offices, a senior citizens center, and a gift shop. Children of both bands attend both and provincial schools.

Among the Alaska Haida, the elders and clan heads are churchgoers and serve as city officials and corporate directors. Extended families are still important, as are Christian churches, especially Presbyterian and the Assembly of God. Schools include classes in native language, drawing, and carving.

Mortuary potlatches and feasting are still part of Haida culture. In the 1980s, Canadian Indians began an initiative to enshrine native rights in the new constitution.

Haihais

See Bella Bella

Hoh

See Quileute

Kikiallus

See Salish, Southern Coast

Klallam

See Salish, Central Coast

Kuitch (Lower Umpqua)

See Coosans

Kwakiutl

Kwakiutl (Kwā gē ` ū tl) was originally the name of a local group and may mean "beach on the other side of the water." Once roughly 30 autonomous tribes or groups, the Kwakiutl did not think of themselves as a people until about 1900. They are sometimes referred to as Kwakwaka'wakw (Kwakiutl-speaking people) or Kwakwala (Kwakiutl language).

Location Many Kwakiutls continue to live in or near their aboriginal territory, which is located around the Queen Charlotte Strait on the central coast of British Columbia.

Population The Kwakiutl population in the early nineteenth century was about 8,000. In 1991, roughly 2,300 Kwakiutl lived on local reserves, and perhaps another 1,800 lived in regional cities and towns.

Language Kwakiutl is a member of the northern (Kwakiutlan) branch of the Wakashan language family. The three related languages were Haisla, Heiltsuk-Oowekyala, and Kwakiutl proper.

Historical Information

History The area around the Queen Charlotte Strait has probably been occupied for 10,000 years or longer. During the last 5,000 years, two distinct cultures arose. One was based on simple obsidian technology and featured a broad-based subsistence economy. People of the second, or Queen Charlotte Strait culture (post–500 B.C.E.), used bone and shell technology and ate mostly salmon, seal, and other marine foods.

Spanish, British, and U.S. explorers arrived in the region in the late eighteenth century. By early in the next century the local sea otter trade was in full swing. The Hudson's Bay Company became active when the sea otter trade diminished, around the 1830s. At that time the Kwakiutl began serving as middlemen in the fur trade. They and many other Indian peoples were frequent visitors to the company's post at Fort Victoria.

Changes in Kwakiutl culture during the fur trade period included the substitution of iron and steel for native materials in tools as well as Hudson's Bay blankets for the older style of robes. Disease epidemics

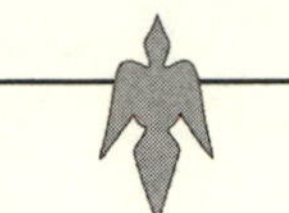

leading to depopulation also took a heavy toll at that time. In the 1850s, several Kwakiutl villages consolidated around a Hudson's Bay Company coal mine at Fort Rupert; this was the genesis of the Kwakiutl tribe. In general, the 1850s and 1860s were terrible years for the Kwakiutl, marked as they were by the destruction of several villages by the British Navy and Bella Coola raiders as well as smallpox epidemics. In the late 1880s, Canada established reserves for some Kwakiutl bands while claiming much of their aboriginal territory.

Aboriginally, trade partners were also often raiding targets. The enforced cessation of intertribal hostilities about 1865 precipitated an explosion of potlatching activity, as all Kwakiutl tribes became part of the system of social alliances and tribal ranking. The potlatch flourished despite legislation outlawing it in 1885 and 1915, as did traditional artistic expression.

Acculturation was proceeding rapidly by the 1880s. The Kwakiutl were giving up their traditional dress, subsistence activities, and many customs and were entering the local wage economy. Around 1900, Alert Bay, site of a cannery, a school, and a sawmill, superseded Fort Rupert as the center of Kwakiutl life. The early twentieth century was a period of economic boom for Kwakiutls owing to the growth of the commercial fishing and canning industries. Another boom in the fishing industry occurred after World War II. Many people abandoned the potlatch and traditional culture during the Depression and converted to the Pentecostal Church. Potlatching was not significantly reestablished until the 1970s.

Religion In traditional Kwakiutl belief, everything had a supernatural aspect that commanded respect from people in the form of individual daily prayer and thanks. Guardian spirits, which provided luck and certain skills, might be obtained through prayer or fasting. Associated with each spirit was a secret ceremonial society, such as Cannibal, Grizzly Bear, and Warrior, as well as specific dances and ceremonies.

Shamans formed an alliance with a supernatural helper and were initiated into their craft by other shamans. The Kwakiutl recognized several degrees of shamanic power, the highest being the ability to cure and cause disease; these most powerful people were usually attached to chiefs. Shamans used songs, rattles, and purification rings (hemlock or cedar) in public curing ceremonies. Witches could harm or otherwise control people without recourse to supernatural power, although knowledge similar to theirs was available to guard against such practices.

The winter ceremonials were based on complex mythological themes and involved representations of supernatural beings and stories of ancestral contact with them. Principal winter ceremonies, including the Cedar Bark Dance and the Weasel Dance, involved feasting, potlatching, entertainment, and theater. Winter was considered a sacred season because the supernaturals were said to be present at that time. People attempted to be on better behavior and even took on sacred names.

Government Each of the roughly 30 autonomous tribes (local groups) had its own hereditary chief, subsistence area, winter village, and seasonal sites. Tribes consisted of between one and seven (usually at least three) kin groups *(numayms)*, each having perhaps 75–100 people aboriginally and roughly 10–15 in the late nineteenth–early twentieth century. In early historic times, some tribes formed joint winter villages without losing their individual identities.

Customs Kin groups (tribes) owned resource areas, myths, crests, ceremonies, songs, dances, house names, named potlatching positions, and some inheritable guardian spirits. Crests, privileges, and rights were transmitted through marriage. The Kwakiutl recognized many forms of permissible marriages. Preserving the existence of crests and privileges remained all important, and rules were bent or broken over time to accommodate this need. There were four traditional classes or status groups: chiefs, nobles, commoners, and slaves. Society became much more equal in the mid–nineteenth century: As the population declined, the number of privileged positions remained constant, so that more people could rise to such positions.

Potlatches, once modest affairs, became highly complex, elaborate, and more culturally central in the late nineteenth century, helping to integrate and drive Kwakiutl society by validating social status

Kwakiutl tribe members participate in a winter initiation ceremony, 1892. The winter ceremonials were based on complex mythological themes and involved representations of supernatural beings and stories of ancestral contact with them. Winter was considered a sacred season because the supernaturals were said to be present at that time.

and reciprocities. The size of a potlatch varied according to the event being marked: Life-cycle events for high-status children and wiping out casual mistakes received small potlatches; receipt of a first potlatch position, dancing the winter ceremonial, and the occasion of girls' puberty received moderate-sized potlatches; and the assumption of a chiefly name and/or position within a kin group, a grease feast, the buying and selling of coppers, the erection of crest memorial poles, and marriage received the largest potlatches. All included feasting, socializing, speeches, songs, displays of wealth and crests, and dances. Such potlatches were occasionally given on credit; that is, on borrowed goods (blankets), usually lent at 100 percent interest.

Traditionally, the Kwakiutl practiced blood revenge, in which one or more people might be killed upon the death of a close relative. Corpses were buried in trees, caves, or canoes (chiefs), although northern groups cremated their dead.

Dwellings Rows of cedar beam and plank houses with shed roofs faced the sea in traditional villages. The central house posts were carved and painted with crests. A sleeping platform extended around walls. Four families of the same kin group occupied most houses, each in a corner with its own

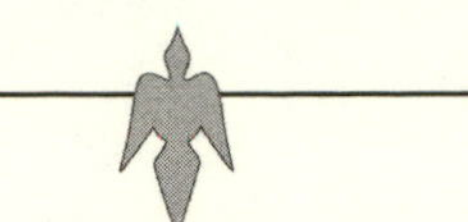

As a people, the Kwakiutl were artists. Wooden objects such as massive house posts, totem poles, masks, rattles, feast dishes, and other objects used for crest displays were carved or painted. On this old house at Alert Bay in British Columbia, the legendary thunderbird is depicted carrying off a whale (1902).

fireplace. Private areas were partitioned off. Each village also had one or more ceremonial houses, similarly constructed. By the late nineteenth century, houses were built with milled lumber and gabled roofs.

Diet The Kwakiutl ate mostly seafood: clams, salmon, halibut, and other marine life. Fish were smoke dried. The people traveled to their widespread resource areas in canoes. Fish (eulachon) oil was also an important dietary supplement. They also ate berries, sea grass, roots, mountain goat, elk, and deer.

Key Technology Fish were taken with dip nets, weirs, and rakes. Harpoons were used for seals and sea lions and bow and arrow for land mammals. Kelp tubes, baskets, wooden boxes, and chests served as containers. In general, men worked wood and women wove fibers. There were no full-time craftspeople. The Kwakiutl had an abundance of material goods such as boxes, mats, spoons, dishes, and canoes. Most craft production took place in winter. A few tools, such as the mortar and pestle, were made of stone.

Trade The Kwakiutl engaged in widespread intertribal trading for specific items such as eulachon oil, dried halibut, and herring roe.

Notable Arts As a people, the Kwakiutl were artists. Even in utilitarian items, visual art was joined with rhetoric, mythology, and performance art to glorify the kin groups. Wooden objects, such as massive houseposts, totem and commemorative poles (nonaboriginal), masks, rattles, feast dishes, and other objects used for crest displays were carved and/or painted. The point of most Kwakiutl art was social—to display ancestral rights—rather than specifically religious, although the two are basically inseparable.

Their basic colors were black and red. The Kwakiutl experienced a golden age of art from about 1890 to 1920. They also produced some excellent twined, spruce root, and cedar bark hats.

Transportation Most travel took place over water in a number of different style of dugout cedar canoes. Skin sails were used from the nineteenth century on.

Dress In warm weather, women wore cedar-bark aprons and men went naked. Women wore waterproof basket caps and cedar-bark ponchos in the rain. Blankets of woven cedar bark, mountain goat wool or dog hair, or tanned, sewn skins served as cold-weather protection. Long yellow cedar-bark robes were particular to Kwakiutl people. Both sexes wore their hair long. Some men let their facial hair grow. Those who could afford them wore abalone nose and ear pendants. Women also wore dentalia bracelets, necklaces, and anklets. People also painted their bodies and faces against sunburn.

War and Weapons The Kwakiutl often fought each other (other Kwakiutl tribes) for revenge and fought neighboring peoples such as the Coast Salish for plunder, land, heads, and slaves. One group, the Lekwiltok, were particularly aggressive. The Kwakiutl had guns as early as the late eighteenth century.

Contemporary Information

Government/Reservations Canadian band councils have municipal power (over roads, water, sewers, and so on) and manage various economic activities. An administrative tribal organization, the Kwakiutl District Council, was organized in 1974. In 1982, four bands (later five) left the council to form the

This carved cedar mask of four bird beaks is almost four feet long. The Kwakiutl Hamatsa Society dancer who wore the mask needed considerable strength and dexterity to manipulate it.

Musga'makw Tribal Council. See "Daily Life" for profiles of individual bands as of 1995.

Economy Various bands are associated with different activities, such as marinas, oyster hatcheries, tourism, laundromats, cafeterias, and shipyards. General band operating funds come from the federal government. Most people also engage in semitraditional seasonal pursuits, such as hunting and commercial fishing. Some jobs are also available within band enterprises.

Legal Status Bands may pass laws binding upon members and visitors; overall law enforcement is assumed by the Royal Canadian Mounted Police.

Daily Life Most Kwakiutl children are educated in provincial schools, although there are some band-administered schools. All have well-established programs to teach traditional language and culture. The Kwaguilth Museum (1979; Cape Mudge, Quadra

Island, British Columbia) and the U'Mista Cultural Center (1980; Alert Bay, British Columbia) both hold ceremonial objects returned by the government in 1978. They also record oral histories, prepare school curricula and display exhibits, and organize classes.

Bands still reflect traditional family alliances and allegiances. Many traditional practices remain, such as potlatches for girls' puberty, memorials, and other purposes; dance societies; and the inheritance of ceremonial prerogatives. The Kwakiutl never experienced a dramatic artistic revival, mainly because their artistry was never significantly interrupted. The elderly now maintain their own households, baptism is common, and most marriages and funerals take place in church. Soccer tournaments are popular, and an annual sports weekend is held in June. English is the first language of most Kwakiutl.

Campbell River Band: Their reserve was established in 1888. Population is 495, of whom 176 live on the reserve. They are governed under the provisions of the Indian Act and are affiliated with the Kwakiutl District Council. Children attend provincial schools. Economic activities include commercial fishing, tourism, logging, pulp and paper, and mining. Facilities include offices and a community hall.

Cape Mudge Band: Five reserves are located on about 665 hectares of land. Population is 761, of whom 314 live on the reserve. They are governed under the provisions of the Indian Act and are affiliated with the Kwakiutl District Council. Children attend band and provincial schools. Economic activities include salmon fishing, commercial fishing, tourism, logging, pulp and paper, trapping, and mining. Facilities include offices, a community hall, a museum, and the Tsaw-Kwa-Luten Resort and Conference Center.

Gwa'sala-Nakwaxda'xw Band: Twenty-six reserves are located on 752 hectares of land near Port Hardy, British Columbia. Population is 502, of whom 374 live in 91 houses on the reserve. They are governed by custom and are affiliated with the Kwakiutl District Council. Children attend band and provincial schools. Economic activities include commercial fishing, forestry, tourism, and mining. Facilities include offices, a community hall, and an arts and crafts building.

Kwa-wa-aineuk Band: Ten reserves are located on 205 hectares of land on Watson Island. The main community is also known as Hopetown. The reserves were allotted in 1916. Population was 28, of whom 19 lived in six houses on the reserve. They are governed by custom and are affiliated with the Musga'makw Tribal Council. Children attend provincial schools. Facilities include offices and a workshop.

Kwakiutl Band: Eight reserves are located on 295 hectares of land near Port Hardy, British Columbia. Population is 536, of whom 279 live in 68 houses on the reserves. They are governed by custom and are affiliated with the Kwakiutl District Council. Children attend band and provincial schools. Economic activities include commercial fishing, forestry, tourism, and mining. Facilities include offices and a community hall.

Kwiakah Band: Two reserves are located on 69 hectares of land. The reserves were allotted in 1886. Most people live on the Campbell River Indian Reserve. Population is 17, of whom none live on the reserve. They are governed by custom and are affiliated with the Kwakiutl District Council.

Kwicksutaineuk-ah-kwaw-ah-mish Band: Ten reserves are located on 172 hectares of land 40 miles east of Port Hardy, British Columbia. The reserves were allotted in 1886. Population is 251, of whom 144 live in 22 houses on the reserves. They are governed under the provisions of the Indian Act and are affiliated with the Musga'makw Tribal Council. Children attend provincial schools. Facilities include offices, a longhouse, and a community hall.

Mamaleleqala-Que'Qua'Sot'Enox Band: Three reserves are located on 233 hectares of land. The reserves were allotted in 1886. This band was formerly known as the Mamalillikulla Band. Population is 295, of whom none live on the reserve. They are governed by custom and are affiliated with the Kwakiutl District Council.

Namgis First Nation, formerly the Nimkish Tribe: Eight reserves are located on 388 hectares of land south of Port NcNeill, British Columbia. The reserves were allotted in 1884. Population is 1,346, of whom 714 live in 121 houses and 15 apartment units on the reserve. They are governed by custom and are affiliated with the Musga'makw Tribal Council.

Children attend band and provincial schools. Economic resources include a salmon hatchery. Facilities include offices, a museum, a longhouse, community buildings, and a community health center.

Oweekeno Band: Three reserves are located on 712 hectares of land on the Wanuk River, British Columbia. Population is 204, of whom 60 live in 23 houses on the reserve. They are governed under the provisions of the Indian Act and are affiliated with the Oweekeno-Nuxalk Tribal Council. Children attend band and provincial schools. Economic resources include logging and salmon enhancement. Facilities include offices, a community center, and a drop-in center.

Quatsino Band: Nineteen reserves are located on 346 hectares of land south of Port Hardy, British Columbia. The reserves were allotted in 1886. Population is 316, of whom 214 live on the reserve. They are governed under the provisions of the Indian Act and are affiliated with the Kwakiutl District Council. Children attend provincial schools. Economic resources include mining, forestry, tourism, and fishing. Facilities include offices, a community center, and a fire station.

Tanakteuk Band: Seven reserves are located on 318 hectares of land 270 kilometers northwest of Vancouver, British Columbia. The reserves were allotted in 1866. Population is 150, of whom 22 live on federal land at Whe-la-la-u, Alert Bay. They are governed by custom and are affiliated with the Kwakiutl District Council. Economic resources include mining, tourism, and fishing. Facilities include offices.

Tlatlasikwala First Nation, formerly known as the Nuwilti Band: Six reserves are located on 3,474 hectares of land. The reserves were allotted in 1916. Population is 37, of whom all live on federal land at Whe-la-la-u, Alert Bay. They are affiliated with the Kwakiutl District Council, the Kwakiutl First Nation Treaty Society, and Kwakiutl Territorial Fisheries. Economic resources include commercial fishing.

Tlowitsis-Mumtagila Band, formerly Turnour Island Band: Eight reserves are located on 188 hectares of land 260 kilometers northwest of Vancouver, British Columbia. The reserves were allotted in 1916. Population is 293, of whom 3 live on the reserve. They are governed by custom and are affiliated with the Whe-la-la-u Area Council and the Musga'makw Tribal Council. Economic resources include forestry, mining, fishing, and tourism.

Tsawataineuk Band: Five reserves are located on 218 hectares of land 290 kilometers northwest of Vancouver, British Columbia. The reserves were allotted in 1886. Population was 447, of whom 113 live in 41 houses on the reserve. They are governed by custom and are affiliated with the Musga'makw/ Tsawataineuk Tribal Council. Children attend band and provincial schools. Economic resources include commercial logging, fishing, and silviculture. Facilities include offices, a community hall, a longhouse, and a church.

Lower Umpqua

See Coosans

Lummi

See Salish, Central Coast

Makah

Makah (Mə `kä) is a Klallam word for "the People." The Makah word for themselves is *Kwe-net-che-chat,* "People of the Point." They were a whaling people, culturally similar to the Nootkans of Vancouver Island.

Location The Makah lived around Cape Flattery on the northwest tip of the Olympic Peninsula, a region of fierce, rainy winters and calm, sunny summers. The Makah Reservation is in Clallam County, Washington, within their aboriginal lands.

Population Makah population was roughly 2,000 in the late eighteenth century. In 1990, 940 Indians lived on the Makah Reservation, and perhaps another 1,000 Makahs lived in regional cities and town.

Language Makah is a southern or Nootkan language of the Wakashan language family.

Historical Information

History People have lived around Cape Flattery for roughly 4,000 years. The Makahs emigrated from Vancouver Island about 500 years ago, although some Makah villages were occupied as early as 1500 B.C.E. The Makahs first encountered non-natives around 1790, when British and Spanish ships entered the area, and the Spanish built a short-lived fort. Around 1809, the Makah detained several shipwrecked Russians and Inuit and also detained three shipwrecked Japanese in 1833. They traded occasionally with Hudson's Bay Company.

Results of early contact included an intensification of trade and the use of non-native goods as well as disease epidemics. By the 1850s, villages were being abandoned as a result of depopulation. The Makah signed the Treaty of Neah Bay in 1855, ceding land in return for "education, health care, fishing rights," and a reservation (subsequently enlarged). The Indian Service soon moved in and tried to eradicate Makah culture. They prohibited the native language and customs in government schools and tried, but failed, to replace maritime traditions with agriculture.

During the 1860s and 1870s, Makahs hunted fur seals for the non-native market. In the 1880s, Makahs were hunting on white-owned ships, at a profit so great that they temporarily abandoned whaling. By the 1890s, some Makahs had their own boats and were hiring both Indian and white crews. At this time, however, the seal population began to decline owing to overhunting. As international treaties began to restrict seal hunting, Makahs turned to poaching and then abandoned the activity altogether. By this time, in any case, many of their maritime-related ceremonies had disappeared.

In 1896, when the boarding school closed, many families moved to Neah Bay, which became the Makahs' primary village. In 1911, a treaty gave the Makah and some other Indian groups the right to hunt seals using aboriginal methods, a practice that continued for several decades. Commercial logging began in 1926. A road connecting the reservation with the outside world opened in the 1930s, as did public schools, which replaced the hated boarding schools. Tourism and the general local cash economy increased. In the 1940s, the Army Corps of Engineers completed a breakwater that provided a sheltered harbor for tourist boats and fishing vessels.

Major postwar economic activities were commercial fishing, logging, and tourism. Makah cultural life began to reemerge with the relaxation of the more severe anti-Indian government policies. In any case, some aspects of traditional culture, such as the potlatch and the language, had never been eradicated. In 1970, archaeological excavations at the village of Ozette revealed much about the aboriginal life of the Makah. This site has yielded over 50,000 artifacts as well as other valuable information and has encouraged many young Makahs to study anthropology.

Religion The acquisition of guardian spirits was central to Makah religion and ceremonialism. Adolescent boys acquired them by fasting in remote places. Shamans, both male and female, who had acquired several guardian spirits cured people and provided ceremonial leadership.

Except for ritual hunting preparations, most ceremonies took place in winter. Carved wooden masks figured prominently in a four-day Wolf ritual, during which members were initiated into the secret *klukwalle* society. A healing ceremony and complex whaling rituals follow Nootka patterns.

Government The Makah lived in five permanent, semiautonomous villages, with one or more lesser satellite village in the same general area.

Customs Social groups included headmen, commoners, and slaves. The headmen regularly affirmed their rank through the institution of the potlatch. Commoners could advance or fall back slightly through marriage or by acquiring privileges. Alliances were formed and privileges and subsistence areas were inherited through ranked patrilineal lineages.

Whaling and fur seal hunting were particularly prestigious occupations. Only the former was an inherited privilege, but both involved substantial ritual components. Only men hunted and fished aboriginally; women gathered shellfish and plants and cleaned, cooked, and otherwise prepared food products.

At the onset of puberty, girls were secluded and observed certain rites. Gifts from the man's to the woman's family constituted a marriage; such gifts were then redistributed to extended family and friends. Corpses were removed through house roofs and buried in boxes, along with possessions. Slaves were sometimes killed when a chief died.

Dwellings Permanent houses were built on wooden frames as large as 60 by 30 by 15 feet high. Platforms along the wall served as sleeping and storage areas. Planks from nearly flat roofs, on which fish drying racks were located, could be easily removed for ventilation. Several families lived in one house. Privacy was provided by removable partitions. House fronts and posts were carved or painted. In summer, some people left the permanent villages for summer residences.

Diet The region supported abundant land and sea life, including mammals, fish and shellfish, birds, and flora. Sea mammals were the most important staple, followed by fish, particularly halibut. Oil, especially from whales and fur seals, was used to flavor dried foods. The Makah ate some land mammals. Plant foods included several varieties of berries, roots (especially sand verbena, surf grass, and buttercup), and greens. Plants were also used medicinally, for raw materials, and in entertainment.

Key Technology Makah women wove spun dog wool or bird skin and fiber cordage on a two-bar loom. Women also made baskets of cedar as well as of cattail, tule, and cherry bark. Whaling equipment included mussel shell–tipped harpoons, line made of whale sinew and pounded cedar boughs, and skin floats for floating the dead whales and towing them ashore. Fishing equipment included hooks and kelp lines, weirs, traps, and gaffs. Land mammals provided additional raw material, such as antler and bone, for manufactured items. Shell was used for cutting and eating tools and for adornment. Mats for canoe sails, blankets, and cargo wrap were made from cedar bark. Wooden implements, such as bent-corner boxes (steamed and bent), bowls, dishes, containers, clubs, harpoon and arrow shafts, and bows, were fashioned from yew, red cedar, spruce, alder, and hemlock.

Trade The Makah were actively involved in trade and social intercourse with all neighbors, including Klallam, Quileute, and Nitinaht. Makahs often served as middlemen, handling items such as dried halibut and salmon, sea otter skins, vermilion, whale and sea oil, dentalium shells, dried cedar bark, canoes, and slaves. They made an especially good profit selling whale oil. Camas, a favorite food, was obtained in trade from the north. They both imported and exported canoes.

Notable Arts Basketry and wood carving were the two most important Makah arts.

Transportation Several different types of canoes were used for hunting marine mammals and for war, trade, carrying freight, and other activities.

Dress Men wore little or nothing in warm weather. Such clothing as men and women did wear was generally made from cedar bark and woven bird down feathers, as were diapers and other such items. Blankets, skins, and cloaks provided warmth in colder weather. People also wore conical hats and bearskin robes in the rain. Personal adornment included nose and ear ornaments and face paint.

War and Weapons Makahs occasionally fought the Quileute, Klallam, Hoh, and others as well as their Nootkan relations to the north. Weapons included bone and horn-tipped clubs, yew-wood bows, arrows with stone or bone tips, knives, spears, and slings.

Contemporary Information

Government/Reservations The Makah Reservation (1855; 27,244 acres) is located in Clallam County, Washington. The tribe accepted the Indian Reorganization Act in 1934 and adopted a constitution and by-laws in 1936. They provide for a five-member tribal council, elected for staggered three-year terms, with various appointed committees. In 1984, the Makah retook possession of Tatoosh and Waadah Islands. A one-square-mile reservation has also been established around the Ozette archaeological site.

Economy The Makah Cultural and Research Center (1979) is home to the Ozette artifacts. This major

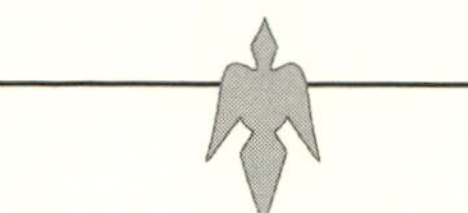

institution administers a highly successful language preservation program and is largely responsible for reinvigorating the Makah language. Commercial fishing, including a side business renting cabins to other fishers, remains important. Other economic activities include some logging and production of olivella-shell jewelry. The government (health services and schools) and local retail businesses provide some stable employment. Unemployment hovers around 50 percent.

Legal Status The Makah Indian Tribe is a federally recognized tribal entity.

Daily Life Radio station KRNB (1975) broadcasts from Neah Bay with some programs in Makah. Makah Days, a two-day celebration, is held at the end of August. The Makah are the only tribe in the United States with a treaty right to hunt whales. In 1995 they took their first whale in 80 years. In October 1997 they received permission from the International Whaling Commission to resume subsistence whaling. Some people still dance the family dances. Most Makahs are literate in their language.

Muckleshoot

See Salish, Southern Coast

Nisqually

See Salish, Southern Coast

Nooksack

See Salish, Central Coast

Nootkans

Nootkans (`Nūt kə ns) were a linguistic group of Vancouver Island Indians consisting of more than 22 tribes, confederacies, or sociopolitical local groups. Captain James Cook, who thought it was the native name for what came to be called Nootka Sound, originated the term.

Location Many Nootkans continue to live in or near their aboriginal territory, which was the western half of Vancouver Island, British Columbia, roughly 125 miles north and south of midcoast. The geography features a rocky coast and a coastal plain ("outside") as well as a series of inlets penetrating deep into the hilly interior ("inside"). The climate is wet and moderate with fierce winter storms.

Population The Nootkan population was at least 15,000 in the mid–eighteenth century. In 1984, roughly 4,700 Nootkans lived in the region.

Language Nootka and Nitinaht, together with Makah, constitute the southern or Nootkan branch of the Wakashan language family.

Historical Information

History Nootkan culture changed relatively little during the 5,000 years preceding contact with non-natives. In the late prehistoric period they had acquired iron and other metals through trade and salvage from shipwrecks. In 1778, Captain Cook remained with the Nootkas for a month, acquiring a large collection of sea otter pelts. Cook's crew later sold the pelts to Chinese merchants at great profit, thereby laying the basis for the northwest maritime fur trade.

A few Nootkan chiefs, such as Maquinna, whose power was maintained in part by the Spanish, became very wealthy by controlling that trade. Partly by means of firearms, they established themselves as intermediaries between whites and other Indian peoples. During that time, Indians began to suffer significant population decline owing to increased warfare (competition over the fur trade) as well as epidemics, including venereal disease. By the end of the century, hunters had so depleted the sea otter stock that the local fur trade was in sharp decline. In its wake, Indians began attacking trade ships, which in turn greatly diminished their contact with non-natives for several decades.

Population decline and general dislocation led to the formation of new tribes and confederacies in the early nineteenth century. Continued Nootkan attacks on trade ships in midcentury brought retaliation from the British navy. Gradually, without

A few Nootkan chiefs, such as Maquinna, pictured here in uniform, became very wealthy by controlling the fur trade. The Nootkan population was at least 15,000 in the mid–eighteenth century. In 1984 roughly 4,700 Nootkans lived in the region.

being formally conquered, the Nootkans became integrated into the new commercial economy. There was a continuing trade in the furs of animals such as deer, elk, mink, marten, and northern fur seal. Throughout the late nineteenth century, Nootkans were important suppliers of dogfish oil, which was used in the logging industry. They also became involved in the pelagic sealing industry, hunting from canoes as well as schooners. Some Nootkans became wealthy during that period and even purchased their own schooners. Commercial fishing was another important local industry, providing jobs and drawing people to canneries from their villages. Crafts for the tourist trade also became important around that time, as did seasonal hop picking in the Puget Sound area.

When British Columbia joined Canada in 1871, Nootkans became part of the federal Indian reserve system. Villages still in use received small reserves in the 1880s, though without having formally surrendered any land to the government. Missionaries arrived to carry out government health and education programs. Such programs included the establishment of Indian boarding schools, where native culture was ruthlessly suppressed.

After World War II, further consolidation and centralization of the Nootkan population paralleled similar trends in the fishing industry. Potlatching and other forms of traditional culture continued, despite government opposition. Beginning in the 1960s and 1970s, Nootkans focused on fostering a positive self-identity and achieving control over their own destinies. In 1978, a political organization called the West Coast District Council (formerly the West Coast Allied Tribes) proclaimed the name *Nuu-chah-nulth* ("all along the mountains") for all Nootkan peoples and renamed the organization the Nuu-chah-nulth Tribal Council.

Religion Numerous categories of spirit and mythological beings were recognized as ubiquitous. They could be obtained and controlled through rituals or by spirit quests. Rituals, especially as practiced by chiefs, helped to ensure bountiful salmon runs, the beaching of dead whales, and other food resources. Long-haired shamans dived to the bottom of the sea to battle soul-stealing sea spirits. Chiefs also engaged in spirit quests (commoners' spirit help came through minor rituals and charms). One obtained power from a spirit being by seizing it, rather than by establishing a relation with it as with a guardian spirit. Such power provided special skills, luck, or other achievements.

Nootkans prayed for power to the Four Chiefs of Above, Horizon, Land, and Undersea. They observed two primary winter ceremonies: the Dancing, or Wolf ritual, and the Doctoring ritual (central and southern Nootkans only). Although the former was an initiation and the latter a curing ceremony, the ultimate purpose of both was to confirm the social order. The Wolf ritual, several of which might be held in a village each winter, involved masks and dramatization.

Government Local groups held defined territories, the legitimacy of which came from a particular legendary ancestor. The chiefly line of descent was the group's nucleus. The highest-ranking man in a local group was its chief; the position was inheritable.

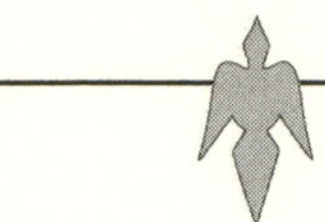

Local groups sometimes united to form tribes, with ranked chiefs and common winter villages and ceremonials. Some northern Nootkan tribes also came together to form confederacies, with each local group retaining its identity, territory, and ceremonies.

Customs Inherited rights formed the basis of social rank and governed the ownership and use of practically everything of value. Inheritance was generally patrilineal. Nootkan social classes consisted of chief, commoners, and slaves. Chiefs did not work; they directed their followers, who in turn supported and were taken care of by them. A chief's close male relations were secondary chiefs (such as war chiefs and speakers). Chiefs received tribute for the use of resource sites. When goods accumulated, they held a feast or a potlatch. Other occasions for potlatches included life-cycle and public events such as status transfer and confirmation. The participation in all life-cycle rituals and ceremonies was commensurate with social rank.

Pregnancy and birth carried numerous rituals and restrictions, especially regarding twins. Infants' heads were flattened to achieve an aesthetic ideal. Children were regularly instructed on correct behavior, such as industry, peacefulness, and social responsibility, and on ritual knowledge. For high-status families, the onset of female puberty was the occasion for a great potlatch. It also entailed rituals and seclusion for the woman herself. Along with warfare, marriage was the means by which local groups sought to maximize access to subsistence areas. As such, it was mostly an alliance between families and was accompanied by great ritual, depending on rank. Although divorce was possible, adultery, unless chronic or within the chief's family, was generally smoothed over.

Corpses were placed in a flexed position and buried away from the village, in boxes or canoes placed in trees or caves. Valuables were also interred, and belongings, including the house, might be burned. Memorial poles were erected to chiefs. Sometimes slaves were killed as companions to the dead.

Dwellings Multifamily cedar houses between 40 and 150 feet long, 30 and 40 feet wide, and 8 and 10 feet high lined the beaches. Planks were removable for use in smaller camp dwellings. Roofs were of both shed (primarily in the south) and gabled style. Individual family areas, each with its own fireplace, were set off from the others by storage chests. Sleeping platforms ringed the walls. Posts and beams were carved with hereditary designs. Local groups had house frames standing at three sites: permanent village, summer fishing and sea hunting areas, and a main salmon stream.

Diet Salmon, smoked and dried, was the staple. Nootkans also ate herring, halibut, cod, snapper, flounder, and other fish. Other important foods included roots, berries, bulbs, ferns, crabapples, and eelgrass; shellfish, mollusks, kelp, and sea cucumbers; waterfowl; and sea mammals such as harbor seals, porpoises, sea lions, sea otters, and whales. The ritual preparation by whalers, who were always chiefs, included bathing, praying, and swimming and began months in advance of the whaling season. Land mammals included deer, elk, black bear, and small mammals. Most food was dried, smoked, steamed in pits, or broiled in wooden boxes with red-hot stones.

Key Technology Fish were taken with dip nets, rakes, floating fences, and weirs; waterfowl with nets, nooses, bow and arrow, and snares; marine invertebrates with yew digging and prying sticks; sea mammals with clubs, harpoons, stakes hidden in seaweed, and nets. Special whaling equipment consisted of harpoons with musselshell blades, two 40- to 60-fathom lines, floats, and lances. Nootkans used six types of canoes, some with cedar bark–mat sails. The uses of wood, a key raw material, included hunting and war tools, canoes, houses, utensils, buckets, and storage boxes. Mattresses and other such items were made of cedar bark.

Trade Nootkans enjoyed a virtual monopoly on dentalia shell, an item highly prized by many peoples along and surrounding the Northwest Coast. They also supplied sea otter pelts and canoes. Their primary trading partners were the Nimpkish Kwakiutl and the Makah. Nootkans received eulachon oil and grease from the Tsimshian, Chilkat goat-hair blankets from the Tlingit, and furs from the Coast Salish (who obtained them from interior peoples).

Notable Arts Music and dance were important Nootkan arts. Vocal music, often containing complicated structures, patterns, and beats, was accompanied by drumming and rattles. Songs were sung for many different occasions, both sacred and secular.

Drama regularly included masks to represent supernatural beings. People told long, complex stories on winter evenings. House posts and fronts and many wooden objects were elaborately carved with crests designs. The decorated conical, onion-domed cedar-bark and spruce-root whaler's hat was a classic Nootkan basketry item. Painting was highly developed in the historic period.

Transportation Red cedar dugout canoes came in various sizes. Paired canoes bridged with house planks served to move large loads.

Dress Men went naked in warm weather. Women wore shredded cedar-bark aprons, and both sexes wore bark robes and conical rain capes as well as hats (which varied according to social class) of tightly woven cedar bark and spruce root. Long yellow cedar-bark robes were distinctive to Nootkan people. Faces were painted for decoration and sunburn protection. Ornaments of dentalium, abalone, horn, and other items were worn in the nose and ears and as bracelets and anklets.

War and Weapons The Nimpkish Kwakiutl and the Makah were regular objects of Nootkan military attention. War chiefs wore elk hide armor with painted designs. Raiding took place primarily to acquire booty, including slaves. Weapons included bone and horn-tipped clubs, yew-wood bows, arrows with stone or bone points, knives, spears, and slings. Many Nootkans had guns as early as the late eighteenth century.

Contemporary Information

Government/Reservations As of 1995, 15 Nootkan bands lived in their traditional territory in British Columbia. The Nuu-chah-nulth Tribal Council is elected by all Nootkans and funded by most bands. See "Daily Life" for summaries of bands.

Economy Economic activities and band resources are described under "Daily Life." Since the nineteenth century, Nootkans have made baskets for commercial sale.

Legal Status All of the following bands are federally and provincially recognized entities.

Daily Life The following are extant Nookan bands (as of 1995):

Ahousaht Band: The band was formed in 1951 from the Ahousaht and Kelsemaht Bands. It controls 25 reserves on 592 hectares of land. The reserves were allotted in 1889. The 1995 population was 1,415, of whom 487 lived in 105 houses on the reserve. The band is governed under the provisions of the Indian Act and is affiliated with the Nuu-chah-nulth Tribal Council. Economic activities and resources include a seabus service, freight services, a bakery, and a campsite. Facilities include a community hall, a church, a cultural center, administrative offices, and two gymnasiums.

Ditidaht Band: The band controls 17 reserves on 727 hectares of land. The reserves were allotted in 1890. The 1995 population was 481, of whom 141 lived in 34 houses on the reserve. The band is governed by custom and is affiliated with the Nuu-chah-nulth Tribal Council. Children attend provincial schools. Economic activities and resources include forestry and a gravel pit. Facilities include a community hall, a cultural center, administrative offices, and recreational facilities.

Ehattesaht Band: The band controls nine reserves on 136 hectares of land. The reserves were allotted in 1889. The 1995 population was 193, of whom 91 lived in 21 houses on the reserve. The band is governed by custom and is affiliated with the Nuu-chah-nulth Tribal Council. Economic activities and resources include fishing, logging, mining, tourism, and aquaculture. Facilities include a community center.

Hesquiaht Band: The band controls five reserves on 320 hectares of land on the west coast of central Vancouver Island. The reserves were allotted in 1886.

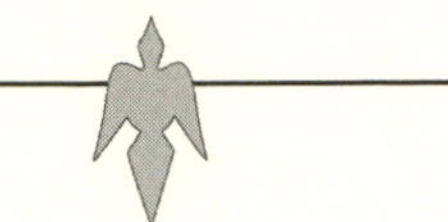

The 1995 population was 543, of whom 149 lived in 24 houses on the reserve. The band is governed by custom and is affiliated with the Nuu-chah-nulth Tribal Council. Economic activities include fishing. Facilities include a community hall, a privately owned store, and a sawmill.

Kyuguot Band: The band controls 20 reserves on 382 hectares of land on northwest Vancouver Island. The reserves were allotted in 1889. The 1995 population was 393, of whom 133 lived in 31 houses on the reserve. The band is governed by custom and is affiliated with the Nuu-chah-nulth Tribal Council. Economic activities include fishing and logging. Facilities include a community hall.

Mowachaht/Muchalaht Band, formerly the Nootka Band: The band controls 17 reserves on 263 hectares of land at the mouth of Nootka Sound. The 1995 population was 390, of whom 119 lived in 28 houses on the reserve. The band is governed by custom and is affiliated with the Nuu-chah-nulth Tribal Council, which administers its schools. Economic activities include forest products and a boat launch. Facilities include offices, a playground, and a tourist center.

Nuchatlaht Band: The band controls 11 reserves on 92 hectares of land on the northwest coast of Vancouver Island. The reserves were allotted in 1889. The 1995 population was 127, of whom 27 lived in eight houses on the reserve. The band is governed by custom and is affiliated with the Nuu-chah-nulth Tribal Council. Economic activities include forestry and fishing. Facilities include offices and a clinic.

Ohiaht Band: The band controls 13 reserves on 816 hectares of land on the southwest coast of Vancouver Island. The reserves were allotted in 1882. The 1995 population was 474, of whom 101 lived in 33 houses on the reserve. The band is governed by custom and is affiliated with the Nuu-chah-nulth Tribal Council. Children attend provincial schools. Economic resources include a campsite. Facilities include offices, a cemetery, and a recreation hall.

Opetchesaht Band: The band controls five reserves on 215 hectares of land near Port Alberni. The reserves were allotted in 1882. The 1995 population was 206, of whom 90 lived in 33 houses on the reserve. The band is governed under the provisions of the Indian Act and is affiliated with the Nuu-chah-nulth Tribal Council. Economic activities and resources include logging and a pulp mill. Facilities include offices, a cemetery, a community hall, and a cultural center.

Pacheenaht Band: The band controls four reserves on 174 hectares of land on the southwest coast of Vancouver Island. The reserves were allotted in 1882. The 1995 population was 214, of whom 82 lived in 24 houses on the reserve. The band is governed under the provisions of the Indian Act and, although unaffiliated, is part of the Nuu-chah-nulth people. Children attend provincial schools. Economic activities and resources include a campsite and a ferry service. Facilities include offices and a longhouse.

Tla-o-qui-aht First Nations (formerly called Clayoquot): The band controls ten reserves on 220 hectares of land near Pacific Rim National Park. The reserves were allotted in 1889. The 1995 population was 618, of whom 264 lived in 60 houses on the reserve. The band is governed under the provisions of the Indian Act and is affiliated with the Nuu-chah-nulth Tribal Council. Economic activities and resources include fishing and tourism. Facilities include offices, a store, an arts and crafts store, a community hall, a clinic, and a marina.

Toquaht Band: The band controls seven reserves on 196 hectares of land on the southwest coast of Vancouver Island. The reserves were allotted in 1882. The 1995 population was 115, of whom 12 lived in eight houses on the reserve. The band is governed by custom and is affiliated with the Nuu-chah-nulth Tribal Council. Economic activities and resources include fishing and building supplies. Facilities include offices.

Tsesaht Band: The band controls eight reserves on 584 hectares of land near Port Alberni. The reserves were allotted in 1882. The 1995 population was 735, of whom 406 lived in 115 houses on the reserve. The band is governed by custom and is affiliated with the Nuu-chah-nulth Tribal Council. Children attend provincial schools. Economic activities and resources include fishing and forestry. Facilities include a community hall, a recreation building, and a cultural center.

Uchucklesaht Band: The band controls two reserves on 232 hectares of land 30 kilometers west of Victoria. The reserves were allotted in 1882. The

1995 population was 135, of whom 25 lived in 13 houses on the reserve. The band is governed by custom and is affiliated with the Nuu-chah-nulth Tribal Council. Economic activities include a water freight service. Facilities include a clinic.

Ucluelet Band: The band controls nine reserves on 199 hectares of land 60 kilometers east of Port Alberni. The reserves were allotted in 1882. The 1995 population was 538, of whom 193 lived in 67 houses on the reserve. The band is governed under the provisions of the Indian Act and is affiliated with the Nuu-chah-nulth Tribal Council. Economic activities include fishing, fish processing, a minimall, a laundromat, and a video arcade. Facilities include a community center, a museum, a nursery school, and a marina.

Oowekeeno

See Bella Bella

Puyallup

See Salish, Southern Coast

Quileute

Quileute (`Kwil ē ūt) is taken from the name of a village at the site of La Push. The Hoh Indians, formerly considered a Quileute Band, now have independent federal recognition.

Location Traditionally, the Quileute lived along the coast from south of Ozette Lake to just south of the Hoh River and west to Mt. Olympus, on the Olympic Peninsula. Most of the region is rain forest. Today, many Quileute live on reservations on the Pacific coast of the Olympic Peninsula, in the state of Washington.

Population In the late eighteenth century, about 500 Quileutes lived on the Olympic Peninsula. Tribal enrollment in the early 1990s was about 875. In 1990, 302 Indians lived on the Quileute Reservation; another 74 on lived on the Hoh Reservation.

Language Quileute is a Chimakuan language.

Historical Information

History In late-prehistoric times, the Quileute were members, with the Hoh and the Quinault, of a confederation that controlled most tribes from Cape Flattery to Grey's Harbor. Quileutes either killed or enslaved the first non-natives they met (Spanish in 1775; British in 1787; Russian in 1808). They had little contact with whites until 1855, when the Indians signed a treaty agreeing to move to the Quinault Reservation. They had not yet moved, however, by 1889, the year the one-square-mile La Push Reservation was created. Four years later, a reservation was established for the people of the Hoh River.

In the interim (1860s–1880s), Quileutes tried as best they could to resist the invading non-natives. Most declined to send their children to an Anglo school that opened at La Push in 1882. Symptomatic of the interracial hostility that reigned during that time was the fire set by a white person at La Push in 1889 that destroyed 26 houses and almost all precontact artifacts.

In 1895, the Quileutes embraced the Indian Shaker religion. In 1912, whites appropriated ancient fishing sites to open a canning industry on the Quillayute River. Indians were declared ineligible to obtain fishing licenses. They gave up whaling in 1904 and sealing in the 1930s. In 1936, shortly after 165 Quileutes were each allotted 80 acres of timbered land on the Quinault Reservation, the tribe adopted a constitution and by-laws.

Religion The Quileute universe was peopled with a creator-transformer and a variety of ghosts, spirits, monsters, and creatures. This interplay gave rise to a rich mythology. Entrée to one of five ceremonial societies—warrior, hunter, whaler, shaman, and fisher—might be obtained by holding a potlatch or showing evidence of an appropriate guardian spirit power. Initiations, which included dances with carved wood masks, took place primarily in winter. Potlatches also accompanied life-cycle events.

Individuals could claim guardian spirits, from nature or ancestors, through special quests or by being adopted by the power. Such powers could also be lost or stolen, perhaps through the intercession of a shaman, or simply depart, in which case a shaman might bring them back (this was the lost soul cure—

shamans could also cure disease). Adolescents quested after spirit powers by fasting and visiting remote places. The Quileute also observed first salmon rites.

Government A village, made up of extended families, was the basic political unit. Each village had two hereditary chiefs.

Customs Quileute society was divided into the hereditary groups that were usual for Northwest Indians: chiefs, commoners, and slaves (acquired in raids or trade). Much social activity was devoted to maintaining and pursuing status. With rank came the rights to names, dances, songs, designs, guardian spirit powers, and membership in certain secret societies.

The traits of cleanliness, moderation, and generosity were especially prized. At puberty, girls were confined to a section of the house for five days. Boys began spirit questing in their late teens. Perhaps because pre- and extramarital sex were taboo, the Quileutes recognized ten different types of marriage, including polygamy. Quileutes intermarried regularly with Makahs and Quinaults. Divorce was common.

Both parents were subject to behavioral restrictions around pregnancy and childbirth. The birth of twins subjected parents to eight months of additional taboos. Babies were kept in cradle boards. Noble families flattened their babies' heads. The dead were wrapped in mats or dog-hair blankets and buried in canoes or hollow logs. Mourners cut their hair and painted their faces. Widows observed special taboos, such as not sleeping lying down. The name of the dead was not spoken for some time, and mourners asked those with similar names to change them. On the second anniversary of death, remains of high-status people were reburied, and a memorial potlatch was given.

Dwellings Winter camps of multifamily, permanent plank houses were located at stream mouths. Houses were roughly 60 feet by 40 feet and had single-pitch roofs, sleeping platforms, and fireplaces for each family. In summer, groups would divide into families and range in hereditary subsistence areas. During this time they lived in cattail-mat or brush lean-tos.

Diet Quileutes ate all five species of salmon. Other important fish included steelhead, halibut, smelt, trout, flounder, dogfish, skate, and octopus as well as shellfish. They gathered 16 types of fruits and berries, roots, sprouts, and seaweed as well as bearberry (kinnikinnick) for smoking. They also hunted marine mammals and land mammals, especially deer and elk, as well as small game and birds, with bow and arrow, snares, and deadfalls.

Key Technology Men and women fashioned most items from spruce roots, hemlock, cedar, willow bark, kelp, reeds, and grasses. Woman made watertight burden and storage twined baskets. They also wove rain hats, mats, skirts, and capes.

Men made bent-corner wooden boxes as well as wooden platters, dishes, bailers, fishhooks, rattles, and masks. When building red-cedar canoes, they used yew-wood wedges to split the trees and adzes to carve and hollow the logs. Hunting equipment included harpoons, lances, bow and arrow, and clubs. Other tools included stone hammers, mortars, and scrapers; mussel shell knives and harpoon points; and antler awls and scrapers.

Trade Trade was primarily with the Makah and the Quinault. The Quileute traded camas and sea mammal blubber for oysters, sockeye salmon, and eulachon grease. They traded Makah dentalia and blankets for Quinault salmon. They also obtained woven blankets of goat wool in trade.

Notable Arts The many Quileute arts and crafts included basketry, weaving, and wood carving.

Transportation Most transportation was by canoe.

Dress Women often wore shredded cedar-bark skirts and capes. Rain gear included spruce-root rain hats. Tattoos and ear and nose ornaments were popular. The nobility flattened their babies' heads.

War and Weapons The Quileute regularly fought their trade partners, the Makah and the Quinault, as well as other coastal peoples, especially over trespass or insult. They retreated to a fortress atop James Island when attacked.

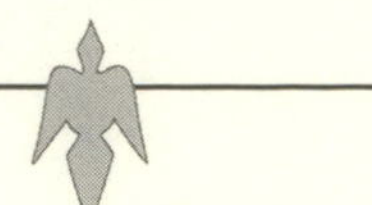

Contemporary Information

Government/Reservations The Quileute (La Push) Reservation (594 [originally 837] acres) was established in 1889. In 1936, the tribe adopted a constitution and by-laws. Members of an elected five-person tribal council serve three-year terms. The tribe has relatively wide legal powers on the reservation.

The Hoh Reservation (443 acres) was created in 1893. That tribe adopted a constitution in 1969. It is governed by a five-member tribal council on which members serve two-year terms.

Economy Important economic activities include a tribally owned fish-buying company, a fish hatchery, a cooperative store, a trailer park, and a fishing gear store. Tourism, including a restaurant and a resort, provides some jobs, as does the logging industry and the tribal government. Many people still fish.

Legal Status The Hoh Indian Tribe and the Quileute Indian Tribe are federally recognized tribal entities.

Daily Life Only a handful of Quileute speakers remain, but a Quileute dictionary and a nationally recognized instructional program are helping people to learn the language. People still practice some traditional crafts, including canoe making. Potlatches, and their accompanying focus on cultural identity and traditions, have become popular again since the 1980s, after having virtually disappeared during the 1960s.

Most Hohs are Protestants or Shakers; their children attend school in nearby Forks. La Push students either attend school in Forks or the tribal school (K-8).

Quileutes have been actively involved in the resurgence of the Northwest cedar canoe culture since the 1980s, which includes regular canoe trips to Seattle and a Heiltsuk festival at Bella Bella. Annual Quileute days are usually held on the first weekend in August. The *Quileute Indian News* is published regularly. Elders Week celebrations are held in May.

Quinault

See Salish, Southwestern Coast

Salish, Central Coast

Central Coast Salish (`Sal ish), a group of Indians that shared a common language family and a related culture. Central Coast Salish tribes and villages included Squamish (at least 16 villages), Nooksack (at least 20 villages), Klallam (about a dozen villages), Halkomelem, and Northern Straits. Halkomelem had three divisions: Island (Nanoose, Nanaimo, Chemainus, Cowichan, and Malahat), Downriver (Musqueam, Tsawwessen, Saleelwat, Kwantlen, Coquitlam, Nicomekl, and Katzie), and Upriver (Matsqui, Sumas, Nicomen, Scowlitz, Chehalis, Chilliwak, Pilalt, and Tait). Northern Straits had six divisions: Sooke, Songhees, Saanich, Semiahmoo, Lummi, Samish. The discussions that follow do not apply to every group or tribe.

Location Traditionally, the lands inhabited by the Central Coast Salish in Canada and the United States included both sides of the southern Strait of Georgia, the San Juan Islands, extreme northwest Washington east of the strait, and parts of the northern Olympic Peninsula. The region is generally wet and moderate, although it includes some drier and cooler regions.

Most contemporary Central Coast Salish Indians live on reserves or reservations in or around their aboriginal lands or in cities of the Northwest.

Population The Central Coast Salish population stood at roughly 20,000 in the mid–eighteenth century. In the 1990s it was around 16,000.

Language Central Coast Salish, which includes the Squamish, Nooksack, Klallam, Halkomelem, and Northern Straits (Lkungen) languages, is a member of the Central division of the Salishan language family.

Historical Information

History Some Central Coast Salish may have had contact with the Spanish explorer Juan de Fuca in 1592, or in 1787 an Anglo fur trader may have been the first non-Indian inside the Strait of Juan de Fuca. Regular Spanish explorations of Coast Salish territory began in the early 1790s. Smallpox epidemics also began about that time, if not earlier.

Land-based Anglo fur traders established themselves at the mouth of the Columbia River in

1811. The Hudson's Bay Company built a fort on the Fraser River in 1827. That post, Fort Langley, became the local center of interracial contact and trade. Indians supplied materials, labor, and goods, and Indian women married or otherwise became involved with Anglo traders. Fort Victoria, built in 1843, drew Indian trade from Puget Sound to as far north as Alaska.

The Treaty of Washington (1846) split Central Coast Salish country between the United States and Canada. The British subsequently created small reserves for every village (which they called bands). On the U.S. side, the Point Elliot and Point No Point Treaties in 1855 ceded Indian land and created a few regional reservations. However, most Indians remained in their own territories rather than remove to the designated reservations. Some groups were left landless by this process. Anglo settlers began trickling in during the 1850s. The trickle turned into a flood in 1858 when gold was discovered in the Fraser River.

Christian missionaries, present since 1841, became more active after 1858. During the following decades a number of bands became thoroughly Christianized. By the 1860s, many Central Coast Salish Indians were working in the new industries: logging, farming, shipping, and commercial fishing. They also found seasonal work picking berries and hops. Nooksacks were expected under the terms of the Point Elliot Treaty to move to the Lummi Reservation, but few did. They continued to function as a tribe, although the government no longer considered them one, and finally received federal recognition in 1973.

The Lummi Reservation was established in 1855. Gold seekers around this time inflicted great personal harm on the Lummi and other tribes. Still, despite pressure to adopt agriculture, many Lummis continued to practice a semitraditional lifestyle based on reef-netting. They lost key lands as a result of white encroachment in 1890s, although by the 1930s they had acquired and cultivated new land. They lost over one-third of their population during the 1950s as a result of the official government policy of relocating reservation Indians to urban areas. In the 1970s they received a land claims settlement for the loss of their reef netting locations, which they have refused to accept because they consider it far too low.

According to the terms of the Point No Point Treaty (1855), Klallams were to remove to the Skokomish Reservation. However, most remained in their traditional villages. In 1874, some Klallam Indians purchased land and called their settlement Jamestown. When the United States purchased about 1,600 acres for the Klallam in 1936, they were separated into the Lower Elwha Tribal Community and the Port Gamble Indian Community (the former sawmill settlement of Little Boston). Some Klallams also went to the Puyallup Reservation.

According to the Point Elliot Treaty (1855), the Samishes were supposed to move onto various local reservations, but few did. Many moved in the 1870s to Guemes Island, built a longhouse (almost 500 feet long) and continued their traditional customs as best they could. By 1912, however, whites had forced them off this land. Some people occupied traditional villages while other simply scattered. Many received allotments on the Swinomish Reservation. They adopted a constitution and by-laws (subsequently revised) in 1926 and were awarded a land claims settlement in 1971, which they refused.

By the turn of the century, Indian material culture had been significantly changed, but some groups retained traditional activities, such as the potlatch. For these Indians, the early twentieth century was marked by economic decline, increased cultural suppression in boarding schools, the spread of the Shaker religion, and the revival of spirit dancing. Meanwhile, the Northwestern Federation of American Indians (formed in Tacoma in 1914) pushed for fulfillment of treaty rights. In *U.S.* v. *Washington* (1974), the U.S. Supreme Court ruled that half of the harvestable salmon and steelhead in Washington waters were reserved for federally recognized, land-based treaty tribes.

Religion Central Coast Salish recognized a mythological time when their legendary ancestors lived. They believed that people are composed of several components, one or more of which might occasionally get lost or lured away and would have to be restored by shamans. In their everyday lives, they made a distinction between what was considered normal and anything that might connote danger or power (such as a deformed person, a menstruating

woman, or a corpse). People sought luck or skills from an encounter with a spirit. An accompanying song provided direct access to the spirit's power.

Shamans' spirit helpers gave special powers. Men and women could be shamans. Curing, the province of shamans, entailed singing, drama, and extracting a harmful entity with the hands and mouth. Some shamans could also foretell the future. Spells or incantations were also believed to carry power. Most people used them to help perform a task, but people highly skilled in such matters could be hired for special occasions.

Intra- and intervillage spirit dances took place in winter. The host provided food, and dancers danced their spirit songs, of which there were several categories. Dances and songs were accompanied by much ritual paraphernalia. Secret societies also held their dances in winter. Their main ceremony was initiating new members; the right to membership was hereditary. Central Coast Salish people also observed first salmon ceremonies (the ritual preparation and consumption of the season's first catch). Cleansing rituals were made both to erase a disgrace and to enhance a festive occasion.

Children at Port Gamble Indian School, a missionary school, in 1910.

Government Each group lived in a number of villages. Heads of the leading or established household served as local group chiefs. As such, they had little or no power to govern; they were wealthy and influential men who entertained guests, made decisions about subsistence activity, and arbitrated disputes.

Customs Several extended families made up a household, which owned particular subsistence areas and tools, such as clam beds and fowl nets. Some particularly prestigious households, or "houses" (in the European sense), descended from a notable ancestor and shared resources, names, ceremonies, and other valuables. Some local groups may have had their own winter villages, although larger villages included several local groups. Members of different households cooperated in some activities such as deer drives, building a salmon weir, ceremonies, and defense, but they were not necessarily culturally homogeneous. There was little intervillage cooperation. Social groups included worthy people (those with wealth, ancestry, manners, and guardian spirits), worthless people, and slaves.

The Central Coast Salish intermarried from within and without. Marriages involved ritual exchanges and promoted trade. They were initiated by men; women could refuse, but they felt pressure to marry "well." A wedding usually entailed the exchange of gifts (material and/or hereditary privileges) and a cleansing ceremony. Exchanges of food and gifts between families-in-law continued throughout the marriage.

From an early age, children were "toughened" by swimming in icy water and running in storms. This process culminated in the adolescent spirit quest. Boys marked puberty by making their first kill. If possible, girls were feted with a feast and a display of hereditary privileges. They were secluded during their periods. Among the Cowichan, a girl undertook a solitary vigil; if she was joined by a boy, and their parents

agreed, they could be married. Corpses were wrapped in blankets and placed in canoes or grave boxes. Among the worthy, bones were rewrapped several years later with an accompanying display of privileges.

Potlatches, as opposed to feasts, were usually held outdoors in good weather. Occasions included life crises and important life-cycle or ceremonial events. Usually all or part of a village held the potlatch, with each house marking its own occasions. Goods were not expected to be returned: The point was status—that is, good relations with neighbors and good marriages for children.

Some hunters, both land and sea, achieved a professional status and spent whole summers hunting. People generally spent the summers traveling in small groups, following seasonal food cycles and living in temporary dwellings. They enjoyed several gambling games, including the hand and disk games. Sports included shinny, races, athletic competitions, and games of skill. Singing for pleasure was common.

Dwellings Winter villages consisted of from one house to several rows of houses built on the beach. Houses were up to several hundred feet long. They had a permanent wooden framework with a shed roof and removable roof and wall planks. Each family had a separate fire. House posts were decorated with painted and carved images of ancestors and spirit powers. These people also built some fortified war refuges (stockades). Other structures included summer mat houses, wooden grave houses, and pole and mat sweat lodges.

Diet Fish, especially salmon (all five species), were the staple food, although they were available to different people in different places at different times of the year. The leaner, fall runs were dried for storage; otherwise they were eaten fresh. Other important foods included sea mammals (seal and porpoise, used mostly for oil; sea lions; whales [Klallam]); shellfish; land mammals such as deer, elk, black bear, mountain goats, and beaver (smaller game as well as grizzlies, cougars, and wolves were generally avoided); waterfowl; and a large variety of plants. Camus, brake fern, wapato, and wild carrots were especially important, but other bulbs, roots, berries, sprouts, and stems were also used. Camus fields were burned and reseeded. Potato husbandry became important after 1800.

Key Technology Fish were taken with reef nets, dip nets, trawl nets, harpoons, gaff hooks, spears, basket traps, weirs, tidal pounds (rows of underwater stakes), hooks, and herring rakes and in rectangular nets suspended between two canoes, a method by which several thousand fish a day might be captured. Harpoons, seal nets, and clubs served as marine mammal hunting equipment; land mammals were taken with pitfalls, snares, bow (2.5 to 3 feet, made of yew) and arrow, and spears. Waterfowl were snagged in permanent nets stretched across flyways. They were also hunted with bow and arrow, flares and nets at night, and snares.

Important raw materials included wood, hides, antler, horn, mountain goat wool, beaver teeth, wood stone, and shell. Wooden items included house materials, canoes, bent-corner boxes, dishes, tools, weapons, and ceremonial items. Shredded bark was used for towels, mattresses, and similar items. Sewn mats of cattail leaves and tule lined interior house walls, covered frames of summer shelters, and were made into mattresses, rain covers, and sitting or kneeling pads. Women made several types of baskets, including wrapped lattice, coiled, twined, and woven. They practiced a distinctive form of weaving, spinning wool from a special breed of dog (now extinct) plus mountain goat wool, waterfowl down, and fireweed cotton on a large spindle and weaving it on a two-bar loom.

Trade All groups engaged in local and regional trade and intermarriage. The Klallam, in particular, were great traders as well as warriors. Salish people imported Chilkat blankets, among other items.

Notable Arts Wooden items such as house posts, canoes, grave monuments, and household and ritual items were artistically carved and/or painted. Designs featured humans, animals, and/or vision powers. Lummi and other women wove cedar-bark baskets and mountain goat and dog wool blankets.

Transportation Most travel was by canoe. There were five distinct types, depending on the activity, not including those obtained in trade.

Dress Men often went naked or wore buckskin shorts or robes (skin or shredded bark). Women wore short aprons or skirts and robes. Some men and women wore conical basketry hats, and some men wore fur caps. In cold weather, both sexes wore down-and-nettle shirts, robes, and perhaps ponchos. There were also fine blankets made of mountain goat and coyote wool as well as plant fibers. Hunters wore hide outfits and moccasins or snowshoes. Ponchos of woven cedar bark or cattail leaves served as rain gear.

Free people had flattened heads. Personal adornments included pierced ears and often pierced noses, tattoos, and body paint (which was also applied against insects). Headgear included women's Plateau-style basketry hats and mushroom-shaped, brimmed spruce-root hats worn by both sexes. Both men and women wore their hair long.

War and Weapons The Central Coast Salish fought wars among themselves, with their neighbors, and with more distant neighbors. Injury and death, intentional or not, demanded compensation. Refusal to pay might lead to fighting, and some groups, such as the Klallam, saw compensation as dishonorable. The Klallam were particularly aggressive; the impaled heads of their foes, often Snohomish, Cowichan, or Duwamish, often decorated their beaches. There was some naval warfare, in which canoes rammed and sank other canoes. At least in the early nineteenth century, the Lekwiltok (Kwakiutl) were a common enemy.

Raids, for loot, territory, vengeance, or a show of power, were led by professional warriors with special powers. Raids featured surprise attacks. Men were killed, and women and children were captured, later to be ransomed or sold as slaves. Warriors wore elk hide armor.

Contemporary Information

Government/Reservations In 1984, 235 reserves (approximately 62,000 acres) were connected with 52 Central Coast Salish bands (approximately 13,000 people) in British Columbia. See "Daily Life" for summary descriptions of selected bands in Canada.

The Nooksack Reservation (12 acres) was created in 1973. Most Nooksacks live in and near Deming, Nooksack, and Everson, Washington. They are governed by a tribal council. A further 60 acres of reservation land is expected. The 1991 tribal population was 1,168.

The Jamestown S'klallam Reservation (1980; 12 acres; population 240) is located at the upper Strait of Juan de Fuca. The Klallam are governed by an elected tribal council. Also, with the Port Gamble, the Lower Elwha Klallams, and the Skokomishes (Twana), the Jamestown S'klallam make up the Point No Point Treaty Council, an administrative body.

The Elwha S'klallam Reservation (1968; 427 acres; 530 population) is located in Clallam County, Washington. The Lower Elwha Tribal Community began in 1936. They adopted a constitution and by-laws in 1968. The Lower Elwha Community Tribal Council is composed of all qualified voters. Members of a business committee are elected to two-year terms.

The Port Gamble Reservation (1936; 1,303 acres; 860 population) is located on the Kitsap Peninsula in Washington. The Port Gamble Indian Community adopted a constitution in 1939. A business committee appoints various standing committees. Many Klallams also live on the Skokomish Reservation.

The Lummi Reservation (1849; 7,073 acres allotted, 12 acres tribally owned) is west of Bellingham, Washington. The Lummi adopted a new constitution in 1970. The 11 members of an elected business council serve three-year terms. The tribal council elects officers and establishes committees. The Lummi are the dominant group on this mixed-group reservation. The enrolled membership in 1992 was 3,200, about half of whom lived on the reservation.

Economy The Lummi run fish hatcheries and an aquaculture program. They also have a salmon-rearing facility, a huge fishing fleet, a restaurant-boating complex, and a fish-processing plant. Nevertheless, the unemployment rate there in the early 1990s approached 70 percent. There are several community-owned businesses, including a gas station, store, and mobile home park, and crafts enterprises on the Port Gamble Reservation. Klallams and Nooksacks are also active in the commercial fishing industry. Other important economic activity includes subsistence gardening, fishing, logging, and seasonal farm work.

Legal Status The Nooksack Indian Tribe has been federally recognized since 1973. The Jamestown Klallam Tribe is a federally recognized tribal entity. The Lower Elwha Tribal Community of the Lower Elwha Reservation (Klallam) is a federally recognized tribal entity. The Port Gamble Indian Community of the Port Gamble Reservation (Klallam) is a federally recognized tribal entity. The Lummi Tribe is a federally recognized tribal entity. The Samish Indian Tribe is seeking federal recognition.

Daily Life Central Coast Salish Indians in both the United States and Canada are still linked socially through festivals, canoe racing, games, winter dancing, and the Indian Shaker Church. The Nooksack have a tribal center complex at Deming. They work closely with federal and state entities to manage local natural resource areas and are engaged in redressing housing and health care shortages. Cultural preservation is carried out mainly by means of identifying and preserving cultural sites. Although these people are largely assimilated, they maintain strong family connections to a greater Indian identity. Funerals, in particular, are important occasions on which to express that identity, as are longhouse ceremonials and local pantribal celebrations.

Most Klallams are Protestant. Their children attend public schools. There are several tribal community programs at Lower Elwha and Port Gamble, including a substance abuse program, health clinic, housing department, hatchery-fisheries department, and a higher adult–vocational education department. The Port Gamble Reservation enforces most of its own laws. The Jamestown Klallam have an annual gathering, "S'klallam Qwen Seyu."

Many of the roughly 600 Samish live on the Tulalip, Lummi, or Swinomish Reservations as well as near the tribal headquarters in Anacortes, Washington. They operate a gift shop as well as an archaeological consulting service and participate in spirit dancing and other local Indian activities.

The Lummi Reservation features childrens' programs as well as a K-8 school and Northwest Indian College. Some Lummi children attend Catholic school. The local Indian Health Service provides medical and dental care. The annual Lummi Stommish water carnival in June features canoe racing. Few speak the tribal language, but some traditional ceremonies and festivals are still held. Some tribes began a revival of blanket weaving in the 1980s. Many Lummis are Christian, although traditional spirit dancing and the Indian Shaker Church are also important.

Selected Central Coast Salish bands in British Columbia (statistics as of 1995):

Chehalis Band controls two reserves on 907 hectares of land 10 miles west of Agassiz. The population is 775, of whom 400 people live on the reserves. The band is governed under the provisions of the Indian Act and is currently unaffiliated. Children attend band and provincial schools. Important economic resources and activities include small businesses, forestry, and fishing. Facilities include two recreation buildings, a cultural center, a longhouse, and offices.

Chemainus Band controls four reserves on 1,225 hectares of land about 30 kilometers south of Nanaimo. The reserves were allotted in 1877. The population is 882, of whom 690 people live on the reserves. The band is governed under the provisions of the Indian Act and is affiliated with the Mid-Island Tribal Council. Children attend band and provincial schools. Important economic resources and activities include a construction company, a campsite, and a general store. Facilities include an administration building and a clinic.

Coquitlam (Kwayhquitlim) Band, formerly part of the Chilliwack Tribe, controls two reserves on 89 hectares of land. The population is 81, of whom seven people live in five houses on the reserves. The band is governed by custom and is currently unaffiliated. Important economic resources and activities include a proposed residential and golf course development.

Cowichan Band controls nine reserves on 2,493 hectares of land near the city of Duncan. The population is 2,972, of whom 1,922 people live on the reserves. The band is governed under the provisions of the Indian Act and is currently unaffiliated. Children attend band and provincial schools. Important economic resources and activities include a construction company, a fish hatchery, land leasing, wood carving, and several small businesses. Facilities include nine recreation buildings, two cultural centers, a community hall, and offices.

Cowichan Lake Band controls one reserve on 39 hectares of land on the north shore of Cowichan Lake. The population is 12, of whom 10 live on the reserve. Elections are by custom. The band is affiliated with the First Nations South Island Tribal Council (FNSITC).

Malahat Band, formerly part of the Saanich Tribe, controls one reserve on 237 hectares of land 40 kilometers north of Victoria. The reserve was allotted in 1877. The population is 220, of whom 81 live in 13 houses on the reserve. Elections are held under the provisions of the Indian Act. The band is affiliated with the FNSITC. Children attend provincial schools. Facilities include a longhouse and a recreation building.

Musqueam Band controls three reserves on 254 hectares of land near the Point Grey area of Vancouver. The population is 925, of whom 454 live in 110 houses on the reserves. Elections are held under the provisions of the Indian Act. Children attend band and provincial schools. Important economic resources include a shipyard and a hotel. Facilities include a community and recreation hall, offices, a longhouse, and a church.

Nanaimo Band controls six reserves on 26 hectares of land near the city of Nanaimo. The reserves were allotted in 1876. The population is 1,089, of whom 409 live in 122 houses on the reserves. Elections are held under the provisions of the Indian Act. The band is affiliated with the Alliance Tribal Council. Children attend band and provincial schools. Important economic activities include forest industries. Facilities include a recreation center, a cultural center, a store, and offices.

Katzie Band controls five reserves on 340 hectares of land west of Port Hammond. The population is 396, of whom 201 people live in 75 houses on the reserves. Elections are held according to custom. The band is affiliated with the Alliance Tribal Council. The economy is based on commercial fishing and land leases. Facilities include offices.

Pauquachin Band, formerly part of the Saanich Tribe, controls two reserves on 319 hectares of land in the southwest part of Vancouver Island. The reserves were allotted in 1877. The population is 265, of whom 177 live in 56 houses on the reserves. Elections are held under the provisions of the Indian Act. The band is affiliated with the FNSITC. Schools are administered by the Saanich Indian School Board. Important economic activities include a recreational vehicle park. Facilities include a recreation center, offices, and a longhouse.

Pehelakut Band controls four reserves on 635 hectares of land near Chemainus, British Columbia. The reserves were allotted in 1877. The population is 657, of whom 421 live in 101 houses on the reserves. Elections are held under the provisions of the Indian Act. The band is affiliated with the Mid-Island Tribal Council. Children attend band and provincial schools. Important economic activities include a general store. Facilities include a community hall, offices, and a longhouse.

Semiahmoo Band controls one reserve on 129 hectares of land southeast of White Rock. The population is 60, of whom 26 live in seven houses on the reserve. Elections are held under the provisions of the Indian Act. The band is unaffiliated. Children attend provincial schools. Economic activities include a campsite. Facilities include a church.

Skwah Band controls four reserves on 342 hectares of land near Chilliwack, British Columbia. The reserves were established in 1879. The population is 354, of whom 171 live in 58 houses on the reserves. Elections are held under the provisions of the Indian Act. The band is unaffiliated. Children attend band and provincial schools. Important economic activities include local agriculture and businesses in Chilliwack. Facilities include a community hall, offices, and a recreation room.

Songhees Band controls three reserves on 126 hectares of land near Esquimault Harbor. The reserves were allotted in 1878. The population is 330, of whom 206 live in 60 houses on the reserves. Elections are held under the provisions of the Indian Act. The band is unaffiliated. Children attend band and provincial schools. Important economic activities include a boat ramp, a mobile home park, and a store. Facilities include a community hall, offices, and a sports field.

Sooke Band controls two reserves on 67 hectares of land on the south end of Vancouver Island. The reserves were allotted in 1877. The population is 160, of whom 78 live on the reserves. Elections are held under the provisions of the Indian Act. The band is affiliated with the FNSITC. Children attend provincial schools. Important economic activities include forestry and off-reservation businesses. Facilities include a community hall, offices, a cultural center, and a park.

Squamish Band controls eight villages from the north shore of Burrand Inlet to the head of Howe Sound. The population is 2,554, of whom 1,627 live in 350 houses. Elections are held by custom. The band is affiliated with the Alliance Tribal Council. Children attend band and provincial schools. Important economic activities include land developed and leased by the band and several small businesses. Facilities include a community hall, a cultural center, a library, an arts and crafts building, a group home, a seniors' home, a longhouse, and offices.

Tsartlip Band, formerly part of the Saanich Tribe, controls three reserves on 324 hectares of land 25 kilometers north of Victoria. The reserves were allotted in 1877. The population is 695, of whom 419 live in 98 houses on the reserves. Elections are held under the provisions of the Indian Act. The band is affiliated with the FNSITC. Schools are administered by the Saanish Indian School Board. Important economic activities include a boat ramp, a campsite, and a store. Facilities include a cultural center and offices.

Tsawout Band, formerly part of the Saanich Tribe, controls two reserves on 258 hectares of land about 30 kilometers north of Victoria. The reserves were allotted in 1877. The population is 567, of whom 402 live in 80 houses on the reserves. Elections are held under the provisions of the Indian Act. The band is affiliated with the FNSITC. Important economic activities include small businesses, hotels, and trailer parks. Facilities include a cultural center, longhouse, community hall, and offices.

Tsawwassen Band controls one reserve on 750 acres of land. The population is 173, of whom 109 live in 55 houses on the reserve. Elections are held under the provisions of the Indian Act. The band is affiliated with the Alliance Tribal Council. Children attend band and provincial schools. Important economic activities include a recreational park and a proposed hotel/marina complex. Facilities include a recreation center, a church, and offices.

Tseycum Band, formerly part of the Saanich Tribe, controls one reserve on 28 hectares of land on Saanich Inlet. The reserves were allotted in 1877. The population is 124, of whom 75 live in 22 houses on the reserves. Elections are held under the provisions of the Indian Act. The band is affiliated with the FNSITC. Important economic activities are mostly off-reserve. Facilities include a cemetery, a sports field, and offices.

Salish, Northern Coast

The constituent groups of the Northern Coast Salish (`Sal ish) included Island Comox, Mainland Comox (Homalco, Klahoose, and Sliammon), Pentlatch, and Sechelt. The Comox called themselves *Catlo'ltx.*

Location Traditional Northern Coast Salish territory, all in Canada, included roughly the northern half of the Strait of Georgia, including east-central Vancouver Island. The climate is wet and moderate. In the 1990s, Northern Coast Salish Indians live in villages and reserves in their traditional territory and in regional cities and towns.

Population The Comox population in 1780 was about 1,800. In 1995, about 2,750 Northern Coast Salish from six bands (Comox, Homalco, Klahoose, Sliammon, Qualicum [Pentlatch], and Sechelt) lived in the region.

Language Northern Coast Salish, which includes the Comox, Pentlatch, and Sechelt languages, is a member of the Central division of the Salishan language family.

Historical Information

History Juan de Fuca may have encountered the Northern Coast Salish in 1752. British and Spanish trade ships arrived in 1792 to a friendly reception. Owing to the lack of sea otter in the Strait of Georgia, however, most Northern Coast Salish did not participate in the local maritime fur trade.

Miners and other non-natives founded Victoria in 1843. By this time local Indians had experienced severe epidemics with some concomitant village abandonment and consolidation. Catholic

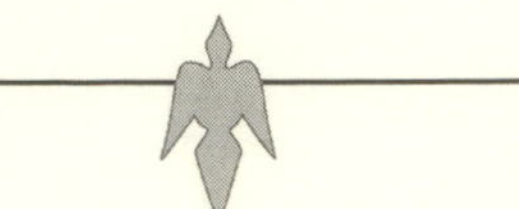

missionaries arrived in the 1860s, and many natives converted and renounced their ceremonials, including potlatching. Some self-sufficient overtly Christian villages were established, complete with a missionary-imposed governing structure. By the end of the century, the missionaries, along with Catholic boarding schools, had largely destroyed the native language and culture.

With their traditional economy severely damaged, many Indian men took jobs as longshoremen, loggers, and migrant farmers. They also worked in commercial fishing, including canneries. Canada officially established Indian reserves in 1876, by which time Indians had already lost much of their aboriginal land. In the early twentieth century, several Indian organizations, such as the Allied Tribes and the Native Brotherhood of British Columbia, formed to pursue title to aboriginal lands. The Alliance of Tribal Councils continued this work in the 1970s and worked to foster a positive self-image as well as political unity. Partly as a result of its activity, in 1986 the Sechelt Band became the first self-governing Indian group in Canada.

Religion People sought guardian spirits (from animate or inanimate objects) to confer special powers or skills. Spirits were acquired in dreams or by fasting or other physical tests. The Northern Coast Salish Indians celebrated two forms of winter ceremonials: spirit dancing, which was inclusive and participatory, and masked dancing, which was reserved for only certain high-status families. Shamans as well as various secret societies provided religious leadership.

Government Villages were headed by chiefs, who were the heads of the leading or established households. Chiefs had little or no power to govern; they were wealthy and influential men who entertained guests, made decisions about subsistence activity, and arbitrated disputes.

Customs Among most groups, the "local group" consisted of members who traced their descent patrilineally from a mythical ancestor; it was identified with and controlled certain specific subsistence areas. The right to hold potlatches and certain ceremonies, including dances and songs, was also inheritable. Northern Coast Salish people were either chiefs, nobles, commoners, or slaves.

Both parents, but especially the mother, were subject to pregnancy and childbirth taboos and restrictions. Infants' heads were pressed for aesthetic effect. Pubescent girls were secluded and their behavior was restricted, but boys were physically and mentally trained to seek a guardian spirit. Those who embarked on extended training and quests became shamans.

People were considered marriageable when they reached adolescence. Men, accompanied by male relatives, first approached women in a canoe. Polygyny was common, and multiple wives resided in the same household. Corpses were washed, wrapped in a blanket, and placed in a coffin that was in turn set in a cave or a tree away from the village. Possessions were burned. The Comox and Pentlatch erected carved and painted mortuary poles.

Dwellings Northern Coast Salish people built three types of permanent plank houses (semiexcavated and with shed and gabled roofs). Planks could be removed and transported to permanent frameworks at summer villages. Some houses were up to 60 or 70 feet long and half as wide. Most were fortified with either stockades or deep trenches. The Pentlatch and Island Comox had enclosed sleeping areas and separate smoke-drying sheds. Structures housed several related households, including extended families and slaves.

Diet Fish was the staple, especially salmon. Fall salmon were smoke dried for winter storage; the catch from summer salmon runs was eaten fresh. The people practiced ritual preparation and consumption of the season's first salmon. They also ate lingcod, greenling, steelhead, flounder, sole, and herring roe.

Other important foods included sea mammals (sea lion, harbor seal, porpoise); shellfish; land mammals, such as deer, bear, and some elk and mountain goat; birds and fowl; and plant foods, including berries, shoots and leaves, roots, bulbs, and cambium.

Key Technology Fish were taken with gill nets, basket traps and weirs, gaffs and harpoons, tidal basins of stakes or rocks, dip nets, and rakes (herring).

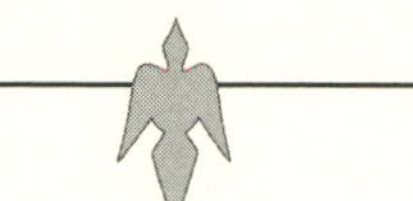

Seal nets, clubs, and harpoons with an identifiable float served as marine mammal hunting equipment. Land mammals were taken with pitfalls, snares, bow (2.5 to 3 feet long, made of yew) and arrow, nets, knives, traps, and spears. Waterfowl were snagged in permanent nets stretched across flyways. They were also hunted with bow and arrow, flares and nets at night, and snares.

Important raw materials included wood, hides, antler, horn, mountain goat wool, beaver teeth, wood, bone, stone, and shell. Wooden items included house materials, canoes, bent-corner boxes, dishes, tools, weapons, and ceremonial items. Shredded bark was used for towels, mattresses, and similar items. Sewn mats of cattail leaves and tule lined interior house walls, covered frames of summer shelters, and were made into mattresses, rain covers, and sitting or kneeling pads. Women made several types of baskets of cedar limb splints or roots, including wrapped lattice, coiled, twined, and woven.

Trade Goods such as fish oil, dentalia, baskets, berries, furs, and deer hides were traded among local groups as well as with neighboring Coast Salish peoples.

Notable Arts Wooden items such as house posts, canoes, grave monuments, and household and ritual items were artistically carved and/or painted. Designs featured humans, animals, and/or vision powers.

Transportation Several different types of red cedar canoes, from narrow trolling canoes to 20-person war canoes, served as water transportation.

Dress Men often went naked in warmer weather and added a woven down and nettle-fiber shirt in winter. Women wore long skirts made of cedar-bark strips and sometimes added a shirt similar to that of the men. Extra clothing, often made of skins, was worn on trips into the interior. The people also made blankets of mountain goat and coyote wool as well as fibers of various plants.

War and Weapons Regular enemies included the Lekwiltok (Kwakiutl) and Nootkans. Wars consisted of armadas of warriors armed with bow and arrow and spears. Warriors wore a long protective robe at least two heavy skins thick.

Contemporary Information

Government/Reservations In 1984, 234 reserves (approximately 25,000 hectares) were connected with 52 Canadian Coast Salish groups. Most Mainland Comox people lived on the Sliammon Indian Reserve. The Sechelt Indian Band Self-governing Act (1986) provided them with municipal constitutional and legislative powers. See profiles of selected bands under "Daily Life."

Economy The people currently engage in various activities. See profiles of selected bands under "Daily Life" for details.

Legal Status Bands listed under "Daily Life" are all federally and provincially recognized.

Daily Life Mainland Comox is still viable and spoken by about one-third of the population. See the following profiles of selected bands for further detail.

Selected Northern Coast Salish Bands in British Columbia (statistics are as of 1995):

Comox Band controls four reserves on 285 hectares of land on the east coast of Vancouver Island. The reserves were allotted in 1877. The population is 243, of whom 103 people live on the reserves. Elections are held under the provisions of the Indian Act. The band is affiliated with the Kwakiutl District Council. Children attend provincial schools. Important economic activities and resources include fishing, logging, and tourism. Facilities include a recreation building, a longhouse, and offices.

Homalco Band controls 11 reserves on 624 hectares of land near Calm Channel. The population is 346, of whom 130 people live on the reserves. Elections are held by custom. The band is affiliated with the Alliance Tribal Council. Children attend provincial schools. Important economic resources include a fish hatchery. Facilities include a recreation building and offices.

Klahoose Band controls ten reserves on 1,357 hectares of land on Cortes Island. The population is 242, of whom 45 people live in 16 houses on the reserves. Elections are held under the provisions of the

Indian Act. The band is affiliated with the Alliance Tribal Council. Children attend provincial schools. Important economic activities include forestry and shell fishing. Facilities include a community center, a church, and offices.

Qualicum Band controls one 77-hectare reserve on the southeast coast of Vancouver Island. The reserve was allotted in 1876. The population is 91, of whom 50 people live in 16 houses on the reserves. Elections are held under the provisions of the Indian Act. The band is unaffiliated. Children attend provincial schools. Important economic resources include a fish hatchery and a campsite/store. Facilities include a sports field and offices.

Sechelt Band controls 33 reserves on more than 1,000 hectares of land 50 kilometers north of Vancouver. The population is 910, of whom 477 people live on the reserves. Elections are held under the provisions of their own constitution. The band is unaffiliated. Economic plans include a marina/hotel complex, a condominium complex, small businesses, and a fish hatchery. Facilities include a preschool.

Sliammon Band controls six reserves on 1,907 hectares of land near Powell River. The population is 775, of whom 569 people live in 165 houses on the reserves. Elections are held under the provisions of the Indian Act. The band is affiliated with the Alliance Tribal Council. Children attend band and provincial schools. Important economic activities and resources include a salmon hatchery, seafood products, forestry, land leases, and small businesses. Facilities include a gymnasium, a movie house, a clinic, group homes, a church, and offices.

Salish, Southern Coast

Southern Coast Salish (`Sal ish) refers to over 50 named, autonomous Indian groups or tribes inhabiting the Puget Sound region and speaking one of two languages. The component groups included (but were not limited to) Swinomish, Skagit (Lower Skagit or Whidby Island Skagits), Upper Skagit, Stillaguamish, Skykomish (perhaps once a subdivision of the Snoqualmie), and Snohomish (speakers of Northern Lushootseed); Steilacoom, Snoqualmie, Suquamish, Duwamish, Puyallup, Nisqually, and Squaxin (speakers of Southern Lushootseed); and Quilcene, Skokomish, and Duhlelip (speakers of Twana). Many of these groups themselves consisted of autonomous subdivisions. Little is known of these Indians' lives before their contact with non-natives.

Location Southern Coast Salish people lived in and around the Puget Sound Basin in Washington. The climate is generally wet and moderate, with the northern areas somewhat drier. Although most of the land was timbered, some was kept open by regular burning practices. Most contemporary Southern Coast Salish Indians live on local reservations or in nearby cities and towns.

Population The precontact population was estimated to be around 12,600. In 1990 there were probably over 20,000 self-identified Southern Coast Salish Indians. See individual entries under "Government/Reservations" under "Contempory Information" for 1990 reservation populations.

Language Southern Coast Salish, which includes the Lushootseed (Northern and Southern dialects) and Twana languages, is a member of the Central division of the Salishan language family.

Historical Information

History The basic Southern Coast Salish culture was in place at least 2,000 years ago. George Vancouver visited the region in 1792. By that time, evidence of metal and smallpox suggested that the Southern Coast Salish might already have encountered Europeans indirectly. Owing primarily to the lack of sea otters in their region, the Salish experienced little further contact for the next 30 years or so.

At least after 1827 and the establishment of the Hudson's Bay Company post on the Fraser River, the Southern Coast Salish were in regular contact with non-native traders. Fort Nisqually was founded in 1833. Among the cultural changes the Indians experienced were the introduction of firearms, the move away from traditional forms of dress, and the beginning of the potato crop. They also experienced new native ideas from remote places, such as the Plateau Prophet Dance.

Catholic missionaries arrived around 1840. The first U.S. settlers followed shortly thereafter, especially after the United States took control of the region by the Treaty of Washington (1846). In 1850, the Donation Land Act of Oregon allowed settlers to invade and claim Indian land. Washington Territory was officially established in 1853.

In 1854 and 1855, Southern Coast Salish Indians signed a number of treaties (Medicine Creek, Point Elliot, and Point No Point) ceding land and creating seven future reservations (Squaxin, Nisqually, Puyallup, Port Madison, Tulalip, Swinomish, and Skokomish). Notable chiefs who signed included Sealth (Suquamish/Duwamish, after whom the city of Seattle was named), Goliah (Skagit), and Patkanin (Snoqualmie). The Nisqually chief Leschi opposed the Medicine Creek Treaty, arguing that his people should settle near the mouth of the Nisqually River and other traditional subsistence areas. He was hanged by the Americans in 1858.

The Steilacooms were denied a reservation because of the planned development of the town of Steilacoom. Most joined other local reservations or remained in their homeland, becoming the ancestors of the modern tribe. Upper Skagits were left landless by the Point Elliot treaty; they later received and then lost several individual allotments.

In 1857, an executive order established the Muckleshoot Reservation (the Muckleshoots were an amalgam of several inland tribes and groups). During subsequent years these lands were whittled away by the Dawes Act and other legal and extralegal coercions (such as the unofficial toleration of illegal whiskey peddlers). Indians rebelled against unfair and dishonest treaty negotiations by engaging in the 1855–1856 Indian war and by refusing to move onto reservations.

However, by the 1850s, most Southern Coast Salish were heavily involved in the non-native economy; most sold their labor, furs, and other resources to non-Indians. Important and growing industries included logging, commercial fishing and canning, and hopyards. Seattle was founded in and grew out of a Duwamish winter village (in 1962, the government paid the members of the Duwamish tribe $1.35 an acre for land that had become the city of Seattle). The Duwamishes moved around the region, refusing to settle on reservations, until some joined the Muckleshoot and Tulalip Reservations. Whites burned them out of their homes in West Seattle in 1893. In 1925, though landless, they adopted a constitution and formed a government. Furthermore, most tribes came under the control of the rigidly assimilationist Bureau of Indian Affairs.

In 1917, the government commandeered most of the 4,700-acre Nisqually Reservation for Camp (later Fort) Lewis. Displaced Nisquallis scattered to various reservations and lands. During the 1960s, clashes between Indians and non-natives over fishing rights sometimes became violent; they were settled in the Indians' favor, however, in the 1970s. Contrary to government desires, they did not farm but maintained their hunting and fishing traditions.

The Puyallups did turn to agriculture during the 1870s. For that reason, they were seen by whites as having made great progress toward civilization. The growth of the adjacent city of Tacoma fueled pressure for the sale of unallotted lands; most of the reservation had been lost by the early twentieth century. The Puyallup were at the forefront of the fishing wars of the 1960s and 1970s. Many Snohomishes left their reservation during the last years of the nineteenth century as a result of overcrowding and oppressive government policies. These Indians, plus those who never moved to the Tulalip Reservation, became the historic Snohomish tribe.

The Tulalip tribes were created in 1855, as was the Tulalip Reservation, which was intended for the Snohomish, Snoqualmie, Stillaguamish, Skykomish, and others. The word "Tulalip" comes from a Snohomish word meaning "a bay shaped like a purse." Many of these Indians refused to settle on the reservation, however, and ended up landless.

By the 1860s, the Squaxins had abandoned their traditional dress but maintained other aspects of their culture. In 1874, about 30 Squaxins went to live at and became assimilated into the Twana community. Some Squaxins also owned allotments on the Quinault Reservation. In 1882, a Squaxin Indian, John Slocum, began the Indian Shaker Church, which emphasizes morality, sobriety, and honesty. This religion soon spread far and wide and continues today. The Snoqualmies were removed to the Tulalip

Reservation after the Indian wars; they slowly assimilated into that and nearby white communities.

Religion According to the Twana, people were possessed of life souls and heart souls. Illness occurred if the former left the body. At death, life souls went to the land of the dead and were eventually reborn, whereas heart souls just disappeared. The people prayed to the sun and the earth, deities concerned with ethics. They also regarded salmon and other animal species as "people in their own country," complete with chiefs and other such conventions.

A mythological age ended when a transformer fashioned this world. Guardian spirits, both regular (lay) and shamanistic, were believed responsible for all luck, skill, and achievement. Shamans received the same powers as lay people, plus two unique powers as well. Spirit helpers and their associated songs were acquired through quests (or occasionally inheritance), which might begin as early as age eight and which consisted of fasting, bathing, and physical deprivation. Following the quest, nothing happened for up to 20 years, at which time the spirit returned (temporarily causing illness), the person sang and danced, and the power was activated. Shamans cured certain illnesses (such as soul loss) and could also cause illness and death, an explanation of why they were sometimes killed.

Southern Coast Salish Indians celebrated several regular ceremonies. The Winter Dance was sponsored by someone who was ill as a result of a returning spirit. There was much ritual connected with a "cure," including dancing, singing, feasting, and gift distribution. The soul recovery ceremony was an

Southern Coast Salish Indians celebrated several regular ceremonies. The soul recovery ceremony was an attempt to recapture a soul from the dead. These performers are singing their spirit songs and dramatizing a canoe search and rescue of a soul.

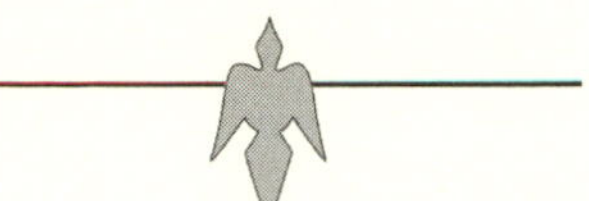

attempt to recapture a soul from the dead. Performers sang their spirit songs and dramatized a canoe search and rescue of soul. The potlatch was given by someone who had encountered a wealthy power and was to become wealthy himself. It was held in summer or early fall. The leading men of nearby villages and their families were invited. Guests brought food and wealth. Potlatches lasted for several days and included games, contests, secular songs, and dances, after which the sponsor gave away gifts and sang his power song.

Among the Twana, Suquamish, and maybe others, the *tamanawas* ceremony initiated new members (adolescents of both sexes with wealthy parents) into a secret religious society.

Government Each local group had one or more winter villages as well as several summer camps and resource sites. Village leaders were generally the heads of the wealthiest households; they had no formal leadership role. In Twana villages, the chief's speaker and village crier delivered brief sermons and awakened people, respectively.

Customs Villages consisted of one or more houses, which in turn sheltered several families, each within its own special section. Village membership may have been more permanent or stable in the south than in the north. Although they were truly autonomous, neighboring groups were linked by intermarriage, ceremonial and customary activities, and the use of common territories. Fishing sites and equipment could be individually or communally owned. Hunting was a profession among many Southern Coast Salish groups.

Classes, or social groups, included upper free (wealthy, high birth, sponsors of feasts and appropriate ceremonies), lower free (less wealth, common birth, fewer and less prestigious ceremonies), and slave (property). Recognition by the intervillage network was required to confirm or alter status. Possessions of woven blankets, dentalia, clamshell-disk beads, robes, pelts, bone war clubs, canoes, and slaves constituted wealth. House posts and grave monuments of high-status people were carved and/or painted. All except slaves and the very poor had their heads flattened in infancy. Popular games included gambling (dice and the disk and hand games) as well as games of skill and athletic contests. More southerly people smoked tobacco (obtained in trade) mixed with kinnikinnick (bearberry).

There were few proper birth ceremonies, although behavior was restricted for a new mother and father. At adolescence, both sexes were expected to seek visions, although a girl was subject to a greater number of behavioral restrictions, including isolation at her first period (and at all subsequent periods). Upper-class girls had "coming out parties" after their first isolation to announce their marriageability. Marriage was arranged by families, usually to people in different villages. It involved the ritual exchange of gifts. Divorce was possible but difficult, especially among the upper class. Death received the most ritualistic treatment. Professional undertakers prepared the body, which was interred in a canoe or an aboveground grave box. After the funeral there was a feast, and the deceased's property was given away.

Dwellings Permanent plank houses had shed roofs (later, gambrel and gabled roofs) and were very similar to those of the Central Coast Salish. Several families (nuclear or extended, possibly including slaves) shared a house. Each family, or sometimes two, had its own fireplace. Co-wives might also share the house and have their own fireplaces. Cedar longhouses might be as large as 200 by 50 feet.

Some houses were built and used by wealthy men as potlatch houses. Temporary summer camp houses consisted of mats covering pole frames. Most villages had at least one sweat house. Stockades protected some villages. The famous "old man house," a Suquamish dwelling, once stood in the village of Suqua. It was about 500 feet long and 60 feet wide. The government ordered it burned in the 1870s.

Diet Fish, especially salmon, was the staple for most groups. They also ate herring, smelt, flatfish, lingcod, sturgeon, and cutthroat and rainbow trout. Sea mammals included seals and beached whales. Of the land mammals, most people ate blacktail deer, black bear, elk, and smaller animals. Dogs were used to help in the hunt. Deer and elk were sometimes hunted in community drives. Other important foods included about 20 species of fowl; shellfish; and plants such as bracken, camus, and wapato as well as other roots, bulbs, sprouts, berries, and nuts. From the mid-1850s on, many of these groups raised potatoes.

Key Technology Fishing equipment included seines, gill nets, weirs, traps, trawl nets, dip nets, lift nets, gaffs, harpoons, and herring rakes. For hunting, people used clubs, harpoons, bow and arrow, pitfalls, snares, nets, and flares (for night hunting). Woodworking was the primary male craft. Men used stone mauls, elk antler, yew wedges, and other tools to make canoes, house planks, utensils, bent-corner boxes, containers, dishes, and spoons.

Women worked with shredded cedar bark and cattail leaves, making cordage, mats (bed, canoe, wall), blankets, and baskets (including coiled cedar-root hard baskets) in various shapes and sizes. They also wove blankets of mountain goat wool, dog fur, and bird and fireweed down. Twana women made soft twined decorated baskets of sedge or cattail leaves. The Nisqually, a more interior people, made elk hide parfleches in which to carry food and store meat.

Trade The Southern Coast Salish regularly traded among themselves and their immediate neighbors as well as with interior groups and Indians east of the Cascade Mountains. Most of their canoes were obtained from outer coast peoples. Items from the east included mountain goat hair and hemp fiber.

Notable Arts Wood carving and painting, weaving, and basket making were the most important arts. All men carved wood, but some were specialized craftsmen. Men also pecked or incised stone, bone, and antler. Boards used in the spirit canoe ceremony (a soul recovery ceremony) were elaborately painted.

Transportation Several types of cedar canoes were employed for purposes such as trolling, hunting, moving freight, and warfare. For major travel (such as travel to and from summer camps), people made a sort of catamaran by lashing some boards between two canoes. Upriver peoples used log rafts for crossing or traveling down streams. Winter hunters walked on snowshoes. Horses arrived in the area in the late eighteenth century, but only inland groups such as the Nisqually and Puyallup used them extensively.

Dress Most clothing was made of shredded cedar bark and buckskin. In warm weather, men wore breechclouts or nothing; women wore a cedar-bark apron and usually a skirt. In colder weather, men and some women wore hide shirts, leggings, and robes of bearskin as well as skins of smaller mammals sewn together. Both wore hide moccasins.

Some groups wore basketry or fur caps. Many wore abalone and dentalia earrings. Women also wore shell, teeth, and claw necklaces as well as leg and chin tattoos. Older men might keep hair on their faces.

War and Weapons Intragroup violence was usually dealt with by compensation and purification. Fighting, usually resulting from revenge, the ambitions of warriors, and slave raids, was usually with nonneighboring groups. Professional warriors did exist, although warfare was largely defensive in nature. Weapons included war clubs, daggers, spears, and bow and arrow (possibly poisoned). Hide shirts were worn as armor. Rather than fight, Twanas might hire shamans to harm other groups.

At least in the early nineteenth century, the Southern Coast Salish had to deal with highly aggressive Lekwiltok Kwakiutl raiders. On at least one occasion the Salish tribes banded together to launch a retaliatory expedition against the Kwakiutl. Some groups, such as the Skagit and Snohomish, had guns before they ever saw non-Indians.

Contemporary Information

Government/Reservations The Skokomish Reservation (1874; 6,300 acres; 431 Indians/183 non-natives) includes Twana, Klallam, and Chimakum Indians. A constitution and by-laws were approved in 1938. They are governed by a tribal council. Their own court regulates hunting, fishing, and other laws.

The Port Madison Reservation (1855; 7,811 acres, less than half of which is Indian owned; 372 Indians/4,462 non-natives) is home to the Suquamish tribe (Suquamish and Duwamish, roughly 800 in the mid-1990s). A 1965 constitution and by-laws call for an elected seven-member tribal council. A large number of non-Indians, not subject to tribal law, live on the reservation. Roughly 400 (1991) Duwamish Indians also live off-reservation.

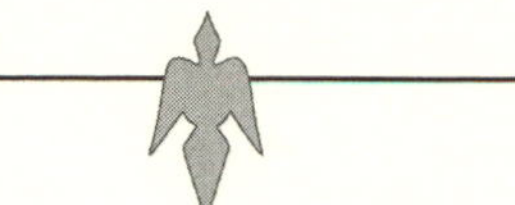

The Muckleshoot Reservation (1857; 1,275 acres; 858 Indians/2,983 non-natives) adopted a constitution and by-laws in 1836, under the Indian Reorganization Act (IRA). Three new members are elected annually to the Muckleshoot Tribal Council. The tribe is a member of the Intertribal Court System (1978).

The Nisqually Reservation (1854; 941 acres; 363 Indians/215 non-natives) approved a constitution and by-laws in 1946. A council governs the Nisqually Indian Community.

The Puyallup Reservation (1855; less than 1,000 acres, almost none of which is Indian-owned; 906 Indians/31,486 non-natives) is governed by the Puyallup Tribal Council. The reservation is also home to some Nisquallis, Cowlitzes, Muckleshoots, Steilacooms, and other Indians.

The Tulalip (formerly the Snohomish) Reservation (1855; 10,667 acres; 1,193 Indians/5,910 non-natives) is home to the Tulalip tribes, who are mostly of Snohomish, Stillaguamish, Snoqualmie, Skykomish, Skagit, and Samish descent. The original constitution and by-laws were approved in 1936. A six-member board of directors is elected every three years.

The Upper Skagit Reservation (1981; roughly 99 acres; 162 Indians/18 non-natives) was purchased by the tribe. The tribe operates under a constitution and by-laws approved in 1974. A chair, elected annually, presides over the seven-member Upper Skagit Tribal Council. The tribe is also a member (with the Swinomish Indian Tribal Community and the Sauk-Suiattles) of the Skagit System Cooperative, which regulates fishing in the Skagit River system, and (with the Lummi, Nooksack, and Swinomish tribes) of the Northwest Washington Service Unit of the Indian Health Service. Tribal enrollment in 1993 was 552 people.

The Swinomish Reservation (1855; 3,602 acres; 578 Indians/1,704 non-natives) is located in Skagit County. Their constitution was adopted in 1936, under the IRA. Governed by the Swinomish Indian Senate, from which the principal tribal officers are elected, the Swinomish Indian Tribal Community (roughly 625 people in 1993) is composed of Swinomish, Kikiallus, Suquamish, Samish, and Upper and Lower Skagit peoples. They are members, with the Upper Skagit Reservation and the Sauk-Suiattles, of the Skagit System Cooperative.

The Squaxin Island Reservation (1854; 971 acres; 127 Indians/30 non-natives on trust lands) has been abandoned; most of the people live in and around Kamilche, the location of their tribal center, and Shelton, Washington. A constitution was accepted in 1965. The people are governed by a tribal council.

The Sauk-Suiattle Reservation (23 acres; 69 Indians/55 non-natives) separated from the Upper Skagits in 1946. Their constitution and by-laws, featuring a seven-member tribal council, were approved in 1975. They are members, with the Upper Skagit Reservation and the Swinomish Indian Tribal Community, of the Skagit System Cooperative.

The Stillaguamish Reservation (60 acres; 96 Indians/17 non-natives) was purchased with proceeds from a 1966 land claims settlement. The tribe of roughly 185 members is governed by a board of directors. It comanages 700 square miles of the Stillaguamish watershed.

The Snohomish Tribe was incorporated in 1927 and 1974. Its by-laws were written in 1928 and its constitution in 1934. It is governed by councils and chairpersons. Tribal enrollment in the early 1990s was about 900 people.

Most of the roughly 600 members of the Steilacoom tribe live in and around Pierce County. The tribal offices, including a museum, are in the town of Steilacoom. Their constitution and by-laws were originally created in the 1930s. They are governed by a nine-member council with three officers. There is also an honorary chieftain. They are largely assimilated.

Economy Fisheries industries predominate, such as aquaculture, hatcheries, and fishing fleets. There are some traditional crafts as well as retail establishments such as stores, marinas, and restaurants. Tribes receive income from trust lands and leases. The Suquamish are involved in clamming, fishing, plant gathering, and bingo. The Muckleshoot are also involved with bingo, as are the Puyallups and Swinomish, and are planning a casino. Tribal governments also provide some employment. Unemployment, however, remains very high on most reservations.

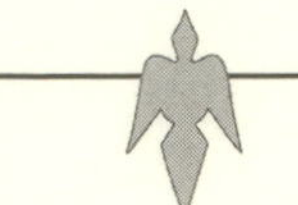

Upper Skagits manufacture replica Northwest Coast bentwood boxes. They and several other tribes recently reached a multimillion-dollar settlement with Seattle City Light for losses sustained to their fisheries by the erection of dams on the Skagit River early in the century.

Tulalip is beginning to reduce its unemployment rate of greater than 40 percent. Part-time work includes fishing, logging, and crop picking. Tribal income is also derived from land leases to non-Indians, a number of small businesses, a bingo operation, and a casino. Economic plans include construction of a golf course, a business park, and a second casino.

Legal Status Fishing rights litigation came to a head in the 1960s and 1970s. The main point of contention was the paucity of the salmon run, which was due primarily to river diversions for power and irrigation. Indians were losing out on the competition for the remaining salmon. When the state of Washington regulated the Puyallup fishery in the name of conservation, the Puyallups fished illegally, justifying that activity by their treaty rights. In the landmark 1974 case of *U.S.* v. *Washington* (the so-called Boldt decision, later upheld almost in its entirety by the U.S. Supreme Court), the court held that traditional tribal fisheries are protected by the 1854 and 1855 treaties.

One result of this decision was that tribal governments began enforcing fishing regulations. Taxes went to support the tribal fisheries industries as well as some social services. The decision also helped to promote Indian identity by refocusing it on fishing as a core activity.

Federally recognized tribal entities include the Upper Skagit Tribe, the Sauk-Suiattle Tribe, the Swinomish Tribal Community (Swinomish, Skagit, Samish), the Skokomish Tribe (Twanas), the Suquamish Tribe, the Muckleshoot Tribe, the Nisqually Indian Community, the Puyallup Tribe, the Tulalip Tribes, the Stillaguamish Tribe, and the Squaxin Island Tribe. The Snoqualmie Tribe received full federal recognition in early 1998.

The Snohomish Tribe is a federally recognized political entity and has applied for tribal recognition. The Kikiallus Tribe, formerly a subdivision of the Skagits; the Steilacoom Tribe; the Duwamish Tribe; and the Snoqualmoo Tribe (derived from the Snoqualmies after a factional split in the 1840s) have petitioned for federal recognition. The Samish Tribe has been denied federal tribal recognition.

Daily Life In general, the Southern Coast Salish people come together regularly for intertribal gatherings around traditional ceremonies and activities, such as winter spirit dancing and games.

The Suquamish Museum and Cultural Center (1980) is a center of that tribe's cultural life. The Suquamishes are predominantly Catholic. Their children attend public school. Chief Seattle Days, held in August in conjunction with the American Legion, celebrates local Indian culture, and other festivals are also open to the public. The Duwamish have formed a nonprofit corporation to foster tribal identity and culture. They still seek federal recognition and fishing rights.

The Muckleshoot Tribe has a community center, library, medical-dental clinic, educational training programs, and police force. Many people are active in the Indian Shaker Church as well as the Pentecostal Church. A land reacquisition program is underway. Their Skopbsh celebration is held in early May.

The Puyallups hold a powwow in late summer. After two physical occupations, they regained title in 1980 to the site of a former Indian hospital. They now operate the Takopid Health Center, which provides a wide range of health care for Indians of hundreds of tribes. They also recently reached a land claims settlement with the government for $112 million for tribal land that illegally became the port of Tacoma. Most Puyallups are Christian, although traditional winter spirit dancing and healing ceremonies are still held. Lushootseed is taught in schools but is not generally spoken.

Numerous services on the Nisqually Reservation include a clinic, programs for the old and young, and a library, trading post, and bingo hall. Nisquallis participate in the Indian Shaker Church and various Christian churches.

Most of the approximately 100 Sauk-Suiattles live in Skagit County. Many work in the fishing and logging industries; unemployment on the reservation exceeds 80 percent. Many also practice spirit dancing, and there are members of the Indian Shaker Church and various Christian denominations.

As a result of dams, diking, and water diversions by public and private interests, the Skokomish lost important pieces of their lands in the twentieth century. They are currently trying to recover some of this land. Most Skokomish children attend public high school, although there is a tribal school for grades K–4. The tribe has native language and curriculum projects, plus a basketry project in conjunction with neighboring tribes. Most Skokomishes are either Pentecostals or Shakers, and some people practice the traditional *tamanawas* religion. The tribe observes several festivals, most connected with traditional activities such as personal naming and the first salmon run.

The Stillaguamish work mainly in Snohomish County. They are assembling a tribal history in order to learn more about their heritage. The tribal center features courses in arts and language, and the tribe operates a fish hatchery. Children of the Swinomish Indian Tribal Community attend public school. Most Swinomishes are Catholics. They hold the Swinomish festival, featuring traditional games, dances, and food, on Memorial Day. They also observe Treaty Days in late January and participate in local canoe races and powwows.

The Steilacoom Tribe is creating an activities learning center on five acres of land they lease from Fort Steilacoom Park (in Pierce County). The center emphasizes both traditional (basketry, wood carving) and modern (such as energy conservation) technology. Fort Steilacoom Community College coordinates programs with the tribe. There is an annual Elders Feast Day.

Most of the 1,000 or so Snoqualmies live on non-Indian lands throughout the Puget Sound area. A very few people still speak the native language. The tribe sponsors arts and crafts classes and trains traditional dancers.

Many Upper Skagits, on the Upper Skagit, the Swinomish, or the Sauk-Suiattle Reservation, retain elements of their traditional culture. The language is still spoken; shamans still practice; and traditional dances, music, and ceremonials, particularly pertaining to funerals, spirit powers, and the giving of inherited Indian names, are still important. A tribal center and a library are on the Upper Skagit Reservation.

Tulalip children attend public schools, including an elementary school on the reservation. Tribal members are attempting to revive the traditional crafts of basketry and wood carving. Instruction in Lushootseed is also offered. They celebrate First Salmon ceremonies as well as other traditional festivals, and much of the traditional social structure remains intact. Primarily as a result of intermarriage, assimilation, and allotment, the Skykomishes no longer constitute an identifiable tribe. The Snohomish continue to seek tribal recognition and a land base.

Squaxin Island people retain the use of the island for various activities. Most are Protestant, although some celebrate the First Salmon ceremony. The tribe is active in local environmental management programs and manages a hatchery and a salmon and steelhead fishery program.

Salish, Southwestern Coast

Southwestern Coast Salish (`Sal ish) is a term used to refer to the speakers of four closely related Salishan languages. Its component groups are Queets, Copalis, and Quinault, who are speakers of Quinault; Humptulips, Wynoochee, Chehalis, and Shoalwater Bay, who are speakers of Lower Chehalis; Satsop and Kwaiailk, or Upper Chehalis, who are speakers of Upper Chehalis; and Cowlitz, who are speakers of Cowlitz.

Location Traditionally, the Southwestern Coast Salish lived along the Pacific coast from just south of the Hoh River delta to northern Willapa Bay, including the drainages of the Queets, Quinault, Lower Cowlitz, and Chehalis River systems, all in the state of Washington. Local environments included rain forest, mountains, open ocean, sheltered saltwater bays, forest, and prairies. Today, most of these Indians live on local reservations or in Northwest cities and towns.

Population There were perhaps 2,500 Quinault and Lower Chehalis and about 8,000 Kwaiailks and (mostly Lower) Cowlitzes around 1800. In 1990, there were roughly 2,000 Southwestern Coast Salish

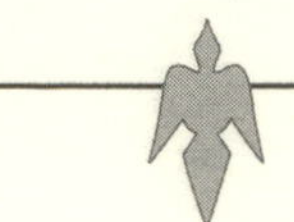

Indians living on reservations (see "Government/ Reservations" under "Contemporary Information") and at least half as many living in local cities and towns.

Language Southwest Salish, which includes the Quinault, Lower Chehalis, Upper Chehalis, and Mountain and Lower Cowlitz languages, is part of the Tsamosan (formerly Olympic) division of the Salishan language family. The Upper and Lewis River Cowlitz spoke dialects of Sahaptian.

Historical Information

History In 1775, Southwestern Coast Salish encountered and killed Spanish explorers and salvaged their ship for iron. By the late 1780s, Indians were used to trading with Europeans and had already experienced population loss from European diseases.

The Lower Chehalises were among the people who traded with Meriwether Lewis and William Clark in 1805–1806. Contact with non-natives was commonplace after Astoria was founded on the Columbia estuary in 1811. The Hudson's Bay Company founded local posts such as Fort Vancouver (1825), Fort Nisqually (1833), and Cowlitz Farm (1839). Some Cowlitz groups became mixed with the Klickitats, an inland group, during the early nineteenth century. As access to European goods increased, Indians also skirmished among themselves for control of the inland trade.

A malaria epidemic devastated Indian populations in the 1830s and resulted in significant village abandonment and consolidation. For instance, the Chinook and Lower Chehalis people combined in a bilingual tribe known as Shoalwater Bay Indians; the Salishan-Chinook language (as well as the tribe's later adoption of Lower Chehalis) eventually died out altogether. The Treaty of Washington (1846) and the Donation Land Act (1850) allowed non-natives to appropriate Indian land. Many Indians, especially inlanders, were driven away, exterminated, and/or had their food resources destroyed or taken.

Cowlitzes refused to sign the 1855 treaty because it did not provide a reservation in their homelands. Along with many other tribes, they fought the United States in the Indian wars of 1855–1856. After inflicting severe dislocations, the government ordered them to remove to the Chehalis Reservation, but they refused, continuing to hold out for their own reservation. Many groups refused to sign treaties or accept goods from Indian agents, fearing that such action would be seen as evidence of forfeiture of land title.

The Quinault River Treaty in 1855 did provide that tribe with a reservation in exchange for vast areas of their traditional lands. In 1864, the Chehalis Reservation was created—without treaties or the formal Indian cession of land—for Chehalis, Cowlitz, and some southern coastal people, but most remained near their homes. These people either became assimilated into white population or joined the Chehalis Confederated Tribes or other tribes. Most Chehalis Reservation land was later reappropriated; the rest was homesteaded by 36 Indians and set aside for school purposes.

The Shoalwater Bay Tribe and Georgetown Reservation were created in 1866. The tribe was composed mainly of Chehalis and Chinook families living on Willapa (formerly Shoalwater) Bay. By 1879, these Indians all spoke the Lower Chehalis dialect.

All reservation Indians experienced pressure to Christianize, take up farming, and give up their culture. Corrupt agents profited on their rations. Of necessity and desire, hunting, fishing, and gathering continued, although Indians increasingly became involved in the cash economy (logging, farming, and railroads).

The Quinaults remained relatively isolated until the late 1880s. During the early twentieth century, a legal ruling allowed members from various non-Quinault tribes to claim allotments on that reservation and to apply for (and receive) status as Quinaults. This process first resulted mostly in environmental degradation and a sharply decreased salmon run as a result of clearcutting and then in the attendant relocation of people off the reservation.

Religion Southwestern Coast Salish religion centered around the relation of individuals, including slaves, to guardian spirits. Spirits lived either in the land of the dead or in animate and inanimate objects. They provided wealth, power, skill, and/or luck. Songs, dances, and paraphernalia were associated with particular spirits. Spirits not properly honored could

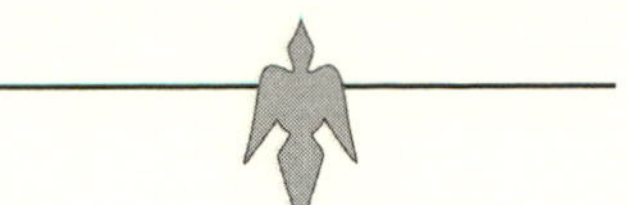

be dangerous. Training (such as bathing, fasting in lonely places, and other physical tests) to acquire a spirit began as early as about age seven and culminated in a formal spirit quest at adolescence.

Shamans, who might be men or women, had especially powerful spirits. They diagnosed and cured disease. They could also cause illness or death and were occasionally hired for this purpose. Feasts involved only local people; potlatches were intertribal. The latter, held in winter, were given at life-cycle events or at the perceived bequest of a spirit. Social status was closely related to potlatching activity.

Spirit song ceremonials were observed in winter, accompanied among some tribes by gift giving. Some coastal groups also had secret societies. Most groups celebrated first salmon rituals during which they burned the salmon's heart and distributed some of the fish to all villagers.

Government Politically independent villages were each composed of between one and ten households, each household consisting of several families. A nonpolitical "tribe" was recognized as several villages that shared a language and a territory. Village leaders tended to come from certain families, with the eldest son often inheriting the leadership position. Leaders were wealthy and often owned several slaves so they would not have to work as hard as others did. Their power was limited to giving advice and settling disputes. In some villages (the Quinault, for example), speakers announced the chief's decisions and negotiated with other villages. This office was obtained by merit. Some villages also had official jokers or buffoons.

Customs Property rights, such as the control of subsistence areas and even the use of particular parts of a whale, were inheritable and carefully controlled. One's work and social activities depended on gender, talent, status, and the possession of an appropriate spirit power. Shamans had especially powerful spirit powers.

The basic social distinction was between slave and free, although some free people were wealthier and more influential than others. Houses were owned by the man who contributed the most labor and materials to its construction. He also directed certain subsistence activities such as weir building. Upon his death, the house would be torn down; it might be rebuilt nearby, or else the former members would each build a new house.

Girls were secluded for up to several months at the onset of puberty. Marriage, especially among the wealthy, began a permanent cycle of mutual gift and food giving. Families of deceased spouses generally provided replacements. Free people were interred in a box or double canoe (one over the other) that was placed in a tree or on posts. Their possessions were either given away or interred with them. The house was purified or destroyed. Among the wealthy, reburial might take place after a year or two.

Dwellings Cedar-planked, gabled houses were arrayed along a river. A door was set at one or both ends. From two to four families, or sometimes more, lived in a house. Partitions divided sections for menstruating women. Sleeping platforms with storage space underneath ran along the interior walls. Shorter benches in front of the houses were used for sitting and as a place for men to talk and work. Interior walls might be lined with mats.

Temporary summer shelters were made of cedar-bark slabs or mat- or bough-covered pole frames. People also occasionally stayed in temporary bark or brush hunting shelters.

Diet Fish, especially all five types of salmon, was the food staple. Besides salmon, the people used sturgeon, trout, eulachon (or smelt), halibut, herring, and cod. Fish were eaten fresh or smoke dried. Eulachon was used mainly for its oil. Other important foods included shellfish; land mammals (especially in the Quinault highlands and among the Kwaiailks) such as deer, elk, and bear; water fowl and birds; sea mammals; and plants, especially inland, such as camas, berries, crabapples, roots, and shoots. Inland people burned prairie land every two to three years.

Key Technology Fishing equipment included nets (trawl, gill, drift, dip), weirs, clubs, traps, harpoons, hook and line, herring rakes, and gaffs. People hunted with bow and arrow, deadfalls, nooses, snares, and nets. Professional woodworkers made most houses and canoes as well as bent-corner and bent-bottom boxes, utensils, and tools. The basic woodworking tool was the adz. Women shredded bark and sewed and twined mats. They also made baskets, mostly of spruce root along the coast.

Trade Neighbors regularly traded and intermarried. Dentalium shells served as currency for durable goods. Food and raw materials were usually exchanged for the same. Canoes were widely exchanged. The Copalises provided many groups with razor clams. The local trading complex stretched from Vancouver Island to south of the Columbia River and also east of the Cascades.

Notable Arts Baskets (especially Cowlitz coiled baskets), carved and painted wooden items, and Quinault spirit masks were the region's most important art objects.

Transportation Canoes were the predominant travel mode. Men made and traded for canoes of varying shapes and sizes, depending on function. Rafts were kept at river crossings. Inland groups acquired horses by at least the early nineteenth century.

Dress Men went naked in the summer; women wore knee-length shredded bark skirts. Both wore fur or skin clothing in colder weather, with robes of dog or rabbit fur or bird skins. The wealthy might wear sea otter–skin robes. Hunters wore leggings and moccasins in winter. Waterproof rainwear was made of cattail fiber. The Quinault wore twined split spruce-root rain hats. Body paint and tattooing were customary, as was infant head flattening, especially with groups nearest the lower Columbia River. Many men along the coast wore mustaches.

War and Weapons Most disputes between villages were usually settled by some form of economic arrangement such as formal compensation or marriage. In general, the Cowlitz were on unfriendly terms with coastal groups, and the Queets fought the Quileute and sometimes the Quinault. The Chehalis killed many Queets and burned their villages around 1800; they also regularly attacked the Copalises. Queets, Quinaults, Hohs, and Quileutes occasionally confederated to oppose the Klallams, Makahs, Satsops, and others.

Fighting was more regulated in the south, and there no slaves were taken. Weapons included mussel-shell knives, whalebone daggers, yew spears with shell or bone points, whale-rib and stone clubs, and the bow and arrow. Elk hide shirts and helmets and cedar shields (Chehalis), as well as slatted wood breastplates, provided protection in war.

Contemporary Information

Government/Reservations In 1990, 942 Quinault, Quileute, Chinook, Hoh, Chehalis, Queets, and Cowlitz Indians lived on the Quinault Reservation, in Taholah, Washington (1855; 340 square miles). These people adopted by-laws in 1922. A new constitution in 1975 gave decision-making powers to an 11-member business committee. Much of the reservation is owned by non-Indian timber and milling companies. Quinault tribal enrollment in the early 1990s was about 2,400.

The Shoalwater (Georgetown) Reservation (1866; 1,035 acres; about 100 residents and 150 enrolled members in 1993) is located in Pacific County, Washington. The people rejected the Indian Reorganization Act but adopted a constitution and became formally organized in 1971. They elected a tribal council shortly thereafter.

In 1990, 307 Chehalis, Quinault, Muckleshoot, Nisqually, Klallam, and other Indians lived on the Chehalis Reservation, Oakville, Washington (1864; 1,952 acres). A constitution and by-laws were adopted in 1939. They are governed by the generally elected Chehalis Community Council, which then elects a business committee.

The Cowlitz Tribe of Indians is an unincorporated association formed to press land claims and maintain traditions. Their constitution and by-laws provide for a five-member executive committee. They have a small (17.5 acres) land base along the Cowlitz River. The tribe divided in 1973 over a $1.55 million land claims settlement when a small group, subsequently calling itself the Sovereign Cowlitz Tribe, preferred to hold out for land. The 1990 population of the Cowlitz Indian Nation was 1,689.

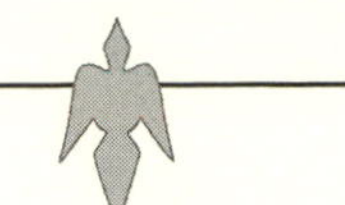

Economy Important economic activities include fishing and related industries, government-related jobs, logging and related industries, building trades, and social services. There is a restaurant at Shoalwater Bay and a bingo parlor at Chehalis. Some income is earned from allotment leases. An arts and crafts manufacturing factory, a fish-processing plant, restaurants, and food markets are on the Quinault Reservation.

Legal Status The Cowlitz Indian Tribe is recognized by the state of Washington and won preliminary approval for federal recognition in early 1998. The Confederated Tribes of the Chehalis Reservation, the Quinault Indian Nation, and the Shoalwater Bay Tribe are federally recognized tribal entities.

Daily Life The Quinaults exercise sovereignty over their territory, participating in a federal self-governance project and rehabilitating depleted and destroyed natural resources. A tribal police force and court system help to maintain order on the Quinault Reservation. There is some dissension over jurisdiction between the tribe and the Quinault Allottees Association, composed of members of other tribes with allotments on the Quinault Reservation. Children attend classes in the Indian-oriented Taholah schools. The contemporary style of Quinault art is influenced by South Sea Island art forms. Although most Quinaults are Protestant, some older members attend the Indian Shaker Church. An annual trout derby, featuring canoe races, is held in late May. Talolah Days take place on the Fourth of July.

The Chehalis Reservation maintains a water system and river clean-up operations. They have a tribal center, a health clinic, a meeting room for the elderly, a library, classrooms, and tribal offices. The county sheriff enforces laws. Most children attend public schools. Programs exist to preserve native language and culture. A tribal history was published in 1980. Tribal Days at the end of May feature games, dances, and feasting. Assembly of God and the Indian Shaker churches have a strong presence on the reservation.

The Shoalwater Bay people run a restaurant and work with non-Indians in the surrounding area. Children attend public school. Funds from a land claims settlement have been invested in reacquiring land. Health care is quite poor. Ongoing traditions include the passing on of hereditary names, annual fishing and gathering, and involvement in the Indian Shaker Church.

Cowlitz Indians have maintained their government and tribal authority since aboriginal times. The native languages have been lost, however, with the possible exception of some Sahaptian among those enrolled on the Yakima Reservation. Recently, they have been involved in several efforts to protect their ancestral lands from the ravages of dams. Many Cowlitzes continue to seek personal spirit guidance through vision quests. The system of extended family networks, so characteristic of traditional life, remains intact.

Samish

See Salish, Central Coast

Sauk-Suiattle

See Salish, Southern Coast

Shoalwater Bay

See Salish, Southwestern Coast

Siltez, Confederated Tribes of

See Coosans; Upper Umpqua

Siuslawans

See Coosans

Skagit

See Salish, Southern Coast

Skokomish (Twana)

See Salish, Southern Coast

Snohomish

See Salish, Southern Coast

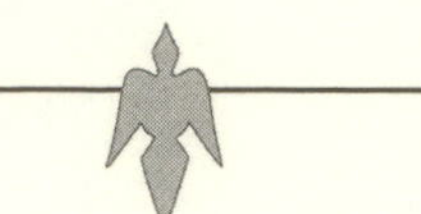

Snoqualmie

See Salish, Southern Coast

Snoqualmoo

See Salish, Southern Coast

Squaxin

See Salish, Southern Coast

Steilacoom

See Salish, Southern Coast

Stillaguamish

See Salish, Southern Coast

Suquamish

See Salish, Southern Coast

Swinomish

See Salish, Southern Coast

Tillamook

Tillamook (ˋTil ə mūk) is a Chinookan word for a Tillamook place-name, possibly meaning "land of many waters" or "People of Nehalem." These people were formerly referred to by other names, such as Calamoxes.

Location The Tillamook traditionally lived along a coastal strip from roughly Tillamook Head to the Siletz River, in present-day Oregon.

Population The Tillamook population stood at about 2,200 in 1805. In 1950 it was under 250. In 1990 roughly 50 Tillamook descendants lived in and around Oregon.

Language Tillamook is a Salishan language. Its dialects included Nehalem, Nestucca, Salmon River (Nechesnan), and Siletz (Tillamook proper).

Historical Information

History History records the first contact between the Tillamook and non-natives as occurring in 1788, although iron knives and smallpox scars told of at least indirect encounters previously. They were also visited by Meriwether Lewis and William Clark. Regular contact with traders began after 1811. Epidemics of malaria, syphilis, smallpox, and other diseases, as well as guns and liquor, diminished the Tillamook population by around 90 percent in the 1830s and greatly reduced the number of their villages.

In 1850, the Donation Land Act opened Tillamook lands for white settlement. Indians ceded land in an unratified 1851 treaty, and the few surviving Tillamooks either remained in place, officially landless, or were removed to the Siletz or Grand Ronde Reservations. Under the leadership of the peaceful Kilchis, Tillamooks refused to participate in the wars of the 1850s. Awards from the Indian Land Claims Commission in 1958 and 1962 did little to reunite a scattered and unorganized people. Congress officially terminated its relationship with the Tillamook in 1956.

Religion Tillamooks attempted to gain power from spirits, whom they believed were more active and closer to humans in winter. Shamans renewed their power in January or February by sponsoring a ceremony that included singing a power song and dispensing food and presents to guests. During the course of this 5- to 15-day ceremony, all other "knowers" (those with spirit powers) sang their songs too. Winter was also the time for relating myth narratives. Mythological characters were particularly important because social status was dependent on one's ability to form a relationship with a mythological personage, a natural feature, or a guardian spirit. Rituals also accompanied the first seasonal consumption of various foods.

Government Society was divided into the many free and the few slave people as well a majority of people who had acquired guardian spirits and a minority of those who had not. The elite were wealthy and experts in doctoring, war, and hunting. Women received status from their own guardian spirits or from those of

their close relatives. Older women were accorded higher status.

Depending on the particular activity, different people, including shamans, headmen, and warriors, played leadership roles in the numerous small villages. Headmen were particularly skilled orators and negotiators. Most disputes, up to and including murder, were settled by arbitration and involved payment. This was often the case even with people from other villages.

Customs After a baby's birth, the mother remained confined and taken care of for 15 days while the father forfeited sleep for 10 nights. Free infants' heads were deformed. Infants were fed on demand and sucked elk sinew pacifiers. Children were formally named at an ear-piercing ceremony; boys also had their nasal septa pierced. This ceremony included feasting and dancing and varied according to the family's wealth. Children were rarely punished corporally. A boy's first food kill and a girl's first gathered food were reserved for the elderly.

Girls were secluded at the onset of puberty and underwent a series of ritual behaviors and food taboos. One such ritual was an all-night guardian spirit vigil in the woods, during which the girl repeatedly bathed in a cold stream. Any spirits gained during this quest remained inactive until middle age. At puberty, boys fasted and undertook guardian spirit quests that also included bathing. A boy's personal power and adult occupation were equated with the spirit song he obtained at that time. Boys, too, activated their spirit powers only at middle age.

Although marriages were arranged, the principals were consulted and respected. Bride and groom prices were commensurate with their family's status. Initial residence was in the groom's parents' village. High-status men might have more than one wife. Infanticide was a common result of illegitimate births.

Corpses were painted, dressed, wrapped in a blanket, and bound with cedar bark. After a two- to three-day wake, they were buried in raised canoes. Wealthy families might reopen the grave after a year, clean the bones, and replace the grave goods.

The Tillamook recognized five types of shamans: healers (men, by drawing with the hands, and women, by sucking), poison doctors (men, with much ritual paraphernalia to send and extract poisons), spirit doctors (men who personally retrieved lost spirits from the spirit world), love doctors (women); and baby diplomats (men who foretold events by conversing with babies).

Dwellings Winter villages were usually built at the mouths of rivers or streams. They typically consisted of several houses, at least one work-and-menstrual hut, sweat houses, and a graveyard. Rectangular houses, which were occupied by up to four families, were constructed of cedar planks tied together with peeled and steamed spruce roots. Roofs were gabled with overlapping planks. Each had several fires in a center pit and sleeping platforms along the sides. Some houses were built aboveground and some were semisubterranean (with a door in the roof and entrance via a ladder). Mat partitions separated families and multiple wives. Floors were covered by ferns and rush mats. Pitch torches or fish-head or whale-oil lamps provided extra light. Roots were kept in pits beneath the floor.

Diet Salmon and other fish were the staples. Other seafood included sea lions, seals, and shellfish. Women gathered salmonberries, huckleberries, strawberries, camas, ferns, and other plant foods. Men hunted elk, beaver, muskrat, bear, and waterfowl. Many foods were either steamed in earth ovens, stone-boiled in baskets or bowls, or dried on racks.

Key Technology Canoes, bone needles and awls, and baskets were among the most important material items. Fish were caught in weirs, traps, and seine and gill nets. They were also clubbed or harpooned.

Trade The Tillamook were part of a flourishing regional trade. In general, they traded tanned beaver hides, canoes, and baskets to northern Columbia River peoples for abalone shell, dentalia, buffalo hides and buffalo horn dishes, and dried salmon. The Tillamook bought wapato roots and other items from Columbia River peoples east of the Coastal Range. They traded and intermarried with the Kalapuyas, and they also raided their southern neighbors for slaves, which they sold in the north.

Notable Arts Women made excellent wrap-twined baskets.

Transportation Canoes of several sizes and shapes were used for travel and fishing. They were single-log dugouts, painted black on the outside and red on the inside, and coated with pitch.

Dress Women wore large grass, tule rush, or shredded-bark back aprons, small front aprons, and buckskin leggings. Men wore fur or basketry caps, breechclouts, buckskin shirts, and hide pants. Beaver and painted buckskin capes and rabbit, bobcat, or sea otter fur blankets kept people warm in the winter. Footgear included both moccasins and snowshoes. Items such as menstrual pads and diapers were made of cedar bark. Both sexes painted their hair part red and wore ear pendants. Men also wore nose pendants. Women wore decorative tattoos, but men's tattoos were only to measure dentalium.

War and Weapons Weapons included hunting equipment as well as elk hide armor. The Tillamook painted themselves for war with red and black stripes. Their enemies may have included the Chinook and the Kalapuyans. Slave raiding may have been a primary object of war.

Contemporary Information

Government/Reservations Since termination, Tillamook descendants have declined to organize or to seek a reversal of their unrecognized status. Some are members of the Confederated Tribes of Siletz and the Grande Ronde community.

Economy Tillamooks have no distinct economic activities.

Legal Status The Tillamook people are not recognized as a distinct native entity by any state government or by the federal government.

Daily Life Tillamooks are integrated within their native and non-native communities. There are few reminders in their daily lives of their Native American heritage.

Tlingit

Tlingit (`Tlēn git or `Klēn kit), meaning "human beings," is taken from the group's name for themselves. The Coastal Tlingit were a "nationality" of three main groups—Gulf Coast, Northern, and Southern—united by a common language and customs. The Interior Tlingit have never considered themselves a cohesive tribe.

Of the three major groups of coastal Tlingits, the Gulf Coast group included the Hoonah of Lituya Bay; the Dry Bay people at the mouth of the Alsek River, who were established in the eighteenth century by a conglomeration of Tlingits and Athapaskans; and the Yakutat, who were composed of Eyak speakers from the Italio River to Icy Bay. In 1910 the Yakutat merged with the Dry Bay people. Northern Tlingits included the Hoonah on the north shore of Cross Sound, the Chilkat-Chilkoot, Auk, and Taku; the Sumdum on the mainland; and the Sitka and Huntsnuwu, or Angoon, on the outer islands and coasts. The Southern Tlingit included the Kake, Kuiu, Henya, and Klawak on the islands and the Stikine or Wrangell, Tongass, and Sanya or Cape Fox along the mainland and sheltered waters.

Location Coastal Tlingit groups lived along the Pacific coast from roughly Icy Bay in the north to Chatham Sound in the south, or roughly throughout the Alaskan panhandle. This country, no more than 30 miles wide, but roughly 500 miles long, is marked by a profusion of fjords, inlets and bays, and islands, most of which are mountainous. The climate is marked by fog, rain, snow, and strong winds in fall and winter. Most Coastal Tlingits live in Alaska and in cities of the greater Northwest.

Interior Tlingits lived along the upper Taku River, although during the nineteenth and twentieth centuries, and in response both to the fur trade and the gold rush, most moved to the headwaters of the Yukon River. Many contemporary Interior Tlingit live in Teslin Village (Yukon Territory) and Atlin (British Columbia). Some also live in Whitehorse (Yukon) and Juneau (Alaska).

Population Total Tlingit population was at least 10,000 in 1740. Inland Tlingits probably never numbered more than 400. In the early 1990s there were roughly 14,000 Tlingits in the United States and 1,200 in Canada.

Language Tlingit is remotely related to Athapaskan languages.

Historical Information

History Humans have lived in Tlingit country for at least 10,000 years; continuous occupation of the region began around 5,000 years ago. People probably came from the south, with Tlingit culture perhaps having its origins near the mouths of the Nass and Skeena Rivers about 800 years ago. The earliest Tlingit villages had disappeared by historic times, however, and a new migration into the area began in the eighteenth century, as the Haida displaced southern Tlingit groups.

Russian explorers in 1741 were the first non-natives to enter the region. Spanish explorers heralded the period of regular interracial contact in 1775. The Russians had established a regular presence in 1790. They built a fort at Sitka in 1799 that fell to the Indians three years later. The Russians rebuilt in 1805, however, and made the fort the headquarters of the Russian-American Company from 1808 until 1867. Although the Tlingits maintained their independence during the Russian period, they did acquire tools and other items. Many fell to new diseases (a particularly severe smallpox outbreak occurred from 1835 to 1839), and some were converted to the Russian Orthodox Church.

In 1839, when the Hudson's Bay Company acquired trading rights in southeastern Alaska from the Russian-American Company, the region saw an influx of European-manufactured goods. The advent of steel tools had a stimulating effect on traditional wood carving. During this time, the Tlingit successfully resisted British attempts to break their trade monopoly with the interior tribes. By the 1850s, Tlingits were trading as far south as Puget Sound and had regular access to alcohol and firearms from the Americans.

Tlingits protested the U.S. purchase of Alaska in 1867, arguing that if anyone were the rightful "owner" of Alaska, it was they and not the Russians. In any case, the soldiers, miners, and adventurers who arrived after the purchase severely mistreated and abused the Indians. For much of the last half of the nineteenth century, U.S. naval authorities persecuted shamans thought to be involved with witches. Although Tlingits owned southeast Alaska under aboriginal title, they were prevented from filing legal claims during, and thus profiting from, the great Juneau gold rush of 1880. The mines ultimately yielded hundreds of millions of dollars worth of gold, of which wealth the Tlingit saw little or none.

Commercial fishing and canning as well as tourism in the area became established in the 1870s and 1880s, providing jobs (albeit at wages lower than those earned by white workers) for the Indians. The Klondike gold rush of 1898–1899 brought more money and jobs to the region. Meanwhile, Christian missionaries, especially Presbyterians, waged an increasingly successful war against traditional Indian culture.

By 1900 many Tlingit had become acculturated. They had given up their subsistence economy and abandoned many small villages. Many worked in canneries in British Columbia or picked hops in Washington. Potlatches began to diminish in number and significance, and many ceremonial objects were sold to museums. Despite this level of acculturation, however, some mid–nineteenth century Tlingit villages continued to exist into the twentieth century.

In 1915, Alaska enfranchised all "civilized" natives, but severe economic and social discrimination continued, including a virtual apartheid system during the first half of the twentieth century. Some villages incorporated in the 1930s under the Indian Reorganization Act and acquired various industries. After World War II the issue of land led to the formation of the Central Council of Tlingit and Haida, which in 1968 won a land claims settlement of $7.5 million ($0.43 an acre).

Despite Tlingit efforts, Alaska schools were not integrated until 1949. The Alaska Native Brotherhood (ANB), founded in Sitka in 1912 by some Presbyterian Indians, was devoted to rapid acculturation; economic opportunity, including land rights; and the abolition of political discrimination. The Alaska Native Sisterhood (ANS) was founded soon after. Both organizations reversed their stand against traditional practices in the late 1960s.

Religion Animals and even natural features had souls similar to those of people. Thus they were treated with respect, in part to win their help or to avoid their malice. Hunters engaged in ritual purification before the hunt, and during the hunt the hunter as well as his family back home engaged in certain formal rules of behavior.

Shamans were very powerful. Most were men. Shamans could cure, control weather, bring success in hunting, tell the future, and expose witches, but only if they were consulted in time and not impeded by another shaman. Their powers came from spirits that could be summoned by a special song. A shaman underwent regular periods of physical deprivation to keep spiritually pure. Neither he nor his wife could cut their hair.

Government The basic political units were matrilineal clans of two divisions, Raven and Eagle. Each clan was subdivided into lineages or house groups. Thus, the tribes, or groups, listed above lacked any overall political organization and were really local communities made up of representatives of several clans. All territory and property rights were held by the clans. Clan and lineage chiefs, or headmen, assigned their group's resources, regulated subsistence activities, ordered the death of trespassers, and hosted memorial ceremonies.

Customs The two divisions served as opposites for marriage and ceremonial purposes. Some clans and lineages moved among neighboring groups such as the Haida, Tsimshian, and Eyak. A clan's crest represented its totem, or the living things, heavenly bodies, physical features, and supernatural beings associated with it. Crests were displayed on house posts, totem poles, canoes, feast dishes, and other items. All present members of an opposite division received payment to view a crest, because in so doing they legitimated both the display and the crest's associated privileges. All clan property could be bought and sold, given as gifts, or taken in war.

In general, spring brought hunting on the mainland, halibut fishing in deep waters, and shellfish and seaweed gathering. Seal hunting began in late spring, about the time of the first salmon runs. Summer activities generally included catching and curing salmon, berrying, and some sealing. Summer was also the time for wars and slave raids. Fall brought some sea otter hunting (land otter were never killed). In the late nineteenth century, fall was also the time for more salmon fishing and curing, potato harvesting, and hunting in the interior. Winter villages were established by November. Winter was the season for potlatches and trading.

Individuals as well as lineages were ranked, from nobility to commoners. Slaves were entirely outside the system. (Slaves were freed after the United States purchased Alaska and were brought into the social system on the lowest level.) Women had high status, probably because they controlled the food supply (not catching fish but the much harder and more laborious jobs of cutting, drying, smoking, and baling it). Any injury to someone in another clan required an indemnity. Clan disagreements were usually but not always settled peacefully. The three important feasts were the funeral feast, memorial potlatch feast, and childrens' feast.

All babies were believed to be reincarnations of maternal relatives. At about age eight, a boy went to live with his maternal uncle, who saw that he toughened and purified himself and learned the traditions and responsibilities of his clan and lineage. Girls were confined in a dark room or cellar for up to two years (according to rank and wealth) at their first period, at which time they learned the traditions of their clan, performed certain rituals, and observed behavior restrictions. At the end of this time their ears were pierced, high-status families gave a potlatch, and girls were considered marriageable.

Only people of opposite divisions but similar clans and lineages could marry. Marriage formalities included mutual gift giving. Southerners erected tall mortuary totem poles near their houses. Death initiated a mourning period and several rituals, including singing and the funeral. Cremation occurred on the fourth day, except possibly longer for a chief. Widows observed particularly restrictive mourning rituals. A person's slaves were sometimes killed. The evening after the cremation, mourners held a feast for their division opposites. Dead slaves were simply cast onto the beach. Burial was adopted in the late nineteenth century.

Dwellings Tlingits usually lived in one main (winter) village and perhaps one or more satellite villages. In the early nineteenth century, the former consisted of a row of rectangular, slightly excavated, gable-roofed planked houses facing the water. Each house could hold 40–50 people, including about six families and a few unmarried adults or slaves. Each family slept on partitioned wooden platforms that could be removed to make a larger ceremonial space.

Other features included a central smoke hole and a low, oval front doorway. The four main house posts were carved and painted in totemic or ancestral designs. Palisades often surrounded houses or whole villages. Other village structures included smokehouses, small houses for food and belongings, sweat houses, and menstrual huts.

In the nineteenth century, Inland Tlingits lived in rectangular houses similar to those of the coastal people. They also built brush lean-tos that could shelter up to 10 or 15 people.

Diet Fish was the staple, especially all five species of salmon, as well as eulachon, halibut, and herring. Fish was boiled, baked, roasted, or dried and smoked for winter. Whole salmon might be frozen for winter use. Other important seafoods included shellfish, seaweed, seal, sea lion, sea otter, and porpoise.

The people also ate land mammals such as deer, bear, and mountain sheep and goat. Dogs assisted in

The Tlingit village of Klukwan in 1895. Tlingits usually lived in one main (winter) village and perhaps one or more satellite villages. In the early nineteeenth century the former consisted of a row of rectangular, slightly excavated, gable-roofed planked houses facing the water.

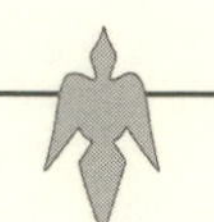

the hunt. Inland Tlingit hunted caribou, moose, and some wood bison. Beaver were speared or netted under ice. Migrating waterfowl provided meat as well as feathers, eggs, and beaks. Some groups gathered a variety of berries, plus hemlock inner bark, roots (riceroot, fern), and shoots (salmonberries, cow parsnips). They began cultivating potatoes after the Russians introduced the food in the early nineteenth century.

People sucked cultivated tobacco mixed with other materials; they began smoking it when the Russians introduced leaf tobacco and pipes in the late eighteenth century.

Key Technology Salmon were caught in rectangular, wooden traps; trapped behind stone walls; or impaled on wooden stakes in low water. Other fishing equipment include hook and (gut) line, harpoons, and copper knives. Men hunted with spears, bow and arrow, a whip sling, and darts. Raw materials included horn (spoons, dishes, containers), wool (blankets), and wood (fire drill, watertight storage and boiling boxes). Tlingits began forging iron in the late eighteenth century, although some iron was acquired from intercontinental trade or drift wreckage in aboriginal times. Some foods were baked in earth ovens.

Trade Imports included walrus ivory from Bering Sea Eskimos, copper from interior tribes, dentalia shell from the south, Haida canoes, Tsimshian carvings, slaves, furs, skin garments decorated with porcupine quills, and various fish products. Exports included Chilkat blankets, seaweed, leaf tobacco, and fish oil. Intragroup trade was largely ceremonial in nature. When the whites came, Tlingits tried to monopolize that trade, even going so far as to travel over 300 miles to destroy a Hudson's Bay Company post.

Inland Tlingit trade partners included the Tahltan, Kaska, Pelly River Athapaskan, and Tagish.

Notable Arts Tlingits excelled at wood carving, especially ceremonial partitions in house chiefs' apartments, bentwood boxes, chests, and bowls, house posts (usually shells fronting the structural posts), masks, weapons and war regalia, and utilitarian and ceremonial items used by nobles.

Chilkat Tlingit blankets were the most intricate and sought-after textiles of the Northwest Coast. They were really ceremonial robes, and the ceremonies, in which myth was dramatized through dance, were fully as artistic as the crafts themselves.

Weaving of shirts, aprons, and leggings may have come originally from the Tsimshian. Rock art probably served functions similar to those of totems. Beadwork was of very high quality. Shamans used many art objects, including carved ivory and antler and bone amulets. Baskets were also an important Tlingit art.

Transportation Tlingits preferred the great Haida canoes that were purchased by wealthy Tlingit headmen. The most common type of canoe was of spruce, except in the south, where they used red cedar. Styles included ice-hunting canoes for sealing, forked-prow canoes, shallow river canoes, and small canoes with upturned ends for fishing and otter hunting. Some Inland Tlingits also used skin canoes, but most used rafts or small dugouts when they could not walk.

The Tlingits' wood-carving expertise is exemplified in these totem poles in front of Chief Kadashan's house in Wrangell, Alaska (1902).

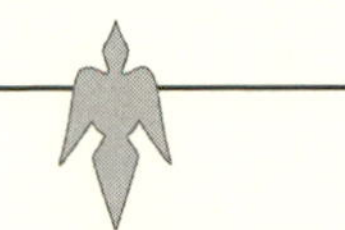

Chilkat Tlingit blankets, such as this one collected on Douglas Island off Alaska's southwest coast in the late nineteenth century, were the most intricate and sought-after textiles of the Northwest Coast. They were really ceremonial robes, and the ceremonies, in which myth was dramatized through dance, were fully as artistic as the crafts themselves.

Tlingits purchased Eyak and Athapaskan snowshoes. They carried burdens using skin packs with tumplines. Only a few coastal groups used Athapaskan-style sleds.

Dress In warm weather, women wore cedar-bark aprons, whereas men went naked. Blankets of woven cedar bark, mountain goat wool or dog hair, or tanned, sewn skins kept people warm in cold weather. Women wore waterproof basket caps and cedar bark ponchos in the rain. Conical twined spruce-root hats also served as prestigious crest objects.

Inland Tlingits wore pants with attached moccasins. Tailored shirts were made of caribou or moose skin. Winter clothing included goat wool pants, hooded sweaters made of caribou or hare skin, and fur robes.

War and Weapons War occurred between clans in different groups or tribes for reasons of plunder or, more often, revenge. Warfare included killing, torture, and the taking of women and children as slaves. Settlement involved the ceremonial kidnapping and ransom of high-ranking individuals, dancing, and feasting. Weapons included daggers, spears, war clubs, and bows and arrows. Fighters also wore hide and rod armor over moose-hide shirts as well as head and neck protection.

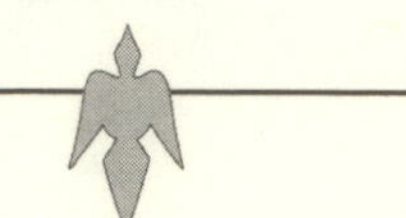

Although a considerable degree of intermarriage took place between the two groups, Interior Tlingits fought with Tahltans and Kaskas in the nineteenth century, mainly over trapping territory.

Contemporary Information

Government/Reservations Many Tlingits live in their traditional villages, although many also live in urban centers in Alaska and the Northwest. In the Yukon, Tlingits form a part of the Carcross Tagish First Nation (Da Ka Nation Tribal Council). The Teslin Tlingit Council Band (part of the Da Ka Nation) controls three reserves on 187 hectares of land in the southwest part of Teslin. The 1993 population was 482 (119 houses). Elections have been mandatory (imposed by the Department of Indian Affairs) since the late 1940s. The clan leadership is composed of a chief and five counselors. Children attend band and provincial schools. Facilities on the reserves include two administration buildings, a longhouse, a clinic, a recreation center, and a drop-in center.

Economy At its founding in the early 1970s, Sealaska Corporation received 280,000 acres of timberland and $200 million. Each native village received surface land rights, and the corporation received subsurface rights to the same land. These corporations became active in logging, fishing, and land development.

Important economic activities of the Teslin Tlingit Council Band include a coin laundry. The band plans to organize a development corporation.

Legal Status The Sealaska Regional Corporation (Tlingit-Haida Central Council) is a federally recognized tribal entity. The council itself is composed of elected delegates from 14 communities in southeast Alaska and of representatives from other communities. The Hydaburg Cooperative Association is a federally recognized tribal entity.

Under the Alaska Native Claims Settlement Act of 1971, 12 regional for-profit corporations (e.g., Sealaska Corporation) and roughly 200 village corporations were created and given nearly $1 billion and fee-simple title to 44 million acres in exchange for the extinction of aboriginal title to Alaska. The not-for-profit Sealaska Heritage Foundation supports a number of cultural activities.

Tlingit and Haida native villages include Angoon, Craig, Hoonah, Hydaburg, Juneau (Juneau Fishing Village), Kake, Klawok, Klukwan, Saxman, Sitka Village, and Yakutat.

The Teslin and Atlin Bands of Tlingit Indians are formally recognized by Canada.

Daily Life Most villages now have full electric service as well as amenities such as satellite television. Every village has a grade school, some have high schools, and all have at least one church. The traditional clan system still exists but has declined in importance. Relatively few people speak the Tlingit language, although it is now being taught in school. Most Tlingits are Christian. Urban Tlingits show a markedly greater level of assimilation than do those away from cities.

The ANB and the ANS now work toward cultural renewal. Some aspects of traditional culture and ceremonialism, such as potlatching (the memorial for the dead), singing and dancing, and crest arts (especially woodworking and carving) have undergone a revival in recent years.

Inland Tlingits became formally linked with the "outside" world when the Alaska Highway opened in the 1940s and again in the 1960s when radio and television became generally available. Most, especially the younger people, speak only English. There is still some traditional potlatching.

Tsimshian

Tsimshian (`Tsim shin, or `Sim shin) is a Coast and Southern Tsimshian self-designation meaning "inside the Skeena River." The Tsimshian were a group of linguistically and culturally related people. Their four major divisions were the Nishga (Nass River), Gitksan (Upper Skeena River), Coast Tsimshian (Lower Skeena River and adjacent coast), and Southern Tsimshian (southern coast and islands). They were culturally similar to the Haida and Tlingit.

Location Northwestern British Columbia, the home of the Tsimshian, is heavily forested, and the climate is wet, with coastal regions marked by numerous fjords

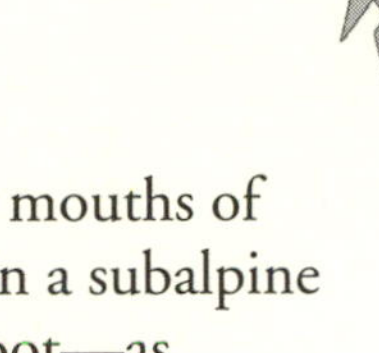

and islands. Most villages were along the mouths of the Nass and Skeena Rivers. Some were in a subalpine zone, where drier land permitted more foot—as opposed to canoe—travel. In the 1990s, Tsimshians live in villages and towns in northwest British Columbia and in cities throughout the Northwest.

Annette Island, on which a reserve is located, is about 16 miles south of Ketchikan, Alaska.

Population The Tsimshian population was about 8,000–10,000 in 1800. In the early 1990s there were about 2,450 Tsimshians in the United States and 4,550 in Canada.

Language The various Tsimshian languages (Coast and Southern Tsimshian, Nishga, and Gitksan) and dialects were not all mutually intelligible.

Historical Information

History Relatively recent arrivals to the Northwest Coast, the Tsimshian began pushing the Tlingit farther north and the Haisla farther south and fighting the Heiltsuk for coastal areas around the mid–eighteenth century. They had already seen European goods when a Southern Tsimshian group met a British trade ship in 1787. Interracial contact remained sporadic until the Hudson's Bay Company founded Fort Simpson in 1831. Many Coast Tsimshian subsequently relocated near the fort in order to strengthen and protect their key role in the local fur trade.

The basic structures of native culture remained intact until the arrival of Christian missionaries. William Duncan, an Anglican, appeared in 1857. Five years later, he and some Indian converts founded the Christian colony of Metlakatla, which grew until it moved in 1887 to Annette Island, Alaska, and was renamed New Metlakatla. Residents there had to renounce traditional life and accept Duncan's utopian principles. Congress established the Annette Island Reserve in 1891. This community prospered until it was beset by factionalism and decline until the 1930s, when it began to recover.

Shortly after the arrival of a Methodist missionary at Fort Simpson in 1874, that community became thoroughly Christianized. As missions spread in the area, Indians replaced many native customs,

William Duncan, an Anglican, and some Indian converts founded the Christian colony of Metlakatla in 1862. Pictured here is the Mission Sunday School of the Reverend William Duncan, a Tsimshian, in Old Metlakatla before 1883.

such as the erection of totem poles, with Euro-Canadian styles and customs. The gold rush of 1867 also brought increased contact with non-natives. Although Indians still practiced some subsistence activities, they also began the switch to a wage economy. The first local salmon cannery was established in 1876, for instance.

During the late nineteenth century, Tsimshian villages became official "bands" with unilaterally imposed reserves under the federal Indian Act. At the end of the century, most coastal bands had been converted to Christianity and the Nass people had abandoned their villages and became largely assimilated into Canadian society; the Gitksan, however, maintained many aspects of traditional culture.

A federal and provincial school system replaced missionary schools in the mid–twentieth century. The enforced enfranchisement of women, air links to the villages (1950s), and television (1960s) and satellite reception (1980s) have generally strengthened the

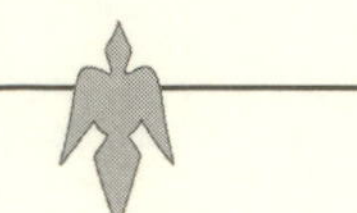

forces of secularization, urbanization, and democratization, although more traditional cultural elements were reestablished after the 1960s.

Religion Potlatches, feasts, and secret society dances, all highly ritualistic, were held in winter. The dances were apparently borrowed from Haisla and Heiltsuk-speaking people in about the seventeenth or eighteenth century. House chiefs also served as religious leaders, ensuring that people showed the proper respect for animals and spirits. They also served as "power," "real," and "great" dancers, in which roles they dramatized and validated the powers of their ancestors and their house and initiated young people into ritual roles.

Religious specialists called blowing shamans complemented the chiefs' activities. Their responsibilities included curing as well as controlling the weather. Witches worked in secret to harm people. They had no recourse to spiritual beings but used items such as bits of corpse to make people unclean and thus unready for a supernatural encounter.

Government Each Tsimshian village was as autonomous from another as it was from a Haida or a Tlingit village. Local groups (26 in the mid–nineteenth century) had permanent winter villages as well as spring and summer fishing villages and camps.

"Houses" (maternal extended families) were presided over by (usually male) chiefs, who, in addition to their religious responsibilities, managed the economic resources of the house. Other house members provided for their economic welfare.

Several houses made up a village. Each group of house chiefs had an established rank order, so that the village chief (a position not present in all villages) was the highest-ranking house chief in the village.

Customs Wolf, Eagle, Raven, and Blackfish or Killer Whale constituted the four matrilineal clans, although traditionally most villages may have had a dual division. The "house" was the basic social unit. It controlled fishing camps and berry and hunting territories and also owned songs, crests, names, and other privileges. Tsimshian people belonged to one of the following groups: chiefs, named families of lesser rank, or free but unnamed people. Slaves were usually imported.

All important life-cycle events necessitated ritual duties and wealth exchanges. Such events included birth, naming, ear (boy) and lip (girl) piercing at about age seven, second naming (and girls' seclusion) at puberty, marriage (arranged with the purpose of advancing social rank), house building, and death. Insults or mistakes, however inadvertent, were occasions for face- (and rank-) saving feasts or potlatches. At puberty, boys sought guardian spirits by bathing and fasting in remote places. Men purified themselves before hunting and fishing. There were also rituals connected with the first seasonal fish catch. Corpses, along with secret society regalia, were generally burned. Ghosts were regarded as possibly being dangerous to the living.

Feasts, such as potlatches, were the glue that held society together; they expressed and maintained the social order, inheritance, and succession. They generally lasted for several days and included dancing, singing, and gift giving. Slaves were often given as gifts; as a wealthy people, the Tsimshian had many of them.

Dwellings Winter longhouses were typical of the area. Post and beam structures constructed of red cedar timbers; gabled roofs covered their roughly 2,500 square feet of living space. Inside were central fireplaces and side platforms for sleeping. Cedar-bark mats provided insulation. The door, which occasionally consisted of holes in totem poles, faced the beach. Chiefs' dwellings became dance houses in winter.

The chief and his immediate family occupied the rear of the house. House fronts were painted with crest designs. Other structures included menstrual huts, summer houses, and sweat lodges.

Diet People ate halibut, salmon, herring spawn, water birds and their eggs, seal, sea lion, sea otter, and shellfish. Eulachon oil ("grease") was obtained by boiling rotting eulachon and skimming the fat. Other important foods included dried seaweed, the cambium of several trees, berries, crabapples, deer, elk, mountain goat, mountain sheep, bear, caribou, and moose.

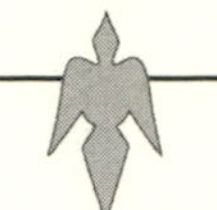

Key Technology Fishing equipment included traps, bent hook and line (of cedar-bark cord), harpoons, and porpoise lures. The yagatl, an underwater net controlled by a ring and pole, was used to catch eulachon. Women wove clothing and other items from the inner bark of red cedar trees. They also wove plaited and twined baskets from cedar (coast) and maple and birch (inland) bark. Men carved wooden items, including totem poles, storage boxes, chests, canoes, tools, cradles, and fishing and hunting gear. Other tools and implements included bark dishes, stone chisel, and goat horn arrow points. Native copper was used for some tools and ceremonial items.

Trade The Tsimshian enjoyed a highly profitable monopoly on the grease (eulachon oil) trade. At a huge regional trade fair held every spring at the mouth of the Nass River, Coast Tsimshian peoples traded grease with interior Tsimshians (Gitksans) for furs, dressed deer and moose skins, and porcupine-quill embroidery, which the latter had obtained from interior tribes such as the Carrier. From the Haida the Tsimshians received canoes, carved boxes, dried halibut, and chewing tobacco. Foods, carved horn spoons, and slaves were also traded.

Notable Arts Carved wood items included painted boxes, rattles, masks and other ceremonial items, and totem poles. House fronts were painted elaborately. Basketry was also an art.

Transportation Transportation between most sites and activities was by sea canoe, often obtained from the Haida, as well as bark canoe or raft.

Dress Women wore Chilkat robes (they may have originated the style and technique), woven from mountain goat wool and yellow cedar bark into colored lineage crest designs. They also wore labrets. Both sexes wore skin aprons, cedar-bark robes, conical spruce basketry hats, and fur or skin robes in winter. Snowshoes were used in winter.

War and Weapons War occurred between clans in different groups or tribes for reasons of plunder or, more often, revenge. Warfare included killing, torture, and the taking of women and children as slaves. Peace settlements involved the ceremonial kidnapping and ransom of high-ranking individuals, followed by dancing and feasting. Enemies included Tlingit, Haida, Kwakiutl, and Salish groups. The people fought with daggers, bone-tipped spears, war clubs, and bows and arrows. Fighters also wore hide and rod armor over moose-hide shirts as well as wooden helmets.

Contemporary Information

Government/Reservations In 1984, 255 reserves (roughly 36,000 hectares) were connected with 17 Tsimshian bands from all four major divisions. See "Daily Life" for profiles of the bands.

Metlakatla has had a city council since 1915. There are 12 democratically elected council members. The Annette Island Reserve (86,471 acres; 1,185 Native Americans in 1990) was established in 1891.

Economy Many households still engage in traditional subsistence activities and eat locally harvested foods. Some bands own logging operations. Other sources of jobs include the commercial fishing and logging industries as well as band government, hatchery projects, and fish farms. There are some individual band enterprises, including crafts for the tourist trade. Tsimshians endure relatively high un- and underemployment.

Legal Status In 1976, the Nisga'a Tribal Council (which represents about 6,000 Nisga'a) began negotiating a comprehensive land claim with the federal government. Provincial officials joined the discussions in 1990. In 1996, the parties reached an Agreement-in-Principle that will form the basis for a final agreement. Provisions include a cash payment of $190 million as well as Indian ownership and self-governance of over 1,900 square kilometers of the Nass River Valley. Also addressed are issues pertaining to taxation, the environment, access to land, land use, mineral rights, and cultural artifacts. This would be the first modern-day treaty in British Columbia.

The Annette Island Reserve is a federally recognized tribal entity. See "Daily Life" for federally and provincially recognized tribal councils.

Daily Life Society and individuals are regulated by a blend of traditional and Anglo institutions. For instance, much ceremonialism was suppressed and replaced over the years by clubs, bands, organizations, and other structures more typical of Anglo society. Tsimshian children receive both English and traditional names, including rank if appropriate. Among some groups, houses still control fishing and hunting places as well as names and privileges.

Most schools contain bilingual-bicultural programs. Port Simpson has the largest concentration of Tsimshian people. Clans still regulate marriage and carry out other roles. Potlatches and other feasts and traditional activities are very much alive. English is the first language for most people.

In 1970, 'Ksan was established, an open-air museum representing a Gitksan village of circa 1800. It also contains an art school and serves as a center for preserving and rebuilding Indian culture. Many of the best contemporary native artists train there. In part because of the existence of 'Ksan, Tsimshian art itself has come back from near obscurity to reclaim its traditions.

Metlakatla remains something of a successful utopian community, based on communal rather than individual values. Since the 1970s, an effort has been underway to reinvigorate traditional culture there.

Tsimshian bands in British Columbia include (statistics are as of 1995):

Gitanmaax Band is located five kilometers west of New Hazelton, British Columbia. The population is 1,632, of whom 665 live in 165 houses on the reserve. Elections are held under the provisions of the Indian Act. Children attend band and provincial schools. The band is affiliated with the Gitksan Wet'suwet'en Local Services Society (GWLSS). Important economic resources and activities include a campground, a taxi service. and lumber activities. Facilities include offices, a community hall, a clinic, an art school, a youth center, and a church.

Gitanyow Band, formerly Kitwancool Band, is located 24 kilometers north of Gitwangah Indian Village. The population is 595, of whom 342 live in 65 houses on the reserve. Elections are held under the provisions of the Indian Act. Children attend band schools. The band is affiliated with the GWLSS. Important economic resources and activities include fishing, logging, and tourism. Facilities include offices, a community hall, a clinic, a longhouse, and churches.

Gitlakdamit Band controls 30 reserves on 2,000 hectares of land 112 kilometers from Terrace. The local community of New Aiyansh was established in 1964. The population is 1,463, of whom 682 live in 178 houses on the reserves. Elections are held under the provisions of the Indian Act. The band is affiliated with the Nisga'a Tribal Council (NTC). Children attend band and provincial schools. Important economic resources and activities include a minimall. Facilities include a newspaper, a radio and local television rebroadcast station, offices, a community hall, a youth center, and a church.

Gitsegukla Band is located 33 kilometers west of New Hazelton. The population is 721, of whom 454 live in 123 houses on the reserve. Elections are held under the provisions of the Indian Act. The band is affiliated with the GWLSS. Children attend band and provincial schools. Important economic resources and activities include a large housing project, logging, and a grocery store. Facilities include offices, a community hall, a clinic, and churches.

Gitwangah Band is located 50 kilometers southwest of New Hazelton. The population is 905, of whom 430 live in 104 houses on the reserve. Elections are held under the provisions of the Indian Act. The band is affiliated with the GWLSS. Children attend band and provincial schools. Important economic resources and activities include a sawmill, logging, fishing, a grocery store, and a gas station. Facilities include offices, a community hall, a clinic, an alcohol treatment center, and churches.

Gitwinksihlkw Band, formerly Canyon City Band, controls six reserves on 655 hectares of land 120 kilometers from Terrace. The on-reserve population lives in 43 houses on the reserves. Elections are held by custom. The band is affiliated with the NTC. Children attend band and provincial schools. Important economic resources and activities include logging and a campground. Facilities include offices, a community hall, and a fire station.

Glen Vowell/Sikokoak Band is located 12 kilometers north of Hazelton. The population is 322, of whom 141 live in 55 houses on the reserve. Elections are held under the provisions of the Indian

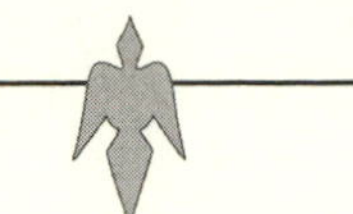

Act. The band is affiliated with the GWLSS. Children attend band and provincial schools. Important economic resources and activities include harvesting wood and an upholstery shop. Facilities include offices, a community hall, a clinic, a fire station, and a church.

Hartley Bay Band controls 14 reserves on 520 hectares of land 144 kilometers south of Prince Rupert. The population is 582, of whom 150 live in 78 houses on the reserves. Elections are held by custom. The band is affiliated with the North Coast Tribal Council and the Tsimshian Tribal Council (TTC). Children attend provincial schools on the reserves. Important economic resources and activities include a freight service, fishing, and a store. Facilities include offices and a nursery school.

Kincolith Band is affiliated with the NTC. The population is 1,250, of whom 370 live on reserve land.

Kispiox Band is located 16 kilometers north of Hazelton. The population is 1,184, of whom 525 live in 153 houses on the reserves. Elections are held under the provisions of the Indian Act. The band is affiliated with the GWLSS. Important economic resources and activities include a fish hatchery, an art studio, a cafe, and three grocery stores. Facilities include offices, a community hall, recreation grounds, and churches.

Kitasoo Band controls 14 reserves on 598 hectares of land on Swindle Island. The population is 423, of whom 319 live in 85 houses on the reserves. Elections are held under the provisions of the Indian Act. The band is affiliated with the Oweekeno/ Kitasoo Nuxalk Tribal Council. Children attend band schools. Important economic resources and activities include a wood shop, a sawmill, a seafood processing plant, a fish farm, a store, and an ice plant. Facilities include offices, a community hall, a drop-in center, and a church.

Kitkatla Band controls 21 reserves on 1,885 hectares of land 72 kilometers southwest of Prince Rupert. The population is 1,304, of whom 407 live in 125 houses on the reserves. Elections are held by custom. The band is affiliated with the North Coast Tribal Council and the TTC. Children attend band and provincial schools. Important economic resources and activities include fishery, video games rental, and a taxi service. Facilities include offices, a community hall, a recreation hall, and churches.

Kitselas Band controls nine reserves on 1,103 hectares of land east of Terrace. The population is 421, of whom 163 live in 36 houses on the reserves. Elections are held according to the provisions of the Indian Act. The band is affiliated with the TTC. Children attend provincial schools. Important economic resources and activities include plans for large tourism and real estate developments. Facilities include offices, a community hall, and a longhouse.

Kitsumkalum Band controls three reserves on 588 hectares of land 5 kilometers west of Terrace. The population is 540, of whom 191 live in 55 houses on the reserves. Elections are held according to the provisions of the Indian Act. The band is affiliated with the TTC. Children attend provincial schools. Important economic resources and activities include a recreational vehicle park, a boat launch, a guide service, a crafts shop, and a motel. Facilities include offices, a recreation center, and a warehouse.

Lakalzap Band controls three reserves on 1,836 hectares of land 144 kilometers from Terrace. The population is 1,375, of whom 617 live in 110 houses on the reserves. Elections are held according to the provisions of the Indian Act. The band is affiliated with the NTC. Children attend band and provincial schools. Important economic resources and activities include a water taxi service, a bus service, and logging. Facilities include offices, a community hall, a warehouse, and a fire station.

Lax Kw'Alaams Band controls 72 reserves on 1,049 hectares of land. The population is 2,404, of whom 1,049 live in 211 houses on the reserves. Elections are held according to the provisions of the Indian Act. The band is affiliated with the TTC. Children attend band and provincial schools. Important economic resources and activities include a store, a video store, and a motel. Facilities include offices, a community hall, and a seniors' home.

Metlakatla Band controls 16 reserves on 162 hectares of land five kilometers from Prince Rupert. The population is 528, of whom 101 live in 47 houses on the reserves. Elections are held according to the provisions of the Indian Act. The band is affiliated with the North Coast Tribal Council. Children attend provincial schools. Important economic resources and

activities include the Metlakatla Development Corporation, a ferry service, industrial real estate, and small businesses. Facilities include offices, a community hall, a museum, and a recreation building.

Tulalip

See Salish, Southern Coast

Tututni

See Tolowa (Chapter 2); Upper Umpqua

Twana

See Salish, Southern Coast

Upper Coquille

See Upper Umpqua

Upper Skagit

See Salish, Southern Coast

Upper Umpqua

Upper Umpqua (`Ump kwä) were one of several Athapaskan-speaking groups of southwest Oregon. The word may have meant "high and low water," "thunder," or "boat over the water." Their self-designation was *Etnemitane.*

Location There were traditionally five bands in southwest Oregon, in the valley of the south fork of the Umpqua River. There were other groups to the west and south, including coastal areas. These included Upper Coquilles (Mishikhwutmetunne), Chetco, Chasta Costa, Tututni (all four so-called Coast Rogue Indians), Galice, and Applegate. Most descendants of these people live on or near reservations in the same area (see "Government/ Reservations" under "Contemporary Information").

Population There were roughly 5,600 Oregon Athapaskans in the late eighteenth century. In 1990 there were roughly 3,000 Grande Ronde Indians as well as 850 Cow Creek Indians. There were around 2,900 enrolled Siletz Indians in the mid-1990s.

Language Upper Umpqua, Galice-Applegate, the Tututni dialects (Mishikhwutmetunne, Tututni, Chasta Costa), and the Chetco dialect of the Tolowa language are all members of the Pacific branch of the Athapaskan language family.

Historical Information

History Non-Indian traders first arrived in the area in the late eighteenth century. The fur trade began around 1818, at which time a group of Umpquas was killed by traders, possibly Iroquois in the service of the North West Company. Hudson's Bay Company established Fort Umpqua in 1836. Around this time, previously unknown diseases began taking a serious toll on the Indians.

Sporadic, trade-based contact continued until the flood of settlers in the late 1840s and the gold rush (Rogue River Valley) of 1852. In 1851, the Tututnis traded 2.5 million acres of land for $28,500. Their bitterness when they subsequently understood the deal fueled their desire to extract revenge. They soon began killing whites and burning settlers' houses. Two years later, when a group of whites attacked some Chetco Indians after persuading them to disarm, the Chetcos attacked some soldiers, and the fighting spread.

Upper Umpquas stayed out of the war, having signed a land cession treaty in 1854 and moved two years later to the Grand Ronde Reservation. Some Upper Umpquas along with villages of different linguistic groups signed a treaty in 1853; in exchange for a land cession of more than 700 square miles, it recognized the existence of and called for a reservation for the Cow Creek Band of the Umpqua tribe. The Rogue River War of 1855–1856 provided an opportunity for whites to destroy game trails and hunting grounds and to appropriate and clear land for farms. Cow Creeks fled the area during this period, hiding in the mountains as refugees.

After the war, local Indians, once fiercely independent, were shattered. Some Upper Umpquas, Tututnis, Chetcos, Coquilles, Chasta Costas, and others were forced to walk over the mountains in

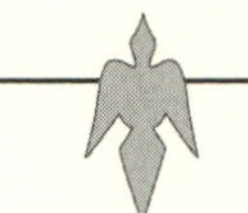

winter to the Grand Ronde Reservation. Other groups straggled in until 1857, when many Indians were moved to the Coast (or Siletz) Reservation, created two years earlier. On the way, and once there, several hundred died from exposure, starvation, and disease. Shamans who failed to cure the diseases were persecuted by their people, which gave the government an excuse to step in and disarm the Indians.

Meanwhile, the Grand Ronde Reservation was created in 1857. A school system designed to eradicate Indian culture was promptly set up. Many people left Grand Ronde for the Siletz Reservation or local communities. Those that remained worked as farmers or loggers.

Disparities between treaty and nontreaty Indians as well as agents' promotion of alcohol and thievery spread discord and exacerbated intertribal conflict. Many Indians escaped during this time but were rounded up by soldiers, who further abused them. Meanwhile, intermarriage further weakened tribal identities.

In 1865, a central strip was removed from the Siletz Reservation and opened for white settlement. The northern part then became the Siletz Reservation and the southern half (Coosans, Siuslawans, and Alseans) became the Alsea Reservation. The Bureau of Indian Affairs (BIA) turned all operations over to the Methodists, who worked to eradicate all vestiges of Indian culture. Indians danced the Ghost Dance in 1871; the variant Earth Lodge cult (locally known as the Warm House Dance) began in 1873. The Indian Shaker Church became popular beginning in the 1890s.

By 1894, most of the Siletz Reservation had been ceded to the public domain, and tribal languages had all but disappeared. Remaining residents worked in subsistence activities or in logging, cutting trees on their plundered reservation. By 1928, as a result of both widespread theft and the allotment processes, most of the land base was gone. Eighteen years later, the Confederated Tribes of the Siletz Reservation voted to accept termination of government recognition and services. The former reservation land base of 1.3 million acres had completely disappeared. Most of the allotments were lost shortly thereafter, mainly owing to nonpayment of taxes. Tribal life for most of the former Siletz tribes virtually disappeared. At the same time, although 537 acres of land had been added to the Grand Ronde Reservation in 1936, it, too, was declared terminated.

Meanwhile, the Cow Creek Band had intermarried extensively with other Indians as well as the French-Canadian population. The group created a formal government around 1918. They pressed their case for land claims litigation, but by the time they learned of the existence of the Indian Claims Commission, they had missed the deadline for filing a claim. Officially terminated in 1956, they were formally restored in 1982. Later in that decade they accepted a land settlement of $1.5 million and, over the objections of the BIA, placed the funds in a permanent endowment.

In 1973, the Siletz formed a new council to work for restoration of tribal status, which was obtained in 1977. The new 3,630-acre Siletz Reservation was created in 1980. Grand Ronde was restored in 1983, with all former rights save those pertaining to subsistence activities. A Tribal Council was formed the same year. Five years later, Congress gave the tribe 9,811 acres of timbered land, the income of which was used to purchase a 100-acre administrative land base.

Religion There were numerous opportunities for feasts and gift giving, such as birth, naming, first kills, puberty, war, death, and the make-doctor dance for new shamans. Feasts included both sacred and secular elements.

Government Each village had a chief who had several wives and slaves. He acted as an arbiter and received a share of all financial transactions as well as a food tithe. The position of chief was generally inherited through the male line.

Customs Although they slept in sweat houses, men and boys ate in the family house, where their mothers or wives cooked for them. Women gathered firewood and plants, made baskets, prepared foods, and carried water. Men fished, hunted, tanned hides, tended tobacco, and made nets, planks, and canoes.

Although society was ranked according to wealth, the divisions were not as rigid as they were farther north. Slaves were usually acquired in raids, although a chief could enslave a villager for improper behavior.

Most shamans were women. They cured by extracting a "pain," a small object filled with the patient's blood. Some groups also had common shamans, who blew smoke and waved a flicker feather over the patient. Unsuccessful cures sometimes led to the identification and murder of evil shamans (sorcerers). However, if the patient then died, a murder compensation had to be paid for the dead shaman. A shaman's fee was often paid to her husband. Shamans' powers derived from guardian spirits. Other powers conferred by certain spirits included the ability to cure rattlesnake bites, talk to herbs to receive remedies and love charms from them, and find lost objects.

Numerous rituals were associated with pregnancy and birth. Girls were secluded when they reached puberty and were not permitted to touch their hair or skin nor to eat anything except dry food for a year. They also had to swim twice a day, and their fathers also underwent certain restrictions. Women were purchased for marriage; children were illegitimate if their mothers were not paid for. Jealousy, meanness, and barrenness were acceptable reasons for divorce. Parents could also buy back their daughter, who then had considerable personal freedom.

The various death customs included the deathbed confession of wrongs, carriage of the corpse to the cemetery on a deerskin, and funeral orations. Mourners cut their hair and wore ashes and pitch on their heads and faces

Dwellings House size corresponded to the status of its residents. The plank house of a wealthy family was 20 by 30 feet, with three inside fires, fern and grass wall mats, and inside drying racks. Men slept in sweat houses, of which each village had at least one. People lived in brush houses in their summer hunting camps and in windbreaks on beaches in their fall fishing camps.

Diet Women dug roots such as camas and wild carrots beginning in early summer. Roots were steamed in large pits and prepared for storage. Women also gathered berries, which were usually eaten fresh. Men caught salmon, trout, and lamprey in summer. In late summer, young men hunted elk and deer in the mountains; the women then dried the meat on racks. Tututnis gathered acorns.

In fall, people moved to fishing camps to catch salmon and smoke salmon eggs. The first few salmon were eaten ritually. The people also burned berry patches in the fall; hunting grounds were burned every five years. Winter fare was soup of leftover bones and dried and rotted salmon heads and eggs. In spring, people ate seagull eggs and yellowjacket grubs, followed by bear and possibly beached whale. There was some local variation in diet, which was leveled out in part by trade.

Key Technology Fishing gear included harpoons, fences, clubs, and nets. In general, raw materials included wood (acorn stirrers, paddles, drying racks, drums, canoes, arrows, bows, spears, traps, fire drills, bowls), animal hides (blankets, aprons, capes, drums, quivers, tobacco pouches), stone (points, blades, fire holders, hammers, pestles), and bone (whistles, men's spoons). Women used their fingers or shells instead of bone spoons. Other items included deer hoof rattles, iris-fiber nets, maple-bark string, tule mats, and baskets.

Trade In general, camas and hides from the interior were exchanged for marine products from the coast. Other important trade items included dentalia shells from Vancouver and obsidian points from the south, both of which were valued as items of wealth.

Notable Arts Baskets, especially from the Chetco, were of particularly fine execution.

Transportation Dugout canoes provided the main mode of transportation.

Dress Women wore buckskin aprons; capes of tule, deerskin, elkskin, or woven rabbit furs; and basketry caps. Girls' aprons were made of maple bark. Men went naked or wore a front apron; they plucked their facial hair. Both sexes kept their hair long and covered their faces with elk or deer grease. Moccasins were only worn when men went into the brush. Chetco women adorned themselves with olivella beads.

War and Weapons Warriors wore very thick elk hide armor, danced a war dance before battle, and fought with bows and arrows. They sometimes paid for a charm to ensure that their arrows might be especially effective. All battlefield deaths were compensated for, a practice that tended to keep the casualty rate down.

Contemporary Information

Government/Reservations The Coquille Tribe, descendants of the Miluk (Lower) Coosans and the Mishikhwutmetunne, was formed in the aftermath of a land claims settlement (1975). In 1993 the tribe of 630 members was headquartered at Coos Bay, Oregon. It elects a seven-member council and owns 6.2 acres of land.

The Grande Ronde Indian Reservation (Confederated Tribes of Grande Ronde Indians: Shasta, Kalapuya, Rogue River, Molalla, Umpqua), created in 1857, comprises 9,811 acres. The confederation began in 1934 under the Indian Reorganization Act, and the group was incorporated in 1935. In 1974 the Confederated Tribes of Grande Ronde Indians grew out of the old Confederated Tribes of the Grande Ronde Community; they incorporated as a nonprofit organization the following year and were restored to federal status in 1983. The reservation is governed by a nine-member elected tribal council as well as tribal courts.

The Confederated Tribes of Siletz Indians were officially rerecognized in 1977 and received 3,630 acres of federal land in 1980. They are governed by a nine-member tribal council. The mid-1990s enrolled population was roughly 2,900.

The Smith River and Elk Valley Rancherias, home to Chetco and Tututni Indians, were terminated in 1960, only to be rerecognized in the 1980s.

The Cow Creek Band owns land in Canyonville, Oregon.

Economy The Coquilles are economically integrated with the local population. Timber revenues are the most important economic resource at Grande Ronde. Under the supervision of the Siletz Tribal Economic Development Corporation (STEDC), the tribe features a smokehouse and timber sales and plans to build a casino. The Cow Creek Band is part-owner of a bingo facility. Its members also work in logging and in the service sector.

Legal Status The Confederated Tribes of Grande Ronde Indians is a federally recognized tribal entity. The Confederated Tribes of Siletz Indians is a federally recognized tribal entity. The Cow Creek Band of Umpqua Indians, a nonprofit organization, is a federally recognized tribal entity (1984).

In 1983, Chetcos and Tututnis (Oregon Tolowas) formed the Tolowa Nation and petitioned the federal government for recognition, which had not been received as of 1997.

Daily Life Among the Oregon Tolowas, the Feather Dance remains important, as does the Indian Shaker Church. The native language remains alive. Facilities include a clinic, a tribal center, and a senior center.

Grande Ronde sponsors many social and economic programs, including student financial assistance and an annual powwow. There is a community center, a dental center, and a seniors' center, and there are plans to build housing on the reservation. Siletz features a tribal center, a housing program, and a clinic.

The Cow Creek Band hosts a week-long powwow in July. Members also gather in midsummer to pick blueberries. Many members are Catholic, but traditional burials and reinterments continue to be practiced.

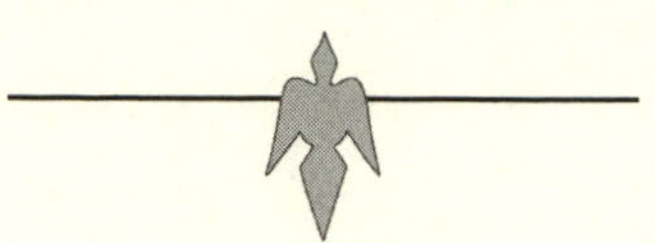

Chapter Four

The Great Basin

Left: A Ute camp near Denver, Colorado.
Right: Paiute men of California's Owens Valley wear ceremonial skirts of magpie feathers and twisted eagle down for a dance.
Far right: A Washoe man weaving a blanket.

Left: Chief Ouray is seated to the right of an unidentified man.

Great Basin

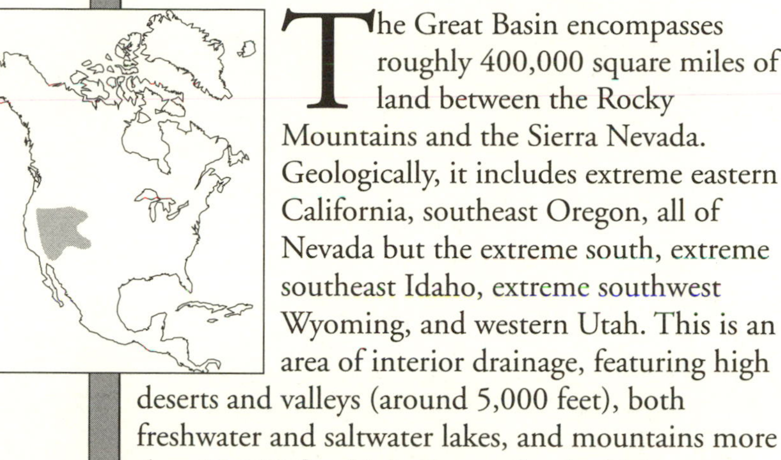

The Great Basin encompasses roughly 400,000 square miles of land between the Rocky Mountains and the Sierra Nevada. Geologically, it includes extreme eastern California, southeast Oregon, all of Nevada but the extreme south, extreme southeast Idaho, extreme southwest Wyoming, and western Utah. This is an area of interior drainage, featuring high deserts and valleys (around 5,000 feet), both freshwater and saltwater lakes, and mountains more than 12,000 feet high. Except for the high mountains, and especially in the south, there is relatively little precipitation.

Although Great Basin Indians share cultural traits and social connections with neighboring groups in other areas, so that the term "Great Basin cultural area" is a somewhat arbitrary convention, sufficient homogeneity existed within a defined region for anthropologists to consider the term legitimate. The boundaries of the Great Basin cultural area considerably exceeded those of the geographical one. Prior to 1600, between 40,000 and 50,000 people lived in an area extending from California east of the Sierra crest into eastern Oregon, central Idaho, extreme southwest Montana, western Wyoming, all of Nevada and Utah, the western two-thirds of Colorado, extreme northern New Mexico, and extreme northern and western Arizona.

Except for the Hokan-speaking Washoe, all late prehistoric Great Basin dwellers spoke dialects of Numic (Shoshonean) languages. Fluidity was a major characteristic of both territory and identity. That is, whereas today we speak of the Western Shoshone or the Northern Paiute, for linguistic and vaguely cultural purposes, these Indians had no such concepts. Since few groups regarded subsistence areas as exclusively controlled, they tended to range over wide distances, mixing and intermarrying with other Numic-speaking and neighboring groups.

Native Americans of the Great Basin

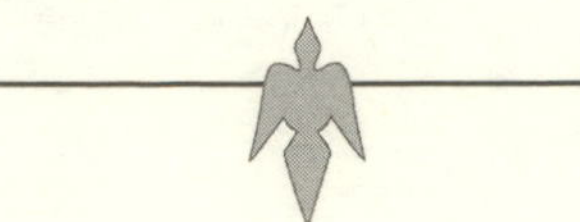

Social and economic organization, and therefore leadership, was decentralized, except in eastern groups after the introduction of the horse.

Residents of the Great Basin adapted very successfully to a large number of microenvironments that changed over time. Hunting and especially gathering were the primary activities. Creosote predominated in the southern and western Great Basin; saltbush and sagebrush, as well as many types of seed grasses, in the high deserts; and juniper, piñon, and other trees in the mountains. A few marshes supported cattails and rushes. The region supported a wide variety of animals, although distribution was uneven.

In general, and with the exception of eastern groups of the posthorse era, Indians of the Great Basin were relatively peaceful. Many groups turned briefly to raiding when faced in the mid–nineteenth century with Anglo attacks and the destruction of their habitat. Afterward, they tried to adjust to the new situation. Many people were able to retain strong elements of traditional culture, particularly religion and social structure. Still, they faced the usual severe discrimination and policies aimed at cultural genocide. Despite land claims victories and mineral leases, the economic and social situation for Great Basin Indians today remains difficult.

Archaeological evidence suggests that people first entered the Great Basin roughly 12,000 years ago, probably arriving from the south. These earliest people were probably not Shoshonean; they were displaced or absorbed by Shoshonean people, perhaps as recently as 1000. The basic hunting and gathering way of life for Great Basin Indians changed relatively little from the Early Archaic period (8000–2000 B.C.E.) through about 1600 C.E. The only exception is in southern Idaho (Snake and Salmon Rivers area), where people hunted now-extinct big game from the thirteenth century B.C.E. until about 6000 B.C.E.

In and around Utah, the typical foraging life was partially replaced from about 400 to 1300 by semisedentary communities based on farming. These Fremont culture people made containers and artistic figurines of clay. Although distinguished in part by their agricultural traditions, they continued to rely on hunting and gathering, especially in the north and west. Fremont cultures began to break up by around 1000, and by about 1350 the Archaic tradition had reestablished itself throughout the Great Basin, remaining more or less intact until the nineteenth century.

Most groups relied heavily on seed-bearing grasses and piñon seeds as well as roots (camas, yampa, bitterroot) and berries (buckberry, wolfberry, chokecherry). Birds, rabbits, deer, pronghorn antelope, rodents, fish, insects, and other nonplant resources probably made up around 25 percent of their diet, on average. For many groups, piñon seeds were the winter staple. Women extracted the seeds, then parched and ground them to make a mush or gruel. Acorns were another important food; after being leached (north and west), roasted, shelled, and ground, they were also stone boiled into a type of gruel. People in and near the southern deserts used plants such as agave, mesquite, and screwbean. Some southern groups also grew a limited amount of corn, beans, and squash.

Great Basin Indian technology was simple but effective. People used twined and coiled baskets, constructed primarily of willow, grasses, and roots, to carry burdens; to beat, winnow, and parch seeds; and to contain cold and boiling water. Pottery generally appeared with the Shoshonean people. Although plants and animals provided most raw materials, people also made tools and utensils out of stone, obsidian, bone, and wood. Nets, traps, snares, flaked stone knives, and bow and arrow were all used in the hunt. Fish were taken with nets, weirs, hook and line, basket traps, spears, and harpoons. The ubiquitous fire-hardened digging stick was the main root-gathering implement. Fire was started with drills, and the embers were often retained for storage and transportation. Some groups also encouraged certain plants by burning brushlands and forests as well as pruning. Some native irrigation was also practiced, especially in Owens Valley.

Both season and location determined the type of shelter. Brush windbreaks were common in warm weather. Winter houses were typically conical, roughly 10 feet high and 10–15 feet in diameter, and built of brush, bark, grass, and/or tule over piñon and/or juniper pole frames. Some northern groups covered the frame with skins. Doorways generally faced east. Caves were also utilized. As for clothing, most people

wore little except in the coldest weather. Women often wore twined sagebrush bark or willow hats and long gowns in winter. Men and women wore fur or twined-bark breechclouts. Fur or sage-bark moccasins were worn in winter, as were twined-bark or skin leggings. Fur (including buffalo) robes and rabbit-skin blankets, consisting of several strips of rabbit skin woven on a frame, were worn as capes during the day and used for coverings at night.

Aboriginal Great Basin society was relatively decentralized. The basic social and economic unit was the camp, or nuclear family, consisting of parents, children, and one or two grandparents, aunts, uncles, or cousins. This group was autonomous and self-governing by consensus, although an older male might be especially influential. Most labor was divided fairly rigidly by gender.

In regions of greater productivity, semipermanent winter villages emerged, which consisted of related family clusters. This type of interaction allowed people to share information about resources, to observe ceremonies and share mythological tales, and to trade. Headmen usually presided over villages; they delivered speeches on and coordinated subsistence activities, but the egalitarian impulse among Shoshonean people rendered their authority tenuous. Some more centralized societies emerged after the introduction of the horse.

Trade routes in the region, featuring Pacific coast shells, appeared at least by 5000 B.C.E. By around 2000 B.C.E., beads, obsidian, and other items were traded in a major network that ran from southern and central California to Nevada and Utah. Shell trade reached its maximum precontact distribution in the Great Basin by 1500. In general, Great Basin Indians exchanged hundreds of items between themselves and their neighbors, especially in the late eighteenth century, including hides, robes, food items, dresses, moccasins, medicinal plants, beads, and horses.

Aboriginal Shoshonean peoples recognized various beings or spirits capable of affecting human existence and may have recognized one or more supreme beings, such as the sun. They practiced both individual and group religious ceremonies. On an individual level, some people acquired supernatural powers, often through dreams or visions, from friendly spirits. Such powers brought them luck or skills. Certain rituals and behavior restrictions were associated with life-cycle events, especially girls' puberty and death. Group activities were mostly associated with the Round Dance. Performed on occasions such as piñon harvests and communal hunts, the Round Dance was associated with fertility, bounty, and rain.

Male or female shamans, although possessing no formal political power, often exercised influence in society owing to their abilities to cure and lead the ceremonies. People formally showed respect for plants and animals they had taken. They ritually disposed of certain animal parts, such as glands or organs, and addressed dead animals in a special way. Plants were often taken with an offering to their spirits and a prayer of thanks. Over 300 plant species were used medicinally. Plants and animals played an important role in mythology and regional cosmology. Rock art as well as small sculptures and figurines, some of which are at least several thousand years old, expressed aspects of prehistoric religion and ritual.

Late-eighteenth-century Spanish explorers of the Great Basin encountered Indians who had already been influenced by Euro-Americans. Utes escaping from Spanish captivity probably brought horses north of the Colorado River by the mid–seventeenth century. By the mid–eighteenth century, many eastern Shoshonean groups had thoroughly adopted the horse and had moved closer—both culturally and physically—to their fellow mounted Indians on the Great Plains. In contrast, some western Shoshoneans, whose environment did not favor mounted exploitation, remained without the horse (except as a food source) until the nineteenth century. Groups like the Goshute Shoshones and the Southern Paiutes became ready targets for Ute and Navajo slave raiders, who in turn were supported by the Spanish and Mexicans into the nineteenth century.

The Spanish explored the region and traded with the Indians, but they did not form colonies. Because of the isolation and relatively harsh environment of the Great Basin, it was the last region in the contiguous United States to be taken over by non-natives. However, change, when it did come, was rapid, largely because the ecology of the region was so fragile. Indians guided and traded with early explorers and trappers; many Indians first received firearms,

alcohol, and new diseases during that period. The first Mormon settlers appeared around the time the United States acquired the Great Basin, in the 1848 Treaty of Guadalupe Hidalgo. Ranchers and farmers soon completed the process, begun by explorers, trappers, emigrants, and miners, of resource degradation and destruction of aboriginal habitat.

Livestock were allowed to compact the soil and overgraze, ruining the seed grasses. Anglos appropriated scarce water sources and converted natural resource–rich lands to farms. They prohibited the Indians from managing grasslands through regular burnings and cut down vital piñon groves for firewood. Game animals, deprived of their own resources and increasingly crowded out, either disappeared or retreated to safer though far less accessible regions. In a relatively few years, the environment that had supported tens of thousands of Indians for millennia was gone. Hungry, weakened by disease, and victims of wanton violence, Indian populations began to decline dramatically.

Survivors responded to this new situation in several ways. Many groups withdrew farther from areas of white activity and tried to carry on as best they could. As these areas became increasingly marginal, the camp groups were forced into greater levels of cooperation. Some briefly formed bands to exploit non-Indian "resources" or even to engage in war. Some remained near the trails and simply begged for food. Some people attached themselves to ranches or farms, working for wages but living apart and trying to retain their identities as Indians. The money around mining towns attracted some Indians, but they were always severely discriminated against and forced to undertake the most menial and low-paying work.

In the 1850s, the government created the first of the Great Basin Indian reservations, on which it planned to transform the Indians into Christian farmers (although without providing adequate land or material or technical support). Native culture was ruthlessly suppressed. Children were kidnapped or otherwise forced to attend culture-killing boarding schools away from the reservation. To make matters worse, the extent of Indian land was gradually whittled away, in part as a result of the Dawes Act of 1886. Many Great Plains Indians (up to 40 percent or more) remained away from the reservations altogether, preferring to take their chances on their own.

The Ghost Dance originated among Northern Paiutes, beginning around 1869. According to the visions of a man named Wodziwob, Indians who danced and sang in a specified way could bring about the return of a precontact golden age, including the return to life of deceased Indians. This movement spread rapidly throughout the Great Basin and into California and lasted from a year or two up to several decades. In 1889, another Northern Paiute, named Wovoka, revived the Ghost Dance religion. His visions instructed Indians to perform the Ghost Dance, live in peace among themselves and with whites, work hard, and avoid alcohol. If they would do these things, they would achieve happiness in the next world. As interpreted by its adherents throughout much of the west, however, the religion promised an immediate salvation.

About the same time as the second Ghost Dance gained popularity, the Ute Bear Dance began to spread into southern Nevada, northern and western Arizona, and southern California. Also, as part of Bear Dance ceremonies, some southwestern Great Basin groups began adapting part of the Yuman mourning ceremony. The "cry," like the Ghost Dances, was probably meant to comfort the living under increasingly desperate conditions.

No Great Basin groups danced the Sun Dance before the nineteenth century, but among the Eastern Shoshone, who adopted it from the Comanche about 1800, it did precede reservation life. At the same time that more western groups were adopting and adapting the Ute Bear Dance, the Utes themselves, along with the Eastern Shoshones, were creating a new, modern Sun Dance. As the Sun Dance spread, its focus shifted away from warfare and buffalo hunting toward transcending contemporary problems such as widespread illness and growing poverty and toward restoring harmony. Christian elements also entered the Sun Dance. The Sun Dance today is very popular as an ongoing expression of interreservation religious life.

The Peyote religion, or Native American Church, also appeared in the Great Basin in the late nineteenth century. Originating in prehistoric Mexico, Peyotism today incorporates elements of Christianity while remaining a pan-Indian affair. It is

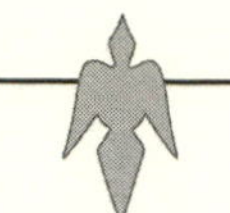

also part of the Traditional-Unity Movement, a recent tradition born of the political struggles of the 1960s and 1970s that incorporates elements of the Sun Dance, Sweat Lodge, and Sacred Pipe ceremonies. This movement and its associated ceremonies are particularly strong at the Fort McDermitt Reservation (Northern Paiute).

By the 1930s, the effort to make Christian farmers out of Great Basin Indians had failed. Instead, Indians had lost much of their land and, even though retaining their Indian identity, were in desperate straits socially and economically. Ranching, a key economic activity, supported only a small minority of reservation Indians. Severe discrimination and lack of language and job skills precluded significant off-reservation employment. Whites succeeded in destroying what viable Indian industry existed, such as the Pyramid Lake fisheries.

Conditions improved marginally into the 1940s as a result of the so-called Indian New Deal, which brought a degree of self-determination as well as increased federal support to the tribes. Land claims victories (over $137 million total) and mineral leases also brought money to selected groups beginning in the late 1930s. However, in a complete reversal of policy, the government began terminating some reservations and treaty responsibilities during the 1950s.

In the 1960s, the government again reversed course and significantly increased support to Indian peoples, helping to alleviate desperate poverty and usher in a renewed period of self-determination. Also, groups like the Northern Paiute and Western Shoshone Indians began a series of actions, such as hunting regardless of local laws and denouncing unfavorable bills before the Nevada legislature, to highlight their push for sovereignty and enforcement of treaty rights. By the 1970s, as a result of federal programs, continued land claims victories, tribal enterprises, and Indian political action, life on Great Basin reservations had improved significantly, if unevenly.

Despite these gains, Great Basin Indians continue to struggle. Chronic poverty and cultural devastation are difficult to overcome. Unemployment, substance abuse, and suicide rates remain high. Health facilities and services remain inadequate. Control over their economic destiny remains elusive. And, as in many Indian tribes, particularly in the west, disagreements between traditionalists and "progressives" divide communities.

Still, pride in Indian identity is at a high point today, as evidenced by the profusion of Indian newspapers and tribal historical and cultural projects. Many tribal governments make decisions in the traditional fashion, by consensus, rather than by majority rule. Traditional activities such as piñon harvesting, ceremonies, and crafts remain important parts of native identity. Women are increasingly participating in tribal government. Tribal businesses include agricultural markets, crafts enterprises, fish hatcheries, and smoke shops. Mineral and ranch leases also provide a large percentage of tribal income, and credit restrictions and cash flows have eased. Despite ongoing challenges, most Great Basin Indians remain committed to prospering as Indians.

Bannock

See Paiute, Northern; Shoshone, Northern

Goshute

See Shoshone, Western

Paiute, Northern

Northern Paiute (`Pī ūt) includes a number of seminomadic, culturally distinct, and politically autonomous Great Basin groups. "Northern Paiute" is a modern construction; aboriginally, these groups were tied together only by the awareness of a common language. Paiute may have meant "True Ute" or "Water Ute" and was applied only to the Southern Paiute until the 1850s. Their self-designation was *Numa,* or "People." Non-natives have sometimes called these people Digger Indians, Snakes (Northern Paiutes in Oregon), and Paviotso. The Bannock Indians were originally a Northern Paiute group from eastern Oregon.

Location. Traditionally, the groups now known as Northern Paiute ranged throughout present-day southeast Oregon, extreme northeast California, extreme southwest Idaho, and northwest Nevada. Bannock territory included southeastern Idaho and western Wyoming (the Snake River region). The highly diverse environment included lakes, mountains, high plains, rivers, freshwater marsh, and high desert. Elements of California culture entered the region through groups living on or near the Sierra Nevada. Presently, Northern Paiutes live on a number of their own reservations (see "Government/ Reservations" under "Contemporary Information"), on other nearby reservations, and among the area's general population.

Population The Paiute population in the early nineteenth century was roughly 7,500, excluding about 2,000 Bannocks. In 1990, about 6,300 Paiutes, including Paiute-Shoshones, lived on reservations.

Language With Mono, Northern Paiute is part of the Western Numic (Shoshonean) branch of the Uto-Aztecan linguistic family.

Historical Information

History People later called the Bannocks, or Snakes, acquired horses as early as the mid–eighteenth century. They soon joined the Northern Shoshone in southern Idaho in developing fully mounted bands and other aspects of Plains culture, including buffalo hunting, extensive warfare, and raiding for horses.

Early Northern Paiute contacts with fur traders such as Jedediah Smith (1827) and Peter Skene Ogden (1829) were friendly, although a party led by Joseph Walker (1833) massacred about 100 peaceful Indians. When reached by whites, the Indians already had a number of non-native items in their possession, such as Spanish blankets, horses, buffalo robes, and Euro-American goods.

In 1887, the Northern Paiute Wovoka, known to whites as Jack Wilson, originated the Ghost Dance religion. It was based on the belief that the world would be reborn with all Indians, alive and dead, living in a precontact paradise. Wovoka is seen seated in this 1923 publicity photo taken during the filming of the silent-era epic *The Covered Wagon.*

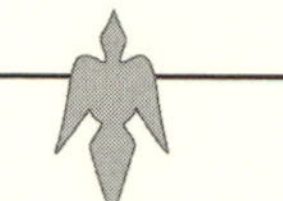

Most Northern Paiutes remained on foot until the late 1840s and 1850s. Around this time, heavy traffic on the Oregon and California Trails (late 1840s) and the gold rush of 1848 brought many non-natives through their territory. These people cut down piñon trees for fuel and housing, and their animals destroyed seed-bearing plants and fouled water supplies. Mining resulted in extensive and rapid resource degradation. New diseases took a heavy toll during this period. Indians responded by moving away from the invaders or attacking wagons for food and materials. White traders encouraged thefts by trading supplies for stolen items and animals. Some Indians began to live at the fringes of and work at white ranches and settlements.

Gold and silver strikes in the late 1850s fueled the cycle of conflict and violence. Local conflicts during this period included the brief Pyramid Lake war in 1860; the Owens Valley conflicts in 1862–1863; and the Coeur d'Alene war (1858–1859), which grew out of the Yakima war over white treaty violations. In the Snake war (1866–1867), Chiefs Paulina and Weawea led the Indians to early successes, but eventually the former was killed and the latter surrendered. Survivors settled on the Malheur Reservation (Oregon) in 1871. Winnemucca, who represented several hundred Northern Paiute in the 1860s and 1870s, participated in the Pyramid Lake war and, with his daughter Sarah, went on to serve as a negotiator and peacemaker. In 1873, he refused to take his band to the Malheur Reservation, holding out for a reservation of their own. The Bannocks, too, rebelled in a short-lived war over forced confinement on the Fort Hall Reservation and white treaty violations.

Beginning in 1859, the United States set aside land for Northern Paiute reservations. Eventually, a number of small reservations and colonies were created, ultimately to lose much of their land to non-Indian settlers. Most Northern Paiutes, however, drifted between reservations, combining traditional subsistence activities with growing dependence on local Anglo economies. Conflict on several reservations remained ongoing for decades (some issues are still pending) over issues such as water rights (Pyramid Lake, Walker River), white land usurpation, and fisheries destruction (Pyramid Lake). Refugees from the Bannock war were forced to move to the Yakima Reservation; from there many ultimately moved to the Warm Springs Reservation.

The government also established day and boarding schools from the late 1870s into the 1930s, including Sarah Winnemucca's school at Lovelock. Sarah Winnemucca, who published *Life Among the Paiutes* in 1884, also worked tirelessly, although ultimately unsuccessfully, for a permanent Paiute reservation. Northern Paiute children also attended Indian boarding schools across the United States. Most traditional subsistence activities ceased during that period, although people continue to gather certain foods. New economic activities included cattle ranching at Fort McDermitt, stock raising, haying, and various businesses.

In 1889, the Northern Paiute Wovoka, known to the whites as Jack Wilson, started a new Ghost Dance religion. It was based on the belief that the world would be reborn with all Indians, alive and dead, living in a precontact paradise. For this to happen, Indians must reject all non-native ways, especially alcohol; live together in peace; and pray and dance. This Ghost Dance followed a previous one established at Walker River in 1869.

Family organization remained more or less intact during the reservation period. By about 1900, Northern Paiutes had lost more than 95 percent of their aboriginal territory. Most groups accepted the Indian Reorganization Act (IRA) and adopted tribal councils during the 1930s. Shamanism has gradually declined over the years. The Native American Church has had adherents among the Northern Paiute since the 1930s, and the Sweat Lodge Movement became active during the 1960s.

Religion Power resided in any animate or inanimate object, feature, or phenomenon. Any person could seek power for help with a skill, but only shamans acquired enough to help, or hurt, others. A power source would expect certain specific behaviors to be followed. Most power sources also had mythological roles.

Shamans, male and female, were religious leaders. Their power often came in a recurring dream. They cured by sucking, retrieving a wandering soul, or administering medicines. Disease could be caused

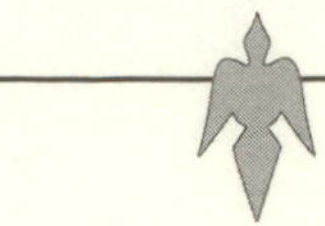

by soul loss, mishandling power, or sorcery. Some shamans could also control weather. Special objects as well as songs, mandated by the power dream, helped them perform their tasks. Power could also be inherited or sought by visiting certain caves.

The sun was considered an especially powerful spirit, and many people prayed to it daily. Some groups celebrated rituals associated with communal food drives or other food-related events.

Government Nuclear families, led (usually) by senior members, were the main political and economic unit. Where various families came together, the local camp was led by a headman who advised, gave speeches on right behavior, and facilitated consensus decisions. The position of headman was often, although not strictly, inherited in the male line. Camp composition changed regularly. Other elders were selected to take charge of various activities such as hunts and irrigation projects.

The traditional headman system was replaced at least in part by the emergence of chiefs during the mounted, raiding years of the 1860s and 1870s. Headmen returned during the early reservation years, however, followed by elected tribal councils beginning in the 1930s.

Customs Extended families came together semiannually (on occasions such as the fall piñon harvest) to form communities with distinct but not exclusive subsistence areas. Groups were generally named with relation to a food that they ate, a particular geographical region, or another category. After contact, some bands were named after local chiefs (e.g., Winnemucca).

Parents suggested marriages for children in their mid to late teens. Sometimes two or more siblings married two or more siblings. An exchange of presents and cohabitation formalized a marriage, with the couple usually living with the wife's family for the first year or so. A man could have more than one wife (additional wives might include his wife's sisters or his brother's widow).

New parents were subject to various food and behavior restrictions. Important ceremonies were the girls' puberty rite and the annual mourning ceremony. The former included running to and from a hill for five to ten mornings and making piles of dry brush along the way, bathing, and ritual food restrictions. Boys performed a ceremony at time of their first large game kill. They stood on a pile of sagebrush and chewed the meat and sage, placing it on their joints to make them strong.

The dead were wrapped in skin blankets and buried with their favorite possessions. Houses and other property were burned. Mourners cut their hair, wailed, and covered their faces with ashes and pitch. The mourning period lasted a year. Suspected witches were burned.

Northern Paiutes held athletic contests and played a number of games, such as the hand game, the four-stick game, and dice games.

Dwellings Dwelling style and type was marked by great seasonal and regional diversity. Wickiups, used mostly in summer, were huts of brush and reeds over willow pole frames. Winter houses in the north were a cone-shaped pole framework covered with tule mats and earth. Some western groups included a mat-covered entryway. All had central fires. In the mountains, people built semisubterranean winter houses of juniper and pine boughs covered with branches and dirt. Dispersed winter camps consisted of two or three related families (roughly 50 people). In late prehistoric times, the Bannock used buffalo skin tipis during winter.

A Bannock family in camp at the head of Medicine Lodge Creek, Idaho, in 1871. Dwelling style and type was marked by great seasonal and regional diversity.

Diet Diet also varied according to specific location. Plants supplied most food needs. They included roots, bulbs, seeds, nuts, rice grass (ground into meal), cattails, berries, and greens. Roots were either eaten raw or sun dried and stored. Pine nuts and acorns were especially important. Animal foods included fowl (and eggs), squirrel, duck, and other small game as well as mountain sheep, deer, buffalo, and elk. Rabbits were hunted in communal drives. Small mammals were either pit roasted, boiled, or dried for storage. Lizards, grubs, and insects were also eaten. Trout and other fish were crucial in some areas, less important in others. Fish were usually dried and stored for winter. Some groups cultivated wild seed-bearing plants. The Bannock fished for salmon in the Snake River and hunted buffalo in the fall.

Key Technology Seed beaters, conical carrying baskets, and twined trays for gathering plant material were just some of the baskets produced by Northern Paiute women. Women shelled and ground seeds and nuts with manos and metates or wood or stone mortars and stone pestles. They used fire-hardened digging sticks to extricate roots. Fish were taken with spears, harpoons, hooks, weirs, nets, basket traps, and poison. Irrigation was carried out with dams of boulders and brush and diversion channels. Diapers and similar items were made of softened bark or cattail fluff.

Some pottery was made after about 1000. Tule and cattails were used for many purposes, such as houses, boats, matting, bags, clothing, duck decoys, and sandals. Hunting technology, which differed according to location, included the bow and arrow, traps, corral, snares, deadfalls, and stone knives. Arrow shafts were straightened, smoothed and polished with stone tools, and kept in skin quivers.

Trade Northern Paiutes obtained some Shoshone mountain sheep horn bows in trade. They also traded fish, moccasins, and beads for pine nuts, fly larvae, and shells. Their trade partners included the Maidu, other Paiute groups, and the Western Shoshone. The Bannock traded for war horses with the Nez Percé.

Notable Arts Rock art in the region is at least several thousand years old. People also made various stone, wood, and/or clay art objects. Baskets, mainly twined, were largely utilitarian.

Transportation Hunters and travelers wore snowshoes in winter. Water transportation was by tule boat. Some groups, especially the Bannock, used horses from the mid–eighteenth century on.

Dress Again, there was much regional variation based on the availability of materials. Women tended to wear tule or skin skirts, aprons, or dresses, with rabbit-skin or hide capes in winter, the edges of which were sometimes fringed and beaded. They also wore tule or hide moccasins and basket caps. Men wove the rabbit-skin blankets on a loom.

Men wore breechclouts, buckskin (or rabbit-skin or twined-sagebrush) shirts, and rabbit-skin or hide robes or capes and caps in winter. Other winter wear included rabbit-skin socks and twined-sagebrush-bark or badger-skin boots. Both sexes wore hide or sagebrush-bark leggings during winter or while hunting. They also wore headbands and feather decorations in their hair. Men plucked their facial hair and eyebrows. Shell necklaces and face and body paint were usually reserved for dances.

War and Weapons Bannock enemies included the Blackfeet and sometimes the Crow and the Nez Percé. They fought with wood and horn bows and stone-tipped arrows, spears, buffalo hide shields, and clubs.

Contemporary Information

Government/Reservations The following are reservations, colonies, and rancherias that have significant Northern Paiute populations:

Duck Valley Reservation, Owyhee County, Idaho, and Elko County, Nevada (1877; Shoshone and Paiute): 289,819 total acres (in Nevada and Idaho); 1,021 Indians (1990); organized under the IRA; constitution and by-laws adopted, 1936; tribal council.

Fallon Reservation and Colony, Churchill County, Nevada (1887; Paiute and Shoshone): 5,540 acres; 356 resident Indians (1990); 900 enrolled members (1992); seven-member tribal council.

Fort McDermitt Reservation, Malheur County, Oregon, and Humboldt County, Nevada (1892;

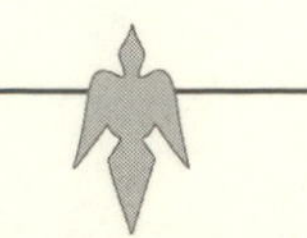

Bannock prisoners at the Snake River Reservation in Fort Hall, Idaho, September 1878.

Paiute and Shoshone): 35,183 acres; 387 resident Indians (1990); 689 enrolled members (1992); eight-member tribal council.

Lovelock Indian Colony, Pershing County, Nevada (1907): 20 acres; 80 resident Indians (1990); 110 enrolled members (1992); five-member tribal council.

Reno-Sparks Indian Colony, Washoe County, Nevada (1917; Washoe and Paiute): 1,984 acres; 262 resident Indians (1990); 724 enrolled members (1992); seven-member tribal council.

Summit Lake Reservation, Humboldt County, Nevada (1913): 10,500 acres; 6 resident Indians (1990); 112 enrolled members (1992); five-member tribal council.

Pyramid Lake Reservation, Lyon, Strorey, and Washoe Counties, Nevada (1874): 475,689 acres, including all of Pyramid Lake; 959 resident Indians (1990); 1,798 enrolled members (1992), almost all of whom live on the reservation; ten-member tribal council.

Walker River Reservation, Churchill, Lyon, and Mineral Counties, Nevada (1871): 323,406 acres; 822 residents (1993); 1,555 enrolled members (1993); seven-member tribal council.

Winnemucca Indian Colony, Humboldt County, Nevada (1971): 340 acres; 17 enrolled members (1992); five-member tribal council.

Yerington Reservation Colony and Campbell Ranch (Yerington Reservation and Trust Lands), Lyon County, Nevada (1916/1936): 1,653 total acres; 354 resident Indians (1992); 659 enrolled members (1992); organized under the IRA; constitution and by-laws adopted, 1937; seven-member tribal council.

Burns Paiute Indian Colony, Burns Paiute Reservation and Trust Lands, Harney County, Oregon (1863): 11,944 acres; 151 resident Indians (1990); 356 enrolled members (1992); five-member tribal council.

Warm Springs Reservation, Clakamas, Jefferson, Marian, and Wasco Counties, Oregon (1855; Confederated Tribes: Northern Paiute, Wallawalla [Warm Springs], and Wasco Indians): 643,507 acres; 2,818 resident Indians (1990); 123 enrolled members (1993). Decisions of the 11-member tribal council are subject to general review by referendum. The IRA

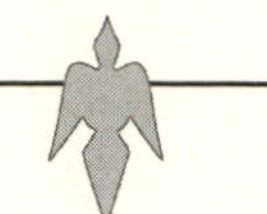

constitution was adopted in 1938 (*see also* Wishram in Chapter 5).

Cedarville Rancheria, Modoc County, California (1914): 17 acres; six resident Indians (1990); 22 enrolled members (1992);

Fort Bidwell Reservation, Modoc County, California (1897): 3,330 acres; 107 resident Indians (1990); 162 enrolled members (1992); five-member community council.

Bridgeport Indian Colony, Mono County, California (1976): 40 acres; 37 resident Indians (1990); 96 enrolled members (1992); five-member tribal council.

Susanville Rancheria, Lassen County, California (1923; Paiute, Maidu, and Pit River Indians): 140 acres; 154 Indians (1990); business council.

Benton (Utu Utu Gwaitu) Paiute Reservation, Mono County, California (1915): 160 acres; 52 resident Indians (1990); 84 enrolled members (1991); five-member tribal council.

Women are generally as active as men on tribal councils.

Economy Economic activities differ at each location. Some have no economic resources at all. Most feature some cattle ranching, agriculture on the larger reservations, and tribal businesses such as smoke shops, minimarts, and especially government (tribal) employment. Fishing and recreational activities dominate the economy at Pyramid Lake. Walker River is a member of the Council of Energy Resource Tribes (CERT). Some Indians work at off-reservation jobs. A few are able to support themselves with crafts work.

Legal Status The following Northern Paiute bands, locations, and peoples are federally recognized tribal entities: Cedarville Rancheria, Bridgeport Paiute Indian Colony, Burns Paiute Indian Colony, Fort Bidwell Indian Community, Fort McDermitt Paiute and Shoshone Tribes, Lovelock Paiute Tribe, Paiute-Shoshone Tribe of the Fallon Reservation and Colony, Pyramid Lake Paiute Tribe, Reno-Sparks Indian Colony, Shoshone-Paiute Tribes of the Duck Valley Reservation, Summit Lake Paiute Tribe, Susanville Indian Rancheria, Utu Utu Gwaitu Paiute Tribe, Walker River Paiute Tribe, Winnemucca Indian Colony, and Yerington Paiute Tribe. The Confederated Tribes of the Warm Springs Reservation is a federally recognized tribal entity. The Pahrump Band of Paiutes has applied for federal recognition, as have the Washoe/Paiute of Antelope Valley, California.

Daily Life Traditional kinship relations remain relatively strong among the Northern Paiute. Although there are various language preservation programs and activities, such as the dictionary and grammar produced by the Yerington tribe, few young Northern Paiute children outside of Fort McDermitt learn to speak their native language. Health, education, and outmigration continue as significant areas of concern.

Most Northern Paiutes are Christians, although some also practice elements of their traditional religion. Others participate in regional religions such as the Native American Church, the Sweat Lodge Movement, and the Sun Dance. The Sun Dance at McDermitt Reservation, introduced in 1981, varies considerably from sun dances held among Utes and Northern and Eastern Shoshones. It includes a pipe ceremony, a peyote ceremony, and a sweat lodge ceremony. Women can dance unless they are menstruating or are pregnant. Men and women pierce themselves. This ceremony is part of the Traditional-Unity Movement.

In 1991, the Truckee River compact confirmed water rights for Pyramid Lake and Fallon; it also granted compensation for water misappropriated earlier.

Paiute, Owens Valley

Owens Valley Paiute (`Pī ūt) is the name given to a number of Paiute groups distinguished in part by their semisettled, cooperative lifestyle as well as their irrigation practices. They were largely responsible for bringing elements of California culture into the southern Great Basin. Non-natives formerly included them with the Monache or Mono Indians. "Paiute" may have meant "True Ute" or "Water Ute" and was applied only to the Southern Paiute until the 1850s. Their self-designation was *Numa,* or "People."

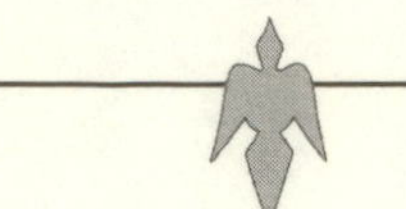

Location Traditionally, the groups now known as Owens Valley Paiute controlled the Owens River Valley, more than 80 miles long and an average of 7 miles wide. The fertile and well-watered region, east of the southern Sierra Nevada, contains a wealth of environmental diversity. Presently, Owens Valley Paiutes live on a number of their own reservations (see "Government/Reservations" under "Contemporary Information"), on other nearby reservations, and among the area's general population.

Population In the early nineteenth century there were about 7,500 total Paiutes (perhaps 1,500–2,000 Owens Valley Paiutes). In the 1990s, about 6,300 Paiutes, including about 2,500 Owens Valley Paiutes, lived on reservations.

Language The Owens Valley Paiutes' dialects of Mono are, with Northern Paiute, part of the Western Numic (Shoshonean) branch of the Uto-Aztecan linguistic family.

Historical Information

History Owens Valley Paiutes first saw non-natives in the early nineteenth century (although they may have seen Spanish explorers earlier). These early explorers, trappers, and prospectors encountered Indians who were already irrigating wild crops.

Military and civil personnel surveyed the region in the late 1850s with an eye toward establishing a reservation for local Indians. The first non-Indian settlers arrived in 1861. These ranchers grew crops that fed nearby miners and other whites. As the white population increased, so did conflicts over water rights and irrigated lands. Whites cut down vital piñons for fuel. Hungry Indians stole cattle, and whites retaliated by killing Indians. As of early 1862, however, the Indians still controlled the Owens Valley, because they formed local military alliances.

Camp Independence was founded in July 1862 as a military outpost. Fighting continued well into 1863, until whites got the upper hand by pursuing a scorched earth policy. Many Indians surrendered but were back in the valley within a few years. By this time, however, whites had taken over most of their best lands, and a diminished Indian population was left to settle around towns, ranches, and mining camps, working mostly as laborers. Indians on newly reserved lands, increasingly including Western Shoshone families, worked mainly as small-scale farmers.

Indian schools opened in the late nineteenth century, although formal reservations were not established until the twentieth. Too small for ranches, the early reservations supported small-scale farming as the main economic activity. However, many Indians still lived on nonreservation lands and on other, non-Paiute reservations.

From the early twentieth century through the 1930s, the city of Los Angeles bought most of Owens Valley, primarily for water rights. This development destroyed the local economy, eliminating the low-level Indian jobs. The city also proposed new ways to dispossess and consolidate the remaining Indians at that time. Ultimately, most Indian people approved of the series of land exchanges (those at Fort Independence rejected the plans). During the 1940s, the federal government built new housing and sewer and irrigation systems on the new Indian lands.

Religion Religious observances centered on round dances and festivities associated with the fall harvest. Professional singers in elaborate dance regalia performed in a dance corral. The girls' puberty ceremony was also important.

The cry was an annual Yuman-derived mourning ceremony for those who had died during the previous year. A ritual face washing (the first time since the death that the face was washed) marked the end of the official spousal year of mourning.

Male and female shamans were primarily doctors and religious leaders. Their power often came in a recurring dream. They cured by sucking, retrieving a wandering soul, or administering medicines. Disease was caused by soul loss, mishandling power, or sorcery. Special objects as well as songs, mandated by the power dream, helped them perform their tasks. They might acquire a good deal of clandestine political power by making headmen dependent on them.

Government Owens Valley Paiutes lived in semipermanent base camps, or hamlets, named for natural features. The camps were semipermanent in that (usually) the same families occupied them intermittently throughout the year and year to year. This level of social organization showed some similarities to California "tribelets." Within the camps families were completely independent. Families might share or coordinate in subsistence activities, but doing so was informal and unstructured.

Hamlets within a given area cooperated in intermarriage, irrigation, rabbit and deer drives, funerals, and the use of the sweat house. The headmen or chiefs directed these communal activities. Their other duties included conducting festivals and ceremonies, overseeing construction of the assembly lodge, and determining the death penalty for a shaman accused of witchcraft. The position was hereditary, usually in the male line.

Customs Although many people maintained the dams, an elected irrigator was responsible for watering a specific area. In summer, most families pursued hunting and gathering activities. They generally occupied their valley dwelling places in spring, the time of irrigation; fall, the time of social activities; and winter, unless the pine nut or Indian rice grass crops failed.

People held athletic contests and played a number of games, such as the hand game, shinny, the four-stick game, hoop and pole, and dice games.

Dwellings The Owens Valley Paiutes built several kinds of structures. The circular, semisubterranean sweat house served as an assembly house, a dormitory for young men, and a place for men to sweat. It was built, under sponsorship and supervision of local chief, of a central ridgepole supported by forked posts. A framework of poles was covered with earth and grass. Heat was by direct fire. The building also contained a central smoke hole, and the doorway faced east.

The winter family dwelling, 15 to 20 feet in diameter, was conical, semisubterranean, and built on a pole framework (no center ridgepole) covered with tule, grass, and sometimes earth. At mountain pine nut gathering winter camps, people built a wooden structure, perhaps with a gabled roof, consisting of poles of dead timber covered with bark slabs and boughs. In summer, ramadas of willow poles supporting a rectangular roof and covered with tule or brush, as well as semicircular brush windbreaks, served as the main living spaces.

Diet Diet also varied according to season and specific location. In general, the staple was pine nuts, harvested in autumn. Other important foods included acorns (prepared California-style); wild seeds, roots, and bulbs; berries; nuts; grasses (such as rice grass, ground into meal); cattails; and greens. Seeds were harvested in summer. Roots were either eaten raw or sand dried and stored. There was also some intentional irrigation of wild roots and seed-bearing plants.

In addition to the all-important plant resources, there was some fishing of suckers, minnows, and pupfish. The larvae and pupae of brine shrimp and fly were gathered, dried, shelled, and stored. People who had the assistance of a supernatural power hunted squirrels, quail, and other small game. The meat of small mammals was either pit roasted, boiled, or dried for storage. Rabbits were hunted in communal drives, deer in hunting teams. Caterpillar larvae were baked and sun dried.

Key Technology For irrigation, Owens Valley Paiutes used temporary dams and feeder streams of summer floodwaters. Their main tool was a long wooden water staff. They used nets to catch rabbits and fish. Fish

The Owens Valley Paiutes built several kinds of structures. Winter dwellings like this (early 1900s) were conical, semisubterranean, and built on a pole framework covered with tule, grass, and sometimes earth.

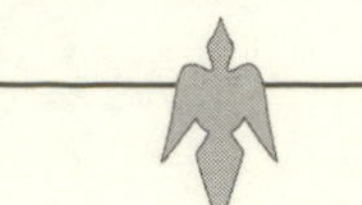

were also speared or poisoned and often dried and stored for winter.

Hunting technology differed according to location, but usually featured a sinew-backed juniper bow, arrows, nets, snares, and deadfalls. Twined and coiled basketry included burden baskets with tumplines for distance (even transmountain) carrying and seed beaters. Fire was made with a drill, and smoldering, cigar-shaped fire matches were used to transport it. Roots were dug with mountain mahogany digging sticks. Nuts were ground and shelled with manos and metates or wood or stone mortars and stone pestles. Some women made pottery, from the mid–seventeenth to the mid–nineteenth century.

Trade The Monache, Miwok, Tubatulabal, and Yokuts of California were important trade, marriage, and ceremonial partners. Strung shell beads served as a medium of exchange. Acorns were usually imported, from the Monache, for example, in exchange for salt and pine nuts. The Owens Valley Paiute also traded shell money to the Western Shoshone for salt and rabbit-skin blankets.

Notable Arts Local rock art is at least several thousand years old. Art objects were also made from a variety of materials, including stone, wood, and clay.

Transportation Some groups plied the lakes and marshes with tule boats.

Dress Type and style of clothing varied according to location. In general, women wore tule or skin skirts, aprons, or dresses. Some women wore relatively large basket caps. Men favored a breechclout and perhaps a buckskin (or rabbit-skin or twined-sagebrush) shirt.

In winter, both sexes wore rabbit-skin or hide capes, hide or sagebrush-bark leggings, tule or hide moccasins, and fur caps. Other winter wear included rabbit-skin socks and twined sagebrush-bark or badger-skin boots. Both sexes wore sagebrush sandals and socks, headbands, and feather decorations in their hair. Men plucked their facial hair and eyebrows.

Men wove rabbit-skin blankets on a vertical frame. Shell necklaces and face and body paint were usually reserved for dances. Diapers and other such items were made of softened bark or cattail fluff.

War and Weapons The aboriginal Owens Valley Paiute seldom fought.

Contemporary Information

Government/Reservations Significant numbers of Owens Valley Paiutes live on the following reservations:

Bishop Colony, Inyo County, California (1912; Owens Valley Paiute-Shoshone): 875 acres; 934 resident Indians (1990); 1,350 enrolled members (1991); five-member tribal council.

Fort Independence Reservation, Inyo County, California (1915; Owens Valley Paiute and Shoshone): 356 acres; 38 resident Indians (1990); 123 enrolled members (1991); three-member business council.

Lone Pine Reservation, Inyo County, California (1939; Owens Valley Paiute-Shoshone): 237 acres; 168 resident Indians (1990); 296 enrolled members (1991); five-member tribal council.

Big Pine Reservation, Inyo County, California (1939; Owens Valley Paiute and Shoshone): 279 acres; 331 resident Indians (1990); 413 enrolled members (1991); five-member tribal council.

Benton (Utu Utu Gwaitu) Paiute Reservation, Mono County, California (1915): 160 acres; 52 resident Indians (1990); 84 enrolled members (1991); five-member tribal council.

Each Owens Valley reservation is governed by a tribal council. Another administrative body, the Owens Valley Paiute-Shoshone Band of Indians (Big Pine, Lone Pine, Bishop, and Fort Independence) administers grant funds and valley-wide programs.

Economy The museum-cultural complex at Bishop provides some employment. Indians are also employed with the tribes and with a number of tribal businesses. Lone Pine, Fort Independence, and Benton have few current economic resources. There is some employment in local mines as well as some tourism.

Legal Status The following Paiute bands, locations, and peoples are federally recognized tribal entities:

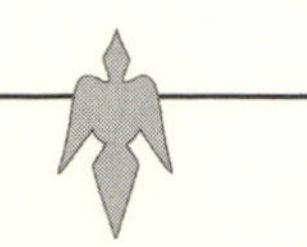

Paiute men of California's Owens Valley wear ceremonial skirts of magpie feathers and twisted eagle down for a dance staged in 1932. Shell necklaces and face and body paint were usually reserved for dances.

Fort Independence Indian Community, Paiute-Shoshone Indians of the Bishop Community of the Bishop Colony, Paiute-Shoshone Indians of the Lone Pine Community, and Utu Utu Gwaitu Paiute Tribe. The Washoe/Paiute of Antelope Valley, California, have petitioned for government recognition.

Daily Life The Bishop Colony maintains a culture center, a museum, and other facilities and programs. With the Owens Valley Paiute-Shoshone Band, they sponsor a summer powwow and rodeo. In the 1980s, elders persuaded the forest services not to apply pesticides against a Pandora moth infestation of nearby piñon pines; the moth's larvae are still gathered and eaten, as are pine nuts and other traditional foods. Much of the Owens River and its watershed has been diverted to Los Angeles. Few people still speak Owens Valley Mono, although individual reservations sponsor cultural awareness and language programs. Other ongoing traditional activities include the cry ceremony, food gathering, and crafts. Outmigration remains a problem, as are poverty, poor health, and the continuing lack of job opportunities.

Paiute, Southern

Southern Paiute (`Pī ūt) is a designation for approximately 16 seminomadic, culturally distinct, and politically autonomous Great Basin groups, such as Kaibab, Kaiparowits, Panguitch, Shivwits, Moapa, Paranigets, and Panaca. Their self-designation was *Nuwu,* or "Person." The Chemehuevi (*see* Chapter 1) were originally a Southern Paiute group. "Southern Paiute" is a modern construction and is more a

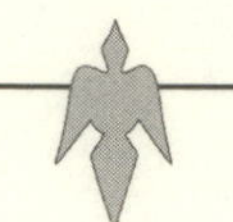

linguistic than a cultural convention. "Paiute" may have meant "True Ute" or "Water Ute" and was applied to the Northern Paiute only after the 1850s. To the north and northeast, some Southern Paiute groups merged with the Western and Southern Ute.

Location Southern Paiutes lived and continue to live in southwest Utah, southern Nevada, northwest Arizona, and southeast California. The San Juan Paiutes lived east of the Colorado River. Southern Paiute territory encompasses a great environmental diversity, including canyons and high deserts of the Colorado Plateau and the Great Basin.

Population The entire early-nineteenth-century Paiute population was roughly 7,500. In 1990, roughly 700 Southern Paiutes lived on reservations.

Language Southern Paiute languages belong to the southern Numic (Shoshonean) branch of the Uto-Aztecan language family. Their languages were mutually unintelligible with those of the Northern Paiutes.

Historical Information

History Numic-speaking Southern Paiutes came into their historic area around 1000, perhaps from around Death Valley. They gradually replaced Hopis in the south and may have learned agriculture from them. They encountered a Spanish expedition in 1776 but adopted neither horses nor much else of Spanish culture. However, diseases and some material items may have preceded actual contact. Some groups were practicing agriculture before 1800.

By 1830, the trail established by the first Spanish explorers was in heavy use. The increased traffic depleted the area's natural resources. The trail also facilitated raiding and trading parties by both Indian and non-native peoples. Mounted Utes and Navajos, and later Spanish expeditions and American trappers, were engaged in raiding and trading for Southern Paiute slaves. Starving Southern Paiutes sometimes sold their children for food. One effect of this situation was the Paiutes' self-removal from areas that were economically productive but close to slave raiders. The loss of a significant percentage of their young also contributed to the population reduction that was well under way by this time.

Mormon settlers arrived in 1847. At first participants in the slave trade, they had it legally abolished by the mid-1850s (although they continued to "adopt" Indian children). However, their practice of establishing settlements and missions on the best land, thereby depleting native resources and squeezing the Indians out, soon left the latter as beggars. Many Mormons alternated between seeing Indians negatively, as did most Americans, and positively, because of a perceived connection to biblical Israelites. About the same time, the Chemehuevi split off and moved down the Colorado River.

Some groups retaliated against whites by raiding their settlements. In a move to head off violence, six Mormon Southern Paiute headmen agreed in 1865 to move their people to the Uintah and Ouray Reservation, the home of their Ute enemies. The treaty remained unratified, however, and was later abandoned. By the 1870s roughly 80 percent of Southern Paiutes had died as a result of starvation and disease (Southern Paiute death rates exceeded birth rates well—in some cases, halfway—into the twentieth century). Survivors had begun the process of acculturation, gathering into larger camps and working in new white towns.

By executive order, a reservation (Moapa) of roughly 3,900 square miles was established in Nevada for the Southern Paiutes in 1872. Although few Indians moved there, it was expanded in 1874 with the idea that Southern Paiutes would be turned into farmers and ranchers. Soon, however, the reservation was greatly reduced in size. When promised federal support was not forthcoming, conditions began rapidly to deteriorate.

Meanwhile, Indians in southern Utah were either seeking wage work or trying desperately to hold on in their traditional locations. In the late 1880s, after a local white rancher persuaded the government to remove the Shivwits from their lands, the Shivwits Reservations was established in southern Utah, Though it was later expanded, the land was never good enough to support the population, even without inevitable conflicts over water and range rights. Many residents eventually moved away. Several small Mormon-affiliated farming communities had also been established by 1885.

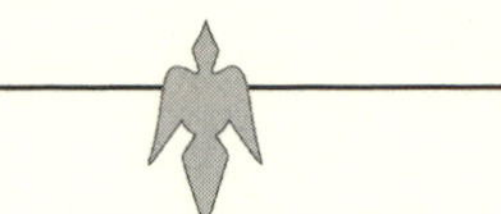

Several reservations were created for Southern Paiutes in the twentieth century (although one, the San Juan Paiute Reservation, was returned to the public domain shortly after an oil company expressed an interest in the parcel). In the mid-1950s, the Utah Paiute (Shivwits, Indian Peaks, Koosharem, and Kanosh Bands) were removed from federal control (terminated), although policy dictated that this would not happen until the people were ready and willing to take care of themselves. (The groups were restored in 1980.) The immediate effects of this action included a tremendous loss of the modest land base (through individual allotment sales and nonpayment of taxes), greater impoverishment, exploitative leases to non-Indians, removal of health services, and greatly increased social problems. When people tried to hunt rabbits again for survival, they discovered that many animals had been poisoned by fallout from the Nevada nuclear test site. Perhaps not surprisingly, many people left the reservation during these years.

In 1965, Southern Paiutes were awarded $8,250,000 ($0.27 an acre) as official compensation for their aboriginal land. The bands used their shares in different ways, but nearly all provided for some direct per capita payments as well as long-term concerns. New federal programs during this time also helped lift many Indians out of dire poverty and provide them with decent housing. During the 1960s, many people were poisoned with the insecticide DDT as a result of government and farmer spraying. Women basket makers, who pulled willow twigs through their teeth, were especially hard hit.

Religion Shamans provided religious leadership; they cured and conducted ceremonies such as the girls' puberty rite. They could be men or women, although women were more often considered evil. Power dreams, perhaps dreamed in a special cave, also provided instructions and songs.

Disease was attributed to sorcerers, a ghost-inspired poisonous object (necessitating the removal of the object by sucking), or soul loss (cured by the shaman's recapturing the soul). The mourning ceremony, or cry, was undertaken by wealthy relatives of a recently (three months to a year) deceased person so they could eat and sleep well. It was a feast at which many items were destroyed.

In general, groups came together for singing (men) and round dancing on occasions such as the harvest and before a war. Some groups danced the 1890 Ghost Dance.

Government Camp groups were composed of between 1 to 10 or 15 households, many of whom were related. They were led by a headman as well as the best hunters and gatherers. Headmen served in an advisory capacity. This position tended to remain in the family and among men but did not necessarily pass from father to son (except for the Chemehuevi and Las Vegas).

Customs The basic unit was the nuclear family. Each group generally gathered food, hunted, and camped together. Each was associated with a specific though nonexclusive geographic territory.

People married early; girls might be pre- or postpubescent. Most marriages were monogamous. Gender-determined rituals over infants' navel stumps underscored the priority placed on hunting for men and industry in domestic chores for women. Both new parents observed postpartum behavior and food restrictions.

Meat that a boy killed was given away to the elderly until he reached puberty. Puberty rites for both sexes included bathing, body painting, hair trimming, and physical endurance. Relatives prepared a corpse, then underwent behavior and food restrictions. Most groups cremated their dead. The dead person's possessions were burned or buried, and his or her house was torn down and moved. Some groups occasionally killed a relative as company for the deceased. There was a permanent taboo on using the name of the dead.

Springs were considered inheritable private property. People commonly gambled on hand and other games such as shinny, four-stick, hoop and pole, and target. Other games included ring and pin as well as athletic contests.

Dwellings Type of residence varied with season and locale. Winter dwellings included caves; conical houses of cedar bark, rushes, or grass over a tree limb framework; and gabled houses of willow and earth over pole frames. Most summer houses were brush

The Southern Paiutes migrated seasonally, following the food supply. Most summer houses were brush shelters, such as the ones depicted in this photograph of a Paiute village encampment.

shelters, shades, and windbreaks. Canvas or skin tipis were adapted from the Ute beginning in the mid–nineteenth century.

Diet Southern Paiutes migrated seasonally, following the food supply. Their diet was based on hunting, gathering, and some agriculture (mostly corn, beans, and squash, using floodplain or ditch irrigation). Tobacco patches and grasslands were burned to encourage growth.

Women gathered wild plants, including goldenrod and grass seeds, roots, pine nuts, yucca dates, cactus fruit, agave, nuts, juniper berries, mesquite, and screwbean. Grasshoppers, caterpillars, ant larvae, and insect grubs were also eaten. Seeds were parched, ground, and eaten as mush or as bread. Men hunted small game, the major source of protein, with the assistance of spirits and/or shamans. Rabbits were especially important. They were hunted individually or driven communally into 100-yard-long nets. Big game included deer, antelope, and mountain sheep. Some groups fished occasionally.

Key Technology Fire-hardened sticks were used to dig roots. Bows were made of cedar, locust, or mountain sheep horn. Basketry was a major craft. Coiled and twined baskets were used for winnowing and parching trays, hats, cradles, burden baskets, and containers. Twined seed beaters were an important gathering implement. Men made nets for hunting and carrying burdens. They also tanned hides, scraping with a sharp bone and rubbing with brain and bone marrow. Some pottery also existed.

Trade Southern Paiutes mainly traded with each other, although there was some intergroup trade as well as intermarriage and economic and ceremonial cooperation with Western Shoshone groups. The Chemehuevi and Las Vegas people were in direct contact with Indians of southern California, partly in connection with the trade in Pacific Coast haliotis shells. Both, but especially the Chemehuevi, took on the Mojave culture in the nineteenth century. They also hunted in Yavapai and Hualapai territory and intermarried with the former.

Other groups traded buckskins, hides, robes, blankets, and other items to Utes, Navajos, and Hopis for items such as blankets, maize, and beads. The Kaibabs traded buckskins and other items to other Paiute groups for agricultural products, horses, dogs, pipes, robes, beads, and other items.

Notable Arts Many Southern Paiutes, especially the Moapa and the Kaibab, made fine baskets. Songs and narratives were also aesthetic arts. Most songs were derived from dreams and sung without accompaniment. Men told tales in winter, including songs and some theater. Local rock art is at least several thousand years old. Art objects were made from a variety of materials, including stone, wood, and clay.

Transportation Women carried burdens in baskets with head tumplines; men used net and chest tumplines. Southern Paiutes traveled widely for

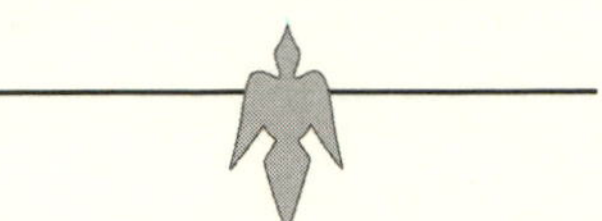

subsistence, trade, and pleasure. Like the Mojave, the Chemehuevi used log rafts and reed balsas.

Dress Although dress varied with location and available materials, women tended to wear double aprons of skin or vegetable fiber and basket caps. Men wore skin breechclouts, if anything, and skin caps. In colder weather, people wore woven rabbit-fur robes, which also served as bedding, as well as twined-bark leggings.

People generally went barefoot or wore bark or yucca sandals. Hunters used snowshoes in winter. Red body paint was used against the sun and also as decoration for life-cycle occasions. Both sexes tattooed their faces. Pierced ears were decorated with stick, stone, and shell earrings.

War and Weapons The Southern Paiutes were generally on friendly terms with each other and with neighboring groups. In early historical times, Utes, Navajos, and non-native New Mexicans aggressively raided Southern Paiutes for slaves. The Chemehuevi–Las Vegas were more warlike. They exterminated the desert Mojave in the late eighteenth century, and the Chemehuevi moved into their territory. Weapons were mostly clubs.

Contemporary Information

Government/Reservations The following colonies and reservations have significant numbers of Southern Paiutes:

Las Vegas Indian Colony, Clark County, Nevada (1911): roughly 3,850 acres; 52 resident Indians (1992); 71 enrolled members (1992); seven-member tribal council.

Moapa River Reservation, Clark County, Nevada (1875): 71,955 acres; 190 resident Indians (1990); 273 enrolled members (1992); six-member business council.

Paiute of Utah Reservation, Iron, Millard, Sevier, and Washington Counties, Utah (1972; Cedar City, Indian Peaks, Kanosh, Koosharem, and Shivwits Bands): 32,458 acres; 323 resident Indians (1990); 609 enrolled members (1992); six-member tribal council.

Kaibab Reservation, Mohave County, Arizona (1913): 120,413 acres; 102 resident Indians (1990); 212 enrolled members (1992); seven-member tribal council.

San Juan Paiute, Arizona and Utah: no reservation currently; 115 Indians live on traditional land (1992); 221 enrolled members (1992); eight-member tribal council.

Pahrump Band of Paiute Indians, Nevada: no reservation currently; 50 Indians live on traditional lands (1992); 70 enrolled members (1992); five-member tribal council.

Although these communities all have constitutions and by-laws, a more traditional decision-making process generally occurs in practice.

Economy Various economic activities on the different reservations and colonies include a cooperative farm, a gift shop, a minimart, a sand and gravel company, and a fireworks and smoke shop at Moapa. The unemployment rate there approaches 90 percent. Promised jobs at a nearby power plant have failed to materialize. Moapa was granted an additional 70,000 acres in the 1980s.

Las Vegas Colony boasts relatively low unemployment, thanks largely to employment in the city as well as a tribal smoke shop and minimart. They received an additional 3,700 acres northwest of the city in 1983, slated for commercial, industrial, recreational, and residential development.

There is a cattle cooperative and tourist center at Kaibab. The Utah Paiutes were granted 4,770 additional acres of land in 1984, plus a multimillion-dollar trust fund. Activities there include farming, mining leases, cattle leases, and cut-and-sew operations. The San Juan Paiutes have revived their traditional excellence in basket making.

Legal Status The following Paiute bands, locations, and peoples are federally recognized tribal entities: Kaibab Band of Paiute Indians, Las Vegas Tribe of Paiute Indians, Moapa Band of Paiute Indians, Paiute Indian Tribe of Utah, and San Juan Paiute Tribe. The Pahrump Band of Paiutes has applied for federal recognition.

Daily Life Although the past remains palpable, many traditional practices have disappeared. Some groups maintain the cry, combining it with funerals,

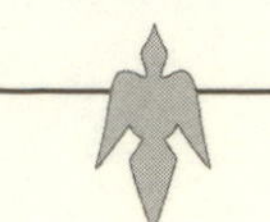

as well as traditional storytelling, the girls' puberty and first child rituals, and some traditional games. A few people still obtain part of their diet from traditional sources. The kinship system remains strong. Except at San Juan, few but the elderly still speak the languages, although there are tribal programs aimed at increasing native language proficiency. Major festive occasions are the Bear Dance, the Ute Sun Dance, and rodeos. Many Kaibabs have been converted to Mormonism. The Utah Paiute endure very high unemployment and many health-related problems, including high cancer rates likely caused by living downwind from the Nevada (nuclear) test site. Most communities have some form of local health care as well as special assistance programs for the elderly.

The San Juan Paiutes struggled for over 100 years with the Navajo and with white authorities over possession of parts of northern Arizona. For much of this period, they were largely forgotten or counted as Navajos, although the people themselves retained their identities. After the death in 1969 of their longtime chief tribal elder, Alfred Lehi, they began taking action to regain their official status. They received federal recognition in 1989 and continue to work for formal landholdings. This community remains relatively traditional.

Shoshone, Eastern or Wind River

Eastern, or Wind River, Shoshone (Shō `shō nē), a group grounded in Great Basin traditions who modified their culture to include elements from Plains and postcontact cultures. The Comanche broke away from the Eastern Shoshone about 1700 and moved south toward Texas (*see* Comanche [Chapter 6]). The term "Shoshone" is of dubious origin and was not a self-designation.

Location The Eastern Shoshone lived in western Wyoming from at least the sixteenth century on, expanded well into the northern Great Plains through the eighteenth century, and then retreated in the nineteenth century. They were loosely divided into two groups: Mountain Sheep Eaters to the north and west and Buffalo Eaters to the east and south. Most Eastern Shoshones now live on the Wind River Reservation, in Fremont and Hot Springs Counties, Wyoming.

Population There were perhaps 3,000 Eastern Shoshones in 1840. In 1990, 5,674 Eastern Shoshones and Arapahos lived on the Wind River Reservation.

Language The Eastern Shoshones spoke dialects of Shoshone, a Central Numic (Shoshonean) language of the Uto-Aztecan language family.

Historical Information

History Beginning at least as early as 1500, the Comanche-Shoshone began expanding eastward onto the Great Plains and adopting wide-scale buffalo hunting. With the acquisition of horses, about 1700, they also began widespread raiding and developed a much stronger and more centralized leadership. It was roughly at this time that the Comanche departed for places south. Armed (with firearms), the Blackfeet and other tribes began driving the Eastern Shoshone off the westward plains beginning in the late eighteenth century. Major smallpox epidemics occurred during that period, and the Eastern Shoshone adopted the Sun Dance introduced around 1800. Extensive intermarriage also occurred with the Crow, Nez Percé, and Métis.

During most of the nineteenth century, the Eastern Shoshone, under their chief, Washakie, were often allied with whites and grew prosperous. During the peak of the fur trade, from 1810 to 1840, the Eastern Shoshone sold up to 2,000 buffalo skins a year. When settlers began pouring into their territory in the 1850s, the Eastern Shoshone, under Washakie, tried to accommodate. In the Fort Bridger Treaty of 1868 they received 44 million acres; this figure was later reduced to fewer than 2 million. During the next 15 or so years they lived in a roughly traditional way on their reservation.

Because the Shoshone fought with the U.S. Army against the Lakota on many occasions, they felt betrayed when the government placed the Arapaho, their traditional enemies, on their reservation in 1878. The disappearance of the buffalo in the 1880s spelled the end of their traditional way of life. From the late nineteenth century and into the mid–twentieth

During most of the nineteenth century, the Eastern Shoshone, under Chief Washakie, were often allied with whites and grew prosperous. Pictured here is Chief Washakie's village near the Sweetwater River in Wyoming, 1870.

century, the Eastern Shoshone, now confined to reservations, experienced extreme hardship, population loss, and cultural decline. They had no decent land, hunting was prohibited, government rations were issued at starvation levels, and they could find no off-reservation employment because of poor transportation and white prejudice. Disease, especially tuberculosis, was rampant. Life expectancy was roughly 22 years at that time. The Indian Service controlled the reservation

A slow recovery began in late 1930s. Land claims victories brought vastly more land as well as an infusion of cash (almost $3.5 million). Concurrently, the tribal council, hitherto relatively weak, began assuming greater control of all aspects of reservation life. By the mid-1960s, the incidence of disease was markedly lower, owing in large part to the diligent efforts of women. Indicators such as housing, diet, economic resources (such as oil and gas leases), education, and real political control had all increased. Life expectancy had risen to 40–45 years. Traditional religious activity remained strong and meaningful. And yet severe and ongoing problems remained, including continuing white prejudice and a corresponding lack of off-reservation job opportunities, outmigration, slow economic development, and fear of the growing strength of the Arapaho.

Religion The Eastern Shoshone knew two basic kinds of religious practice. One was aimed at an individual's obtaining the assistance of supernatural powers from spirits. In exchange for power, such spirits, which could also be dangerous, demanded adherence to strict behavioral taboos. Power was gained either through dances or by sleeping in sacred places. Success in obtaining power was marked by a vision through which the power transferred skills or

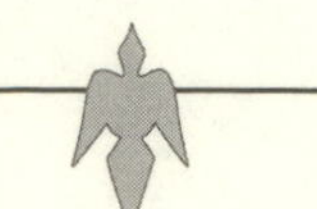

protections as well as songs, fetishes, and taboos. Power might also be transferred from one shaman to another by blowing. Should a person's power depart, a shaman had to recapture it lest the person die. Shamans did not so much control power as they were dependent on it.

The other kind of religious practice was designed to ensure the welfare of the community and nature as a whole by the observance of group ceremonials. The Father, the Shuffling (Ghost), and the Sun Dances were all addressed toward beneficent beings. The first two, during which men and women sang sacred songs, often took place at night in any season except summer. The Shuffling Dance was particularly important to Mountain Sheep Eaters.

The four-night and three-day Sun Dance was held in summer and featured exhaustion owing to dancing and lack of water. Introduced from the Plains around 1800, it symbolized the power and cohesion of the tribe and of the generations. It was an occasion for demonstrating virility, courage, and supernatural powers. Male dancers first participated in ritual sweats and other preparations, which began as early as the preceding winter. The ceremony itself, held around ten outer poles encircling a buffalo head mounted on a center pole, was followed by a great feast of buffalo tongues. Little boys were charged with grabbing the tongues.

Spirit places, things, and people were inherently dangerous and included ghosts, whirlwinds, old or menstruating women, death, and illness. Illness was seen as coming from either a breach of taboo or malevolent spirits. Sacred items and activities included sweating, burning certain grasses and wood, smoking wild tobacco, eagle feathers, paints, and certain songs. The peyote cult began on the reservation around 1900.

Government Centralization was the key to successful buffalo hunting and warfare and thus to eighteenth- and nineteenth-century Eastern Shoshone survival. During prosperous times (for instance, those with strong chieftainships) and when they came together seasonally as a tribe (for instance, for the spring buffalo hunt and the summer Sun Dance), the Eastern Shoshone numbered between 1,500 and 3,000.

A chief was at least middle-aged and of military or shamanistic training. He had authority over hunting, migration, and other issues. He and his assistants controlled the two military-police societies. His several distinctions included possessing a painted tipi and a special feathered headdress. He also acted as chief diplomat for external disputes.

The Eastern Shoshone separated into between three and five bands in winter, camping mainly in the Wind River Valley. Each band had a chief as well as military societies. Bands were loosely identified with particular geographic regions. Membership fluctuated, with extended family groups joining different Shoshone bands or perhaps even bands of other tribes such as the Crow.

Customs Women were in general subordinate to men, chiefly because menstruation set them apart as sources of ritual pollution. The younger wife or wives usually suffered in instances of polygyny. Widows were dispossessed. At the same time, women gained status as individuals through their skills as gatherers, crafters, gamblers, midwives, and child care providers. Particularly during the fur trade, alliances with white trappers and traders were made with daughters and sisters, leading to important interethnic ties.

Social status positions were earned through the use (or nonuse) of supernatural power, except that age and sex also played a role. Infants and small children were not recognized as sexually different. Boys began their search for supernatural power around adolescence. "Men" were those who were married and members of a military society.

Girls helped their mothers until marriage, which was arranged shortly after the onset of puberty. Menstrual restrictions included gathering firewood (a key female chore) and refraining from meat and daytime sleeping. A good husband was a good provider, although he might be considerably older.

Wealth and prestige accrued to curers; midwives; good gamblers; hunters and traders; and fast runners. Property was often destroyed or abandoned at death. Generosity was a central value: Giveaways for meritorious occasions were common. Men cared for war and buffalo horses, women for packhorses. High-stakes gambling games included the hand and four-

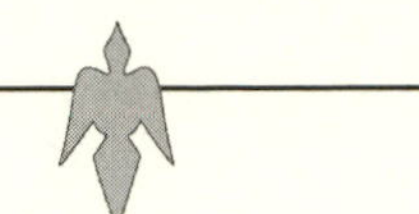

stick dice game, double-ball shinny (women), and foot races.

Dwellings After the move onto the Plains, women made buffalo skin tipis according to a strenuous, time-consuming procedure. Men decorated the tipis. Beds, a central fireplace, and parfleches filled the inside. The master bed had a decorated antelope hide or two.

Diet Bands engaged in small-scale hunting and gathering in summer; buffalo were hunted communally in spring and especially in fall. Staples included buffalo, elk, beaver, mule deer, antelope, mountain sheep, moose, bear, jackrabbit, and smaller game. The winter diet relied heavy on dried buffalo (pemmican). Trout and other fish, caught in spring, were also a staple. Fish were eaten fresh or sun dried or smoked for storage. Important plants included camas, wild onion, berries, and sunflower seeds.

Key Technology Most goods were made from animal (especially the buffalo) and plant materials as well as minerals such as flint, obsidian, slate, and steatite. Every part of the buffalo was used, including the dung (for fuel). In the historic period, iron from non-native traders became very important.

Fishing equipment included traps, weirs, dams, and spears. Roots in particular were cooked in earth ovens. Food was kept in leather parfleches. Men prepared shields, hide drums, and rattles; women made most other leather work, such as tipis, clothing, containers, and trade items. They also made coiled baskets.

With counting sticks, Eastern Shoshones could keep track of numbers up to 100,000.

Trade Perhaps the largest regional intertribal trade gathering was held in midsummer at Green River, Wyoming.

Notable Arts Art objects were made from a variety of materials, including stone, wood, and clay. Leather goods included tipis, parfleches, shields, and other items. Elkhides were painted to depict important events such as Sun Dances, buffalo hunts, and warfare. The best-made goods were often decorated with beads or drilled elk's teeth. People made pictographs at the sites of particularly sacred places.

Transportation Eastern Shoshones had the horse from about 1700 on. A horse (formerly dog)-drawn travois transported the infirm as well as households. Dogs aided in transportation, hunting, and war. Snowshoes were worn for winter hunting.

Dress Most clothing and blankets were made of buffalo and other hides. With their eastern expansion, the Eastern Shoshone adopted Plains fringed-and-beaded styles.

War and Weapons Beginning in the eighteenth century, the state of war was more or less continuous, and warfare took a great toll on the Eastern Shoshone. There were two military societies. About 100–150 brave young men were Yellow Brows. The recruitment ritual included backwards speech (no for yes, for example). This fearless society acted as vanguards on the march. They fought to the death in combat and had a major role keeping order on the buffalo hunt. Their Big Horse Dance was a highly ritualistic preparation for battle. Logs were older men who took up the rear on the march. Both groups were entitled to blacken their faces.

Shamans participated in war by foretelling events and curing men and horses. As many as 300 men might make up a war party. Traditional enemies included the Blackfeet and later the Arapaho, Lakota, Cheyenne, and Gros Ventre. During the mid– to late nineteenth century, the principal ally of the Shoshone was the U.S. Army.

Spring and especially fall were the time for war. At these times the Eastern Shoshone generally fought as a tribe. Men made handle-held shields from thick, young buffalo bull hide. Rituals and feasting accompanied their manufacture. Each was decorated with buckskin and fringed with feathers. Weapons included sinew-backed bows, obsidian-tipped arrows, and clubs. Successful warriors were entitled to paint black and red finger marks on their tipi. Warriors occasionally committed suicide in combat.

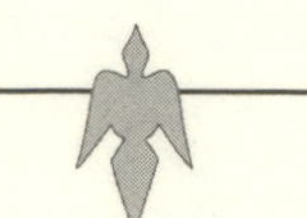

Contemporary Information

Government/Reservations The Wind River Reservation (1863; Shoshone and Arapaho Tribes), Fremont and Hot Springs Counties, Wyoming, has 2,268,008 acres and a population of 5,674 Indians (1990). Both tribes have business councils.

Economy Major activities are ranching, crafts, and clerical jobs. Some people regularly hunt and fish. There is income from mineral leases; the Eastern Shoshone tribe is a member of the Council of Energy Resource Tribes (CERT). Un- and underemployment is chronically high.

Legal Status The Arapaho Tribe of the Wind River Reservation and the Shoshone Tribe of the Wind River Reservation are federally recognized tribal entities.

Daily Life Quasi-traditional religion remains important. The Sun Dance has been explicitly Christianized and is now intertribal. Only a few Mountain Sheep Eaters practice the Shuffle Dance. Peyotism is popular. Giveaways, formerly related to public coup counting, are now associated with other occasions. Shoshone language courses are taught at the Wyoming Indian High School, located on the reservation. Housing, most of which consists of modern "bungalows," is considered generally inadequate. The people use canvas tipis for ceremonial purposes.

High rates of substance abuse and suicide plague the reservation; accidents have replaced disease as primary killers. Outmigration remains a problem. Women have more freedom as well as political and social power, obtained in part through their participation in certain musical ceremonies. Wyoming Indian High School is Arapaho-dominated; most Shoshone attend off-reservation public high schools. Traditional games such as the hand game, with its associated gambling, remain popular, especially at powwows. Many people still speak the language.

Shoshone, Northern

Northern Shoshone (Shō `shō nē) is a modern, anthropological term used to distinguish a region of Shoshone culture. The Northern Shoshone and Bannock (originally a Northern Paiute group) shared a number of cultural traits with the Paiute and the Ute Indians as well as with so-called Eastern or Wind River Shoshones (there was no aboriginal distinction between Shoshone groups) and Northern Paiutes. Northern Shoshones incorporated elements of Great Basin, Plateau, and Great Plains culture. The term "Shoshone" first surfaced in 1805. Other Indians and non-Indians sometimes referred to some Shoshone and Northern Paiute groups, particularly mounted bands, as Snake Indians (sedentary Shoshone and Northern Paiutes were often referred to as Diggers), but their name for themselves was *Nomo,* or "People."

Location In the early nineteenth century, Northern Shoshones lived mostly in Idaho south of the Salmon River or on the Snake River plains and the mountains to the north. This region, on the border of the Columbia Plateau, has a relatively dry climate. It contains the Sawtooth and Bitterroot Mountains, valleys, river highlands, and the Snake and other rivers and creeks. Today, most Northern Shoshones live in and around Bannock, Bingham, Caribou, and Power Counties, Idaho.

Population The precontact population of up to 30,000 had been cut by 90 percent by the mid–nineteenth century. In 1990, the Fort Hall Reservation population was 3,035 Indians.

Language Shoshone is part of the central Numic (Shoshonean) division of the Uto-Aztecan language family. The Bannocks spoke western Numic, also a Shoshonean language, although mutually unintelligible with central Numic.

Historical Information

History The Paiute-speaking Bannock were among the first local groups to acquire horses, in the late seventeenth century. At that time, they migrated from eastern Oregon to Shoshone territory near the Snake River and organized fully mounted bands and engaged in group buffalo hunts. They and the Northern Shoshones also began to raid for horses and assumed many other aspects of Plains culture, such as

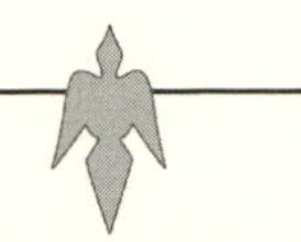

Sacajawea, a Shoshone woman, served as a guide on the Lewis and Clark expedition of 1804. In this early-twentieth-century painting by Charles M. Russell, Sacajawea uses sign language to communicate with Chinook Indians. Her diplomatic and navigational skills saved the party on more than one occasion.

tipis and warrior societies, yet the Bannock continued to interact with their Northern Paiute relatives. Sacajawea, a Shoshone woman, served as a guide on the Lewis and Clark expedition of 1804. Her diplomatic and navigation skills saved the party on more than one occasion.

Continuing their move east to the western extremity of the northern Plains, the Shoshone were soon (mid–eighteenth century) driven back by the gun-wielding Blackfeet. Some Northern Shoshone groups did not become mounted until the nineteenth century or used the horse only as a pack animal. Such groups, particularly those away from the centers in the Snake and Lemhi River Valleys (for example, the so-called Sheepeaters), lived in scattered settlements and remained sedentary and peaceful.

The Lewis and Clark party (1804–1806) may have been the first non-Indians in the area. Anglos soon opened trading posts at Pend Oreille Lake (British, 1809) and the Upper Snake River (Northwest Company, 1810). Throughout the 1810s and 1820s, white trappers ranged across Shoshone territory, destroying all beaver and buffalo west of the Rockies. Other game suffered as well, as did the traditional Northern Shoshone way of life. Indians also acquired much non-native technology during this

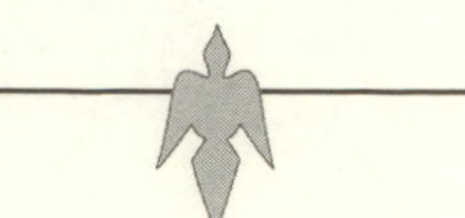

time, including firearms, iron utensils, and alcohol, and new diseases took a heavy toll.

By the 1840s, the fur trade had collapsed. Non-Indians began arriving en masse after the California gold rush and the opening of the Oregon Trail, further stressing the delicate local ecology. In 1847, the Mormons arrived. By the 1860s, the buffalo had all but disappeared. Relatively quickly, many Northern Shoshone groups faced starvation. They began to raid white settlements and wagons in retaliation, an activity that quickly brought counterraids. This kind of conflict persisted throughout the 1860s and 1870s, although the Fort Hall Reservation (originally 1.8 million acres) was created by treaty in 1868.

The Bannocks, however, had resisted confinement to Fort Hall. Some peoples' resistance was a direct influence of the Dreamers cult founded about 1860 by the Wanapum Smohalla. The continued destruction of their way of life—led by the wholesale slaughter of the buffalo, inadequate rations, white ranchers' crowding, and violence committed against them when they continued subsistence activities guaranteed by treaty—led to a major revolt in 1878. Its immediate cause was Anglo hog herding in a camas root area forbidden to them by treaty. The Bannocks and some Northern Paiute bands, under the Bannock chief Buffalo Born and the Paiutes Egan and Oytes, engaged the soldiers for several months that summer. Ultimately, the Paiutes were settled among the Yakima in Washington, and the Bannocks, held as prisoners of war for a while, were permitted to return to Fort Hall.

The Sheepeater war also took place in 1878, when roughly 50 central Idaho Bannocks and Shoshones, who lived primarily on mountain sheep, began raiding settlers who were encroaching on their subsistence area. At first eluding the army, they were eventually captured and placed at Fort Hall. Other Shoshones, too, fought to retain their traditions; most ended up at Fort Hall.

The United States created the Lemhi Valley Reservation in 1875, but its people were moved to Fort Hall when the reservation was terminated in 1907. Meanwhile, the Fort Hall Reservation itself shrank by more than two-thirds as a result of encroachments by the railroads, timber, mining, highway, and other interests. Dawes Act (1887) allotments further reduced it in size. Life at Fort Hall was marked by irrigation problems; major projects in the early twentieth century benefited white farmers only. Other serious problems included the flooding of good bottomlands by the American Falls Reservoir. Major economic activities during that time included sheep and cattle ranching. A phosphate mine opened after World War II.

Fort Hall Indians acquired the Sun Dance from Plains Indians, via the Wind River Shoshone, during the 1890s. Some also adopted the Native American Church in 1915. The government awarded them a land claims settlement of more than $8.8 million in 1964; another, smaller settlement was received in 1971 by the Lemhi Valley descendants.

Religion Northern Shoshones used dreams and visions to acquire helping spirits. Such spirits instructed people on the use of medicines with which to activate their power. Certain food and other restrictions might also be imposed. Spirits might cure illness, protect an individual from arrows, or hurt other people.

Most or all men could cure, although there were also professionals. Their methods included herbs, charms, and sweats. They gained their supernatural power through dreams, visions, and visits to remote, spirit-dwelling places.

There was a concept of a creator, but creative agency was proscribed to mythological characters such as wolf and coyote. Ceremonial occasions that featured round dances included the spring salmon return, the fall harvest, and times of adversity.

Government Loosely organized groups were characteristic of Great Basin culture. Traditionally, the Northern Shoshone were organized into seminomadic bands with impermanent composition and leadership. Some bands had chiefs; others, particularly in the west, had neither bands nor chiefs.

Life on the Plains called for higher forms of organization, both to hunt buffalo and to defend against enemies. In the fall, for instance, the Snake and Lemhi River–area bands came together for councils, feasts, and buffalo hunts. During these times, the more eastern bands were led by a principal chief and several minor chiefs. However, these offices were still nonhereditary, loosely defined, and somewhat transitory. Also, with more complex social organization, band councils arose to limit the power of the chiefs. Some "police" or soldier societies may also have existed to keep order during hunts and dances.

Customs Equality and individual autonomy were cardinal Shoshone values. Just as social organization was fairly undeveloped, especially to the west, there was also little barrier to social interaction. Many groups often intermarried, visited, and shared ceremonies and feasts. Social networks were wide and strong.

Local groups were named by the foods they ate, but the same band might have several names, and the same name might apply to several bands. Most marriages were monogamous. Both marriage and divorce were simple and common. The dead were wrapped in blankets and placed in rock crevices. Mourners cut their hair, gashed their legs, and killed one of the deceased's horses. Some private property (such as tools and weapons) was recognized, but private ownership of land or subsistence areas was not.

Dwellings Fort Hall and Lemhi people lived in Plains-style tipis after about the eighteenth century. Otherwise, Northern Shoshones typically built conical dwellings of sagebrush, grass, or woven willow branches. A similar structure was used for sweat lodges and menstrual huts.

Diet Roots (such as prairie turnips, yampa root, tobacco root, bitterroot, and camas) were steamed in earth ovens for several days or boiled. Berries (such as chokecherries and service berries), nuts, and seeds were also important foods, as were grasshoppers, ants and other insects, lizards, squirrels, and rabbits.

Big game included antelope, deer, elk, and mountain sheep. Buffalo were native to parts of the region but became especially important in the seventeenth century, when people would travel for the fall hunt to the Plains (east of Bozeman) and then back to the Snake River in winter or early spring.

Salmon was the most important fish. In fact, the salmon fishery was one of the key distinguishing features between the Northern Shoshone and the Eastern Shoshone. People also caught sturgeon, perch, trout, and other fish on Columbia and Snake River tributaries.

Key Technology Fish were caught with nets, weirs, basket traps, harpoons, and spears. They were also attracted at night with torches. Steatite (soapstone) was used for items such as bowls and pipes. Women made coiled and twined sagebrush-bark and -root baskets and containers. They applied pitch to the interior to make them watertight. Boiling was accomplished by dropping hot stones into water baskets. Rawhide containers, perhaps painted with geometric designs, were also used.

Women carried willow stick and buckskin cradle boards on their backs. Digging sticks were hardened and sharpened by fire, which was in turn made with a drill. The Bannock used some pottery, horn utensils, and salmon-skin bags.

Trade Trade was extensive in the area. Many Plateau as well as northern Plains Indians received the horse by way of the Shoshone. Their main trade partners were the Flathead, Nez Percé, Crow, Umatilla, and Cayuse, with whom they traded buffalo skins, salmon, horses, and mules. There were also friendly relations and trade with the Northern Paiute. Annual trade fairs occurred at places like the Green River (Wyoming), the Cache Valley (Utah), and Pierre's Hole (Idaho).

Notable Arts The chief art, especially in the late prehistoric and historic periods, was rawhide painted with geometric designs. The Northern Shoshone and Bannock also made beadwork with geometric designs. Their petroglyphs are at least several thousand years old. Various other art objects have been made from a variety of materials, including stone, wood, and clay.

Transportation Horses arrived in the mid– to late seventeenth century; before that, dogs helped with transporting goods. Hunters used snowshoes in winter. The Bannock used tule rafts.

Dress After they entered the mounted period, people dressed similarly to Plains Indians. They wore

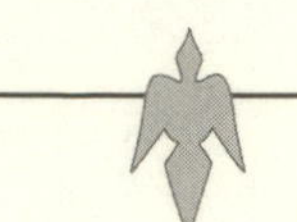

elk-skin clothing decorated with quillwork or beadwork in summer. Men wore leggings and fringed shirts, and women wore dresses, knee-length leggings, and elk-tooth necklaces. In the winter both sexes wore buffalo-skin, elk-skin, or deerskin moccasins as well as antelope, deer, buffalo, or mountain sheep robes. Otherwise, the traditional dress was breechclouts and rabbit-skin robes. Feathered headdresses were worn for ceremonial purposes.

War and Weapons Weapons included cedar, elk, or sheep horn bows; poison-tipped arrows kept in otterskin quivers; and stone war clubs. Obsidian was used for knives and arrowheads. Defensive equipment included antelope-skin armor and buffalo-skin shields. Among the peoples' traditional enemies were the Blackfeet and possibly the Nez Percé. In later aboriginal times, the Shoshone acquired Plains war customs such as counting coup and taking scalps. Their Scalp Dance was also acquired from Plains groups.

Contemporary Information

Government/Reservations Fort Hall Reservation, Bannock, Bingham, Caribou, and Power Counties, Idaho (1868; Bannock and Northern Shoshone), contains 523,917 acres. The 1990 Indian population was 3,035. A constitution and by-laws were approved in 1936, and a corporate charter was ratified the following year. Government is provided by an elected business council. Most of the land is in Indian hands.

Duck Valley Reservation, Owyhee County, Idaho, and Elko County, Nevada (1877; Shoshone and Paiute), contains 289,819 acres. The 1990 Indian population was 1,021. An Indian Reorganization Act–based constitution and by-laws were adopted in 1936. Government is provided by a tribal council.

The Northwestern Band of Shoshoni Indians (roughly 400 population in 1995) live near Fort Hall, Idaho, although their land base, the Washakie Reservation (184 acres) is in Utah.

Economy At Fort Hall, important economic activities include public fishing and hunting, high-stakes bingo, tribal income from leases and mineral rights, several small businesses, and some agriculture. The tribe operates a 20,000-acre irrigation project. Many people also work for the tribal government. The people also receive interest and investments from a $15.7 million land claims award to the Northern and Eastern Shoshone in 1968. A proposal to open a casino is tied up in court. Un- and underemployment is a major problem.

Legal Status The Bannock Tribe (Shoshone-Bannock), the Shoshone Indians, and the Northwestern Band of the Shoshoni Nation are federally recognized tribal entities.

Daily Life Despite centuries of intermarriage, many people still identify themselves as Bannock or Shoshone. Both languages are still spoken. Children attend public schools. A new clinic opened in 1990. The museum and library at Fort Hall are just two of the ways by which the people stay in touch with their Indian identities. Other ways include bilingual education, a weekly newspaper, and active religious observances such as the Sun Dance and the Peyote cult. The reservation runs adult education and youth recreation programs. It also hosts many traditional festivals, including a week-long celebration in August and an all-Indian rodeo.

Shoshone, Western

Western Shoshone (Shō `shō nē) were a number of Shoshonean-speaking groups generally inhabiting a particular area. Many groups were known to whites as Diggers. Their self-designation was "*Newe.*" The Goshute (Gosiute) are ethnic Shoshones, despite considerable intermarriage with the Ute and the existence of a 1962 court ruling legally separating them from the Western Shoshone. Little pre-1859 scientific ethnographic data exist on the Western Shoshone.

Location Most Western Shoshone bands lived in harsh environments such as the Great Salt Lake area (Goshute) and Death Valley (Panamint). Their territory stretched from Death Valley through central Nevada into northwestern Utah and southern Idaho. Most Western Shoshones today live on a number of reservations within their aboriginal territory. They also live in nearby and regional cities and towns.

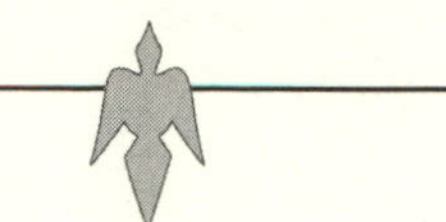

Population The aboriginal population of Western Shoshones may have numbered between 5,000 and 10,000, although it had declined to roughly 2,000 by the early nineteenth century. In 1990, 3,815 Paiute-Shoshones, Goshute Shoshones, and Shoshones lived on reservations. This figure does not include 2,078 Te-Moak Shoshones (1992).

Language The Western Shoshone spoke three central Numic languages—Panamint, Shoshone, and Comanche—all members of the Numic (Shoshonean) branch of the Uto-Aztecan language family. Since all Shoshones (Western, Northern, and Eastern or Wind River) spoke Shoshone, the term Shoshone is an ethnic rather than a linguistic one.

Historical Information

History Western Shoshones were first visited by non-natives—the Jedediah Smith and Peter Skene Ogden parties—in the late 1820s. Other trappers and traders passed through during the next 20 years. Despite the willingness of some groups, such as the Walker party, to massacre Indians, the latter were relatively unaffected by early contacts with non-natives.

The Mormons, who ultimately had a huge impact on the Goshute Shoshone, began arriving to stay in 1847. The white presence increased throughout 1840s and 1850s, but the discovery of the Comstock Lode in 1857 turned the stream into a flood. By then, degradation of the natural environment was well under way. New diseases also stalked the region, severely affecting both human and animal populations. Indians responded by either retreating farther from white activity or, less often, by raiding, stealing, and begging.

The Pony Express, established in 1860, passed through the center of Western Shoshone country. Supply depots at important springs displaced Indians, which encouraged attacks and then army reprisals. By 1860, Mormons had invaded Goshute territory, and miners and ranchers were closing in on the rest of Western Shoshone lands. Grazing, plowing, and wood cutting (piñon and juniper pine) destroyed subsistence areas and forage land. Indians began to work for settlers as wage laborers to fend off starvation. Euro-American clothing, technology, and shelter quickly replaced the traditional variety.

Federal negotiations with Great Basin tribes began in the 1850s, in part to check sporadic violence against settlers. The first treaties with Western Shoshone groups were signed in 1863. They called for Indians to give up hostilities, settle down eventually, and receive goods annually worth a total of $50,000. In return, the settlers could stay. Significantly, the Indians never actually ceded any land.

The army soon began rounding up Indians. When no reservations near good land with water were established during the 1870s, some Shoshones joined Northern Paiutes and Bannocks in their wars of resistance. In 1879, Shoshones refused an order to move to the Western Shoshone (Duck Valley) Reservation. Despite the extreme disruption of their lives, elements of traditional culture survived, such as religious beliefs (largely excepting the Goshute) and limited subsistence patterns. Most Shoshones still lived unconfined after 1900.

The percentage of Western Shoshones living on reservations peaked at 50 in 1927. Most carried out semitraditional subsistence activities combined with seasonal or other wage work in mines and on ranches and farms. In an effort to enlarge the reservation population, the United States encouraged Northern Paiutes to settle at Duck Valley. Finally, accepting the fact that most Western Shoshones did not and would not live at Duck Valley, the government created a series of "colonies" during the first half of the twentieth century.

In 1936, the Paiutes and most Shoshone groups organized the Paiute-Shoshone Business Council. Chief Temoak and his descendants were considered the leaders of this effort. The U.S. government refused to recognize the traditional Temoak council, however, and instead organized their own Te-Moak Bands Council. This split culminated when the traditionalist-backed United Western Shoshone Legal Defense and Education Association (1974) argued that the Te-Moak Bands Council did not represent Western Shoshone interests and, further, that the Western Shoshones never ceded their land. The courts rejected their claim in 1979 and ordered them paid $26 million in compensation. In 1985, the Supreme Court ruled that the 1979 payment

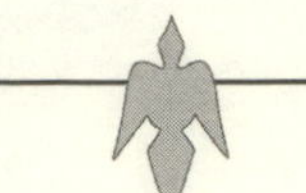

legally extinguished their title to the disputed 24 million acres.

Religion Apo, the sun, was a principal deity. Anyone could obtain supernatural powers through dreams and visions, although medicine men *(bugahant)* served as religious leaders. Most groups recognized three kinds of shamans: curers of specific ailments, general curers, and self-curers or helpers. Curing was effected by sucking and the laying on of hands. In theory, men and women could both be shamans, although only men may have practiced curing. Shamans were also capable of capturing antelopes' souls and helping to drive them into corrals. Some groups may not have had shamans at all.

People used several hundred herbal remedies to cure nonsupernatural ailments such as cuts and bruises. The round dance was basic to ceremonial celebration. In some areas the dance was associated with courtship or rainmaking. Festivals were often held in times of plenty.

Government Groups in small winter villages were composed of family clusters and named for an important food resource or a local geographic feature. Thus, the territory and not the composition of the group was definitive. Group membership was not fixed and groups were not bands per se. Chiefs or headmen had little authority other than directing subsistence activity.

Customs Ritual activity focused on birth, girls' puberty, and death. Girls' puberty rituals included isolation as well as instruction on hard work and other proper behaviors. Corpses were cremated or buried in caves or rock slides. Some groups observed an annual mourning ceremony that included singing, speech making, and destroying the deceased's property. Mourners cut their hair and waited at least a year before remarriage. Shamanistic midwives offered supernatural assistance to ensure a baby's welfare. Some infanticide was practiced, especially in the west.

Good hunters might take more than one wife. Groups west of the Humboldt River practiced the bride price. Marriages were meant to establish close family ties. Divorce and remarriage were common. In the Reese River Valley, piñon groves were owned by individual families. Games included shinny, ball race (men), hoop and pole, dice, and four-stick. Most of these games involved betting. Shinny had some religious significance. People also played with jacks and string games. The elderberry flute was the only widespread musical instrument.

Dwellings Relatively little subsistence activity in winter meant less population mobility and the chance to establish villages of several families. Winter houses for about six people were conical huts of bark-covered pole frame. The smoke hole served as an entrance. People also lived in caves, brush sun shades, and domed wickiups. Sweat houses were domed in the north and conical in the south. Most groups also built menstrual huts.

Diet The main economic activity was foraging in families or groups of families from spring through fall. Staple plant foods included grasses, pine nuts, seeds, berries, spring greens, and roots. The Panamint ate mesquite pods and screwbeans. Seeds were threshed, roasted on parching trays, winnowed, ground, and boiled. They could then be eaten or cached. Mesquite pods were ground and eaten as cakes. Other desert foods included salvia seeds, cactus, agave, and gourds.

Meat, some of which was dried for winter, included bighorn sheep, antelope, deer, jackrabbits, and rodents. Dogs assisted in summer sheep hunts. Groups of people drove antelope and rabbits into corrals and nets. Antelope were also hunted individually using masks and disguises. Other food sources, depending on location, included fish, birds, waterfowl, larvae, grasshoppers, and crickets.

Key Technology In general the Western Shoshone adapted very successfully to a relatively harsh environment. They used sticks to beat grasses and dig roots, as well as using seed beaters of twined willow. Coiled and twined baskets were important in grass collection, as was a twined winnowing tray. Waterproof baskets allowed people to forage far from water.

Other tools and equipment included stone metates for grinding seeds; snares, traps, and deadfalls to hunt cottontails and rodents; bows of juniper and

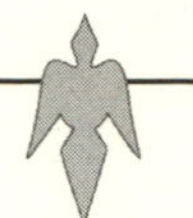

mountain mahogany; wildcat skin quivers; stone or horn arrow straighteners; and some pottery.

Trade Western Shoshones traded items such as salt and rabbit-skin blankets to Owens Valley Paiutes for shell money and buckskins.

Notable Arts Baskets were of very high quality. The people also made rock art for at least several thousand years as well as art objects from a variety of materials, including stone, wood, and clay.

Transportation Western Shoshones possessed few horses even after other Shoshones acquired them (horses competed for their staple grasses).

Dress Boys and some girls remained nude, especially in summer. Otherwise girls wore a front apron. Even in winter many people wore few clothes other than fur robes. What clothing existed was made of rabbit skin and/or the hides of bighorn sheep, antelope, or deer. If these materials were scarce, people used bark or grass as clothing materials. Women wore twined sage-bark or willow hats and a skin gown in winter. Both sexes wore fur or sage-bark moccasins in winter. They pierced their ears and wore ear and neck ornaments of shell and bone. Face and body painting and tattooing were common, especially among young adults.

War and Weapons Other than some historic-era conflict over the Ute propensity to sell Goshutes into slavery, the Western Shoshone practiced little warfare.

Contemporary Information

Government/Reservations The following reservations and colonies have a significant Western Shoshone presence:

Duck Valley Reservation, Owyhee County, Idaho, and Elko County, Nevada (1877; Shoshone and Paiute): 289,819 acres; 1,701 enrollment (1990); organized under the Indian Reorganization Act (IRA); constitution and by-laws approved 1936; governed by a business council.

Duckwater Reservation, Nye County, Nevada (1940; Shoshone): 3,815 acres; 288 enrollment (1990); governed by a tribal council.

Ely Indian Colony, White Pine County, Nevada (1931; Shoshone): 111 total acres; 274 enrollment (1990); organized under the IRA; constitution and by-laws approved 1966; governed by a council.

Fallon Reservation and Colony, Churchill County, Nevada (1887; Paiute and Shoshone): 69 (colony) and 3,480 (tribal, plus 4,640 allotted) acres; 506 Indians (1990); governed by a business council.

Fort McDermitt Reservation, Humboldt County, Nevada, and Malheur County, Oregon (1892; Shoshone and Paiute): 16,354 tribal acres in Nevada plus almost 19,000 acres of tribal land in Oregon; 387 Indians (1990); governed by a tribal council.

Big Pine Reservation, Inyo County, California (1939; Paiute and Shoshone): 279 acres; 331 Indians (1990).

Bishop Indian Colony, Inyo County, California (1912; Paiute-Shoshone): 877 acres; 934 Indians (1990); governed by a tribal council.

Death Valley Indian Community, Death Valley, California (1982; Timbi-sha Shoshone): 40 acres; 199 Indians (1992).

Fort Independence Reservation, Inyo County, California (1915; Paiute and Shoshone): 234 acres; 38 Indians (1990).

Lone Pine Reservation, Inyo County, California (1939; Paiute-Shoshone): 237 acres; 168 Indians (1990); governed by a tribal council.

Yomba Reservation, Nye County, Nevada (1937; Yomba Shoshone): 4,718.46 acres; 192 Indians (1992).

Goshute Reservation, White Pine County, Nevada, and Juab and Tooele Counties, Utah (1863): 7,489 acres; 98 Indians (1990); 413 enrolled members (1993), 1940 constitution and by-laws; governed by a business council.

Battle Mountain Reservation, Battle Mountain, Nevada (1917; Te-Moak Band of Western Shoshone): 700 acres; 553 Indians (1995); governed by a tribal council.

Elko Indian Colony, Elko, Nevada (1918; Te-Moak Band of Western Shoshone): 193 acres; 1,326 Indians (1995); governed by a band council.

Ruby Valley (Te-Moak) Trust Lands, Elko, Nevada (1887; Te-Moak Western Shoshone Indians):

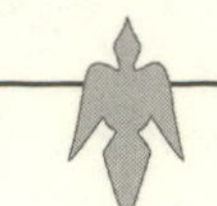

15,000 acres; approximately 30 Indians (1998); governed by a tribal council.

South Fork and Odgers Ranch Indian Colony, Lee, Nevada (1941; Te-Moak Band of Western Shoshone): 13,050 acres; 257 Indians (1995); governed by South Fork Tribal Council.

Wells Indian Colony (1980; Te-Moak Tribe of Western Shoshone): 80 acres; 182 Indians (1995); governed by a band council.

Skull Valley Reservation, Tooele County, Utah (1917; Goshute Tribe): 17,444 acres; 32 Indians (1990); 111 enrolled members (1993); no constitution.

Economy In addition to employment with federal and tribal entities and income from leases and land claims funds, significant economic activities on the various reservations include enterprises such as smoke shops, motels, gas stations, and other small businesses. Several reservations and colonies remain in the cattle and farming business. Un- and underemployment are generally very high.

Outside of limited cattle and hay ranching, there are no employment opportunities on the Goshute Reservation. Skull Valley leases land to Hercules (aerospace), and some tribal members work there as well as at a convenience store and a seasonal water project.

Legal Status The following are federally recognized tribal entities: the Death Valley Timbi-sha Shoshone Band (since 1982), the Duckwater Shoshone Tribe, the Fort McDermitt Paiute and Shoshone Tribes, the Paiute-Shoshone Indians of the Bishop Community, the Paiute-Shoshone Tribe of the Fallon Reservation and Colony, the Paiute-Shoshone Indians of the Lone Pine Community, the Shoshone-Paiute Tribes of the Duck Valley Reservation, the Yomba Shoshone Tribe, the Confederated Tribes of the Goshute Reservation, and the Skull Valley Band of Goshute Indians of Utah. The constituent bands of the Te-Moak tribe of Western Shoshone Indians make up a federally recognized tribal entity.

Daily Life Tribal gatherings (fandangos) feature traditional round dances, prayers, and games. Most groups have instituted language preservation programs. In confederation with other Great Basin tribes, several Western Shoshone groups opposed siting the MX intercontinental ballistic missile system on treaty lands. Western Shoshones have rejected the 1985 Supreme Court land claims decision (see "History" under "Historical Information"), holding that by the terms of the 1863 treaty they retain formal title to 24 million acres of aboriginal land. Negotiations are currently in progress.

Communications remain difficult on the remote Goshute and Skull Valley Reservations. Those Goshute Reservation children not attending boarding schools are bused 60 miles to high school; the ride is 16 miles at Skull Valley. Both the Native American Church and the Mormon Church are popular among Goshutes. Reservation crafts include beadwork, basketry, and making buckskin items.

Shoshone, Wind River

See Shoshone, Eastern

Ute

Ute (Yūt), roughly 11 autonomous Great Basin bands. In the eighteenth century, eastern bands included the Uncompahgre (or Tabeguache), Yampa and Parusanuch (or White River Band), Mouache, Capote, and Weeminuche, and western bands included the Uintah, Timpanogots, Pahvant, Sanpits, and Moanunts. The word "Utah" is of Spanish derivation, probably borrowed originally from an Indian word. Their self-designation was *Nunt'z,* "the People."

Location Aboriginally, Utes lived in most of present-day Utah, except the far western, northern, and southern parts; Colorado west of and including the eastern slopes of the Rockies; and extreme northern New Mexico. Today, the three Ute reservations are in southwest Colorado, the Four Corners area, and north-central Utah.

Population From roughly 8,000 in the early nineteenth century, the Utes declined to about 1,800 in 1920. In 1990 approximately 5,000 lived on

Many Utes came to Washington in 1868 to discuss the creation of the tribe's first two reservations. Chief Ouray is seated to the right of an unidentified man. The U.S. government considered Ouray "head chief of the Utes," paid him an annual salary, and supplied him with expensive goods.

reservations, and roughly another 2,800 lived in cities and towns.

Language With Southern Paiute, Ute is a member of the southern Numic (Shoshonean) division of the Uto-Aztecan language family. All dialects were mutually intelligible.

Historical Information

History The Utes and their ancestors have been in the Great Basin for as many as 10,000 years. They lived along Arizona's Gila River from about 3000 B.C.E. to about 500 B.C.E. At that time, a group of them began migrating north toward Utah, growing a high-altitude variety of corn that had been developed in Mexico. This group, who grew corn, beans, and squash and also hunted and gathered food, is known as the Sevier Complex. Another, related group of people, known as the Fremont Complex, lived to the northeast.

In time, Fremont people migrated into western Colorado. When a drought struck the Great Basin in the thirteenth century, the Fremont people moved into Colorado's San Luis Valley, where they later became known as the Utes. They became one of the first mounted Indian peoples when escaped Spanish captives brought horses home in the mid–seventeenth century. Communal buffalo hunts began shortly thereafter. Mounted warriors brought more protection, and larger camps meant more centralized government and more powerful leaders as well as a rising standard of living. Utes also facilitated the spread of the horse to peoples of the Great Plains.

Southern and eastern Ute bands raided New Mexico Indians and hunted buffalo on the Plains during the seventeenth into the nineteenth centuries. Utes also raided Western Shoshones and Southern Paiutes for slaves (mostly women and children), whom they sold to the Spanish. Moreover, they were forced to defend some hunting territory against the Comanche (formerly an ally) and other Plains tribes around that time. As a result of relentless Comanche attacks, the Southern Utes were prevented from developing fully on the Plains. Driven back into the mountains, they lost power and prestige, and the northern bands, enjoying a more peaceful and prosperous life, increased in importance.

A Spanish expedition in 1776 was the first of a line of non-native explorers, trappers, traders, slavers, and miners. Non-natives established a settlement in Colorado in 1851, and a U.S. fort (Fort Massachusetts) was built the following year to protect that settlement. Utes considered non-native livestock grazing on their (former) land fair game. In the midst of growing conflicts, treaties (which remained unratified) were negotiated in the mid-1850s.

The flood of miners that followed the 1858 Rockies gold strikes overwhelmed the eastern Utes. At the same time, Utes were allied with the Americans and Mexicans against the Navajo. Mormons, fighting the western Utes for land from late 1840s on, had succeeded by the mid-1870s in confining them to about 9 percent of their aboriginal territory. The United States created the Uintah Reservation in 1861

on land the Mormons did not want. They made most Utah Utes, whose population had been decimated, settle there in 1864.

In 1863, some eastern bands improperly signed a treaty ceding all bands' Colorado mountain lands. Five years later, the eastern Utes, under Chief Ouray, agreed to move west of the continental divide provided about 15 million acres was reserved for them. Soon, however, gold discoveries in the San Juan Mountains wrecked the deal, and the Utes were forced to cede an additional 3.4 million acres in 1873 (most of the remainder was taken in 1880). The U.S. government considered Ouray "head chief of the Utes," paid him an annual salary, and supplied him with expensive goods.

The Southern Ute Reservation was established on the Colorado–New Mexico border in 1877. At that time, the Mouache and Capote Bands settled there, merged to form the Southern Ute tribe, and took up agriculture. Resisting pressure to farm, the Weeminuche, calling themselves the Ute Mountain tribe, began raising cattle in the western part of the Southern Ute Reservation (the part later called the Ute Mountain Reservation).

In the late 1870s, a new Indian agent tried to force the White River Utes to give up their traditional way of life and "become civilized" by setting up a cooperative farming community. His methods included starvation, the destruction of Ute ponies, and encouraging the government to move against them militarily. When the soldiers arrived, the Indians made a defensive stand and a fight broke out, resulting in deaths on both sides (including Agent Nathan Meeker and U.S. Army Commander Thomas Thornburgh). Chief Ouray helped prevent a general war over this affair. The engagement was subsequently called by whites the Thornburgh "ambush" and the Meeker "massacre" and led directly to the eviction of the White River people from Colorado.

By 1881, the other eastern bands had all been forced from Colorado (except for the small Southern and Mountain Ute Reservations), and the other eight bands, later known as the Northern Ute, were assigned to the Uintah and Ouray Reservation in northern Utah (the Uintah Reservation was expanded in 1882 to include the removed Weeminuche Band).

Government attempts to force the grazing-oriented Ute to farm met with little success, owing in part to a lack of access to capital and markets and in part to unfavorable soil and climate. Irrigation projects begun early in the twentieth century mainly benefited non-Indians who leased, purchased, or otherwise occupied Ute land. The government also withheld rations in an effort to force reservation Utes to send their children to boarding school. During the mid-1880s, almost half of the Ute children at boarding schools in Albuquerque died. In 1911, the Ute Mountain Utes increased their acreage while ceding land that became Mesa Verde National Park.

The last traditional Weeminuche chief, Jack House, assumed his office in 1936 and died in 1971. Buckskin Charley led the Southern Utes from Ouray's death in 1880 until his own in 1936. His son, Antonio Buck, became the first Southern Ute tribal chair. During the 1920s and 1930s, Mountain Utes formed clubs to promote leadership and other skills. Disease remained a major killer as late as the 1940s.

By 1934, the eastern Utes controlled about .001 percent of their aboriginal lands. In 1950, the Confederated Ute Tribes (Northern, Southern, and Mountain) received $31 million in land claims settlements. During the 1950s, Ute Mountain people began to assume greater control over their own money, and mineral leases provided real tribal income. Funds were expended on a per capita basis and invested in a number of enterprises, mostly tourist related. The 1960s brought federal housing programs and more land claims money, but the effectiveness of tribal leadership declined considerably. A group of mixed bloods, called the Affiliated Ute Citizens, were legally separated from the Northern Utes in 1954.

Religion Utes believed that supernatural power was located within all living things. Curing and weather shamans, both men and women, derived additional power from dreams. A few shamans, influenced by Plains culture, undertook vision quests.

One of the oldest of Ute ceremonies, the ten-day Bear Dance was a welcome to spring. Bear is a mythological figure who provides leadership, wisdom, and strength. Perhaps originally a hunting ritual, the dance, directed by a dance chief and his assistants, signaled a time for courtship and the renewal of social ties. It was also related to the end of the girls' puberty ceremony. An all-male orchestra played musical rasps to accompany dancers. The host band sponsored feasting, dancing, gambling, games, and horse racing.

The Sun Dance, of Plains origin, was held in midsummer.

Government Before the mid–seventeenth century, small Ute hunting and gathering groups were composed of extended families, with older members in charge. There may also have been some band organization for fall activities such as trading and hunting buffalo.

With the advent of horses, band structure strengthened to facilitate buffalo hunting, raiding, and defense. Each band now had its own chief, or headman, who solicited advice from constituent group leaders. By the eighteenth century, the autonomous bands came together regularly for tribal activities. Each band retained its chief and council, and within the bands, family groups retained their own leadership.

Customs Western Utes were culturally similar to the Paiutes and Shoshones, whereas eastern Utes adopted many Plains traits. The southeastern Utes, in turn, were influenced by the Pueblos and the Jicarilla Apache. Resource areas were owned communally. Games included shinny (women), hoop-and-pole, and dice.

People chose their own spouses with some parental input. Divorce was easy and common. In general, men could have multiple wives. There were various taboos and food restrictions during and immediately after pregnancy for both men and women. Minor rituals were meant to ensure a child's industriousness. Although children were welcomed, twins were considered an unlucky sign, and one or both were often allowed to die. Naming might take place any time, and names were not fixed for life. Nicknames were common.

A menstruating woman was secluded and observed several behavioral restrictions, including the common one of not being allowed to scratch herself with her own hands. There were few puberty customs per se, although girls sometimes danced the Bear Dance, and boys could not eat their first kill. Corpses were wrapped in their best clothes and buried in rock crevices, heads to the east. Their possessions were destroyed (or occasionally given away), and their horses were killed or had their hair cut.

Dwellings The western Utes lived year-round in domed willow houses. Weeminuches used them only in summer, and all groups also used brush and conical pole-frame shelters 10–15 feet in diameter, covered with juniper bark or tule. Sweat houses were of similar construction and heated with hot rocks. In the east, after the seventeenth century, people lived in buffalo (or elk) skin tipis, some of which were up to 17 feet high.

Diet Bands generally regrouped into families to hunt and gather during spring and summer. Important plant foods included seeds, pine nuts, yampa, berries, and yucca. Some southeastern people planted corn in the late prehistoric period. Some groups burned areas to encourage the growth of wild tobacco.

Buffalo were native to the entire area and were important even before the horse. Other important animal foods included elk, antelope (stalked or driven over cliffs), rabbit (hunted with throwing sticks or communally driven into nets), deer, bear, beaver, fowl, and sage hens. Meat was eaten fresh, sun dried, or smoked. Coyote, wolf, and bobcat were hunted for their fur only.

Other important foods included crickets, grasshoppers, and locusts (dried with berries in cake form). Some western groups ate lizards and reptiles.

A Ute camp near Denver, Colorado.

Some bands also fished, especially in the west, using weirs, nets, basket traps, bow and arrow, and harpoons. Important fish included cutthroat trout, whitefish, chubs, and suckers.

Key Technology Musical instruments included flutes, rasps, and drums. Later prehistoric eastern groups obtained shelter, food, clothing, glue, containers, tools, bow strings, and more from the buffalo. Baskets, often made of willow and squawbush twigs, were used for a variety of purposes, especially in seed and berry gathering and preparation. Wood, stone, and horn were other common raw materials. People made cedar, chokecherry, or sheep horn bows, flint knives, and coiled pottery, mostly in the west. They wove tule sleeping mats and made cordage of various barks and plant fibers.

Trade Some southeastern bands traded at Taos and Pecos, perhaps exchanging meat and buckskin for agricultural products. Utes traded with the Spanish when they were not at war. They also acquired blankets and other items from the Navajo for buckskins and buffalo parts.

Notable Arts Fine and performing arts included music, especially singing and drumming; basket making; leather tanning (by women); rock art; and assorted art objects made from materials such as stone, wood, and clay.

Transportation Dogs pulled small travois before horses arrived in the region. Later, goods were moved on full-sized horse-pulled travois made from tipi poles. Winter hunters wore snowshoes, and some western groups used tule rafts or balsas.

Dress Eastern groups wore tanned buckskin clothing. Shirts were plain before increased contact with Plains groups added beads, fringe, and other designs. Twined sagebrush bark was the preferred material in the west. Blankets were made especially of rabbit and buffalo (especially in the east). Men protected their eyes against the sun with rawhide eye shields. They also wore beaver or weasel caps, and both sexes wore hard-sole moccasins over sagebrush socks in winter. Personal decoration included face painting (mostly for special occasions) tattooing, ear ornaments, and necklaces.

War and Weapons Before the horse, warfare was generally defensive in nature. Utes became mounted raiders in the late seventeenth century. Their usual targets were Pueblo, Southern Paiute, and Western Shoshone Indians. Weapons included a three- to four-foot bow (chokecherry, mountain mahogany, or mountain sheep horn was preferred) and arrows. Eastern Utes also used spears as well as buffalo-skin shields.

Some bands were allied with the Jicarilla Apache and the Comanche against both the Spanish and the Pueblos. Utes had generally poor relations with the Northern and Eastern Shoshone, although they were generally friendly with the Western Shoshone and Southern Paiute, especially before they began raiding these groups for slaves in the eighteenth century. Navajos were alternately allies and enemies. Eastern Utes observed ceremonies before and after raids.

Contemporary Information

Government/Reservations The Southern Ute Reservation is located in Archuleta, La Plata, and Montezuma Counties, Colorado. Established in 1873, it contains 310,002 acres. The 1990 Indians population was 1,044. A constitution adopted in 1936 provides for an elected tribal council.

The Uintah and Ouray Reservation is located in Carbon, Duchesne, Grand, Uintah, Utah, and Wasatch Counties, Utah. Founded in 1863, it contains 1,021,558 acres and had a 1990 Indian population of 2,647. It is governed by a business council.

The Ute Mountain Reservation, including the White Mesa Community, is in La Plata and Montezuma Counties, Colorado; San Juan County, New Mexico; and San Juan County, Utah. Created in 1873, it contains 447,850 acres. The 1990 Indians population was 1,262. A 1940 constitution provides for a tribal council.

Economy Important economic activities include oil and gas leases (all Ute reservations are members of the Council of Energy Resource Tribes), stock raising (Ute Mountain and Uintah and Ouray), some timber sales,

Utes became mounted raiders in the late seventeenth century. Before the advent of the horse, warfare was generally defensive in nature.

interest on tribal funds, tribal and government agencies and programs, and tourism, especially on the Southern Ute and Uintah and Ouray Reservations. The Southern Utes are planning a casino and gambling complex. They have also purchased and operate natural gas wells.

The Ute Mountain high-stakes casino joins a bingo hall and pottery cooperative as important economic activities. Ute Mountain has also been able to restore some of its some year-round hunting rights and to negotiate model mineral leases, including provisions for job training. The Ute Mountain Tribal Park features Anasazi ruins. On the Southern Ute Reservation, the Sky Ute Convention Center has had trouble showing a profit. Up to one-half of Utes work for the tribal or federal government. Unemployment remains high on all Ute reservations, and household incomes remain well below those of neighboring non-natives.

Legal Status The Southern Ute Indian Tribe, the Ute Mountain Tribe, and the Ute Indian Tribe (of the Uintah and Ouray Reservation) are federally recognized tribal entities.

Daily Life The Ute language is still widely spoken, although less so among the Southern Ute and among young people in general. There are annual performances of the Bear and Sun Dances. Most housing on all reservations is relatively modern and adequate, although it is considered insufficient on the Southern Ute Reservation. The Southern Ute Reservation also holds a fair and a rodeo and features a newspaper, a library, and a Head Start program. It is the most acculturated of the three communities.

All tribes have scholarship programs for college-bound young people. The White Mesa people at Ute Mountain have become mixed with Navajos and Paiutes. Water there has been contaminated by nearby uranium mills. Most White Mesa people are Mormons. At Ute Mountain, life expectancy remains below 40 years, and alcoholism rates may approach 80 percent. Job discrimination remains a formidable obstacle to employment. Basketry and beadwork remain important artistic activities.

The Animas–La Plata water settlement may mean considerable additional water resources for drinking and possibly farming for the Southern and Mountain Utes. The Native American Church is active among the Southern and Mountain Utes. Factionalism based on tribal membership requirements and deep-seated political disputes, many based on government policy, still threatens the tribes. The quasi-official Affiliated Ute Citizens, with low blood quantums, remain ineligible for most tribal benefits.

Washoe

Washoe (`Wä shū), a word derived from *Washiu,* or "Person," their self-designation. Though lacking any formal institutional structures, the Washoe considered themselves a tribe, or a distinct people.

Location Washoes lived and continue to live around Lake Tahoe, from Honey Lake in the north to about 40 miles north of Mono Lake in the south, on both sides of the California-Nevada border. This mountainous and environmentally rich region was relatively compact (most groups lived within an area of 4,000 square miles, although their range exceeded 10,000 square miles). The Washoe shared many cultural traits of both California and Great Basin Indians.

Population The Washoe population was at least 1,500 in the early nineteenth century. In 1991, over 1,000 lived on reservations and at least 500 lived off-reservation.

Language Washoe is a Hokan language.

Historical Information

History Ancestors of the Washoe arrived in the region roughly 6,000 years ago. Unbroken cultural continuity lasted from around 500 up to about 1800. Although Washoes may have met Spaniards in the late eighteenth century, they were fairly removed from contact with non-Indians until the 1848 California gold rush brought people through their lands. Anglos established trading posts and settlements, complete with fenced lands and water resources, in the 1850s. Indian demands for compensation were met with refusal and/or violence.

When Anglos blamed the Washoe for Northern Paiute resistance, the Indians were forced to turn for protection to the whites who were appropriating their lands. The 1858 discovery of the Comstock silver lode brought a flood of people to nearby Virginia City. They cut the pine forests, and their cattle ate all the wild grasses and scared off the game. Barely ten years after their first substantive contact with white people, around 1850, the Washoes' subsistence areas, and thus the basis for their traditional lives, had been virtually destroyed.

Commercial fishing began in Lake Tahoe by the 1860s. Washoes danced the Ghost Dance in the 1870s. The government repeatedly refused to grant them a reservation on the grounds that there was no good land to give them and that, in any case, their disappearance was imminent. The Washoe were pushed farther and farther into the margins, trying to stay alive as best they could. By the late nineteenth century, whites thought of the "Washoe Tribe" as those groups around Carson City and the Carson Valley; other Washoe groups were unknown or ignored.

The Washoes eventually bought or were allotted some small plots of marginal land. Land for "colonies" was donated or purchased with government funds around 1917 and again in the 1930s. The land was always of poor quality, with little or no water. Some Washoe men worked as ranch hands, women as domestic laborers. Well into the twentieth century, desperate poverty was made even worse by white efforts to repress their culture. The Indians suffered severe discrimination and had no legal civil rights.

Some Washoes embraced the Peyote religion in 1932. Its strenuously opposition by whites and by some traditional shamans brought factionalism to the community. In 1935, the tribe accepted the Indian Reorganization Act and ratified a constitution and bylaws. However, tribal leadership remained ineffective through the 1960s. Throughout the period, most Washoes lived marginally in Carson Valley and around Carson City, although some small groups continued to live in their traditional territory. Public facilities, including schools, were desegregated in the 1950s. The Washoes were awarded a land claims settlement of $5 million in 1970.

Religion Spirits could be related to myths and legends as well as death; those related to death were seen as sources of illness and bad luck. The Pine Nut Dance was the most important ceremony. It was a harvest ceremony that featured prayers, feasting, dances, and games. Other ceremonies were also related to communal subsistence activities.

Male and female shamans acquired supernatural powers through dreams and refined them through apprenticeships. The power imposed strict behavioral and dietary regulations. Shamans used their powers to cure, often by sucking after singing and praying for four days. They also used certain paraphernalia, such as rattles, feathers, and whistles. Shamans collected a fee for curing and participated in hunting and warfare by using their powers. However, they were also regarded with suspicion as potential sorcerers and were regularly killed.

Government In general, the Washoe maintained a strong impulse toward egalitarianism. Small, autonomous, occasionally permanent settlements were composed of family groups. These settlements were fluid in composition, since families regularly moved from one group to another. Each family group was led by temporary headmen (occasionally headwomen) who exercised wider (settlement-wide) influence only occasionally and by dint of accomplishment. Their role as diplomats was assisted by having several wives who might remain with their relatives and establish various family alliances.

Hunt leaders also played leadership roles, and shamans might acquire unofficial influence. Although some concept of a regional community did exist (in the form of local groups that occasionally cooperated), there was probably no formal division into bands, even into the twentieth century when white-imposed leadership created such a perception.

Customs A weak dual division structure may have existed in camps and for games. Marriage partners were generally arranged. Marriage or sexual relations between relatives was strictly taboo. An exchange of gifts between two families constituted a marriage. Couples generally lived with the woman's family until after the first child was born. Separation and divorce were easily obtained.

The dead were cremated, their unburned bones placed in a creek. They were also buried under logs or left in the open. Mourners cut their hair, and houses of the dead were either burned or abandoned. The Washoe had no concept of exclusive territoriality. Some intermarriage with Northern Paiute groups as well as with Miwoks, Maidus, and Nisenans led to irregular cooperation between various subgroups for purposes of trade, visiting, and defense.

Women gathered, processed, and cooked most foods (although both sexes cooperated in gathering acorns and pine nuts and in some fishing and hunting). There were many life-cycle rites and rituals, all connected with ensuring both individual and community health and well-being. Husbands were not present at birth, although they shared some of their wives' postpartum restrictions. Women nursed babies for up to five years. Babies received their names, which were usually derived from some personal behavior, at around age one. Games, which usually included gambling, included the hand game, races, and athletic contests.

The four-day girls' puberty ceremony was a major event. The young women observed several food restrictions, performed many chores on little sleep, and were prohibited from combing their own hair or scratching themselves. Women friends and relatives chanted songs by a fire while dancing a "jumping dance." Afterward, men and women danced a round dance. The dancing continued throughout the night and was followed by a formal conclusion ceremony. The whole was repeated at a woman's second period, after which she was considered marriageable.

Dwellings Mountain winter villages were occupied by at least some members of the family year-round. A conical pole framework between 10 and 15 feet in diameter and set in a shallow pit supported slabs of bark tied on with cordage or sinew. Thatching may also have been used. Doorways faced east. Houses could hold up to about seven people. Temporary, dome-shaped brush shelters, as well as windbreaks and lean-tos, served as seasonal housing while people were away fishing, gathering, or hunting.

Diet Most people moved seasonally with the food supply, but that supply was generally abundant and in predictable locations. Washoes faced little regular hunger until non-natives destroyed their way of life. Each unit made its own decisions about when and where to procure food. The only exceptions to this rule were foods taken collectively, such as acorns, pine nuts, fish, and some animals.

Fish, including trout, suckers, whitefish, and chub, was a staple. Ice fishing was practiced in winter. Fish were caught both individually and communally and were prepared either by pit roasting, stone boiling (in baskets), or drying. Other staples usually included acorns, which were shelled, ground into flour, and leached before being used to make dumplings. Pine nuts, gathered in late fall, were made into flour for soup.

Washoe women gathered a great variety of wild plants, including roots, grasses, seeds, nuts, berries, and bulbs, for food as well as medicine. Tule and cattails were especially important. Women gathered plants with digging sticks. Family groups had traditional harvesting areas. Some rituals were associated with gathering activities.

Deer, antelope, and rabbit were hunted communally in drives. Rabbits, the most important dietary animal, were driven into corrals or over cliffs. The people also hunted mountain sheep and other large and small game, birds, and waterfowl. They collected insects, especially locusts, grasshoppers, and grubs. Men and sometimes women smoked wild tobacco or used it for poultices. Golden eagles were never killed; bears only rarely.

Key Technology Fishing equipment included harpoons, nets, dams, weirs, basket traps, and hook and line. Men used the bow and (sometimes poisoned) arrows for hunting. Other technological items included twined and coiled baskets; stone mortars and pestles, metates and manos, and knives; sandstone pipes and arrow smoothers; wooden utensils and cooking items; fire drills; and looms for making beadwork and weaving rabbit-skin blankets.

Trade The Washoe traded mostly among themselves. When they did trade "outside the family," mainly with groups such as the Miwok, Nisenan, and Northern Paiute, they generally exchanged items such as salt, obsidian, pine nuts, and rabbit skins for sea shells, redbud bark (for baskets), hides, and food items.

Notable Arts Basketry was utilitarian in form and style but, fueled by white demand, reached artistic heights in the late nineteenth century. Rock art was at least several thousand years old. Art objects were made from a variety of materials, including stone, wood, and clay.

Transportation People built cedar-bark and tule rafts for lake fishing and river crossings, circular manzanita or piñon snowshoes for winter hunting, and wooden skis for marsh or snow walking.

Dress The basic clothing materials were skins, usually deerskin, and sagebrush bark. Men generally wore breechclouts, plus capes and leggings in winter. They also plucked their facial hair. Women wore aprons, adding capes in winter. Both sexes wore moccasins of deer hide lined with sage in winter, although people usually went barefoot. Rabbit-skin blankets or robes were also important for clothing and bedding. Both sexes wore tattoos as well as ornaments of many materials and pierced their ears.

War and Weapons Intergroup relations were generally peaceful and cooperative. Most wars (with Maidus, Northern Paiutes, or Miwoks) concerned conflict over the use of subsistence areas. They were small and relatively insignificant. The Achumawi and Atsugewi sometimes raided northern Washoe camps. War leaders were selected for periods of conflict.

For the Washoe who lived in the high and often cold deserts of California and Nevada, rabbit-skin blankets and robes were important for clothing and bedding. The Washoe man pictured here is weaving a blanket.

Contemporary Information

Government/Reservations The Washoe Tribe of Nevada and California has 4,300 acres, plus over 60,000 acres of assorted parcels. These include the Wade Property, California (388 acres); Silverado Parcel, Nevada (160 acres); Upper Clear Creek, Nevada (157 acres); and Lower Clear Creek, Nevada (209 acres). They also have public domain allotments. The tribe serves the residential communities of Dresslerville, Carson, and Stewart, Nevada, and Woodfords, California. It is governed by a 14-member tribal council according to a constitution adopted in 1966.

Woodfords Community, Alpine County, California (1970), 80 acres, 338 resident Indians (1991), is governed by a community council.

Carson Colony, Carson City County, Nevada (1917), 160 acres, 275 resident Indians (1991), is governed by a community council.

Dresslerville Colony, Douglas County, Nevada (1917), 90 acres, 348 resident Indians (1991), is governed by a community council.

Stewart Community, Nevada (1990), 2,960 acres, 90 resident Indians (1991), is governed by a community council.

Washoe Reservation (Ranches), Douglas County, Nevada (1982), 794 acres, 65 Indians (1990), is governed by a tribal council.

Reno-Sparks Indian Colony, Washoe County, Nevada (1917; Washoe and Paiute), 1,984 acres, 262 resident Indians (1990), 724 enrolled members

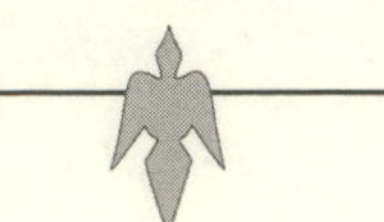

(1992), is governed by a seven-member tribal council.

Susanville Rancheria, Lassen County, California (1923; Maidu, Pit River, and Washoe), 150 acres, 154 Indians (1990), is governed by a seven-member tribal council.

Economy There is still some subsistence acorn and pine nut gathering as well as deer and rabbit hunting. Women make baskets and rabbit-skin blankets. Tribal businesses include a smoke shop, crafts shop, park with camping facilities, construction company, and an aquaculture facility.

Legal Status The Washoe Tribe of Nevada and California (Carson Colony; Dresslerville, Woodfords, and Stewart community councils), the Reno-Sparks Indian Colony, and the Susanville Indian Rancheria are federally recognized tribal entities. The Washoe-Paiute of Antelope Valley, California, have petitioned for government recognition.

Daily Life The Washoe have succeeded in keeping many aspects of their cultural heritage alive. The language is still spoken, although mostly by older people. The girls' puberty rite is still an important ceremony. The tribe hosts an annual tribal picnic, publishes a newsletter, and operates a health center, senior center, housing authority office, and police force. It has jurisdiction of the deer herd as well as other natural resources within their territory. The Stewart Colony maintains a library and archives, and a cultural center is in progress at Lake Tahoe along land long disputed. Children take classes in a wide range of tribal traditions, customs, and arts. The tribe is still creating a land base and seeks to identify sacred sites.

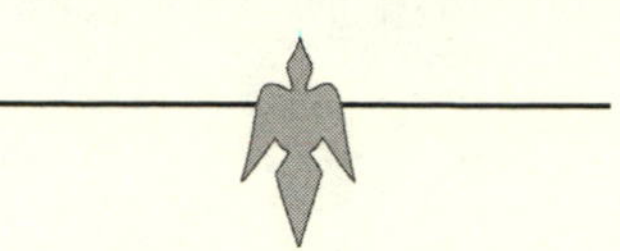

Chapter Five

The Plateau

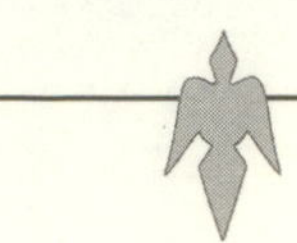

Left: A Wishram bride wears a loop necklace, a dress with six broad rows of lazy-stitch beading on the yoke.
Below right: A Colville woman wears a Hudson's Bay blanket.

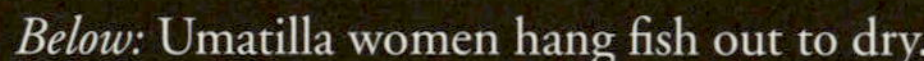

Below: Umatilla women hang fish out to dry.

Above: Chief Joseph, legendary spokesman for the united bands of the Nez Percé.

Native Americans of the Plateau

Plateau

The Plateau region is physically defined by two major river systems, the Columbia and the Fraser. Some 240,000 square miles of land east of the Coast Range (British Columbia) and the Cascade Range (Washington and Oregon) are drained by these rivers. Plateau Indian territory encompassed present-day eastern Washington; eastern Oregon; extreme northeastern California; northern Idaho; extreme western Montana; and interior portions of British Columbia. Aboriginal population estimates for the Columbia Plateau range between 50,000 and 60,000 people.

Climatically, the Plateau is a land of extremes. The northern, or Canadian, Plateau is heavily forested and receives significantly more rain than does the semiarid southern, or Columbia, Plateau. Summer temperatures may approach those of the deserts, whereas near-Arctic cold regularly grips the region in winter.

Most Plateau tribes spoke dialects of either Sahaptian or Interior Salishan languages; the former, along with Wasco-Wishram (Upper Chinookan [Kiksht]) and Modoc/Klamath, are sometimes grouped as Penutian languages. The Kootenai spoke a linguistically isolated language. Owing to trade and familial considerations, however, many groups were functionally multilingual. Athapaskan-speaking Indians such as the Carrier and Chilcotin, considered Subarctic peoples in this book, are occasionally grouped within the Plateau area.

A dependence on inland fish, particularly salmon, as well as roots and berries, was a defining characteristic of Plateau Indian life. Other typical traits included the use of semisubterranean pit earth houses as well as aboveground mat longhouses, the production of a wide variety of grass baskets, individual relationships with guardian spirit helpers, an appreciation of individual dignity and autonomy,

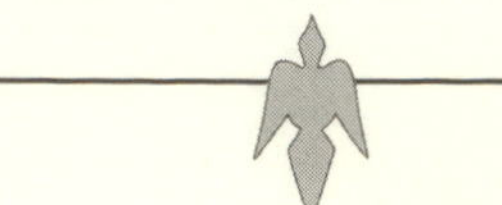

and a reluctance (at least before the early eighteenth century) to engage in warfare.

In the eighteenth and nineteenth centuries, acquisition of the horse made buffalo hunters and raiders out of many groups. Not surprisingly, contact with non-Indians resulted in enormous population and territorial losses as well as significant cultural loss. With the help of land claims awards, favorable legal rulings concerning subsistence rights, and an increasingly well-educated population, Plateau tribes today are attempting with increasing success to rebound from the relative misery of the past 150 years.

People have lived in the Plateau region continuously for at least 10,000 years. Cultural and linguistic continuity dates back at least several thousand years. During much of this period there was no effective cultural boundary between the Plateau and adjacent parts of other regions such as the Great Basin. Although technology changed through the centuries (for example, people adopted specialized grinding tools circa 3000 B.C.E. and the bow and arrow circa 500 B.C.E. at the latest), the basic lifestyle remained similar from the earliest days to the arrival of the horse in the late prehistoric period.

Although salmon and other fish were a staple food for most groups, Plateau Indians also gathered plant foods such as camas, kouse root, bitterroot, and a variety of berries. Roots were often cooked in earth ovens. Plants provided essential medicines and raw materials. Hunting provided additional nourishment: Depending on location, game included deer, elk, antelope, mountain sheep, and bear as well as rabbit, squirrels, and other small game. Most Plateau groups followed a regular migratory route to obtain foods at their greatest productivity. The purpose of Plateau food acquisition was both to meet immediate needs and to built up a surplus for the lean winter months and for trade.

Winter villages, usually located along waterways, were occasionally occupied all year, although generally the dwellings were dismantled and their mats used in temporary summer shelters. Houses generally consisted of semisubterranean lodges (roughly 5 feet deep and 10–16 feet in diameter) of grass, brush, and earth over planks (probably an older style). Roofs were either flat or dome shaped. Entrance was gained

Secretary of the Interior Harold Ickes accepts the new constitution and by-laws from leaders of Montana's Flathead Reservation, October 29, 1935.

through the smoke hole. In summer and perhaps later in time people lived in rectangular tule mat–covered structures with inverted V roofs. Shared hearths ran along the center. These reached lengths of up to 60 feet and accommodated from two to eight families.

In the Thompson River region, circular winter pit houses generally had pyramidal roofs through which one entered and descended on notched ladders. These houses, 20–40 feet in diameter, accommodated 15 to 30 people. Sweat lodges were generally constructed of grass and earth over a wooden frame. Food was stored in pits or on wooden platforms.

Twined "Indian hemp" and tule were two of the most important raw materials for Plateau Indians. The former (along with sagebrush and willow bark) was used to make cordage, baskets, hats, bedding, and nets for fishing and hunting rabbits. Tule, a type of bulrush, was used in the manufacture of mats, which were in turn used as house coverings, flooring, and corpse shrouds. Twined and coiled baskets, often made of spruce or cedar root, were ubiquitous on the Plateau. People used them for household utensils, cooking vessels (boiling by placing heated stones in liquid), water and burden containers, drinking cups, cradles, and numerous other purposes. Bark containers were also used.

Basket weavers and bone carvers, in particular, sometimes reached levels of artistic excellence. Some baskets were decorated with geometric designs,

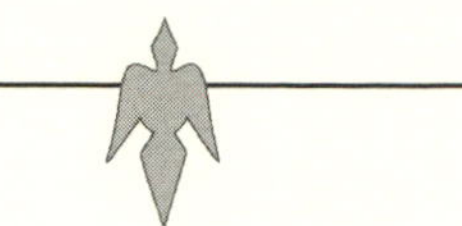

especially in the Thompson River region. In the Middle Columbia region (Sahaptian speakers), Northwest Coast influence revealed itself during the late prehistoric period in art motifs of humans and animals.

The bow and arrow was the principal hunting tool and weapon. Spears were also used and, in war, clubs and armor of rawhide or wooden slats. Arrows were straightened with an elk bone wrench and smoothed with sandstone tools. Fish were speared, netted with weirs and traps, or, especially in the north, caught with hook and line. Women used a stick, sometimes tipped with antler, to dig roots. Other tools, such as pestles and mauls, were made from stone (basalt and granite), bone, and other materials. Dugout as well as bark canoes served as water transportation. Some Indians also regularly burned certain areas to make them more productive and attractive to game.

Before the equestrian tradition became established, clothing was generally made from bark, grass, and fur. Men and women wore breechclouts or aprons and ponchos. Men wore fur leggings in winter; those of women were made of hemp. Ornaments were fashioned from a number of materials, including olivella and dentalium shells from the Pacific Ocean, river clam shells, and various bones.

Plateau Indians traded widely as part of a huge regional network. The largest and most important trading center was located at the Dalles and Celilo Falls, at the head of the Columbia gorge. Surplus salmon—dried, pounded into meal, and stored in salmon skin and cattail bags—was one of the main trade items. Groups from hundreds of miles around brought their specialties: Dentalium and other shells, obsidian, baskets, meat, animal products, clothing, and later slaves and horses were among the most important items. The trade fairs were also centers of cultural exchange.

At least before the advent of the horse, most Plateau societies were relatively egalitarian. That is, villages were politically autonomous, and the authority of village chiefs lay more in their ability to persuade and adjudicate than in their power to make rules and enforce decisions. Women as well as men could be chiefs of many bands. Specialized leaders such as salmon and war chiefs exercised leadership in specific situations. Slavery was hereditary only in far western groups with close ties to Northwest Coast Indians.

In general, Plateau society was held together less by authoritarian means than by an ethic of sharing and obligation as well as by kinship and trade networks and associations. Because people rarely married within their own village, these networks were quite extensive throughout the Plateau. Furthermore, marriage networks generally survived even death, as a widow or widower often married her or his spouse's sibling. Plateau Indians practiced a sexual division of labor, in which women gathered plants, processed and prepared food, and took care of young children, and the men fished, hunted, and had a greater voice in politics, diplomacy, and military affairs.

Aboriginal Plateau religion centered around the relationship between individuals and spirits of animate or inanimate natural things (animals, plants, phenomena, or physical features). Pubescent or prepubescent boys and girls undertook quests in remote places, at which time they often entered into a relationship with a spirit and obtained its song and power, which were revealed indirectly years later. In exchange for respect, which included honor during the winter dances, the spirit was thought to bestow important powers or skills. Shamans, salmon chiefs, and other highly skilled leaders were thought to have attracted one or more particularly powerful spirit helpers.

Non-native influence in the Plateau region appeared with the introduction of the horse, from Shoshone peoples to the south, as early as 1730. Use of the horse influenced life on the Plateau in many ways. It allowed people to migrate over greater distances and to transport larger quantities of dried food. It generally favored political centralization and the formation of tribal structures. Although most groups, especially those on the Canadian and Upper Columbian Plateau, retained their traditional subsistence patterns, others began to hunt buffalo on the Great Plains (or greatly increased their buffalo-hunting activity) and to adopt other aspects of Plains culture, including full-scale raiding.

The historical period among Plateau Indians began with the 1804–1806 Lewis and Clark expedition. However, as was almost universally true, by the time non-Indians actually appeared, Indian

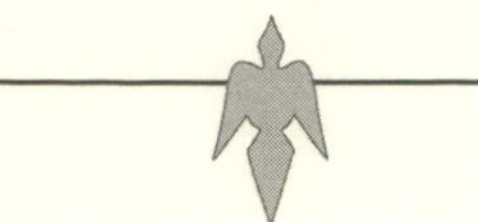

populations had declined substantially (up to 90 percent in some cases) owing to the advance arrival of previously unknown diseases such as smallpox and malaria. Disease epidemics among Indians continued well into the twentieth century. Fur traders followed on the heels of Lewis and Clark, and right behind them came missionaries. Initial relations between Plateau Indians and non-natives were generally friendly.

By the early 1840s, the fur trade in the region had come to an end, and the great tide of non-Indian invaders began to pour in. One of the first major interracial conflicts occurred in 1847 when Cayuse Indians attacked the Waiilatpu Mission and killed its founders, Marcus and Narcissa Whitman, as well as several other whites. The motive behind this action was apparently that the Cayuse held the missionaries responsible for all the sickness and death among the Indians. They also saw the missionaries as symptomatic of the rapidly increasing assault on Indian land and the growing attacks on Indian traditions.

In 1855, several Indian groups, mostly Sahaptian speakers, ceded millions of acres of land in exchange for reservations, financial considerations, and certain subsistence rights (such as fishing) guaranteed in perpetuity. Other Plateau reservations were established by executive order. Between 1855 and 1858, the Yakima and other Plateau groups fought in desperate wars of resistance with the U.S. Army and volunteers. Twenty years later, a Nez Percé band, in a famous and nearly successful act, chose flight to Canada rather than accept the loss of their beloved homeland and a greatly diminished reservation. British Columbia did not establish tribes and reservations per se, but rather created dozens of very small reserves for the individual bands. Although this process allowed most Indians to remain in their traditional territory, it left them with less land overall and discouraged social and political cohesiveness.

Meanwhile, the rise of new Indian religions reflected the extent to which native culture was being altered by the new situation. Around 1860, a Wanapum (Columbia River) Indian named Smohalla had a vision while recovering from a wound. He spoke of the coming end of the world and the resurrection of the Indian dead. He urged Indians to resist Euro-American culture and reservation life and focus instead on attaining salvation through traditional beliefs and practices, including sacred singing and dancing. Smohalla attracted groups of defiant, antireservation Indians to his community near Priest Rapids. He was often jailed for opposing U.S. efforts to encourage farming among Indians.

The teachings of Smohalla and other Plateau prophets were a direct response to the unprecedented destruction of Indian population and traditional lifestyle. They were as well an attempt to bridge the gulf between Indian religion and Christianity, past and present. These beliefs spread rapidly throughout the Plateau and formed the core of the *Wáashat,* Dreamer, Seven Drums, or Longhouse religion.

Few Indians of British Columbia were conquered militarily, nor did they formally surrender title to their land. In 1884, 13 years after British Columbia joined the Canadian Confederation, the Canadian government simply discounted Indian landownership and passed its first Indian Act, under which it appropriated land and exercised legal control over Indians within Canada. Roughly 200 small reserves were created to accommodate the different bands. The thinking was to permit Indians to remain self-sufficient as they made the transition to the capitalist economy, whereas in the United States policymakers forced various groups of Indians to live together on large reservations, where they were strongly encouraged to become farmers and abandon their traditional identities.

Like most North American Indians, Plateau tribes saw increasing difficulty in the late nineteenth and early twentieth century. Few treaty provisions that protected Indians were enforced. For instance, selling alcohol to Indians was prohibited, but offenders were never punished. Indians' land base continued to shrink, sometimes dramatically, owing to a combination of strategies that included the infamous Dawes Act as well as unilaterally imposed "boundary negotiations."

By that time, Indian culture was under full-scale assault at the hands of missionaries and Bureau of Indian Affairs (BIA) boarding schools. Most groups, previously independent and self-sufficient, sank into dependency and poverty. Government officials failed to transform these fishers, gatherers, and hunters into

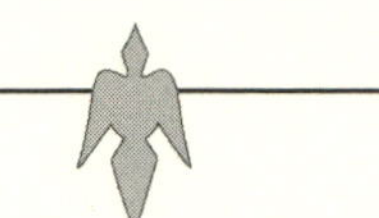

farmers. Job opportunities were minimal, and legal and social discrimination was rampant. Overall health on the reservations was poor.

The tide began to change, ever so slowly, in the mid-1930s, with the passage of the Indian Reorganization Act (IRA). Although many tribes rejected its provisions, the act provided tribes with an opportunity to form governments recognized by the United States (even if the structures were largely alien to native tradition) and to begin to assume greater control over their lives. Unfortunately, the official termination policies of the 1950s undid much of the good of the IRA, and the general postwar economic recovery excluded most Indian reservations.

Revitalization began again in the 1960s, a period of increased federal support to tribes as well as the emergence of a renewed identification with and pride in Indian heritage. In 1974, the issue of fishing rights came to a dramatic head with the so-called Boldt decision reaffirming Indians' right to an active, vital fishery. Corollary concerns such as the effect on native fisheries of potentially destructive actions such as logging, pollution, and dams remain controversial. Fisheries issues may be seen as part of the larger and still controversial question of overall tribal sovereignty. This in turn is bound up with the still deplorable economic situation on most reservations: Although individuals and tribes receive income from timber, mining, grazing leases, and tourism, poverty and its concurrent social ills remain endemic.

On an individual level, many Indians participate in traditional cultural practices. The *Wáashat* (Longhouse or Seven Drums) religion is particularly strong among Sahaptian speakers. Services are conducted in the Sahaptian language, and the religion is an important means for transmitting and affirming Indian identity. The Native American (Peyote) Church and various Christian churches are also represented on the reservations. Like many Native Americans, Plateau Indians face the challenge of retaining a meaningful Indian identity within a culture that cares little about such things. As the tribes become more important decision makers in regional economic matters, this challenge will assume growing importance and poignancy.

Cayuse

Cayuse (`Kī ūz) is a word derived from the French *cailloux,* meaning "People of the Stones or Rocks." Their self-designation was *Waiilatpus,* "Superior People." The Cayuse were culturally similar to the Nez Percé and Wallawalla.

Location In the eighteenth century, Cayuse Indians lived along the headwaters of the Walla Walla, Umatilla, and Grande Ronde Rivers, in present-day Oregon and Washington. Today, most Cayuse live in Umatilla County, Oregon, and in regional cities and towns.

Population The Cayuse population was about 500 in the eighteenth century. In 1990, 1,028 Cayuse, Umatilla, and Wallawalla Indians lived on the Umatilla Reservation.

Language Cayuse, or Waillatpuan, may have been associated with the Sahaptian division of the Penutian language family. However, many Cayuse adopted the Nez Percé language in the nineteenth century.

Historical Information

History The Cayuse may have lived with the Molala Indians, on the John Day River, until the early eighteenth century. At that time the Cayuse acquired horses, and by the nineteenth century they owned many horses and were very strong and dominating for the size of the tribe. They expanded northward and eastward, into the Grande Ronde and Walla Walla Valleys, subjugating the Wallawalla tribe in the process. They also regularly hunted buffalo on the Great Plains, adapting many Plains cultural attributes.

Largely because of their enormous herds of horses, the Cayuse became so wealthy during this period that they no longer bothered to fish, trading instead for fish and other necessities. They welcomed the Lewis and Clark expedition in 1806 and welcomed as well the fur traders who entered their territory shortly thereafter. They were not especially interested in furs but rather in the goods of non-Indian manufacture that they might trade for. Their openness to non-natives was also due in part to their luck at having so far escaped most of the disease epidemics that ravaged other Indian peoples.

The first Presbyterian missions in the area opened in 1836. In 1843, the first emigrants traveled on the Oregon Trail. In 1847, relations between the Cayuse and whites, hitherto friendly, took a dramatic turn for the worse when a group of Indians destroyed the local mission and killed its founders, Marcus and Narcissa Whitman, and others. They blamed the missionaries for the disease epidemics that were destroying their people. They also resented the Whitmans for their intolerance to the Indians and their new wealth based on sales of former Indian land.

The Whitman "massacre" was the opening salvo in a constant struggle (the Cayuse war) with non-natives that lasted until about 1850. Tiloukaikt, a band chief and former friend of non-native traders, was a leader in this conflict. The tribe was ultimately defeated, and some of its members were hanged by the U.S. government. By this time, disease, warfare, and intermarriage with the Nez Percé had greatly reduced the tribe. Although the Cayuse kept up sporadic resistance into the 1850s, they were assigned by treaty to the Umatilla Reservation in 1855 and most were removed there in 1860. Some Cayuses took up farming on the reservation. Some joined the Yakimas (1855), Nez Percés (1877), and Bannocks (1878) in their various wars against the whites, but some also served with the U.S. Army during these wars.

Religion Individuals acquired and maintained relationships with helping nature spirits. Such spirits were obtained during adolescent quests; their powers, which facilitated various skills, were revealed many years later. Shamans acquired particularly strong guardian spirits. They led religious ceremonies and cured illness by blowing, sucking, and chanting. They were also regularly killed for misusing or stealing power. The main religious ceremonies were related to guardian spirits (winter ceremonies), food, and battle.

Government At least in early historic times, each of three autonomous bands was led by a chief and occasionally a war chief. The three chiefs made up a tribal council. Chiefs usually owned many horses and were responsible in part for lecturing their people on proper behavior. The bands, composed of families, were seminomadic. Most subsistence activity was carried out at the family level. By the mid–nineteenth century a single chief had replaced the tripartite structure.

Customs Wealthy men could have more than one wife. The Cayuse regularly intermarried with the Nez Percé. There were strict sanctions against adultery. Infants' heads were shaped for aesthetic purposes. Twins were often killed at birth. In the eighteenth century, the Cayuse became highly skilled horsepeople and adopted the Plains philosophy of war and raiding.

Dwellings Typical Plateau woven reed and mat summer huts and semisubterranean earth-covered winter lodges gave way to hide tipis in the eighteenth century.

Diet Salmon and other fish were the staples. This was supplemented by various plant foods, especially camas and other roots, and berries. Large and small game also contributed to the Cayuse diet.

Key Technology Woven reed mats and baskets played a major role in Cayuse material culture.

Trade Particularly after the early eighteenth century, the Cayuse dominated trade at the Dalles, site of the region's premier trade fair, as well as at other trade locations. Among other items, salmon products and shells came from the west, and elk and buffalo products came from the east. Horses became the most important trade item: In the early nineteenth century, the Cayuse commonly exchanged beaver and horses for guns and ammunition. The Cayuse also collected tribute from weaker tribes.

Notable Arts Cayuse Indians were known for their fine baskets and, later, horse equipment.

Transportation Horses arrived in Cayuse country about 1750. In the early nineteenth century, each person had from 10 to 15 to up to as many as 2,000 horses.

Dress Plateau-style clothing of bark and fur breechclouts, aprons, and ponchos were replaced in the eighteenth century by Plains-style clothing such as long dresses for women, shirts and leggings for men, and moccasins. This late-prehistoric clothing was made of tanned skins, especially antelope and elk, and decorated with fringe and quillwork.

War and Weapons In common with most Plateau groups, the Cayuse engaged in little raiding or warfare until they acquired horses. At that time, they quickly subjugated neighbors such as the Umatilla and the Wallawalla. Plains-style raiding for booty and glory became very important, as did secret war societies and ceremonial preparations for combat. Women and children, particularly Shastas and Klamaths, were

Cayuse finery in this early 1900s photograph shows two styles of warbonnets: The horseman wears a halo style with bison horns, and a standup warbonnet is worn by the man holding the heavily fringed rifle scabbard. In common with most Plateau groups, the Cayuse engaged in little raiding or warfare until they acquired horses. The prebattle ceremony included fasting, sweating, praying, and dancing.

taken as slaves, and captured men were killed. The prebattle ceremony included fasting, sweating, praying, and dancing. Western Shoshones were traditional enemies of the Cayuse, whereas the Nez Percé were longtime allies.

Contemporary Information

Government/Reservations Most Cayuses live on the Umatilla Reservation, Umatilla and Union Counties, Oregon (1855; Umatilla, Cayuse, Wallawalla). The reservation contains 95,273 acres; in 1990, its Indian population was 1,028 people. The reservation is governed by a nine-member elected tribal council plus several active committees. The constitution and bylaws were adopted in 1949.

The Umatilla Reservation is a member of the Umatilla Basin Project, the Columbia River Intertribal Fish Commission, the Basalt Waste Isolation Project, the Hanford Environmental Dose Reconstruction Project, the Columbia Gorge Commission, and other environmental and planning organizations.

Economy In the 1960s, each member of tribe was paid almost $3,500 as compensation for fishing sites lost to the Dalles Dam. There have been other land claims settlements as well. The reservation is developing an Oregon Trail Interpretive Center. There is income from farm leases. Tribal programs provide credit as well as seasonal and regular employment. The tribes also own a forest, a range, a store, and a lake (facilities for camping and fishing).

Legal Status The Confederated Tribes of the Umatilla Reservation is a federally recognized tribal entity.

Daily Life The Confederated Tribes of the Umatilla Reservation value both traditional and modern education. There are some language preservation programs as well as a college scholarship fund. Facilities include a day care center, an arts and crafts organization, and health education and substance abuse programs. Activities include the annual Pendleton Round-up (dances, crafts fair, rodeo) and an annual Indian festival of the arts. The Seven Drum religion is a major force in cultural revitalization. Traditional first salmon and roots ceremonies are also celebrated. The tribes' role in regional economic and political affairs continues to grow.

Coeur d'Alene

Coeur d'Alene (ˋKir də ˋlā n), French for "awl heart," is reportedly a reference by an Anglo trader to the trading skills of these Indians. Their self-designation was *Skitswish,* perhaps meaning "foundling."

Location In the eighteenth century, the Coeur d'Alene lived along the Spokane River upstream from Spokane Falls, including Lake Coeur d'Alene. The region of over four million acres is fertile and well watered. In the early nineteenth century the tribe lived in central Idaho, eastern Washington, and western Montana; the mountains in this area helped to protect their horses against raiders from the Plains. Today's Coeur d'Alene Reservation is located in Benewah and Kootenai Counties, Idaho.

Population The aboriginal (early-eighteenth-century) population of roughly 2,000 had declined to about 500 by 1850. In 1990, 749 Coeur d'Alene and Spokan Indians lived on the reservation, and another 500 or so lived off-reservation.

Language Coeur d'Alene Indians spoke an Interior Salish dialect. They also used a local sign language.

Historical Information

History Like all Salish peoples, the Coeur d'Alenes probably originated in British Columbia. They migrated to the Plateau during their prehistoric period, keeping some Pacific Coast attributes even after they adopted Plateau culture. They acquired the horse around 1760, at which time they gave up their semisedentary lives to hunt buffalo, Plains-style.

Their traditional antipathy toward outsiders made it difficult for trappers to penetrate their territory. A Jesuit mission was established in 1842, however, foreshadowing the significant role the Jesuits were to play in their later history. At this time, the Jesuits successfully influenced the Indians to give up buffalo hunting and begin farming.

In the meantime, intermittent warfare with Indians and non-Indians, plus disease and crowding, had dropped their population by about 85 percent by 1850. In 1858 they fought the ill-fated Coeur d'Alene war (1858) with the help of tribes such as the Northern Paiute, Palouse, and Spokan. Although the immediate cause of this conflict was white treaty violations, it may be seen as an extension of the Yakima war (1855–1856) and the general Plateau Indian resistance struggle during that time.

The roughly 600,000-acre Coeur d'Alene Reservation was created in 1873, at which time the Indians ceded almost 2.4 million acres. However, pressure from miners soon forced the tribe to cede almost 185,000 more acres in the late 1880s. Most of the rest of their land was lost to the allotment process in the early twentieth century. In 1894, 32 Spokan families joined the reservation. Most Coeur d'Alene Indians became Catholics, farmers, and stock breeders. In 1958, the tribe was awarded over $4.3 million in land claims settlements.

Religion Mythical creatures and spirits were all around and in many different forms. Everyone could potentially obtain guardian spirits through vision quests. Furthermore, people prayed for luck to forces of nature. Shamans cured with the help of especially powerful guardians. The few group festivals were held at the beginning of the food season.

Government There were originally three geographical divisions of Coeur d'Alene Indians: Coeur d'Alene River, Spokane River, and Coeur d'Alene Lake. Each was composed of autonomous bands, which were in turn composed of groups of several families, each led by an elected chief. There was no overall tribal organization until the mid–nineteenth century.

Customs Coeur d'Alenes were fiercely independent. Band territorial rights merited a high degree of respect. The people practiced some polygyny. Descent and residence were generally patrilineal. The dead were wrapped in blankets and buried in the ground or under rocks. In addition, the Coeur d'Alenes engaged in giveaways reminiscent of the coastal potlatch.

Dwellings Semiexcavated conical mat houses held between one and three families. Larger, aboveground structures were used for communal activities. Sweat houses were made of bark or grasses over a willow-stick frame. As the tribe became more nomadic, skin tipis gradually replaced mat lodges.

Diet In addition to salmon and other fish, deer was a staple before the time of large-scale buffalo hunting. Other important animal foods included elk, antelope, moose, sheep, bear, and small game. Dogs provided assistance in the hunt. Camas, bulbs, roots, seeds, and berries rounded out the diet.

Key Technology Fishing technology included assorted gaffs, hooks, traps, and nets. A variety of coiled baskets served different functions. Many utensils were made of stone and bone. Pipes were carved of soapstone. Bows were made of mountain sheep horn.

Trade The Coeur d'Alene traded in coiled baskets, rabbit-skin clothing, and, especially after the mid–eighteenth century, horses and buffalo-derived items. They were known for their shrewd trading practices.

Notable Arts Artistic expression may be seen especially in the manufacture of coiled baskets.

Transportation Cedar-bark canoes were used to traverse lakes and navigate rivers. Horses were in general use from about 1760 on.

Dress Traditional clothing was made of woven rabbit skin and the skins of deer, elk, or antelope. Women wore aprons, and men wore leggings, breechclout, and shirt. Beginning in the late eighteenth century, beads and quillwork were added to many clothes. Both sexes wore moccasins and robes in cold weather.

War and Weapons Aboriginally, the people enjoyed good relations with their neighbors, only occasionally

fighting with the Nez Percés or the Spokan. After they acquired the horse, the Coeur d'Alene were allied with the Nez Percé, the Flathead, and the Kootenai against Plains tribes such as the Crow, Lakota, and Blackfeet. Coeur d'Alenes generally won few wars.

Contemporary Information

Government/Reservations The Coeur d'Alene Reservation (1873) is located in Benewah and Kootenai Counties, Idaho. It contains 69,176 acres and had a 1990 population of 749 Indians. The constitution, approved in 1949, calls for a seven-member tribal council elected for three-year terms. Reservation residents are mostly Coeur d'Alene but also include some Kalispel, Spokan, and other Indians. The tribe is a member of the Upper Columbia United Tribes and the Affiliated Tribes of Northwest Indians. Some Coeur d'Alene Indians also live on the Colville Reservation (*see* Colville).

Economy Farming, grazing, and lumbering constitute the most important economic activities. There are also a large tribal farm, a shopping center, a medical center, a construction company, and a service station. Unemployment is chronically high (around 50 percent). Some Indians continue to hunt, fish, and gather foods on and around the reservation. A gambling establishment has been proposed. The tribe received almost $174,000 in land claims settlements in 1981, money that helps the tribe in its goal to purchase lost tribal land.

Legal Status The Coeur d'Alene Tribe is a federally recognized tribal entity. The people are currently contesting the U.S. claim to Coeur d'Alene Lake.

Daily Life Most Coeur d'Alene Indians are Catholics. Little traditional culture remains, although some language preservation programs have recently been instituted. Children attend a mission school or public schools. People celebrate various Catholic and quasi-traditional ceremonies. There is a tribal college scholarship fund. The tribe is reacquiring non-Indian owned land in order to unify its land base. It is currently engaged in environmental reclamation projects to mitigate the effects of mining devastation. Whaa-laa Days, in July, feature traditional games and contests.

Columbia

See Sinkiuse

Columbia River Indians

See Colville; Umatilla; Yakima

Colville

Colville (`Kōl vil) is a name derived from the Colville River and Fort Colville (a Hudson's Bay Company trading post), which in turn were named for Eden Colville, a governor of the company. Whites also called these Indians "Basket People," after their large salmon fishing baskets, and "Chaudière" (kettles), after depressions in the rocks at Kettle Falls and a corruption of their self-designation, *Shuyelpee.* They were culturally similar to the Okanagon and Sanpoil Indians.

Location In the eighteenth century, the Colville Indians lived in northeastern Washington, around the Kettle and Columbia Rivers. Today, most live in Ferry and Okanogan Counties, Washington, and in nearby cities and towns.

Population The eighteenth-century Colville Indian population stood at roughly 2,000. The Colville population reportedly declined to six or seven in 1882. In 1990, 3,782 Indians lived on the reservation.

Language Colville Indians spoke a language from the Okanogan group of the Interior division of the Salish language family.

Historical Information

History As early as 1782, a smallpox epidemic destroyed large numbers of Colville Indians. Colville Indians became involved with the fur trade shortly after the arrival in the area of the first non-Indians around 1800. By the mid–nineteenth century they were suffering from a sharply declining population and a deteriorating way of life due to new diseases,

This woman is wearing a Hudson's Bay blanket, a popular trade item for the Colvilles. The name of this tribe is derived from the Colville River and Fort Colville, a Hudson's Bay Company (HBC) trading post, which in turn took their names from Eden Colville, an HBC governor.

anti-Indian violence, land theft, and severe disruption of their subsistence habits. Missionaries arrived in 1838. Non-Indian miners flooded into the area in the mid-1850s. Colvilles did not participate in the wars of that time.

Two Colville reservations were established in 1872 for local nontreaty tribes. One, created in April, was considered by local whites to have too-fertile lands, so another reservation with less desirable land was established in July. The early reservation years were marked by conflict with non-Indians and among the tribes. Many Colville Indians converted to Catholicism in the later nineteenth century. In 1900, they lost 1.5 million acres, over half of their reservation. Even so, non-natives continued to settle on the truncated reservation in large numbers until 1935.

The Confederated Tribes of the Colville Reservation were formed in 1938. The government restored some land in 1956. The tribe divided over the issue of termination through the 1950s and 1960s but ultimately decided against it. The tribe won significant land claims settlements in the later twentieth century.

Religion Colvilles believed in the presence of spirits in all natural things, animate and inanimate. Individuals sought guardian spirits and their associated songs through the traditional means of singing, fasting, praying, and performing feats of endurance. Prepubescent boys generally undertook a series of one-night vigils. Shamans' especially powerful spirits allowed them to cure illness and perform other particularly difficult tasks.

The five-day first salmon ritual, held under the direction of the salmon chief, was the most important ceremony. Other important religious occasions included the midwinter spirit dances and the first fruits rite. The midwinter dances served the additional purposes of bringing people together and releasing winter tensions.

Government Autonomous villages were each led by a chief and a subchief; these lifetime offices were hereditary in theory but were generally filled by people possessing the qualities of honesty, integrity, and diplomacy. The authority of chiefs to serve as adviser, judge, and general leader was granted mainly through consensus. As judge, the chief had authority over crimes of nonconformity such as witchcraft, sorcery, and assault.

An informal assembly of all married adults confirmed a new chief and oversaw other aspects of village life. All residents of the village were considered citizens. Other village leaders included a messenger, a speaker, and a salmon chief (often a shaman, with the salmon as a guardian spirit, who supervised salmon-related activities). By virtue of their ability to help or hurt people, shamans also acquired relative wealth and power from their close association with chiefs, who liked to keep them friendly.

Customs Colvilles regularly intermarried with other Salish people. They also very occasionally practiced a

form of potlatch. Local villages had associated, nonexclusive territories or subsistence areas. Winter was a time for visits and ceremonies. During that season, women also made mats and baskets, made or repaired clothing, and prepared meals while men occasionally hunted or just slept, gambled, and socialized.

Pacifism, generosity, and interpersonal equality and autonomy were highly valued. Girls fasted and were secluded for ten days at the onset of puberty, except for a nighttime running regime. The exchange of gifts between families constituted a marriage, a relationship that was generally stable and permanent. Corpses were wrapped in tule mats or deerskin and buried with their possessions. The family burned the deceased's house and then observed various taboos and purification rites. Mourners cut their hair and wore old clothes.

Dwellings Traditional winter dwellings were semisubterranean, circular pit lodges, with grass, brush, and earth covering a pole frame; they had flat or conical roofs. Entrance was through a ladder in the smoke hole. In the late prehistoric period, the people began building rectangular tule-mat houses. Each of the two to eight families in the house paired off to share a fire in the center of the building.

Diet Food was much more often acquired by the family than by the village. Fish, especially salmon, played a central role in the diet (groups were able to net up to 3,000 a day at Kettle Falls). Men caught four varieties of salmon as well as trout, sturgeon, and other fish. They fished from May through October. Although women could not approach the actual fishing areas, they cleaned and dried the fish. Dried fish and sometimes other foods made up much of the winter diet. People generally ate two meals a day in summer and one in winter.

Women gathered shellfish, salmon eggs, bulbs, roots, nuts, seeds, berries, and prickly pear. Camas was eaten raw or roasted, boiled, or made into cakes. A short ceremony was performed over the first gathered crop of the season. Men hunted most large and small game in the fall. They prepared for the hunt by sweating and singing. Meat was roasted, boiled, or dried. Women came along to help dress and carry the game. Men also hunted birds and gathered mollusks.

Key Technology Twined and coiled basketry items were heavily represented. These included utensils, cooking tools, containers, bags, and hats. Some items were decorated with geometric designs. Women sewed tule mats with Indian hemp. Hunting tools included spears and the bow and arrow. People also used sandstone arrow smoothers and elk rib arrow straighteners. Fish were speared, netted, and caught in weirs and traps. Women used a slightly curved digging stick with an antler or wood cross handle.

Trade Trade fairs were held at Kettle Falls and at the mouth of the Fraser River. The level of trade increased with the acquisition of horses.

Notable Arts Artistic expression was seen mainly in coiled baskets with geometric designs as well as mat weaving. Rock painting had been practiced for thousands of years.

Transportation Before the horse, people used two kinds of dugout canoes and snowshoes.

Dress Standard traditional attire was a bark breechclout or apron, a bark poncho, winter leggings (fur for men, hemp for women), and fur robes. Skin garments became popular beginning in the late prehistoric period. For decoration, people wore Pacific Coast shell ornaments as well as animal teeth and claws.

War and Weapons Men used their hunting tools as weapons, plus rawhide or wooden armor. War chiefs were selected on an ad hoc basis. Colvilles were occasionally allied with Okanagon Indians against the Nez Percé and Yakima.

Contemporary Information

Government/Reservations The Colville Reservation (1872) is located in Ferry and Okanogan Counties, Washington. It comprises 1,011,495 acres and had a 1990 Indian population of 3,782. An Indian Reorganization Act constitution approved in 1938 calls for a 14-member business council and various

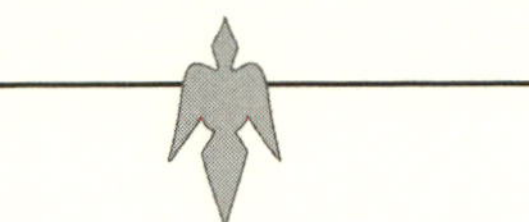

committees. The Confederated Tribes is a member of the Affiliated Tribes of Northwest Indians and other intertribal organizations.

Colville Indians are also members of the Columbia River Indians, a group who lives primarily in Priest Rapids, Cooks Landing, Billieville, and Georgeville, Washington; Celilo, Oregon; and non-Indian communities. The Council of Columbia River Chiefs meets at Celilo, Oregon. The community at Priest Rapids is directly descended from that of Smohalla, a founder of the Dreamer or Longhouse religion.

Economy The reservation economy is largely built around stock raising, farming, logging (including a sawmill) and reforestation, and seasonal labor. There is some mining as well as a meat-packing plant, a log cabin sales business, and tourism-related businesses such as a trading post and gambling enterprises. There is potential for development of hydroelectric resources.

Legal Status The Confederated Tribes of the Colville Reservation is a federally recognized tribal entity. The Columbia River Indians are not federally recognized.

Daily Life Colville Indians are largely acculturated. Language preservation programs are hindered by the lack of a common aboriginal language. Recent efforts to reinvigorate disparate tribal cultures and religions include the presence of the Chief Joseph Band of Nez Percé Indians with their Seven Drum Religion, the Indian Shaker Church, and the Native American Church. The reservation hosts an annual powwow and a circle celebration. There is also a program of reacquiring and consolidating the land base and a goal to increase the general levels of education. The Colville Business Council wields growing power in regional and statewide issues.

Flathead

See Salish

Kalispel

Kalispel (`Kal ə s pel), "Camas People," from the name of an important plant food. They are also known as the Pend d'Oreilles, French for "ear drops," a term referring to the Indians' personal adornment. These people were grouped aboriginally into two divisions, lower (Kalispel proper) and upper.

Location In the eighteenth century, the Kalispel lived around Pend d'Oreille Lake and River. Today, most live on their reservation in Pend Oreille County, Washington. Kalispels also live on the Colville and Flathead Reservations.

Population The eighteenth-century Kalispel population was approximately 1,600. In 1990, some 250 Kalispels lived on reservations and in regional cities and towns.

Language Kalispels spoke a dialect of Interior Salish.

Historical Information

History Like other Salish peoples, the Kalispel probably came from British Columbia. The upper division may have moved east and south onto the plains of Montana before the Blackfeet pushed them back, in the eighteenth century, to the Pend d'Oreille Lake region. They especially joined with other Plateau groups to hunt buffalo and organize war and raiding parties after the introduction of the horse.

The North West Trading Company opened a trading post in Kalispel country in 1809. The first Catholic mission opened in 1846 and relocated in 1854 with the Upper Kalispels to the Lake Flathead area. Kalispels were forced into a major land cession in 1855, and the upper division was assigned to the Flathead Reservation, in Montana, but the lower division refused to relocate, asking instead for a reservation of their own. They remained relatively isolated until 1863, when the British Columbia gold rush brought many miners through their territory.

In 1887, one of the two Lower Kalispel bands moved to the Flathead Reservation. The other, under Marcella, remained in the Pend d'Oreille Valley. Their reservation was created by executive order in 1914: It consisted of 4,629 acres, of which only 150 acres of tribal land remained after individual allotments and white encroachments. The tribe was awarded $3 million in land claims settlements in 1960, and another $114,000 in 1981.

Religion Individuals obtained guardian spirits in dreams and visions to provide them with luck and success. Boys began vision quests around the onset of puberty with fasting and praying. Shamans' powerful spirits let them cure illness, see the future, and influence hunting. To honor their spirits, men sang their spirit songs and danced during a midwinter festival. The Kalispel also celebrated other, food-related festivals.

Government In the eighteenth century there were two geographical divisions, Upper Pend d'Oreilles and Lower Pend d'Oreilles, or Kalispelem. The latter were further divided into Lower Kalispel (Kalispel proper), Upper Kalispel, and Chewelah (perhaps a separate tribe). Each division was composed of related families and was led by a chief selected on the basis of merit. Later, a tribal chief presided over a council made up of the band chiefs.

Customs Games almost always included gambling. Marriage was usually monogamous. People cultivated some tobacco. The dead were dressed in robes, sewn in blankets, temporarily placed on a platform, and then buried. Their possessions were given away, and their names were never spoken again.

Dwellings The basic structure was semiexcavated and cone shaped, built of mat and earth covering a wood frame. A larger one was used for communal and ceremonial use, and smaller ones, holding one to three families, for living. Kalispels also built cedar-bark lodges and temporary brush shelters. Decorated hide tipis replaced mat dwellings during the eighteenth century.

Diet Fish was the staple, especially trout, salmon, and whitefish. Important plant foods included camas (from which the Indians made a distinctive bread), bitterroot, other roots, and berries. Some buffalo hunting took place on the Plains after the eighteenth century; other important animal foods included antelope, deer, elk, and small game. Most food was boiled with hot stones in baskets.

Key Technology In addition to the usual Plateau technological items, Kalispels specialized in making white pine canoes, birch-bark baskets, and woven skin bags.

Trade Kalispels traded for smoked salmon and other items with people from the west.

Notable Arts Artistic expression was found mainly in basketry.

Transportation The Kalispel were masters of their white pine canoes. The lower division had distinctive low-riding canoes to meet the winds on Pend d'Oreille Lake. Although they were excellent horsemen, they had relatively few horses, even in the mid–nineteenth century.

Dress Most clothes were made from rabbit or deer skins. Men wore breechclouts and shirts, and women wore dresses. Both wore moccasins, caps, robes, leggings, and shell earrings.

War and Weapons The Kalispel were generally peaceful, although they were occasionally allied with the Spokan against the Kootenai.

Contemporary Information

Government/Reservations The Kalispel Reservation (1914) is located in Pend Oreille County, Washington. It contains 4,557 acres; the 1990 Indian population was 91. The tribal charter and constitution were approved in 1938. The Kalispel Indian Community is descended from Lower Kalispels.

Some Kalispel also live on the Salish-Kootenai Reservation, Montana, as well as on the Colville Reservation, Washington (*see* Colville; Salish).

Economy Tribal businesses include Kalispel Caseline, Kalispel Agricultural Enterprise, and Kalispel Tribal Bingo. Grazing also provides some income. Other projects, such as a tribal store and a fish and game business, are under consideration. The Kalispel are also attempting to reacquire several thousand acres of land. Income levels on the reservation are chronically low.

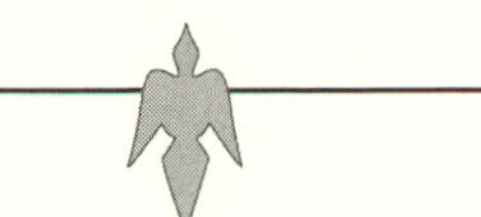

Legal Status The Kalispel Indian Community is a federally recognized tribal entity.

Daily Life Kalispels are trying to remain economically competitive into the twenty-first century while retaining their tribal identity. Kalispel Powwow Days are held in August.

Klamath

Klamath (`Klam uth) is a word of uncertain derivation. The Klamaths' self-designation is *Maklak*, "People." The Klamath were culturally similar to the Modoc and other northern California Indian peoples.

Location In the early nineteenth century, Klamath people lived on 20 million acres in south-central Oregon and northeastern California. The land included forests and mountains of the Cascade Range, highland lakes and marshes, and the headwaters of the Klamath River. Today the descendants of these people live mostly in Klamath County, Oregon, and in regional cities and towns.

Population Perhaps 1,200 Klamath Indians lived in the early nineteenth century. In 1958, on the eve of termination, the tribal rolls stood at 2,133. In 1993, the tribe had about 2,700 enrolled members.

Language Klamath is a dialect of Lutuami, a Penutian language.

Historical Information

History Klamath Indians were probably spared direct contact with non-natives until the arrival in 1829 of Peter Skene Ogden. The white invasion of the 1850s also brought disease and scattered the game, destroying traditional subsistence patterns. In an 1864 treaty, the Klamath and Modoc people ceded over 13 million acres of land for a 1.1-million-acre reservation on former Klamath lands in southern Oregon. In addition to Klamaths and Modocs, the reservation included Pit River Indians, Shastas, Northern Paiutes, and other groups. These Indians agreed to end the practice of slavery at that time.

Some Modocs left the reservation in 1870 because of friction between themselves and the Klamaths. The latter remained aloof from the 1872–1873 Modoc war. By the end of the nineteenth century, all Indians on the Klamath Reservation were known as the Klamath tribe. In 1901, the government agreed to pay the tribe $537,000 for misappropriated lands. Other land claims settlements, for millions of dollars, followed during the course of the century.

In 1958 the U.S. government terminated the Klamath Reservation. Although the government had long coveted the timber-rich reservation, whereas many Klamaths were strongly against it, termination was hastened by a tribal leader at the time. In 1958, 77 percent of the tribe voted to withdraw from the collective entity and take individual shares of the land proceeds. In 1974, the remaining 23 percent agreed to sell the rest of the reservation for per capita shares. At that time, the Klamaths lost the last of their land base. Termination has had a profoundly negative effect on members of the tribe.

Religion Male and female shamans acquired power through fasting, visions, and prayer. The most powerful shamans, able to cure illness as a result of their possession of very strong spirit power, were generally men. Curing itself was dramatic in a literal sense. Shamans also controlled weather, accompanied war parties, affected hunting, and found lost items. They held winter seances to demonstrate their power.

People sought spiritual help at puberty and at other times by going to remote places to fast, pray, and swim. Powers came from spirits that were associated with nature. Spirits conferred power and songs, which might provide luck and skills, in dreams and visions.

Government Traditionally, the Klamath were organized into from four to seven autonomous subdivisions or tribelets. Each tribelet may have consisted of about ten winter hamlets. Each had a chief (chosen either as a consequence of wealth or the ability to provide leadership in war), but shamans probably wielded more authority.

Customs Acquiring wealth and prestige was the basic goal, although the concept was nowhere near as developed as it was along the Northwest Coast. Klamaths collected items such as skins, food, shells, and weapons. Industriousness and acquisitiveness were valued, and the people practiced little hospitality or sharing. The tribelets were as likely to feud as to intermarry.

Summer was a time for gathering, hunting, and warfare. Exchanging gifts (the bride price) constituted a marriage. Divorce was not uncommon, although it was complicated by property arrangements. Klamaths flattened their babies' foreheads. Corpses were wrapped in tule mats and, with their possessions, carried by canoe to a funeral pyre. The house was also burned. Following the ceremony, relatives of the deceased sweated in the sweat lodge for purification. Dances were generally nonceremonial in nature.

Dwellings Permanent winter hamlets were generally built on lake shores and near marshes. Houses were semisubterranean, circular multifamily structures, covered with earth on a wood frame. Entrance was through the roof. Several nuclear families might live in one lodge. Circular, mat-covered wood frame houses served in summer or on hunting trips. Winter and summer sweat lodges were built in a style similar to that of the dwellings.

Diet Fish, mostly freshwater whitefish and suckers, was the food staple. The Klamaths also ate waterfowl. In summer, women gathered roots, berries, and other plant foods, and men hunted deer, antelope, and small game. Wild waterlily seeds *(wokas)* were harvested in late summer; they were eventually ground into flour.

Key Technology Fishing equipment consisted of nets, traps, and spears. Bows were made of juniper or yew; arrowheads were of obsidian or stone. Twined baskets and mats served a large variety of purposes.

Trade Klamath Indians participated in local trade patterns. With the arrival in the region of horses, the Klamath engaged in large-scale raiding for slaves and goods, which they then traded in the north for horses.

Notable Arts Basketry was well developed into a fine art.

Transportation Klamath Indians used both dugout canoes and snowshoes.

Dress Women wore basketry caps, and moccasins were made of tule before the switch to buckskin. Men and women wore fiber skirts, as well as tule leggings, sandals, and fur mittens in winter. After the Plains influence became stronger, in the nineteenth century, they switched to fringed fiber or buckskin aprons. They also pierced their ears and noses for dentalia shells and wore tattoos.

War and Weapons War leaders were selected on an ad hoc basis. The Klamath were frequently at war with the Achumawi, Shasta, and Kalapuya. They raided these groups, especially in the early nineteenth century, for slaves and goods, which they traded in the north for horses. Raiding parties might consist of men from different tribelets, since war was the main activity that brought people together (women sometimes accompanied war parties). Revenge was a major cause of war. Offensive and defensive equipment included fine bows and arrows and elk hide and slat armor, clubs, and spears. The main strategy lay in surprise attacks. After victory, warriors would collect booty and slaves, mutilate and dismember the dead, and perform a scalp dance that lasted for several nights.

Contemporary Information

Government/Reservations The Klamath Reservation is located in Chiloquin, Oregon. The General Council (total enrolled adult population) chooses an eight-member business committee. A constitution, originally adopted in 1929, was reestablished in 1975.

Economy At least 70 percent of Klamaths live below the poverty level (before termination, Klamaths were one of the most self-sufficient of all U.S. tribes).

Legal Status The Klamath Indian Tribe is a federally recognized tribal entity (rerecognized in 1986). In the 1970s, federal courts recognized Klamath hunting and fishing rights, despite the absence of a land base.

Daily Life The Klamath tribe has a new dental facility and plans for new tribal offices and a cultural center. Cultural revitalization programs include an annual sucker ceremony, basket-weaving classes, and native-language textbooks. Klamath people also practice such traditional crafts as beadwork and bone work. They host an all-Indian basketball tournament in February and March and a powwow on December 31. Treaty Days in August celebrate the restoration of tribal status.

Klikitat

Klikitat (`Klik i tat) is derived from a Chinook term meaning "beyond" (the Cascade Mountains). Their self-designation was *Qwulh-hwai-pum,* "Prairie People." The Klikitat were culturally similar to the Yakima.

Location Klikitats lived and continue to live in the vicinity of Mt. Adams in south-central Washington.

Population The precontact population was roughly 700. Today Klikitat descendants constitute roughly 8 percent of the population of the Confederated Tribes and Bands of the Yakima Indian Nation (about 500 people).

Language Klikitat was a member of the Sahaptian division of the Penutian language family.

Historical Information

History The Klikitat may have originated south of the Columbia River, moving north in the prehistoric period to become skilled horsepeople and fighters after they acquired horses around 1700. The 1805 encounter with Meriwether Lewis and William Clark, on the Yakima and Klikitat Rivers, was friendly all around.

Skilled with firearms, the Klikitat sometimes acted as mercenaries for other Indian tribes, taking women and horses as pay. Their effort during the 1820s to expand south of the Columbia was repulsed by the Umpqua. Later, the Klikitats had their revenge by helping whites to conquer the Umpqua. They also scouted for the U.S. Army in the 1850s.

In 1855, the United States asked Klikitats and other local Indians, including Yakimas, to cede 10.8 million acres of land. Most tribes accepted a 1.2-million-acre reservation in exchange. Although Indians retained fishing and gathering rights at their usual off-reservation places and were given at least two years to relocate, the governor of Washington declared their land open to non-Indians 12 days after the treaty council ended.

In anger at this betrayal, a few Yakimas killed some whites. When soldiers arrived, a large group of Indians drove them away. In retaliation for the treacherous murder of a Wallawalla chief and negotiator, the Wallawalla, Klikitat, Cayuse, and Umatilla Indians joined the Yakimas in fighting non-Indians. Yakimas agreed to settle on a reservation in 1859, after the war ended and 24 of their number were executed. The future Yakima Indian Nation included, in addition to Yakima bands, the Klikitat, Wanapam, Wishram, Palus (Palouse), and the Wenatchi.

Reservation Yakimas entered a brief period of prosperity but were soon pressured to sell land; most people were forced into poverty, obtaining some seasonal work at best. In 1891, about one-third of the reservation land had been allotted to individuals, but the Yakima Nation, under Chief Shawaway Lotiahkan, was able to retain the "surplus" usually sold to non-Indians in such cases. Still, many of the individual allotments, including some of the best irrigated land, were soon lost. Around the turn of the century as much as 80 percent of the reservation was in non-Indian hands.

As a result of twentieth-century dam construction (Bonneville, 1938; Grand Coulee, 1941; Dalles, 1956), the number of salmon and steelhead that returned to spawn to the Yakima River declined by between 98–99 percent. The issue of fishing rights remained an important and controversial one from the beginning of the reservation period through its resolution in 1974. Well into the twentieth century, Yakima Nation people continued much of their traditional subsistence and ceremonial activities.

Religion Klikitats believed in a supreme creator and many other deities as well. Adolescent boys undertook spirit quests in the mountains. Shamans, recipients of particularly powerful guardian spirits, cured illness but were sometimes killed themselves if their patient died.

Government Nomadic bands were led by nonhereditary chiefs with advisory powers. Before the historic period, the tribe created two divisions, eastern and western, of which the latter mixed with Cowlitz Indians west of the Cascades to become Taitnapams.

Customs Dogs and women carried most burdens before the horse's arrival. Burial took place in rock slides and gravel pits lined with cedar planks. Occasionally a corpse, along with tools and ornaments, was cremated in such a pit. Klikitats were skilled horse riders.

Dwellings Klikitats traditionally lived in typical Plateau-style semisubterranean circular pit houses with conical earth-covered roofs. Aboveground, mat-covered houses partially replaced the pit houses around 1800.

Diet Fish, especially salmon, was the dietary staple. Various berries, roots, bulbs, and other plant foods were also important. Men also hunted deer, elk, antelope, and various large and small game.

Key Technology The reed mat served a number of purposes, as did coiled and twined baskets. Containers were made out of bark as well as reeds. Hunting weapons included spears and the bow and arrow. Spears, nets, and weirs were used in fishing. Other tools included stone drills, scrapers, and knives. Antler wedges were used to split wood. Bone was used to make awls and needles.

Trade Skilled traders, Klikitats served as intermediaries between Northwest Coast and Plateau peoples.

Notable Arts Women made fine baskets that were sometimes decorated with geometric patterns. Beginning in the late prehistoric period, they also made clothing decorated with quillwork, shells, and feathers, as well as fine beaded blankets.

Transportation The people used dugout canoes and snowshoes. They acquired horses around 1700.

Dress Bark and fur breechclouts, aprons, and ponchos were replaced by Plains-style clothing in the eighteenth century. Women wore twined basket hats.

War and Weapons Weapons of war were generally the same as hunting weapons, with the addition of stone clubs. Klikitat bows and arrows were of particularly high quality.

Contemporary Information

Government/Reservations The Yakima Reservation and Trust Lands (1859) are located in Klikitat, Lewis, and Yakima Counties, Washington. They consist of roughly 1.4 million acres. The 1992 enrolled Indian population was 8,315 (of a total reservation population of well over 27,000). The reservation is governed by a 14-member tribal council.

Some Klikitats also live on the Siletz Reservation (*see* Upper Umpqua in Chapter 3).

Economy Timber and its associated industries, including a furniture manufacturing plant, are the nation's main income producer. The reservation also owns extensive range and farmland, although 80 percent of irrigated land remains leased by non-Indians. The Wapato Project provides control over their own water. The Yakima-Klikitat Fish Production Project, a cooperative effort between the Yakima Nation and Washington State, is a major fishery restoration/conservation venture.

In addition to fishing and small business enterprises, the nation owns an industrial park containing Indian and non-Indian industries. The Yakima Land Enterprise operates fruit orchards and stands and a recreational vehicle park. Government and the tribe provide other jobs. Still, unemployment fluctuates between about 30 and 60 percent, and up to 75 percent of the people live below the poverty level.

Legal Status The Confederated Tribes and Bands of the Yakima Indian Nation is a federally recognized tribal entity.

Daily Life Klikitats are no longer distinct as a tribe. In 1972, the United States restored about 22,000 acres of land, including the sacred Pahto (Mt. Adams). The Longhouse (Seven Drums) religion is active on the reservation, as are sweat house customs and first foods feasts. The longhouse serves as the locus of Indian identity. Longhouse families throughout the Plateau

region are tied together, mostly through marriage. The Indian Shaker religion is also active on the reservation, as are Christian churches.

In addition to religious practice, Yakimas maintain many aspects of traditional culture, including family customs, service, and leadership. The language is alive and well, especially as part of religious ceremonies and among more traditional people. There are language classes for adults and childrens. Yakima basketry is still an important art and craft.

The nation operates a huge, full-service cultural center, museum, and restaurant in addition to two community centers and an elders' retirement center. As part of an overall emphasis on education, the nation provides incentives such as scholarships and summer programs. Children attend public school on the reservation. There is also a tribally run school as well as a private, four-year liberal arts college on the reservation. The nation publishes newspapers and operates a radio station. It also hosts an annual summer all-Indian rodeo, a powwow, a huckleberry festival, and basketball tournaments. Lawsuits over water use from the Yakima River system are pending.

Kootenai

Kootenai (`Kūt ə nā), a nomadic people geographically divided into upper and lower divisions after their exodus from the northern Great Plains. The Upper Kootenai remained oriented toward the Plains, whereas the Lower Kootenai assumed a more Plateau-like existence. Their self-designation was *San'ka,* "People of the Waters."

Location The Kootenai may once have lived east of the Rockies, perhaps as far east as Lake Michigan. In the late eighteenth century, the Kootenai lived near the borders of British Columbia, Washington, and Idaho. Today, most live on the Kootenai Reservation, Boundary County, Idaho; on the Flathead Reservation, Flathead, Lake, Missoula, and Sanders Counties, Montana; and on several reserves in British Columbia.

Population The immediate precontact population was about 1,200. In 1990, roughly 900 Kootenai Indians lived in the Northwest, including several hundred intermarried with Salish people. The 1991 Canadian Kootenai population was around 550.

Language Kutenaian is unrelated to any language family except possibly Algonquian.

Historical Information

History During the eighteenth century, the Kootenai acquired the horse and began hunting buffalo on the Plains, adopting much of Plains culture. Shortly after initial contact around 1800, Canadian traders built Kootenai House, a trading post. More traders, including Christianized Iroquois, as well as missionaries soon followed. Despite the Kootenais' avoidance of much overt conflict with whites, they suffered dramatic population declines during these years, primarily as a result of disease and alcohol abuse. The formal establishment of the international boundary in 1846 divided the tribe over time.

The Flathead Reservation was established in 1855 for the Salish and Kootenai people. Some Kootenai refused to negotiate the loss of their land, however, and did not participate in these talks. Some moved to British Columbia rather than accept reservation confinement. When the Kootenai Reservation was established in 1896, about 100 Kootenai Indians moved to the Flathead Reservation. Of the ones who refused to move, those near Bonners Ferry were granted individual allotments in 1895. The tribe won a $425,000 land claims settlement in 1960, and the Kootenai Reservation was officially established in 1974.

Religion People believed that every natural thing has a spirit and that there is one master spirit, perhaps the sun. Everyone hoped to acquire the help of guardian spirits they sought on adolescent vision quests. Male and female shamans provided religious leadership, acquiring spirit powers in dreams that allowed them to cure and foretell the future. Curing involved singing power songs, chanting, and shaking rattles. Ceremonies such as the midwinter festival, the Sun Dance, and the War Dance were related to soliciting and/or honoring spirits. There were three religious societies: Crazy Dogs, Crazy Owls, and Shamans.

Government Each of roughly eight autonomous bands was led by a chief and an assistant chief, such as a war, fish, and hunting chief. The chieftainship was hereditary into the historic period, when leadership qualities began to assume the most importance. A council of shamans chose the upper division chief. Decision making was by consensus.

Customs Games almost always included gambling. Prisoners of war were enslaved. Marriage was usually monogamous. People cultivated some tobacco. The dead were dressed in robes, sewn in blankets, temporarily placed on a platform, and then buried. The family moved the deceased's tipi, gave away all former possessions, and never spoke the person's name again. Kindness was a highly valued quality.

Dwellings The Kootenai traditional dwelling, summer and winter, was conical (especially the lower division), made of rushes and mats or hemp over pole frames. During the eighteenth century, that style switched, especially among the upper division, to buffalo-skin or mat tipis. They also used oblong, semisubterranean communal festival houses of mats on a pole frame.

Diet Although they lived in the mountains west of the continental divide, upper division Kootenais remained oriented toward Great Plains buffalo, whereas the lower division ate mostly fish (trout, salmon, and sturgeon), small game, and roots. Both divisions also hunted big and small game, and both gathered roots and berries, especially bitterroots. Most foods were dried and stored for winter.

Key Technology Men fished using weirs, basket traps, and spears. Women made a variety of baskets, including ones that could hold water. Hunting equipment included cherry and cedar bows, clubs tipped with antler points, stone knives, and slingshots. Buffalo were hunted with a bow and arrow or by driving them off cliffs. Leather items were prominent, especially among the upper division, whereas the lower division primarily made items of Indian hemp and tule. Kootenais also made carved wood bowls, clay pots, and stone pipes.

Trade Kootenais participated in regional trading complexes and began trading with non-native trappers about 1807.

Notable Arts Upper division people especially became very skilled leather workers.

Transportation The Lower Kootenai were oriented toward rivers and lakes, and their water transportation was accomplished by use of bark and dugout canoes. Hunters used snowshoes in winter. Upper division people acquired horses in the eighteenth century.

Dress Lower division Indians wore bark, mat, and hemp clothing, whereas upper division people used mostly skins. They switched to Plains-style clothing, including dresses, breechclouts, shirts, and leggings that were decorated with fringe, feathers, quills, and beadwork, in the eighteenth century. Both groups wore moccasins and fur robes.

War and Weapons Although the Kootenai were not especially militaristic, the war chief reigned in the upper division and was second in importance in the lower division. The Blackfeet, Lake, Assiniboine, and Cree were traditional enemies. Hunting equipment was used as weapons.

Contemporary Information

Government/Reservations The Kootenai Reservation (1974) is located in Boundary County, Idaho. It contains roughly 2,680 acres, most of which are allotted. The 1990 Indian population was 61, of roughly 200 tribal members, most descended from Lower Kootenais. Residents are closely related to the Kootenai community at Creston, British Columbia. The 1947 constitution calls for a four-member elected tribal council. The Kootenai Tribe is a member of the Upper Columbia United Tribes Organization and the Affiliated Tribes of Northwest Indians.

The Flathead Reservation (1855; Confederated Salish and Kootenai Tribe, which includes Flathead, Kalispel, and Kootenai) is located in Flathead, Lake, Missoula, and Sanders Counties, Montana. It contains 627,070 acres and is governed by a ten-member tribal council. The 1990 Indian population was 5,110; most Kootenais are descended from the upper division. Just

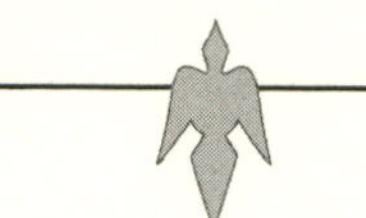

under half of the land base is non-Indian owned, and over 80 percent of the reservation population is non-Indian. Kootenais live mainly in the northern part of the reservation.

Four bands (Columbia Lake, Lower Kootenai, Saint Mary's, Tobacco Plains) live on various reserves in British Columbia (see their profiles under "Daily Life").

Economy On the Flathead Reservation, forestry and associated enterprises as well as ranching are important economic activities. Tourism, including the KwaTaqNuk resort on Blue Bay on Flathead Lake, is also important. The tribes lease the Kerr Dam for $10 million annually and will assume the dam's operating license in 2015. S&K Electronics provides some jobs. Most tribal members work for the tribes. High unemployment (about 50 percent in the late 1980s) remains chronic.

There are a crafts shop, a motel, and a fish hatchery at Bonners Ferry (Kootenai Reservation). Some people continue to hunt, fish, and gather plant foods.

Legal Status The Confederated Salish and Kootenai Tribes of the Flathead Reservation is a federally recognized tribal entity. Legal jurisdiction over Flathead Reservation Indians belongs to the tribes. The Kootenai Tribe of Idaho is a federally recognized tribal entity. The four Canadian bands are federally and provincially recognized.

Daily Life Despite serious economic, social, and health problems on the Flathead Reservation, people try to retain their Indian culture and to transmit it to the younger generations. Salish and Kootenai College and a tribal high school were created around 1977. The reservation hosts two large powwows in July.

The establishment of the Kootenai Reservation in 1974 led to paved roads, improved housing, and a community center. Traditional culture, religion, and language remain strong among the Bonners Ferry Kootenai.

There are four Kootenai bands in Canada (statistics are as of 1995):

Lower Kootenai Band controls eight reserves on 2,443 hectares of land. The reserves were allotted in 1906. The population is 156, of whom 77 live in 32 houses on the reserves. Election is by custom, and the band is affiliated with the Ktunaxa/Kinbasket Tribal Council. Children attend band and provincial schools. Important economic resources and activities include trapping, hay ranching, a bird sanctuary, and small businesses. Facilities include offices, a community hall, and a recreation center.

St. Mary's Band controls four reserves on 7,446 hectares of land. The reserves were allotted in 1884. The population is 231, of whom 163 live in 54 houses on the reserves. Election is by custom, and the band is affiliated with the Ktunaxa/Kinbasket Tribal Council. Children attend band schools. Important economic resources and activities include livestock ranching, a museum, arts and crafts, and individual hay farms. Facilities include offices, a recreation center, a garage, and a church.

Tobacco Plains Band controls one reserve on 4,227 hectares of land. The reserve was allotted in 1884. The population is 138, of whom 88 live in 24 houses on the reserve. Election is by custom, and the band is affiliated with the Ktunaxa/Kinbasket Tribal Council. Important economic resources and activities include livestock ranching, logging, farming, a restaurant, and a duty-free shop. Facilities include offices, a garage, and a fire station.

Columbia Lake Band controls one reserve on 3,401 hectares of land. The reserve was allotted in 1884. The population is 199, of whom 111 live in 44 houses on the reserves. Election is by custom, and the band is affiliated with the Ktunaxa/Kinbasket Tribal Council. Important economic resources and activities include a campground and an individually owned dude ranch. Facilities include a recreation hall and a ceramics shop.

Lake

See Okanagon

Lillooet

Lillooet (`Lil wet), a name meaning "wild onion" or "end of the trail" and once applied only to the lower division of the tribe. The Lillooet exhibited marked characteristics of Northwest Coast culture.

Location Most Lillooets lived traditionally and continue to live in southwest British Columbia, Canada.

Population The eighteenth-century population of approximately 4,000 has recently been exceeded (about 4,500 in 1995).

Language Lillooet is an Interior Salish language.

Historical Information

History Indian groups of the Plateau, including Interior Salishan speakers, have been living in their historic regions for a long time, probably upward of 9,000 years. Early (circa 1809) intercourse with non-native traders was generally friendly, although some non-native diseases had struck the people even before the beginning of the actual contact period. The people were able to live in a relatively traditional way until they were devastated by smallpox epidemics accompanying the gold rushes of the mid–nineteenth century. To make matters worse, famine followed the disease epidemics, striking with particular severity in the mid-1860s. Survivors gradually resettled on reserves delineated by the government of British Columbia.

Religion Special guardian spirits helped shamans cure and recover lost souls. Carved wooden masks representing mythological clan ancestors were displayed at clan dances.

Government Lillooets were organized into upper and lower divisions, with each division composed of named bands of one or more villages. In aboriginal times, each village represented a single clan with one hereditary chief. Other leaders included war chiefs, hunting chiefs, orators, and wealthy and generous men.

Customs Adolescents prepared for adulthood by fasting and engaging in feats of physical endurance. They also sought guardian spirits through vision quests or dreams to give them luck and skills. Girls were isolated at the time of their first menstrual periods. Like coastal groups, the Lillooet observed a caste system and kept slaves. Potlatches commemorated special life-cycle events, at which the host enhanced his prestige by giving away gifts. The dead were wrapped in woven grass or fur robes and placed in painted grave boxes or in bark- or mat-lined graves. Graves were often marked with mortuary poles carved with clan totems (spirit and mythological associates).

Dwellings Men built circular winter lodges of cedar bark and earth on a wood frame. Lodges were excavated to a depth of around 6 feet and ranged between about 20 and 35 feet in diameter. The floor was covered with spruce boughs. The clan totem was carved on the center pole or on an outside pole (lower division). Larger log and plank dwellings housed between four and eight families. Oblong or conical mat-covered houses served as shelter in summer.

Diet Salmon and other fish were the food staples. Men hunted both large and small game, including bear, beaver, rabbit, raccoon, and mountain goat. Hunters rubbed themselves with twigs to disguise their human scent. Women gathered assorted roots and berries and dried the foods for storage.

Key Technology The basic raw materials were bark, tule, and wood in addition to skins and other animal parts. Fishing equipment included nets, weirs, spears, and traps. Men, sometimes assisted by dogs, hunted with bow and arrow, traps, deadfalls, and snares. Many items and utensils were carved from wood. Bags were of bark, twined grasses, or skin. Digging sticks were made of sheep horn or deer antler.

Trade The Lillooet were great traders in the lower Fraser River region. They served as the main intermediary for coastal trade. Exports included animal skins, cedar bark, berries, hemp, and goat's wool. Imports included sea products, especially shells and salmon, as well as dugout canoes and slaves.

Notable Arts Men were known for their skill at wood carving. Stone, often soapstone, was also carved for artistic purposes, most often in the shape of a seated person holding a bowl. Women decorated clothing with porcupine quillwork. They also made

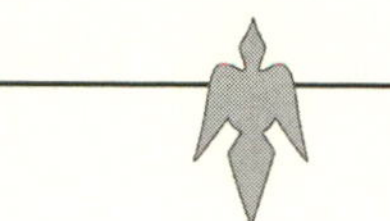

excellent coiled baskets decorated with geometric motifs and colorful dyes.

Transportation People used both bark and cedar dugout canoes to navigate local waterways. They used snowshoes for winter travel. Most Interior Salish people acquired horses in the mid–eighteenth century.

Dress Most clothing was made from cedar bark or skins. Men wore deerskin breechclouts in summer and added skin leggings and short shirts in winter. Women probably wore wraparound skirts, plus leggings in winter. Moccasins were generally plain. Some people used thongs to tie pieces of fur or hide to their feet. Women wove robes of rabbit skin or goat wool. Personal decorations included dentalium shell ornaments and face paint. Men wore long looped necklaces, often decorated with abalone shell. Women tended to wear abalone in their braids and tattoo their wrists and arms.

War and Weapons Lillooets fought with Thompsons and other Salish groups. Defensive equipment included armor of elk skin or rods as well as large shields.

Contemporary Information

Government/Reservations See "Daily Life" for profiles of contemporary Lillooet bands (all statistics are as of 1995).

Economy Economic activities center around forestry, fishing, hay ranching, and land development.

Legal Status The bands described under "Daily Life" are federally and provincially recognized.

Daily Life Anderson Lake Band controls 804 hectares of land at the head of Anderson Lake. The reserve was established in 1881. The population is 213, of whom 134 live on the reserve. Elections are held under the provisions of the Indian Act, and the band is affiliated with the Coast Mountain Development Council. Children attend provincial schools. Important economic activities and resources include a campsite, a boat launch, a fast food restaurant, an investment corporation, logging, a sawmill, and a fish factory. Facilities include offices, a community hall, and a church.

Bridge River Band controls three reserves on 3,940 hectares of land. The reserve was established in 1881. The population is 303, of whom 111 live on the reserve. Elections are held under the provisions of the Indian Act, and the band is affiliated with the Lillooet Tribal Council. Children attend band and provincial schools. Important economic activities and resources include forestry management and a hay cooperative. Facilities include offices, a community hall, and a garage.

Cayoose Creek Band controls three reserves on 687 hectares of land near the town of Lillooet. The reserve was established in 1881. The population is 150, of whom 85 live on the reserves. Elections are held by custom, and the band is affiliated with the Lillooet Tribal Council. Children attend band and provincial schools. Important economic activities and resources include a partnership in Lillooet Salish Enterprise, ranching, arts and crafts, and forestry. Facilities include offices and a church.

Fountain Band controls 17 reserves on 1,572 hectares of land north of the town of Lillooet. The population is 706, of whom 489 live in 82 houses on the reserves. Elections are held by custom, and the band is currently unaffiliated. Children attend band and provincial schools. Important economic activities and resources include ranching, arts and crafts, forestry, and a small boat factory. Facilities include offices, a community hall, a day care center, and a church.

Lillooet Band, formerly part of the Fraser River Band, controls six reserves on 700 hectares of land west of the town of Lillooet. The population is 290, of whom 163 live in 44 houses on the reserve. Elections are held by custom, and the band is affiliated with the Lillooet Tribal Council. Children attend band and provincial schools. Important economic activities and resources include land leases and commercial property rentals. Facilities include offices, a community hall, a recreation center, a kindergarten, and a church.

Mount Curie Band controls ten reserves on 2,929 hectares of land 6 miles south of Pemberton. The population is 1,515, of whom 1,053 live in 276 houses on the reserves. Elections are held under the

provisions of the Indian Act. Children attend band and provincial schools. The Mount Curie Band has instituted a five-year economic development plan that includes agriculture, forestry, and tourism. Facilities include offices, a community hall, and a group home.

Pavilion Band controls seven reserves on 1,112 hectares of land north of the town of Lillooet. The reserves were established in 1861. The population is 380, of whom 253 live in 43 houses on the reserves. Elections are held by custom, and the band is affiliated with the Lillooet Tribal Council. Children attend band and provincial schools. Important economic activities and resources include a limestone plant and small businesses. Facilities include offices, a recreation center, and a church.

Samahquam Band controls five reserves on 183 hectares of land on Douglas Portage. The population is 220, of whom 12 live in two houses on the reserves. Elections are held by custom, and the band is affiliated with the Coast Mountain Development Council. Children attend provincial schools. Important economic activities and resources include the Coast Mountain Development Corporation. There are no facilities on the reserves.

Seton Lake Band controls six reserves on 1,802 hectares of land on the north shore of Seton Lake. The population is 512, of whom 230 live in 71 houses on the reserves. Elections are held by custom, and the band is affiliated with the Lillooet Tribal Council. Children attend band and provincial schools. Important economic activities and resources include forestry, a sawmill, a store, a restaurant, and a wood products manufacturing shop. Facilities include offices, a community hall, a church, and a garage.

Skookum Chuck Band, formerly part of the Lillooet River Band, controls ten reserves on 676 hectares of land on Douglas Portage. The population is 305, of whom 25 live in 16 houses on the reserves. Elections are held by custom, and the band is affiliated with the Coast Mountain Development Council and the In-SHUCK-ch Council. Important economic activities and resources include the Coast Mountain Development Council. Facilities include offices, a community hall, a church, and a diesel power station.

Modoc

Modoc (`Mō dok), from *Moatokni,* or "Southerners" (Klamath). Their self-designation was *Maklaks,* or "People," as was that of their neighbors and linguistic cousins, the Klamath.

Location Traditionally, Modocs lived around Goose, Clear, Tule, and Klamath Lakes, in northern California and southern Oregon. Today, Modocs live mostly around Oregon and in Northwest cities as well as in Oklahoma.

Population The eighteenth-century Modoc population was roughly 500. There were almost 600 enrolled Modocs in 1990, roughly two-thirds of whom lived in or near Chiloquin, Oregon.

Language With the Klamath, the Modoc spoke a dialect of the Lutuami division of the Penutian language family.

Historical Information

History Modocs obtained horses early in the nineteenth century, about the time they encountered non-natives, and by the 1830s they were aggressively raiding their neighbors for horses, slaves, and plunder. Major disease epidemics in 1833 and 1847 reduced their population considerably. Wagon trains began coming through their territory during the late 1840s, scaring the game away and disrupting their natural cycles. Hungry now, and anxious and resentful, they began attacking the intruders, as well as neighboring Indians, for slaves. When gold was found near their territory in 1851, miners flocked in and simply appropriated Indian land, killing Indians as they liked.

The 1860s Ghost Dance brought them little comfort, and they, especially the women, drifted into debauchery during this period. In 1864, Modocs and Klamaths ceded most of their land and moved to the Klamath Reservation. The Modoc were never comfortable there, however, and matters became worse when a food scarcity exacerbated the level of conflict. They petitioned several times for their own reservation, but to no avail. In 1870, about 300 Modocs under Kintpuash (Captain Jack) reestablished a village in their former homeland on the Lost River.

In 1870, about 300 Modocs under Kintpuash (Captain Jack) reestablished a village in their former homeland on the Lost River. Increasing conflict with white settlers soon led to a military confrontation. Pictured here are prisoners Captain Jack, Wheum, and Buckskin Doctor.

Increasing conflict with white settlers soon led to a military confrontation, after which the Indians escaped to nearby lava beds.

Meanwhile, another group of Modocs under Hooker Jim also fled to the lava beds south of Tule Lake after attacking several ranches in revenge for an unprovoked army attack on their women and children. In a confrontation early in 1873, about 80 Indians held off 1,000 U.S. soldiers and irregulars. At a peace parley later that year, the Modocs killed the U.S. general and one of his negotiators. Later, another white attack was repulsed, but the Indians killed some soldiers during negotiations. However, Modoc unity was failing, and their food was running out. Hooker Jim was captured and betrayed his people, leading troops to the hideout of Kintpuash, who was forced to surrender. At his trial, Hooker Jim's testimony against Kintpuash and others resulted in their being hanged. Most surviving Modocs were sent to the Quapaw Reservation in the Indian Territory (Oklahoma).

The Oklahoma Modoc became farmers and ranchers, and many adopted Christianity. Modoc tribal land ownership in Oklahoma ended in 1890 when their land was allotted to individuals. A group of 47 Modocs returned to the Klamath Reservation around 1905, but that reservation was terminated in 1954. Its lands were sold in 1964 and 1971. The Oklahoma Modocs lost their tribal status in 1956 as well, but they were restored in 1978.

Religion Shamans, usually men, provided religious leadership. They dreamed spirit dreams for five nights and then performed a five-day quest, acquiring a number of guardians and powers. They could cure illness, interpret dreams, control the weather, and harm people at will. Curing was generally accomplished by sucking out a disease object. Adolescent boys and girls also undertook spirit quests.

Government Each of about 25 Modoc villages was led by a civil and a war chief. Civil chiefs were selected on the basis of their wealth as well as their leadership and oratory skills; there were also some hereditary chiefs. An informal community assembly decided most legal matters.

Customs Corpses were wrapped in deerskin and cremated. The house and possessions were also burned, and the deceased's name was no longer spoken. Widows cut their hair and covered their faces with pitch and ash. Modocs practiced infant head flattening.

Dwellings Winter dwellings were permanent, semiexcavated lodges made of willow poles covered with tule mats and earth. Width averaged between 12 and 20 feet. People entered through a smoke hole in the roof. Temporary mat-covered structures were used at seasonal camping sites. Sweat houses were heated with steam; they were a place for cleansing as well as praying.

Diet Modocs followed the food supply in three seasons. They ate fish, especially salmon, trout, perch, and suckers. Men hunted a variety of large animals as well as rabbits and other small game. Antelope were driven into brush corrals. Fowl were taken with nets and decoys. Women gathered camas and other roots, greens, berries, and fruits. Seeds, especially those of the waterlily *(wocus),* were also important; they were gathered in the fall and ground into flour.

Key Technology Fishing equipment included nets, spears, hook and line, and basket traps. Many items were made of tule or bulrushes, such as twined baskets, mats, cradles, rafts, and moccasins. The people used stone mullers and metates for grinding seeds, stone arrow straighteners, and basketry seed beaters.

Trade Modoc Indians were actively involved in the regional trade. They especially obtained horses for slaves and plunder at the Dalles.

Notable Arts Women made particularly fine baskets.

Transportation Traditional means of transportation included cedar dugout canoes, snowshoes, and tule and lashed-log rafts. Horses were acquired in the early nineteenth century.

Dress Men and women wore skin, grass, or tule aprons. They also wore tule moccasins, leggings, fur robes, and hats in winter. Charcoal black on the face protected against sun and snow. They flattened their infants' heads for aesthetic purposes.

War and Weapons The war chief was coleader of the village. Modocs' traditional enemies were the Achumawi and the Shasta.

Contemporary Information

Government/Reservations The Modoc Tribe of Oklahoma is located in Miami, Oklahoma. Their constitution was approved in 1991. They own an administrative building, a church, a cemetery, and just over nine acres of land.

Many Modoc descendants also live on the Klamath Reservation in Chiloquin, Oregon. The General Council (total enrolled adult population) chooses an eight-member business committee.

Economy Modoc descendants participate in the local economy.

Legal Status The Modoc Tribe of Oklahoma is a federally recognized tribal entity.

Daily Life Oklahoma Modocs are engaged in a major project to document their history and recover their language and traditions. Some Oklahoma Modocs regularly attend ceremonies with their relatives in the Northwest. They are also involved with pan-Indian activities in Oklahoma.

Nespelem

See Sanpoil

Nez Percé

Nez Percé (`Nā Pūr `sā, `Nez Pur`sā, or Nez Pūrs), French for "pierced nose," was a name bestowed by non-Indian traders in the nineteenth century. Ironically, the Nez Percé did not generally pierce their noses as many other local Indians did. Their Salishan neighbors called them *Sahaptin,* or *Shahaptin.* Their self-designation was *Nimipu,* "the People," or *Tsoop-Nit-Pa-Loo,* "the Walking Out People." Their early historic culture also contained Great Plains and Northwest Coast elements.

Location Before contact with non-Indians, the Nez Percé lived on about 17 million acres between the Blue and the Bitterroot Mountains in southeast Washington, northeast Oregon, and southwest Idaho. Today, most live in Clearwater, Idaho, Lewis, and Nez Percé Counties, Idaho; Ferry and Okanogan Counties, Washington; and in regional cities and towns.

Population The early-nineteenth-century Nez Percé population was about 6,000. In 1990, roughly 3,000 enrolled Nez Percés lived in Idaho.

Language Nez Percé is a member of the Sahaptian division of the Penutian language family.

Historical Information

History Somewhere around 1730, the Nez Percé acquired horses and began their dramatic transformation from seminomadic hunters, fishers, and gatherers to Plains-style buffalo hunters. They quickly became master horse riders and breeders. Several decades of peaceful hunting and trading ended around 1775, when the Blackfeet Indians, armed with guns they received through the fur trade, began a long period of conflict in western Montana. By 1800 or so, Nez Percé Indians had been exposed to Euro-American technology and had heard rumors of a very powerful people to the east.

Their first encounter with non-Indians was with the Lewis and Clark expedition (1805). The Indians welcomed these white people as well as the hundreds of traders, missionaries, and others who poured in in subsequent years. The Nez Percé were involved in fur trade during the 1820s and 1830s; they even helped to outfit settlers in the 1840s. Meanwhile, epidemics were taking a tremendous toll on their population.

In 1855, the Indians ceded several million acres of land but kept over eight million acres for a reservation. Non-Indian miners and other intruders ignored the restrictions and moved in anyway, precipitating a crisis among the Indians over the issue of loyalty toward whites. Following gold strikes in 1860, whites wanted the Wallowa and Grande Ronde Valleys, land that equaled more than 75 percent of the reservation. In 1863, only one chief, with no authority to sell Nez Percé land, signed a treaty. The United States then used that document as an eviction notice, ending years of friendship and cooperation between the Nez Percés and whites. In the meantime, the Dreamer religion had begun influencing the Nez Percé, among others, to resist non-native imperialism.

In 1877, the Wallowa Band were unilaterally given 30 days to leave their homeland. In response to this ultimatum, some younger Indians attacked a group of whites. Young Joseph, chief with his brother, Ollikut, reluctantly sided with the resisters. When soldiers came, firing on an Indian delegation under a flag of peace, the Indians fired back. Joseph's band, about 450 Indians under the leadership of Looking Glass, knew that they could never return home or escape punishment at the hands of the United States. They decided to head for Canada.

Chief Joseph, legendary spokesman for the united bands of the Nez Percé (1903).

During their two-month flight, the group traveled 1,700 miles, constantly evading and outwitting several thousand U.S. Army troops. They did fight several battles during their journey but never were defeated. They also passed through Yellowstone National Park at one point, encountering tourists but leaving them in peace. Joseph was just one of the leaders of this flight, but he became the most important and well known. Many Indians died along the way.

Tired, hungry, and cold, the group was forced to surrender in early October just 30 miles from Canada. Joseph and other Nez Percé were never allowed to return to their homeland. Those who survived were exiled to Kansas and the Indian Territory (Oklahoma), where many died of disease, and finally to the Colville Reservation in Washington.

The sharply rising death rate among the Nez Percé from tuberculosis after the 1870s stemmed largely from the replacement of their traditional mat

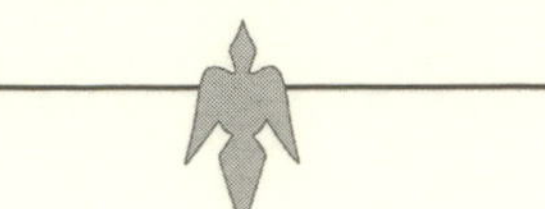

houses by "modern" wooden ones. Heavy missionization had by the end of the nineteenth century resulted in factionalism and considerable loss of tribal heritage. In 1971, Nez Percés received land claims settlements of $3.5 million.

Religion Spirits were inherent in all of nature. After years of instruction, adolescents sought their protection and power by fasting and visiting remote places. Men and women shamans, with especially strong, heavenly oriented guardian spirits, provided religious leadership. They cured illness, controlled the weather, and presided at ceremonies. They might also inflict harm. Curing methods included smoking, sweats, and herbal medicines. Dreams were also connected to good and evil events. During the winter religious ceremonies, participants dressed as their spirits and sang their spirit songs. There were many intertribal festivals and ceremonials as well, such as scalp dances.

Government Small, local bands each had one or more villages and fishing areas. Civil chiefs led the bands, although war chiefs exercised temporary power during periods of conflict. Chiefs were generally elected, although sons often followed fathers, and wealth (in horses) became more important in the late prehistoric period. They had no power in purely personal matters. Women could neither be nor elect chiefs. Chiefs and old men made up the village and tribal councils; decisions were taken by consensus. Ultimately, tribal cohesion grew out of the necessity to defend against fighters from the Great Plains.

Customs Bands were called by the names of streams. Each group contained at least one permanent winter village and a number of temporary fishing camps. Some subsistence areas were considered tribal property. All handmade items were the property of the maker, except that the male was entitled to all property in unusual cases of separation or divorce.

Menstruating and late-term pregnant women were strictly segregated. Young, unmarried men slept in the sweat lodges. Young men and women, especially the latter, were married by about age 14. Brides were commonly purchased, and polygamy was common. Abortion was rare, as was birth out of wedlock. Adultery was a capital crime. Women did most domestic work, including dressing skins; men's work revolved around hunting and war.

Immediately after death, corpses were dressed in good clothes and had their faces painted. After several days, they were wrapped in deerskin and buried with their former possessions. Boulders and cedar stakes marked grave sites. The family in mourning cut their hair and wore poor, dirty clothing.

Pipe smoking was an important part of burial and other rites and ceremonies. The murder of a tribe member usually required blood revenge or at least blood money. Theft was punished by public disgrace. Other serious crimes or infractions included adultery, rape, and lying. Prisoners of war might be used as slaves, but their children were free, and the adults were also frequently adopted into the tribe. Some names and songs ran in the male line. Typical games included archery, dice, hoop-and-pole, and the hand game; most included betting. Childrens' games included tops and string games.

Dwellings Permanent settlements were located along rivers. Winter dwellings were semisubterranean, circular wood frame structures covered with cedar bark, sage, mats, grasses, and earth. The roof was flat or conical. Mats covered the floors. There were also tipi-like communal longhouses, up to 150 feet long, of similar construction. These houses held up to 50 families. People slept along inner walls and shared fires along the center.

Older boys and unmarried men slept and sweated in grass- and earth-covered sweat lodges; others were built for men and women to sweat in. Circular, underground menstrual huts were about 20 feet in diameter. In summer, people built temporary brush lean-tos. Some groups adopted hide tipis in the eighteenth century.

Diet Nez Percés were seminomadic, moving with the food supply. Fish, especially salmon, was a staple, along with trout, eel, and sturgeon. Salmon was broiled, baked, or boiled or dried, smoked, and stored. Animal food included elk, deer, moose, mountain sheep, rabbits, and small game. After the Nez Percé acquired the horse, parties traveled to the Plains to hunt buffalo. Some meat was "jerked" for

winter. Deer were run down or shot, as were other game, with a bow and arrow or killed with a spear. Some animals were hunted with use of decoys.

Women gathered plant foods such as camas, kouse, bitterroot, wild carrot, wild onion, and berries. Camas, dug in midsummer, was peeled and baked in a pit oven. Most berries were dried and stored for winter. Other food included fowl, eggs, and birds. People ate horses, lichens, and tree inner bark when there was nothing else to eat. Most food was either boiled, steamed in pits, or roasted in ashes.

Key Technology Fish were speared from platforms and caught using nets, spears, small traps, and weirs. Men used various nooses, snares, nets, and deadfalls for hunting as well as bows made of mountain sheep horn. Women made a range of woven and coiled baskets, some watertight, as well as woven reed bags. They also made cups, bowls, winnowing baskets, women's caps, and mats of cattails and tule. Many baskets were made of Indian hemp, bear grass, and other grasses.

Other important raw materials included bone, horn, and wood. Many tools and items, such as mortars, pestles, knives, and mauls, were made of chipping and flaking stone and also obsidian. Mattresses were cottonwood inner bark or dry grass, blankets were elk hides, and folded skins served as pillows.

Nez Percé Indians also used a fire-hardened digging stick, a fire drill, and board and buckskin cradles. Musical instruments included rattles, flageolets, whistles, and drums. They also used a 12-month calendar and named four seasons.

Trade Relatively early acquisition of horses gave the Nez Percé a trade advantage, although they also traded widely before they had the horse. They acquired items made as far away as British Columbia and the Mississippi Valley. Abalone was among the items they acquired from coastal Indians, as were carved wooden items, dried clams, dentalium shells, and wapato root. Also, by the eighteenth century, the Nez Percé were trading east of the Bitterroots for buffalo products and other Plains items.

Notable Arts Traditional arts included woven baskets, wallets, petroglyphs, and blankets and tipi skins decorated with pictographs. In the historical period they were known for porcupine-quill embroidery, rawhide painting, and cornhusk basketry.

Transportation After acquiring the horse in the mid–eighteenth century, the Nez Percé went on to develop first-rate stock through selective breeding. They also used snowshoes and dugout canoes.

Dress Clothing was made of cedar bark and the untailored skin of deer, elk, and buffalo. Men wore moccasins, leggings, breechclouts, shirts, and highly decorated robes. Women wore moccasins, fringed gowns, and basket hats, replaced in the historic period with skin caps decorated with fringe and elks' teeth. People cleaned their clothes with white clay. Men plucked their facial hair. People painted their faces and bodies for decoration and against snow blindness. Tailored, Plains-style skin clothing became popular in the eighteenth century.

War and Weapons In general, raiding and war, for booty, glory, and revenge, were very important to the Sahaptians. By virtue of their being the most powerful Plateau tribe, the Nez Percé played a central role in regional peace and war. At least after the late eighteenth century, they fought with the Flathead, Coeur d'Alene, and Spokan against the Blackfeet, Gros Ventre, Crow, and other Plains tribes. They also sometimes fought against these allies. The Cayuse, Umatilla, Yakima, and Wallawalla were also allies against the Shoshone, Bannock, and other northern Great Basin tribes.

Men held intertribal dances before wars and buffalo hunts. Weapons included cedar, ash, or mountain sheep horn bows; obsidian or jasper-tipped arrows, sometimes dipped in rattlesnake venom; and spears. Elk-skin shields, helmets, and armor were used for defense. The eagle-feather war bonnet may or may not have come originally from the Plains. Men and horses were painted and decorated for war.

Contemporary Information

Government/Reservations The Nez Percé Reservation (1855) is located in Clearwater, Idaho, Lewis, and Nez Percé Counties, Idaho. It contains 92,685 acres; the 1990 Indian population was 1,860.

Nez Percé warriors on horseback. By virtue of their being the most powerful Plateau tribe, the Nez Percé played a central role in regional peace and war. Men and horses were painted and decorated for war.

A tribal committee is elected every three years, according to the constitution adopted in 1948. A nine-member executive committee serves staggered three-year terms. The Nez Percé Tribe is a member of the Columbia River Intertribal Fish Commission, the Affiliated Tribes of Northwest Indians, and other state and regional organizations.

The Colville Reservation (1872) is located in Ferry and Okanogan Counties, Washington. It contains 1,011,495 acres and had a 1990 Indian population of 3,782. Under the Indian Reorganization Act constitution approved in 1938, the reservation is governed by a 14-member business council plus various subcommittees. The Confederated Tribes is a member of the Affiliated Tribes of Northwest Indians as well as other intertribal organizations.

Economy The Nez Percé tribe is currently undertaking a major land reacquisition program. Most income comes from farm and timber, and the tribe runs a printing plant, a marina, and a limestone quarry. Their economic development plans include a forestry management program and gambling and tourist facilities, including the Nee-Mee-Poo Trail and an expansion of the Nez Percé National Historical Park. With other Idaho tribes, they are negotiating for a favorable settlement of the water rights issue. A large percentage of the reservation is leased to non-Indians.

Important economic activities on the Colville Reservation include stock raising, farming, logging (including a sawmill) and reforestation, seasonal labor, mining, and tourism. The reservation contains the potential to develop hydroelectric resources. The tribe owns a meat-packing plant, a log cabin sales business, and various gambling enterprises.

Legal Status The Nez Percé Tribe of Idaho is a federally recognized tribal entity. The Confederated Tribes of the Colville Reservation is a federally recognized tribal entity.

Daily Life The Nez Percé tribe makes an effort to preserve their native language, since few people under age 30 speak it well. There are dictionaries and other texts in the Nez Percé language. Other ongoing aspects of native culture include traditional dances, root feasts, traditional games, and Seven Drums Society ceremonies. The tribe has attained legal jurisdiction on the reservation. It is actively involved in nuclear and other regional environmental issues, including efforts to reinstate local salmon and steelhead runs. The tribe administers a scholarship fund for deserving students. Among the festivals observed on the reservation are Lincoln's birthday, a spring root festival in May, a Presbyterian camp meeting in early summer, and Pi-Nee-Wau Days in August.

Colville people are largely acculturated. Language preservation programs are hindered by lack of a common language. The Chief Joseph Band of Nez Percés, with their Seven Drum religion, have taken the lead in recent efforts to reinvigorate disparate tribal cultures and religions. The Indian Shaker Church and the Native American Church are also active on the reservation. There is a program to reacquire and consolidate the land base. Educational levels are on the rise. The Colville business council wields growing power in regional and statewide issues.

Okanagon

Okanagon (Ō kən `ä gən), "seeing the top, or head," or *Isonkva'ili,* "Our People." They were the main tribe of a culturally related group of Indians also including the Senijextee (Lake), Colville, and Sanpoil Indians. They are occasionally known today as the Northern Okanagon (Canada) and the Sinkaietk (United States).

Location Okanagons traditionally lived in the Okanagon and Similkameen River Valleys, including Lake Okanagon, in Washington and British Columbia. Today, most Okanagons live on the Colville Reservation, on reserves in British Columbia, and in regional cities and towns.

Population The late-eighteenth-century Okanagon population was about 2,500. Today roughly 2,000–2,500 Okanagon Indians live mostly in Canada.

Language Okanagon Indians spoke a dialect of Interior Salish.

Historical Information

History Okanagons undertook a gradual northward expansion following their acquisition of horses in the mid–eighteenth century. They first encountered non-native traders in the early nineteenth century and Catholic Indians and missionaries shortly thereafter. The tribe was artificially divided when the international boundary was fixed in 1846. The Sinkaietks did not participate in the Yakima war (1855–1856), although some did join in fighting the United States later in that decade.

A gold strike on the Fraser River in 1858 brought an influx of miners and increased the general level of interracial conflict. Most U.S. Okanagons settled on the Colville Reservation in 1872. The Canadian Okanagon were assigned to several small reserves.

Religion Okanagons believed in a chief creator deity as well as the presence of spirits in all natural things, animate and inanimate. Guardian spirits could be acquired by adolescents through physical training, fasting, and seclusion. Shamans' especially powerful spirits allowed them to cure illness and perform other particularly difficult tasks. Okanagon Indians celebrated a girls' puberty ceremony, a first fruits ceremony, and a midwinter spirit festival and dances as well as war, scalp, marriage, and sun dances, some of which were acquired in the historical period.

Government Two geographical divisions, the Similkameen and the Okanagon proper, were each composed of between 5 and 10 autonomous bands. Each band was led by a (usually hereditary) chief with advisory powers. The true locus of authority was found in a council of older men. War, hunt, and dance chiefs were selected as needed.

Customs Corpses were wrapped in matting or robes and then buried in the ground or in rock slides. Sometimes canoes or carvings were placed over the grave site. Mourners cut their hair and wore old

clothes. A pleasant land of the dead was recognized as existing to the south or west. Okanagons regularly intermarried with other Interior Salish people, especially Spokan and Thompson Indians. They practiced polygamy. They also very occasionally practiced a form of potlatch.

Dwellings Winter dwelling were of two types. One was a conical, semisubterranean, pole frame lodge covered with earth. This type was about 10–16 feet in diameter, and entrance was gained through the roof. The people also built rectangular, mat-covered, multifamily lodges. In summer they used conical, tule mats on pole frames and, later, skin tipis. Men and women used domed sweat houses for purification; the structures were also used as living quarters for youths in spirit training.

Diet Salmon was the main staple. Large and small game, including elk, bear, bighorn sheep, and marmot, was also important. Dogs sometimes assisted in the hunt, in which animals were often surrounded and/or driven over a cliff. Meat was roasted, boiled, or dried. Buffalo was always part of the diet but became more important when groups began using horses to hunt buffalo on the Great Plains. Important plant foods included camas, bitterroot, berries, and nuts.

Key Technology Men caught fish with dip nets, seine nets, traps, weirs, spears, and hook and line. Stone, bone, and antler provided the raw material for most tools. Women made cedar-bark or woven spruce root-baskets with geometric designs. Some baskets were woven tight enough to hold water. Women also specialized in making woven sacks. They sewed tule mats with Indian hemp.

Trade Trade fairs were held at Kettle Falls and at the mouth of the Fraser River. The level of trade increased with acquisition of horses.

Notable Arts Basketry and tanning were especially well developed. Rock painting had been practiced for thousands of years.

Transportation Water transportation methods included bark, especially birch-bark, canoes and rafts. People used snowshoes during winter travel. Horses were acquired in the mid–eighteenth century.

Dress Beginning in the eighteenth century, dressed skins provided the main clothing material. Men wore shirts and breechclouts, and women wore aprons. Both wore moccasins, leggings, sewn or woven caps, and goat wool or woven rabbit-fur blankets and robes.

War and Weapons War chiefs were selected on an ad hoc basis. Weapons included juniper bows and flint-tipped arrows. Okanagons were occasionally allied with Colville Indians against the Nez Percé and Yakima.

Contemporary Information

Government/Reservations The Colville Reservation (1872) is located in Ferry and Okanogan Counties, Washington. It covers 1,011,495 acres and had a 1990 Indian population of 3,782. An Indian Reorganization Act constitution approved in 1938 calls for a 14-member business council and various committees. The Confederated Tribes is a member of the Affiliated Tribes of Northwest Indians and other intertribal organizations.

Okanagon bands in Canada live on a number of different reserves. See "Daily Life" for profiles of some of these bands (all statistics are as of 1995).

Economy The reservation economy is built largely around stock raising, farming, logging (including a sawmill) and reforestation, and seasonal labor. There is some mining as well as a meat-packing plant, a log cabin sales business, and tourism-related businesses such as a trading post and gambling enterprises. There is potential for development of hydroelectric resources. The economies of the Canadian bands center on agriculture, farming, forestry, and small businesses.

Legal Status The Confederated Tribes of the Colville Reservation is a federally recognized tribal entity. All of the bands described under "Daily Life" are federally and provincially recognized.

Daily Life Colville Indians are largely acculturated. Language preservation programs are hindered by the

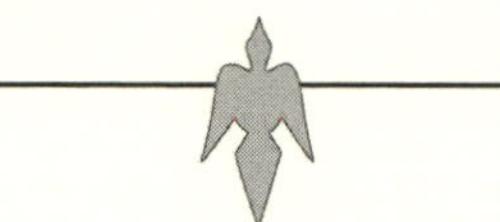

lack of a common aboriginal language. Recent efforts to reinvigorate disparate tribal cultures and religions include the presence of the Chief Joseph Band of Nez Percé Indians with their Seven Drum religion, the Indian Shaker Church, and the Native American Church. The reservation hosts an annual powwow and a circle celebration. There is also a program of reacquiring and consolidating the land base and a goal to increase the general levels of education. The Colville Business Council wields growing power in regional and statewide issues.

The Lower Similkameen Band controls 11 reserves on 15,276 hectares of land. The reserves were allotted in 1876. The population is 313, of whom 275 live in 64 houses on the reserves. Elections are by custom, and the band is affiliated with the Similkameen Administration. Children attend band and provincial schools. Important economic resources and activities include agriculture, farming, forestry, and small businesses. Facilities include offices and a church.

The Okanagon Band, composed of seven different communities, controls five reserves on 10,603 hectares of land. The reserves were allotted in 1877. The population is 1,367, of whom 676 live in 224 houses on the reserves. Elections are under the provisions of the Indian Act, and the band is currently unaffiliated. Children attend band and provincial schools. Important economic resources and activities include haying and small businesses. Facilities include offices, a community hall, a fire station, and a church.

The Osoyoos Band controls two reserves on 13,052 hectares of land. The reserves were allotted in 1877. The population is 316, of whom 223 live in 86 houses on the reserves. Elections are under the provisions of the Indian Act, and the band is currently unaffiliated. Children attend band and provincial schools. Important economic resources and activities include a vineyard, a campsite, farming, and land leases. Facilities include offices, a community hall, a church, and a garage.

The Penticton Band controls two reserves on 18,691 hectares of land. The population is 675, of whom 397 live in 120 houses on the reserves. Elections are by custom, and the band is currently unaffiliated. Children attend band and provincial schools. Important economic resources and activities include land leases, forestry, a gravel pit, a billiard hall, and individual hay ranches. Facilities include offices, a community hall, a heritage center, and a church.

The Upper Similkameen Band controls seven reserves on 2,602 hectares of land. The population is 41, all of whom live in 14 houses on the reserves. Elections are held under the provisions of the Indian Act, and the band is affiliated with the Similkameen Administration and the Okanagon Tribal Council. Children attend provincial schools. Important economic resources and activities include a campsite, ranching, and a hairdressing business.

Pend d'Oreille

See Kalispel

Salish

Salish (`Sal ish), or Flathead, from the fact that they did not, like many neighboring peoples, shape their babies' foreheads (they left them "flat"). Their self-designation was *Se'lic,* or "People."

Location Traditionally, the Salish lived in western Montana, around the Rocky and Little Belt Mountains. Today, most live in Flathead, Lake, Missoula, and Sanders Counties, Montana.

Population The precontact population of Salish Indians may have been between 600 and 3,000. In 1990, the reservation Indian population, including Kalispel and Kootenai people, was 5,110, with several hundred Salish Indians also living away from the reservation.

Language The Salish spoke a dialect of Interior Salish.

Historical Information

History All Salish-speaking Indians probably originated in British Columbia. From their base in western Montana, the Salish may have moved farther east onto the Plains before being pushed back around 1600 by the Blackfeet. The Salish continued moving westward, into north-central Idaho, throughout the following two centuries.

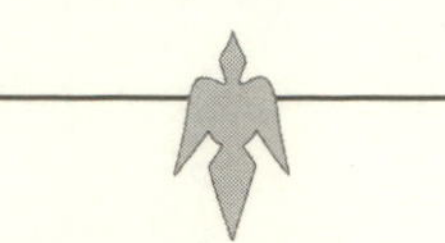

Two women on horseback at Flathead Reservation, July 1906. Around 1700 the Salish acquired horses and assumed a great deal of the culture of Plains Indians (including buffalo hunting, stronger tribal organization, and raiding).

Around 1700 they acquired horses and assumed a great deal of the culture of Plains Indians (including buffalo hunting, stronger tribal organization, and raiding). Ongoing wars with the Blackfeet as well as several smallpox epidemics combined in the eighteenth century to reduce their population significantly. They also encountered Christian Iroquois Indians during this time.

Although disease preceded their physical arrival, non-Indians began trading in Salish country shortly after the 1805 visit of the Lewis and Clark expedition. The missionary period began in 1841. In 1855, a major land cession (the Hellgate Treaty) established the Flathead, or Jocko, Reservation, but most Salish Indians avoided confinement until at least 1872, in part owing to their friendliness with the Americans. During these years, other tribes were placed on the reservation, and the buffalo herds diminished rapidly. Charlot, the leader of one Salish band, held out in the Bitterroot Mountains until 1891, when his people finally joined the Flathead Reservation.

The government considered terminating the reservation in the 1950s but was successfully opposed by tribal leaders. In 1960, the tribe won roughly $4.4 million in land claims settlements.

Religion People sought luck from guardian spirits in dreams and visions. Preadolescent spirit quests included fasting and praying. Spirits also conferred songs and objects that became a person's medicine.

Chief Charlot at Flathead Reservation in the late nineteenth century. Chief Charlot and his people finally joined the Flathead Reservation in 1891.

Shamans' strong guardians let them cure illness, confer hunting success, and see the future. The many dances and ceremonies of the early historic period included the Sun Dance, Medicine Dance, Hunting Dance, first fruit ceremony, Woman's Dance, and war dances. Seasonal religious ceremonies were generally related to food or guardian spirits.

Government Various bands were formed of several related families. Each band was led by a chief and an assistant chief, chosen by merit. The chieftainship may have been hereditary in earlier times. Beginning in the late prehistoric period, as tribal cohesiveness increased, the band chiefs formed a tribal council to advise a tribal chief, and later the band chiefs themselves were relegated to the status of minor chiefs or subchiefs. In addition, individuals were selected as needed to lead various activities such as hunting and war.

Customs Rule or law breakers were punished by public whipping and/or ridicule. Premarital sexual relations were frowned on; the woman could be whipped if discovered. Marriage was arranged by families, although some people also eloped. It was formalized by cohabitation as well as a formal ceremony. Polygamy was common. Women were responsible for all domestic tasks.

The dead were buried dressed in skins and robes. A mourning feast followed the funeral; it included the disposal of the dead person's former possessions. The mourning period could last a year.

Dwellings Winter dwellings were of two types. One was partially excavated, conical mat (cedar bark, hemp) houses on wooden frames; the other was long communal and ceremonial lodges. Brush shelters sufficed during camping and mountain hunting trips. Bark or skin tipis gained popularity after the horse turned the Salish into buffalo hunters.

Diet Beginning in the eighteenth century, buffalo, hunted on the Great Plains, became a key food item. Before this period, however, the Salish ate a number of animals including elk, deer, antelope, and small game. Fish, including trout, salmon, and whitefish, formed an important part of their diet. Plant foods included camas, bitterroot, other bulbs, roots, and berries.

Key Technology Men used hook and line, nets, traps, and weirs to catch fish. Women made birch-bark and woven skin containers as well as coiled cedar baskets. They also made twined grass spoons.

Trade Salish Indians participated in the regional trade, particularly with the Kalispel. They imported Nez Percé baskets and traded in stolen horses from the early eighteenth century on. They became involved in the fur trade in the early nineteenth century.

Notable Arts Women decorated their well-made baskets with geometric designs.

Transportation Pole rafts served as water transportation. The horse arrived after about 1700, and the Salish soon learned to handle this animal expertly.

Dress Most clothes were made from rabbit or deer skins. Men wore breechclouts and shirts, and women wore dresses. Both wore moccasins, caps, robes, leggings, and shell earrings.

War and Weapons The Salish fought few wars before they acquired horses, at which time warfare became common and serious. They often fought the Blackfeet and Crow with the help of the Kalispel and Nez Percé. Capturing an enemy without using weapons was considered a great coup. Dances preceded and followed wars. War captives became slaves.

Contemporary Information

Government/Reservations The Flathead Reservation (1855; Flathead, Kalispel, and Kootenai) is located in Flathead, Lake, Missoula, and Sanders Counties, Montana. It contains 1,244,000 acres. The 1990 Indian population was 5,110. Just under half of the land base is non-Indian owned, and over 80 percent of the reservation population is non-Indian. There is a ten-member tribal council.

Economy Forestry, including sawmills, and ranching are important reservation industries.

Tourist facilities include the KwaTaqNuk resort on Flathead Lake. The tribe receives $10 million on an annual lease for Kerr Dam, on the Lower Flathead River; it will assume the operating license in 2015. Many people work for the tribe, including its tourist resort on Flathead Lake and its facilities at Hot Springs. S&K Electronics provides some jobs. Income is also generated by gravel sales. Unemployment remains quite high (about 50 percent in the late 1980s).

Legal Status The Confederated Salish and Kootenai Tribes is a federally recognized tribal entity. Legal jurisdiction over reservation Indians belongs to the tribes.

Daily Life Despite considerable intermarriage with non-Indians, the tribes attempt to retain their culture and transmit it to the young by means of a cultural heritage project. The reservation is plagued with the serious social ills that often accompany poverty, including substance abuse. Salish Kootenai College and a tribal high school were created around 1977. The tribes hold two large powwows in July and various other activities.

Sanpoil

Sanpoil, or San Poil (Sän pō `ēl), is derived from a native word possibly referring to what may have been their self-designation, *Sinpauelish (Snpui'lux).* They were culturally and linguistically similar to the neighboring Nespelem Indians.

Location Late-eighteenth-century Sanpoils lived near the Columbia and the Sanpoil Rivers, in north-central Washington. The environment is one of desert and semidesert. Today, most Sanpoils live in Ferry and Okanagon Counties, Washington, and in regional cities and towns.

Population The Sanpoil population around 1775 was approximately 1,600. Today, perhaps several hundred Indians claim Sanpoil descent.

Language With the Nespelem, the Sanpoil spoke a particular dialect of Interior Salish.

Historical Information

History Severe epidemics in the late eighteenth century, and again in the late 1840s and early 1850s, depleted the Sanpoil population considerably. Sanpoils were among the Indians who visited Catholic missionaries at Kettle Falls in 1838. By avoiding the wars of the 1850s and by consciously eschewing contact with non-Indians, they managed to remain free until 1872, when they were moved to the Colville Reservation. Even after confinement, the Sanpoil refused government tools, preferring to hunt, fish, and gather by traditional means and to conduct small-scale farming.

Religion Individuals sought guardian spirits through the traditional means of singing, fasting, praying, and performing feats of endurance. Such spirit quests were considered mandatory for men and optional for women. Prepubescent boys generally undertook a series of one-night vigils. Many people acquired between three and six spirit helpers.

The spirits in question were those of animals; they assured the seeker of luck and various skills. Songs often accompanied received powers, which were generally called upon well after the quest: When one had settled into an adult life, the returning spirit power caused an illness that had to be cured by a shaman.

Male shamans outnumbered female shamans. Their powerful spirits helped them to cure illness; they could also harm people if they chose. Among the causes of illness, in addition to a returning spirit, were breaking taboos and suffering bewitching. Shamans were paid for successful cures.

The five-day first salmon ritual was the most important ceremony. It was held under the direction of the salmon chief. Other important religious occasions included the midwinter spirit dances and the first fruits rite. The midwinter dances served the additional purposes of bringing people together and releasing winter tensions.

Government Autonomous villages were each led by a chief and a subchief; these lifetime offices were hereditary in theory but were generally filled by people possessing the qualities of honesty, integrity, and diplomacy. Unlike some other Plateau groups, only men could be chiefs. The authority of Sanpoil chiefs to serve as adviser, judge, and general leader was granted mainly through consensus. As judge, the chief had authority over crimes of nonconformity such as witchcraft, sorcery, and assault. His penalty usually consisted of a fine and/or lashes on the back.

An informal assembly of all married adults confirmed a new chief and oversaw other aspects of village life. All residents of the village were considered citizens. Village size averaged about 30–40 people, or roughly three to five extended families, although some villages had as many as 100 people. Other village leaders included a messenger, a speaker, and a salmon chief (often a shaman, with the salmon as a guardian spirit, who supervised salmon-related activities). By virtue of their ability to help or hurt people, shamans also acquired relative wealth and power from their close association with chiefs, who liked to keep them allied.

Customs Local villages had associated, nonexclusive territories or subsistence areas. Any person was free to live anywhere she or he wanted; that is, family members could associate themselves with relatives of their settlement, relatives of a different settlement, or a settlement where they had no relatives. Winter was a time for visits and ceremonies. During that season, women also made mats and baskets, made or repaired clothing, and prepared meals while men occasionally hunted or just slept, gambled, and socialized.

People rose at dawn, winter and summer, and began the day by bathing in the river. In spring, groups of four or five families left the village for root-digging areas; those who had spent the winter away from the main village returned. The old and the ill generally remained in camp.

Pacifism, generosity, and interpersonal equality and autonomy were highly valued. Girls fasted and were secluded for ten days at the onset of puberty, except for a nighttime running regime. The exchange of gifts between families constituted a marriage, a relationship that was generally stable and permanent. Corpses were wrapped in tule mats or deerskin and buried with their possessions. The family burned the deceased's house and then observed various taboos and purification rites. The land of the dead was envisioned as being located at the end of the Milky Way.

Dwellings Sanpoil Indians used the typical Plateau-style winter houses. One was a single-family structure, circular and semisubterranean, about 10–16 feet in diameter, with a flat or conical roof. People covered a wood frame with planks or mats and then a layer of grass, brush, and earth. Entrance was gained through the smoke hole, which could be covered by a tule mat. The interior was also covered with a layer of grass.

They also built communal tule-mat houses consisting of a pole framework covered by grass, earth, and tule mats. These houses were about 16 feet wide, between 24 to about 60 feet long, and about 14 feet high, with gabled roofs. Entrance was through matted double doors. Each family had an individual tule-covered section, but they shared a number of fireplaces in the central passage.

Summer houses were similar in construction but smaller, single-family structures. Some more closely resembled a mere windbreak. Some groups built adjoining rectangular, flat-roofed summer mat houses/windbreaks. Mat houses were always taken down after the season. Men also built sweat lodges of grass and earth over a willow frame.

Diet Food was much more often acquired by the family than by the village. Fish was a staple. Men caught four varieties of salmon as well as trout, sturgeon, and other fish. They fished from May through October. Although women could not approach the actual fishing areas, they cleaned and dried the fish. Dried fish and sometimes other foods made up much of the winter diet. People generally ate two meals a day in summer and one in winter.

Women gathered shellfish, salmon eggs, bulbs, roots, nuts, seeds, berries, and prickly pear. Camas was eaten raw or roasted, boiled, and made into cakes. A short ceremony was performed over the first gathered crop of the season. Men hunted most large and small game in the fall. They prepared for the hunt by sweating and singing. Women came along to help dress and carry the game. Men also hunted birds and gathered mollusks. Venison and berries were pounded with fat to make pemmican.

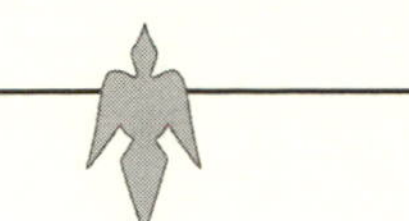

Key Technology Fish were caught using traps, nets, spears, and weirs. Spearing required the construction and use of artificial channels and platforms. Utensils were carved from wood. Women made woven cedar, juniper, or spruce root baskets, including water containers and cooking pots. Women also made the all-important mats, of tule and other grasses, whose uses included houses, bedding (skins were also used), privacy screens, waterproofing, holding food, and wrapping corpses. There was also some sun-dried pottery covered with fish skin.

Trade The Sanpoil engaged in extensive local trade, communication, visiting, and intermarriage.

Notable Arts Artistic expression was seen mainly in carved wood items, coiled baskets with geometric designs, and mat weaving.

Transportation Dugout canoes served as water transportation. Horses arrived about the mid–eighteenth century.

Dress The Sanpoil wore surprisingly little clothing. Woven bark and, later, dressed buckskin provided breechclouts, ponchos, and aprons. Women also wore woven caps. Men wore fur leggings in winter; women's leggings were generally made of hemp. Some winter clothing, such as mittens, caps, woven blankets, and robes, was made from the fur of rabbits and other animals. Men plucked their facial hair. Both sexes plucked their eyebrows and wore earrings, necklaces, and face paint.

War and Weapons The Sanpoil were known for their general pacifism, even in the face of attacks by the Shuswap, Coeur d'Alene, and Nez Percé.

Contemporary Information

Government/Reservations The Colville Reservation (1872) is located in Ferry and Okanogan Counties, Washington. It consists of 1,011,495 acres. The 1990 Indian population was 3,782. An Indian Reorganization Act constitution, approved in 1938, calls for a 14-member business council and various committees. The Confederated Tribes are members of the Affiliated Tribes of Northwest Indians and other intertribal organizations.

Economy The reservation economy is built largely around stock raising, farming, logging (including a sawmill) and reforestation, and seasonal labor. There is some mining as well as a meat-packing plant, a log cabin sales business, and tourism-related businesses such as a trading post and gambling enterprises. There is potential for development of hydroelectric resources.

Legal Status The Confederated Tribes of the Colville Reservation is a federally recognized tribal entity.

Daily Life Confederated Colville Indians are largely acculturated. Language preservation programs are hindered by the lack of a common aboriginal language. Recent efforts to reinvigorate disparate tribal cultures and religions include the presence of the Chief Joseph Band of Nez Percé Indians with their Seven Drum religion, the Indian Shaker Church, and the Native American Church. The reservation hosts an annual powwow and a circle celebration. There is also a program of reacquiring and consolidating the land base and a goal to increase the general levels of education. The Colville Business Council wields growing power in regional and statewide issues.

Shuswap

Shuswap (Shus wäp): "to know, or recognize" or "to unfold, or spread." The word may also refer to relationships between people. They may once have called themselves *Xatsu'll,* "on the cliff where the bubbling water comes out." The people currrently refer to themselves as the Great Secwepemc Nation.

Location Shuswaps continue to live in and near their aboriginal territory in the Fraser and North and South Thompson River valleys, British Columbia.

Population The early-nineteenth-century Shuswap population was about 7,000. In 1991 it stood at almost 5,000.

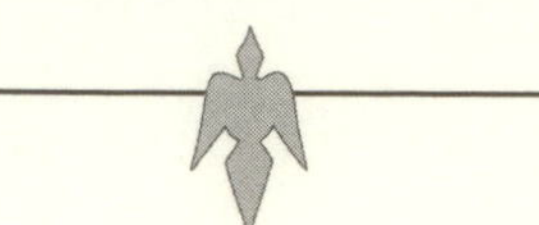

Language Shuswap is a dialect of the Interior division of the Salishan language family.

Historical Information

History Interior Salishan people settled in their historic areas roughly 9,000 years ago. Hudson's Bay Company posts were established in the early nineteenth century. The people soon became active in the fur trade. Intertribal warfare ended in the early 1860s. About that time, the Shuswap were decimated by epidemics, in part brought by gold miners flooding the region. Non-natives squatted on and then claimed the land of the ailing Shuswap. A Shuswap reserve of 176 square miles was created in 1865; it was soon reduced to 1 square mile. A second reserve was created in 1895. In 1945, with the Chilcotin and other groups, the Shuswap founded the British Columbia Interior Confederation to try to persuade provincial and federal officials to be more responsive to their needs.

Religion Adolescent boys sought guardian spirits for luck and skills through fasting, praying, and visiting remote places. Shamans' powerful guardians allowed them to cure illness and restore lost souls. Their methods included massage, blowing, sprinkling water, and prescribing taboos. Feasting, dancing, singing, drumming, and tobacco smoking were included in most religious ceremonies. Masked dances reenacted a person's vision quest.

Government The Shuswap were divided into about seven autonomous bands. All had hereditary chiefs who advised, lectured on correct behavior, and coordinated subsistence activities. There were also specialized chiefs for war, hunt, dance, and other activities.

Customs Bands were more or less nomadic, according to their food sources. By the nineteenth century, northern and western bands had adopted the Northwest Coast pattern of social stratification. The nobility belonged to hereditary crest groups, and commoners belonged to nonhereditary associations. Slaves were generally acquired in battle or trade. At puberty, boys undertook guardian spirit quests, whereas girls were secluded and practiced basket making and other skills. They also fasted and prayed, and they went out at night to run, exercise, and bathe. Corpses were buried in sand banks or rock slides with their possessions; small mourning houses were sometimes built by the grave.

Dwellings Men built circular winter lodges of cedar bark and earth on a wood frame. Lodges were excavated to a depth of around 6 feet and ranged between about 20 and 35 feet in diameter. The floor was covered with spruce boughs. The clan totem was carved on the center pole or on an outside pole (lower division). Larger log and plank dwellings had several rooms and housed between four and eight families. Oblong or conical mat-covered houses served as shelter in summer.

Diet Fish, especially salmon, was the staple in some areas. People away from rivers depended on large and small game and fowl. All groups ate roots and berries.

Key Technology Men caught fish with nets, basket traps, spears, weirs, and hooks. Hunting equipment included bow and arrow, traps, and spears. Utensils and some baskets were made of birch bark, coiled baskets were fashioned from cedar or spruce roots, and many tools were made of stone. People also made skin or woven grass bags. Digging sticks had wood or antler cross-handles.

Trade All bands traded for slaves. Other major trade items included dentalium shells, hemp, cedar bark, moose and deer skins, roots, and salmon products.

Notable Arts Women wove geometric designs into their well-crafted baskets. They also decorated clothing with porcupine quillwork.

Transportation People plied the rivers and lakes in bark and dugout canoes. They used snowshoes in winter. Horses arrived in the late eighteenth century.

Dress Most clothing was made from cedar bark or skins. Men wore deerskin breechclouts in summer and added skin leggings and short shirts in winter. Women probably wore wraparound skirts, with leggings in winter. Moccasins were generally plain. Some people

used thongs to tie pieces of fur or hide to their feet. Women wove robes of rabbit skin or goat wool. Fringe, bone, teeth, and shell decoration was used on some items. Personal decorations included dentalium shell ornaments and face paint. Men wore long looped necklaces, often decorated with abalone shell. Women tended to wear abalone in their braids and tattoo their wrists and arms. In the nineteenth century, many people switched to Plains-style skin clothing.

War and Weapons All bands acquired slaves by raiding and in war. At least by the eighteenth century, warfare had become a regular band activity. The Shuswap fought at one time with most of their neighbors, including bands of Okanagon, Thompson, Cree, Chilcotin, and Carrier. Defensive equipment included rod armor, elk-skin vests, and shields. Weapons included the bow and arrow; short spears; wood, bone, and stone clubs; and bone knives.

Contemporary Information

Government/Reservations Some eighteen Secwepemc bands live in British Columbia. Total reserve land equals roughly 59,000 hectares. See selected profiles under "Daily Life." (All statistics are as of 1995 unless otherwise noted.)

Economy Hunting, trapping, and fishing remain important. See profiles under "Daily Life" for additional activities.

Legal Status The bands profiled under "Daily Life" are federally and provincially recognized.

Daily Life The Adams Lake Band controls seven reserves on almost 3,000 hectares of land. The reserve, then called the Sahkaltkum Band Reserve, was allotted in 1877. The population is 570, of whom 363 live on the reserves. The band is affiliated with the Shuswap Nation Tribal Council. Children attend band and provincial schools. Important economic activities and resources include forestry, land leases, and a laundromat. Facilities include offices, a community hall, a fitness and cultural center, a clubhouse, and a church.

The Bonaparte Band controls six reserves on 1,332 hectares of land. The reserve was allotted in 1878. The population is 631, of whom 204 live on the reserves. Elections are held under the provisions of the Indian Act, and the band is affiliated with the Shuswap Nation Tribal Council.

The Canim Lake Band (Tsqescen) controls six reserves totaling 2,029.6 hectares of land. They are part of the Lake Division of the Shuswap Tribe. Band population in 1996 was 517 members, nearly three-quarters of whom lived on tribal land. The band is affiliated with the Cariboo Tribal Council. Facilities include a K-12 school. The band itself employs between 50 and 150 people, depending on the season. In addition to educating its members, the band operates many social programs, several businesses, and health services. Shuswap is taught in the school.

The Canoe Creek Band includes the communities of Dog Creek and Canoe Creek. The band controls 5,880.4 hectares of relatively poor land; the best local land is owned by non-native ranchers. The band is affiliated with the Cariboo Tribal Council. Fewer than half of the band's 650 members live on the reserve. Housing and jobs are in short supply. Dog Creek children attend public school; Canoe Creek operates a K-3 school. Facilities in Dog Creek include administrative offices, a store/gas station/post office, a gymnasium/community center, and a skating rink. Canoe Creek has the school, a community center, and a church. Band members operate their own small businesses. Sports are popular, as are hunting, gathering, and fishing.

The High Bar Band controls three reserves on 1,506 hectares of land on the Fraser River. The reserve was allotted in 1871. The population is 49, of whom two live in one house on the reserves. Elections are held according to custom, and the band is currently unaffiliated. There is a cattle ranch on the reserve.

The Kamloops Band controls five reserves on 13,249 hectares of land near the city of Kamloops. The reserve was allotted in 1877. The population is 832, of whom 491 live in 138 houses on the reserves. Elections are held according to custom, and the band is affiliated with the Shuswap Nation Tribal Council. Children attend provincial schools. Important economic activities and resources include

forestry, mining, ranching, a development corporation, an industrial park, land leases, a museum, and cattle and hay ranching. Facilities include offices and a garage.

The Little Shuswap Band controls five reserves on 3,135 hectares of land. The population is 258, of whom 157 live in 53 houses on the reserves. Elections are held according to custom, and the band is unaffiliated. Children attend band and provincial schools. Important economic activities and resources include forestry, land leases, a resort, and logging. Facilities include offices, a community hall, a boat house, and a machine shop.

The Neskonlith Indian Band controls three reserves. They are currently in the process of forging a ten-year plan for community building and economic development. Along with the Adams Lake and Little Shuswap Bands, they are working on land claims arising from their original 1862 reservation.

The Shuswap Band controls one reserve on 1,106 hectares of land. The reserve was allotted in 1884. The population is 205, of whom 113 live in 49 houses on the reserves. Elections are held according to the provisions of the Indian Act, and the band is affiliated with the Ktunaxa/Kinbasket Tribal Council. Children attend band and provincial schools. Important economic activities and resources include a sand and gravel company, a hay ranch, a recreational vehicle park, and small businesses. Facilities include offices and a community center.

The Skeetchestn Band, formerly Dead Man's Creek Band, controls one reserve consisting of 7,908 hectares of land. The population is 383, of whom 135 live in 45 houses on the reserve. Elections are held according to custom, and the band is affiliated with the Shuswap Nation Tribal Council. Children attend band and provincial schools. Important economic activities and resources include a campsite, a store, tourism, and individual ranches. Facilities include offices, a recreation center, a church, and a community center.

The Soda Creek Band (Xatsu'll First Nation) occupies two reserves totaling about 2,048 hectares. The present population is between 250 and 300 people, almost all of whom are Secwepemc. The band is affiliated with the Cariboo Tribal Council. Economic activities include logging and tourism. The people have received little or no compensation for non-native utility and natural resource extraction on tribal lands.

The Spallumcheen Band controls three reserves on 3,095 hectares of land at Enderby. The reserves were allotted in 1877. The population is 574, of whom 309 live in 84 houses on the reserves. Elections are held according the provisions of the Indian Act, and the band is affiliated with the Shuswap Nation Tribal Council. Children attend band and provincial schools. Important economic activities and resources include logging, a gas station, a grocery store, and arts and crafts.

The Whispering Pines/Clinton Band controls three reserves on 565 hectares of land 18 kilometers north of Kamloops. The population is 97, of whom 60 live in 11 houses on the reserves. Elections are held according the provisions of the Indian Act, and the band is affiliated with the Shuswap Nation Tribal Council. Children attend provincial schools. Important economic activities and resources include cattle and hay ranching and a rodeo grounds.

The Williams Lake Band has roughly 1,927 hectares of land. Over 60 percent of the approximately 350 band members live on-reserve. The band is affiliated with the Cariboo Tribal Council. Economic activities include agriculture and timber as well as small businesses. Children attend public schools. Members enjoy indoor and outdoor recreational facilities.

Sinkaietk

See Okanagon

Sinkiuse

Sinkiuse (`Sin ku yūs), "between people," also known as Columbia, Isle de Pierre, and Moses Band.

Location In late prehistoric times, the Sinkiuse lived mainly along the east bank of the Columbia River, although they ranged throughout the plateau south and east of the river. Today, their descendants live on the Colville Reservation, Ferry and Okanogan Counties, Washington, and in cities and towns around central Washington.

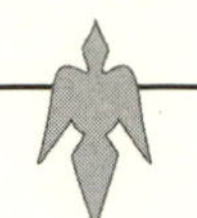

Population The late-eighteenth-century Sinkiuse population was at least 800. In 1990, 3,782 Indians lived on the Colville Reservation, perhaps 10 percent of whom were Sinkiuse descendants.

Language The Sinkiuse spoke a dialect of Interior Salish.

Historical Information

History Sinkiuses may have come either from the lower Columbia River area or from a more northerly location. They encountered non-Indians and joined the fur trade in 1811. They fought the United States in the 1850s under their chief, Moses, but adopted a peaceful stance after the war. The Columbia Reservation was established in 1879 and was abolished several years later. Four bands followed Chief Moses to the Colville Reservation; others accepted allotments and lost their geographic identity.

Religion Individuals sought guardian spirits through the traditional means of singing, fasting, praying, and performing feats of endurance. The spirits assured the seeker of luck and various skills. Songs often accompanied received powers, which were generally called upon well after the quest: When one had settled into an adult life, the returning spirit power manifested itself by means of an illness that had to be cured by a shaman.

Shamans' powerful spirits helped them to cure illness; they could also harm people if they chose. Among the causes of illness, in addition to a returning spirit, were breaking taboos and suffering bewitchment. Shamans were paid for successful cures.

Important religious occasions included the first salmon ritual, the midwinter spirit dances, and the first fruits rite. The midwinter dances served the additional purposes of bringing people together and releasing winter tensions.

The Dreamer Cult, a mid-nineteenth-century phenomenon, was a revivalistic cult that celebrated traditional Indian religious beliefs. Although it was explicitly antiwhite, the religious doctrine also contained elements of Christianity. Its adherents thus attempted to remain faithful to their Indian traditions while taking steps to adapt to non-Indian culture.

Government Autonomous villages were each led by a chief and a subchief; these lifetime offices were hereditary in theory but were generally filled by people possessing the qualities of honesty, integrity, and diplomacy. The authority of chiefs was granted mainly through consensus.

An informal assembly of all married adults confirmed a new chief and oversaw other aspects of village life. All residents of the village were considered citizens. Other village leaders included a messenger, a speaker, and a salmon chief (often a shaman, with the salmon as a guardian spirit, who supervised salmon-related activities). By virtue of their ability to help or hurt people, shamans also acquired relative wealth and power from their close association with chiefs, who liked to keep them allied.

Customs The Sinkiuse were seminomadic for nine months a year; during the other three they lived in permanent winter villages. Winter was a time for visits and ceremonies. During that season, women also made mats and baskets, made or repaired clothing, and prepared meals; men occasionally hunted or just slept, gambled, and socialized.

In spring, groups of four or five families left the village for root-digging areas; those who had spent the winter away from the main village returned. People rose at dawn, winter and summer, and began the day by bathing in the river. Men's realm was toolmaking, war, hunting, fishing, and, later, horses.

Pacifism, generosity, and interpersonal equality and autonomy were highly valued. Girls fasted and were secluded for ten days at the onset of puberty, except for a nighttime running regime. The exchange of gifts between families constituted a marriage, a relationship that was generally stable and permanent. Corpses were wrapped in tule mats or deerskin and buried with their possessions. The family burned the deceased's house and then observed various taboos and purification rites.

Dwellings The Sinkiuse built typical Plateau-style, semiexcavated, cone-shaped wood frame houses covered with woven matting and/or grass. Longer, lodge-style structures of similar construction were used for communal activities. Villages also contained mat-covered sweat lodges. Temporary brush shelters

served as summer houses. Later, skin tipis replaced the aboriginal structures.

They also built communal tule-mat houses consisting of a pole framework covered by grass, earth, and tule mats. These houses were about 16 feet wide, between 24 to about 60 feet long, and about 14 feet high, with gabled roofs. Entrance was through matted doors. Each family had an individual tule-covered section, but they shared a number of fireplaces in the central passage.

Diet Food was much more often acquired by the family than by the village. Fish was a staple. Men caught four varieties of salmon as well as trout, sturgeon, and other fish. They fished from May through October. Women cleaned, dried, and stored the fish. Dried fish and sometimes other foods made up much of the winter diet. People generally ate two meals a day in summer and one in winter.

Women gathered shellfish, salmon eggs, bulbs, roots, nuts, seeds, and berries. Camas was eaten raw or roasted, boiled, and made into cakes. A short ceremony was performed over the first gathered crop of the season. Men hunted most large and small game in the fall. They prepared for the hunt by sweating and singing. Women came along to help dress and carry the game. Men also hunted birds and gathered mollusks.

Key Technology Men caught fish with nets, weirs, traps, and hook and line. Utensils were carved of wood. Women made coiled baskets of birch bark and/or cedar root; they also wove wallets and bags of woven strips of skin, and they sewed tule mats and other items.

Trade The Sinkiuse engaged in extensive local trade, communication, visiting, and intermarriage.

Notable Arts Artistic expression was seen mainly in carved wood items, coiled baskets with geometric designs, and mat weaving.

Transportation Dugout canoes and some pole rafts served as water transportation. Horses arrived about the mid–eighteenth century.

Dress The Sinkiuse wore surprisingly little clothing for such a northern climate. Woven bark and, later, dressed buckskin provided breechclouts, ponchos, and aprons. Women also wore woven caps. Men wore fur leggings in winter; women's leggings were generally made of hemp. Some winter clothing, such as mittens, caps, woven blankets, and robes, was made from the fur of rabbits and other animals. Both sexes plucked their eyebrows and wore earrings, tattoos, necklaces, and face paint.

War and Weapons Sinkiuse were generally friendly with their Interior Salish neighbors.

Contemporary Information

Government/Reservations The Colville Reservation (1872) is located in Ferry and Okanogan Counties, Washington. It comprises 1,011,495 acres and had a 1990 Indian population of 3,782. An Indian Reorganization Act constitution approved in 1938 calls for a 14-member business council and various committees. The Confederated Tribes is a member of the Affiliated Tribes of Northwest Indians and other intertribal organizations.

Economy Important economic resources and activities include stock raising, farming, logging (including a sawmill) and reforestation, seasonal labor, mining, a meat-packing plant, a log cabin sales business, tourism, and gambling enterprises. The tribe plans to develop its hydroelectric potential.

Legal Status The Confederated Tribes of the Colville Reservation is a federally recognized tribal entity.

Daily Life Although a small number of Colville residents claim Sinkiuse descent, most people are largely acculturated. Language preservation programs are hindered by the lack of a common language, and few people still speak Sinkiuse (Columbia). Recent efforts to reinvigorate disparate tribal cultures and religions include the Seven Drum religion, the Indian Shaker Church, and the Native American Church. The tribe has undertaken a program of reacquiring and consolidating their land base. Education levels are increasing. The Colville

Business Council wields growing power in regional and statewide issues.

Spokan

Spokan (Spō `kan), a Plateau tribe having three geographic divisions: upper, lower, and southern, or middle. The Spokan have also been known as Muddy People, as well as Sun People, probably after a faulty translation of their name. Their self-designation was *Spoqe'ind,* "round head."

Location Spokan Indians lived in the mid–eighteenth century along the Spokane River, in eastern Washington and northern Idaho. Today they live on reservations in Washington and Idaho as well as in regional cities and towns.

Population The early-nineteenth-century Spokan population was very roughly 2,000. In 1990, about 2,100 enrolled Spokan Indians lived on the Spokane Reservation as well as on the Coeur d'Alene, Flathead, and Colville Reservations and in regional cities and towns.

Language Spokan is a dialect of the Interior division of the Salishan language family.

Historical Information

History The Spokan Indians probably originated in British Columbia along with other Salish groups. After they acquired horses from Kalispel Indians, around the mid–eighteenth century, they began hunting buffalo on the Great Plains. This was especially true of the upper division. By the time they encountered the Lewis and Clark expedition in 1805, their population had already declined significantly as a result of smallpox epidemics.

Following the Lewis and Clark visit, the North West, Hudson's Bay, and American Fur Companies quickly established themselves in the area. Missionaries arrived in the 1830s: They found the Spokan to be reluctant converts, and the influence of Christianity acted to create factionalism among the tribe. Interracial relations declined sharply in the late 1840s with the Whitman massacre and the closing of the Protestant mission (*see* "History" under Cayuse). Severe smallpox epidemics in 1846 and in 1852 and 1853 helped spur the rise of the Prophet Dance and the Dreamer Cult.

After miners had effectively dispossessed the Spokan from their territory, they joined with Coeur d'Alenes, Yakimas, Palouses, and Paiutes in the short-lived 1858 Coeur d'Alene, or Spokan, war. Spokan Indians then remained on their land as best they could or settled on various reservations. Despite pleas from Chief Joseph, they remained neutral in the 1877 Nez Percé war. In that year, the lower division agreed to move to the Spokan Reservation (1881; 154,898 acres). Ten years later, the other two divisions, as well as some remaining lower Spokans, agreed to move to either the Flathead, Colville, or Coeur d'Alene Reservations. The local fort, Fort Spokan, became an Indian boarding school from 1898 to 1906. There were also conflicts over land with non-natives in and around the city of Spokane at this time.

In the early twentieth century, much tribal land was lost to the allotment process as well as "surplus" land sales to non-Indians. Dams built in 1908 (Little Falls) and 1935 (Grand Coulee) ruined the local fishery. Uranium mining began in the 1950s. The Spokan tribe successfully fought off termination proceedings begun in 1955. In 1966, the tribe received a land claims settlement of $6.7 million.

Religion Preadolescents acquired spirit helpers, through quests and in dreams and visions, to provide them with essential skills. Shamans' particularly strong spirits allowed them to cure illness, foresee the future, and assist hunters. Spokan Indians celebrated the midwinter (spirit) and midsummer religious ceremonies as well as first fruits and harvest ceremonies.

The Dreamer Cult, a mid-nineteenth-century phenomenon, was a revivalistic cult that celebrated traditional Indian religious beliefs. Although it was explicitly antiwhite, the religious doctrine also contained elements of Christianity. Its adherents thus attempted to remain faithful to their Indian traditions while taking steps to adapt to non-Indian culture.

Government Each division was composed of a number of bands, which were in turn composed of groups of related families. Bands were led by a chief

and an assistant chief, who were selected on the basis of leadership qualities. The office of band chief may once have been hereditary. Several bands might winter together in a village and at that time select an ad hoc village chief. Decisions were taken by consensus. In the historic period, as authority became more centralized, there was also a tribal chief.

Customs The Spokan were seminomadic for nine months a year; during the other three they lived in permanent winter villages. Men's realm was tool making, war, hunting, fishing, and, later, horses. The dead were covered with skins and robes and buried after spending some time on a scaffold. A pole marked the grave site.

Dwellings The Spokan built typical Plateau-style, semiexcavated, cone-shaped wood frame houses covered with woven matting and/or grass. Longer, lodge-style structures of similar construction were used for communal activities. Villages also contained mat-covered sweat lodges. Temporary brush shelters served as summer houses. Later, skin tipis replaced the aboriginal structures.

Diet Fish, especially salmon, was the staple. Trout and whitefish were also important. These were mostly smoked, dried, and stored for the winter. Men hunted local big game and, later, buffalo on the Plains. A favorite hunting technique was for many men to surround the animal. Important plant foods included camas, bitterroot and other roots, bulbs, seeds, and berries.

Key Technology Men caught fish with nets, weirs, traps, and hook and line. Women made coiled baskets of birch bark and/or cedar root; they also wove wallets and bags of woven strips of skin, and they sewed tule mats and other items.

Trade Spokan Indians traded coiled baskets, woven wallets and caps, and tule mats, among other items, with local tribes, particularly the Coeur d'Alene.

Notable Arts Women wove geometric designs into their well-made baskets. They also decorated clothing with porcupine quillwork.

Transportation Spokan Indians used pole rafts for river travel. They acquired horses around the mid–eighteenth century.

Dress Clothing was made of bark and fur until the advent of widespread buffalo hunting, when styles took on Plains characteristics. Both men and women tattooed their bodies.

War and Weapons Spokans were generally friendly with their Interior Salish neighbors, especially the Kalispel. The Coeur d'Alene were occasional enemies until the mid–eighteenth century, when they became allies in wars against the Crow and Blackfeet. As part of these wars, the Spokan counted coups, took scalps, and held war dances.

Contemporary Information

Government/Reservations The Spokane Reservation (1881) is located in Lincoln and Stevens Counties, Washington. It contains 133,302 acres. The 1990 Indian population was 1,229. The reservation is governed by an elected tribal council.

Economy There is a tribal store on the Spokane Reservation. Income is also generated by land leases, a post mill, a lumber mill, farming, and a fish hatchery. The reservation suffers from chronic high unemployment. There is a casino on the Colville Reservation.

Legal Status The Spokane Tribe is a federally recognized tribal entity.

Daily Life Spokan Indians are essentially assimilated, although there are some language preservation programs operating through a cultural center on the reservation. Efforts to revitalize traditional religion are controversial owing to the concurrent introduction of religious elements from Great Plains cultures. Water rights, gaming, and control of resource areas remain ongoing issues. The reservation has both Catholic and Protestant churches as well as a community center. It hosts an annual festival over Labor Day weekend.

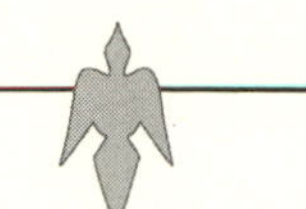

Thompson

The Thompson (`Tom sun) Indians are also known as *Ntlakyapamuk.*

Location The Thompson Indian homeland is the Fraser, Thompson, and Nicola River Valleys in southwest British Columbia.

Population The late-eighteenth-century Thompson population was about 5,000. It was approximately 5,700 in 1995.

Language Thompson is a dialect of the Interior division of the Salishan language family.

Historical Information

History Several trading companies became established in Thompson country following the initial visit of non-Indians in about 1809. Miners flooded in after an 1858 gold strike, taking over land, disrupting subsistence patterns, and generally forcing the Indian population to the brink of ruin. Disease, too, took a heavy toll during the nineteenth century, killing as many as 70 percent of the precontact Indian population. The government of British Columbia confined the Thompson Indians to reserves in the late nineteenth century.

Religion Guardian spirits, acquired in youth through fasting and seclusion, provided luck and various skills. Shamans cured illness with the help of their especially powerful spirits. Thompson Indians celebrated the arrival of the season's first salmon as well as the Ghost or Circle Dance.

Government Thompson Indians recognized two geographical divisions, located downstream and upstream of about the location of Cisco on the Fraser River. Within the divisions, bands were autonomous, consisted of related families, and were led by hereditary chiefs whose powers were largely advisory. A council of older men wielded real authority.

Customs The girls' puberty rite consisted of daily prayers, bathing, and rubs with fir branches. The dead were buried in sand pits or rock slides; graves were marked with stakes or posts. People's former ornaments and tools were buried with them. In a reflection of their cultural proximity to Northwest Coast people, slavery was hereditary among the Thompson.

Dwellings In winter, people lived in circular, earth-covered pole-frame lodges built in pits. Each lodge was about 20–40 feet in diameter and could hold between 15 and 30 people. Entry was gained via a notched ladder inserted through the smoke hole. In summer, people used oblong or circular lodges consisting of rush mats over a pole frame. Both men and women used domed sweat houses for purification. Sweat houses were also homes for youths during their spirit quest period.

Diet Thompson Indians subsisted on the typical Plateau diet of fish, especially salmon; some large and small game; and plant foods that included many roots, berries, and nuts (especially camas and bitterroot).

Key Technology Men caught fish by using weirs, seine nets, traps, dip nets, and hook and line. They also carved soapstone (steatite) pipes. Bows were often made of juniper. Women made cedar-root or birch-bark baskets decorated with geometric designs, as well as birch and spruce bark containers. Some were woven tight enough to hold water. Women also wove blankets of goat wool or strips of rabbit fur, and they sewed tule mats with Indian hemp cord. Digging sticks featured antler or wood cross-handles. Other tools and utensils were also made of stone, antler, and bone.

Trade Thompson Indians traded especially with the Okanagon, Lake, Colville, and Sanpoil people. They received dentalium shell from north of Vancouver Island, across the mountains, and down the Fraser River.

Notable Arts Women made fine baskets decorated with geometric motifs and natural dyes. The Thompson people developed a distinctive form of "negative" body painting, which involved removing pigment from a painted surface. Deer jaws were used to scratch parallel lines.

Transportation Thompson men made both birchbark and dugout canoes. Snowshoes were worn in winter. Horses arrived around the mid– to late eighteenth century.

Dress Traditionally, most clothing, such as breechclouts, ponchos, skirts, and robes, was made from cedar bark and fur. Dressed skin clothing, including leggings, breechclouts, and tunics, probably reflected the later influence of the Great Plains. Moccasins were generally plain. Women wove robes of rabbit skin or goat wool. Fringe, bone, teeth, and shell decoration was used on some items. Personal decorations included jewelry of dentalium shell, bone and animal teeth, and face paint. Men wore long looped necklaces, often decorated with abalone shell. Women tended to wear abalone in their braids.

War and Weapons Thompsons selected temporary war chiefs, as needed. Stuwiks were a traditional enemy until the Thompsons absorbed them by about 1800, although the people also fought regularly with other Salishan groups. Weapons used in regular raiding included the bow and arrow; spears; wood, bone, or stone clubs; bone daggers; and wooden slat armor.

Contemporary Information

Government/Reservations Thompson Indians are organized into roughly 16 bands located on about 200 reserves in British Columbia. Their total land base is roughly 42,500 hectares. See band profiles under "Daily Life" (all statistics are as of 1995).

Economy Wage labor and basket sales complement farming, hunting, fishing, and gathering.

Legal Status All of the bands discussed under "Daily Life" are federally and provincially recognized.

Daily Life The Boston Bar Band, originally the Koia'um Village, controls 12 reserves on 609 hectares of land. The reserves were allotted in 1878. The population is 182, of whom 64 live in 20 houses on the reserves. Elections are held according to the provisions of the Indian Act, and the band is affiliated with the Nlaka'pamux Nation Tribal Council. Children attend provincial schools. Important economic resources include a campsite.

The Boothroyd Band, formerly known as Chomok Band, controls 19 reserves on 1,122 hectares of land. The population is 244, of whom 84 live in 29 houses on the reserves. Elections are held according to the provisions of the Indian Act, and the band is affiliated with the Nlaka'pamux Nation Tribal Council. Children attend provincial schools. Facilities include a church.

The Cook's Ferry Band controls 24 reserves on 4,048 hectares of land. The reserves were allotted in 1878. The population is 267, of whom 75 live on the reserves. Elections are held according to custom, and the band is currently unaffiliated. Children attend provincial schools. Important economic activities include ranching. Facilities include a community hall, a fire station, and a garage.

The Kanaka Bar Band (formerly part of the Lytton Band) was originally composed of gold miners from the Hawaiian Islands. The Kanakas were employed by the Hudson's Bay Company, which had established a trading post in Honolulu in 1834. Many Hawaiians traveled on company ships to the Northwest Coast. Some stayed, especially to mine gold, and intermarried with the Native Americans. The band controls six reserves on 229 hectares of land. The reserves were allotted in 1881. The population is 147, of whom 55 live in seven houses on the reserves. Elections are held according to custom, and the band is affiliated with the Fraser Canyon Indian Administration. Children attend provincial schools. Silviculture is an important economic activity.

The Lower Nicola Band controls nine reserves on 7,096 hectares of land. The reserves were allotted in 1878. The population is 807, of whom 470 live in 121 houses on the reserves. Elections are held according to the provisions of the Indian Act, and the band is affiliated with the Nicola Valley Tribal Council. Children attend band and provincial schools. Important economic activities and resources include an irrigation system, cattle ranching, logging/forest products, and small businesses. Facilities include a community hall, a church, and a cultural club.

The Lytton Band controls 54 reserves on 5,980 hectares of land near the Fraser and Thorpe Rivers. The reserves were allotted in 1881. The population is 1,480, of whom 714 live in 228 houses on the reserves. Elections are held according to the provisions of the Indian Act, and the band is affiliated with the Nklaka'pamux Nation Tribal Council. Children attend band and provincial schools. Important economic activities and resources include a hardware store, a motel, and individual ranches and businesses. Facilities include a community hall, a seniors' home, a group home, a womens' shelter, and an arts and crafts store.

The Neskonlith Band, a South Thompson band, is located six kilometers south of Chase, British Columbia. The reserve was allotted in 1877. The population is 499, of whom 223 live in 54 houses on the reserves. Elections are held according to the provisions of the Indian Act, and the band is affiliated with the Shuswap Nation Tribal Council. Children attend band and provincial schools. Important economic activities and resources include a development corporation, a demonstration farm and silviculture program, and small farms and businesses. Facilities include a community hall, a fire station, and a church.

The Nicomen Band controls 15 reserves on 1,175 hectares of land. The population is 85, of whom 53 live in 14 houses on the reserves. Elections are held according to the provisions of the Indian Act, and the band is affiliated with the Fraser Canyon Indian Administration. Children attend provincial schools. Important economic activities and resources include ranches.

The Nooaitch Band controls two reserves on 1,693 hectares of land. The reserves were allotted in 1878. The population is 171, of whom 116 live in 27 houses on the reserves. Elections are held according to the provisions of the Indian Act, and the band is affiliated with the Nicola Valley Tribal Council. Children attend provincial schools. Important economic activities and resources include small businesses. Facilities include offices, a church, and a fish hatchery.

The North Thompson Band controls five reserves on 1,521 hectares of land 24 kilometers north of Barnere. The reserves were allotted in 1877. The population is 512, of whom 217 live in 71 houses on the reserves. Elections are held according to the provisions of the Indian Act, and the band is affiliated with the Shuswap Nation Tribal Council. Children attend band and provincial schools. Important economic activities and resources include a feed lot, haying, logging, a fish hatchery, farming, a construction company, and a sawmill. Facilities include offices, a recreation hall, a women's club, a church, and an elders' home.

The Oregon Jack Creek Band controls six reserves on 823 hectares of land 17.5 kilometers west of Cache Creek. The reserves were allotted in 1878. The population is 49, of whom 11 live in six houses on the reserves. Elections are held according to custom, and the band is affiliated with the Nlaka'pamux Nation Tribal Council. Important economic activities and resources include cattle and hay ranching.

The Shakan Band controls two reserves on 3,874 hectares of land. The reserves were allotted in 1878. The population is 112, of whom 68 live in 22 houses on the reserves. Elections are unofficially held according to custom as well as according to the provisions of the Indian Act. The band is affiliated with the Nicola Valley Tribal Council. Children attend band and provincial schools. Important economic activities and resources include a campground and individual ranches. Facilities include a community hall and a church.

The Siska Band controls 11 reserves on 319 hectares of land. The reserves were allotted in 1876. The population is 231, of whom 78 live in 24 houses on the reserves. Elections are held according to custom, and the band is currently unaffiliated. Children attend band and provincial schools. Important economic activities and resources include a grocery store and a convenience store. Facilities include a community hall and offices.

The Skuppah Band controls eight reserves on 211 hectares of land. The population is 56, of whom 40 live in 12 houses on the reserves. Elections are held according to custom, and the band is affiliated with the Fraser Canyon Indian Administration. Children attend band and provincial schools. Important economic activities and resources include livestock, a café-restaurant,

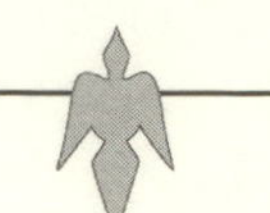

and individual hay and cattle ranches. Facilities include a community hall.

The Spuzzum Band controls 16 reserves on 636 hectares of land. The population is 152, of whom 37 live in 13 houses on the reserves. Elections are held according to custom, and the band is affiliated with the Fraser Canyon Indian Administration. Children attend provincial schools. Important economic activities and resources include an individual backhoe business. Facilities include offices.

The Upper Nicola Band (Thompson and Okanagon) controls eight reserves on 12,503 hectares of land. The reserves were allotted in 1878. The population is 715, of whom 431 live in 96 houses on the reserves. Elections are held according to custom, and the band is affiliated with the Nicola Valley Tribal Council. Children attend band and provincial schools. Important economic activities and resources include a store, a gas station, a cattle company, and individual small businesses. Facilities include offices, a hotel, a community hall, and a church.

Umatilla

Umatilla (Ū mä `til ä) is a name derived from a village name meaning "many rocks." This group is culturally similar to other Sahaptian people, such as Klikitat, Nez Percé, Wallawalla, and Yakima.

Location The Umatilla homeland was located along the lower Umatilla River and the Columbia River west of the mouth of the Walla Walla River. Today, most Umatillas live in Umatilla and Union Counties, Oregon, and in regional cities and towns.

Population The late-eighteenth-century Umatilla population was roughly 1,500. In 1990, over 1,000 Umatillas, Cayuses, and Wallawallas lived on the Umatilla Reservation, and approximately 700 Umatillas lived off-reservation. The Confederated Tribes of the Umatilla Reservation had a combined enrollment of around 1,900 in the mid-1990s.

Language Umatilla was a member of the Sahaptian division of the Penutian language family.

Historical Information

History As with other regional Indian groups, the Umatillas first encountered non-natives when the Lewis and Clark expedition passed through their territory around 1805. Fur traders quickly moved in shortly thereafter. Severe epidemics began in the mid–nineteenth century, about the same time Catholic and Protestant missionaries flocked to the region.

The Umatillas enjoyed a peaceful relationship with non-Indians until the late 1840s. In 1851 a Catholic mission, previously established in 1847 and then abandoned, was rebuilt. At that time the Umatillas sent warriors to support the Cayuses in their war against whites from the Willamette Valley. In the mid-1850s they were forced, with the Wallawallas and the Cayuses, to cede over four million acres and accept the creation of a reservation. The Umatillas joined the Yakima war of resistance from 1855 to 1856. However, two decades later, they fought against the Indians in the Bannock war. Umatillas were responsible for the death in that war of the Paiute chief Egan. Despite the Indians' possible hopes for better treatment at the hands of the whites, the original reservation of over 245,000 acres was quickly pared to under 100,000 by the process of allotment and sales of "surplus" to non-Indians.

Religion After years of instruction, adolescents sought the protection and power of spirits in nature by fasting and visiting remote places. Men and women shamans, with especially strong, heavenly-oriented guardian spirits, provided religious leadership. They cured illness, controlled the weather, and presided at ceremonies. They might also inflict harm. Dreams were also connected to good and evil events. During the winter religious ceremonies, participants dressed as their spirits and sang their spirit songs. Most important ceremonies centered on the first gathered fruit and salmon catch of the season.

Government Small, local bands each had one or more villages and fishing areas. Civil chiefs led the bands, although war chiefs exercised temporary power during periods of conflict. Chiefs were generally selected by a combination of merit, heredity, and wealth. Chiefs and old men made up the village and tribal councils; decisions were taken by consensus. The bands came together under a single chief in times of celebration and danger.

Customs Each band contained at least one permanent winter village and a number of temporary fishing camps. Some subsistence areas were considered tribal property. Menstruating and late-term pregnant women were strictly segregated. Young, unmarried men slept in the sweat lodges. Young men and women, especially the latter, were married by about age 14. Brides were commonly purchased, and polygamy was common. Abortion was rare, as was birth out of wedlock. Adultery was a capital crime. Women did most domestic work, including dressing skins; men's work revolved around hunting and war.

Immediately after death, corpses were dressed in good clothes and had their faces painted. After several days, they were wrapped in deerskin and buried with their former possessions. Boulders and cedar stakes marked grave sites. The family in mourning cut their hair and wore poor, dirty clothing.

Pipe smoking was an important part of burial and other rites and ceremonies. The murder of a tribe member usually required blood revenge or at least blood money. Theft was punished by public disgrace. Other serious crimes and infractions included adultery, rape, and lying. Typical games included archery, dice, hoop-and-pole, and the hand game; most included betting. Childrens' games included tops and string games.

Dwellings Permanent settlements were located along rivers. Winter dwellings were semisubterranean, circular wood frame structures covered with cedar bark, sage, mats, grasses, and earth. The roof was flat or conical. Mats covered the floors. These houses, up to 60 feet long, held up to 50 families. People slept along inner walls and shared fires along the center. In summer, people built temporary brush lean-tos. Some groups adopted hide tipis in the eighteenth century.

Diet Umatillas moved with the food supply. Fish, especially salmon, was the staple, along with trout, eel, and sturgeon. Salmon was broiled, baked, boiled, or dried, smoked, and stored. Animal food included elk, deer, moose, mountain sheep, rabbits, and small game. Parties also traveled to the Plains to hunt buffalo. Some meat was "jerked" for winter. Deer were run down or shot, as were other game, with a bow and arrow or killed with a spear. Some animals were hunted with the use of decoys.

Women gathered plant foods such as camas, kouse, bitterroot, wild carrot, wild onion, and berries. Camas, dug in midsummer, was peeled and baked in a pit oven. Most berries were dried and stored for winter. Other food included shellfish, fowl, eggs, and birds. People ate horses, lichens, and tree inner bark when there was nothing else to eat. Most food was either boiled, steamed in pits, or roasted in ashes.

Key Technology Fish were speared from platforms and caught using nets, spears, small traps, and weirs. Men used various nooses, snares, nets, and deadfalls for hunting as well as bows made of mountain sheep horn. Women made a range of woven and coiled baskets, some watertight, as well as woven reed bags. They also made cups, bowls, winnowing baskets, women's caps, and mats of cattails and tule. Many baskets were made of Indian hemp, bear grass, and other grasses.

Other important raw materials included bone, horn, and wood. Many tools and items, such as mortars, pestles, knives, and mauls, were made of chipping and flaking stone and also obsidian. Mattresses were cottonwood inner bark or dry grass, blankets were elk hides, and folded skins served as pillows. The ubiquitous digging stick was fire-hardened with a wood or antler cross-handle.

Trade Relatively early acquisition of horses gave the Umatilla a trade advantage, although they also traded widely before they had the horse. They acquired items made as far away as British Columbia and the Mississippi Valley. Abalone was among the items they acquired from coastal Indians, as were carved wooden items, dried clams, dentalium shells, and wapato root.

Notable Arts Traditional arts included woven baskets, wallets, petroglyphs, and blankets and tipi skins decorated with pictographs.

The Umatilla moved with the food supply. Fish, especially salmon, was the staple, along with trout, eel, and sturgeon. Salmon was broiled, baked, and boiled or dried, smoked, and stored. These women are hanging fish out to dry (1887).

Transportation The Umatilla used snowshoes and dugout canoes. They acquired the horse in the early eighteenth century.

Dress Clothing was made of cedar bark and the untailored skin of deer, elk, and buffalo. Men wore moccasins, leggings, breechclouts, shirts, and highly decorated robes. Women wore moccasins, fringed gowns, and basket hats, replaced in the historic period with skin caps decorated with fringe and elks' teeth. People painted their faces and bodies for decoration and against snow blindness. Tailored, Plains-style skin clothing became popular in the eighteenth century.

War and Weapons To counter the threat of attack from Paiutes, their most feared enemy, Umatillas formed a war alliance with the Nez Percés. They often took refuge on Blalock Island, now under water.

Contemporary Information

Government/Reservations The Umatilla Reservation (1855; Umatilla, Cayuse, Wallawalla) is located in Umatilla and Union Counties, Oregon. It contains roughly 172,000 acres, most of which are individually allotted. The 1990 Indian population was 1,028. The constitution and by-laws, adopted in 1949, call for an elected nine-member Board of Trustees.

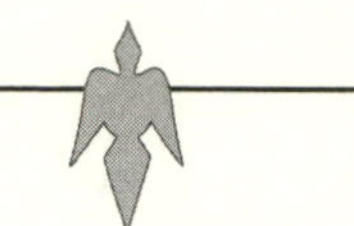

Umatilla Indians are also members of the Columbia River Indians, who live primarily in Priest Rapids, Cooks Landing, Billieville, and Georgeville, Washington; in Celilo, Oregon; and in non-Indian communities. The Council of Columbia River Chiefs meets at Celilo, Oregon. The community at Priest Rapids is directly descended from that of Smohalla, a founder of the Dreamer or Longhouse religion.

The tribes are also members of the Umatilla Basin Project, the Columbia River Intertribal Fish Commission, the Basalt Waste Isolation Project, the Hanford Environmental Dose Project, the Columbia Gorge Commission, and other environmental and planning organizations.

Economy In 1953, the tribe received almost $4 million in compensation for fishing sites lost to the Dalles Dam. The tribe has won other land claims settlements as well. It is currently developing an Oregon Trail interpretive center. Other sources of income include farm leases as well as a tribally owned forest, range, resort, trailer court, grain elevator, store, and lake (camping and fishing). A golf course and entertainment park are planned. Tribal programs provide credit as well as seasonal and regular employment.

Legal Status The Confederated Tribes of the Umatilla Reservation is a federally recognized tribal entity. The Columbia River Indians are not federally recognized.

Daily Life The tribe values both traditional and modern education. There are some language preservation programs, and there is a college scholarship fund. The Seven Drum religion is a major force in cultural revitalization. People's religious practices also include traditional salmon and roots ceremonies. Facilities include a day care center and an arts and crafts organization. The tribe also operates health education and substance abuse programs. It sponsors an annual Pendleton Round-up, including dances, crafts fair, and rodeo, and an annual Indian festival of the arts. The regional political and economic effectiveness of the Umatillas continues to grow.

Wallawalla

See Umatilla

Warm Springs Reservation, Confederated Tribes of the

See Paiute, Northern (Chapter 4); Umatilla; Wishram

Wasco

See Wishram

Wishram

Wishram (ˋWish rəm), or *Tlakluit,* a Plateau group with many cultural attributes of Northwest Coast Indians. They were culturally similar to the neighboring Wasco people.

Location Wishram Indians lived along the north bank of the Columbia River, several miles above and below the Dalles. Today, their descendants live on local reservations, especially the Yakima, and in regional cities and towns.

Population The eighteenth-century Wishram population was about 1,500. A 1962 census listed 10 Wishrams in Washington. The contemporary population is part of the Warm Springs and Yakima Reservation communities.

Language Wishram was a member of the Chinookan (Kiksht) division of the Penutian language family.

Historical Information

History Owing to their physical location at the Dalles, the most important trading area in the Northwest, the Wishram traditionally enjoyed favorable trade relations with many neighboring tribes. In the early nineteenth century, however, non-Indian traders threatened this position while at the same time the Wishram population was declining rapidly due to disease. Conflict with traders was one result. Ongoing intertribal warfare also took a population toll.

In 1855, the Wishram and Wasco were forced to sign treaties ceding most of their land (roughly 10 million acres); the treaties established the Warm Springs Reservation in north-central Oregon. Wishram Indians also became part of the Yakima Indian Nation on the Yakima Reservation. A key treaty provision allowing the Indians to fish "at all . . . usual and accustomed stations in common with the citizens of the United States . . ." served as the basis for a landmark legal ruling in 1974 that protected the Northwest Coast Indian fishery. In the 1860s members of the Warm Springs Reservation organized informally into linguistic and cultural divisions: There were Sahaptian-speaking people ("Warm Springs Indians"); Upper Chinookan–speaking Wascos and Wishrams; and Northern Paiutes after 1879.

In 1891, about one-third of Yakima Reservation land was allotted to individuals, but the Yakima Nation, under chief Shawaway Lotiahkan, retained the "surplus" usually sold to non-Indians in such cases. Still, much land that was allotted to Indians was soon lost, including some of the best irrigated land. Around the turn of the century as much as 80 percent of the reservation was in non-Indian hands.

The Warm Springs Boarding School opened in 1897; designed to eradicate Indian culture, it fell short of its goal before it closed in the 1960s. Dams, however (Bonneville, 1938; Grand Coulee, 1941; Dalles, 1956), destroyed the native fisheries. Although the tribes were compensated financially for the fisheries, the spiritual and cultural loss was devastating. During the course of the twentieth century the number of salmon and steelhead that returned to the Yakima River to spawn declined by about 99 percent. The issue of fishing rights remained an important and controversial one from the beginning of the reservation period through its resolution in 1974. Well into the twentieth century, Yakimas continued much of their traditional subsistence and ceremonial activities.

Religion Adolescent boys sought guardian spirits by fasting and performing feats of skill or daring associated with remote places. Shamans' guardian spirits, usually several animals, helped them cure the sick. Important ceremonies included first salmon rites as well as midwinter guardian spirit dances.

Government Each of several villages was led by a hereditary chief.

Customs Wishram Indians observed the system of social stratification typical of Northwest Coast Indians: There were nobles, middle-class, commoners, and slaves; the slaves were acquired in war or trade. Slavery was also hereditary. Marriage was formalized by an exchange of gifts and family visits. Infants were occasionally betrothed for purposes of creating or cementing family alliances. Corpses were wrapped in buckskin and interred in plank burial houses. Remarriage to the dead spouse's sibling was common. Fishing areas were privately owned and inheritable by groups of families.

Dwellings Wishrams probably built plank houses characteristic of the coastal style. Beginning about the eighteenth century, they also built circular winter houses, holding between one and six families. These were built of a pole framework over a six-foot pit, covered with mats of grass and dirt or cedar bark. Entrance was through the smoke hole. Bed platforms were located around the walls. In summer, people built gabled-roof mat lodges with several fireplaces. Hunters and mourners purified themselves, and the sick healed, in sweat lodges.

Diet Fish, especially salmon, pike, eels, sturgeon, and smelts, was the most important food. Salmon eggs were also eaten. Fish were either eaten fresh or dried or smoked and ground for long-term storage. Important plant foods included roots, bulbs (especially camas), wild onions, wild potatoes, acorns, and various nuts and berries. Men hunted game to supplement the diet.

Key Technology In addition to nets, weirs, traps, and spears for fishing, men made a variety of carved wood tools and utensils. Women made twined baskets and bags decorated with geometric figures.

Trade The Dalles, or Five Mile Rapids, in Wishram territory was the most important trading location in the Northwest; several thousand Northwest Coast and Plateau Indians traded there during various trade fairs. Wishram and Wasco people acted as intermediaries in

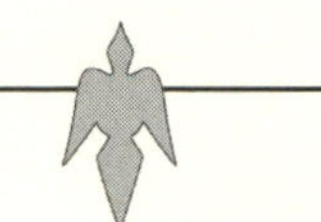

the trade of a huge amount and variety of items, including blankets, shells, slaves, canoes, fish and animal products, dried roots, bear grass, and, later, horses. Trade connections stretched from Canada to Mexico and from the Rocky Mountains west to the ocean.

Notable Arts Baskets and some carved wood items were exceptionally well made.

Transportation Men built and traded for dugout canoes and snowshoes.

Dress Most clothing was made of skins. Men wore breechclouts; women wore aprons and basket caps. People also painted their faces and wore dentalium shell ornaments. Plains-style clothing became popular in the nineteenth century.

War and Weapons At least in the early to mid–nineteenth century, the Wishram and Wasco fought Northern Paiutes, Bannocks, and Northern Shoshones.

Contemporary Information

Government/Reservations The Yakima Reservation and Trust Lands (1859) are located in Klikitat, Lewis, and Yakima Counties, Washington. They contain roughly 1.4 million acres. The 1990 Indian population was 6,296, of a total population of well over 27,000. The Yakima Nation is governed by a 14-member tribal council.

The Warm Springs Reservation (1855; Wasco/Wishram, Wallawalla [Warm Springs], and Northern Paiute) is located in Clakamas, Jefferson, Marian, and Wasco Counties, Oregon. It contains 643,507 acres. The 1990 Indian population was 2,818. The 1993 tribal enrollment was 3,410. Decisions of the 11-member tribal council are subject to general review by referendum. An Indian Reorganization Act constitution was adopted in 1938.

Economy Warm Springs features the Kah-Nee-Ta resort; the Warm Springs Forest Products Industries, which includes logging, a plywood plant, and a sawmill; herds of wild horses; a salmon hatchery; a tribally owned hydroelectric plant; a museum; a

A Wishram bride wears a loop necklace, a dress with six broad rows of lazy-stitch beading on the yoke. She has three strands of white disk shell beads, used as currency, as a necklace. The front of her wedding cap has a row of Chinese coins.

casino; and two radio stations. Tribal government is also a major provider of jobs. The tribe's economy is significantly self-sufficient and reservation based.

Timber is the Yakima Nation's main income producer; its forest products industry includes a furniture manufacturing plant. The nation maintains extensive range and farmland. However, 80 percent of irrigated land remains leased by non-Indians. The Wapato Project provides the Indians with control over their own water.

The Yakima-Klickitat Fish Production Project, a cooperative effort between the Yakima Nation and Washington State, is a major fishery restoration/conservation venture. An industrial park contains Indian and non-Indian industries. The Yakima Land Enterprise operates fruit orchards and stands and a

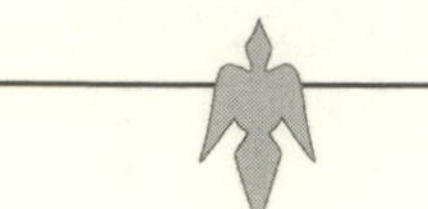

recreational vehicle park. Other employment is provided by the government and the nation as well as by small business enterprises. Still, unemployment fluctuates between about 30 and 60 percent, and up to 75 percent of the people live below the poverty level.

Legal Status The Confederated Tribes and Bands of the Yakima Nation and the Confederated Tribes of the Warm Springs Reservation are both federally recognized tribal entities. Lawsuits over water use from the Yakima River system are pending.

Daily Life The Warm Springs Sahaptians remain the most traditional group on the reservation; this language is spoken on ceremonial occasions. Few people still speak Wishram. Warm Springs children attend public grade school on the reservation and public high school off the reservation. The Seven Drum religion, conducted in Sahaptian, provides a link to other Plateau Sahaptian communities. The Feather Dance religion, which emphasizes ritual healing, is also active on the Warm Springs reservation.

On the Yakima Reservation, many people follow the Longhouse (Seven Drums) religion as well as sweat house customs and first foods feasts. The longhouse serves as the locus of Indian identity and is used for ceremonial occasions. Longhouse families throughout the Plateau region are linked together, mostly through marriage. The Indian Shaker religion is also active on the reservation, as are several Christian churches.

Yakimas maintain many aspects of traditional culture, including family customs, service, and leadership. The language is alive and well, especially as part of religious ceremonies and among more traditional people. Adults and children may take classes to strengthen their native language skills. Yakima basketry is still an important art and craft.

The Yakima Reservation boasts a huge, full-service tribal cultural center, museum, and restaurant in addition to two community centers. There is an emphasis on education, with the tribe providing incentives such as scholarships and summer programs. Children attend public school on the reservation. The reservation also sponsors a tribally run school; a private, accredited, four-year liberal arts college; tribal newspapers; and a radio station. It hosts an annual all-Indian rodeo, a powwow, a huckleberry festival, and several basketball tournaments. In 1972, the government restored about 22,000 acres of land to the Yakima Nation, including the sacred Pahto (Mt. Adams).

Yakima

Yakima (`Ya ku mu), "runaway," the common name for the people who called themselves *Waptailmim,* "People of the Narrow River." The Yakima people may have originated from members of neighboring tribes such as the Palouse and Nez Percé.

Location The Yakima homeland is located along the Columbia, Wenatchee, and Yakima Rivers in southern Washington. It includes lands from the Cascade summits to the Columbia River.

Population The late-eighteenth-century (precontact) population was about 7,000. By 1805 the population had fallen to half of that. A 1910 reservation census noted the population at 1,362. Today, Yakimas are among the over 6,000 Indians enrolled in the Yakima Nation. Yakimas also live off-reservation and in regional cities and towns.

Language Yakima is a member of the Sahaptian division of the Penutian language family.

Historical Information

History Yakima bands acquired horses by the early eighteenth century and began hunting buffalo on the Great Plains. Horses brought them wealth, but even though the people acquired certain aspects of Plains culture, they did not become wholesale buffalo hunters as some other Plateau tribes did. In 1805 the Lewis and Clark expedition arrived; many trappers, missionaries, and traders soon followed. The missionaries found reluctant converts. By the early to mid–nineteenth century, the Yakima had suffered dramatic population reductions owing to disease as well as to warfare with the Shoshone.

In 1855, the governor of Washington forced local Indians to cede 10.8 million acres of land. Most

tribes agreed to accept a 1.2-million-acre reservation. Shortly thereafter, gold was discovered north of the Spokane River. Although Indians retained fishing and gathering rights at their usual off-reservation places and were given two to three years to relocate after they signed the 1855 treaty, the governor declared their land open to non-Indians 12 days after the treaty council.

Friction was inevitable at this point. Miners killed some Yakimas, and the Indians retaliated in kind. When soldiers arrived, a large group of Indians drove them away. In response to the treacherous murder of a Wallawalla chief and negotiator, the Wallawalla, Palouse, Cayuse, and Umatilla Indians joined the Yakimas in fighting non-Indians. The war spread in 1856. Seattle was attacked, and southern Oregon tribes joined the fighting; that part of the conflict was called the Rogue River war. The Coeur d'Alene war of 1858, in which Yakimas also participated, was essentially another part of the same conflict.

In 1859, following the end of the fighting and the execution of 24 Yakimas, the Indians agreed to settle on a reservation. The future Yakima Indian Nation included, in addition to the Yakima bands, the Klickitat, Wanapam, Wishram, Palus (Palouse), and the Wenatchi. Reservation Yakimas entered a brief period of relative prosperity under a worthy Indian agent. Soon, however, facing the usual pressures to sell their land, most Indians were forced into poverty, mitigated in part by some seasonal work.

By 1891, about one-third of the reservation land had been allotted to individuals, but the Yakima Nation, under Chief Shawaway Lotiahkan, retained the "surplus" usually sold to non-Indians in such cases. Still, much land that had been allotted to Indians was soon lost, including some of the best irrigated land. Around the turn of the century as much as 80 percent of the reservation was in non-Indian hands. Some Indians also established homesteads on original village sites off of the reservation. Despite government attempts to eradicate it, Indians retained their *Wáashat* (Longhouse) religion.

Dams (Bonneville, 1938; Grand Coulee, 1941; Dalles, 1956) destroyed the native fisheries. During the course of the twentieth century, the number of salmon and steelhead that returned to spawn in the Yakima River declined by about 99 percent. The issue of fishing rights remained an important and controversial one from the beginning of the reservation period through its resolution in the Boldt decision of 1974.

Well into the twentieth century, Yakimas continued much of their traditional subsistence and ceremonial activities. In the 1950s, their long-standing fishing place, Celilo Falls, was lost to a dam. A tribal renaissance began around that time, however. It included the development of several tribal industries such as a furniture factory, clothing manufactures, and a ceramic center as well as an all-Indian rodeo.

Religion Yakima Indians believed in a creator as well as the existence of animal spirits. The latter could be helpful in life and were sought in remote places by adolescent boys. Shamans' powerful spirits allowed them to cure illness. Most important ceremonies had to do with first food (salmon, root, berry) feasts.

Government Autonomous bands were led by leaders selected partly by merit and also by heredity. The bands came together under a head chief in times of celebration and danger.

Customs Groups of families lived together in permanent winter villages, where they raced, gambled, and held festivals. During the rest of the year individual families dispersed to hunt, fish, and gather food. Corpses were buried in pits where they were sometimes cremated as well. Graves were marked by a ring of stones. More than one individual may have been buried and cremated at a time. Burials also occurred in rock slides, where they were marked with stakes.

Dwellings The winter lodge consisted of a semisubterranean, rectangular, pole-frame structure covered with mats and earth. Skin-covered tipis were adopted during the eighteenth century.

Diet Fish, especially salmon (five kinds), steelhead trout, eel, and sturgeon, was the staple. Fish was eaten fresh or dried, ground, and stored. People also ate game, roots, berries, and nuts.

Key Technology Men fished using platforms, weirs, dip nets, harpoons, and traps. They hunted using bow and arrow and deadfalls. Other technological items included skin bags, baskets (some watertight), and carved wooden utensils.

Trade Yakimas participated in aboriginal trade activities as well as the early-nineteenth-century fur trade. Prominent trade items included skins, shells, beads, feathers, baskets, and reed mats.

Notable Arts Fine arts included tanned skins, decorated with shells, beads, and feathers, as well as baskets and reed mats.

Transportation People negotiated their territory using dugout canoes and snowshoes. Horses arrived in the early eighteenth century.

Dress Breechclouts, aprons, vests, and moccasins were made of skins. Fur robes were added in cold weather. Plains-style leggings and dresses became popular in the eighteenth century.

War and Weapons In the early nineteenth century the Yakima fought many wars with the Shoshone.

Contemporary Information

Government/Reservations The Yakima Reservation and Trust Lands (1859) are located in Klikitat, Lewis, and Yakima Counties, Washington. They contain roughly 1.4 million acres. The 1990 Indian population was 6,296, of a total population of well over 27,000. The Yakima Nation is governed by a 14-member elected tribal council of both sexes.

Yakima Indians are also members of the Columbia River Indians, who live primarily in Priest Rapids, Cooks Landing, Billieville, and Georgeville, Washington; in Celilo, Oregon; and in non-Indian communities. The Council of Columbia River Chiefs meets in Celilo, Oregon. The community at Priest Rapids is directly descended from that of Smohalla, a founder of the Dreamer or Longhouse religion.

Economy Timber is the Yakima Nation's main income producer; its forest products industry includes a furniture manufacturing plant. The nation maintains extensive range and farmland. However, 80 percent of irrigated land remains leased by non-Indians. The Wapato Project provides the Indians with control over their own water. The tribe has spent over $50 million to purchase former lands.

The Yakima-Klickitat Fish Production Project, a cooperative effort between the Yakima Nation and Washington State, is a major fishery restoration/conservation venture. An industrial park contains Indian and non-Indian industries. The Yakima Land Enterprise operates fruit orchards and stands and a recreational vehicle park. Other employment is provided by the government and the nation as well as by small business enterprises. Still, unemployment fluctuates between about 30 and 60 percent, and up to 75 percent of the people live below the poverty level.

Legal Status The Confederated Tribes and Bands of the Yakima Indian Nation is a federally recognized tribal entity. The Columbia River Indians are not federally recognized. Lawsuits over water use from the Yakima River system are pending.

Daily Life Many people follow the Longhouse (Seven Drums) religion as well as sweat house customs and first foods feasts. The four reservations longhouses serve as the locus of Indian identity and are used for ceremonial occasions. Longhouse families throughout the Plateau region are linked together, mostly through marriage. The Indian Shaker religion is also active on the reservation, as are several Christian churches.

Yakimas maintain many aspects of traditional culture, including family customs, service, and leadership. Although most live in nuclear families, elders remain of key importance to Yakima society. The language is alive and well, especially as part of religious ceremonies and among more traditional people. Adults and children may take classes to strengthen their native language skills. Yakima basketry is still an important art and craft.

The Yakima Reservation boasts a huge, full-service tribal cultural center, museum, and restaurant in addition to two community centers and an elders' retirement center. There is an emphasis on education, with the tribe providing incentives such as scholarships and summer programs. Children attend public school on the reservation. The reservation also sponsors a tribally run school; a private, accredited, four-year liberal arts college; tribal newspapers; and a radio station. It hosts an annual all-Indian rodeo, a powwow, a huckleberry festival, and several basketball tournaments. In 1972, the government restored about 22,000 acres of land to the Yakima Nation, including the sacred Pahto (Mt. Adams).